THE CANADIAN YEARBOOK OF INTERNATIONAL LAW

INTERNATIONAL LAW

1993

ANNUAIRE CANADIEN DE DROIT INTERNATIONAL

The Canadian Yearbook of International Law

VOLUME XXXI 1993 TOME XXXI

Annuaire canadien de Droit international

Published under the auspices of
THE CANADIAN BRANCH, INTERNATIONAL LAW ASSOCIATION
AND
THE CANADIAN COUNCIL ON INTERNATIONAL LAW
*with the financial support of the Social Sciences
and Humanities Research Council of Canada*

Publié sous les auspices de
LA SECTION CANADIENNE DE L'ASSOCIATION DE DROIT INTERNATIONAL
ET
LE CONSEIL CANADIEN DE DROIT INTERNATIONAL
*avec l'appui financier du Conseil de recherches
en Sciences humaines du Canada*

UBC Press

VANCOUVER, B.C.

Printed in Canada on acid-free paper ∞

ISBN 0-7748-0496-3
ISSN 0069-0058

Canadian Cataloguing in Publication Data

The National Library of Canada has catalogued this publication as follows:

The Canadian yearbook of international law — Annuaire canadien de droit international

Annual.
Text in English and French.
"Published under the auspices of the Canadian Branch, International Law Association and the Canadian Council on International Law."
ISSN 0069-0058

1. International Law — Periodicals. I. International Law Association. Canadian Branch. II. Canadian Council on International Law. III. Title: Annuaire canadien de droit international. JX21.C3   341'.05   CS75-34558-6

Donnés de catalogage avant publication (Canada)

Annuaire canadien de droit international — Canadian yearbook of international law

Annuarie.
Textes en anglais et en français.
"Publié sous les auspices de la Branche canadienne de l'Association de droit international et le Conseil canadien de droit international."
ISSN 0069-0058

1. Droit international — Périodiques. I. Association de droit international. Section canadienne. II. Conseil canadien de droit international. III. Titre: The Canadian yearbook of international law. JX21.C3   341'.05   CS75-34558-6

UBC Press
University of British Columbia
6344 Memorial Road
Vancouver, BC V6T 1Z2
(604) 822-3259
Fax: (604) 822-6083

The Board of Editors, the Canadian Branch of the International Law Association, the Canadian Council on International Law, and the University of British Columbia are not in any way responsible for the views expressed by contributors, whether the contributions are signed or unsigned.

Les opinions émises dans le présent *Annuaire* par nos collaborateurs, qu'il s'agisse d'articles signés, ou non signés, ne sauraient en aucune façon engager la responsabilité du Comité de rédaction, de la Section canadienne de l'Association de droit international, de la section canadienne du Conseil canadien de droit international ou de l'Université de Colombie Britannique.

Communications to *The Yearbook* should be addressed to:

Prière d'adresser les communications destinées à l'*Annuaire* à:

THE EDITOR, THE CANADIAN YEARBOOK OF INTERNATIONAL LAW
FACULTY OF LAW, COMMON LAW SECTION
UNIVERSITY OF OTTAWA
57 LOUIS PASTEUR
OTTAWA, ONTARIO K1N 6N6 CANADA

Contents / Sommaire

BOOK REVIEWS / RECENSIONS DE LIVRES

TRIBUTE TO
Charles B. Bourne

CHARLES BOURNE was the founding Editor-in-Chief of this *Yearbook* in 1963, and he remained in that capacity until last year — a span of thirty years. For international lawyers in Canada and around the world the name of *The Canadian Yearbook of International Law* will be indelibly associated with his name.

A graduate of the University of Toronto, Cambridge, and Harvard, Charles Bourne has had a lifelong commitment to the field of international law, as a professor at the University of British Columbia, as a scholar widely renowned for his work on the law relating to international water resources, and as Editor-in-Chief of this *Yearbook*. His approach to international legal issues and to his work as Editor-in-Chief has been characterized by intellectual rigour, a strong sense of legality and of the rule of law, and by pragmatism and common sense. That is why his scholarly works continue to have relevance and why the *Yearbook* has always held a respected position among international legal publications.

Charles Bourne a eu une influence remarquable sur une génération de juristes canadiens qui pratiquent en droit international. Ses étudiantes et étudiants diplômés se souviendront toujours "qu'une thèse doit avoir une *thèse*." En outre, les normes qu'il a établies pour l'*Annuaire* et qu'il a respectées pendant les trente ans où il a été rédacteur en chef sont maintenant l'aune à laquelle les recherches canadiennes en droit international sont mesurées. Il a assuré la continuité tout en favorisant le changement. Au fil des ans, l'*Annuaire* a reflété les opinions des juristes canadiens et étrangers sur les questions qui touchent la collectivité mondiale et la place du Canada dans cette collectivité.

En tant que premier universitaire en résidence à la Direction des affaires juridiques du ministère des Affaires extérieures du gouvernement du Canada, Charles Bourne a toujours essayé de faire en sorte que l'*Annuaire* satisfasse aussi bien les besoins des chercheurs et chercheuses que ceux des praticiens et praticiennes. Bien qu'il soit ancré dans le monde universitaire, Charles Bourne a néanmoins adopté une approche du droit international, et de la publication de l'*Annuaire*, qui tenait compte de la réalité de la pratique des États. Les sections de l'*Annuaire* qui traitent de la pratique du Canada en droit international ont été beaucoup consultées et elles sont devenues un modèle pour d'autres publications de droit international.

The Editors are honoured to pay tribute to Charles Bourne for a contribution to international legal scholarship that is unparalleled in Canada, and rarely equalled elsewhere in the world. As colleagues we have been enriched by our association with him, and as international lawyers we know that we speak on behalf of a far-ranging international community that is indebted to Charles Bourne for his outstanding contribution to the field.

THE EDITORS

Preface

A CHANGE IN THE EDITORSHIP OF THE *Canadian Yearbook of International Law* after thirty years of the hand of Charles Bourne as its editor-in-chief is an event that cannot go without note. As his successor, I am acutely aware of the standard Charles Bourne set and of the contribution that he has made through the *Yearbook*.

An important element in any change is continuity, and thus the *Yearbook* will continue its commitment to international legal scholarship and to encouraging the dissemination of the writings of international lawyers in Canada, as well as to contributing to a wider knowledge of the legal practices of Canada in international affairs.

The present volume reflects the traditional characteristics of the *Yearbook*. There are articles by established scholars as well as by those entering the field. There are topics that relate uniquely to Canada's position in the world community and those of more universal concern. There are articles that deal with legal theory and those that deal with specific problems of the practice of international law. In all, the thirty-first volume presents a picture of the state of international law and international legal scholarship in Canada as it was in 1993.

A yearbook must also reflect its times. That is what Charles Bourne was so successful in doing. It is now up to me and my associates to provide the editorial guidance that will ensure that the *Yearbook* responds to the present and to the times that are ahead. The task is a challenging one and I enter upon it with a deep sense of responsibility and with excitement and enthusiasm.

DONALD M. McRAE

THE CANADIAN YEARBOOK OF INTERNATIONAL LAW

1993

ANNUAIRE CANADIEN DE DROIT INTERNATIONAL

Changing Relations between the International Court of Justice and the Security Council of the United Nations

R. ST. J. MACDONALD*

INTRODUCTION

THIS ARTICLE CONSIDERS A few of the questions that were raised but left largely unanswered in the decision of the International Court of Justice in *Questions of Interpretation and Application of the 1971 Montreal Convention Arising from the Aerial Incident at Lockerbie.*[1] The main issue of jurisprudential interest that emerged in that case was the relationship between the International Court of Justice and the Security Council in situations where both organs are concurrently dealing with the same matter. It will be suggested in this article that the key to understanding the relationship is to recognize the distinctness of the legal and political processes. In earlier decisions, the Court, recognizing that distinctness, concluded that the Court and the Security Council could perform separate but complementary functions with respect to the same events. In *Lockerbie*, however, the Court, perhaps fearing that the two organs might arrive at inconsistent decisions, took a somewhat tentative approach. This article seeks to demonstrate that differences in legal

* Professor of International Law, University of Toronto; Judge at the European Court of Human Rights, Strasbourg; Honorary Professor in the Law Department, Peking University, Beijing. The author wishes to recognize with pleasure as well as gratitude the assistance of Alistair Crawley and Angus Gunn in the preparation of this paper.

1 (*Libyan Arab Jamahiriya* v. *United States of America*; *Libyan Arab Jamahiriya* v. *United Kingdom*), Provisional Measures, Order of Apr. 14, 1992, [1992] ICJ Rep. 114 [hereinafter *Lockerbie*]. References in this text are to *Libya* v. *U.S.*, [1992] ICJ Rep. 114.

and political decisions in respect of the same matter are more a reflection of distinct legal and political processes than of disagreement and conflict between the respective decision-making organs of the United Nations. Once this fact is recognized, any inconsistencies in the decisions of the two bodies will cause less concern.

The background to the *Lockerbie* case is well known and tragic. The "aerial incident at Lockerbie" was the explosion of Pan American Airliner 103, which killed all 259 passengers and crew and a further eleven residents on the ground. Three years after the bombing and following an extensive investigation, two Libyan nationals were accused of perpetrating the atrocity. In the face of demands from the United States and the United Kingdom that Libya surrender the two suspects for trial, the Libyan government appointed a Supreme Court justice to head an inquiry into the charges and indicated its willingness to co-operate with authorities in the United States and the United Kingdom. Unfortunately, an impasse was reached. On the one hand, Libya claimed that the matter should be dealt with in accordance with the Convention for the Suppression of Unlawful Acts against the Safety of Civil Aviation, done at Montreal on September 23, 1971 (the "Montreal Convention of 1971"),[2] to which Libya, the United Kingdom, and the United States were all parties. On the other hand, the United Kingdom and the United States expressed the view that Libya was using the Convention as a diversionary tactic and demanded that Libya surrender the two suspects for trial, accept responsibility for the actions of Libyan officials, and pay appropriate compensation.

Libya's application to the Court was a request for an indication of provisional measures to protect the rights that Libya claimed to possess under the Montreal Convention of 1971 and under general principles of international law. Before the hearing, the Security Council had adopted Resolution 731 (1992), which condemned the Libyan government for failing to accede to the requests of the United States and the United Kingdom and urged a full and effective response to those requests. However, when the Court issued its order it was found to contain no determination on whether the rights that Libya claimed *prima facie* existed and warranted the protection of provisional measures. The reason for the omission was that, three days after the hearing had closed, the Security Council adopted Resolution 748 (1992), which deter-

[2] Reprinted in 10 ILM 1151 (1971).

mined that the failure of the Libyan government to demonstrate by concrete actions its renunciation of terrorism and in particular its continued failure to respond fully and effectively to the requests in Resolution 731 (1992) constituted "a threat to international peace and security." Acting under Chapter 7 of the Charter of the United Nations, the Security Council decided that Libya must comply with the requests of the United States and United Kingdom referred to in Resolution 731 (1992) and that all states must comply with the resolution notwithstanding the existence of any rights or obligations conferred or imposed by any international agreement.

On the basis of Resolution 748 (1992), the Court declined to award the provisional measures requested by Libya. The order of the Court did not state whether Libya's application would have been successful in the absence of Resolution 748 (1992). Also, the order left it unclear whether provisional measures were declined because the Court was not prepared to make an Order contrary to a decision of the Security Council or whether the basis of the refusal was that the legal effect of any measures would have been negated by the Security Council resolution. The order was also silent on the question of the lawfulness of Resolution 748 (1992), which had been questioned by Libya in its observations on the effect of the resolution made pursuant to Article 62 of the Rules of Court.

As a result of these omissions, the decision of the Court is notable for the number of questions of far-reaching jurisprudential significance that it left unanswered. Must the Court avoid making a decision that will conflict with a binding decision of the Security Council? Should the Court draw back from the full exercise of its judicial power if the effects of its determinations will be annulled by a resolution of the Security Council? Are there limits on the decision-making powers of the Security Council? Although little guidance can be found in the order of the Court, the separate and dissenting opinions cast some light on how these issues may be handled in the future. The discussion will proceed in three stages. First, the distinctive features of legal reasoning and judicial decision-making will briefly be outlined and contrasted with those of political decision-making. Second, the discussion will focus on the allocation of functions between the organs of the United Nations within the framework of the Charter, and on the management of the concurrent exercise of the judicial and political functions of the

Court and the Security Council before the *Lockerbie* case.[3] Third, the *Lockerbie* case will be examined in an attempt to show how the Court was inclined to dispose of the issues raised.

JUDICIAL DECISION-MAKING

The International Court of Justice is the principal judicial organ of the United Nations. Its status as a "principal" organ places it on an equal footing with the other organs of the United Nations.[4] As the principal "judicial" organ, its sphere of responsibility is necessarily defined by a conception of what is "judicial." Within the institutional framework of the United Nations organization, this entails a distinction between judicial functions, which under the Charter are the responsibility of the Court, and political and administrative functions, which are the responsibility of other organs of the organization. It is inevitable that, in carrying out the work of the organization, these organs will occasionally focus on the same matter. When this occurs, the relationship between these organs and the scope of their respective functions becomes an issue of considerable importance. If the International Court of Justice is to maintain its distinct identity, "its judicial character and the integrity of the judicial process" must, as Rosenne emphasizes, be preserved at all costs.[5] Only a clear conception of the traditionally accepted difference between political and legal decision-making will enable the Court's distinct identity to be preserved. It will be suggested that this is the key to resolving the issue raised by the dispute in the *Lockerbie* case.

It is generally thought to be philosophically unfashionable to attempt to distinguish legal from political issues. Jurisprudential endeavours to do so in the domestic context are often associated with legal formalism, by which law is perceived to have an innate character that manifests an "intelligible moral order," in contrast to political issues, which concern more open-ended disputes about

[3] See, generally, Stephen M. Schwebel, "Relations Between the International Court of Justice and the United Nations," in *Mélanges Michel Virally* (Paris: Pedone, 1991), 431-44. And for a very useful detailed study see Tetsuo Sato, "An Emerging Doctrine of the Interpretative Framework of Constitutional Instruments as the Constitutions of International Organizations," 21 Hitotsubasti J. Law & Politics 1-64 (1993).

[4] Shabtai Rosenne, *The World Court* 28 (4th ed., Dordrecht: Martinus Nijhoff, 1989).

[5] *Ibid.*

the basic terms of social life.[6] The formalist's apolitical conception of law has been vigorously challenged since early in this century, and a decisive intellectual victory has been widely claimed by its opponents.[7] Accepting for the moment that, perhaps, no meaningful *philosophical* distinction can be made between law and politics, our institutional experience tells us nevertheless that some matters are considered to be appropriate for judicial and others for political determination.

The mistake of traditional theories of legal formalism (or at least the popular interpretations of them) lay in the attempt to distinguish law from politics by reference to some quality of the legal rules and norms themselves. The distinctiveness of law lies instead in the particular *style* of reasoning and the way in which rules are used. In an insightful analysis of the subject, Friedrich Kratochwil expresses this view: "If the constraints for legal decision-making do not lie in the type of norms, such constraints can still lie in the way norms are *used* i.e. in the decision-making *style* which distinguishes legal from other modes of decision-making."[8] The distinguishing features of legal reasoning are attributable to institutional expectations about the use of rules. For example, if one contrasts a legal "rule" with a "policy," it will be seen that a policy leaves the relevant decision-maker with a considerable measure of discretion as to the time, place, and method of implementation, whereas a legal rule provides "relative firm guidance with respect to ends but also *to the means* to be adopted, to the contexts or settings of application, and to admissible and inadmissible exceptions."[9] Further, one speaks of "violating" a legal rule in contrast to "changing" a policy. These features all relate to the contextual specificity of legal rules. Because of the specificity of legal contexts, the finding of the "truth" in legal proceedings is subordinate to what counts as "proof" and what is admissible as evidence.

Legal reasoning is geared to third-party decision-making. In this respect, judicial decision-making is shaped by role expectations. It

---

6 Roberto Unger, "The Critical Legal Studies Movement," 96 Harv. L. Rev. 561 at 565 (1983).

7 Richard Rorty, "The Banality of Pragmatism and the Poetry of Justice," 63 So. Cal. L. Rev. 1811 at 1811-1812 (1990).

8 Friedrich V. Kratochwil, *Rules, Norms, and Decisions* 205 (Cambridge: Cambridge University Press, 1989).

9 *Ibid.*, 206.

is expected that legal rules (and policies) will be applied fairly and consistently. Their application is not a deductive process of subsuming facts within a rule, but is instead a matter of "weighing" or "balancing" the persuasiveness of opposing cases. This touches on one of the key aspects of legal reasoning and judicial decision-making — namely, the way in which a legal issue or case is conceived. A "case" is initially formed by the assertion of one party and the response of another. It takes further shape through the pleadings of the parties and through the decisions of pre-trial procedures. The case itself is largely rhetorical. Each advocate presents a favourable interpretation of the relevant rules and norms and gathers support from previous decisions and other sources of legal authority. Ultimately the judge must make a "decision" and present reasons in support as to which case is the more compelling. The judge's decision is based on the relative persuasiveness of each case rather than on demonstrative reasoning.

These distinguishing features of legal reasoning and judicial decision-making are evident in the rules and procedures of the courts in various jurisdictions. For example, the German Federal Constitutional Court has declared that all judicial rulings must be "founded on rational argumentation." As regards the International Court of Justice, the Rules of Court (1978) contain detailed provisions on the presentation of pleadings and submissions. Article 38 of the Statute of the Court specifies the sources of law that the Court is bound to apply (and which limit the jurisdiction of the Court), and Article 56(1) requires the Court to state the reasons for its decision. Sir Robert Jennings, President of the International Court of Justice, has recently noted some of the defining characteristics of the judicial process of the Court. Addressing the issue of what constitutes a dispute under Article 38 of the statute of the International Court of Justice — a key factor in determining the jurisdiction of the Court — Sir Robert observes that:

. . . the *kind* of legal dispute that the Court can deal with is much affected by the practices and processes of written and oral pleadings; and especially of the requirement of "submissions." Art. 60 of the ICJ Rules, is designed to reduce the whole case to a series of quite specific issues of fact or law, or both, for the Court to determine. The processing of the case, this reduction, or refinement, is practically a concomitant of an adversarial process. A "legal dispute" in a technical and realistic sense is accordingly, one which has thus been processed, or reduced, into a form suitable for decision by a court of law; i.e. a series of specific issues for decision.[10]

Like Kratochwil, Sir Robert Jennings identifies the *form* or *style* of legal proceedings as the critical distinguishing characteristic. It is the form that imposes real substantive constraints on the matters that are appropriate for judicial determination by the International Court of Justice. Sir Robert illustrates his point by reference to the *United States Diplomatic and Consular Staff in Tehran* case, in which the Iranian government, in a letter to the Court, argued that the case brought by the United States was but a secondary aspect of the larger problem of twenty-five years of United States interference in Iran, and hence should not be determined in isolation.[11] The Court rejected Iran's argument, but not because it did not raise a legitimate legal dispute. The rejection was solely due to the failure of Iran to reduce its general claim to specific and particular issues: that is, into a form appropriate for judicial determination.[12] In other words, unless a general contention is particularized into a case that consists of arguments on specific points of fact or law, it is not possible for a court to evaluate opposing positions in the fashion required by a judicial process. It was not, therefore, possible to distinguish the legal dispute from the broader political context.

THE DEMARCATION OF THE COURT'S JUDICIAL FUNCTIONS

To date the International Court of Justice has demonstrated its resolve to preserve the integrity of its judicial functions. The *Hostages* case is an important example of a case in which the Court refused to hold that a legal dispute was non-justiciable on the grounds that it was only one aspect of a broader political problem. In the opinion of the Court:

. . . never has the view been put forward before that, because a legal dispute submitted to the Court is only one aspect of a political dispute, the Court should decline to resolve for the parties the legal questions at issue between them. Nor can any basis for such a view of the Court's functions or jurisdiction be found in the Charter or the Statute of the Court; if the Court were, contrary to its settled jurisprudence, to adopt

10 Sir Robert Jennings, "Reflections on the Term Dispute" in R. St. J. Macdonald (ed.), *Essays in Honour of Wang Tieya on His Eightieth Birthday* 401 at 403 (Dordrecht: Martinus Nijhoff, 1994).

11 *Case Concerning United States Diplomatic and Consular Staff in Tehran (United States of America v. Iran)*, [1980] ICJ Rep. 3 [hereinafter *Hostages*].

12 Jennings, *supra* note 10.

such a view, it would impose a far-reaching and unwarranted restriction upon the role of the Court in the peaceful solution of international disputes.[13]

As Sir Robert Jennings points out, it was the view of the Court that once an issue has been clearly specified and refined so that it is appropriate for rational argument and capable of proof, it is suitable for judicial determination.[14] Because the function of the Court under the Charter and under its own statute is to decide in accordance with international law such disputes as are submitted to it, there is no apparent reason why the Court should declare a matter to be non-justiciable merely because the outstanding legal issue is part of a broader political question. To hold otherwise might effectively, and quite wrongly, eliminate the possibility of a judicial process, because legal issues are frequently situated in a wider political context.[15]

The Court had again to consider the demarcation of its judicial responsibilities in the *Nicaragua* case, in which the United States contested the admissibility of Nicaragua's application to the Court on several grounds.[16] One such ground was that a judicial determination of the issues presented to the Court by Nicaragua would affect the rights and interests of other states in the area that were not parties to the proceedings and that it was "fundamental to the jurisprudence of the Court that it cannot determine the rights and obligations of States without their express consent or participation."[17] Recognizing that in certain circumstances its jurisdiction is indeed limited, the Court referred to its decision in the *Monetary Gold* case as an illustration of jurisdiction having been declined on that basis.[18] In the *Nicaragua* case, however, the Court held that its judgment would bind only the parties and, further, that no indication was made by other states that they intended to initiate separate

---

13 *Supra* note 11 at 20.

14 *Supra* note 10 at 404.

15 Edward Gordon, "'Legal Disputes' Under Article 36(2) of the Statute" in Lori Fisler Damrosch (ed.), *The International Court of Justice at a Crossroads* 183 at 185 (New York: Transnational Publishers Inc., 1987).

16 *Case Concerning Military and Paramilitary Activities in and Against Nicaragua (Nicaragua v. United States of America)*, Jurisdiction and Admissibility, [1984] ICJ Rep. 392 [hereinafter *Nicaragua*].

17 *Ibid.*, 430. Costa Rica, El Salvador, and Honduras were mentioned in this respect.

18 *Monetary Gold Removed from Rome in 1943*, [1954] ICJ Rep. 32 [hereinafter *Monetary Gold*].

proceedings or seek to intervene, steps that they were free to take if they perceived that their interests were being compromised.

A second ground on which the United States contested the admissibility of Nicaragua's application was that the situation at hand involved an ongoing armed conflict which could not, therefore, be resolved effectively without overstepping proper judicial bounds. That was to argue, in effect, that a matter concerning ongoing armed conflict was an inherently political matter. The United States argued that:

> The resort to force during ongoing armed conflict lacks the attributes necessary for the application of the judicial process, namely a pattern of legally relevant facts discernible by the means available to the adjudicating tribunal, establishable in conformity with applicable norms of evidence and proof, and not subject to further material evolution during the course of, or subsequent to, the judicial proceedings.[19]

In rejecting this argument the Court held that:

> A situation of armed conflict is not the only one in which evidence of fact may be difficult to come by, and the Court has in the past recognized and made allowance for this. . . . Ultimately, however, it is the litigant seeking to establish a fact who bears the burden of proving it; and in cases where evidence may not be forthcoming, a submission may in the judgment be rejected as unproved, but it is not to be ruled out as inadmissible *in limine* on the basis of an anticipated lack of proof.[20]

The Court's exposition emphasizes that the judicial process is self-limiting. Provided that a court pays due attention to standards of argument and proof, a matter unsuited for judicial determination will reveal itself once an applicant attempts to formulate a legally persuasive case. On the basis of the preceding discussion, and without in any way asserting that capacious decision-making is in general any more acceptable in the political than in the judicial realm, it seems that it is nevertheless possible to distinguish legal from political decision-making and, consequently, legal from political issues, even when legal and political disputes comprise the same general dispute.

CONCURRENT JUDICIAL AND POLITICAL DECISION-MAKING

A matter of greater controversy arises when the political organs of the United Nations, particularly the Security Council, address the

---

[19] *Supra* note 16 at 436.

[20] *Ibid.*, 437.

same general matter that is before the Court. In that situation, a sharper demarcation must be made between the respective functions of each organ.

While for practical purposes it is possible, indeed necessary, to distinguish legal from political decision-making, as indicated above, the institutional context in which a separation of judicial and political responsibilities occurs may make it more appropriate for some matters to be resolved by either political or judicial means. On this ground it has been argued that the International Court should abstain from determining matters of which the Security Council is seized. The argument is based on the allocation of responsibilities between the organs of the United Nations within the constitutive framework of the United Nations Charter. In particular, the fact that Article 24 of the Charter confers on the Security Council "primary responsibility for the maintenance of international peace and security" raises the question of whether any issue of which the Security Council is seized in respect of the maintenance of international peace and security is the Council's exclusive responsibility. Needless to say, this is an issue of great importance for the future of constitutional development within the United Nations organization.

Before proceeding to examine this question in more detail, it is important to recognize that in general terms there is nothing wrong with the Security Council and the Court acting concurrently in respect of the same matter. The International Court addressed this point and laid it to rest in the *Hostages* case, in which the Court and the Security Council did in fact proceed simultaneously. After the Court had entertained the United States request for an indication of provisional measures, the Security Council, which was already actively seized of the matter, adopted Resolution 461 (1979), of which the preamble expressly took account of the Court's order. Noting this fact, the Court observed:

. . . it does not seem to have occurred to any member of the Council that there was or could be anything irregular in the simultaneous exercise of their respective functions by the Court and the Security Council. Nor is this any cause for surprise. Whereas Article 12 of the Charter expressly forbids the General Assembly to make any recommendation with regard to a dispute or situation while the Security Council is exercising its functions in respect of that dispute or situation, no such restriction is placed on the functioning of the Court by any provision of either the Charter or the Statute of the Court. The reasons are clear. It is for the Court, the principal judicial organ of the United Nations, to resolve any legal questions that may be in issue between parties to a dispute; and the resolution of such questions by the Court may be an important, and sometimes decisive, factor in promoting the peaceful settlement of the dispute.[21]

The Court also referred to paragraph 3 of Article 36 of the Charter, which provides that: "In making recommendations under this Article the Security Council should also take into consideration that legal disputes should as a general rule be referred by the parties to the International Court of Justice in accordance with the provisions of the Statute of the Court."

It is thus clear that in general there is nothing irregular about the International Court determining legal disputes that are part of a political issue being dealt with by the Security Council. Indeed, in respect of the pacific settlement of disputes under Chapter 6 of the Charter, that appears to be the ideal. Whether this is the case when the Security Council is seized of a matter under Chapter 7 of the Charter is more controversial.

In the *Nicaragua* case, the United States argued that, because Nicaragua's allegations amounted to claims that the United States was employing unlawful armed force against Nicaragua, the matter was one that, under the United Nations Charter, properly belonged to the political organs of the organization. In support of this contention, the United States referred to Article 24 of the Charter, which allocates to the Security Council primary responsibility for the maintenance of international peace and security. The essence of the United States argument was that an issue concerning the ongoing use of armed force is inherently a Chapter 7 matter, there being no reference in the Charter to the resolution of such matters other than politically through the Security Council.[22] The United States position was that Nicaragua's complaint amounted to an allegation of aggression and armed conflict envisaged by Article 39 of the Charter, that being a matter that could be dealt with only by the Security Council under Chapter 7, and not by the Court under Chapter 6. In addition, and in support of that general contention, the United States claimed that any judicial determination of the allegations in Nicaragua's application would require the Court to adjudge whether the United States was exercising an inherent right to self-defence under Article 51 of the Charter. Article 51 provides a role only for the Security Council. The United States emphasized that a determination by the Court on that point would mean that

---

[21] *Supra* note 11 at 21-22.

[22] *Supra* note 16 at 432.

the Court and the Security Council would be acting in respect of "virtually identical" claims, since Nicaragua had brought the same allegations before the Security Council before instituting judicial proceedings. The United States argued that, in these circumstances, Nicaragua's application to the Court amounted to an appeal from an adverse determination by the Security Council.[23]

Faced with this complex series of arguments, the Court made an extremely interesting general observation to the effect that the argument of the United States was "an attempt to transfer municipal-law concepts of separation of powers to the international plane" and that "these concepts are not applicable to the relations among international institutions for the settlement of disputes."[24] The Court then referred to its observations in the *Hostages* case, discussed above, which made it clear that there is nothing wrong in principle with the judicial and political organs of the United Nations exercising their jurisdiction concurrently. In respect of the more specific argument about determinations under Article 51, the Court held that the allegations of fact failed to bring Article 51 into play but that, even if they had done so, there was nothing in the provision requiring that determinations under that article be the exclusive responsibility of the Security Council.[25] The Court also held that Nicaragua's allegations did not amount to claims that there was an ongoing conflict between itself and the United States. Further, the Security Council had given no notification that the matter was being dealt with under Chapter 7 of the Charter. Accordingly the matter was held to require peaceful settlement within the terms of Chapter 6. As outlined above, Chapter 6, specifically Article 36, refers to the determination of legal disputes by the Court.

Because the Court found that there was no ongoing armed conflict, that an allegation of unlawful armed force is not necessarily a Chapter 7 matter, and that Article 51 was not applicable on the facts of the case, there was no need to rule on the question of the Court and the Security Council proceeding concurrently when the Security Council is seized of a matter under Chapter 7. Unlike Chapter 6, Chapter 7 of the Charter does not expressly recognize a role for the Court when the Security Council is addressing a matter deemed to constitute a threat to international peace and security. Nevertheless, there is in principle no reason why the relationship

23 *Ibid.*, 432-33.
24 *Ibid.*, 433.
25 *Ibid.*

between the Security Council and the Court should differ in the two situations. This fact was recognized by the Court, which emphasized that Article 24 of the Charter confers on the Security Council the *primary*, not the *exclusive*, responsibility for the maintenance of international peace and security.[26] It was further observed that:

While in Article 12 there is a provision for a clear demarcation of functions between the General Assembly and the Security Council . . . there is no similar provision anywhere in the Charter with respect to the Security Council and the Court. The Council has functions of a political nature assigned to it, whereas the Court exercises purely judicial functions. Both organs can therefore perform their separate but complementary functions with respect to the same events.[27]

The Court made it clear that even if the matter in issue involves the use of armed force, and even if the Security Council is seized of the matter under Chapter 7 of the Charter, the Council and the Court will perform "separate but complementary functions with respect to the same events."

The question of the legitimacy of the concurrent exercise of the functions of the Court and the Security Council when the Council is seized of a matter under Chapter 7 was raised in the recent case concerning the *Application of the Convention on the Prevention and Punishment of the Crime of Genocide (Bosnia and Herzegovina v. Yugoslavia (Serbia and Montenegro))*.[28]

In the *Bosnia-Herzegovina* case, the International Court was faced with an application from Bosnia-Herzegovina for an order of provisional measures against Yugoslavia (Serbia and Montenegro) in respect of alleged violations of Article 9 of the Genocide Convention, "as well as matters which Bosnia-Herzegovina maintains to be connected therewith." Although Bosnia-Herzegovina sought to ground the jurisdiction of the Court on Article 9 of the Genocide Convention, it requested the Court to judge and declare that Yugoslavia (Serbia and Montenegro) had violated and was continuing to violate various articles of the Universal Declaration of Human Rights, obligations under general and customary international law, and obligations under the United Nations Charter, both in respect of the human rights of the people of Bosnia and Herzegovina, and also by using force against Bosnia and

---

26 *Ibid.*, 434.

27 *Ibid.*, 435.

28 Provisional Measures, Order of Sept. 13, 1993, [1993] ICJ Rep. 325 [hereinafter *Bosnia-Herzegovina*].

Herzegovina and intervening in its internal affairs. As a consequence of the latter allegation, Bosnia-Herzegovina sought a
declaration that Security Council Resolution 713 (1991), imposing
a weapons embargo on former Yugoslavia, did not impair Bosnia-
Herzegovina's right of individual or collective self-defence under
Article 51 of the United Nations Charter.

The Security Council had adopted numerous resolutions concerning the former Yugoslavia. It had made decisions intended to be
binding under Article 25 of the Charter and it had expressly indicated that it was acting under Chapter 7. On this basis, Yugoslavia
contended that, in view of these relevant circumstances, "it would be
premature and inappropriate for the Court to indicate provisional
measures, and certainly provisional measures of the type which have
been requested."[29] The Court understood this objection to relate to
the matters raised by Bosnia-Herzegovina that went beyond those
within the scope of the Genocide Convention. Quite rightly, the
Court declined to indicate provisional measures in respect of any of
those matters, because its jurisdiction in the case at hand extended
only to a consideration of the matters within the scope of the Genocide Convention. However, in response to Yugoslavia's objection,
the Court quoted the passage set out above from the *Nicaragua* case,
indicating that, in the event that the Court's jurisdiction had not
been so restricted, the Court and Security Council could perform
their "separate but complementary functions with respect to the
same events," even though the Security Council was seized of the
matter under Chapter 7 of the Charter.

THE DECISION IN THE *Lockerbie* CASE

The *Lockerbie* case obviously troubled the Court. Explaining why
the case posed problems that the Court had not directly encountered to date, Judge Bedjaoui observed as follows:

. . . if the concomitant exercise of concurrent but not exclusive powers
has thus far not given rise to serious problems, the present case, by
contrast, presents the Court not only with the grave question of the
possible influence of the decisions of a principal organ on the consideration of the same question by another principal organ, but also, more
fundamentally, with the question of the possible inconsistency between
the decisions of the two organs and how to deal with so delicate a
situation.[30]

29 *Ibid.*
30 *Supra* note 1 at 143.

The *Lockerbie* case certainly presented a situation in which the binding determinations of the Court and the Security Council could conflict in respect of the same matter. The political processes of the Security Council had produced a decision (Resolution 748) that obliged Libya to extradite the two suspects. A judicial pronouncement on the interpretation of the Montreal Convention of 1971 could conceivably have held that Libya was under no legal obligation to extradite the suspects contrary to its domestic law. Understandably this scenario was perceived to be problematic.

There appear to have been three ways in which the apparent conflict could have been avoided. First, the application before the Court could have been considered non-justiciable. Second, the determination of the Security Council could have been considered *ultra vires*. Third, provided that the matter was justiciable and that the determination of the Security Council was *intra vires*, the conflicting effects of the determinations of the two organs could have been resolved by recognizing that precedence was to be accorded to the enforcement of the decisions of one of them. I will consider the first and third possibilities first because they contain the substantive basis of the judgments of the Court.

JUSTICIABILITY

Earlier observations in this article indicate that in principle there is nothing wrong with the Court and the Council concurrently making determinations in respect of the same matter. In *Lockerbie* this fact was expressly recognized in Judge Ni's declaration, in the separate opinions of Judges Lachs and Shahabuddeen, and in the dissenting opinions of Judges Bedjaoui, Weeramantry, Ajibola, and El-Kosheri. Nothing in the order of the Court, the declaration of Judge Oda, or the joint declaration of Judges Evensen, Tarassov, Guillaume, and Aguilar is contrary to that conclusion. It follows that, if one accepts the legitimacy of the concurrent exercise of the jurisdiction of the Court and the Council, one must also recognize that there is a possibility for conflict between their determinations. Certainly nothing in the Charter or in the statute of the Court indicates that the Court is constrained to avoid any and every disagreement with the Security Council. Indeed it might be argued that any such constraint would be contrary to the allocation of judicial and political functions expressly provided for in the Charter.

Since the decision-making processes of the Court and the Council are different, there is no reason why contrary determinations should undermine the integrity of the decisions of either body. In *Lockerbie* the Court need not, in principle, have been overly concerned to avoid a determination that might conceivably conflict with resolutions of the Security Council; the integrity of Security Council resolutions is based more on a political than a judicial process. As explained above, the style of political decision-making is somewhat different from that of legal decision-making. This view is shared by Tomuschat:

> The World Court is no second-rate organ of the international community. The Charter has not subordinated it to the Security Council. Rather, both organs are duty-bound to co-operate and mutually respect their areas of competence, taking into account their different nature: the Security Council is an action-oriented political organ, whereas the Court is a judicial organ whose function is limited to evaluating in strict legal terms disputes or other legal questions submitted to it.[31]

The distinctness of the political and legal processes is underlined by the fact that the Security Council, when acting under Chapter 7 of the Charter, need not always act in accordance with the usually applicable rules of international law — in fact, the measures that the Council may adopt under Articles 41 and 42 in response to a threat to international peace and security would be unlawful if taken by one state against another.[32] In his dissenting opinion in the *Nicaragua* case, Judge Schwebel expressed this point with lucidity:

> . . . while the Security Council is invested by the Charter with the authority to determine the existence of an act of aggression, it does not act as a court in making such a determination. It may arrive at a determination of aggression — or, as more often is the case, fail to arrive at a determination of aggression — for political rather than legal reasons. However compelling the facts which could give rise to a determination of aggression, the Security Council acts within its rights when it decides that to make such a determination will set back the cause of peace rather than advance it. In short, the Security Council is a political organ which acts for political reasons. It may take legal considerations into account but, unlike a court, it is not bound to apply them.[33]

In the event of conflicting determinations by the Court and the Council the main conclusion to be drawn is that one determination is more legal, the other more political. The fact of difference does

---

[31] Christian Tomuschat, "The Lockerbie Case Before the International Court of Justice," 48 Int'l Comm. Jur. Rev. 38 at 41 (1992).

[32] *Ibid.*, 46.

[33] *Military and Paramilitary Activities in and Against Nicaragua*, Merits, [1986] ICJ Rep. 14 at 290.

not, in itself, tell us anything about the merits of either determination. This point was recognized by Judge Bedjaoui in *Lockerbie*. He pointed out that there was a legal dispute and a political dispute. The legal dispute concerned the interpretation and application of the Montreal Convention of 1971. The Court was asked to determine whether by the terms of the Convention Libya was under a legal obligation to extradite the two suspects. Judge Bedjaoui noted that in parallel with "this very precise legal dispute," the Security Council was being asked to resolve a political dispute in which the United Kingdom and the United States accused Libya of "being implicated in terrorism in general and in the Lockerbie bombing in particular." In his opinion, the disputes were distinct:

> . . . the first dispute concerns the extradition of two Libyan nationals and is being dealt with, legally, by the Court at the request of Libya, whereas the second dispute concerns, more generally, State terrorism as well as the international responsibility of the Libyan State and is being dealt with, politically, by the Security Council, at the request of the United Kingdom and the United States.[34]

Judge Bedjaoui elaborated the distinction by pointing out that the Court was not being requested to pass judgment on state terrorism or on the international responsibility of Libya. Heavily underlining the focus of the legal dispute, he rightly emphasized that, in contrast to the political dispute and solution, a judicial solution would require adherence to higher procedural standards, such as the production of evidence, adversary proceedings, and respect for the due process of the law.[35]

In essence, it is misconceived to treat the decisions of the Court and the Council as conflicting determinations. There is simply no common standard by which a comparison can be made. The *apparent* conflict is with respect to the *effects* of the determinations if they are enforced. The question of what happens as a result of enforcing inconsistent decisions of the Court and the Council is distinct from the question of whether the matter in issue is justiciable. To declare a matter non-justiciable in this context is to deny the *possibility* of determinations with conflicting effects. That, however, is to

---

[34] *Supra* note 1 at 144.

[35] For Judge Bedjaoui's treatment of the *Lockerbie* case and its relation to the ICJ's earlier advisory opinion in the *Monetary Expenses* case, see his "Du contrôle de légalité des actes du Conseil de Sécurité" in *Bibliothèque de la faculté de droit de l'Université Catholique de Louvain*, Tome XXII, 106-107 (Bruxelles: Bruylant, 1993).

constrain the Court in the exercise of its judicial functions. Once the conflict is seen as occurring, if at all, on the level of effects, its resolution has no impact on the capacity of the International Court of Justice or of the Security Council to discharge their respective responsibilities.

CONFLICTING RESULTS

The conflicting results of determinations of the Court and the Security Council relate to the enforcement of orders and decisions. It was on the basis of the priority accorded the decisions of the Security Council acting under Chapter 7 and pursuant to Article 25 of the Charter that the Court refused to prescribe the provisional measures requested by Libya in the *Lockerbie* case.

The potential for conflicting results arose because Security Council Resolution 748 (1992) required Libya to extradite the two suspects. The Court might have contradicted this requirement if it had prescribed provisional measures to protect Libya's rights, conferred *prima facie* by the Montreal Convention of 1971, before the hearings on the merits to determine Libya's rights and obligations under that same Convention and under general international law. As suggested above, this possibility should not raise questions as to the justiciability of the issue. Presuming for the moment that Resolution 748 (1992) was lawful, it clearly bound Libya under Article 25 of the Charter and, pursuant to Article 103 of the Charter, the obligation contained in the restriction would take priority over Libya's rights and obligations under the Montreal Convention of 1971. The potential conflict in the results of the decisions of the Security Council and the Court was easily resolvable, because the status of Resolution 748 was such that it negated the effects of the determination of the Court. This particular analysis was forcefully presented by Judge Bedjaoui, with whom Judge Shahabuddeen agreed.[36] Judge Bedjaoui concluded that "it should have been imperative for the Court to indicate provisional measures on the basis of the facts of the case submitted to it — even if the *effects* of that decision might have been negated by Resolution 748 (1992)."[37]

It is respectfully submitted that the basis of the Court's refusal to indicate provisional measures is perhaps not as clear as it might

---

36 "[T]he Court must take account of the resolution in so far as it affects the *enforceability* of the rights for the protection of which Libya is seeking interim measures": *supra* note 1 at 140.

37 *Supra* note 1 at 158.

have been. The orders of the Court noted that Resolution 748 (1992), which was assumed to have been valid, imposed obligations on the parties that took precedence over any rights or obligations that may have existed pursuant to the Montreal Convention of 1971. The Court held that "whatever the situation previous to the adoption of that resolution, the rights claimed by Libya under the Montreal Convention cannot now be regarded as appropriate for protection by the indication of provisional measures."[38] The rationale of the decision could have been either that an indication of the provisional measures requested would have had no effect or that the Court felt that it should avoid making a determination that would conflict with a binding resolution of the Security Council. It is unclear from the orders on which of these grounds the Court based its decision. Judge Oda's declaration indicates that any incompatibility between Resolution 748 and a decision of the Court would be in respect of their effects.[39] Judge Shahabuddeen, in his separate opinion, was adamant that the orders were based on the former consideration. He stated:

In this case, it happens that the decision which the Court is asked to give is one which would directly conflict with a decision of the Security Council. That is not an aspect which can be overlooked. Yet, it is not the juridical ground of today's Order. This results not from any collision between the competence of the Security Council and that of the Court, but from a collision between the obligations of Libya under the decision of the Security Council and any obligations which it may have under the Montreal Convention. The Charter says that the former prevail.[40]

On the other hand, Judge Lachs's separate opinion attempted to justify the Court's order on the ground that the Court had a responsibility to act in "harmony" with the Security Council in respect of its binding decisions, and therefore, "[t]he Order made should not . . . be seen as an abdication of the Court's powers . . . rather a reflection of the system within which the Court is called upon to render justice."[41] This is perhaps an indication that the Court was eager to avoid conflict with the Security Council. Further to such evidence is the statement in the Orders that an indication of provisional measures "would be likely to impair" the rights

[38] *Ibid.*, 126-127.

[39] *Ibid.*, 129.

[40] *Ibid.*, 141.

[41] *Ibid.*, 139.

prima facie enjoyed by the United Kingdom and the United States by virtue of Resolution 748 (1992). It appears that the Court was reluctant to make a decision that might undermine the effects of Security Council Resolution 748 (1992). Judge Bedjaoui certainly interpreted the Court's orders in that way:

The two Orders do not appear to be an expression of the Court's discretionary power to refrain from indicating provisional measures; on the contrary, they are a result of a power "constrained" by a decision of the Security Council which, among other things, concerned the very object of the legal dispute submitted to the Court.[42]

Despite these hints of an underlying fear of treading on the toes of the Security Council, the Court did not suggest that the matter was non-justiciable for that reason. This raises the question whether, assuming that the matter was justiciable and that the Court had jurisdiction, the failure to determine the rights claimed by Libya under the Montreal Convention and to determine whether in the circumstances those rights warranted the protection of provisional measures meant that the Court shied away from the full discharge of its judicial responsibilities. If the main reason for refusing to indicate provisional measures was that their effect would undoubtedly be negated by Resolution 748 (1992), would it not have been helpful for the Court to have said just that and then to have gone on to explain why that result justified it in not making a decision? In the opinion of Judge Bedjaoui, it was unsatisfactory for the Court to "refrain from exercising its judicial duty and to bow to the Security Council in order to avoid any conflict with it."[43] This is an issue that the Court should have addressed.

The foregoing reservations were shared by other members of the Court. Acting-President Oda found it necessary, in a declaration, to point out that he was not in agreement with the Court basing its decision solely on the ground of Resolution 748 (1992). He said that the Court should have refused to award provisional measures regardless of Resolution 748 (1992) because there was a "mismatch between the object of the Application and the rights sought to be protected."[44] Judge Ni expressed the view that provisional measures should be declined "on the sole ground" that the temporal requirement in Article 14(1) of the Montreal Convention

---

[42] *Ibid.*, 150.

[43] *Ibid.*, 154.

[44] *Ibid.*, 131.

had not been satisfied by Libya; that is to say, that the Court did not have jurisdiction to hear the case.[45] In the opinion of Judge Shahabuddeen, the Court had no choice but to conclude as it did because, "in finding the applicable law, the Court must take account of the resolution in so far as it affects the enforceability of the rights for the protection of which Libya is seeking interim measures."[46] On this point it should be noted that, while the resolution, if valid, undoubtedly bound the parties to the case, it did not constitute the applicable law. In fact, the resolution made no pronouncement whatsoever about the state of the law.

THE LAWFULNESS OF RESOLUTION 748 (1992)

It will be recalled that the settlement of a potential conflict between Resolution 748 (1992) and a decision of the Court indicating provisional measures raised three possibilities. First, the matter could have been considered non-justiciable either because the Court should avoid collisions with the Security Council when the Council is seized of a matter under Chapter 7 of the Charter — a "political" decision — or because any judicial determination would have been unenforceable in the circumstances. Second, the Security Council resolution could have been considered to have been unlawful either because it was *ultra vires* the powers of the Council as conferred by the Charter of the United Nations or because it was otherwise contrary to international law. Third, the decisions of the Court and the Council could have been considered valid within their respective domains and conflicting effects would have been resolved at a later stage.

In *Lockerbie* the Court did not find it necessary to consider the first two possibilities. In particular, the Court found it unnecessary to examine the legality of Security Council Resolution 748 (1992). That issue will not be considered, if at all, until a hearing takes place on the merits.[47] In these circumstances, Resolution 748 (1992) had

---

45 *Ibid.*, 135.

46 *Ibid.*, 140.

47 See Thomas M. Franck, "The 'Powers of Appreciation': Who is the Ultimate Guardian of United Nations Legality?" 86 A.J.I.L. 519 (1992). Art. 103 trumps any rights Libya might have for the purposes of an application for interim measures: see paragraphs 42 and 43 of the order of the Court, *supra* note 1; *contra* Michael W. Reisman "The Constitutional Crisis in the United Nations," 87 A.J.I.L. 83 at 91 (1993).

to be regarded, *prima facie*, as lawful and binding; indeed, it was so regarded in the two orders of the Court. This fact was recognized by the dissenting judges, with two exceptions. Judge Bedjaoui, while recognizing that Security Council Resolution 748 (1992) was in general to be presumed lawful and binding at the stage of the preliminary hearings, nevertheless stated that, if the object of the resolution had been to prevent the Court from exercising its judicial function pursuant to the Charter, it would have been necessary to review the legality of the resolution even at the stage of provisional measures.[48] Judge El-Kosheri paid closer attention to the question of the legality of the resolution; he concluded that it had no legal effect on the jurisdiction of the Court and that, accordingly, the application for provisional measures was to be evaluated in accordance with the "habitual pattern."[49]

Although the Court found it unnecessary to question the legality of Resolution 748 (1992) at the stage of interim measures, Judges Oda and Shahabuddeen indicated that the resolution may indeed be open to question in other circumstances,[50] and Judges Weeramantry, Bedjaoui, and El-Kosheri disclosed a number of issues that may arise at the hearing on the merits and in future cases. A review of the legality of Security Council Resolution 748 (1992) will involve an examination of the limits, if any, on the decision-making powers of the Security Council when the Council acts under Chapter 7 of the Charter. Needless to say, the Security Council enjoys extensive powers once it makes a determination at its discretion that a particular matter presents a threat to international peace and security pursuant to Article 39, thus bringing a matter within the scope of Chapter 7. A decision of the Security Council under Chapter 7 is binding on all members of the United Nations pursuant to Article 25, and pursuant to Article 103 that decision overrides the obligations that states have under other international agreements. In the opinion of some distinguished scholars, the Security Council has the last word when it comes to interpreting the scope of its own powers under the United Nations Charter; the Security Council is infallible, they suggest, not because it is wise but

---

48 *Supra* note 1 at 156, n. 1.

49 *Ibid.*, 212.

50 *Ibid.*, 129 *per* Judge Oda: "a decision of the Security Council, properly taken in the exercise of its competence cannot be summarily reopened." See also *ibid.*, 142 *per* Judge Shahabuddeen.

because it is final.[51] There is some merit in that view, because no organ of the United Nations is specifically authorized by the Charter or by any other authoritative text to review the decisions of the Security Council to ensure that they conform with the Charter and with international law.[52]

Nevertheless, certain provisions in the Charter suggest that the powers of the Security Council are indeed limited. For example, Article 24(2) of the Charter states that "[i]n discharging these duties the Security Council shall act in accordance with the Purposes and Principles of the United Nations." Article 1(1) of the Charter sets out the purposes and principles of the United Nations as follows:

To maintain international peace and security, and to that end: to take effective collective measures for the prevention and removal of threats to the peace, and for the suppression of acts of aggression or other breaches of the peace, and to bring about by peaceful means, and in conformity with *the principles of justice and international law*, adjustment or settlement of international disputes or situations which might lead to a breach of the peace. (Emphasis added.)

An obvious interpretation of Article 24(2), therefore, is that the Security Council is bound to act in accordance with fundamental principles of justice and international law. Judges Weeramantry and Bedjaoui specifically referred to these provisions and expressed the opinion that they require the Security Council to respect the principles of international law.[53] As noted above, Judge Bedjaoui also suggested that Article 24(2) prevents the Security Council from acting in any way that adversely affects the International Court in the discharge of its responsibilities. He observed that each of the United Nations organs is to "carry out its task fully and not to abdicate any part of it." In particular:

---

51 Louis Henkin, "The Security Council During the Decade of International Law: Politics and Law," in B. G. Ramcharan (ed.), *Proceedings* (New York: June 22, 1992). On Art. 103, see R. St. J. Macdonald, "Reflections on the Charter of the United Nations," in Jekewitz, Klein, Kuhne, et al. (eds.), *Festschift fur Karl Josef Partsch* 29-46 (Berlin: Duncker & Humblot, 1989).

52 See Reisman, *supra* note 47 at 93.

53 *Supra* note 1 *per* Judge Weeramantry at 171; *per* Judge Bedjaoui at 155-56. See also Ian Brownlie, "The Decisions of Political Organs of the United Nations and the Rule of Law" in R. St. J. Macdonald (ed.), *Essays in Honour of Wang Tieya on His Eightieth Birthday*, 91 (Dordrecht: Martinus Nijhoff, 1994).

Article 92 of the Charter states that the Court is the principal judicial organ of the United Nations and Article 36 of the Court's Statute, which is an integral part of the Charter, confers upon the Court the power to settle "all legal disputes concerning (a) the interpretation of a treaty, (b) any question of international law."[54]

It would thus appear that there are at least two potential limitations on the powers of the Security Council: (1) the Council must act in accordance with principles of international law, and (2) the Council must not prevent any organ of the United Nations from exercising its responsibilities under the Charter.

It is instructive to observe that Judges Bedjaoui and El-Kosheri also drew on the *Namibia* case, in which the Court expressed views on the potential limits of the decision-making powers of the Security Council.[55] In their dissenting opinions in that case, Judges Gros and Fitzmaurice commented on the Security Council's exercise of its discretion to characterize a situation as a threat to international peace and security, as a result of which the matter is brought within the scope of Chapter 7 of the Charter. Referring to the Security Council's exercise of its discretion in that case, Judge Gros stated that it was another attempt to modify the principles of the Charter as regards the powers vested by states in the organs they instituted. To assert that a matter may have a distant repercussion on the maintenance of peace is not enough to turn the Security Council into a world government.[56] Sir Gerald Fitzmaurice expressed the view that "the Security Council can act in the preservation of peace and security, provided the threat said to be involved is not a mere figment or pretext."[57] Furthermore (he continued), "limitations on the powers of the Security Council are necessary because of the all too great ease with which any acutely controversial international situation can be represented as involving a latent threat to peace and security, even where it is really too remote genuinely to constitute one."[58] Sir Gerald Fitzmaurice went on to say that it was possible for the Security Council to act beyond its competence and, therefore, to be *ultra vires*.

54 *Supra* note 1 at 155.

55 *Legal Consequences for States of the Continued Presence of South Africa in Namibia (South West Africa) notwithstanding Security Resolution 276 (1970)*, Advisory Opinion, [1971] ICJ Rep. 6 [hereinafter *Namibia*].

56 *Ibid.*, 340.

57 *Ibid.*, 293.

58 *Ibid.*, 294. To like effect, see Renata Sonnerfeld, *Resolutions of the United Nations Security Council*, 105 (Dordrecht: Martinus Nijhoff, 1988).

The opinions of Judges Gros and Fitzmaurice are essentially based on a construction of the United Nations Charter. In their view, the determinations of the Security Council regarding the conditions that are necessary for it legally to exercise its powers must be made reasonably. The *Lockerbie* decision, while not expressly addressing that issue at the stage of interim measures, nevertheless leaves open the possibility that the Court can and will review the decisions of the Security Council. Thomas Franck expresses the opinion that the majority and dissenting opinions tacitly agree that there are limits to the competence of the Security Council and that these limits cannot be left exclusively to the Security Council to interpret. Franck concludes that:

The legality of actions by any UN organ must be judged by reference to the Charter as a "constitution" of *delegated* powers. In extreme cases, the Court may have to be the last-resort defender of the system's legitimacy if the United Nations is to continue to enjoy the adherence of its members. This seems to be the tacitly acknowledged judicial common ground.[59]

While this may be the case in theory, it must be recognized that no text in the Charter authorizes any organ to review the reasonableness of the determinations of the Security Council. In this vein, Reisman notes that, while the past exercise of the Court's advisory jurisdiction in the *Expenses* case and in the *Namibia* case may serve as precedents for the legitimacy of a general power of judicial review, "finding criteria to be applied in such review that might limit the Security Council in its peace and security functions is another matter."[60] Reisman concludes that:

Hard substantive and procedural standards for review of Chapter 7 actions are difficult to pinpoint in the Charter. Their very absence, in a context where so much power is assigned to the Council, is telling. A judicial review function, in view of the formal Charter regime, seems somewhat difficult.[61]

Other commentators are unable to accept this view. Tomuschat argues that, if the Court is called upon to apply a resolution of the Security Council, it must be satisfied that the resolution complies with the requirements of lawfulness as established by the United

---

[59] Franck, *supra* note 47 at 523.

[60] Reisman, *supra* note 47 at 92.

[61] *Ibid.*, 93.

Nations Charter.[62] That appears to be a reasonable proposition.[63] In this respect, it is helpful to look at the German constitutional model, in which the German Constitutional Court is the final interpreter of the Federal Republic's constitution. Franck, in reviewing the decisions of government in respect of foreign policy, examines the German model to contrast the role of the courts in Germany with that of the courts in the United States.[64] In the United States, the courts have to some extent abdicated their judicial review function under the famous "political questions" doctrine. Like the United States constitution, the German basic law neither requires nor precludes judicial reticence in foreign relations. Unlike the United States courts, however, the German courts have always exercised their judicial review function. Nevertheless, in conducting that review, the courts (probably in recognition of the distinctiveness of political decision-making) require that a very high onus be satisfied to establish illegality. In general, judges ask whether (1) the policy of the government is a means to a constitutionally sanctioned objective; and (2) it is at least rationally defensible as a means in attaining that objective.[65]

The use of these presumptions in favour of the legality of political decisions may be sufficient to answer the disquiet of those who fear that judicial review of the Security Council's decisions will undermine its ability to respond quickly and effectively to threats to international peace and security. Perhaps in this respect a closer study of the jurisprudence of the Federal Constitutional Court of Germany and of the doctrine of the margin of appreciation developed by the European Court of Human Rights may be useful.[66]

In *Namibia*, Sir Gerald Fitzmaurice suggested that the powers of the Security Council are limited by principles of international law. The Security Council resolutions to which he was referring con-

---

[62] *Supra* note 31 at 48.

[63] *Supra* note 1 at 129, *per* Judge Oda: "a decision of the Security Council, *properly taken in the exercise of its competence*, cannot be summarily reopened" (emphasis added).

[64] Thomas M. Franck, *Political Questions/Judicial Answers*, 107 (Princeton: Princeton University Press, 1992).

[65] *Ibid.*, 118.

[66] See further R. St. J. Macdonald, "The Margin of Appreciation," in R. Macdonald, F. Matscher, and H. Petzold (eds.), *The European System for the Protection of Human Rights*, 83-125 (Dordrecht: Martinus Nijhoff, 1993).

cerned South Africa's rights under its mandate to administer the territory of South West Africa. He observed that:

Even when acting under Chapter 7 of the Charter itself, the Security Council has no power to abrogate or alter territorial rights, whether of sovereignty or administration. . . . [T]his is a principle of international law that is as well-established as any there can be . . . and the Security Council is as much subject to it (for the United Nations is itself a subject of international law) as any of its individual member States are.[67]

Sir Gerald added that: "[I]t was to keep the peace, not to change the world order, that the Security Council was set up."[68] The implication of his view is that the decision-making powers of the Security Council are constrained by the Council's institutional role, which is to react to bona fide threats to international peace and security. While it may, on occasion, be necessary to disregard the rights enjoyed by states on the basis of international law, the action of the Security Council cannot normally extinguish those rights; it merely suspends their enforcement until the threat is no more. If, for its part, the International Court of Justice is called upon to make a determination on the legal rights of a particular state, its judicial responsibilities may require it to point out that decisions of the Security Council purporting to extinguish or seriously alter the legal rights of the state in question do not in fact go that far.[69] In *Lockerbie,* the Court did not discuss whether the Security Council is limited in any way by principles of international law, apart from making passing reference to Article 24(2) of the Charter and to the Court's advisory opinion in *Namibia.* An answer to the question whether the International Court of Justice enjoys an inherent power to review the legality of the actions of the Security Council in accordance with international law awaits another day, probably another case. In the opinion of the present writer it is reasonable to suggest that the Court enjoys an inherent capacity to decide according to the broad values that inform the system of international co-operation embodied mainly but not exclusively by the United Nations Charter.

A powerful argument may be made for such an inherent power of review. One may plausibly contend that the powers conferred on the Security Council by the United Nations Charter need to be interpreted according to the canons of the general corpus of international law. The Charter begs *some* form of interpretive context, if

---

[67] *Supra* note 55 at 294.

[68] *Ibid.,* 294.

[69] See the separate opinion of Judge Onyeama, *ibid.,* 143-44.

broad purposes such as that of "maintain[ing] international peace and security" are to be given precise content. The favourable reference in Article 1(1) of the Charter to the principles of international law suggests that this body of law provides an appropriate interpretive framework for the Charter. If a proper understanding of the powers conferred on the Security Council does indeed require reference to the canons of international law, then the International Court of Justice seems to be the appropriate forum for determining the rightful limits of the Council's authority. The Court's familiarity with international law affords it a special appreciation of the *legal* limits of the Council's powers. Only the Court has the institutional expertise to integrate the Charter into the broader legal totality of which it forms a part. This argument is, of course, open to the rejoinder that the United Nations Charter is a special instrument that must be understood in the light of its own special imperatives, as to which an institution such as the Court has no singular insight.

We are left with an interesting question. By what principles or standards could the Court review the legality of decisions of the Security Council, presuming that the Court is vested with such a power? That is an issue about which very little has been written. On the basis of the discussion in this article and of the scholarly opinions that have been cited, it is possible to identify three different types of standards.

First, in respect of any decision of the Security Council it may be questioned whether the decision is *intra vires* the powers of the Council. The Council's powers are considerable when it acts under Chapter 7 of the Charter. However, as Sir Gerald Fitzmaurice observed in *Namibia*, when the Council exercises its judgment as to whether a matter should be dealt with under Chapter 7, pursuant to Article 39, it must act reasonably and respond only to bona fide threats to international peace and security.

Second, the Security Council, in making its decisions, must comply with standards of procedural fairness. In particular, it should not condemn particular states without giving those states a fair hearing and taking steps to have the relevant facts ascertained objectively. In the political as in the judicial arenas, sound decision-making implies rational justification.[70]

[70] Felice Morgenstern "Legality in International Organizations," 48 Brit. Y. B. Int'l L. 241 at 253 (1976-77); see also Rule 37 of the Rules of Procedure of the Security Council.

The third type of standard is more substantive and less precise. In *Namibia*, Sir Gerald Fitzmaurice referred to the fact that the Security Council has no power to alter "territorial rights." Territorial rights are an example of rights that are recognized at international law, that may be temporarily suspended by decision of the Security Council in order to respond to a threat to international peace and security, but that cannot be extinguished. Any decision by the Council that purports to do so cannot be considered to be legally binding. An example of such a decision was the Security Council's purported settlement of a disputed boundary between Iran and Kuwait. The Council simply has no authority to determine boundaries, since the procedures for doing so are firmly entrenched in international law. Examples of other legal rights may be human rights[71] and rights concerning extradition, such as those that arose in *Lockerbie*. Respect for this type of legal right is arguably essential if the Security Council is to act within the bounds of international law.

CONCLUSION

Despite the need for caution in the context of a delicate political dispute, it would seem that the path was nevertheless clear for the Court to have made a determination on Libya's legal rights pursuant to the Montreal Convention of 1971 and on whether, *prima facie*, those rights warranted the protection of provisional measures. It is true that political events overtook the judicial proceedings and that at the stage of the hearings on interim measures the Court was not in a position to question the legality of Security Council Resolution 748 (1992). An indication of provisional measures as sought by Libya was bound to be of no effect. However, in choosing not to decide, the Court adopted an unnecessarily conservative stance.

In the final analysis it remains unclear just what Libya's legal rights were. Was Libya acting in accordance with the Montreal Convention of 1971? Was Libya legally entitled to refuse to accede to the demands of the United States and the United Kingdom? Although the adoption of Resolution 748 (1992) might make this uncertainty seem unimportant, it is arguable that if the effect of the resolution was to suspend or override the legal rights that Libya would ordinarily enjoy at international law, the Court should have made this fact explicit in its reasoning. If the Security Council is to

71 See Brownlie, *supra* note 53.

be allowed to invoke its extensive powers under Chapter 7 of the Charter to override the legal rights of a state, this is a fact that should be openly recognized.

Sommaire

Le changement des relations entre la Cour internationale de justice et le Conseil de sécurité des Nations Unies

Cet article examine les implications des opinions exprimées dans l'affaire Lockerbie et arrive à la conclusion que les décisions du Conseil de sécurité ne seront pas, dans toutes les circonstances, en dehors de la compétence inhérente de la Cour internationale de justice en matière de révision.

L'initiative juridique canadienne sur la pêche en haute mer

PAUL FAUTEUX*

INTRODUCTION

LE 22 DÉCEMBRE 1992, la 47e session de l'Assemblée générale des Nations Unies décidait la convocation en 1993 d'une conférence intergouvernementale sur les stocks de poissons dont les déplacements s'effectuent tant à l'intérieur qu'au-delà de zones économiques exclusives (stocks chevauchants) et les stocks de poissons grands migrateurs, dont les travaux devraient se terminer avant la 49e session[1] qui se tiendra à l'automne 1994. C'était là un point tournant dans le déroulement d'une initiative juridique sur la pêche en haute mer que menait alors le Canada depuis plus de trois ans.

La Conférence a tenu deux sessions en 1993[2] et en tiendra deux autres en 1994.[3] Il nous a par conséquent semblé utile de faire le point à mi-chemin de ses travaux et de les situer dans le cadre des efforts multiples que déploie le Canada pour briser l'inertie de la

---

* Actuellement Directeur adjoint des Opérations juridiques au Ministère des Affaires étrangères du Canada. Les opinions exprimées ici sont celles de l'auteur et ne représentent pas nécessairement celles du Gouvernement canadien.

---

1 Résolution de l'Assemblée générale des Nations Unies 47/192 du 22 décembre 1992, au para. 1.

2 Une session d'organisation s'est déroulée du 19 au 23 avril, suivie d'une session de fond du 12 au 30 juillet. Voir à cet égard le document A/48/479 du 7 octobre 1993, aux paras. 6 et 8.

3 La résolution 48/72 du 21 décembre 1993 de l'Assemblée générale des Nations Unies prévoit en son paragraphe 3 que la Conférence se réunirait du 14 mars au 1er avril et du 15 au 26 août 1994.

communauté internationale face à la surexploitation des ressources biologiques de la haute mer. Avant de ce faire il nous faut cependant exposer les principaux paramètres du problème, notamment au plan juridique.

II LE CADRE JURIDIQUE

Un nouveau régime juridique a émergé de la troisième Conférence des Nations Unies sur le droit de la mer. La zone précédemment connue sous le nom de haute mer a été considérablement circonscrite par l'extension de la juridiction maritime des États côtiers, jusqu'à 200 millês marins des lignes de base à partir desquelles est mesurée la largeur de la mer territoriale. La liberté de la haute mer et les droits correspondants des États de pêche lointaine ont été restreints par le nouveau droit de la mer. Le concept de zone économique exclusive (ZEE) a été créé et les droits, les obligations et les intérêts de l'État côtier en ce qui a trait aux ressources biologiques de cette zone ont été reconnus.

La Convention des Nations Unies sur le droit de la mer[4] n'est toujours pas en vigueur.[5] Cependant, de l'avis de la majorité des auteurs la pratique des États démontre que la plupart de ses dispositions relatives à la conservation des ressources halieutiques font aujourd'hui partie du droit international coutumier.[6] La Convention prévoit notamment un cadre de coopération en ce qui concerne la conservation et la gestion des ressources biologiques de la haute mer qui débordent des limites nationales. Malheureusement, elle est floue quant aux garanties juridiques et aux obligations concernant les stocks chevauchants et les stocks de grands migrateurs. Les stocks chevauchants, qu'on appelle aussi parfois transzones ou transfrontaliers, sont des stocks de poisson qui se trouvent à la fois dans la ZEE et dans un secteur de la haute mer adjacent à cette zone. Les grands migrateurs sont des espèces de poisson énumérées à l'Annexe I de la Convention, dont près de la moitié

---

[4] Faite à Montego Bay (Jamaïque) le 10 décembre 1982, document A/CONF.62/122 du 7 octobre 1982.

[5] Selon son article 308, la Convention entre en vigueur douze mois après la date de dépôt du soixantième instrument de ratification ou d'adhésion. Cet instrument ayant été déposé par la Guyana le 16 novembre 1993, elle entrera donc en vigueur le 16 novembre 1994.

[6] Voir par exemple Miles et Burke, "Pressures on UNCLOS of 1982 Arising from New Fishing Conflicts: The Problem of Straddling Stocks," (1989) 20 Ocean Dev. & Int'l L. 354.

sont des variétés de thon. Les droits des États côtiers à l'égard de ces deux types de stocks et les obligations qui en découlent pour les États qui les pêchent en haute mer ne sont que vaguement ébauchés dans la Convention.

Ces droits et obligations sont prévus à la Partie VII de la Convention, qui porte sur la haute mer, ainsi qu'à la Partie V sur la ZEE. L'article 87 apparaît dans la section 1 de la Partie VII, qui en contient les dispositions générales. Il énonce dans les termes suivants le principe traditionnel de la liberté de pêche en haute mer, consacré dans la Convention sur la haute mer[7] et bien établi en droit international coutumier:[8]

1. La haute mer est ouverte à tous les États, qu'ils soient côtiers ou sans littoral. La liberté de la haute mer s'exerce dans les conditions prévues par les dispositions de la Convention et les autres règles du droit international. Elle comporte notamment pour les États, qu'ils soient côtiers ou sans littoral. . . .
e) La liberté de la pêche, sous réserve des conditions énoncées à la section 2. . . .
2. Chaque État exerce ces libertés en tenant dûment compte de l'intérêt que présente l'exercice de la liberté de la haute mer pour les autres États. . . .

La section 2 de la Partie VII, que mentionne la disposition précitée, porte sur la conservation et la gestion des ressources biologiques de la haute mer. L'article 116, qui se trouve au début de cette section, énonce comme suit le droit de pêche en haute mer, auquel il apporte d'importantes restrictions:

Tous les États ont droit à ce que leurs ressortissants pêchent en haute mer, sous réserve:
(a) de leurs obligations conventionnelles;
(b) des droits et obligations ainsi que des intérêts des États côtiers tels qu'ils sont prévus, entre autres, à l'article 63, paragraphe 2, et aux articles 64 à 67; et
(c) de la présente section.

Le droit de pêche en haute mer n'est donc pas absolu. D'une part, la formule "ont droit à ce que leurs ressortissants pêchent en haute mer" ne garantit pas la pêche dans toutes les zones de la

---

7 Faite à Genève le 29 avril 1958, en vigueur le 30 septembre 1962, 450 R.T.N.U. 83, art. 2. Le Canada a signé cette Convention le jour de sa conclusion mais ne l'a jamais ratifiée.

8 *Le régime actuel de la pêche en haute mer: situation actuelle et perspectives*, Nations Unies, Bureau des affaires juridiques, Division des affaires maritimes et du droit de la mer, (1992) au para. 9.

haute mer à un moment quelconque.[9] D'autre part, ce droit s'exerce expressément "sous réserve" d'un certain nombre de conditions et notamment "des droits, des obligations et des intérêts des États côtiers" que prévoient certaines dispositions spécifiées de la Convention. L'article 116 rend ainsi le droit de pêche en haute mer tributaire d'obligations relatives à la conservation, qui doivent tempérer le régime du libre accès afin d'assurer la viabilité des stocks de poisson. Il reconnaît en outre que, vu le caractère artificiel de la ligne qui sépare la ZEE d'un État côtier de la haute mer, les intérêts de cet État dans sa ZEE peuvent être affectés par la pêche en haute mer de stocks chevauchants ou des stocks de grands migrateurs.[10]

Le paragraphe 2 de l'article 63, auquel se réfère l'article 116 et qui apparaît dans la Partie V de la Convention, concerne les stocks chevauchants. Il stipule que:

Lorsqu'un même stock de poissons ou des stocks d'espèces associées se trouvent à la fois dans la zone économique exclusive et dans un secteur adjacent à la zone, l'État côtier et les États qui exploitent ces stocks dans le secteur adjacent s'efforcent, directement ou par l'intermédiaire des organisations sous-régionales ou régionales appropriées, de s'entendre sur les mesures nécessaires à la conservation de ces stocks dans le secteur adjacent.

La Convention n'impose donc aux États intéressés qu'une obligation de moyens, puisque par définition une obligation de "s'efforcer de s'entendre" n'exige pas qu'on y parvienne. En outre, elle ne fixe à cette obligation aucune limite de temps et ne prévoit à son égard aucun mécanisme obligatoire[11] de règlement des différends dans l'éventualité où les États ne parviennent pas à s'entendre.

À la troisième Conférence des Nations Unies sur le droit de la mer certains États côtiers avaient tenté à plusieurs reprises, mais en vain, de faire reconnaître leur intérêt spécial[12] en ce qui concerne

---

[9] *Ibid.* au para. 11.

[10] *Ibid.* au para. 12.

[11] Le mot "obligatoire" est employé ici au sens de l'expression anglaise "compulsory and binding," c'est-à-dire qu'il existe une obligation de recourir à un mécanisme de règlement des différends et que la décision qui en résulte est elle-même obligatoire pour les parties au différend.

[12] Ce principe est reflété comme suit dans la *Convention sur la pêche et la conservation des ressources biologiques de la haute mer,* 29 avril 1958, 559 R.T.N.U. 285, art. 6, alinéa 1: "Tout État riverain a un intérêt spécial dans la productivité des ressources biologiques dans toute partie de la haute mer adjacente à sa mer territoriale." L'article 7 autorise l'État riverain dans certaines circonstances à

les stocks chevauchants dans la partie de la haute mer adjacente à leur ZEE.[13] Leur ultime projet d'amendement aurait libellé ainsi le paragraphe 2 de l'article 63 de la Convention:

Lorsqu'un même stock de poissons ou des stocks d'espèces associées se trouvent à la fois dans la zone économique et dans un secteur adjacent à la zone, l'État côtier et les États qui exploitent ces stocks adoptent, par accord mutuel conclu directement ou par l'intermédiaire des organisations sous-régionales ou régionales appropriées, les mesures éventuellement nécessaires à la conservation de ces stocks dans le secteur adjacent. Si l'accord ne peut se faire sur ces mesures dans un délai raisonnable et une procédure est engagée devant le tribunal compétent conformément à l'article 286, ledit tribunal détermine les mesures à appliquer dans le secteur adjacent pour la conservation de ces stocks. Si des mesures définitives ne peuvent être arrêtées dans un délai raisonnable, le tribunal, à la demande de l'un quelconque des États intéressés, prescrit pour ledit secteur des mesures conservatoires. En instituant des mesures définitives ou des mesures conservatoires, le tribunal prend en considération les mesures que l'État côtier applique aux mêmes stocks de poissons dans sa zone économique exclusive et les intérêts des autres États qui exploitent ces stocks.[14]

Déposée vers la fin de la Conférence, cette proposition fut retirée à la demande pressante de son Président[15] le 26 avril 1982, vu l'absence de consensus à son sujet et l'état avancé des travaux. La revendication des États côtiers, visant à faire reconnaître leur intérêt spécial dans la partie des stocks chevauchants située à l'extérieur de leur zone de juridiction exclusive en matière de pêche, n'a donc pas été satisfaite. Les problèmes que pose aujourd'hui la pêche en haute mer, du moins en ce qui concerne ces stocks, sont largement attribuables à ce fait.

---

adopter unilatéralement des mesures de conservation pour cette partie de la haute mer. Le Canada a signé cette Convention le jour de sa conclusion mais ne l'a jamais ratifiée.

13 Pour un exposé détaillé de la genèse du paragraphe 2 de l'article 63, voir Meseguer, "Le régime juridique de l'exploitation de stocks communs de poissons au-delà des 200 milles," (1982) 28 Ann. fran. dr. int. 885; voir également Burke, "Fishing in the Bering Sea Donut: Straddling Stocks and the New International Law of Fisheries" (1989) 16 Ecology L. Q. 285 aux pp. 300-2.

14 Il s'agit du document A/CONF.62/L.114 du 13 avril 1982, présenté par l'Australie, le Canada, le Cap-Vert, l'Islande, les Philippines, Sao Tomé-et-Principe, le Sénégal et le Sierra Leone.

15 R. Applebaum, "The Straddling Stock Problem: The Northwest Atlantic Situation, International Law, and Options for Coastal State Action" dans H. A. Soons, dir., *Implementation of the Law of the Sea Convention Through International Institutions* (1990) à la p. 283.

L'article 64, qui constitue également une restriction au droit de pêche en haute mer aux termes de l'article 116, concerne les grands migrateurs et son paragraphe 1 se lit comme suit:

L'État côtier et les autres États dont les ressortissants se livrent dans la région à la pêche de grands migrateurs figurant sur la liste de l'annexe I coopèrent, directement ou par l'intermédiaire des organisations internationales appropriées, afin d'assurer la conservation des espèces en cause et de promouvoir l'exploitation optimale de ces espèces dans l'ensemble de la région, aussi bien dans la zone économique exclusive qu'au-delà de celle-ci. Dans les régions pour lesquelles il n'existe pas d'organisation internationale appropriée, l'État côtier et les autres États dont les ressortissants exploitent ces espèces dans la région coopèrent pour créer une telle organisation et participer à ses travaux.

L'obligation imposée par cette disposition est donc de "coopérer," ce qui est sans doute plus contraignant que de simplement "s'efforcer de s'entendre" mais pas beaucoup plus. Encore une fois, la Convention ne prévoit ici ni limite de temps ni règlement obligatoire des différends.

Des lacunes semblables caractérisent l'article 117, qui stipule que: "Tous les États ont l'obligation de prendre les mesures, applicables à leurs ressortissants, qui peuvent être nécessaires pour assurer la conservation des ressources biologiques de la haute mer, ou de coopérer avec d'autres États à la prise de telles mesures." La portée de cette obligation est en effet limitée, puisqu'elle n'exige pas qu'un accord soit conclu sur le contenu des mesures qu'elle prescrit.[16]

Il en va de même pour l'article 118, qui traite ainsi de la coopération des États à la conservation et à la gestion des ressources biologiques en haute mer:

Les États coopèrent à la conservation et à la gestion des ressources biologiques en haute mer. Les États dont les ressortissants exploitent des ressources biologiques différentes situées dans une même zone ou des ressources biologiques identiques négocient en vue de prendre les mesures nécessaires à la conservation des ressources concernées. À cette fin, ils coopèrent, si nécessaire, pour créer des organisations de pêche sous-régionales ou régionales.

Bref, les États "coopèrent" et "négocient" mais ils n'arrivent pas nécessairement à s'entendre sur les mesures nécessaires à la conservation des ressources biologiques en haute mer, qui peut alors être sérieusement compromise. Même dans ce cas, aucun mécanisme de

---

[16] W. T. Burke, "U.S. Fishery Management and the New Law of the Sea" (1982) 76 AJIL 48.

règlement obligatoire des différends ne pourra pallier à l'incapacité des États concernés d'en venir à un accord et mettre un frein à la surexploitation qui en découle.

Les obligations générales de conservation et de coopération respectivement énoncées aux articles 117 et 118 sont explicitées dans les termes suivants à l'article 119, qui porte sur la conservation des ressources biologiques de la haute mer:

1. Lorsqu'ils fixent le volume admissible des captures et prennent d'autres mesures en vue de la conservation des ressources biologiques en haute mer, les États:
(a) S'attachent, en se fondant sur les données scientifiques les plus fiables dont ils disposent, à maintenir ou rétablir les stocks des espèces exploitées à des niveaux qui assurent le rendement constant maximum, eu égard aux facteurs écologiques et économiques pertinents, y compris les besoins particuliers des États en développement, et compte tenu des méthodes en matière de pêche, de l'interdépendance des stocks et de toutes normes minimales internationales généralement recommandées au plan sous-régional, régional ou mondial;
(b) Prennent en considération les effets de ces mesures sur les espèces associées aux espèces exploitées ou dépendant de celles-ci, afin de maintenir ou de rétablir les stocks de ces espèces associées ou dépendantes à un niveau tel que leur reproduction ne risque pas d'être sérieusement compromise.
2. Les informations scientifiques disponibles, les statistiques relatives aux captures et à l'effort de pêche et les autres données concernant la conservation des stocks de poisson sont diffusées et échangées régulièrement par l'intermédiaire des organisations internationales compétentes, sous-régionales, régionales ou mondiales, lorsqu'il y a lieu, et avec la participation de tous les États concernés.
3. Les États concernés veillent à ce que les mesures de conservation et leur application n'entraînent aucune discrimination de droit ou de fait à l'encontre d'aucun pêcheur, quel que soit l'État dont il est ressortissant.

Les obligations qu'impose cet article à tous les États, s'agissant de la conservation des ressources biologiques de la haute mer, sont similaires à celles qu'impose l'article 61 aux États côtiers, s'agissant de la conservation des ressources biologiques de la ZEE. Dans les deux cas l'objectif fondamental est d'assurer la pérennité de stocks permettant un rendement constant maximum et d'éviter de compromettre les espèces associées ou dépendantes. Cependant, l'article 61 contient une référence aux "besoins économiques des collectivités côtières vivant de la pêche" qui n'a pas d'équivalent à l'article 119. En outre, le premier établit clairement que c'est l'État côtier qui fixe le volume admissible des captures dans la ZEE. Le second n'en confie la responsabilité en ce qui concerne la haute mer ni à un État particulier, ni à un groupe d'États donnés, mais seulement aux "États."[17]

Ce n'est pas par hasard si les dispositions de la Convention relatives à la conservation et à la gestion en haute mer sont si lacunaires. C'est parce que la création des ZEE a placé plus de 90% des ressources halieutiques de la planète sous la juridiction des États côtiers.[18] Par conséquent, de 1975 à 1982 les négociations sur la pêche ont essentiellement porté sur la ZEE. Le régime de la pêche en haute mer n'a pas réellement été modifié par rapport à ce que prévoyait la première ébauche de la Convention, le texte unique de négociation officieux.[19] C'est ce qui explique que les articles 61 et 62, qui portent respectivement sur la conservation et l'exploitation des ressources de la ZEE, comportent chacun cinq paragraphes alors que les articles 63 et 64 n'en comptent que deux.

De fait, la Convention établit clairement les modalités de la réglementation des pêches à l'intérieur de la ZEE. Il s'agit, pour les États côtiers, d'adopter des mesures qui permettront de pêcher de manière durable. C'est ce que signifie l'article 61, qui prévoit notamment que "l'État côtier . . . prend des mesures appropriées . . . pour éviter que le maintien des ressources biologiques dans sa zone économique exclusive ne soit compromis par une surexploitation" et ajoute que "ces mesures visent aussi à maintenir ou rétablir les stocks des espèces exploitées à des niveaux qui assurent le rendement constant maximum." La Convention établit ainsi une autorité unique pour la gestion et la conservation des ressources biologiques de la ZEE. Les États côtiers qui ont la chance d'en avoir les moyens ont assumé cette responsabilité et se sont dotés de régimes de conservation et de gestion des pêches, qui leur ont d'ailleurs coûté très cher. Bien sûr, on remarque à l'occasion des faiblesses ou des erreurs dans l'exercice du pouvoir de réglementation de la pêche dans la ZEE. Néanmoins, en ce

17 Nations Unies, *supra* note 8 aux paras. 16-17.

18 Selon les plus récentes estimations de l'Organisation des Nations Unies pour l'alimentation et l'agriculture (FAO), en 1989 les flottilles opérant en haute mer ont récolté environ 8% de la production mondiale des pêches maritimes. Voir FAO, *Rapport sur les pêches No 484 Supplément*, Documents présentés à la Consultation technique sur la pêche en haute mer, Rome, 7-15 septembre 1992, au para. 1.

19 Nations Unies, *supra* note 8 au para. 5.

qui concerne son fondement juridique la Convention est parfaitement claire.[20]

On ne peut malheureusement pas en dire autant pour la partie des océans qui s'étend au-delà de 200 milles des côtes. C'est là que règne la liberté de pêcher, là où la Convention n'établit aucune autorité pour la gestion et la conservation des ressources biologiques. Certes, cette liberté n'est pas illimitée, mais nous avons vu les faiblesses des restrictions qui y ont été imposées par la Convention.[21] Comme on peut le lire dans un récent rapport de l'Organisation des Nations Unies pour l'alimentation et l'agriculture, mieux connue sous son sigle anglais de FAO:

Les aspects juridiques des pêches hauturières ne sont pas traités de manière exhaustive par la Convention sur le droit de la mer et lorsque les questions concernant les pêches hauturières sont abordées, on constate, en général, un manque de clarté sur des matières aussi importantes que l'application des mesures de conservation et d'aménagement. Il est donc urgent d'examiner et d'éclaircir ces questions, de manière à adopter un cadre d'aménagement international des pêches hauturières.[22]

Entre temps,

L'exploitation effrénée de peuplements communs au-delà des 200 milles marins peut rendre ineffectives [sic] les mesures, quelles qu'elles soient, prises à l'intérieur de la zone exclusive de 200 milles pour gérer ces peuplements.[23]

III LA SURPÊCHE EN HAUTE MER

Cette faille majeure dans le cadre juridique international nuit à la conservation d'importants stocks de poisson dans diverses régions

[20] Notes pour une allocution de l'Honorable John C. Crosbie, Ministre des Pêches et des Océans et Ministre responsable de l'Agence de promotion économique du Canada Atlantique, devant les représentants de pays réunis le 22 janvier 1993 à St. John's (Terre-Neuve), en prévision de la Conférence des Nations Unies sur la pêche en haute mer (ci-après cité comme discours Crosbie I), à la p. 3.

[21] Ces faiblesses sont telles que les Nations Unies affirment, *supra* note 8 à la note 12, que la relation existant entre les restrictions au droit de pêche en haute mer et les obligations de coopération et de conservation, que la Convention de 1982 a précisée davantage, "ne constitue pas un changement important par rapport aux obligations conventionnelles préexistantes et au droit international coutumier."

[22] FAO, *Situation des pêches dans le monde*, Document préparé pour la Conférence Internationale sur la Pêche Responsable, Cancun, Mexique, 6-8 mai 1992, au para. 35.

[23] Nations Unies, *supra* note 8 au para. 62.

du monde: merlu et calmar dans l'Atlantique sud-ouest, sur la plate-forme patagonienne au large de l'Argentine; hoplostète orange sur le plateau Challenger, au large de la Nouvelle-Zélande; thon dans les océans Atlantique et Pacifique; carangue et poutassou dans les parties centrale et méridionale de l'est du Pacifique, au large du Pérou et du Chili; goberge dans le "Donut Hole," au centre de la mer de Béring, et le "Peanut Hole," au centre de la mer d'Okhotsk, au large de la côte orientale de la Russie; hareng et saumon dans le "Donut Hole" de l'Atlantique nord-est, entre la Norvège, les îles Féroé, l'Islande, l'île de Jan Mayen, le Groenland et l'archipel de Svalbard; morue et aiglefin dans le "Loop Hole" de la mer de Barents, entre la Norvège et la Russie; morue, poissons plats et sébaste sur les Grands Bancs de Terre-Neuve, dans un secteur adjacent à la zone canadienne de 200 milles dans l'Atlantique nord-ouest.[24]

Dans ce dernier secteur, d'importants stocks de poisson sont administrés par l'Organisation des pêches de l'Atlantique nord-ouest (OPANO). On doit également souligner l'existence d'un important stock de morue du nord dans la zone dite 2J3KL au large de la côte nord-est de Terre-Neuve. Ce stock, qui est géré par le Canada, peut être exploité dans une certaine mesure en haute mer.[25]

Dans le cas des eaux qui bordent la côte est du Canada, la surpêche pratiquée au-delà de la limite de 200 milles a contribué sensiblement à réduire les stocks qui chevauchent cette limite.[26] Pendant longtemps cette surpêche était essentiellement le fait de la Communauté économique européenne (CEE). À partir de 1985 celle-ci s'est prévalue de la procédure prévue à l'article XII de la Convention de l'OPANO[27] pour s'objecter à la plupart des mesures de gestion adoptées à chaque année par la Commission des pêches

---

[24] Allocution de l'Ambassadeur Louise Fréchette de la mission permanente du Canada à la quarante-septième session de l'Assemblée générale des Nations Unies, Point 79: Rapport de la Conférence des Nations Unies sur l'environnement et le développement, New York, le 22 décembre 1992, Communiqué de presse no 28 (ci-après cité comme discours Fréchette), à la p. 1; Gouvernement du Canada, "Le Canada participera à la séance d'organisation d'une conférence de l'ONU," communiqué C-AC-93-36F du 16 avril 1993, à la p. 2.

[25] Sur l'OPANO et la morue du 2J3KL, voir P. Fauteux, "L'Organisation des pêches de l'Atlantique nord-ouest et le conflit Canada-CEE" (1994) 2 Revue de l'Institut du droit économique de la mer, à paraître.

[26] Discours Fréchette, *supra* note 24 à la p. 1.

[27] *Convention sur la future coopération multilatérale dans les pêches de l'Atlantique nord-ouest*, 24 octobre 1978, R.T. Can. 1979 no 11, en vigueur le 1er janvier 1979.

de l'Organisation.[28] Elle a ensuite adopté ce qu'elle a appelé des "quotas autonomes" pour certains stocks gérés par l'OPANO et a permis à ses navires d'en pêcher d'autres sans restriction aucune. La majorité de ces quotas étaient supérieurs aux prises tradition-nelles des États membres de la CEE. Au fil du temps certains d'entre eux en vinrent même à dépasser le niveau des prises réali-sées par les navires de la CEE alors qu'ils n'étaient soumis à aucune réglementation communautaire. Ces quotas étaient en fait si élevés qu'ils n'avaient plus aucun rapport avec un quelconque système de contrôle.[29] Tout cela a fait que les prises de la CEE ont très large-ment dépassé les quotas qui lui étaient attribués par l'OPANO. Ses prises ont même parfois excédé le montant des "quotas auto-nomes" qu'elle s'était fixés,[30] voire la totalité du TAC pour certains stocks.[31]

Suite à l'effondrement de la morue du 2J3KL en 1992, qui forçait le Canada à interdire complètement à ses navires de pêcher ce

28 Applebaum, *supra* note 15 à la p. 286. Celui-ci situe le début du problème en 1986, année au cours de laquelle s'appliquaient les mesures adoptées en 1985 et auxquelles s'était objectée la CEE. L'article XII de la Convention de l'OPANO prévoit que les membres de la Commission des pêches peuvent présenter des objections aux propositions que celle-ci a adoptées. Les proposi-tions visées deviennent alors des mesures exécutoires pour toutes les Parties contractantes, sauf pour celles qui s'y sont objectées.

29 Pêches et Océans Canada, Notes for an address by Dr. Peter Meyboom, Deputy Minister of Fisheries and Oceans, to the Northwest Atlantic Fisheries Organiza-tion, Ottawa, September 13, 1988 (cité ci-après comme discours Meyboom), aux pp. 10-11. À titre d'exemple, voir Commission des Communautés euro-péennes (CCE), Proposition de Règlement (CEE) du Conseil relatif à la conclusion de l'accord sous forme d'échange de lettres entre la Communauté économique européenne, d'une part, et le gouvernement du Canada, d'autre part, concernant leurs relations dans le secteur de la pêche, document COM(93) 214 final, Bruxelles, 17 mai 1993. Le tableau annexé à ce document démontre qu'en 1988 la Communauté a unilatéralement fixé ses quotas pour l'année suivante à 156,590 tonnes, soit plus de 11 fois ceux que lui avait attribués l'OPANO, alors que ses prises pour l'année en cours n'étaient que de 65,939 tonnes.

30 Le tableau annexé au document de la CCE (*supra* note 29) démontre qu'en 1986 les quotas attribués à la CEE par l'OPANO (le document dit "proposés") s'élevaient à 25,360 tonnes, alors que ses prises étaient de 151,404 tonnes, soit 5.9 fois plus. Ces prises étaient 18.8% plus élevées que les "quotas autonomes" que la CEE avait fixés à 127,440 tonnes. En 1987, 88 et 89, le rapport entre les prises de la CEE et les quotas que lui avait attribués l'OPANO était respective-ment de 5.6, 3.4 et 6.2.

31 Discours Meyboom, *supra* note 29 à la p. 9.

stock, la CEE a consenti à "réintégrer le cadre de la NAFO."[32] À la réunion annuelle de l'OPANO cette année-là elle déposait conjointement avec le Canada une proposition interdisant la pêche à la morue du 3L dans la Zone de réglementation[33] en 1993, qui fut adoptée à l'unanimité. De plus, la CEE acceptait tous les quotas de l'OPANO pour la première fois depuis 1985 et affirmait qu'elle n'établirait pas de quotas plus élevés pour ses membres en 1993.[34] Mais d'autres navires ont continué de surexploiter les ressources de la Zone de réglementation. Il s'agit de navires battant les pavillons d'États non-membres de l'OPANO, notamment de la Corée du Sud, et de navires espagnols et portugais réimmatriculés sous des pavillons de complaisance afin de les soustraire aux mesures internationales de conservation adoptées par cette Organisation.

Pourquoi certains pays tolèrent-ils que des navires battant leur pavillon ou que leurs ressortissants pratiquent la surpêche en haute mer? Parce que cela rapporte beaucoup d'argent, tout simplement. L'appât du gain est particulièrement grand lorsque les ressources d'un État font l'objet de mesures de conservation. En effet, ironiquement, tant que des États conserveront les ressources à l'intérieur de leur ZEE, la surexploitation de ces mêmes ressources à l'extérieur de cette zone par d'autres États sera une solution "viable," du moins à court terme. Cependant, tout bascule lorsque le taux de surexploitation dépasse la capacité de reconstitution de la ressource.[35]

Dans l'état actuel des choses, la tentation est simplement trop grande pour certains États de remplir leurs cales pendant que les autres agissent de manière responsable, sous l'égide d'une organisation régionale de conservation des pêches. C'est exactement ce qui s'est passé dans l'Atlantique nord-ouest.[36] À ce propos, les

[32] CCE, *supra* note 29 à la section I, para. 5.

[33] Selon l'article premier, paragraphe 2, de la Convention de l'OPANO, *supra* note 27, la "Zone de réglementation" désigne la partie de la Zone de la Convention qui s'étend au-delà des régions dans lesquelles les États côtiers exercent leur juridiction en matière de pêche. Les coordonnées géographiques de la "Zone de la Convention" sont définies au paragraphe 1 du même article.

[34] Pêches et Océans Canada, "L'OPANO adopte à l'unanimité l'interdiction, pour 1993, de pêcher la morue de la division 2J3KL en dehors de la limite de 200 miles," communiqué C-AC-92-76F du 18 septembre 1992. Le tableau annexé au document de la CCE (*supra* note 29) confirme que le Conseil européen n'a pas adopté de "quotas autonomes" pour 1993.

[35] Discours Crosbie I, *supra* note 20, aux pp. 4-5.

[36] *Ibid.* à la p. 5.

chiffres suivants sont éloquents: de 1986 à 1992 les États membres de l'OPANO ont réduit l'ensemble des TAC pour les stocks autres que le calmar dans la Zone de réglementation de 167,965 à 153,365 tonnes,[37] soit une diminution de 8.5%. Au cours de la même période, les prises des États non-membres réalisées à partir de ces mêmes stocks sont passées de 19,300 tonnes, alors qu'elles représentaient 11.5% des TAC, à 42,600 tonnes ou 27.7%.[38] Autrement dit, pendant que les membres réduisaient leur ponction sur la ressource, les non-membres augmentaient l'importance relative de la leur de 140%.

Dans les régions où aucun contrôle n'est exercé, la situation est encore pire. C'est chacun pour soi, puisque ce que vous ne prenez pas quelqu'un d'autre le prendra. C'est ce qui s'est passé dans le Donut Hole et ce qui s'est ensuite répété dans le Peanut Hole: les navires des États de pêche lointaine, obligés d'abandonner le premier secteur qu'ils avaient vidé de sa ressource, se sont rabattus sur le second situé à relative proximité et encore riche en poisson. Que la pêche soit ou non gérée par une organisation régionale, la surpêche appauvrit fatalement la ressource et celle-ci finit par s'effondrer.[39] Tout État côtier dans les eaux duquel évoluent des stocks chevauchants ou des stocks de grands migrateurs est par conséquent susceptible de devenir la prochaine victime des pillards de la haute mer, toujours en quête d'une nouvelle ressource à surexploiter.

IV DES ÉLÉMENTS DE SOLUTION MULTIPLES

Comment faire pour que les États de pêche lointaine respectent leur obligation de coopérer entre eux et avec les États côtiers intéressés à la conservation des stocks de poisson de la haute mer? Le Canada a choisi de travailler sur plusieurs fronts pour y arriver, afin de faire échec à la surpêche dans la Zone de réglementation de l'OPANO.

[37] Northwest Atlantic Fisheries Organization (NAFO), Meetings and Decisions 1979-1992 (1993) 359 et 365.

[38] NAFO, Meeting of the Standing Committee on Fishing Activities of Non-Contracting Parties in the NAFO Regulatory Area (STACFAC), Dartmouth, Canada, 28-30 April 1993, Data on Non-Contracting Parties Activities in the NAFO Regulatory Area, NAFO/GC Doc. 93/2, 7.

[39] Discours Crosbie I, *supra* note 20, à la p. 5.

A   L'OPANO

Depuis la création de cette Organisation en 1978, le Canada cherche par son entremise à contrôler la pêche hors de sa zone de 200 milles. Malheureusement, l'OPANO n'a pas réussi à résoudre des aspects clés du problème de la surpêche sur les Grands Bancs. Il aura fallu que le stock de morue du 2J3KL s'effondre pour que la CEE consente enfin à respecter ses mesures de conservation. L'Organisation n'a pas non plus pu faire obstacle à la pêche non réglementée par des navires battant des pavillons d'États non-membres de l'OPANO, dont plusieurs ont des équipages composés de ressortissants d'États membres de la Communauté.

Il n'en demeure pas moins que toute amélioration apportée au fonctionnement de l'OPANO contribuera à rendre plus durables les pêcheries dont celle-ci est responsable et c'est pourquoi le Canada cherche à la renforcer. Par exemple, il a proposé d'amender la Convention de l'OPANO pour limiter le recours à la procédure d'objection prévue par son article XII, afin de faire en sorte que les membres de l'Organisation respectent les quotas qu'elle établit.[40] Il coopère également avec les autres membres pour mettre un terme à la surpêche par les États non-membres dans la Zone de réglementation. C'est ainsi qu'à la réunion annuelle de 1993 le Canada, le Japon, la CEE et la Russie se sont entendus pour constituer une délégation de haut niveau chargée de faire pression sur les États non-membres. Le but de cette démarche collective était de faire en sorte que les États en question retirent de cette Zone les

[40] Documents NAFO GF/92-279 du 15 juin 1992 et GF/92-308 du 13 juillet 1992. Voir à ce sujet *supra* la note 28 et le texte l'accompagnant. Les amendements canadiens auraient limité les motifs pour lesquels une Partie contractante pourrait présenter une objection à une proposition adoptée par la Commission des pêches. Dans le cas d'une proposition relative aux quotas dans la Zone de réglementation, celle-ci devrait ne pas tenir suffisamment compte de la part traditionnelle de la Partie qui s'objecte ou de l'attention particulière à laquelle a droit l'État côtier en vertu de l'alinéa 4 de l'article XI de la Convention de l'OPANO. Dans le cas de toute autre proposition, celle-ci devrait ne pas être conforme aux dispositions de la Convention ou créer une discrimination de forme ou de fait à l'encontre de la Partie qui s'objecte. Ces amendements auraient en outre établi pour toutes les Parties contractantes le droit de contester une objection présentée par l'une d'entre elles et un mécanisme obligatoire de règlement des différends qui pourraient surgir à cet égard. Aucun accord n'ayant pu se faire sur le fond de la proposition canadienne, il fut convenu d'en reporter l'examen à une date indéterminée. Voir NAFO, *supra* note 37, à la p. 296.

navires battant leur pavillon ou qu'ils retirent à ces navires le droit de battre ce pavillon.[41]

B L'ACCORD AVEC LA CEE

Une entente bilatérale avec la CEE représenterait évidemment une bonne partie de la solution du problème dans l'Atlantique nord-ouest. Le Canada a été très encouragé lorsque au cours de l'été 1992 la CEE a ordonné à ses navires de cesser de pêcher dès que les quotas étaient atteints. Cette décision contrastait avec les années précédentes où même ses quotas unilatéraux avaient été dépassés.[42] La "réintégration du cadre" de l'OPANO par la CEE en septembre de la même année a constitué un autre signe encourageant.[43] Enfin, toujours en 1992, la Commission européenne a proposé d'apporter des changements importants à la politique commune sur les pêches. Ces changements auraient soumis les navires communautaires à des contrôles plus stricts et auraient permis de s'attaquer plus efficacement au problème de la pêche par les navires d'États non-membres de l'OPANO.[44]

C'est cette nouvelle attitude de la Communauté qui a permis le paraphe à Bruxelles le 17 décembre 1992 d'un Accord sur ses relations de pêche avec le Canada. Le Conseil des ministres des Pêches de la CEE l'a approuvé le 20 décembre 1993. Il ouvrait ainsi la voie à la signature de l'accord et à son entrée en vigueur qui mettront officiellement un terme à sept ans de guerre du poisson entre les deux parties. L'élément essentiel de cet Accord, c'est le retour par la CEE au respect des quotas et des autres décisions de l'OPANO qu'elle a pratiqué jusqu'en 1985. S'y ajoutent notamment la fixation par le Canada d'un TAC pour la morue du 2J3KL et la limitation des prises de ce stock par les États membres de l'OPANO autres que le Canada à l'extérieur de sa zone de 200 milles à 5% du TAC. Il prévoit en outre des modalités renforcées de contrôle de la pêche par les navires communautaires et une volonté

---

41 Pêches et Océans Canada, "Les décisions de l'OPANO: des pas dans la bonne direction," communiqué C-AC-93-80F du 10 septembre 1993, à la p. 2.

42 Notes pour une allocation de l'Honorable John C. Crosbie, Ministre des Pêches et des Océans et Ministre responsable de l'Agence de promotion économique du Canada Atlantique, au sujet d'une entente conclue avec la Communauté européenne en matière de pêches, le 21 décembre 1992 (ci-après cité comme discours Crosbie II), à la p. 2.

43 Voir *supra* les notes 32 à 34 et le texte les accompagnant.

44 Discours Crosbie II, *supra* note 42, à la p. 3.

de coopérer avec le Canada pour résoudre le problème de la pêche par les États non-membres de l'OPANO et élaborer un mécanisme de règlement des différends pour empêcher le recours abusif à la procédure d'objection. En échange le Canada traitera la CEE sur le même pied que tous les autres États qui coopèrent avec lui en matière de conservation. Cette égalité de traitement s'appliquera à l'accès à ses ports, à l'octroi de quotas de poisson excédentaire dans sa zone de pêche et à la coopération commerciale.[45]

C   LES ÉTATS NON-MEMBRES

Une troisième voie suivie par le Canada a consisté à exiger de manière bilatérale le retrait par les États non-membres de l'OPANO de leurs navires de pêche de la Zone de réglementation de l'Organisation. Le Canada a également exercé des pressions auprès des États qui délivrent des pavillons de complaisance pour qu'ils imposent de lourdes amendes aux navires qui, battant leur pavillon, pêchent dans cette Zone sans quota attribué par l'OPANO. Ces démarches ont déjà remporté un certain succès.

Ainsi, suite à des pressions répétées du Canada, la République de Corée a retiré ses navires de la Zone réglementaire de l'OPANO à la fin d'avril 1993. Les navires de ce pays, qui à l'époque n'était pas membre de l'OPANO et n'en recevait par conséquent aucun quota, pêchaient néanmoins dans cette Zone depuis plusieurs années. On estime qu'ils y ont pris environ 24,000 tonnes de morue, de sébaste, de plie et de flétan en 1992 seulement.[46]

En 1992 le Panama a convenu d'agir sur la base de rapports officiels canadiens sur les activités de navires immatriculés chez lui. Il s'est engagé à imposer aux contrevenants des sanctions sévères, notamment des amendes ou le retrait de l'immatriculation, afin de garantir le respect des mesures de conservation telles que celles de l'OPANO.[47] Il a en outre fait de l'engagement de se conformer à de

---

[45] Pour plus de détails au sujet de cet Accord, voir Fauteux, *supra* note 25.

[46] Pêches et Océans Canada, "La pêche étrangère hors de la zone canadienne de 200 milles," Fiche d'information, septembre 1993, à la p. 1. La République de Corée a accédé à la Convention de l'OPANO le 21 décembre 1993.

[47] Gouvernement du Canada, communiqué du 14 avril 1992. Ce document reprend le texte d'un communiqué conjoint émis à l'occasion de la visite au Panama de l'Honorable John C. Crosbie, ministre des Pêches et des Océans du Canada. Ce document parle de "garantir le respect des mesures de conservation, telles les mesures de l'OPANO, adoptées par la République du Panama de concert avec d'autres pays." La formule est étrange et ne reflète

telles mesures une condition de l'immatriculation des navires de pêche.[48] D'avril 1992 à décembre 1993 le Panama a mis à l'amende 19 de ses navires et a retiré leur immatriculation à 5 d'entre eux.[49]

Le Canada a également obtenu du Venezuela qu'il retire le permis de pêche de deux navires battant son pavillon. Le Maroc, le Sierra Leone et le Vanuatu ont retiré l'immatriculation de certains de leurs navires ou leur ont interdit de pêcher dans la Zone de réglementation de l'OPANO. Malgré cela au cours de l'année 1993 une trentaine de navires battant le pavillon d'États non-membres de l'OPANO pêchaient toujours sans quota dans cette Zone.[50] Le Canada a annoncé son intention de poursuivre ses efforts jusqu'à ce qu'ils en aient tous été retirés.[51]

D L'ACCORD DE LA FAO

Un des principaux obstacles au contrôle de la pêche en haute mer est l'adoption par certains navires de pavillons de complaisance pour se soustraire aux mesures internationales de conservation et de gestion comme celles qu'adopte l'OPANO. Environ 20 % des navires de pêche opérant en haute mer à travers le monde sont inscrits dans ce qu'il est convenu d'appeler des "registres ouverts." Cela leur permet notamment de réduire les taxes et les autres coûts d'opération et de contourner les normes nationales et internationales du travail. Au cours des dernières années on en est venu à considérer cette pratique comme l'expression d'une volonté de contourner également les quotas de pêche.[52] Ce constat a conduit à la négociation sous l'égide de la FAO de l'Accord visant à favoriser le respect par les navires de pêche en haute mer des mesures

---

vraisemblablement pas l'intention des parties puisque, n'étant pas membre de l'OPANO, le Panama ne peut pas participer à l'adoption de ses mesures de conservation.

48 *Ibid.*

49 Pêches et Océans Canada, *supra* note 46, à la p. 1.

50 Interview réalisée le 29 décembre 1993 avec M. Bob Applebaum, Directeur général des Affaires internationales au ministère des Pêches et des Océans du Canada (ci-après citée comme interview Applebaum). Dès l'origine M. Applebaum a été intimement mêlé à la conception et à la mise en oeuvre de l'initiative juridique canadienne sur la pêche en haute mer.

51 Pêches et Océans Canada, *supra* note 46, aux pp. 1-2.

52 FAO, "Adoption d'un projet d'accord sur le respect par les navires de pêche en haute mer des mesures de conservation et de gestion des ressources biologiques marines," communiqué PR 93/47 C/20 du 23 novembre 1993, à la p. 2.

internationales de conservation et de gestion,[53] à laquelle le Canada a activement participé.

Les principales dispositions de cet Accord sont les suivantes. Tout d'abord:

> Chaque Partie prend les mesures qui peuvent être nécessaires pour s'assurer que les navires autorisés à battre son pavillon n'exercent aucune activité susceptible de compromettre l'efficacité de mesures internationales de conservation et de gestion.[54]

Les États non-membres de l'OPANO ne sont pas juridiquement liés par la Convention créant cette Organisation et par les mesures de conservation et de gestion qu'elle adopte. En devenant Parties à l'Accord de la FAO, ils seraient néanmoins tenus de faire en sorte que les navires autorisés à battre leur pavillon "n'exercent aucune activité susceptible de compromettre l'efficacité" de ces mesures. Cette obligation exigerait notamment que ces navires s'abstiennent de pêcher sans quota dans la Zone de réglementation de l'Organisation. Du point de vue du Canada, le principal intérêt de l'Accord de la FAO est donc le fait que, par son entremise, les mesures de conservation et de gestion de l'OPANO deviendraient indirectement applicables aux États non-membres.

L'Accord prévoit en outre qu'

> aucune Partie ne permet à un navire de pêche autorisé à battre son pavillon d'être utilisé pour la pêche en haute mer à moins qu'il n'ait été autorisé à être ainsi utilisé par la (ou les) autorité(s) compétente(s) de ladite Partie. Un navire de pêche ainsi autorisé doit pêcher en se conformant aux conditions de l'autorisation.[55]

Il ajoute que:

> Chaque Partie prend des mesures d'exécution à l'encontre des navires autorisés à battre son pavillon qui contreviendraient aux dispositions du présent Accord, y compris, s'il y a lieu, des mesures visant à assurer que de telles contraventions constituent une infraction au regard de la législation nationale.[56]

Enfin, chaque Partie doit tenir un fichier des navires de pêche autorisés à battre son pavillon et à être utilisés pour la pêche en

---

[53] Document C 93/LIM/26 de la vingt-septième session de la Conférence de la FAO, tenue à Rome du 6 au 25 novembre 1993, annexe G (ci-après cité comme Accord FAO).

[54] *Ibid.* art. III, para. 1(a).

[55] *Ibid.* art. III, para. 2.

[56] *Ibid.* art. III, para. 8.

haute mer.[57] Elle met à la disposition de la FAO, pour ce qui concerne chaque navire de pêche inscrit dans ce fichier, des informations détaillées et à jour.[58] Elle lui fournit également les détails pertinents concernant toute activité de navires de pêche, qu'ils soient ou non autorisés à battre son pavillon, qui compromet l'efficacité de mesures internationales de conservation et de gestion.[59] La FAO communique ces informations à toutes les Parties et individuellement, sur demande, à chaque Partie.[60]

Cet Accord a été élaboré avec une exceptionnelle rapidité, reflétant l'importance du problème et la volonté de la communauté internationale d'y apporter une solution. Suite à une proposition faite par les États-Unis, une recommandation en ce sens a d'abord été faite par la Consultation technique sur la pêche en haute mer tenue par la FAO en septembre 1992.[61] Le Conseil de la FAO est convenu en novembre de la même année qu'un accord international était nécessaire sur les navires de pêche battant pavillon de complaisance pour éviter de se conformer aux mesures de conservation et de gestion.[62] Un petit groupe officieux d'experts s'est réuni du 1 au 5 février 1993 à Rome pour élaborer un projet d'un tel accord.[63] Les États membres de la FAO en furent saisis en mars dans le cadre de son Comité des Pêches. Un Groupe de travail à composition non limitée formé pour examiner le projet d'Accord n'a alors pas été en mesure d'en mettre le texte définitivement au point.[64] En juin un Comité technique à composition non limitée du Conseil de la FAO a rédigé une version révisée de l'Accord, dont un certain nombre de dispositions n'ont cependant pas été pleinement approuvées.[65]

---

[57] *Ibid.* art. IV.

[58] *Ibid.* art. VI, paras. 1, 2, 3, 5, 6, 7 et 9.

[59] *Ibid.* art. VI, para. 8.

[60] *Ibid.* art. VI, paras. 4 et 10.

[61] FAO, Rapport sur les pêches no 484, Rapport de la Consultation technique sur la pêche en haute mer, Rome, 7-15 septembre 1992, paras. 42-45.

[62] FAO, document CL 102/REP, Rapport du Conseil de la FAO, cent deuxième session, Rome, 9-20 novembre 1992, paras. 58 et 59.

[63] FAO, document COFI/93/10, Comité des pêches, vingtième session, Rome, 15-19 mars 1993, annexe 2.

[64] FAO, document CL 103/7, Conseil, cent troisième session, Rome, 14-25 juin 1993, paras. 77-82 et annexe F.

[65] FAO, document CL 103/REP, Rapport du Conseil de la FAO, cent troisième session, Rome, 14-25 juin 1993, para. 68.

Des consultations informelles se sont tenues à ce sujet en juillet, en marge de la Conférence des Nations Unies sur les stocks de poissons chevauchants et les stocks de poissons grands migrateurs. Un accord officieux y a été réalisé sur la quasi-totalité des dispositions restées jusqu'alors entre crochets.[66] Sur la base d'observations soumises par des membres de la FAO, le Comité des questions constitutionnelles et juridiques a étudié le texte révisé par le Comité technique en octobre et y a proposé un certain nombre d'amendements.[67] D'autres observations ayant été reçues par la suite, un Comité technique à composition non limitée du Conseil de la FAO s'est réuni les 2 et 3 novembre et est parvenu à un consensus sur une version révisée de l'Accord.[68] Le Conseil l'a approuvée à l'unanimité[69] et la Conférence de la FAO l'a adopté le 24 novembre 1993,[70] à peine un an après la décision du Conseil qui avait lancé le processus.

Cet Accord "constitue une réussite considérable et un événement marquant dans la gestion internationale des pêches en haute mer."[71] Il est ouvert à l'adhésion des membres ou membres associés de la FAO, ainsi que des États membres de l'Organisation des Nations Unies (ONU) ou de l'Agence internationale de l'énergie atomique.[72] Il entrera en vigueur à la date de réception par le Directeur général de la FAO du vingt-cinquième instrument d'adhésion.[73] Le Canada a été le premier Etat à déposer un tel instrument le 20 mai 1994.

V L'INITIATIVE JURIDIQUE

Par ailleurs, le Canada souhaite une solution mondiale au problème de la surpêche en haute mer. Il cherche à faire établir des

[66] FAO, document CCLM 61/3, Comité des questions constitutionnelles et juridiques, soixante-et-unième session, Rome, 4-6 octobre 1993, annexe II.

[67] FAO, document CL 104/3, Rapport de la soixante-et-unième session du Comité des questions constitutionnelles et juridiques, Rome, 4-6 octobre 1993, para. 17.

[68] FAO, document CL 104/REP, Rapport du Conseil de la FAO, cent quatrième session, Rome, 2-5 novembre 1993, para. 92.

[69] *Ibid.* au para. 93.

[70] FAO, *supra* note 52. Ce communiqué soulignait l'adoption de l'Accord en Commission le 23 novembre. La Conférence y a procédé en plénière le lendemain.

[71] Résolution 15/93 du 24 novembre 1993 de la Conférence de la FAO, para. 2.

[72] Accord FAO, *supra* note 53, art. X, para. 1.

[73] *Ibid.* art. XI, para. 1.

règles et des mécanismes internationaux efficaces pour assurer la conservation et la gestion des ressources halieutiques au-delà de la limite de 200 milles. Autrement dit, il veut faire adopter des règles conformes au droit de la mer, auxquelles tous les États pêchant en haute mer acceptent de se plier, et capables de mettre un terme à la surexploitation de ces ressources.[74] L'établissement de règles contraignantes, qui préciseraient les dispositions vagues de la Convention sur le droit de la mer et donneraient de la substance à l'obligation qu'elle impose aux États de coopérer entre eux afin de conserver et de gérer les ressources biologiques de la haute mer, tel est l'objectif de l'initiative juridique canadienne.

Cette initiative était au départ un des trois volets de la stratégie mise au point en 1989 par les autorités canadiennes pour mettre un terme à la surpêche pratiquée par les navires communautaires dans la Zone de réglementation de l'OPANO. Il y avait également une initiative diplomatique, faite de représentations au niveau politique, y compris par le Premier ministre du Canada, auprès des autorités européennes. S'y ajoutait enfin une initiative de relations publiques, qui prévoyait des contacts suivis avec les médias, surtout européens, pour expliquer le point de vue du Canada dans cette affaire.[75] Même si ces deux initiatives devaient à court terme être couronnées de succès, il était dès le départ entendu que l'initiative juridique serait poursuivie. Celle-ci visait en effet à mettre définitivement fin à la surpêche, par le biais de règles contraignantes plutôt que par un arrangement politique ponctuel.[76]

L'initiative juridique se déroule actuellement dans le cadre de la Conférence des Nations Unies sur les stocks de poissons chevauchants et les stocks de poissons grands migrateurs. Avant de passer en revue les travaux de la Conférence et d'examiner ses chances de succès, rappelons tout d'abord les principaux événements qui ont mené à sa convocation.

---

[74] Gouvernement du Canada, L'initiative juridique du Canada, document d'information, décembre 1992.

[75] Interview réalisée le 14 décembre 1993 avec M. Serge April, alors Haut-Commissaire adjoint du Canada à Londres (ci-après citée comme interview April). Jusqu'en 1992 M. April était Directeur général des Affaires juridiques au ministère des Affaires extérieures, auquel titre il a été intimement mêlé à la conception et à la mise en oeuvre de l'initiative juridique canadienne sur la pêche en haute mer.

[76] Interview Applebaum, *supra* note 50.

A   ST. JOHN'S-RIO ALLER-RETOUR

1   La voie coutumière

En 1989 la meilleure façon d'élaborer des règles nouvelles de droit international pour empêcher la surpêche en haute mer n'était pas évidente. Formellement, il aurait fallu convoquer de nouveau la troisième Conférence des Nations Unies sur le droit de la mer afin de préciser le contenu des normes floues de la Convention qu'elle a adoptée. Or, rouvrir le texte de la Convention aurait été inacceptable à la grande majorité des États. Cela était particulièrement vrai tant que n'étaient pas réglées les difficultés relatives à sa Partie XI, portant sur l'exploitation des ressources minérales des grands fonds marins, qui avaient inhibé sa ratification par la quasi-totalité des États industrialisés[77] et ainsi retardé son entrée en vigueur.[78]

À défaut de pouvoir négocier des changements à la Convention sur le droit de la mer, la seule voie qui s'ouvrait alors au Canada était de favoriser l'émergence de normes coutumières, entreprise évidemment aléatoire et surtout de longue haleine. Les responsables de la mise en oeuvre de l'initiative juridique canadienne se mirent par conséquent à consulter des collègues de pays amis, à publier des articles, à participer à des réunions d'experts et même à en convoquer. Tout ceci était fait dans l'espoir que l'accumulation des textes et des opinions puisse un jour former un corps de doctrine que, avec la pratique des États qu'il aurait par hypothèse contribué à orienter, le Canada pourrait opposer aux États qui pratiquent la surpêche en haute mer.[79]

2   St. John's I

C'est dans ce contexte que le Canada a convoqué la Conférence sur la conservation et la gestion des ressources biologiques en haute mer à St. John's, Terre-Neuve, du 5 au 7 septembre 1990. Cette Conférence internationale a rassemblé des experts juridiques et

---

[77] Au 1er janvier 1994 l'Islande était le seul État industrialisé à avoir déposé un instrument de ratification ou d'adhésion.

[78] Le Secrétaire général de Nations Unies à mené pendant plusiers années des consultations informelles pour surmonter ces difficultés. Ces consultations sont débouché sur l'Accord relatif à la Partie XI de la Convention des Nations Unies sur le droit de la mer de 1982, adopté par la résolution 48/263 de l'Assemblée générale des Nations Unies des 28 juillet 1994 et signe par le Canada le 29 juillet 1994.

[79] Interview April, *supra* note 75.

scientifiques de seize pays ainsi que des observateurs de l'ONU et de la FAO. Elle devait se pencher sur les problèmes de la haute mer, à la lumière des dispositions pertinentes de la Convention sur le droit de la mer. Selon le Secrétaire d'État aux Affaires extérieures de l'époque, le très honorable Joe Clark, elle avait pour objectif d'"intensifier la sensibilisation et la coopération internationale qui s'imposent si l'on veut régler une fois pour toutes ces graves problèmes."[80] Elle a été présidée par le premier Ambassadeur du Canada pour la conservation des pêches, M. J. Alan Beesley. Celui-ci avait dirigé la délégation canadienne à la troisième Conférence des Nations Unies sur le droit de la mer et présidé le Comité de rédaction de cette Conférence.

Les experts réunis à St. John's ont convenu de certains principes fondamentaux, à savoir:

— les membres de la communauté internationale dont les ressortissants pêchent en haute mer doivent coopérer entre eux et avec les États côtiers adjacents pour la conservation, ce qui implique des mesures d'application et le règlement des différends;
— les membres d'organisations régionales de gestion des pêches ont le devoir de s'assurer que leurs ressortissants observent toutes les mesures de conservation et n'usent pas d'artifices comme la réimmatriculation des navires pour échapper aux contrôles;
— les États éloignés doivent voir à ce que la pêche pratiquée par leurs ressortissants en haute mer n'ait pas de conséquence néfaste sur les ressources vivantes relevant de la compétence des États côtiers;
— le régime de gestion appliqué en haute mer aux stocks chevauchants et aux stocks de grands migrateurs[81] devrait concorder avec le régime de gestion adopté et mis en oeuvre pour ces mêmes stocks par les États côtiers dans leur ZEE.[82]

---

80 Gouvernement du Canada, "La Conférence de St. John's recherche des solutions juridiques à la surpêche en haute mer," communiqué no 188 du 4 septembre 1990.

81 Dès la Conférence de St. John's il était clair que, si certains pays partageaient la préoccupation du Canada à l'égard des stocks chevauchants, l'intérêt principal de la majorité des États côtiers concernait les stocks de grands migrateurs et devrait être pris en considération. Voir Ministère des Affaires extérieures, Bureau des Affaires juridiques, *Quelques exemples de questions courantes de droit international d'une importance particulière pour le Canada*, octobre 1993, 19.

82 Gouvernement du Canada, *supra* note 74. Ces quatre paragraphes correspondent aux conclusions 4, 10, 11, 14 et 15 de la Conférence de St. John's (International Conference on the Conservation and Management of the Living Resources of the High Seas, St. John's, Newfoundland, 5-7 September 1990, Conclusions). Notons toutefois que, contrairement aux treize premières, les

Les conclusions de la Conférence de St. John's reflétaient des opinions partagées par un nombre croissant d'États sur la façon d'interpréter et d'appliquer la Convention sur le droit de la mer. Au premier chef, on y trouve le principe voulant qu'une compréhension et une coopération internationales accrues avec les États côtiers, pour tout ce qui touche à la pêche dans les secteurs adjacents à leur ZEE, soient des conditions essentielles pour garantir une conservation et une gestion efficaces des stocks chevauchants et des stocks de grands migrateurs.

3   La route de Rio

L'étape suivante vers un contrôle efficace des pêches en haute mer a été franchie à l'occasion d'une réunion d'experts sur le droit de la mer convoquée par l'ONU à Santiago en mai 1991. Les experts du Chili, de la Nouvelle-Zélande et du Canada ont alors préparé une série de mesures et de principes s'inspirant des conclusions de St. John's et que l'on a baptisé le texte de Santiago.[83] Au nombre des principes énoncés dans ce document figuraient notamment les trois suivants: l'intérêt spécial de l'État côtier à l'égard des stocks chevauchants et des stocks de grands migrateurs; la concordance entre les mesures de conservation applicables à ces stocks en haute mer avec celles que leur applique l'État côtier dans sa ZEE; et l'absence d'impact négatif de la pêche en haute mer sur les ressources dans la ZEE.

Ce document fut révisé à l'occasion d'une autre rencontre d'experts sur la conservation des ressources de la haute mer, organisée sous l'égide de l'ONU à New York en juin 1991.[84] L'expert de l'Argentine y a manifesté son adhésion aux idées défendues par ceux du Canada, du Chili et de la Nouvelle-Zélande. Ensemble ces quatres experts ont réussi à rallier autour du texte de Santiago ceux de plusieurs autres États côtiers.

La prochaine étape consistait à soumettre le texte de Santiago à une tribune multilatérale plus large, où se réuniraient des représentants des États et non plus des experts s'exprimant à titre personnel.

---

conclusions 14 et 15, qui portent toutes deux sur le principe de concordance et respectivement sur les stocks chevauchants et les stocks de grands migrateurs, commencent par les mots "la plupart des participants sont convenus que."

[83] *Ibid.*

[84] Cette réunion avait été convoquée pour discuter d'une première ébauche de ce qui allait devenir le document des Nations Unies, cité *supra* la note 8.

En 1989 l'Assemblée générale avait décidé la convocation de la Conférence des Nations Unies sur l'environnement et le développement (CNUED), prévue pour juin 1992.[85] Celle-ci devait notamment adopter Action 21, un programme d'action pour le développement durable au vingt-et-unième siècle, dont le projet comportait une section sur la conservation des ressources biologiques de la mer. L'occasion était belle d'insérer dans ce document les principes du texte de Santiago sur la conservation des pêches en haute mer, afin d'en faire un autre élément du corps de doctrine que le Canada cherchait à établir.[86]

Dans la foulée des réunions de Santiago en mai et de New York en juin, la troisième session du Comité préparatoire de la CNUED se tenait à Genève du 12 août au 4 septembre 1991. À cette occasion le texte de Santiago révisé fut déposé par un groupe de dix-sept États côtiers[87] et prit le nom de document L.16. C'était la première fois que se constituait un groupe d'États appuyant formellement les thèses canadiennes. Parmi ceux-ci figurait l'Islande, qui avait rejoint l'Argentine, le Chili et la Nouvelle-Zélande au sein du petit groupe de pays avec lesquels le Canada coordonne depuis sa stratégie dans cette affaire.

L'opposition des États pratiquant la pêche lointaine, notamment européens, empêcha que le document L.16 ne soit reflété dans le projet révisé d'Action 21 autrement qu'entre crochets.[88] À la fin de la réunion de Genève les stocks chevauchants et les stocks de grands migrateurs étaient une des cinq questions en suspens dans la section sur les ressources biologiques marines du chapitre 17 d'Action 21, portant sur la protection des océans, de toutes les sortes de mers, y compris les mers fermées et semi-fermées, et des zones côtières et la protection, l'utilisation rationnelle et le développement de leurs ressources biologiques.[89] Déjà il était clair que les principes fondamentaux d'intérêt spécial, de concordance et

---

85 Résolution de l'Assemblée générale des Nations Unies 44/228 du 22 décembre 1989.

86 Interview April, *supra* note 75.

87 Document A/CONF.151/PC/WG.II/L.16 du 15 août 1991, présenté par l'Argentine, la Barbade, le Canada, le Chili, la Guinée, la Guinée-Bissau, l'Islande, Kiribati, la Nouvelle-Zélande, le Pérou, le Samoa, les Îles Salomon et le Vanuatu.

88 Interview April, *supra* note 75.

89 International Institute for Sustainable Development (IISD), Earth Negotiations Bulletin, volume 7, number 1, July 12, 1993, à la p. 1.

d'absence d'impact négatif que défendait le Canada se heurtaient à une véhémente opposition de la part de certaines délégations, dont au premier chef celle de la CEE. Il était par conséquent peu probable qu'ils soient reflétés dans Action 21, dont l'adoption était prévue par consensus.[90]

Afin de ne pas rater ce qu'Yves Fortier, alors Représentant permanent du Canada à l'ONU, avait appelé "une occasion unique d'obtenir l'appui de la communauté internationale dans ce dossier,"[91] le Canada ajusta alors sa stratégie pour Rio. John Crosbie, le ministre des Pêches et des Océans de l'époque, annonçait que la surpêche étrangère était un des sujets prioritaires que le Canada entendait y aborder et que son objectif était double: faire approuver par les leaders mondiaux réunis au Sommet de la Terre certains principes et mesures, d'une part, et solliciter une conférence de suivi pour examiner ces questions plus en détail, d'autre part.[92] Cette nouvelle exigence, à l'effet que la tenue d'une conférence des Nations Unies consacrée exclusivement à la pêche en haute mer de stocks chevauchants et de stocks de grands migrateurs devrait faire partie du suivi de Rio, s'appuyait également sur la diversité des sujets confiés à la CNUED et le fait qu'il devait en résulter une série de recommandations non contraignantes.[93]

Quelques jours plus tard le ministre Crosbie faisait comprendre en des termes à peine voilés que l'initiative juridique du gouvernement fédéral canadien sur la pêche en haute mer était en fait une alternative aux appels pressants que lui adressaient les provinces de l'Atlantique, et en particulier celle de Terre-Neuve, pour qu'il règle le problème de la surpêche étrangère sur le "Nez" et la "Queue" des Grands Bancs en étendant unilatéralement sa juridiction en matière de pêche au-delà de la limite des 200 miles.[94] Le ministre

[90] Interview April, *supra* note 75.

[91] Gouvernement du Canada, Le Canada fait part aux Nations Unies de ses préoccupations concernant la surpêche, communiqué no 284 du 12 décembre 1991.

[92] Pêches et Océans Canada, "Le Canada accroît ses efforts pour mettre fin à la surpêche étrangère," communiqué C-AC-92-01F du 3 janvier 1992.

[93] Gouvernement du Canada, *supra* note 74.

[94] Le rapport de l'Étude indépendante sur l'état des stocks de morue du nord (Rapport Harris), préparé en février 1990 à l'intention de l'honorable Thomas E. Siddon, Ministre des Pêches et des Océans, contenait une recommandation 5 libellée comme suit:

Que le Canada conclue une entente internationale lui accordant la gestion de tous les stocks de poissons indigènes du plateau continental canadien qui

s'exprimait ainsi à Londres, devant le Royal Institute of International Affairs:

Le gouvernement est de plus en plus pressé par les Provinces atlantiques à agir unilatéralement à l'extérieur des 200 milles. Cette démarche et ses conséquences possibles sont des solutions qu'aucun pays ne veut envisager.

Le temps presse pour les ressources surexploitées et pour les collectivités de pêche qui en tirent leur subsistance. Des progrès réels devront être faits en 1992, sinon il faudra penser sérieusement à d'autres options.[95]

C'est donc avec ce genre de pressions à l'esprit que les représentants du Canada ont abordé la quatrième session du Comité préparatoire, tenue à New York du 2 mars au 3 avril 1992. Celle-ci était

---

se déplacent hors de la zone de 200 milles; et, s'il ne peut atteindre cet objectif, qu'il prenne des mesures unilatérales en vue d'acquérir les droits de gestion conformément aux dispositions du Traité sur le droit de la mer.

En répondant à cette recommandation le gouvernement fédéral observa que:

À ce stade, le droit international ne permet pas à un État côtier de prendre des mesures unilatérales de gestion au-delà de la zone de 200 milles.

Voir Pêches et Océans Canada, Réponse du gouvernement aux recommandations formulées dans l'Étude indépendante sur l'état des stocks de morue du nord, 7 mai 1990, à la p. 7.

Le 1er mai l'Honorable Walter Carter, ministre des Pêches de Terre-Neuve, avait rendu public par l'entremise du Newfoundland Information Service le contenu d'une lettre qu'il venait d'adresser à l'Honorable Bernard Valcourt, ministre des Pêches et des Océans du Canada, dans laquelle il se disait profondément déçu par le rejet fédéral de la recommandation précitée, à son avis trop hâtif. M. Carter y ajoutait que le problème de la surpêche étrangère était un des plus sérieux auxquels faisait face l'industrie de la pêche de sa province et que celle-ci ne pouvait pas attendre éternellement pour y trouver une solution négociée.

Les déclarations publiques de membres du Gouvernement de Terre-Neuve de ce genre se sont multipliées et intensifiées au cours des années suivantes. Ainsi, en avril 1992 le Premier ministre Wells affirmait lors d'une visite en Belgique qu'à défaut d'un règlement multilatéral rapide et efficace, le Canada devrait envisager l'imposition de la "gestion fiduciaire" (*custodial management*) des stocks chevauchants "afin d'assurer l'avenir de cette ressource pour toutes les nations." Selon M. Wells une décision unilatérale du Canada en ce sens lui permettrait de gérer efficacement les ressources du Nez et de la Queue des Grands Bancs "pour protéger les intérêts des utilisateurs internationaux". Voir Notes for an address by the Honourable Clyde K. Wells, Premier of Newfoundland and Labrador, to the Royal Institute of International Affairs, April 28, 1992, Brussels, Belgium, à la p. 9.

95 Pêches et Océans Canada, "Crosbie dit à un auditoire étranger qu'il faut agir vite dans la crise de la surpêche étrangère," communiqué du 10 janvier 1992.

saisie d'un projet de chapitre 17 préparé par le Secrétariat qui ne contenait aucune référence à la pêche en haute mer, tellement le sujet avait été source de division à Genève.[96] Suite à une série de représentations auprès des délégations participantes le document L.16 fut co-parrainé par 40 États,[97] ce qui correspondait à la majorité de ceux qu'intéressait le problème de la surpêche.

Au cours de ces représentations la délégation canadienne s'est vite rendue compte de la valeur de l'argument environnemental à l'appui de sa cause. En effet, ses arguments juridiques ne convainquaient pas. Ils donnaient au contraire l'impression que le Canada ne cherchait en réalité qu'à étendre sa juridiction contrairement à la Convention sur le droit de la mer et à s'accaparer plus de poisson aux dépens des autres. De même, ses arguments économiques, basés sur l'impact de la surpêche étrangère sur les revenus des pêcheurs de Terre-Neuve, n'étaient pas de nature à impressionner les représentants d'États en développement. Par contre, en dénonçant le pillage et l'épuisement d'une ressource biologique et alimentaire appartenant à l'humanité tout entière, le Canada cessait de passer pour un égoïste. Ce sont ses adversaires qui dès lors semblaient vouloir continuer de piller sans vergogne.[98]

Un groupe de contact sur les ressources biologiques marines (domaines d'activité C et D du chapitre 17) se réunit à huis clos pendant presque quatre des cinq semaines disponibles pour tenter de trouver un consensus, mais en vain.[99] La plupart des principes du document L.16 furent reflétés d'une façon ou d'une autre, sauf les trois qui étaient fondamentaux pour le Canada mais, comme à Genève, inacceptables pour les États hauturiers. Au début de la cinquième semaine le blocage était total. Le Canada fit alors savoir par l'entremise de la présidence américaine du groupe de contact qu'il serait prêt à ne pas insister sur l'approbation des principes qui lui tenaient à coeur par la CNUED, à condition que celle-ci con-

[96] IISD, *supra* note 89.

[97] Document A/CONF.151/PC/WG.II/L.16/Rev.1 du 16 mars 1992, présenté par Antigua-et-Barbuda, l'Argentine, les Bahamas, la Barbade, le Bélize, le Canada, le Chili, les Comores, les îles Cook, le Costa Rica, le Cuba, la Dominique, le Fidji, la Gambie, la Guinée, la Guinée-Bissau, la Guyana, l'Islande, la Jamaïque, le Kenya, le Kiribati, les Maldives, les îles Marshall, la Mauritanie, l'Île Maurice, la Nouvelle-Zélande, la Papouasie-Nouvelle-Guinée, le Pérou, les Philippines, le Saint-Kitts-et-Nevis, la Sainte-Lucie, les Îles Salomon, le Samoa, le Sri Lanka, la Tanzanie, les îles Tonga et le Vanuatu.

[98] Interview April, *supra* note 75.

[99] IISD, *supra* note 89.

vienne de la convocation d'une conférence des Nations Unies qui les examinerait en détail (et qui lui permettrait de continuer à se battre pour l'adoption des principes en question, plutôt que de les voir définitivement annihilés par le droit de veto que conférait en pratique à ses opposants la règle du consensus qui prévalait à la CNUED). Cette idée d'une conférence fut appuyée par tous les États de pêche lointaine, qui y voyaient un compromis raisonnable, sauf la CEE. La plénière adopta par conséquent le chapitre 17 avec des crochets autour des paragraphes relatifs aux stocks chevauchants et aux stocks de grands migrateurs et la question fut référée au Sommet de Rio pour y être résolue au niveau politique.[100]

Entre temps les efforts du Canada et de son ministre des Pêches et des Océans mettaient de plus en plus l'accent sur la convocation d'une conférence des Nations Unies. Au cours des mois précédents le Canada avait notamment cherché à obtenir l'appui de l'URSS,[101] du Japon[102] et des États membres de la CEE[103] à ses thèses. Ces dernières tentatives n'avaient apparemment pas été fructueuses. En effet, au moment où M. Crosbie transportait en mai sa "croisade contre la surpêche étrangère"[104] à la Conférence de Cancun sur les pêches responsables, il déclarait que, parmi les 66 pays participants, seule la CEE s'opposait à la tenue d'une conférence sur les pêches hauturières.[105]

Poursuivant ses efforts pour surmonter cette opposition, quelques semaines plus tard le ministre canadien se rendait à Washington pour solliciter l'appui des États-Unis. Comme il l'avait fait

---

100 Interview April, *supra* note 75.

101 Pêches et Océans Canada, "MM. Valcourt et Kotlyar signent une déclaration d'intention sur la conservation en haute mer," communiqué C-AC-90-036F du 22 août 1990.

102 Gouvernement du Canada, "Crosbie demande au Japon d'appuyer les mesures visant à mettre fin à la surpêche en haute mer," communiqué C-AC-92-05F du 17 janvier 1992.

103 Pêches et Océans Canada, "Au cours d'une conférence en Espagne, le ministre exigera la fin de la surpêche," communiqué C-AC-91-059-F du 5 septembre 1991.

104 Pêches et Océans Canada, "Le ministre Crosbie transporte sa croisade contre la surpêche étrangère à Cuba et au Panama," communiqué C-AC-92-28F du 10 avril 1992.

105 Pêches et Océans Canada, "M. Crosbie est fier de la réussite du Canada à Cancun," communiqué C-AC-92-37F du 11 mai 1992.

avant de se rendre à Cancun,[106] à la veille de son départ il rappelait qu'en plus de décider de la convocation d'une conférence sur la pêche en haute mer, le Canada voulait que la CNUED reconnaisse:

les droits et les responsabilités spéciaux des États côtiers en vertu du Droit de la mer, pour conserver les stocks qui migrent au-delà de la limite et sont capturés en haute mer.[107]

Autrement dit, le Canada cherchait toujours à obtenir à Rio ce qu'il n'avait pas pu avoir à la troisième Conférence des Nations Unies sur le droit de la mer: la consécration de l'intérêt spécial de l'État côtier dans la partie des stocks chevauchants qui se trouve dans un secteur de la haute mer adjacent à sa ZEE.[108]

4   Le Sommet de la Terre

La veille de l'ouverture de la CNUED la CEE annonçait qu'elle suspendait sa pêche au stock de morue du 2J3KL dans le secteur de la haute mer adjacent à la ZEE canadienne. Cela faisait sept ans qu'elle pêchait ce stock en dépit du moratoire de l'OPANO dont il faisait l'objet.[109] Les déclarations antérieures du Canada, qui avait à maintes reprises caractérisé la surpêche en haute mer comme "un problème environnemental global qui exige une solution globale,"[110] n'y étaient sans doute pas étrangères. On pouvait en effet penser que cette annonce reflétait la volonté de la CEE d'éviter un débat potentiellement gênant sur ses pratiques de

---

[106] Pêches et Océans Canada, "M. Crosbie mettra l'accent sur l'environnement et la surpêche au Mexique," communiqué C-AC-92-035F du 4 mai 1992.

[107] Pêches et Océans Canada, "M. Crosbie demande aux États-Unis d'appuyer les objectifs canadiens à la CNUED," communiqué C-AC-92-041F du 26 mai 1992.

[108] Voir à ce propos *supra* les notes 13 à 15 et le texte s'y rapportant.

[109] Reuter, EC to suspend fishing for cod off Canada, Brussels, June 1, 1992. Cette dépêche précisait que la CEE s'était fixée un quota de 27,000 tonnes de morue pour l'année en cours et qu'il avait déjà été presque complètement pris. L'annonce par la Commission européenne dont elle se faisait l'écho avait elle-même été précédée par une déclaration des autorités espagnoles le 28 mai à l'effet qu'elles retireraient une partie de leur flotte de pêche du Nez des Grands Bancs de Terre-Neuve à titre de "geste pour le Canada." Cette déclaration avait été faite à l'occasion de la visite en Espagne d'une délégation composée de représentants de l'industrie de la pêche et de parlementaires des provinces de l'Atlantique du Canada, qui s'inscrivait dans le cadre de l'initiative de relations publiques mentionnée dans le texte accompagnant la note 75. Voir Canadian Press, Canada-Spain-Cod, Madrid, May 28, 1992.

[110] Voir par exemple Pêches et Océans Canada, *supra* note 106.

pêche dans l'Atlantique nord-ouest. L'hypothèse est particulièrement plausible dans une enceinte aussi médiatisée que la CNUED
où chacun des participants s'efforçait de paraître aussi "écologique-
ment correct" que possible.

Le texte présenté à Rio du domaine d'activité C du chapitre 17
d'Action 21, qui traite de l'utilisation durable et de la conservation
des ressources biologiques marines en haute mer, comportait tous
les éléments du document L.16. Cependant les principes d'intérêt
spécial, de concordance et d'absence d'impact négatif auxquels
s'opposait toujours la CEE y étaient exprimés entre crochets.
Pour sa part la délégation canadienne avait fait savoir qu'elle était
prête à reprendre publiquement la bataille sur ces trois principes.
En outre, le ministre canadien des Pêches et des Océans Crosbie
et le Premier ministre Wells de Terre-Neuve arrivaient à la fin
de la première semaine. Il était clair que, pour des raisons de
politique intérieure, les deux hommes n'hésiteraient pas en cas de
besoin à dénoncer une fois de plus les pratiques de pêche de la
Communauté.[111]

Lorsque la question fut débattue en Comité plénier, tous les
intervenants cherchèrent par conséquent à inciter la Communauté
à accepter le compromis mis de l'avant par les États-Unis à New
York. On se rappellera que ce compromis prévoyait la convocation
d'une conférence des Nations Unies sur la pêche en haute mer à
laquelle seraient débattus les trois principes prônés par le Canada.
Le Président du Comité plénier et ancien Président du Comité
préparatoire, l'Ambassadeur Tommy Koh de Singapour, conclut ce
bref débat en demandant au représentant américain de poursuivre
ses consultations informelles et de lui faire rapport.[112]

La CEE proposa alors ce qu'elle présenta comme un nouveau
texte de compromis, lequel comportait trois points. Premièrement,
la Conférence serait convoquée à la lumière d'études scientifiques
et techniques menées par la FAO. Deuxièmement, elle ne pourrait
d'aucune façon modifier ou remettre en cause les dispositions de la
Convention sur le droit de la mer. Troisièmement, outre les stocks
chevauchants et les stocks de grands migrateurs, elle porterait
également sur l'accès au reliquat du volume admissible des captures. Ce dernier aspect de la proposition communautaire se révéla
inacceptable à un grand nombre d'États parce qu'il aurait amené le
mandat de la Conférence à empiéter sur les droits souverains des

---

111 Interview April, *supra* note 75.

112 *Ibid.*

États côtiers dans leur ZEE. En conséquence la CEE n'insista pas sur ce point et concentra ses efforts sur les deux autres.[113]

La première proposition de la CEE reflétait son avis que la FAO, et plus particulièrement son Comité sur les pêches, constituait l'enceinte appropriée pour traiter le problème des stocks chevauchants et des stocks de grands migrateurs. Le Canada considérait pour sa part que la FAO devait se limiter aux aspects scientifiques et techniques de la question et qu'une conférence des Nations Unies était nécessaire pour débattre de ses aspects juridiques, politiques et institutionnels. La CEE acceptait désormais qu'une telle conférence soit convoquée. Le Canada n'avait donc aucune difficulté à admettre que celle-ci doive tenir compte d'études menées par la FAO dans ce qu'il estimait être son domaine de compétence.[114]

La seconde proposition communautaire, qui demandait une reconnaissance explicite du fait que la conférence ne pourrait d'aucune façon modifier ou remettre en cause les dispositions de la Convention sur le droit de la mer, était plus lourde de sens. La CEE cherchait ainsi à se protéger contre ce qu'elle croyait être l'ordre du jour caché du Canada, à savoir l'extension subreptice de sa juridiction (*creeping jurisdiction*) en matière de pêche au-delà de la limite des 200 milles marins prévue par la Convention.[115] La CEE fondait cette crainte sur les pressions qu'exerçait le Gouvernement de Terre-Neuve sur le Gouvernement fédéral canadien pour qu'il règle de cette façon le problème de la surpêche étrangère sur le Nez et la Queue des Grands Bancs.[116]

En réalité, dès le départ le Gouvernement canadien avait conçu son initiative juridique comme une alternative à l'extension de juridiction et non pas comme un moyen détourné d'y parvenir. Outre les obstacles juridiques auxquels elle n'aurait pas manqué de se heurter, une telle attitude de sa part aurait été politiquement improductive. Ses alliés potentiels chez les États côtiers n'auraient pas toléré une quelconque atteinte à la Convention, de peur que l'accord global (*package deal*) qui lui avait permis de voir le jour[117] ne s'effondre, entraînant avec lui tous les avantages qu'ils en avaient

---

[113] *Ibid.*

[114] Interview Applebaum, *supra* note 50.

[115] Interview April, *supra* note 75.

[116] Voir à cette égard *supra* la note 94 et le texte s'y rapportant.

[117] Voir à ce sujet Caminos et Molitor, "Progressive development of international law and the package deal" (1985) 79 AJIL 871.

retirés.[118] C'est pourquoi le Canada a toujours pris soin de présenter son objectif comme étant de donner pleinement effet aux dispositions pertinentes de la Convention et non pas de remettre en cause les fondements du régime juridique qu'elle a établi, en particulier la fixation à 200 milles marins de l'étendue maximale de la ZEE.[119]

Les assurances répétées qu'il avait données à cet effet n'ayant manifestement pas suffi à convaincre la CEE, le Canada a facilement accepté le second aspect du "compromis" proposé par celle-ci à Rio, puisqu'il correspondait à sa position de départ. Il l'a accepté avec d'autant plus d'empressement que, contrairement au but visé par le troisième élément de sa proposition, à cause du second la CEE ne pourrait pas amener la conférence à adopter des règles relatives à la partie des stocks chevauchants et des stocks de grands migrateurs située à l'intérieur de la ZEE, puisqu'en vertu de la Convention celle-ci est soumise à la juridiction exclusive de l'État côtier.[120] Autrement dit, en croyant faire renoncer le Canada à l'extension de juridiction, la CEE renonçait en principe à empiéter sur les droits souverains dans la ZEE.[121]

Il ne fallut par conséquent pas plus de vingt-quatre heures aux États-Unis pour élaborer un texte de compromis sur les stocks chevauchants et les stocks de grands migrateurs. Ce texte, qui devint le paragraphe 17.49 (e) d'Action 21, se lisait comme suit:

[118] Interview April, *supra* note 75.

[119] Voir à titre d'exemple la lettre du 9 mars 1993 du Représentant permanent du Canada près les Communautés européennes au Commissaire européen chargé des pêches, dont les extraits pertinents sont reproduits dans ce volume de l'Annuaire.

[120] Le principe de cette juridiction est posé à l'article 56 de la Convention sur le droit de la mer, *supra* note 4:
   (1) Dans la zone économique exclusive, l'État côtier a:
     (a) des droits souverains aux fins d'exploration et d'exploitation, de conservation et de gestion des ressources naturelles, biologiques ou non biologiques, des eaux surjacentes aux fonds marins, des fonds marins et de leur sous-sol, ainsi qu'en ce qui concerne d'autres activités tendant à l'exploration et à l'exploitation de la zone à des fins économiques, telles que la production d'énergie à partir de l'eau, des courants et des vents. . . .

Les modalités d'exercice en sont explicitées aux articles 61 et 62 de la Convention, qui portent respectivement sur la conservation et l'exploitation des ressources biologiques de la ZEE.

[121] Interview April, *supra* note 75.

17.49. Les États doivent prendre des mesures efficaces, notamment dans le cadre de la coopération bilatérale et multilatérale, le cas échéant aux niveaux sous-régional, régional et mondial, pour veiller à ce que *la pêche hauturière* soit gérée conformément aux dispositions de la Convention des Nations Unies sur le droit de la mer. Ils devraient notamment . . .
(e) Convoquer, dès que possible, une conférence intergouvernementale sous les auspices de l'ONU, compte tenu des activités pertinentes menées aux niveaux sous-régional, régional et mondial, afin de promouvoir l'application efficace des dispositions de la Convention des Nations Unies sur le droit de la mer sur les stocks de poisson qui chevauchent la zone de 200 milles et les grands migrateurs. La conférence, se fondant notamment sur des études scientifiques et techniques de la FAO, devrait identifier et évaluer les problèmes liés à la préservation et à la gestion de ces stocks, et étudier les moyens d'améliorer la coopération sur les pêches entre les États et formuler des recommandations appropriées. Les travaux et les résultats de la conférence devraient être pleinement conformes aux dispositions de la Convention des Nations Unies sur le droit de la mer, en particulier les droits et obligations des États côtiers et des États menant des activités de pêche en haute mer.[122]

Quelques heures à peine avant l'arrivée du ministre Crosbie,[123] un texte généralement acceptable avait donc été convenu aux termes duquel le Canada obtenait la Conférence qu'il souhaitait. M. Crosbie dit voir dans le fait que 188 pays avait unanimement appuyé la convocation de cette Conférence le signe d'un appui grandissant de la communauté internationale pour mettre fin à la surpêche en haute mer. Reconnaissant que la Conférence ne pourrait pas résoudre des problèmes dans l'immédiate, il souligna qu'elle pourrait servir de base à une action commune pour des résultats à plus long terme.[124]

5   *La 47e session de l'Assemblée générale des Nations Unies*

La CNUED pouvait recommander la tenue d'une conférence sur la pêche en haute mer mais seule l'Assemblée générale pouvait formellement la convoquer. C'est ce qu'a fait la résolution 47/192, une des cinq grandes résolutions sur le suivi de Rio négociées à

---

122 Nations Unies, Rapport de la Conférence sur l'environnement et le développement, Rio de Janeiro, 3-14 juin 1992, document A/CONF.151/26, chapitre I, résolution 1, annexe II, para. 17.49 (e). Les soulignés sont de nous.

123 Interview April, *supra* note 75.

124 Pêches et Océans Canada, "Le ministre Crosbie demande l'appui de la communauté internationale pour mettre fin à la surpêche en haute mer," communiqué C-AC-92-49F du 8 juin 1992.

l'automne 1992,[125] qui a été adoptée par consensus le 22 décembre 1992 après plusieurs mois de négociations souvent difficiles. Ces difficultés étaient largement attribuables aux positions prises par la CEE, notamment en ce qui concerne le mandat de la Conférence et sa durée.

Pour ce qui est du mandat, la résolution ne fait que reprendre celui adopté par la CNUED, ce qui avait été dès le départ l'intention du Canada et des autres co-auteurs du document L.16. Tout au long de l'automne la CEE a tenté de rédiger ce mandat de façon à englober la gestion par les États côtiers des stocks chevauchants et des stocks de grands migrateurs à l'intérieur de leur ZEE, comme elle avait tenté sans succès de le faire à Rio. Il est cependant clair, à la lecture de l'ensemble de la résolution,[126] que la Conférence devra s'employer à résoudre le problème de la surpêche en haute mer. Elle n'a pas à débattre des obligations des États dans les eaux soumises à leur juridiction exclusive en matière de pêche, une question réglée depuis longtemps par la Convention sur le droit de la mer.

Quant à la durée de la Conférence, la CEE, qui avait été la dernière à s'y rallier à Rio, voulait éviter sa pérennisation et souhaitait en particulier qu'elle ne se réunisse pas après 1993. Le texte finalement adopté stipule que les travaux de la Conférence "devraient se terminer avant la quarante-neuvième session de

---

125 Les autres sont les résolutions 47/188 (Création d'un comité intergouverne-mental de négociation pour l'élaboration d'une convention internationale sur la lutte contre la désertification dans les pays gravement atteints par la sécheresse et/ou par la désertification, en particulier en Afrique), 47/189 (Convocation d'une conférence mondiale sur le développement durable des petits États en développement insulaires), 47/190 (Rapport de la Conférence des Nations Unies sur l'environnement et le développement) et 47/191 (Arrangements institutionnels pour le suivi de la Conférence des Nations Unies sur l'environnement et le développement), également adoptées le 22 décembre 1992.

126 À cet égard le dernier paragraphe de la résolution est particulièrement pro-bant. C'est celui qui décide d'inscrire à l'ordre du jour provisoire de la quarante-huitième session de l'Assemblée générale, au titre d'une question intitulée "Application des décisions et recommandations de la Conférence des Nations Unies sur l'environnement et le développement," un alinéa intitulé "Utilisation durable et conservation des ressources biologiques *en haute mer*: Conférence des Nations Unies sur les stocks de poissons dont les déplacements s'effectuent tant à l'intérieur qu'au-delà de zones économi-ques exclusives et les stocks de poissons grands migrateurs." Les soulignés sont de nous.

l'Assemblée générale,''[127] qui se tiendra à l'automne 1994. L'expression "devraient se terminer," par opposition à "se termineront," réserve en principe la possibilité d'une prolongation des travaux au-delà de 1994 en cas de besoin.

La résolution précise que la Conférence tiendra en 1993, au siège de l'ONU à New York, une session d'organisation de cinq jours au maximum pour élire son président et les autres membres de son bureau et pour organiser ses travaux.[128] Elle ajoute que la Conférence tiendra en juillet 1993, toujours au siège de l'ONU, une session d'une durée de trois semaines pour traiter des questions de fond.[129] La résolution ne dit mot du calendrier des travaux pour 1994, qui devait par conséquent être décidé à l'automne 1993 par la quarante-huitième session de l'Assemblée générale, à la lumière du rapport que devait lui soumettre le Secrétaire général.[130] Enfin elle invite les organisations non gouvernementales (ONG) compétentes à contribuer aux travaux de la Conférence, dans leurs domaines de compétence ou de spécialisation respectifs, en suivant la procédure d'accréditation utilisée pour la CNUED.[131]

6   La Consultation technique de la FAO

Du 7 au 15 septembre 1992 le Canada a participé à la Consultation technique sur la pêche en haute mer organisée à Rome par la FAO.[132] La Consultation a mis l'accent sur la recherche scientifique, les systèmes de gestion et les pratiques de pêche, fournissant à cet égard des éléments techniques et factuels pour servir de base aux travaux de la Conférence des Nations Unies. Se félicitant de l'issue de la Consultation, le ministre Crosbie a dit y voir:

> une autre étape réussie d'un long processus qui a débuté par la Conférence de St. John's sur les pêches en haute mer de septembre 1990, s'est poursuivi par la Conférence des Nations Unies sur l'environnement et le développement, tenue à Rio de Janeiro en juin dernier, et qui

[127] Résolution de l'Assemblée générale des Nations Unies 47/192 du 22 décembre 1992, au para. 1.

[128] *Ibid.* au para. 5.

[129] *Ibid.* au para. 7.

[130] *Ibid.* au para. 13.

[131] *Ibid.*

[132] Le rapport de cette Consultation est cité *supra* note 61.

donnera lieu, l'été prochain, à une conférence des Nations Unies sur les aspects juridiques des pêches en haute mer.[133]

Employant une formule dans laquelle on pouvait lire la recette du succès remporté par la délégation canadienne à Rio, le ministre ajoutait que "[l]e Canada a intégré ses initiatives juridiques et écologiques à l'encontre de la surpêche étrangère." Faisant alors le point sur ces initiatives, il concluait en ces termes:

La route sera encore longue, mais nous avons accompli beaucoup en faisant reconnaître l'existence du problème et (en) amorçant le processus de . . . définition des solutions au niveau international. Les efforts consentis par le Canada iront en augmentant à mesure que nous nous préparerons en fonction de la conférence juridique de l'été prochain.[134]

7 *St. John's II*

L'étape suivante de ces préparatifs a été la Réunion de pays d'optique commune sur la pêche en haute mer, dont le Canada a été l'hôte à St. John's, Terre-Neuve, du 20 au 24 janvier 1992. Contrairement à la conférence d'experts tenue à St. John's en 1990, il s'agissait cette fois-ci d'une véritable réunion intergouvernementale. Les 39 autres co-auteurs du document L.16 y avaient été conviés, ainsi qu'un certain nombre de pays qui, comme les États-Unis, la Russie, l'Australie et le Maroc, éprouvaient de la sympathie pour les objectifs poursuivis par ce texte même s'ils n'étaient pas en mesure d'adhérer à chacun de ses éléments. En tout 56 pays étaient représentés à la réunion,[135] dont 8 par le biais de l'Agence des pêches du Forum du Pacifique Sud.

En annonçant la tenue de la Réunion le ministre Crosbie avait présenté le but des participants comme étant de convenir entre eux des objectifs de la Conférence des Nations Unies et de coordonner leur stratégie. Ce faisant il avait énoncé comme suit l'objectif qu'entendait y poursuivre le Canada:

133 Pêches et Océans Canada, "Le ministre Crosbie qualifie de nouvelle étape réussie la conférence technique de l'ONU sur la gestion des pêches en haute mer," communiqué C-AC-92-74F du 16 septembre 1992, à la p. 1.

134 *Ibid.* à la p. 2.

135 Pêches et Océans Canada, "Le Canada accueillera une réunion préparatoire à la conférence sur la pêche en haute mer," communiqué C-AC-93-06F du 18 janvier 1993, à la p. 1. Ce communiqué annonçait que 57 pays avaient convenu de participer mais la Lituanie a été empêchée de le faire pour des raisons techniques.

Nous comptons faire en sorte que la conférence établisse un régime de gestion efficace de la pêche en haute mer qui lie tous les pays et respecte les principes de conservation et de développement durable.[136]

Au cours de la Réunion le ministre précisa cet objectif en exhortant les participants "à collaborer à la conclusion d'une entente internationale sur la conservation des ressources halieutiques en haute mer."[137] Il était cependant conscient du fait que l'adoption par la Conférence des Nations Unies d'un instrument juridique obligatoire ne faisait pas l'unanimité parmi les pays représentés. C'est pourquoi le même jour il nuançait ses propos en invitant ceux-ci à "apaiser les craintes des nations qui sentent leurs intérêts menacés." Il leur suggéra également d'éviter "les prises de position juridiques contre-productives," tout en faisant en sorte que "toutes les nations sentent le besoin de sauver les ressources vivantes de la mer."[138]

La Réunion s'est articulée autour de quatre documents de travail préparés par le Canada et d'un cinquième soumis par la Nouvelle-Zélande. Les thèmes traités par ces documents étaient les suivants:

— principes de gestion pour la conservation de stocks chevauchants et de stocks de grands migrateurs en haute mer;
— problèmes liés à la pêche par des États qui ne sont pas membres de l'organisation régionale de conservation pertinente ou qui en sont de nouveaux membres;
— surveillance, contrôle et application de la loi en haute mer;
— mesures correctives;
— problèmes particuliers des pays en développement.

La réunion s'est achevée avec la lecture par M. Randolph Gherson, le second Ambassadeur du Canada pour la conservation des pêches, de ses conclusions orales à titre de Président. La plus importante de ces conclusions fut reprise en conférence de presse par le ministre Crosbie dans les termes suivants:

Les participants s'entendent sur la nécessité d'agir à l'égard de toutes les questions soulevées dans les documents de travail. On perçoit également une volonté concertée de voir la Conférence des Nations Unies aboutir à la mise en place d'un régime efficace de conservation et de gestion des

---

[136] *Ibid.* à la p. 2.

[137] Pêches et Océans Canada, "Le ministre Crosbie demande la conclusion d'une entente internationale pour mettre fin à la surpêche en haute mer," communiqué C-AC-93-10F du 22 janvier 1993, à la p. 1.

[138] Discours Crosbie I, *supra* note 20 à la p. 7.

stocks chevauchants et des grands migrateurs, le mot "efficace" signifiant qui produit dans la pratique les effets attendus.[139]

C'est donc en insistant sur l'efficacité du futur régime que l'Ambassadeur Gherson a contourné la difficulté posée par le débat toujours irrésolu sur le caractère juridiquement contraignant ou non des éventuels résultats de la Conférence. Le mandat recommandé par la CNUED et entériné par l'Assemblée générale ne tranche pas la question. En effet, en formulant des "recommandations appropriées" la Conférence pourrait recommander à l'Assemblée générale l'adoption tant d'une convention internationale en bonne et due forme que de principes ou de lignes directrices sous forme de résolution. Toutefois, à St. John's partisans et adversaires d'une convention sur la pêche en haute mer ont convenu que ce qui importe c'est d'établir un régime "efficace." Ce consensus tendrait par conséquent à imposer le fardeau de la preuve à ceux qui estiment que cette efficacité pourrait être garantie par un instrument qui n'aurait pas valeur obligatoire en droit international.

B   LA CONFÉRENCE DES NATIONS UNIES

1   La session d'organisation

À sa première séance, tenue le 19 avril 1993, la Conférence a élu Président par acclamation l'Ambassadeur Satya Nandan de Fiji.[140] Celui-ci a participé activement, à titre de rapporteur de la deuxième commission de la troisième Conférence des Nations Unies sur le droit de la mer, à la rédaction des dispositions que la Conférence sur les stocks chevauchants et les stocks de grands migrateurs a aujourd'hui pour mandat d'interpréter. De plus, de 1983 à 1992 l'Ambassadeur Nandan a exercé les fonctions de Secrétaire général adjoint pour les affaires maritimes et le droit de la mer et de Représentant spécial du Secrétaire général pour le droit de la mer.

Le 23 avril la Conférence élisait par acclamation trois Vice-Présidents représentant les États et les groupes régionaux suivants: la

139 Gouvernement du Canada, Notes pour une allocution de l'Honorable John C. Crosbie, Ministre des Pêches et des Océans et Ministre responsable de l'Agence de promotion économique du Canada Atlantique, à la clôture d'une réunion internationale organisée en prévision de la Conférence des Nations Unies sur la pêche en haute mer, le 24 janvier 1993 à St. John's (Terre-Neuve), (ci-après cité comme discours Crosbie III), à la p. 2.

140 Nations Unies, document A/CONF.164/9 du 2 juin 1993, au para. 3.

Mauritanie (Afrique), l'Italie (États d'Europe occidentale et autres États) et le Chili (Amérique latine). Elle décidait également de remplacer le poste de rapporteur par un poste supplémentaire de Vice-Président et de reporter l'élection du dernier membre du bureau à sa session de fond en juillet.[141]

Le 22 avril la Conférence avait désigné sans difficulté neuf États pour siéger à la Commission de vérification des pouvoirs. En revanche son Règlement intérieur, adopté le même jour, avait exigé des consultations officieuses et occupé l'essentiel du temps dont disposait la session d'organisation. Les trois questions les plus controversées ont été résolues de la façon suivante.

En ce qui concerne tout d'abord la participation de la CEE, il a été convenu que ses représentants participeraient à la Conférence pour les questions relevant de sa compétence, mais sans droit de vote. L'article pertinent du Règlement intérieur précise que "Cette représentation n'entraîne en aucun cas une représentation supérieure à laquelle les États membres pourraient autrement prétendre."[142] La grande méfiance qu'inspirait cette question chez les États non-membres de la CEE est illustrée par la note de bas de page dont fait l'objet le titre de cet article[143] et par la consécration d'un autre article à l'invocation de certains articles du Règlement intérieur par la CEE et ses États membres.[144]

---

[141] *Ibid.* au para. 5. Cette dernière décision avait été prise en raison de l'incapacité du groupe des États d'Europe de l'Est de s'entendre sur un représentant, la Russie s'étant opposée à la candidature de la Pologne en raison de l'activité de navires battant son pavillon dans le "Peanut Hole" de la mer d'Okhotsk. Ce différend n'a pas pu être résolu en juillet et le bureau de la Conférence compte toujours seulement quatre membres.

[142] Nations Unies, document A/CONF.164/6 du 3 mai 1993, art. 2.

[143] Cet article a été adopté pour tenir compte du fait qu'en ce qui concerne la conservation et la gestion des ressources de la pêche maritime, les États membres de la Communauté économique européenne ont transféré leur compétence à la Communauté, et ne constitue d'aucune manière un précédent pour d'autres instances des Nations Unies où il n'y a pas eu de transfert analogue de compétences. Voir Déclaration de la Communauté économique européenne lors de la signature de la Convention des Nations Unies sur le droit de la mer. Traités multilatéraux déposés auprès du Secrétaire général (ST/LEG/SER.E/10, 87).

[144] Nations Unies, document cité *supra* note 142, art. 30:

Aucun représentant de la Communauté économique européenne n'invoquera les articles 20 (motions d'ordre), 24 (ajournement du débat), 25 (clôture du débat), 26 (suspension ou ajournement de la séance), 28

La participation des ONG à la Conférence a également suscité la controverse, en dépit de la décision de l'Assemblée générale de leur appliquer les mêmes règles qu'à la CNUED.[145] Face aux réticences d'un certain nombre d'États en développement, le Canada a plaidé en faveur de l'ouverture. Il a ainsi obtenu un accord à l'effet que les représentants des ONG pourront participer en qualité d'observateurs aux séances publiques de la Conférence et de ses organes subsidiaires. Ces observateurs pourront faire de brefs exposés oraux sur les questions qui sont de leur compétence particulière. Cependant, si leurs demandes de prise de parole sont trop nombreuses, la Conférence pourra leur demander de constituer des groupes ayant chacun un porte-parole.[146] La méfiance de certaines délégations a survécu à cet accord. Dans un ultime effort pour tenter de la dissiper le Président déclara après l'adoption du Règlement intérieur que, "compte tenu du caractère intergouvernemental de la Conférence, les organisations non gouvernementales ne disposeront pas d'un pouvoir de négociation dans le cadre de ses travaux."[147]

Enfin, le mode de prise de décision de la Conférence a fait l'objet d'une vive discussion. Celle-ci opposait essentiellement les États côtiers qui, étant les plus nombreux, voulaient des décisions adoptées à la majorité des voix, aux États de pêche lointaine qui, conscients de former une minorité, souhaitaient au contraire que celles-ci ne puissent se prendre que sur la base d'un consensus. Le compromis final est au même effet que celui qui avait gouverné la prise de décision au cours de la troisième Conférence des Nations Unies sur le droit de la mer,[148] à savoir que le con-

---

séance), 28 (présentation des propositions et des amendements de fond) et 29 (retrait d'une proposition ou d'une motion) si ceux-ci ont déjà été invoqués, sur la même question, par l'un quelconque des États membres de la Communauté. Aucun représentant d'un État membre de la Communauté n'invoquera l'un quelconque des articles précités si un représentant de la Communauté l'a déjà fait à propos de la même question.

145 Voir *supra* le texte accompagnant la note 131.

146 Nations Unies, *supra* note 142, art. 60.

147 Nations Unies, *supra* note 140 au para. 20.

148 Voir à cet égard B. Buzan, "Negotiating by Consensus: Developments in Technique at the United Nations Conference on the Law of the Sea" (1981) 75 AJIL 329-35.

sensus serait la règle mais que l'on pourrait recourir au vote en cas de besoin.[149]

Toujours à sa séance du 22 avril, la Conférence a adopté son ordre du jour. Celui-ci ne comprend qu'un seul point de fond, qui est l'examen de la question visée au paragraphe 2 de la résolution 47/192 de l'Assemblée générale, qui reprend le mandat convenu à Rio.[150] La délégation péruvienne déclara à cette occasion qu'elle avait accepté l'ordre du jour:

> étant entendu que l'utilisation du terme "recommandations" figurant dans la résolution 47/192 ne préjugeait pas du résultat final de la Conférence qui, si elle en décidait ainsi, pourrait adopter un accord international ayant force obligatoire, conforme aux dispositions de la Convention des Nations Unies sur le droit de la mer et complémentaire de celles-ci.[151]

Le 23 avril la Conférence a décidé de l'organisation des travaux relatifs à sa session de fond. Un débat général de trois jours a notamment été prévu et le Président a été prié d'établir un document présentant la liste des sujets et des questions de fond que la Conférence pourrait examiner. À cet égard les délégations ont été priées de faire connaître leurs vues au Président afin de faciliter l'établissement de ce document.[152] La session d'organisation s'est terminée avec la lecture par le Président d'une déclaration où il a relevé le climat de coopération dans lequel s'étaient déroulés ses travaux. Il a également exprimé l'espoir que le même esprit de conciliation marquerait la prochaine étape des activités de la Conférence.[153]

[149] Nations Unies, *supra* note 142, art. 33:

> La Conférence devrait conduire ses travaux sur la base d'un consensus général. Elle ne procède à un vote conformément à l'article 35 qu'après avoir fait le maximum pour parvenir à un consensus général. Le Président informe la Conférence auparavant que le maximum a été fait pour parvenir à un tel consensus.
>
> Sur l'importance du mode de prise de décision de la Conférence pour le Canada, voir *supra* le texte accompagnant la note 100.

[150] Nations Unies, document A/CONF.164/5 du 26 avril 1993, point 8. À la demande de certaines délégations qui n'avaient pas suivi de près les débats entourant l'adoption de cette résolution, une note de bas de page fut ajoutée citant son paragraphe 2. Celui-ci est basé sur le paragraphe 17.49 e) d'Action 21, cité *supra* dans le texte accompagnant la note 122.

[151] Nations Unies, *supra* note 140 au para. 18.

[152] Nations Unies, document A/CONF.164/3 du 22 avril 1993, au para. 4.

[153] Nations Unies, document A/CONF.164/8 du 11 juin 1993.

2 La première session de fond

Répondant à l'appel du Président, au cours des semaines suivant la fin de la session d'organisation de nombreuses délégations lui ont soumis leurs vues sur les questions que la Conférence devrait examiner. Plusieurs d'entre elles ont souhaité faire connaître ces vues à l'ensemble des participants par l'entremise de documents de la Conférence qui ont été distribués au début de sa première session de fond.[154]

La contribution du Canada à cette phase préliminaire des travaux de la Conférence est reproduite dans le document L.5. On y lit que son objectif est d'assurer l'application des dispositions pertinentes de la Convention sur le droit de la mer pour résoudre les problèmes urgents posés par l'épuisement des stocks chevauchants et des stocks de grands migrateurs en haute mer. À cette fin la Conférence devrait instaurer un régime efficace de conservation et de gestion de ces deux types de stocks, ce qui exige des obligations ayant force exécutoire. Il faudrait donc élaborer une convention internationale qui définirait les éléments et les mesures nécessaires pour la mise en place d'un tel régime, sous-tendu par une surveillance et un contrôle effectifs et un mécanisme de règlement des différends. Suivent un certain nombre de propositions sur ces éléments et mesures, présentées dans des documents séparés. Le document canadien conclut en soulignant qu'il serait important qu'un consensus se dégage sur le fond avant que ne s'engage un débat sur la structure juridique à adopter.[155]

Cette dernière mise en garde reflétait la persistance du différend sur l'opportunité pour la Conférence d'élaborer une convention internationale[156] et la volonté canadienne de voir celle-ci se concentrer d'abord sur les questions de fond plutôt que de forme. Cette préoccupation était partagée par le Président, qui a lors de la

154 Il s'agit des documents A/CONF.164/L.1 (Pérou), L.2 et Corr.1 (Russie), L.3 (États-Unis), L.4 (Colombie), L.5 (Canada), L.6 (Japon), L.7 (République de Corée), L.8 (CEE), L.9 (Australie), L.10 (Argentine) et L.12 (Cuba).

155 Nations Unies, document A/CONF.164/L.5 du 4 juin 1993.

156 Dans leurs contributions respectives, *supra* note 154, les États-Unis ont déclaré qu'il ne serait pas indiqué — voire possible — que la Conférence tente de rédiger un instrument ayant force obligatoire, parce qu'une telle entreprise ne pourrait sans doute être menée à bien qu'après de longues années; le Japon s'est dit d'avis que le bilan des travaux de la Conférence ne devrait pas avoir force obligatoire, mais prendre la forme de recommandations ou de directives; et la CEE a opiné que les résultats de la Conférence devraient se présenter comme des recommandations ou des déclarations.

première session de fond studieusement évité la question de la valeur juridique du résultat de la Conférence dans ses déclarations publiques et dans les documents qu'il lui a soumis.

Conformément au programme de travail adopté à la session d'organisation, les trois premiers jours de la session de fond ont été consacrés à des déclarations générales. À cette occasion M. Ross Reid, ministre des Pêches et des Océans dans le gouvernement Campbell, a prononcé une allocution. Il y a souligné à la fois la situation particulière du Canada face à la surpêche en haute mer et le caractère universel de ce problème:

> Le Canada accorde la plus haute importance au succès de cette conférence, parce qu'aucun pays n'a autant souffert de l'absence d'un régime international efficace de conservation et de gestion des ressources halieutiques de la haute mer; parce que les sacrifices que font les pêcheurs canadiens pour la reconstitution des stocks ne doivent pas être faits en vain; et parce que la surpêche en haute mer est un problème planétaire qui appelle une solution internationale pour le bien du genre humain. . . .[157]
>
> Nous devons aborder les problèmes qui nous occupent comme des problèmes relatifs à notre patrimoine commun, et non pas dans la perspective étroitement juridique de l'application des droits et obligations des États en vertu du droit de la mer. Nous devons nous y attaquer avec une éthique écologiste fondée sur l'intérêt commun et non pas avec le désir de tirer son épingle du jeu en prenant plus de ressources que son voisin. Nous devons faire en sorte d'accroître la solidarité internationale pour une cause commune; car, si nous n'y parvenons pas, le résultat sera le même pour toutes les nations: la destruction des ressources entraînée par la surpêche en haute mer.[158]

À la conclusion du débat général le 15 juillet le Président a constaté qu'il y avait accord général sur un certain nombre de problèmes clés. Il a aussi déclaré que la Conférence s'était acquittée de la première partie de son mandat, qui était de "recenser et évaluer les problèmes liés à la préservation et à la gestion" des stocks chevauchants et des stocks de poissons grands migrateurs. Elle devait ensuite s'atteler aux deux autres aspects de son mandat définis au paragraphe 2 de la résolution 47/192, dans laquelle il lui a été demandé de "délibérer des moyens d'améliorer la coopéra-

---

157 Gouvernement du Canada, Notes pour une allocution de l'honorable Ross Reid, ministre des Pêches et des Océans et ministre responsable de l'Agence de promotion économique du Canada atlantique, à la Conférence des Nations Unies sur les stocks chevauchants et les grands migrateurs, à New York, le 12 juillet 1993 (ci-après cité comme discours Reid), à la p. 5.

158 *Ibid.* à la p. 2.

tion entre les États dans le domaine de la pêche" et de "formuler des recommandations appropriées."[159]

Le lendemain la Conférence abordait l'examen des questions présentées dans le "Guide des questions dont est saisie la Conférence établi par le Président."[160] Le même jour le Canada déposait sous la cote L.11 un projet de Convention sur la conservation et la gestion des stocks chevauchants et des stocks de poissons grands migrateurs en haute mer. Ce texte était co-parrainé par l'Argentine, le Chili, l'Islande et la Nouvelle-Zélande.[161] Une lettre au Président de la Conférence précisait qu'il regroupait les propositions énoncées par le Canada dans le document L.5, modifiées par ses co-auteurs pour tenir compte de commentaires formulés lors de consultations officieuses.[162]

Un communiqué canadien publié à l'occasion de son dépôt[163] soulignait certaines des principales dispositions du projet de convention. On y relevait notamment l'obligation qu'il ferait aux États qui y deviendraient parties de respecter les décisions internationales prises en matière de conservation[164] et le mécanisme obligatoire de règlement des différends qu'il prévoit. Le communiqué notait également les principes d'intérêt spécial, de concordance et d'absence d'impact négatif, dont on se souviendra que le Canada avait accepté à Rio d'en reporter la discussion à la future conférence sur la pêche en haute mer. Il citait enfin le ministre Reid, selon lequel "il est nécessaire de formuler des obligations qui lient légalement les parties pour que le contrôle de la pêche en haute mer soit efficace." Le ministre ajoutait que le Canada allait "pousser l'adoption de ce projet de convention lors de la Conférence des Nations Unies."

Néanmoins, vu les divergences d'opinion précédemment mentionnées et afin d'éviter une polarisation de la Conférence, le Canada et les autres co-auteurs convinrent de ne pas insister sur une discussion immédiate de leur proposition. Le Président a donc

---

159 Nations Unies, document A/CONF.164/12 du 21 juillet 1993.

160 Nations Unies, document A/CONF.164/10 du 24 juin 1993.

161 Nations Unies, document A/CONF.164/L.11 du 14 juillet 1993.

162 Nations Unies, document A/CONF.164/L.13 du 16 juillet 1993.

163 Gouvernement du Canada, "Le Canada dépose une ébauche de convention sur la pêche en haute mer à la Conférence des Nations Unies," communiqué NR-HQ-93-68F du 16 juillet 1993.

164 Il s'agit d'une disposition très semblable à l'article III, paragraphe 1 (a), de l'Accord de la FAO. Voir *supra* le texte accompagnant la note 54.

pu diriger les travaux de la Conférence en se servant du guide des questions qu'il avait établi à son intention.[165] Au cours de ces travaux les co-auteurs du L.11 s'y sont fréquemment référés pour attirer l'attention de la Conférence sur les réponses qu'il apporte aux questions dont elle est saisie. Les débats consacrés à ces questions se sont déroulés en plénière et ont été résumés par la suite au cours de consultations officieuses, sur la base d'une série de documents de travail officieux soumis par le Président.[166]

Ce processus a éventuellement permis au Président de rédiger un texte de négociation[167] qu'il a soumis à la Conférence le dernier jour de sa première session de fond. Ce texte s'inspire dans une large mesure du projet de convention déposé par le Canada,[168] dont une version révisée a également été diffusée en fin de session pour refléter les commentaires recueillis au cours de consultations menées en marge des travaux de la Conférence.[169] Le

[165] Ministère des Affaires extérieures, *supra* note 81 à la p. 20.

[166] Nations Unies, document A/48/479 du 7 octobre 1993, au para. 14.

[167] Nations Unies, document A/CONF.164/13 du 29 juillet 1993. Le texte de négociation comporte au les onze parties suivantes: (I) Nature des mesures de gestion et de conservation à mettre en place dans le cadre de la coopération; (II) Les mécanismes de coopération internationale; (III) Organismes ou accords régionaux de gestion de la pêche; (IV) Responsabilités des États du pavillon; (V) Observation et application des mesures de conservation et de gestion des ressources halieutiques de la haute mer (A. Observation et application par les États du pavillon; B. Arrangements régionaux pour l'observation et l'application des mesures); (VI) États du port; (VII) États non-parties aux accords ou arrangements sous-régionaux ou régionaux; (VIII) Règlement des différends; (IX) Compatibilité et cohérence des mesures nationales et internationales de conservation d'un même stock; (X) Besoins particuliers des pays en développement; et (XI) Examen de l'application des mesures de conservation et de gestion. Il comprendait en outre deux annexes, portant l'une sur les données minimales requises aux fins de la conservation et de la gestion des stocks chevauchants et des stocks de grands migrateurs et l'autre sur l'arbitrage.

[168] Ministère des Affaires extérieures, *supra* note 81 à la p. 20.

[169] Nations Unies, document A/CONF.164/L.11/Rev.1 du 28 juillet 1993. Le projet de convention révisé comportait huit parties et 26 articles qui se présentent comme suit: (Partie I) Dispositions générales: (Article 1) Définitions, (Article 2) Application, (Article 3) Objectif; (Partie II) Conservation et gestion: (Article 4) Mesures de conservation et de gestion, (Article 5) Mesures préventives, (Article 6) Communication d'information; (Partie III) Surveillance et contrôle: (Article 7) Mesures de surveillance et de contrôle; (Partie IV) Mise en oeuvre: (Article 8) Autorisation donnée par l'État du pavillon, (Article 9) Infractions commises par des navires ou des nationaux,

texte de négociation servira de base aux futurs travaux de la Conférence, parce que "à la différence des autres conférences de ce type, celle-ci n'était pas saisie d'une proposition ou d'un texte de base."[170]

Le Président a fait une déclaration de clôture dans laquelle il a notamment constaté que la Conférence s'était acquittée de la deuxième tâche que lui avait confiée l'Assemblée générale. Il a aussi estimé qu'elle avait fait des progrès considérables en vue de l'accomplissement de la troisième, c'est-à-dire la formulation de recommandations appropriées, à laquelle elle procéderait à sa prochaine session.[171] La Conférence a recommandé à l'Assemblée générale la tenue de deux autres sessions en 1994, au printemps et en été.[172] Le Président a dit qu'il pensait qu'une révision de son texte de négociation serait publiée à l'issue de la session de printemps. Il serait alors distribué aux États pour examen "afin que la Conférence puisse l'adopter à la session de clôture, sous la forme dont il pourra être convenu."[173]

(Article 10) Attribution du pavillon, (Article 11) Pouvoirs de l'État du port, (Article 12) Coopération internationale, (Article 13) Arraisonnement, inspection et saisie en haute mer, (Article 14) Pouvoirs des Parties à l'encontre de navires non-immatriculés, (Article 15) Pouvoirs des Parties à l'encontre de navires refusant d'indiquer leur signalement, (Article 16) Information sur la suite donnée aux cas; (Partie V) Organismes et accords régionaux en matière de ressources halieutiques: (Article 17) Circonstances régionales, (Article 18) Normes minimales, (Article 19) Nouveaux participants, (Article 20) Mers fermées et semi-fermées, (Article 21) Zones non-réglementées de la haute mer, (Article 22) Évaluation internationale; (Partie VI) Pays en développement: (Article 23) Renforcement de l'aptitude des pays en développement à remplir leurs obligations, (Article 24) Coopération technique avec les pays en développement; (Partie VII et Article 25) États non Parties; (Partie VIII et Article 26) Règlement des différends. Il comprend en outre trois annexes: (I) Stocks de poissons grands migrateurs, (II) Quelques mesures préventives en haute mer (Stocks nouvellement découverts et Pêcheries existantes) et (III) Arbitrage. S'y ajoute une note explicative indiquant les sources utilisées dans la rédaction du projet de convention, dont la Convention des Nations Unies sur le droit de la mer, d'autres accords internationaux, l'Accord de la FAO et les règlements de la CEE. En revanche il ne comprend encore ni préambule ni clauses finales.

[170] Nations Unies, *supra* note 166 au para. 15.

[171] Nations Unies, document A/CONF.164/16 du 17 août 1993, au para. 22.

[172] *Ibid.* au para. 25(a).

[173] *Ibid.* au para. 26.

C   LA 48E SESSION DE L'ASSEMBLÉE GÉNÉRALE DES NATIONS UNIES

Tel que mentionné précédemment,[174] l'Assemblée générale devait décider les dates des réunions de la Conférence en 1994. Suite aux discussions animées de la première session de fond, la plupart des participants souhaitaient éviter une répétition des débats acerbes qui avaient précédé l'adoption de la résolution 47/192. Ils voulaient donc faire en sorte que la résolution pertinente de la 48e session se limite à des questions de procédure. C'est ce que faisait le projet initial préparé par le Président de la Conférence à la fin du mois d'octobre.[175]

Au cours de consultations officieuses présidées par l'Ambassadeur Nandan, plusieurs amendements à ce projet furent proposés et acceptés. À titre d'exemple, la CEE a obtenu que soit éliminée une référence à "tous les États intéressés" (au motif qu'elle n'est pas un État). On lui a également accordé l'addition d'un paragraphe rappelant que, conformément à la résolution 47/192, la Conférence devrait compléter ses travaux avant la 49e session de l'Assemblée générale. Avec l'appui de la CEE, la République de Corée a fait ajouter un paragraphe reprenant une recommandation de la Conférence priant la FAO d'établir deux documents d'information. L'un d'eux portera sur l'adoption d'une approche prudente pour la gestion des pêcheries et l'autre sur la notion de rendement constant maximal.[176]

Cependant, la CEE a également fait une proposition d'amendement qui n'a pas fait l'objet d'un accord, visant à éliminer le dernier paragraphe du projet de résolution. Celui-ci prévoyait l'inscription à l'ordre du jour provisoire de la 49e session de l'Assemblée générale, au titre d'une question intitulée "Application des décisions et recommandations de la Conférence des Nations Unies sur l'environnement et le développement," d'un alinéa intitulé "Utilisation durable et conservation des ressources biologiques en haute mer: Conférence des Nations Unies sur les stocks de poissons dont les déplacements s'effectuent tant à l'intérieur qu'au-delà de zones économiques exclusives et les stocks de poissons grands migrateurs."

---

174 Voir *supra* le texte accompagnant la note 130.

175 Ce projet a été distribué informellement sous la cote A/RES/48/L . . . en date du 29 octobre.

176 Nations Unies, document A/48/479 du 7 octobre 1993, au para. 17(c).

Le but poursuivi par la CEE en mettant de l'avant cet amendement était clair. Comme elle avait tenté sans succès de le faire à Rio[177] et à la 47e session de l'Assemblée générale,[178] il s'agissait de modifier le mandat de la Conférence pour y inclure la gestion et la conservation de la partie des stocks chevauchants et des stocks de grands migrateurs située à l'intérieur des ZEE des États côtiers. Cette proposition de fond se heurta par conséquent à une vive opposition. D'autant plus que le paragraphe en question était tiré de la résolution 47/192, adoptée par consensus en 1992, et qu'il faisait partie du format commun à toutes les résolutions sur les conférences de suivi de Rio.

La CEE maintint néanmoins sa proposition, en dépit de l'isolement dans lequel la plaçait son insistance et du fait que tous ses autres amendements avaient été acceptés. Les négociations se prolongèrent pour cette raison au cours des mois de novembre et décembre. La CEE proposa de manière informelle des formules alternatives pour le paragraphe auquel elle s'opposait, qui omettaient toutes les mots "haute mer." Aucune de ces formules ne fut retenue.

Le 12 décembre la Deuxième Commission de l'Assemblée générale adoptait la résolution relative à la Conférence sans que son dernier paragraphe ait été changé. Dans un ultime effort pour répondre aux préoccupations de la CEE, cette adoption avait été précédée par la déclaration suivante du Président de la Commission:

Il est entendu que la Conférence doit également résoudre la question du lien entre la gestion et la conservation saines des ressources halieutiques concernées en haute mer et dans les zones soumises à la juridiction nationale à la lumière de l'unité biologique de ces stocks et des droits et obligations des États tels qu'énoncés dans la Convention des Nations Unies sur le droit de la mer de 1982.[179]

Le Canada avait préalablement donné son accord au libellé de cette déclaration, qui protège sa position à la Conférence. En effet, le Canada reconnaît sans peine l'unité biologique des stocks chevauchants et des stocks de grands migrateurs. C'est elle qui est à l'origine de l'impact négatif à l'intérieur de sa zone de 200 milles

177 Voir *supra* le texte accompagnant les notes 113 à 122.

178 Voir *supra* la note 126 et le texte l'accompagnant.

179 Cette déclaration a été faite en anglais et la traduction est de nous. Elle sera reproduite dans le compte-rendu de séance de la Deuxième Commission à paraître sous la cote A/C.2/48/SR.47.

qu'a la surpêche dans le secteur de la haute mer adjacent à cette zone. Le Canada souhaite que la Conférence "résolve la question du lien" entre la conservation et la gestion de ces stocks à l'intérieur et à l'extérieur de la ZEE. C'est pourquoi il a tant milité en faveur de sa convocation. Enfin, le Canada attache la plus haute importance aux droits et obligations des États énoncés dans la Convention sur le droit de la mer. C'est la raison pour laquelle il veut que le lien susmentionné soit résolu par le biais d'un accord international sur les principes d'intérêt spécial, de concordance et d'absence d'impact négatif.

Le 21 décembre l'Assemblée générale adoptait la résolution 48/194 sur la recommandation de la Deuxième Commission. Lors d'une déclaration faite après son adoption, la CEE a critiqué ce qu'elle a décrit comme un manque d'esprit de compromis pour en arriver à une formule acceptable pour le dernier paragraphe de la résolution. Elle a dit y voir un mauvais augure pour la Conférence et a réitéré que celle-ci devait se pencher sur la protection des stocks chevauchants et des stocks de grands migrateurs à travers toute leur aire de migration.[180]

Le Canada a répondu que depuis le début de novembre sept amendements avaient été proposés au projet de résolution pertinent et que six d'entre eux avaient été retenus. La formule dont se plaignait la CEE avait été adoptée par consensus l'année précédente. La vaste majorité des États était convenue qu'elle devait figurer de nouveau dans la résolution de l'année en cours, qui se limitait à des questions de procédure. Il était par conséquent injuste d'accuser les États côtiers d'inflexibilité, ce que démentait l'historique des négociations. Pour sa part le Canada entendait continuer à travailler de façon constructive pour amener la Conférence à adopter une convention qui établisse un régime international pour la gestion efficace des stocks chevauchants et des stocks de grands migrateurs en haute mer.

VI CONCLUSION

Lorsque le Canada est parti en campagne contre la surpêche en haute mer en 1989, il était le seul pays à exiger un régime plus

---

[180] Delegation of the Commission of the European Communities to the United Nations, Forty-eighth session of the United Nations General Assembly, Statement of the European Commission on resolution A/C.2/48/L.44 concerning straddling and highly migratory fish stocks under agenda item 99(c), New York, December 21, 1993.

efficace de conservation et de gestion des ressources halieutiques hauturières de la planète. Qui plus est, il n'avait même pas de tribune d'où il aurait pu réclamer les changements qu'il prônait.[181] Les efforts qu'il a déployés depuis ont porté fruit puisque cette tribune est maintenant une réalité. À la Conférence des Nations Unies sur les stocks de poissons chevauchants et les stocks de poissons grand migrateurs le Canada n'est plus seul à réclamer des changements. Il peut désormais y présenter, en compagnie de plus de 50 autres États, un solide plaidoyer contre le pillage qui s'exerce sous couvert de la liberté de la haute mer.

C'est ce qui faisait dire en juillet 1993 à Perrin Beatty, alors Secrétaire d'État aux Affaires extérieures, que:

> Tout porte à croire que les travaux de la Conférence, qui se termineront en 1994, seront couronnés de succès. De plus en plus d'États et d'organismes non gouvernementaux du monde entier accordent leur appui à une convention exécutoire visant à réglementer les pêches en haute mer.[182]

Ces États et ces ONG appuient aujourd'hui la position canadienne à l'effet que:

> le cadre légal international ne pourra autoriser la conservation et la gestion efficaces des ressources en haute mer que lorsque seront acceptés des principes et des mesures destinés à donner un effet concret aux obligations juridiques des États de coopérer entre eux à cette fin.[183]

Ils acceptent également que, pour donner un effet concret à des obligations juridiques, un instrument juridiquement contraignant s'impose.

Pour relatifs qu'ils soient, les succès remportés par le Canada à ce étaient stade largement dûs à la caractérisation de la surpêche en haute mer comme un problème environnemental de portée mondiale. Le Canada a présenté ce problème "à travers le filtre d'une morale environnementale fondée sur l'intérêt partagé."[184] C'est ainsi qu'il a pu obtenir l'appui des États côtiers, des médias et des ONG pour amener les États de pêche lointaine à accepter la nécessité, ou du moins le caractère inévitable, de règles pour la gestion et

---

181 Discours Crosbie III, *supra* note 139 à la p. 2.

182 Gouvernement du Canada, "Perspectives de succès à la Conférence des Nations Unies sur la pêche en haute mer," communiqué C-AC-93-70F du 30 juillet 1993.

183 Discours Crosbie I, *supra* note 20 à la p. 6.

184 Discours Crosbie I, *supra* note 20 à la p. 7.

la conservation des stocks chevauchants et des stocks de grands migrateurs en haute mer qui soient compatibles avec le concept de développement durable,[185] dans le cadre de coopération créé par la Convention sur le droit de la mer.

Paradoxalement, les initiatives diplomatique et de relations publiques du Canada sur la pêche en haute mer, dont il attendait des résultats à court terme, n'ont pas été déterminantes dans l'immédiat. C'est son initiative juridique qui a obtenu le retrait des navires communautaires d'une partie du secteur de la haute mer adjacent à sa zone de 200 milles,[186] parce qu'elle avait été aiguillée sur la voie environnementale dans le cadre de la CNUED. L'initiative de relations publiques y a contribué, mais dans la mesure où elle a été mise au service de l'initiative juridique.

Cette dernière était conçue à l'origine comme une entreprise de longue haleine, puisqu'elle visait initialement à favoriser le développement de règles de droit international coutumier. C'est d'ailleurs dans cette perspective qu'elle a été insérée au départ dans le processus préparatoire de la CNUED.[187] Le tournant décisif à cet égard a été pris au moment où le Canada a constaté qu'il ne réussirait pas à faire adopter par la CNUED les trois principes qu'il souhaitait élever à terme au rang de normes coutumières. C'est alors qu'il a commencé à militer en faveur de la convocation d'une conférence des Nations Unies sur la pêche en haute mer. Cette conférence, qui contrairement à la CNUED aurait la possibilité d'adopter un instrument juridiquement obligatoire, faisait donc passer l'initiative juridique canadienne de la voie coutumière à la voie conventionnelle.

Même si l'on avait disposé à Rio du temps nécessaire à cette fin, il n'eut sans doute pas été politiquement possible d'obtenir un accord sur un mandat législatif clair pour la Conférence sur les stocks chevauchants et les stocks de grands migrateurs. D'où l'emploi du terme "recommandations" dans le mandat agréé par la CNUED et entériné par l'Assemblée générale. S'il ne garantit pas que la Conférence débouchera sur une convention, ce terme a à

---

185 La Commission Bruntland a défini ce concept comme "un développement qui répond aux besoins du présent sans compromettre la capacité des générations futures de répondre aux leurs." Voir Commission mondiale sur l'environnement et le développement, *Notre avenir à tous* (1989) à la p. 51.

186 Voir *supra* le texte accompagnant les notes 109 et 110.

187 Voir *supra* le texte accompagnant la note 86.

tout le moins le mérite d'en réserver la possibilité.[188] En revanche, cette ambiguïté inhérente au mandat de la Conférence explique que, comme l'a noté son Président, "à la différence des autres conférences de ce type, celle-ci n'est pas saisie d'une proposition ou d'un texte de base."[189]

Cette absence de texte de base préalablement agréé comme tel a au moins deux conséquences pour les chances de succès de l'initiative juridique du Canada. D'une part, elle soulève le doute sur la possibilité matérielle de négocier une convention internationale sur la conservation et la gestion des stocks chevauchants et des stocks de grands migrateurs en haute mer dans les délais impartis à la Conférence.[190] À cet égard le précédent de l'Accord de la FAO, négocié en à peine un an, n'est qu'imparfaitement applicable. En effet, contrairement à celle de New York, la négociation de Rome avait bénéficié à la fois d'un accord préalable à l'effet qu'une convention internationale sur la réimmatriculation des navires de pêche était nécessaire et d'un texte de base élaboré par un groupe d'experts.

La résolution 47/192 réserve implicitement à l'Assemblée générale la possibilité de prolonger la Conférence.[191] Toutefois il est clair que les pays de pêche lointaine, et particulièrement la CEE qui a tant insisté sur sa volonté d'en réduire le plus possible la durée, seraient portés à s'y opposer. Ces pays sont conscients que, tant qu'elle dure, la Conférence maintient l'attention internationale, tant gouvernementale que non-gouvernementale, sur le problème de la surpêche en haute mer. Elle contribue de ce fait à accroître la pression en vue d'y mettre un terme.[192] Voilà pourquoi ils souhaitent qu'elle se termine au plus tôt.

D'autre part, c'est en invoquant l'absence de texte de base préalablement agréé que le Président de la Conférence a justifié sa décision de faire de son texte de négociation la base de la suite des travaux de la Conférence.[193] Cette décision se justifiait également

---

[188] Voir à ce propos la déclaration péruvienne aitée *supra* dans le texte accompagnant la note 151.

[189] Nations Unies, *supra* note 166 au para. 15.

[190] Cet argument a notamment été invoqué par les États-Unis, qui ne se sont cependant pas dits en principe hostiles à la négociation d'une telle convention. Voir *supra* note 156.

[191] Voir *supra* le texte accompagnant la note 127.

[192] Gouvernement du Canada, *supra* note 74.

[193] Voir *supra* le texte accompagnant la note 170.

par le différend relatif à l'opportunité pour la Conférence d'élaborer une convention. Elle ne facilitera pas pour autant la tâche aux co-auteurs du document L.11/Rev.1, qui souhaiteraient d'autant plus que la Conférence se penche sur leur projet de convention qu'ils sont conscients du peu de temps qu'il lui reste pour compléter ses travaux.

En décembre 1993, la partie était donc loin d'être jouée. Les discussions ardues qui ont entouré l'adoption des résolutions 47/192 et 48/194 et les débats animés auxquelles avaient donné lieu les deux premières parties du mandat de la Conférence laissent entrevoir la difficulté de négocier le texte de "recommandations appropriées." Les négociateurs canadiens allaient en outre devoir tenir compte de l'aggravation de la crise des pêcheries de l'Atlantique[194] et de la détermination de leur nouveau gouvernement à mettre fin coûte que coûte à la surpêche étrangère au large de sa zone de 200 milles, par voie d'accord si possible et unilatéralement si nécessaire.[195] Néanmoins, les activités du Canada dans le cadre de l'OPANO, ses démarches auprès des États non-membres de cette Organisation, l'Accord de pêche paraphré avec la CEE et l'Accord de la FAO qu'il avaient contribué à façonner lui permettaient d'aborder la phase finale de son initiative juridique avec un optimisme modéré.

[194] Le 20 décembre 1993 Brian Tobin, ministre des Pêches et des Océans, annonçait que d'importantes pêcheries de morue du Canada atlantique seraient fermées en 1994 et que les quotas de la plupart des autre espèces de poisson de fond seraient radicalement réduits. Voir Pêches et Océans Canada, "Le ministre Tobin annonce le plan de gestion du poisson de fond de l'Atlantique et des changements aux programmes d'aide," communiqué C-AC-93-93F du 20 décembre 1993. Les causes de cette crise sans précédent, parmi lesquelles figure la surpêche étrangère de stocks chevauchants sur le Nez et la Queue des Grands Bancs, sont énumérées aux pages 24 et 25 de Changement de cap: Les pêches de l'avenir, Rapport du Groupe d'étude sur les revenus et l'adaptation des pêches de l'Atlantique, publié par le ministère des Pêches et des Océans en novembre 1993.

[195] Gouvernement du Canada, Notes pour une allocution de l'honorable Brian Tobin, ministre des Pêches et des Océans, à la Conférence nationale sur la professionnalisation des pêcheurs, Moncton (Nouveau-Brunswick), le 16 novembre 1993, à la p. 5.

Summary

The Canadian Legal Initiative on High Seas Fishing

On December 22, 1992, the United Nations General Assembly decided to convene a conference on straddling fish stocks and highly migratory fish stocks. This decision was a turning point for a legal initiative on high seas fishing that Canada had been working on for more than three years. This article discusses the work of the conference in 1993 and places it in the context of Canada's numerous efforts to break through the inertia of the international community in dealing with the over-exploitation of high seas living resources. After setting out the legal framework for high seas fishing, the author describes the extent of overfishing on the high seas and elements of a possible solution to this problem. The origins and the evolution of the Canadian legal initiative are recalled, including the lead-up to the United Nations Conference on Environment and Development, the discussions in Rio de Janeiro preceding the adoption of the mandate of the UN conference on high seas fishing and those in New York leading to the General Assembly's decision to convene the conference. The organizational and substantive sessions held by the conference in 1993 are subsequently reviewed, as well as the debate on the conference at the forty-eighth session of the General Assembly. In conclusion, the author notes the relative success of this initiative at this stage, which he attributes in large measure to the identification of overfishing on the high seas as a global environmental problem, and highlights the difficulties that remained to be resolved as the conference moved into the final phase of its work.

Interpretation and Naming: The Harmonized System in Canadian Customs Tariff Law

MAUREEN IRISH*

I IMPLEMENTATION OF THE HARMONIZED SYSTEM

O N JANUARY 1, 1988, Canada repealed its existing customs tariff and replaced it with the Harmonized Commodity Description and Coding System.[1] The Harmonized System (HS) is contained in an international convention that entered into force on that date.[2] The Harmonized System was built on the Customs Co-operation Council Nomenclature,[3] previously in use by most of the major

---

* Faculty of Law, University of Windsor. This article is based on a chapter from "The Harmonized System and Tariff Classification in Canada," my thesis for a D.C.L. degree granted by McGill University. I would like to express my continuing gratitude to Professor A.L.C. de Mestral for his kind supervision of both this thesis and a previous LL.M. thesis. Funding for doctoral research was provided by the Foundation for Legal Research and the Ontario Law Foundation (University of Windsor Law Faculty Grant). Thanks are also due to Ms. Cindy Dickinson, a 1993 graduate of the Faculty of Law, University of Windsor, for assistance in the checking of footnotes.

---

1 *Customs Tariff*, R.S.C. 1985 (3rd Supp.), c. 41 (S.C. 1987, c. 49).

2 *International Convention on the Harmonized Commodity Description and Coding System*, Can. T.S. 1988, No. 38, done at Brussels June 14, 1983, amended by Protocol of Amendment June 24, 1986, in force Jan. 1, 1988. See Customs Co-operation Council, *The International Convention on the Harmonized Commodity Description and Coding System* (Brussels: 1989), Annex C, Annex D.

3 *Convention on the Nomenclature for the Classification of Goods in Customs Tariffs* (CCCN), signed Dec. 15, 1950, 347 UNTS 127, amended by Protocol of Amendment July 1, 1955, 347 UNTS 143, in force Sept. 11, 1959. The CCCN was called the Brussels Tariff Nomenclature (BTN) until the name was changed in 1974 to avoid confusion with institutions of the European Union. For background on the history of tariff nomenclatures, see: Customs Co-operation Council, *The International Convention on the Harmonized Commodity Description and Coding*

trading nations of the world except the United States and Canada. Development of the Harmonized System led to membership for both Canada and the United States, which implemented the system on January 1, 1989. As of June 30, 1992, there were sixty-seven contracting parties to the HS, including a number of developing countries.[4]

To assist in interpretation, the Harmonized System contains section, chapter, and subheading notes that form part of the nomenclature. For matters that are not settled in these specific clarifications, the HS provides six general rules for interpretation. These rules, as well as the section, chapter, and subheading notes, are legally binding. There are also two supplementary sources for interpretation — explanatory notes and classification opinions — that are not officially binding within the Harmonized System.[5]

The first general rule for interpretation gives primary attention to the headings and legal notes. Rule 2(a) treats goods as finished or assembled so long as they have the "essential character" of the complete product. Rules 2(b) and 3 classify mixtures of materials by the component that gives the goods their "essential character." When no other heading applies, Rule 4 opts for the description of goods to which the imports "are most akin."

These rules emphasize the physical characteristics of imported goods, particularly their state of assembly and material composition.

System, Brussels, 1989; Customs Co-operation Council, *The CCC Nomenclature for the Classification of Goods in Customs Tariffs: Its Origins, Characteristic Features, Development and Application*, Brussels, 1979; Howard L. Friedenberg, *The Development of a Uniform International Tariff Nomenclature from 1853 to 1967, with Emphasis on the Brussels Tariff Nomenclature*, TC Publication 237 (Washington: United States Tariff Commission, 1968).

[4] An additional 35 administrations were using an HS-based tariff: Customs Co-operation Council, *Annual Report: The Activities of the Council, July 1991 to June 1992*, Bulletin No. 37 at 7, 61-62. Only Malawi had elected in favour of the partial application allowed to developing countries under Art. 4 so that they need not administer all the detailed subheadings. Other contracting parties must apply the HS in its full version, because reservations are prohibited by Art. 18 of the convention.

[5] The legal notes and general rules for interpretation were implemented as part of Canadian customs legislation. The supplementary sources — explanatory notes and classification opinions — are issued and revised from time to time by the Customs Co-operation Council. Canadian courts are directed to have regard to these two supplementary sources in interpretation: *Customs Tariff*, R.S.C. 1985 (3rd Supp.), c. 41, s. 11.

Interpretation is to be objective, rejecting extrinsic circumstances such as industrial origin, destination, and use, which may not be apparent on observation at the border. When the criteria are less concrete — the "essential character" of the imported goods or the identification of other goods "to which they are most akin" — the Customs Co-operation Council worries that interpretation will vary "according to the viewpoint of the person" making the decision. Such abstract matters are seen as too subjective, too influenced by the "personal appreciation" of the interpreter.[6] To ensure uniformity, it is assumed that interpretation must concentrate on concrete facts.

Physical features of goods, however, were not the only criteria on which the HS was drafted. Other considerations, including function and purpose ("footwear," "headgear," etc.), were relevant for some chapters, as was the case in the previous Customs Co-operation Council Nomenclature.[7] The thesis of this article is that interpretation should not be limited to the physical features intrinsic in goods, but should take account of other commercially relevant factors — in particular, the use. It is artificial to assume that a description of a good should answer only the questions "What does this look like?" or "What is it made of?" and never "What is this for?" There is no reason to think that the physical features of goods announce their real identity, while any hint of human intervention concerning them is somehow extraneous and unreliable. The Harmonized System, and the goods themselves, were produced to serve a commercial context. Attention to that context will not make application less uniform.

It is argued throughout that objectivism and the observation model do not provide certainty, even for a task as basic as the naming of concrete goods. Interpretation of the Harmonized System — and of any other treaty — will be affected by the perspectives of interpreters. To arrive at shared understandings, it is necessary to consider shared views and experiences. Interpretation of the Harmonized System requires an appreciation of the use of goods in application.

II THESIS: METAPHYSICS AND COGNITION

This study is a test of the objectivist assumptions behind the idea of pointing to a concrete object and naming it. Those assumptions

---

6 Customs Co-operation Council, *The International Convention on the Harmonized Commodity Description and Coding System*, 1989 at 38.

7 Howard L. Friedenberg, *supra* note 3 at 23; Michael Lux, *The Harmonized Commodity Description and Coding System*, Eurostat, undated but probably 1981 at 29.

are tested in a context where decisions have serious financial consequences and where those working in the field think that description should depend on qualities in the object itself. The idea that identity exists in the physical object raises a classic question in metaphysics about whether there is a real world out there or whether we just imagine it to be so. The claim made for qualities intrinsic in goods is, in fact, wider than the four primary qualities that John Locke thought to be in the object (solidity, extension, figure, and mobility), while others were in the observer.[8] This study does not quarrel with the existence of concrete objects. Attention, rather, is directed to the link between objects and the human mind, or, more precisely, the link between objects and human language.

The conclusion is that this link does not work in the way the Customs Co-operation Council and the observation model assume. Description is a very complicated process, especially if that description is to apply around the world in many different languages. Successful interpretation requires a more participatory model, incorporating the perspectives of users of the Harmonized System. When human perception is acknowledged, more attention will be paid to the function and purpose for which goods are produced.

The observation of colour has been studied by linguists. Different languages code colour in different ways. In other languages, the word that translates the English term "red" might also cover colours that English-speakers call brown, pink, orange, or yellow.[9] It has been suggested that there are about eleven universal basic colours, described in various ways in different languages. English calls them white, black, red, green, yellow, blue, brown, purple, pink, orange, and grey. Not all languages have all eleven. Some might have as few as two or three.[10] It is not necessary to decide the

---

[8] John Locke, *An Essay Concerning Human Understanding*, 1690, Book 2, Ch. 8, Para. 9, 46-47 (Chicago: Gateway Edition, 1956). These are sometimes listed as five — size, shape, solidity, numerability, mobility: Marcus Long, *The Spirit of Philosophy*, 68 (New York: W.W. Norton, 1953).

[9] Bernard Harrison, *An Introduction to the Philosophy of Language*, 16 (London: Macmillan Press, 1979), citing Brent Berlin and Paul Kay, *Basic Color Terms* (Berkeley: University of California Press, 1969). See also Richard L. Gregory, *Mind in Science*, 50 (Middlesex: Penguin Books, 1981); W. Haas, "The Theory of Translation" in G. H. R. Parkinson (ed.), *The Theory of Meaning* 86 at 97-98 (London: Oxford University Press, 1968).

[10] Geoffrey Leech, *Semantics*, 233-34 (2d ed., Middlesex: Penguin Books, 1981). The list of eleven comes from Berlin and Kay, *supra* note 9. Since the publication of *Basic Color Terms*, Paul Kay apparently has proposed that there are

debate about the existence of these universal basics to see that descriptions of colour will not match from one language to another. The effect of language structure has been tested in experiments involving English and Tarahumara, a language of Northern Mexico which has one word for the English terms "blue" and "green." In one experiment, subjects were shown several sets of colour chips, all either blue or green. Each set contained three chips, with one outside chip greener, one bluer, and the centre chip somewhere in the intervening range. Subjects were asked to pick out the chip that was most different from the other two — in effect, the outside chip that was further in colour from the centre chip. It was hypothesized that English-speakers might be influenced by colour labels in English when the set contained one outside chip in the range identified as "green" in English and the other outside chip in the range identified as "blue." The results bore out this hypothesis. For those sets, English-speaking subjects thought that a green centre chip was closer to the green outside chip and a blue centre chip was closer to the blue outside chip. Tarahumara-speakers demonstrated no such tendency to push colours apart at the border, but gave responses that generally matched the distances as measured scientifically according to wavelengths.

The experiment was then modified so that the tester would initially suggest to English-speakers that the centre chip was both blueish and greenish. Subjects then viewed the centre-left and centre-right pairs separately and were asked which colour difference was larger. In that situation, the English-speakers produced results very similar to those of the Tarahumara-speakers. The researchers concluded that actual perception was the same for the two groups, but when colour labels were available to be used, English-speakers were influenced by them.[11] If this result is applicable for other terms, it means that not only is there difficulty agreeing on names when perception is the same, but different names can actually cause us to think we see different things. It is an illustra-

---

actually only ten, with blue and green classified as one. There have also been suggestions that there are languages with twelve basic colours — including French, which has two terms "brun" and "marron" for what in English is called brown (Leech at 236).

11 The experiments are from Paul Kay and Willett Kempton, "What is the Sapir-Whorf Hypothesis?" 86 American Anthropologist 65 (1984). See discussion by Clark D. Cunningham in "A Tale of Two Clients: Thinking About Law as Language," 87 Michigan L. Rev. 2459 at 2475ff. (1989).

tion of how the classification system affects what we perceive and describe. What counts is not the object, but the linguistic reaction.

For the description of colour, which should be a fairly basic process, the observation model is insufficient. It is also, overall, seriously incomplete as an explanation of general names for concrete objects. In experiments, general names do not describe categories that consist unproblematically of things having the same features. When, for example, subjects were asked to rank certain birds and animals according to their degree of "birdiness," the answers consistently produced the following hierarchy: (1) robins, (2) eagles, (3) chickens, ducks, and geese, (4) penguins and pelicans, and (5) bats. Subjects seemed to classify by resemblance to a best example, about which there was widespread agreement.[12] The observation model does not explain how these prototypes arise. If general names are like colours, in that we understand them by fitting them into patterns, we should examine the criteria on which this is done.

George Lakoff has suggested that categories are determined by human imagination and not by the characteristics of objects themselves. In his theory, called experiential realism, basic-level categories ("chair," "table") are sized for human interaction. More general names ("furniture") reflect human purposes and uses. Categories are structured in complex ways through metaphor, metonymy, and imagery ("chair back," "table leg") rather than from detached observation of shared features. He concludes that there is no direct, unmediated link between language and the world as it exists outside human perception. It is therefore pointless to expect names to be a mirror representation of nature, unaffected by perspectives and cultures.[13]

In the early to mid part of this century, objectivism encountered heavy weather. The idea that one can verify through observation was attacked by W. V. O. Quine in "Two Dogmas of Empiricism," first

[12] Experiments by Eleanor Rosch (Eleanor Heider), discussed in George Lakoff, "Hedges: A Study in Meaning Criteria and the Logic of Fuzzy Concepts," 2 Journal of Philosophical Logic 458 (1973). See further Frederick Bowers, *Linguistic Aspects of Legislative Expression* 139 (Vancouver: UBC Press, 1989)

[13] George Lakoff, *Women, Fire and Dangerous Things: What Categories Reveal about the Mind* (Chicago: University of Chicago Press, 1987). The title of the book comes from a category in Dyirbal, an Aboriginal language of Australia, which provides links quite different from those in western cultures (Lakoff at 92ff.).

published in 1951. In that paper, he took issue with the notion that synthetic truths (grounded in fact) are different from analytic truths (grounded in meaning). Both are simply grounded in usage, according to Quine, and derive their truth from the overall network of beliefs.[14] The supposed method of verifying a synthetic truth through observation does not provide a secure link to reality. When a non-English-speaker points to what looks like a rabbit and says "gavagai," I can never know for sure what exactly the name means. It may mean "rabbit," "rabbit part," "rabbit colour," "small animal," "sacred beast," which includes rabbits and one other rare species, or any number of possibilities. Even if it is established that the word is a noun for a general kind, empirical observation cannot of itself prove the truth of the assertion, "that is a gavagai." The next instance could be the one in which the rabbit is missing an ear, and I find out that I have misunderstood the term all along.[15] Our whole network of beliefs may impinge on reality at the edges, as Quine suggested, but within the network what we take to be facts are surprisingly underdetermined. One cannot classify concrete objects simply by pointing a finger and naming.[16]

If there is no certainty in concrete objects, then attention shifts away from the relationship between objects and the human mind to the question of communication among minds.[17] In the preface to *The Order of Things*, Michel Foucault quotes the following classification of animals from Jorge Luis Borges, purportedly taken from an ancient Chinese encyclopedia:

14 W. V. O. Quine, "Two Dogmas of Empiricism" in Quine, *From a Logical Point of View*, 20 at 43 (Cambridge: Harvard University Press, 1964) ("Any statement can be held true come what may, if we make drastic enough adjustments elsewhere in the system."). The second dogma was the idea that all meaningful statements can be reduced to terms that refer to immediate experience. See further Friedrich Waismann, "Verifiability" in G. H. R. Parkinson (ed.), *supra* note 9 at 37 (paper first published 1945).

15 Example from W. V. O. Quine, *Word and Object*, 29ff. (Cambridge: MIT Press, 1960). See further Harrison, *supra* note 9 at 17-19, 96, 104-26.

16 Michael Devitt and Kim Sterelny, who are in the naturalist school of thought, make fun of this counter-intuitive argument in their text *Language and Reality: An Introduction to the Philosophy of Language*, 229 (Cambridge: MIT Press, 1987): "When the naturalistic philosopher points his finger at reality, the linguistic philosopher discusses the finger." Anthony D'Amato does just that, thoroughly, in "Aspects of Deconstruction: The Failure of the Word 'Bird,'" 84 Nw.U.L.Rev. 536 (1990).

17 Harrison, *supra* note 9 at 203.

(a) belonging to the Emperor, (b) embalmed, (c) tame, (d) sucking pigs, (e) sirens, (f) fabulous, (g) stray dogs, (h) included in the present classification, (i) frenzied, (j) innumerable, (k) drawn with a fine camelhair brush, (l) *et cetera*, (m) having just broken the water pitcher, (n) that from a long way off look like flies.[18]

The very difficulty of imagining such a system highlights the assumptions of rationality and human control behind the classic tabulation.[19] Foucault's (or Borges's) categories are quite distant from the organized, hierarchical headings and subheadings of the Harmonized System, in which any given object is to have one and only one correct classification. A coding system for objects depends not on qualities of the objects themselves, but on the human assumptions behind the system.

But does this mean that everything is subjective and uniform interpretation impossible? This paper suggests the use of goods as a factor to be considered, but use is not immune from interpretation either. Attention to basic assumptions means that we concentrate less on the objects and more on the interpreters. The issue is how uniformity is created, how interpreters agree about the prototype for "bird" or for anything else.

Thomas Kuhn, in *The Structure of Scientific Revolutions*, examines major shifts of assumptions in the scientific community, such as followed the discovery of oxygen or X-rays. Some fundamental ideas changed, but adjustments would normally be made and the network rewoven. Much of ordinary scientific activity continued in the usual way. Students still learned acquired knowledge through a combination of experiments and textbook examples. The training still provided a common way of seeing things, so that recognition of patterns would become automatic. New problems would be seen as similar to previous examples, and there would be widespread expectation of assent within the professional community.[20] Even major flaws in the observation model, identified with the develop-

18 Michel Foucault, *The Order of Things: An Archaeology of the Human Sciences*, xv (New York: Vintage Books, 1973, translation of *Les mots et les choses*, 1966).

19 See Hubert L. Dreyfus and Paul Rabinow, *Michel Foucault: Beyond Structuralism and Hermeneutics*, 19-20 (2d ed., Chicago: University of Chicago Press, 1983).

20 Thomas S. Kuhn, *The Structure of Scientific Revolutions*, 176-207 (2d ed., Chicago: University of Chicago Press, 1970). See Barry Barnes, "Thomas Kuhn" in Quentin Skinner (ed.), *The Return of Grand Theory in the Human Sciences* (Cambridge: Cambridge University Press, 1985) at 83. Jay M. Feinman discusses legal education as a similar sort of learning process: "Jurisprudence of Classification," 41 Stan.L.Rev. 661 (1989).

ment of quantum mechanics at the beginning of this century,[21] have not undermined shared community interpretations. Jeremy Campbell, writing in 1982, reports as an "often repeated *bon mot*" among scientists the quip that "[t]here is no such thing as an immaculate perception."[22] The abandonment of certainty in concrete objects does not imply the impossibility of shared understandings.

It is the thesis of this study that classification criteria come not from the objects themselves but rather from the observers. The human mind organizes according to factors relevant for human convenience.[23] In particular, for commodities in commercial trade, this study argues that use is a key concept. Natural kinds such as "bird" may be determined mainly by physical features, but for manufactured goods, function and purpose are central. Part of the idea of "vehicle" is that it is "for transporting goods or people."[24] Part of the idea of "cup" is that it "is used for drinking out of."[25] The emphasis on use will be particularly marked for products of new technology, which may accomplish the same thing as older goods but have different physical characteristics. Since the introduction of transistors and Walkmans, for example, what is a radio?[26]

21 Gary Zukav, *The Dancing Wu Li Masters: An Overview of the New Physics* (New York: Bantam Books, 1979). Note, in particular, the discussion of the wave/particle controversy at 45-66.

22 Jeremy Campbell, *Grammatical Man: Information, Entropy, Language and Life* 49 (New York: Simon and Schuster, 1982).

23 "To return to general words, it is plain . . . that general and universal belong not to the real existence of things; but are the inventions and creatures of the understanding, made by it for its own use, and concern only signs, whether words, or ideas": John Locke, *An Essay Concerning Human Understanding*, 1690, Book 3, Chapter 3, para. 11, 145 (Chicago: Gateway Edition, 1956). See the criticism of the jump from this theory to the question of essences, in Harrison, *supra* note 9 at 34-37.

24 Bowers, *supra* note 12 at 141.

25 Leech, *supra* note 10 at 120. See further: Harrison, *supra* note 9 at 202-6 (at 206: "The introduction of bean-bags into the extension of 'chair,' again, surely has something to do with the fact that 'chair' is an artifact term, and so ultimately defined, somehow or other, in terms of function"); Lakoff, *supra* note 13 at 51, 270.

26 With appreciation to Gordon Irish for this suggestion. See further Bowers, *supra* note 12 at 148, discussing legislation to regulate emerging technology in transportation and factory production from about 1850 to 1950. He notes that, in statutory interpretation, increased attention was paid to the function of goods, to context, and to technical language.

The sections below first discuss decisions under the Canadian customs tariff before the Harmonized System was implemented, with some references to more recent Canadian cases.[27] The rules of the Harmonized System are then examined in decisions drawn both from Canada and from the European Union, which has had long experience with the predecessors of the HS. The conclusion argues in favour of an interpretation that takes into account the perspectives of users of the Harmonized System, in both domestic and international applications.

III NAMING PRINCIPLE

A GENERAL

The most basic principle in tariff classification law is that of specificity: an import will be classified under the tariff item that describes it most specifically. In the *Accessories* appeal, which went to the Supreme Court of Canada in 1957, the Tariff Board, the Exchequer Court, and the Supreme Court all found that a replacement motor imported for a power shovel was more specifically classified under "[e]lectric motors . . . n.o.p." than as a part of the power shovel.[28] In summarizing the Board's decision, the Exchequer Court said:

It is clear from the Board's decision that in solving this problem it came to the conclusion that Parliament in setting up a tariff item for "electric motors" . . . dealt with them in a specific way by giving them an *eo nomine* classification, thereby removing them from the more general and unspecific designation of "all machinery . . . n.o.p., and complete parts of the foregoing." . . . In the Board's opinion there was nothing in the words "parts of the foregoing" . . . which in any way pointed directly to "electric motors"; the word "parts" was therefore inadequate to destroy or overcome the *eo nomine* classification that Parliament had seen fit to confer on "electric motors."[29]

The naming or *eo nomine* principle thus says that the best description is the one that seems to point most directly to the goods

---

27 The decisions are mainly from the Tariff Board and from the Canadian International Trade Tribunal, which replaced the Board for tariff classification appeals at the beginning of 1989: Canadian International Trade Tribunal Act, R.S.C. 1985 (4th Supp.), c. 47.

28 *Accessories Machinery Ltd.* v. *DMNRCE* (1955), 1 T.B.R. 221 (T.B. App. 331), aff'd [1956] Ex. C.R. 289, 1 T.B.R. 223, aff'd [1957] S.C.R. 358, 1 T.B.R. 229.

29 *Ibid.* at 227 (T.B.R.).

imported. This does not explain exactly how the description points to the goods.

The observation model for tariff classification focuses on the physical characteristics of goods at the time of importation, with the idea that they determine the name. It is argued throughout this study that interpretation should be done instead on a participatory model, in which attention is also directed to the interpreters and to the use of goods in application. If a motor is designed for one particular commercial application, then the context could show that it is more specifically described as a part of a machine than as a motor. The better description, then, might not actually be the name that on its surface seems to refer to the smaller class of goods.

This section is divided into several parts. The first one examines the basic *eo nomine* principle and the term "n.o.p." ("not otherwise provided"). The second looks at the question of specialized meaning in a trade or commercial context. The next part deals with naming according to essential components. Decisions on naming according to use are then reviewed. The last part discusses the purposive or teleological approach to naming.

It is argued throughout that description according to intrinsic, observable characteristics should not be treated as the primary way to approach classification, and that the best theory of description will take account of the natural tendency to describe goods according to their use. It is further argued that this does not necessarily imply narrow purposive interpretation as it is usually understood by legal scholars, since the Harmonized System is intended to have global application, and the Canadian customs tariff is not the only context in which it will be interpreted.

B   EO NOMINE AND N.O.P.

When two tariff items might be applicable, the choice between the two sometimes seems to be made according to which item is more specific on its surface. One item might cover a whole category of goods, while the other is more narrow. Or one item may be unrestricted, while another is limited by "n.o.p." ("not otherwise provided"[30]). In *Pascal Hotel*, for example, utensils for cooking were found to be "spoons" rather than "manufactures . . . of iron or

---

30 This was the definition in s. 2 of the previous Customs Tariff Act, R.S.C. 1985, c. C-54, which was repealed R.S.C. 1985 (3rd Supp.), c. 41. The phrase in French was "non dénommé (n.d.)." For an early application, see *Dress Manufacturers Guild of Toronto v. DMNRCE* (1949), 1 T.B.R. 2 (T.B. App. 160).

steel . . . n.o.p."[31] In *Tripar,* steel strips coated first with brass and then with resin were classified as "coated with metal or metals other than lead, zinc or tin" rather than under an item for steel strips "coated n.o.p."[32] And in the *BCL X-Ray Canada* appeal, a fluoroscopic TV camera to be used in medical X-ray diagnosis was found to be "X-ray apparatus" rather than "television apparatus, n.o.p."[33] As was stated in the *Okanagan Gift* appeal: "When an article is within the description of goods in more than one tariff item, one of which specifically names the article while the other includes a more general description with an n.o.p. provision, the former is to be preferred."[34]

This sort of surface or grammatical analysis is undoubtedly helpful and draws attention to considerations that cannot be ignored in interpretation. But it does not provide guidance for complete answers. The *Pascal Hotel* decision really dealt with whether the word "spoons" had to be interpreted as only for tableware, given that other goods listed in the same item were so limited. Tariff Board member Gorman wrote a separate concurring judgment in which he pointed out that there was no qualifying adjective for "spoons" as there was for "table knives" and "table forks." In *Tripar,* the Board said that "coated with metal" was not only a more specific phrase, but was also a better description of the goods than simply "coated n.o.p."; the question of which coating was applied last was therefore less significant. And "X-ray apparatus" was held to be both more specific and also a better description of the camera in question in *BCL X-Ray Canada,* which presented the information in a usable form since the X-ray screen itself was too small and had too high a voltage to be viewed directly. While the surface, grammatical analysis is

---

[31] *Pascal Hotel Supplies Inc.* v. *DMNRCE* (1984), 9 T.B.R. 116, 6 C.E.R. 179 (T.B. App. 1985). For a similar decision that found souvenir spoons to be "spoons" rather than "electro-plated ware n.o.p.," see *Okanagan Gift & Souvenir* v. *DMNRCE* (1984), 9 T.B.R. 82, 7 C.E.R. 4 (T.B. App. 2035). *Pascal Hotel* was applied in *Johnson-Rose Inc.* v. *DMNRCE* (1985), 10 T.B.R. 22, 8 C.E.R. 204 (T.B. App. 2165).

[32] *Tripar Inc.* v. *DMNRCE* (1983), 8 T.B.R. 605, 5 C.E.R. 217 (T.B. App. 1913).

[33] *BCL X-Ray Canada Inc.* v. *DMNRCE* (1987), 12 T.B.R. 35, 13 C.E.R. 212 (T.B. App. 2530).

[34] *Okanagan Gift & Souvenir* v. *DMNRCE* (1984), 9 T.B.R. 82 at 85, 7 C.E.R. 4 (T.B. App. 2035). See also *Commander R.D.C. Sweeney* v. *DMNRCE* (1981), 8 T.B.R. 12, 3 C.E.R. 348 (T.B. App. 1687). For examples under the HS that seem to use a superficial approach to specificity, see: *Éditions Panini du Canada Ltée* v. *DMNRCE,* [1993] C.I.T.T. No. 38 (QL) (AP-92-018); *Praher Canada Products Ltd.* v. *DMNRCE,* [1993] C.I.T.T. No. 99 (QL) (AP-92-112).

necessary, it is not a sufficient explanation of the factors that determine classification decisions. And the grammatical analysis does not help in situations where there are no obvious surface indications, such as the *B.L. Marks* appeal, in which the Board had to determine whether toaster pastries were biscuits or confections.[35]

It may be noted that in the early *Accessories* appeal, the *eo nomine* item for electric motors had priority despite the fact that it was an "n.o.p." item and the mention of parts in the machinery item was not "n.o.p."[36] The *eo nomine* aspect meant that the goods were more specifically electric motors than parts of the power shovel. The item would have given way to another item describing the goods more narrowly as motors or as motive power, but did not give way to the parts item. It was thus possible that an *eo nomine* item could have priority despite being n.o.p., if the competing description was not as good. In another example, in the *Underwood* appeal, a machine that added and multiplied automatically was classified as "calculating . . . machines . . . n.o.p." rather than under an item for "adding machines," since adding machines were construed as a smaller, more limited class of calculating machines taken out of the wider item. Since the imported good could also multiply automatically, it was not in the smaller class.[37]

C ORDINARY MEANING, TRADE MEANING

In *Parke Davis*, the first appeal to the Exchequer Court under the Customs Act, it was established that ordinary meaning would have priority in the interpretation of the tariff. In the words of Mr. Justice Thorson:

35 *B. L. Marks Sales Co.* v. *DMNRCE* (1986), 11 T.B.R. 216, 11 C.E.R. 314 (T.B. App. 2199), aff'd 14 C.E.R. 56 (F.C.A.). The Board looked to dictionary definitions and commercial advertising to determine that the goods were in fact better described as confections.

36 *Accessories Machinery Ltd., supra* note 28.

37 *Underwood Ltd.* v. *DMNRCE* (1966), 3 T.B.R. 310 (T.B. App. 831). See also *Les Publications Étrangères au Canada* v. *DMNRCE* (1978), C. Gaz. 1978.I.5375 at 5380 (T.B. Apps. 1306, 1320); *Thomas J. Lipton Inc.* v. *DMNRCE* (1985), 10 T.B.R. 145, 9 C.E.R. 102 (T.B. App. 2204), in which the majority held herbal teas to be "vegetable materials for use as flavourings, n.o.p.," rather than under 71100-7 "prepared . . . beverages . . . for human consumption," in part because of the residual nature of the 71100-7 item. In another decision, however, the Tribunal relied on an "n.o.p." designation to classify goods as parts of semiconductors rather than as "electric apparatus designed for welding, n.o.p.": *Eev Canada Ltd.* v. *DMNRCE*, [1991] C.I.T.T. No. 55 (QL) (App. 2372).

[I]n the absence of a clear expression to the contrary, words in the Customs Tariff should receive their ordinary meaning but if it appears from the context in which they are used that they have a special technical meaning they should be read with such meaning.[38]

In the appeal, the Court upheld the Board's decision to classify penicillin as a "biological product" because that was in accordance with the technical meaning in the pharmaceutical industry at the time. Evidence concerning this technical meaning was to be based solely on testimony of experts before the Board, and Mr. Justice Thorson criticized the dissenting Board member for basing his opinion on his own technical knowledge as a chemist.

The ordinary meaning approach was confirmed by the Supreme Court of Canada in the *Pfizer* case, which had to do with the importation of various forms of the antibiotic oxytetracycline. If the goods were within "tetracycline and its derivatives," they were subject to duty; otherwise they would be duty free, under a general exemption for antibiotics. The appellant argued that, since the goods could not actually be produced from tetracycline itself, they were not "derivatives" of tetracycline and thus were not dutiable. The Tariff Board and the majority of the Federal Court of Appeal both decided in favour of the Crown, on evidence that showed a possible wider meaning of "derivative" in the industry, covering substances with closely related chemical structures, even if they could not actually be prepared from the basic substance. This wider meaning was rejected by the Supreme Court of Canada, which decided in favour of the appellant and found the goods to be duty free.[39] The judgment of the Supreme Court, written by Mr. Justice Pigeon, confirms the primacy of the ordinary language approach:

The rule that statutes are to be construed according to the meaning of the words in common language is quite firmly established and it is applicable to statutes dealing with technical or scientific matters. . . . Of course, because "tetracycline" designates a specific substance the composition of which has been determined in terms of a chemical formula, resort may be had to the appropriate sources for ascertaining its

---

38 *DMNRCE* v. *Parke Davis & Co.* (1953), [1954] Ex. C.R. 1, 1 T.B.R. 12 at 21, aff'g (1949), 1 T.B.R. 10 (T.B. App. 195). See also *ETF Tools Ltd* v. *DMNRCE* (1962), 3 T.B.R. 50 (Ex. Ct.); *DMNRCE* v. *First Lady Coiffures Ltd.* (1986), 13 C.E.R. 42, 71 N.R. 76 (F.C.A.). For earlier adoption of trade usage in a different procedural setting, see *Dominion Bag Co.* v. *R.* (1894), 4 Ex. C.R. 311.

39 *Pfizer Co.* v. *DMNRCE*, (1971), 5 T.B.R. 223 (T.B. App. 963), aff'd [1973] F.C. 3, 5 T.B.R. 236 (F.C.A.), rev'd (1975), [1977] 1 S.C.R. 456, 5 T.B.R. 257.

meaning. In my view, this does not imply that "derivative" is to be construed as it might be in a scientific publication. The question concerns the meaning of "derivative" not of "tetracycline."[40]

The decision of the Supreme Court appears to mirror the approach in *Parke Davis*, but is actually more restrictive in how much territory it is prepared to cede to specialized technical usages. The Exchequer Court in *Parke Davis* accepted the technical meaning of "biological product," even though both words could be said to be individually part of general linguistic competence. The Supreme Court of Canada, on the other hand, was not prepared to give up supervision of "tetracycline and its derivatives," even though the phrase is probably not part of everyday speech for the average citizen.

The Supreme Court decision involved as well an assertion of literal interpretation and a rejection of the purposive approach.[41] At the time, there were no manufacturers of oxytetracycline in Canada, but there was one manufacturer of chlortetracycline, a directly competitive antibiotic. The majority of the Federal Court of Appeal below had rejected the narrow meaning of "derivative" in part because it seemed to lead to an improbable result. As Chief Justice Jackett stated:

[T]he result of such an interpretation . . . would be that the only protection afforded to the manufacturer in Canada of chlortetracycline and its salts would be against the importation of the salts of tetracycline. Not only would there be no protection against the importation of oxytetracycline or its salts but there would be no protection against the importation of chlortetracycline or its salts.

It does seem improbable that it would have been intended to afford a chlortetracycline manufacturer protection against tetracycline and its salts but not against chlortetracycline itself or its salts.[42]

While the narrow meaning requiring actual production of one substance from the other existed in both ordinary and specialized usage, the Board and the Court of Appeal were willing to adopt the wider meaning found in some technical usage in order to give effect to the legislator's presumed purpose.

Mr. Justice Pigeon in the Supreme Court clearly rejected this sort of reasoning and opted instead for a literal reading, which reduced

[40] *Ibid.* at 261 (T.B.R.).

[41] The decision was also based on questions of onus and the interpretation of bilingual legislation.

[42] *Supra* note 39 at 237-38 (T.B.R.).

the relevance of the commercial context and at the same time gave the Court full jurisdiction over the task of interpretation.[43]

The Tariff Board had relied heavily on dictionary definitions, since the expert witnesses were evenly divided on technical usage. Dictionaries can, of course, be read just as easily by judges on review as by the members of the Tariff Board. The Federal Court of Appeal had been reluctant to re-do the interpretative work of the Board below, but the Supreme Court had no such hesitation. Even if there had been a finding of fact based on the expert testimony as to what industry usage permitted, the approach taken by Mr. Justice Pigeon meant that the Court would still have had jurisdiction to reinterpret. Since the ordinary meaning of "derivative" was the one to use, the judges — not the technical experts — were in control.

There is obviously more than protection of turf in the approach taken by the Supreme Court. Removed from arguments about the proper role of judges in relation to administrative agencies, the trade meaning/ordinary meaning split becomes a generalized question of who should decide. In the context of the Harmonized System applied on a wide geographic basis, this becomes less a question of justifying the supervisory power of the judiciary and more a simple question of how much should be determined by each user. In most contexts, those making classification decisions would be within the particular trade or industry and would automatically adopt the trade usage without giving the matter any particular thought. Manufacturers of antibiotics, for example, could be expected to use the vocabulary of their industry automatically without wondering whether an ordinarily competent speaker of the language in question would agree. The issue is basically how much has to be universal in order for the HS to function as it was intended — that is, how much has to be common for the classifications to be translatable across geographic regions. From a global perspective, trade meaning is not necessarily the specialized meaning, but could in fact have wider acceptance than ordinary Canadian meaning.

The Supreme Court decision in *Pfizer* was the high-water mark of the ordinary meaning approach. In some contexts, ordinary meaning will quite naturally have priority. It would normally be used, for example, in the classification of common, everyday objects such as

---

43 In part, Mr. Justice Pigeon was also giving effect to the presumption that taxing legislation should be interpreted in favour of the taxpayer. As well, it should be noted that the goods had previously been free of duty as chemicals of a kind not produced in Canada. The question was how much the new scheme was intended to change.

socks,[44] tool bags,[45] hats,[46] bread,[47] or cooking apparatus.[48] The context, however, can indicate that the ordinary, everyday meaning is not the one intended. In *Adams Brands*, for example, when the Tariff Board cited an old popular song about chewing gum as evidence of the ordinary meaning of "gums and blends consisting wholly or in chief part of gums, n.o.p.," the Federal Court of Appeal reversed. According to the Court of Appeal, the surrounding tariff items indicated that this one was intended to refer only to natural gums, not to synthetic chemical products like the goods in question.[49]

Furthermore, despite the Supreme Court judgment in *Pfizer*, it is still quite possible to apply trade meaning to the interpretation of the customs tariff. In *Denbyware*, an unreported Federal Court of Appeal decision, the Court dismissed an appeal from a Tariff Board

44 *Trimark Athletic Supplies Inc.* v. *DMNRCE* (1984), 9 T.B.R. 311, 7 C.E.R. 41 (T.B. App. 2121).

45 *Cavalier Luggage Ltd.* v. *DMNRCE* (1987), 12 T.B.R. 69, 13 C.E.R. 243 (T.B. App. 2573)(pencil cases were not included).

46 *Greisman & Son (Canada) Ltd.* v. *DMNRCE* (1957), 2 T.B.R. 107 (T.B. App. 439); *Midway Industries Ltd.* v. *DMNRCE* (1959), 2 T.B.R. 167 (T.B. App. 486); *Neckwear Ltd.* v. *DMNRCE* (1962), 2 T.B.R. 272 (T.B. App. 582). The definitions established in these appeals were followed in *Beco Industries Ltd.* v. *DMNRCE* (1980), 7 T.B.R. 220, 2 C.E.R. 318 (T.B. App. 1540); *Kate's Millinery Ltd.* v. *DMNRCE* (1982), 8 T.B.R. 103, 4 C.E.R. 76 (T.B. App. 1660), aff'd F.C.A., June 13, 1984 (see [1984] 1 F.C. 1157).

47 *B. L. Marks Sales Co.* v. *DMNRCE* (1977), C.Gaz. 1977.I.2821 (T.B. App. 1186). For a decision under the HS in which trade and ordinary meanings were in agreement, see *Little Bear Organic Foods* v. *DMNRCE* (1992), 5 T.C.T. 1107 (C.I.T.T., AP-89-214).

48 *Food Machinery of Canada Ltd.* v. *DMNRCE* (1959), 2 T.B.R. 118 (T.B. App. 443), aff'd (*sub nom. Campbell Soup Co.* v. *DMNRCE*) (1960), 2 T.B.R. 120 (Ex. Ct.); *Zuccarini* v. *DMNRCE* (1959), 2 T.B.R. 201 (T.B. App. 512). See also *J. H. Ryder Machinery Co.* v. *DMNRCE* (1952), 1 T.B.R. 66 (T.B. App. 255); *A. P. I. Laboratory Products Ltd.* v. *DMNRCE* (1983), 8 T.B.R. 730, 5 C.E.R. 514 (T.B. App. 1948).

49 *Adams Brands* v. *DMNRCE* (1981), 7 T.B.R. 288, 3 C.E.R. 71 (T.B. Apps. 1485 etc.), rev'd (1984), 7 C.E.R. 153 (F.C.A.), reheard (1984), 9 T.B.R. 280, 7 C.E.R. 7 (T.B. Apps. 1485 etc.). The Federal Court of Appeal did not, however, mean that any human intervention in the production process would disqualify goods from being "natural gums": *Kelco Specialty Colloids Ltd.* v. *DMNRCE* (1985), 10 T.B.R. 10, 8 C.E.R. 191 (T.B. App. 2129), rev'd (1987), 13 C.E.R. 345 (F.C.A.). For further examples of context overriding common, everyday meaning, see *Consolidated Sand and Gravel Ltd.* v. *DMNRCE* (1951), 1 T.B.R. 42 (T.B. App. 2299); *I. D. Foods Corp.* v. *DMNRCE* (1986), 11 T.B.R. 55, 13 C.E.R. 90 (T.B. App. 2526).

declaration that had adopted trade usage concerning pottery and porcelain. Mr. Justice Urie of the Court of Appeal said:

A customs tariff being for commercial usage in respect of the conditions of admission of goods to Canada, the terms used in it should be given the meaning which the term used is generally given in the trade concerned with the production and sale of the goods in question.[50]

This particular passage was quoted in *Olympia Floor*, a later judgment of the Federal Court, when it allowed an appeal from a Tariff Board decision and directed the Board to follow trade meaning rather than ordinary meaning. The dispute had to do with imported ceramic building tile, which the Deputy Minister had classified as "earthenware tiles n.o.p." The appellant argued that these tiles were less porous and less water-absorbent than the tiles known in the industry as earthenware tiles. Since there was no other item providing a better description, the appellant said the goods should be classified as "manufactures of clay n.o.p." The Tariff Board majority, following one of the Board's earlier declarations,[51] said that the goods were earthenware tiles according to the ordinary meaning of that phrase. Tariff Board member Martin dissented on the ground that the appellant had presented adequate evidence to support its argument concerning the specialized trade meaning, and this was the meaning that should be applied.[52]

The Federal Court of Appeal adopted this dissent when it allowed the appeal. Referring to the judgment of Mr. Justice Pigeon in *Pfizer*, the Court implied that the use of the trade meaning here was like relying on the technical meaning for interpreting the word "tetracycline," and that it was trade meaning that should be followed. Speaking for the Court, Mr. Justice Ryan said:

[I]f the term "earthenware tiles" carries a recognized trade meaning, it must be read in that sense. I have no doubt that a legislature could

---

[50] *Denbyware Canada Ltd.* v. *DMNRCE*, Reasons for Judgment, p. 2 (15 May 1979), A-274-78 (F.C.A.) (also noted 5 C.E.R. 566), aff'g (1978), 6 T.B.R. 620 (T.B. App. 1304). The Supreme Court of Canada refused leave to appeal the Court of Appeal decision in *Denbyware*: (1979), 31 N.R. 172. See also *Josiah Wedgwood and Sons (Canada) Ltd.* v. *DMNRCE* (1982), 8 T.B.R. 154, 4 C.E.R. 164 (T.B. App. 1634); *Anglo-Canadian Mercantile Co.* v. *DMNRCE* (1984), 9 T.B.R. 345, 7 C.E.R. 116 (T.B. App. 2116).

[51] *Tilechem Ltd.* v. *DMNRCE* (1976), C.Gaz. 1977.I.2810 (T.B. App. 1102).

[52] *Olympia Floor and Wall Tile Co.* v. *DMNRCE* (1982), 8 T.B.R. 31, 4 C.E.R. 10 (T.B. Apps. 1526 etc.).

specify that, even though a term has a special meaning in a trade with which a statute deals, it must nevertheless be read in another sense; and if that can be done expressly, it can certainly be done by implication. But I do not read [the tariff item in question], whether alone or in context, as being intended to require giving to "earthenware tiles" a non-trade meaning where, as here, a trade meaning is proved.[53]

In the result, the matter was referred back to the Tariff Board which held the goods to be "manufactures of clay n.o.p."[54]

This decision is not as easily reconciled with the Supreme Court judgment in *Pfizer* as the Federal Court of Appeal seems to imply, although it is quite consistent with the approach in *Denbyware* and with the judgment of the Exchequer Court in *Parke Davis.* If ceramic tiles, porcelain, and penicillin are all to be classified according to trade usage, why not also derivatives of tetracycline? The Supreme Court's enthusiasm in *Pfizer* for interpretation by the non-specialist seems out of place. And, given the Court's refusal to grant leave to appeal in *Denbyware*, it may be that *Pfizer* no longer represents the definitive position on the question.

Perhaps the best solution is to take the suggestion of the Federal Court of Appeal and concentrate on the context in which each term is used:

It seems reasonably clear that, if a term used in the *Customs Tariff* has a particular meaning in a trade, it should be interpreted in that sense. But there are, of course, many words used in the *Customs Tariff* which are quite ordinary words, words used in ordinary conversation in an everyday way; such words are to be read in their ordinary sense.[55]

As an illustration of this approach, the Court cites an earlier decision of the Exchequer Court, *Hunt Foods*, in which that court had to interpret "lard compound and similar substances, n.o.p." The Court followed trade meaning for "lard compound" but said that "similar substances" should be interpreted according to its ordi-

---

53 *Olympia Floor and Wall Tile Co.* v. *DMNRCE* (1983), 5 C.E.R. 562 at 575, 49 N.R. 66 (F.C.A.).

54 *Olympia Floor and Wall Tile Co.* v. *DMNRCE* (1984), 9 T.B.R. 169, 6 C.E.R. 218 (T.B. Apps. 1526 etc.); see also *Olympia Floor* v. *DMNRCE* (1984), 9 T.B.R. 308, 7 C.E.R. 27 (T.B. Apps. 1617 etc.). The appellant was again successful when the Department reclassified further imports of the goods after a slight change in the tariff item: *Olympia Floor and Wall Tile Co.* v. *DMNRCE* (1987), 12 T.B.R. 479, 15 C.E.R. 137 (T.B. Apps. 2548, 2642).

55 *Olympia Floor, supra* note 53 at 565.

nary meaning since it did not have a specialized trade sense.[56] In form at least, this is reminiscent of the technique in *Pfizer.* The difference is the implication that trade meaning should have priority if it is shown that a specialized trade usage exists.

If the question is determined by who the expected audience would be, it probably does make sense to follow trade meaning, since most users of the customs tariff or of the Harmonized System would be business users already operating within the context of that trade. It would be an artificial and unnecessary imposition to expect them to disregard accepted trade terminology and always ask themselves whether a particular interpretation would agree with that of the ordinarily competent speaker.

After the Federal Court of Appeal judgments in *Denbyware* and *Olympia Floor,* the Tariff Board was quite willing to adopt trade usage where relevant. In *Beaulieu,* for example, the Board looked to the commercial context and decided that imported jute yarn was not "twine" because it would not be so classified in trade usage. The goods might perhaps have met a dictionary definition of the term. In the trade, however, twine was a more processed yarn used for binding, while the imported goods were a less expensive, less refined yarn used for the structural backing of rugs. Citing a previous declaration which in turn had referred to *Olympia Floor,* the Board decided that the imported goods were not twine but jute yarn, and thus eligible for duty exemption under the General Preferential Tariff.[57] At this point, it may probably be said that trade

---

[56] *Hunt Foods Export Corp.* v. *DMNRCE,* [1970] Ex. C.R. 828, 4 T.B.R. 333, rev'g (1969), 4 T.B.R. 328 (T.B. Apps. 907, 908 909). A Tariff Board reference was held as a result of the Exchequer Court decision in this appeal: C.Gaz. 1975.I.573. For other declarations interpreting the item, see *Consumers Foodcraft Corp.* v. *DMNRCE* (1955), 1 T.B.R. 237 (T.B. App. 343); *Les Entreprises Mair Fried Enrg.* v. *DMNRCE* (1978), C.Gaz. 1979.I.3048 (T.B. App. 1220); *Frito-Lay Canada Ltd.* v. *DMNRCE* (1978), 6 T.B.R. 634 (T.B. Apps. 1241 etc.), aff'd (1980), 2 C.E.R. 143 (F.C.A.).

[57] *Beaulieu of Canada Inc.* v. *DMNRCE* (1987), 12 T.B.R. 27, 13 C.E.R. 206 (T.B. App. 2386), citing *British Steel Canada Inc.* v. *DMNRCE* (1984), 9 T.B.R. 240, 7 C.E.R. 230 (T.B. App. 2067). In a decision under the Harmonized System, the Canadian International Trade Tribunal also followed the Court of Appeal judgment in *Olympia Floor* and opted for trade meaning: *Diamant Boart Truco Ltd.* v. *DMNRCE* (1992), 5 T.C.T. 1315 (C.I.T.T., AP-90-166).

usage is followed in just as routine a fashion as before the Supreme Court judgment in *Pfizer*.[58]

When trade meaning is applied, it is the meaning as understood by those knowledgeable in the trade.[59] As the Tariff Board said in *Carl Zeiss*:

> In an issue relating to the interpretation of a statute such as the *Customs Tariff*, neither the technical usage of a particular science or art nor the use current among the uninformed should prevail over the commercial or trade usage common among those informed persons conversant with the subject matter.[60]

It is not the technical or laboratory sense that governs, but rather the terminology of those who deal with the goods as articles of

---

58 See *Ocelot Chemicals* v. *DMNRCE* (1985), 10 T.B.R. 286, 10 C.E.R. 208 (T.B. App. 2019); *Fisher Scientific Ltd.* v. *DMNRCE* (1987), 12 T.B.R. 457, 15 C.E.R. 114 (T.B. App. 2650); *Jagenberg of Canada Ltd.* v. *DMNRCE* (1988), 17 C.E.R. 296 (T.B. App. 2686); *Cassidy's Ltd.* v. *DMNRCE* (1989), 2 T.C.T. 1043 (C.I.T.T. Apps. 2914 etc.); *Burroughs Wellcome Inc.* v. *DMNRCE* (1989), 2 T.C.T. 1054 (C.I.T.T. App. 2673); *International Cordage Systems Ltd.* v. *DMNRCE* (1989), 2 T.C.T. 1193 (C.I.T.T. App. 3085). For declarations after *Denbyware* but before *Olympia Floor*, see *Turmac Electronics Ltd.* v. *DMNRCE* (1979), 6 T.B.R. 931, 1 C.E.R. 292 (T.B. App. 1401); *C. J. Rush Ltd.* v. *DMNRCE*, (1979), 6 T.B.R. 902, 1 C.E.R. 231 (T.B. App. 1422); *Wilson Machine Co.* v. *DMNRCE* (1979), 6 T.B.R. 895, 1 C.E.R. 226 (T.B. App. 1402), which cites the F.C.A. judgment in *Pfizer*, but not the Supreme Court decision. For a few earlier examples of routine application of trade usage, see *J. H. Ryder Machinery Co.* v. *DMNRCE* (1956), 1 T.B.R. 252 (T.B. App. 371); *Reference re Tall Oil Fatty Acids* (1959), 2 T.B.R. 184 (T.B. App. 497); *American-Standard Products (Canada) Ltd.* v. *DMNRCE* (1960), 2 T.B.R. 220 (T.B. App. 529); *Industrial Textiles Ltd.* v. *DMNRCE* (1961), 2 T.B.R. 226 (T.B. App. 538); *Bomac Electrotype Co.* v. *DMNRCE* (1965), 3 T.B.R. 243 (T.B. App. 785); *Beloit Sorel Ltd.* v. *DMNRCE* (1966), 3 T.B.R. 321 (T.B. App. 839). Trade usage also seems to be readily adopted when it has to do with measurement: *Anglophoto Ltd.* v. *DMNRCE* (1979), 6 T.B.R. 767, 1 C.E.R. 61 (T.B. App. 1397); *Auto Radiator Manufacturing Ltd.* v. *DMNRCE* (1979), 6 T.B.R. 857, 1 C.E.R. 194 (T.B. App. 1424). For decisions under the Harmonized System, see *Crosby Valve Ltd.* v. *DMNRCE* (1991), 5 T.C.T. 1003 (C.I.T.T. AP-90-179); *Esden Ltd.* v. *DMNRCE* (1992), 5 T.C.T. 1078 (C.I.T.T. AP-90-006); *MLG Enterprises Ltd.* v. *DMNRCE* (1992), 5 T.C.T. 1134 (C.I.T.T. AP-89-170); *D. Dyck Industries Ltd.* v. *DMNRCE* (1992), 5 T.C.T. 1396 (C.I.T.T. AP-91-157); *F. W. Woolworth Co.* v. *DMNRCE*, [1993] C.I.T.T. No. 63 (QL) (AP-92-007); *Apotex Inc.* v. *DMNRCE*, [1993] C.I.T.T. No. 112 (QL) (AP-92-087); *Gilmour Sports Ltd.* v. *DMNRCE*, [1993] C.I.T.T. No. 132 (QL) (AP-92-102, AP-92-354).

59 *W. J. Elliott & Co.* v. *DMNRCE* (1968), [1969] Ex. C.R. 67, 4 T.B.R. 86; *R.* v. *Planters Nut and Chocolate Co.* (1951), 1 T.B.R. 271 (Ex. Ct.).

60 *Carl Zeiss Canada Ltd.* v. *DMNRCE* (1967), 4 T.B.R. 31 at 37 (T.B. App. 849).

commerce.[61] The meaning as understood by users of the goods in ordinary commerce[62] is, in a sense, the ordinary or regular meaning.

In each case, it is a question of deciding what should be the relevant context. In a given context, trade meaning and ordinary meaning might be the same,[63] or at least the evidence might be insufficient to establish a distinctive trade use.[64] And it may be that, even if a distinctive trade usage could be proved, the ordinary meaning would still be the one to apply, particularly for goods in common household use.[65] In *Perley-Robertson*, for example, instant coffee was classified as an extract of coffee in accordance with ordinary meaning, despite the fact that the coffee trade studiously avoided the word "extract" due to its association with an earlier inferior product that had been marketed unsuccessfully. The suppression of the term within the industry had not been so pervasive as to change the ordinary meaning, and ordinary meaning governed.[66] It is really a question of looking each time to the context to decide whether specialist or non-specialist meaning should govern. The context for most discussions about instant coffee, for example, is likely to be different from the context for most discussions about derivatives of tetracycline. Both before and after the implementation of the Harmonized System, trade meaning has been applied in tariff classification appeals where required by the context.

D   COMPOSITION

In the customs tariff before the Harmonized System was implemented, goods could be classified by composition without having to

---

[61] *Reference re Dehydrated Grasses* (1958), 2 T.B.R. 175 (T.B. App. 493); *Cosmos Imperial Mills Ltd.* v. *DMNRCE* (1957), 2 T.B.R. 99 (T.B. App. 421); *Sherwin-Williams Co. of Canada* v. *DMNRCE* (1950), 1 T.B.R. 35 (T.B. App. 215).

[62] *Aries Inspection Services Ltd.* v. *DMNRCE* (1980), 7 T.B.R. 18, 2 C.E.R. 25 (T.B. App. 1446); *Mine Equipment Co.* v. *DMNRCE* (1970), C.Gaz.1971.I.2829 at 2831 (T.B. App. 948); *Mount Bruno Floral Co.* v. *DMNRCE* (1949), 1 T.B.R. 6 (T.B. App. 167).

[63] *Sefer Ltd.* v. *DMNRCE* (1970), 5 T.B.R. 52 (Ex. Ct.).

[64] *Universal Fur Dressers and Dyers Ltd.* v. *DMNRCE* (1951), 1 T.B.R. 43 (T.B. App. 231); *Quebec Photo Service Inc.* v. *DMNRCE* (1980), 7 T.B.R. 185, 2 C.E.R. 282 (T.B. App. 1463); *Johnson & Johnson Ltd.* v. *DMNRCE* (1982), 8 T.B.R. 147, 4 C.E.R. 146 (T.B. App. 1653).

[65] *Grand Specialties Ltd.* v. *DMNRCE* (1987), 12 T.B.R. 60, 13 C.E.R. 233 (T.B. App. 2565).

[66] *Perley-Robertson* v. *DMNRCE* (1962), 2 T.B.R. 274 (T.B. App. 586).

be composed entirely of only one element. In the *Dow Chemical* appeal, the Tariff Board held that the imports did not have to be 100 per cent ethylene glycol in order to be classified as this, since 100 per cent purity was rarely available; all that was necessary was that the product be "of such degree of purity as not to be confused in either technical or commercial language" with various blends of ethylene glycol that were for sale on the market.[67] Similarly, the goods in *Toronto Refiners* were old lead scrap even though they contained some tin,[68] the mirrored sliding doors in *Monarch Mirror* were mirrors despite the presence of tracks and nylon rollers,[69] and the fruit syrups in *Imported Delicacies* were still fruit syrups even though they contained a small quantity of stabilizer in addition to the fruit juice and sugar.[70] The meaning of the language in use governed, whether in ordinary or in trade usage. In the *Bic* appeal, for example, the Tariff Board held that cigarette lighters were nickel-plated even though they were not 100 per cent nickel-plated; the goods would not have worked if they had been. The Federal Court of Appeal agreed, accepting as a finding of fact that there was sufficient plating to justify the classification.[71]

If goods could thus be classified as consisting of one element when other substances might actually be present, how was it determined which component set the description? How did usage show

67 *Dow Chemical of Canada Ltd.* v. *DMNRCE* (1953), 1 T.B.R. 109 (T.B. App. 284). See: *Reference . . . as to Classification of Dehydrated Grasses* (1958), 2 T.B.R. 175 (T.B. App. 493); *Canadian Titanium* v. *DMNRCE* (1975), C.Gaz. 1976.I.1558 (T.B. App. 1097); *Degussa Canada Ltd.* v. *DMNRCE* (1987), 12 T.B.R. 279, 14 C.E.R. 235 (T.B. App. 2545). Note also the declaration in *Perley-Robertson* v. *DMNRCE* (1962), 2 T.B.R. 283 (T.B. App. 591), in which the goods were classified as tea even though they did not contain the whole tea leaf. For a decision under the Harmonized System, see *Upjohn Inter-American Corp.* v. *DMNRCE* (1992), 5 T.C.T. 1052 (C.I.T.T. AP-90-197 and AP-90-146), in which the addition of starch did not disqualify goods from classification as estrogens and progestogens.

68 *Toronto Refiners and Smelters Ltd.* v. *DMNRCE* (1983), 8 T.B.R. 537, 5 C.E.R. 152 (T.B. App. 1861). Goods did not have to be worthless in order to be "waste": *Cloudfoam Ltd.* v. *DMNRCE* (1963), 3 T.B.R. 54 (T.B. App. 636); *Oliver-MacLeod Ltd.* v. *DMNRCE* (1977), C.Gaz. 1978.I.663 (T.B. Apps. 1226, 1227).

69 *Monarch Mirror Door Co.* v. *DMNRCE* (1980), 7 T.B.R. 13, 2 C.E.R. 19 (T.B. App. 1458).

70 *Imported Delicacies Ltd.* v. *DMNRCE* (1980), 7 T.B.R. 207, 2 C.E.R. 302 (T.B. App. 1541).

71 *Bic Inc.* v. *DMNRCE* (1985), 10 T.B.R. 58, 8 C.E.R. 280 (T.B. App. 2170), aff'd (1987), 13 C.E.R. 277 (F.C.A.).

what the "essence" was? One criterion sometimes suggested was that of the component of chief value, but this was not a frequent test in Canadian tariff law. It was listed in the residual item 71100-1, which had applied before the Harmonized System was implemented, when goods were not covered by any other tariff item.[72] Where the tariff item gave no specific directions, however, the chief value test was not a significant factor. It was applied in the *Microsonic* appeal, against the argument of counsel for the Deputy Minister who said that function and use should govern instead. The appeal had to do with calculators that had been attached to rulers for sale as desk ornaments. The Department had classified them as rulers, but the Tariff Board disagreed, holding that the goods were electronic data processing apparatus. The calculators represented about 90 per cent of the value of components, and the Board specifically adopted chief value as the test, while mentioning that the primary usage of the goods also related to data processing rather than to the ruler functions.[73] The *Microsonic* appeal contradicted on this point an earlier decision that had dealt with Pac-man watches. That appeal, *Waltham Watch,* had similarly found goods to be electronic data processing apparatus rather than watches, but the reasoning was based on function rather than on the component of chief value. The toy watches relied on microchip processing for both the game (95 per cent of capacity) and the timekeeping functions (5 per cent of capacity). Classification as data-processing apparatus thus covered both functions and best reflected the essential nature of the goods. The relative value of the various components was not the determining factor.[74]

---

[72] *Alcock, Downing & Wright Ltd.* v. *DMNRCE* (1958), 2 T.B.R. 158 (T.B. App. 473); *Union Carbide Canada Ltd.* v. *DMNRCE* (1964), 3 T.B.R. 69 (T.B. Apps. 652, 769); *Cavalier Luggage Ltd.* v. *DMNRCE* (1987), 12 T.B.R. 69, 13 C.E.R. 243 (T.B. App. 2573). Under the item, if the goods had consisted only of the component of chief value and if that component would have been classified at a higher rate of duty, then the higher rate applied. The component of chief value was the component that exceeded in value any other single component.

[73] *Microsonic Digital Systems Ltd.* v. *DMNRCE* (1985), 10 T.B.R. 210, 9 C.E.R. 259 (T.B. App. 2274). The relative value of components was also mentioned in *Monarch Mirror Door Co.* v. *DMNRCE, supra* note 69 at 17 (T.B.R.).

[74] *Waltham Watch Co. of Canada* v. *DMNRCE* (1984), 9 T.B.R. 388, 8 C.E.R. 133 (T.B. App. 2117), aff'd (1987), 15 C.E.R. 159 (F.C.A.). See also *Jewel Radio Co. of Canada* v. *DMNRCE* (1953), 1 T.B.R. 104 (T.B.); *General Instrument* v. *DMNRCE* (1957), 2 T.B.R. 40 (T.B. App. 282).

Classification by component of chief value was specifically rejected in *Reference on Cotton and Plastic*[75] and in *Jossal Trading* concerning classification of a needlework kit.[76] The use of relative costs was also rejected as a criterion in the *Kelley* appeal which had to do with an antique barge made more than fifty years before it was imported, but modified somewhat in the interim. The question was whether the modifications prevented the goods from qualifying as an "article . . . produced more than fifty years prior to the date of importation." The figures on relative value showed the restorations to be about one-quarter of total value, but the Board did not adopt this as a test:

The cost of alterations, particularly in the case of restorations, bears a relationship only to the difficulty of maintaining or restoring the integrity or usefulness of the original article and the fragility, inherent or technological, of the original. . . . The article must be readily recognizable and indeed identifiable with the original product despite any alterations and regardless whether any restoration was well or badly done, the current cost of these in relation to the cost of the original more than fifty years previous being totally irrelevant.[77]

Since the essence of the vessel had remained the same and the original qualities were still present,[78] the Board held that the barge qualified as an article produced more than fifty years previously. This decision points out some of the difficulties involved in application of a test that depends on the component of chief value. Costs could easily have changed over time and the information required might not be readily available. If we look only to prices of components before they are incorporated into the finished product, we ignore the changes that the transformation may have effected. The addition of a relatively inexpensive element may be the key factor that makes the finished product suitable for its purpose and gives it commercial value. The chief value criterion, can therefore be inconvenient and risks being somewhat artificial, judging not the imported good itself but rather the situation that existed before the good was created.

75 *Reference on Cotton and Plastic Combination Materials* (1956), 1 T.B.R. 243 at 245-46 (T.B. App. 362).

76 *Jossal Trading Ltd.* v. *DMNRCE* (1977), C.Gaz. 1978.I.7547 at 7549 (T.B. App. 1243). The appellant had been arguing that the goods came under the residual item 71100-1, which would have made the criterion relevant.

77 *Kelley* v. *DMNRCE* (1985), 10 T.B.R. 70 at 79, 9 C.E.R. 236 (T.B. App. 2082).

78 The Board, unfortunately, phrased this as "those essential qualities that gave it its original value": *Ibid.* at 78 (T.B.R.).

A further criterion used in classifying some tariff items was that of the relative weight of components, but this criterion suffers from the same defects as relative value. It was not normally applicable unless required by the terms of the item.[79] When weight was mentioned, it could be difficult to decide whether this meant the weight of components before processing or the weight when the imported goods were subsequently analysed.[80]

Normally, the main criterion used to determine which component set the description related in some way to the use of the goods. The description had to apply to the whole of the goods, not just a part.[81] It also had to be relevant to the main purpose of the goods, preferably to the component that gave the goods their commercial value, or to the "active ingredient" that other elements simply enhanced.[82] In the *Alcock, Downing, and Wright* appeal, for example, a combination of asphalt and woven fibreglass was held to be plasticized asphalt rather than a coated fabric, because it was used as an asphalt coating to protect pipes from corrosion, and the fibreglass component was merely a carrier to reinforce the asphalt.[83]

[79] *Bic Inc.* v. *DMNRCE* (1987), 13 C.E.R. 277 (F.C.A.), aff'g (1985), 10 T.B.R. 58, 8 C.E.R. 280 (T.B. App. 2170). But see *Monarch Mirror Door, supra* note 69, in which the Board indicated that the track and rollers did not affect classification of mirrored sliding doors, because they were of minimal value and weight relative to the mirrors. Under the Harmonized System, see *Canadian Thermos Products Inc.* v. *DMNRCE,* [1993] C.I.T.T. No. 4 (QL) (AP-92-015), concerning note 5 to section 15, which adopts the relative weight criterion.

[80] See, e.g., *Sealed Air of Canada Ltd.* v. *DMNRCE* (1982), 8 T.B.R. 208, 4 C.E.R. 235 (T.B. App. 1726), in which the Board was trying to decide whether goods contained more than 50 per cent by weight of polyether polyols. Since it was not possible to analyse after the goods were processed, the Board used the weight of elements before processing. The decision was subsequently reversed by the Federal Court of Appeal, which determined that the criterion relating to weight did not apply to this paragraph of the tariff item: *DMNRCE* v. *Sealed Air of Canada Ltd.* (1983), 5 C.E.R. 584 (F.C.A.).

[81] *Rema Tip Top Remaco Ltd.* v. *DMNRCE* (1968), 4 T.B.R. 181 (T.B. App. 880).

[82] *A.M. Meincke & Son Inc.* v. *DMNRCE* (1952), 1 T.B.R. 65 (T.B. App. 254).

[83] *Alcock, Downing & Wright Ltd.* v. *DMNRCE* (1958), 2 T.B.R. 158 (T.B. App. 473). See, *contra, Andrew Gilchrist Ltd.* v. *DMNRCE* (1964), 3 T.B.R. 188 (T.B. App. 745), in which the goods were a combination of textile and plastic, but the Board refused to accept the function of the goods as the basis for classification. The Board may have been influenced in *Gilchrist* by a number of previous appeals that had found similar goods to be coated textiles rather than plastics, based in large part on trade usage. See, e.g., *Reference . . . on Cotton and Plastic Combination Materials* (1956), 1 T.B.R. 243 (T.B. App. 362); *Lewis Specialties Ltd.*

In the *Garant* appeal, the importance of function was so great that the functioning part of an axe, the axe head, was classified under an item for axes even though the item did not mention parts. The Board reasoned that, since the axe head gave the tool its special quality, the head was the essence of the axe, and the handle was only secondary. The tariff item for axes would apply, therefore, whether or not the imported goods had a handle.[84]

Attention to components could mean that the description depended in some way on what the raw materials were before they were processed into the imported goods. In the *Power Cranes Reference*, Board Vice-Chairman Leduc added a note in which he listed the principal types of tariff items at the time:

[I]n the Canadian Tariff, the commodity may be specifically designated by name (eo nomine); or by the nature of its components (manufactures of rubber, etc. . . .); or by the end use to which it is to be put; or, as one of a number of related commodities under a generic term (entering in the cost of production, etc.); or in many instances, left to fall within the ambit of the "basket" item of the Tariff Schedule, No. 711.[85]

Goods could thus be classified by component under a "manufactures of" item, which would normally be n.o.p. In this sense, classification by component was a secondary approach, used when some other item did not apply.[86]

Goods did not need to be composed 100 per cent of only one element to be a "manufacture of" it, but the presence of that element had to be substantial.[87] In *DeBell*, metal binders did not

v. *DMNRCE* (1958), 2 T.B.R. 151 (T.B. App. 469); *Wm. Gladstone Ltd.* v. *DMNRCE* (1962), 2 T.B.R. 291 (T.B. App. 596). The *Reference* was followed in *Crown Wallpaper Co.* v. *DMNRCE* (1967), 4 T.B.R. 3 (T.B. App. 825). See further *Crown Wallpaper Co.* v. *DMNRCE* (1974), C.Gaz. 1975.I.1589 (T.B. App. 1080); *Reed Decorative Products Ltd.* v. *DMNRCE* (1980), 7 T.B.R. 177, 2 C.E.R. 261 (T.B. App. 1375).

84 *Garant Inc.* v. *DMNRCE* (1984), 9 T.B.R. 190, 6 C.E.R. 233 (T.B. App. 2085).

85 *Reference . . . regarding . . . Power Cranes and Shovels* (1953), 1 T.B.R. 90 at 94 (T.B. App. 272).

86 See, e.g., *Garden Research Laboratories Ltd.* v. *DMNRCE* (1964), 3 T.B.R. 225 (T.B. App. 766); *Acme Slate and Tile* v. *DMNRCE* (1966), 3 T.B.R. 314 (T.B. App. 835); *Chinmei Enterprises Ltd.* v. *DMNRCE* (1986), 11 T.B.R. 542, 13 C.E.R. 53 (T.B. App. 2454).

87 *Clorox Co. of Canada* v. *DMNRCE* (1977), 6 T.B.R. 544 (T.B. App. 1246). See also *Nortesco Inc.* v. *DMNRCE* (1984), 9 T.B.R. 164, 6 C.E.R. 211 (T.B. App. 2004), in which goods were manufactures of cork because cork was the most substantial element both by volume and by use.

qualify as manufactures of aluminum since they contained both aluminum and steel.[88] In *Union Carbide*, goods were neither manufactures of regenerated cellulose nor manufactures of paper when they contained elements of both. The Board would have permitted some light treatment of either paper or cellulose "to give or to enhance some ancillary characteristic" of the goods, but held that when the two elements were substantially combined, the resulting product was "essentially neither one nor the other," and the tariff classification had changed.[89]

In summary, goods could be classified by composition even if they contained more than one element. The principal component was usually linked to the use of goods in some way. Relative value and weight of components were not determinative unless the item in question adopted those criteria.

E USE: FUNCTION AND PURPOSE

An interpretation that emphasizes the function or purpose of goods under an *eo nomine* item pays special attention to the context in which language operates. The attention directed to use implies that naming involves the imposition of a human pattern of thought in which goods are arranged according to categories set by human society. Naming is not done simply by observable characteristics, since those characteristics may not have real meaning. It may not matter, for example, whether the object is green or blue, so long as it fulfils the purpose. The argument is that use is a fundamental criterion for naming.

The use factor may be seen as defining a best example, or prototype, of what the term means, against which the imports in question can be judged. An illustration of how this works appeared in the *Beco Imports* appeal, dealing with the classification of stainless steel flatware knives designed for use with meals on airplanes. The Department had classified them as "table knives." The appellant said that fold-down trays on aircraft were not tables, and the knives should therefore be classified as "knives n.o.p." The Tariff Board agreed with the Department and found the knives to be "table knives," since:

[88] *DeBell Industries* v. *DMNRCE* (1962), 2 T.B.R. 320 (T.B. App. 635).

[89] *Union Carbide, supra* note 72. See also *Kenneth Field* v. *DMNRCE* (1985), 10 T.B.R. 39, 8 C.E.R. 252 (T.B. App. 2066), in which the imported goods were classified as manufactures of marble despite having a small quantity of mother-of-pearl.

The term "table knife" refers to an eating instrument used to reduce portions of food to bite size. That is clearly the function of the subject goods. . . . . Even if it had been established that a fold-down food tray is not a "table" in the broadest sense, a table knife is defined by its function, not its place of use.[90]

The goods, in other words, met the functions of the typical table knife and were to be classified as such even if the trays in question were not strictly "tables."

In commercial application, attention to use can manifest itself as the wish to give priority to trade meaning. The trade vocabulary brings with it certain automatic assumptions about looking at goods according to their suitability for particular purposes, even for items that are not end-use items. The *Beaulieu* appeal discussed above under trade meaning is a good example of this sort of interpretation. The imported goods could be classified as either jute yarn or jute twine. The Department examined them, found that they consisted of two plys twisted together in opposite directions, and determined that they therefore met the dictionary definition of "twine." The appellant did not dispute the Department's empirical findings, but denied that this was what twine meant in the trade. In the rugmaking business, the jute used for backings was only slightly processed and contained impurities. It was known as jute yarn and was much cheaper than the more processed goods known as jute twine, which had general use for binding. Although the tariff item did not mention end use, the Board found for the appellant and interpreted according to suitability for particular purposes:

The substantial difference in cost clearly reflects the difference shown to exist between the two products, one of which is obviously produced for and suitable only for use as backing weft in the manufacture of goods such as rugs and carpets, while the other is a product to be used by consumers for tying or binding and is far too expensive for industrial use in the manner described above. . . . The goods are clearly yarns for use in the weaving of rugs and carpets and are so regarded in the trade rather than twines which are a different, more costly product, produced for use in tying and binding.[91]

The goods were therefore classified according to their suitability for the rug-making business, which was presumed to represent their chief use. Although the item was not an end-use one, the classifica-

90 *Beco Imports Reg'd.* v. *DMNRCE* (1985), 10 T.B.R. 202 at 203, 9 C.E.R. 253 (T.B. App. 2215).

91 *Beaulieu of Canada Inc.* v. *DMNRCE* (1987), 12 T.B.R. 27 at 34, 13 C.E.R. 206 (T.B. App. 2386).

tion decision was taken in commercial context according to the language and assumptions of those dealing with the goods in regular transactions. In a sense, this is treating the customs tariff as a "users' tariff" rather than as a "customs officers' tariff."

Beco and *Beaulieu* also neatly illustrate the two principal categories of naming according to use: naming by actual functions (table knives in *Beco*) and naming by suitability for particular purposes (jute yarn in *Beaulieu*). The cases below are arranged to deal first with naming according to actual function and then with naming according to suitability for given purposes.

When naming was done by function, decisions would depend on whether the goods matched a typical model that the words of the tariff item were thought to describe.[92] In *Texas Electroniques,* for example, the imported deep fryer with an automatic basket lifting device did not qualify under "fryers equipped with automatic conveyors," because this was just a small piece of equipment intended for use in snack bars, not a large fryer with extensive conveyor systems for full-scale commercial processing. Although the goods did actually move food a short distance automatically, this was not what an "automatic conveyor" was taken to mean in the customs tariff.[93] Similarly, the signboards imported in an unassembled condition in *Ontario Outdoor Advertising* did not qualify as "signs," since they did not yet have a message to convey and thus did not do what a typical sign was supposed to do.[94] A typical "dental instrument"

---

[92] Certain tariff items mentioned the required function. For them, the analysis was done directly without reference to a typical model. See *Mannesmann Tube Co.* v. *DMNRCE* (1959), 2 T.B.R. 149 (T.B. App. 467) ("strength-testing machines"); *Atlas Asbestos Co.* v. *DMNRCE* (1961), 2 T.B.R. 186 (T.B. App. 498) ("strength-testing machines"); *Corning Canada Inc.* v. *DMNRCE* (1982), 8 T.B.R. 188, 4 C.E.R. 214 (T.B. App. 1711) ("high thermal shock resisting glassware"); *Montreal Interglass Corp.* v. *DMNRCE* (1982), 8 T.B.R. 283, 4 C.E.R. 365 (T.B. Apps. 1784 etc.) ("high thermal shock resisting glassware"); *Canada Printing Inc.* v. *DMNRCE* (1986), 11 T.B.R. 125, 11 C.E.R. 97 (T.B. App. 2326) ("lubricating oils, composed wholly or in part of petroleum").

[93] *Texas Electroniques (Canada Inc.)* v. *DMNRCE* (1986), 11 T.B.R. 351, 12 C.E.R. 94 (T.B. App. 2391). See *La Coopérative de Croustilles* v. *DMNRCE* (1988), 17 C.E.R. 347 (T.B. App. 2870). Similarly, a labelling machine was not a printing press in *Soabar Canada Ltd.* v. *DMNRCE* (1986), 11 T.B.R. 397, 12 C.E.R. 131 (T.B. Apps. 2322 etc.).

[94] *Ontario Outdoor Advertising Ltd.* v. *DMNRCE* (1958), 2 T.B.R. 137 (T.B. App. 448). The relevant time is the time of importation. The goods will be classified according to the functions that they meet at that time: *Cytrigen Energy Products & Services Ltd.* v. *DMNRCE* (1986), 11 T.B.R. 338, 12 C.E.R. 85 (T.B. App. 2540).

was "a device used and manipulated by the dentist, in part within the mouth of the patient, in treating the teeth,"[95] and a typical "surgical instrument" was "a device required to execute an operation."[96] Even in the *Whiteco* decision, in which the Board said that "classification [of the import] must not be made solely in regard to its function or usage but must take into account its own nature and essential characteristics,"[97] use was the fundamental criterion. The goods were silver nitrate applicators for cauterization and the removal of warts. While the procedure itself was surgical, the goods were not "surgical instruments" because the cauterization was simply a chemical reaction and the disposable applicators did not have an active part in the process.[98]

In naming by function, the best description will be the one that most accurately reflects all of the significant functions of the imported good.[99] When choices have to be made, it can also be important to determine which functions are actually crucial to the

95 *Weil Dental Supplies Ltd.* v. *DMNRCE* (1967), 4 T.B.R. 41 at 49 (T.B. App. 856). See also *Dentists' Supply Co. of New York* v. *DMNRCE* (1957), 2 T.B.R. 86 (T.B. App. 415), aff'd (1960), 2 T.B.R. 87 (Ex.Ct.); *University of Manitoba* v. *DMNRCE* (1968), 4 T.B.R. 184 (T.B. App. 882). In a later appeal, Weil Dental was unable to have this definition applied to cotton rolls, since the latter were not seen as "devices" even though they met the required function: *Weil Dental Supplies Ltd.* v. *DMNRCE* (1973), C.Gaz. 1973.I.3049 (T.B. Apps. 1038, 1044).

96 *Instrumentarium* v. *DMNRCE* (1981), 7 T.B.R. 254, 3 C.E.R. 12 (T.B. App. 1557), which held that this did not cover plastic eye shields used during recovery. See also *First Lady Coiffures Ltd.* v. *DMNRCE* (1985), 10 T.B.R. 26, 8 C.E.R. 228 (T.B. App. 2126), varied (1986), 13 C.E.R. 42, 71 N.R. 76 (F.C.A.); *Sherwood Medical Industries (Canada) Ltd.* v. *DMNRCE* (1986), 11 T.B.R. 520, 13 C.E.R. 30 (T.B. App. 2397); *Geo. S. Trudell Co.* v. *DMNRCE* (1988), 13 T.B.R. 239, 16 C.E.R. 257 (T.B. App. 2712); *M.& S. X-Ray Services Ltd.* v. *DMNRCE* (1989), 2 T.C.T. 1184 (C.I.T.T. App. 3018); *M.& S. X-Ray Services Ltd.* v. *DMNRCE* (1992), 5 T.C.T. 1121 (C.I.T.T. App. 3058).

97 *Whiteco* v. *DMNRCE* (1986), 11 T.B.R. 94 at 97, 11 C.E.R. 48 (T.B. App. 2252).

98 See also *Imax Systems Corp.* v. *DMNRCE* (1986), 11 T.B.R. 460, 12 C.E.R. 219 (T.B. App. 2259), in which the Board stated that the end-use tail should not wag the dog to be kennelled in the item (at 471 T.B.R.), but nevertheless looked to end-use factors such as the need for a specialized theatre to decide that the film in question was a moving picture film n.o.p. rather than a news feature or recording of a current event.

99 *Waltham Watch Co.*, *supra* note 74; *Magnasonic Inc.* v. *DMNRCE* (1986), 11 T.B.R. 407, 12 C.E.R. 142 (T.B. App. 2389); *Canadian General Electric Co.* v. *DMNRCE* (1988), 13 T.B.R. 15, 15 C.E.R. 345 (T.B. App. 2878). See further *Jutan International Ltd.* v. *DMNRCE* (1988), 13 T.B.R. 68, 16 C.E.R. 39 (T.B. Apps. 2626, 2648), aff'd (1989), 2 T.C.T. 4320 (F.C.A.).

description. In *Montreal Children's Hospital,* for example, the imported cradle warmers were classified as incubators even though they did not control oxygen or humidity, since these features were not seen as essential to the definition.[100] Even if the usual name of the goods met the words of the tariff item, they might not be classified under that item if they did not have the essential functions of the typical model. Wooden handles for pickaxes did not qualify as handles for axes in the appeal, since a pickaxe is a "digging tool quite different in design and use" from the typical model of an axe.[101] A "switch" was defined by its function to open and close an electric or electronic circuit[102] and a video disc player could not be classified under a tariff item for turntables because its technology and functions were much more complex than those of the typical turntable in a stereo sound system.[103]

In the *Musicstop* appeal, Tariff Board member Beauchamp cited the *Beco* decision (concerning table knives for airplanes) as authority for the proposition that the specificity requirement in naming emphasized function and purpose. *Musicstop* dealt with the classification of a digital keyboard, which could have been either electronic data processing apparatus or "musical instruments of all kinds, n.o.p." Since the keyboard was created for musicians, was sold in music stores, and was used to produce music, the Board

[100] *Montreal Children's Hospital* v. *DMNRCE* (1966), 3 T.B.R. 293 (T.B. App. 818); *Mansoor Electronics Ltd.* v. *DMNRCE* (1987), 12 T.B.R. 157, 14 C.E.R. 120 (T.B. Apps. 2514, 2515).

[101] *Tiefenbach Tool & Handle Ltd.* v. *DMNRCE* (1981), 7 T.B.R. 247 at 251, 3 C.E.R. 15 (T.B. App. 1553).

[102] *Volkswagen Canada Ltd.* v. *DMNRCE* (1972), 5 T.B.R. 322 (T.B. App. 980), aff'd [1973] F.C. 643, 5 T.B.R. 330 (F.C.A.). For other decisions on the functioning of goods, see *Cullen Detroit Diesel Allison Ltd.* v. *DMNRCE* (1979), 6 T.B.R. 832, 1 C.E.R. 165 (T.B. App. 1380); *ITT Barton Instruments* v. *DMNRCE* (1982), 8 T.B.R. 408, 5 C.E.R. 49 (T.B. App. 1803); *Astrographic Industries Ltd.* v. *DMNRCE* (1987), 12 T.B.R. 235, 14 C.E.R. 166 (T.B. App. 2579). For decisions under the Harmonized System, see *Esden Ltd.* v. *DMNRCE* (1992), 5 T.C.T. 1078 (C.I.T.T., AP-90-006); *Callpro Canada Inc.* v. *DMNRCE* (1992), 5 T.C.T. 1322 (C.I.T.T., AP-91-165); *Takara Co. Canada Ltd.* v. *DMNRCE*, [1993] C.I.T.T. No. 48 (QL) (AP-92-139); *F. W. Woolworth Co.* v. *DMNRCE*, [1993] C.I.T.T. No. 63 (QL) (AP-92-007, dissenting opinion of Tribunal member Blouin); *Weil Co. Ltd.* v. *DMNRCE*, [1993] C.I.T.T. No. 64 (QL) (AP-92-096); *Procedair Industries Inc.* v. *DMNRCE*, [1993] C.I.T.T. No. 87 (QL) (AP-92-152); *Gilmour Sports Ltd.* v. *DMNRCE*, [1993] C.I.T.T. No. 132 (QL) (AP-92-102, AP-92-354).

[103] *Philips Electronics Ltd.* v. *DMNRCE* (1982), 8 T.B.R. 173, 4 C.E.R. 204 (T.B. App. 1719).

opted for the musical instruments item even though it was n.o.p. In his concurring opinion, Board member Beauchamp stated:

Clearly . . . the goods qualify for both . . . tariff items. Of the two, the more specific is musical instruments of all kinds which categorizes as well according to function or end use rather than according to the goods' constitution.[104]

In the *Tractor Reference*, when the Board was asked to set the criteria for classification of "internal combustion tractors," the main focus was on the function of the typical goods that the item was thought to describe. The Board decided that a tractor would be self-propelled and would accomplish its work by "the traction or pulsion of vehicles, devices or objects by its own locomotion."[105] Decisions in subsequent appeals then applied these criteria, classify-

---

104 *Musicstop Ltd.* v. *DMNRCE* (1986), 11 T.B.R. 356 at 362, 12 C.E.R. 97 (T.B. App. 2490). An earlier decision on the electronic data-processing apparatus item had opted in favour of that item because it best reflected the goods' dual functions as computer games and as timepieces: *Waltham Watch Co. of Canada* v. *DMNRCE* (1984), 9 T.B.R. 388, 8 C.E.R. 133 (T.B. App. 2117), aff'd (1987), 15 C.E.R. 159 (F.C.A.). For other decisions giving a wide interpretation to the EDP item, see *Reference re Electronic Apparatus for Use in the Home* (1983), 8 T.B.R. 587, 5 C.E.R. 150 (T.B. App. 1907); *General Datacomm Ltd.* v. *DMNRCE* (1984), 9 T.B.R. 78, 7 C.E.R. 1 (T.B. Apps. 1983 etc.); *Manitoba Telephone System* v. *DMNRCE* (1984), 9 T.B.R. 177, 6 C.E.R. 223 (T.B. App. 2045); *Digital Equipment of Canada Ltd.* v. *DMNRCE* (1986), 11 T.B.R. 58, 11 C.E.R. 5 (T.B. App. 2262); *Nevco Scoreboard Co.* v. *DMNRCE* (1986), 11 T.B.R. 342, 12 C.E.R. 88 (T.B. App. 2435), aff'd (1988), 13 C.E.R. 343 (F.C.A.); *Par T Golf (Alberta) Ltd.* v. *DMNRCE* (1987), 12 T.B.R. 300, 14 C.E.R. 261 (T.B. App. 2670); *IBM Canada Ltd.* v. *DMNRCE* (1991), [1992] 1 F.C. 663 (F.C.A.), rev'g *ROLM Canada Inc.* v. *DMNRCE* (1988), 17 C.E.R. 264 (T.B. Apps. 2600, 2625); *IBM Canada Ltd. (formerly Rolm Canada Inc.)* v. *DMNRCE*, [1993] C.I.T.T. No. 123 (QL) (Apps. 2700, 2701). The item would not apply, however, when goods were more specifically described elsewhere: *Foxboro Canada Inc.* v. *DMNRCE* (1986), 11 T.B.R. 384, 12 C.E.R. 118 (T.B. App. 2418), aff'd (1988), 17 C.E.R. 1 (F.C.A.); *IMS International Mailing Systems Ltd.* v. *DMNRCE* (1988), 18 C.E.R. 57 (T.B. Apps. 2612, 2616).

105 *Reference . . . as to What Criteria Should be Applied in Determining Whether Equipment Should be Classified as an Internal Combustion Tractor* (1966), 3 T.B.R. 259 at 270 (T.B. App. 795) (with a list of more extensive criteria). The reference was undertaken after the decision in *J.M.E. Fortin Inc.* v. *DMNRCE* (1963), 3 T.B.R. 107 (T.B. App. 700), aff'd (1964), 3 T.B.R. 112 (Ex. Ct.), which found certain heavy forestry machinery to be within the terms of the item.

ing goods according to whether they were[106] or were not[107] designed to operate primarily by pushing or pulling. Although the criteria did not always produce predictable results,[108] the Board reaffirmed them in a reference dealing with the classification of riding lawnmowers.[109]

In the *Lawnmower Reference*, the Board indicated that naming by function was quite a concrete exercise and did not involve speculation about intentions, which the Board felt would be difficult to determine. In rejecting as irrelevant the Department's mention that the goods were all designed for cutting grass, the Board quoted its earlier words from the *Tractor Reference*:

The concept of primary purpose or design gives the Board anxiety. The determination of primacy of purpose or design is fraught with great difficulty; if it is to be determined by knowledge of the mind of the designer then, in the absence of clear and acceptable documentary evidence, this presents many problems . . . if it is to be determined by actual use there is a clear possibility of use for purposes remote from those which motivated the original design; if it is to be determined by speculation, howsoever skilled, from the apparent characteristics of the machine there are evident seeds of conflict already clearly apparent in the thousand pages of the transcript of proceedings in this appeal; if it is to be determined by weighing the consideration said to be uppermost in the importer's or the exporter's mind the Board is apprehensive of the degree to which their views might be coloured by variations in rates of duty. . . . Primacy of purpose appears to be a subjective criterion, difficult to determine and replete with perplexity and conflict for all concerned.[110]

This quote indicates the fear of uncertainty that is associated with a classification based on factors external to the goods themselves.

[106] *Macleod's Lawn Equipment Ltd.* v. *DMNRCE* (1979), 6 T.B.R. 924, 1 C.E.R. 249 (T.B. App. 1431); *Rokon Distributors* v. *DMNRCE* (1984), 9 T.B.R. 212, 7 C.E.R. 155 (T.B. App. 2063).

[107] *Massot Nurseries Ltd.* v. *DMNRCE* (1974), C.Gaz. 1975.I.335 (T.B. App. 1073); *J. R. Macdonald* v. *DMNRCE*, (1980), 7 T.B.R. 156, 2 C.E.R. 228 (T.B. App. 1493).

[108] A snow-grooming machine, for example, was not a tractor in *Mont Sutton Inc.* v. *DMNRCE* (1972), C.Gaz. 1972.I.1927 (T.B. App. 983), but was a tractor in *Universal Go-Tract Ltd.* v. *DMNRCE* (1981), 7 T.B.R. 392, 3 C.E.R. 239 (T.B. App. 1683), aff'd (1982), 4 C.E.R. 381 (F.C.A.).

[109] *Reference . . . Regarding the Tariff Classification of Certain Self-propelled Lawn Grooming Riding Machines and Related Attachments* (1986), 11 T.B.R. 440, 12 C.E.R. 171 (T.B. App. 2294). See also, concerning the issue of whether the tractor and attachment might be classified together as an integrated machine: *Canadiana Garden Products Inc.* v. *DMNRCE* (1981), 7 T.B.R. 400, 3 C.E.R. 244 (T.B. Apps. 1761, 1762).

[110] *Supra* note 105.

The attitude seems to be that anything that looks beyond the actual functioning and observable structure of the imported goods is inevitably ambiguous. It is presumed that external circumstances are all as problematic as the intent of the designer or the importer, and thus all should be avoided.

While the subjective intent of the parties involved may indeed be difficult to determine, and while the Board could not monitor the end uses of goods after importation, the question of "speculation from apparent characteristics" should be viewed quite differently. Throughout this article it is argued that such speculation is not only desirable for sensible classification, but is an inherent part of the activity. When classification involves fitting physical objects into established categories of human thought, it is next to impossible to avoid wondering about the intended purpose of goods. A classification methodology that prohibits asking the question "What is this for?" will be artificial and limited in application. In its own decisions involving the "tractor" item, the Board had speculated about primary purpose,[111] major function,[112] and whether the import in question was "designed to and does function primarily as a tractor in the pushing and pulling of a variety of implements."[113] When the item for self-propelled power lawnmowers came before it on an appeal, the Board decided that the goods were to be classified under that item rather than as tractors. In a distinct change of heart, the Board noted that, while the goods qualified as tractors, they were "more specifically described as self-propelled power lawn mowers, the primary function for which they are intended, designed, sold, and used."[114] The decision was affirmed by the Court of Appeal, which stated:

It is, of course, true that the majority [of the Board], on several occasions . . . referred to the use which was made of the subject goods. This does

111 *Mont Sutton Inc., supra* note 108 at 1929 (T.B. App. 983).

112 *Massot Nurseries Ltd.* v. *DMNRCE* (1974), C.Gaz. 1975.I.335 at 338 (T.B. App. 1073).

113 *Universal Go-Tract Ltd.* v. *DMNRCE* (1981), 7 T.B.R. 392 at 399, 3 C.E.R. 239 (T.B. App. 1683), aff'd (1982), 4 C.E.R. 381 (F.C.A.). See also *Macleod's Lawn Equipment Ltd.* v. *DMNRCE* (1979), 6 T.B.R. 924 at 930, 1 C.E.R. 249 (T.B. App. 1431); *Rokon Distributors* v. *DMNRCE* (1984), 9 T.B.R. 212 at 216, 7 C.E.R. 155 (T.B. App. 2063).

114 *John Deere Ltd.* v. *DMNRCE* (1988), 13 T.B.R. 33 at 51, 16 C.E.R. 22 (T.B. Apps. 2247 etc.). See also *Springhouse Trails Ltd.* v. *DMNRCE* (1989), 2 T.C.T. 1235 (C.I.T.T. App. 2954). On procedures, note *MTD Products Ltd.* v. *Tariff Board* (1986), 13 C.E.R. 123 (F.C.T.D.).

not mean that they viewed tariff item 42505-1 as an "end use" item but simply that use was one of the many aspects of the subject goods which the Board looked at in order to determine their true nature. Not only is this no error but it would seem to me that use, along with the other matters mentioned by the Board, is an important and essential consideration to be taken into account whenever the Board is faced with a classification problem. In every such case the Board must ask itself the question "what are the subject goods" and the use to which the goods are designed to be put is unquestionably relevant to that inquiry.

Indeed, far from construing item 42505-1 as an "end use" item, the Board, in my view, did just the opposite; it determined that, because the goods before it were in their true nature power lawn mowers, they should be classified as such even though they might incidentally be used for other purposes than cutting grass.[115]

The fact that parties may disagree as to purpose does not mean that purpose must be ignored. The disagreement may have to be resolved, perhaps by choosing one purpose as primary or perhaps even by deciding that there are really two or more categories present. But acknowledgment of purpose is nevertheless essential if the classification system is to be properly linked to reality.

The attribution of purpose in a classification exercise is in fact so fundamental that it is the basis of the second type of naming by use, in which naming depends on suitability of the goods for their intended purpose. A prime example of this type of naming is the *Beaulieu* decision mentioned at the beginning of this section, in which goods were classified as jute yarn rather than as twine, since they were for use in rug making.[116]

Suitability for purpose was quite frequently used in *eo nomine* classification decisions, in which the Board did not emphasize the subjective intentions of the various parties but rather deduced the primary purpose or chief use from characteristics of the goods themselves. In the *Lily Cups* appeal, the suitability of the imported cup stock for use in the making of paper cups was the crucial factor in classification. The Department had classified the goods as fibreboard. The appellant maintained that they were instead printing papers since they could carry printing on one side. The Board rejected the fibreboard item, which was mainly for building materials. The Board also rejected the appellant's argument, however, since it did not centre on the chief use of the goods:

---

115 *John Deere Ltd.* v. *DMNRCE* (1990), 3 T.C.T. 5097 at 5099 (F.C.A.).

116 *Beaulieu, supra* note 57.

The Board notes that the product in issue in this appeal, cup stock, is designed specifically for the manufacture of drinking cups, and no evidence was adduced to show that it is used for any other purpose. It is coated with polyethylene for the purpose of waterproofing and this coated surface is placed on the inside of the cup. The product must be white, made of virgin fibre and must meet certain bacteriological standards, all for the purpose of making it suitable for a drinking cup. The fact that this product may have the quality of printability does not, in the Board's view, make it a printing paper. . . . As was stated in evidence, almost every form of paper or board . . . is capable of carrying print.[117]

Printability was an undisputed characteristic of the goods, but it was not sufficiently central to their main purpose. It could not be presumed that every form of paper or board was to be covered under the "printing papers" item when this was not descriptive of the intended use. In the result, the Board opted for the Department's alternate choice, "paper of all kinds, n.o.p."

In *Control Data*, as well, printability was not seen as crucial for the goods in issue, and they were classified under the general "paper of all kinds" item. In explaining its reasoning, the Board said:

Considering the evidence and the exhibits, it seems clear . . . that the basic characteristics for tabulating card stock relate to its prime use in computer processing. The quality of printability may be such that it may be used to impart information to the person looking at the card, and this may have some additional commercial use. This, however, is not necessary for the card to function in the computer for which these cards are designed and for the most part used. . . . The evidence is that the properties essential for tabulating card stock do not relate to properties required for printing paper.[118]

In these appeals, the Board was trying to restrict the potential scope of the "printing papers" item, and did this by assuming that the basic characteristics of imported goods would relate in some way to their primary purpose.[119]

---

117 *Lily Cups* v. *DMNRCE* (1977), 6 T.B.R. 503 at 509 (T.B. App. 1162). See also *Delta Printing and Advertising Ltd.* v. *DMNRCE* (1978), C.Gaz. 1978.I.5369 (T.B. Apps. 1265 etc.).

118 *Control Data Canada Ltd.* v. *DMNRCE* (1978), C.Gaz. 1978.I.5924 at 5927-28 (T.B. App. 1184). See also *Rolph-Clarke Stone Ltd.* v. *DMNRCE* (1978), C.Gaz.1979.I.984 (T.B. App. 1343).

119 See also *McCall Pattern* v. *DMNRCE* (1975), C.Gaz.1976.I.2085 (T.B. App. 1093,), which classified dressmakers' patterns as "manufactures of paper, n.o.p." rather than under an item for "other printed matter, n.o.p." Printing was only incidental to the intended use as an outline model for dressmakers. The "manufactures of paper, n.o.p." item was thus more specific. Under the

Purpose was significant in an appeal by the Institute for Development Education Through the Arts that concerned a hand-carved sculpture in the form of a chair. Since the work was too intricate and delicate (as well as too uncomfortable) to be used for sitting, the Tariff Board rejected the Department's classification of the chair as house furniture and ruled that it was instead original sculpture.[120] In *Reich*, model cars were similarly classified under their chief use as toys, rather than as ornaments or decorations as the appellant had argued. Although the cars were "reasonably attractive," they were "unlikely to excite the attention of the adult collector or the interior decorator — whether professional or amateur — by reason of their value or their beauty."[121] They were intended to be used as playthings for children and classification was thus determined by that purpose.[122]

When naming was done by purpose, it was the main purpose or chief use that counted, and incidental functions of the goods were generally ignored.[123] The miniature railway cars at issue in the *Association Montréalaise d'Action Récréative* appeal, for example, did

---

Harmonized System, see *Éditions Panini du Canada Ltée* v. *DMNRCE*, [1993] C.I.T.T. No. 38 (QL) (AP-92-018). For a decision in which the purpose of the printing made the "printed matter" item more specific, see *P.F. Collier & Son Ltd.* v. *DMNRCE* (1987), 12 T.B.R. 285, 14 C.E.R. 239 (T.B. App. 1950), dealing with an educational kit for children.

120 *Institute for Development Education Through the Arts* v. *DMNRCE* (1985), 10 T.B.R. 234, 10 C.E.R. 109 (T.B. App. 2257). See also *Field* v. *DMNRCE* (1985), 10 T.B.R. 39, 8 C.E.R. 252 (T.B. App. 2066), in which classification of an ornamental marble plaque as a table top was similarly rejected, since it clearly was not for use as household furniture.

121 *Reich Bros. Ltd.* v. *DMNRCE* (1961), 2 T.B.R. 273 at 274 (T.B. App. 584).

122 For an appeal in which it was decided that toys could also be for adults, see *International Games of Canada Ltd.* v. *DMNRCE* (1983), 9 T.B.R. 41, 6 C.E.R. 132 (T.B. App. 2024). The Tariff Board in another appeal stated that the definition of "toy" was "elastic . . . ranging according to perception from the rich man's yacht or Ferrari to a baby's hand-held rattle": *Reference re Classification of Electronic Apparatus* (1983), 8 T.B.R. 587 at 588, 5 C.E.R. 150 (T.B. App. 1907). For HS decisions in which purpose was relevant, see *Industrial Adhesives, Division of Timminco Ltd.* v. *DMNRCE* (1992), 5 T.C.T. 1163 (C.I.T.T., AP-90-075); *Nygard International Ltd.* v. *DMNRCE*, [1993] C.I.T.T. No. 84 (QL) (AP-92-105).

123 *Diversified Research & Sales Ltd.* v. *DMNRCE* (1953), 1 T.B.R. 124 (T.B. App. 287); *Mansoor Electronics Ltd.* v. *DMNRCE* (1987), 12 T.B.R. 157, 14 C.E.R. 120 (T.B. Apps. 2514, 2515); *Ener-Gard Energy Products Inc.* v. *DMNRCE* (1987), 12 T.B.R. 531, 15 C.E.R. 180 (T.B. App. 2524).

not qualify as amusement riding devices, since their main purpose was to transport visitors around a floral exhibition, and it was not relevant that some passengers might find the ride itself entertaining.[124] In a few decisions, classification was based on a secondary purpose, particularly if there was no more specific item relating to the primary purpose. In *Mrs. Smith's Pie*, for example, pie plates were classified as kitchen hollow-ware rather than as manufactures of aluminum, even though the fact that they were re-usable was secondary to their primary purpose of acting as containers for commercially sold pies.[125]

The intended purpose for goods was a significant factor in many Tariff Board decisions. In *Coles Book Stores*, the Board held that a 1908 Sears Roebuck catalogue was no longer a catalogue when it was reproduced and sold in 1975. The articles listed were no longer for sale and the purpose had clearly changed:

[T]he purpose of this publication in its present form is solely to provide the prospective reader with a documentary presentation of life and tastes as they existed in the United States during the early 1900s. No commercial intent is apparent, other than the income to be earned from the sale of the publication itself.[126]

In many instances, the Board could determine purpose as it did in *Coles Book Stores* from the characteristics of the goods as imported. In the *Publications Étrangères* appeal, for example, the Board examined the contents of the periodicals in question to determine that they were "illustrated advertising periodicals" rather than "periodical publications," since they were intended for

124 *Association Montréalaise d'Action Récréative et Culturelle* v. *DMNRCE* (1984), 9 T.B.R. 126, 6 C.E.R. 186 (T.B. App. 2048).

125 *Mrs. Smith's Pie Co. (Canada)* v. *DMNRCE* (1978), C.Gaz. 1979.I.688 (T.B. App. 1362). See also *Parsons-Steiner Ltd.* v. *DMNRCE* (1950), 1 T.B.R. 32 (T.B. App. 209); *Glennie* v. *DMNRCE* (1962), 2 T.B.R. 326 (T.B. App. 679); *Pyrotronics Canada Ltd.* v. *DMNRCE* (1980), 7 T.B.R. 55, 2 C.E.R. 78 (T.B. App. 1414). Both *Glennie* and *Pyrotronics* cite as authority the Supreme Court of Canada judgment in *Javex Co.* v. *Oppenheimer*, [1961] S.C.R. 170, 2 T.B.R. 35, in which Clorox bleach qualified for an end use item covering "preparations . . . for disinfecting" in the absence of a more specific item relating to the primary function of bleaching.

126 *Coles Book Stores Ltd.* v. *DMNRCE* (1978), C.Gaz. 1978.I.3948 at 3950 (T.B. App. 1270).

advertising within the trade.[127] Sometimes the Board also looked to treatment of the goods or statements made about them by the importer or persons linked to the importer. The fact that the goods were sold through music stores was used in favour of the appellant's argument that they were musical instruments in the *Musicstop* appeal.[128] In *Colgate-Palmolive-Peet,* the fact that the goods had been advertised as laundry soap was used to defeat the appellant's argument that they should be classified instead as toilet soaps.[129] Advertising is not necessarily limited to the intended purpose of the goods, of course, but can also be used to indicate other factors such as their function[130] or their composition.[131] Advertising evidence was presented to prove purpose in the *General Mills* appeal, in which the Department tried unsuccessfully to maintain the classification of granola bars as confectionery. Although the bars were advertised as snacks and were sold at candy counters, the Board opted instead for evidence of composition and accepted the appellant's argument that they were "prepared cereal food."[132]

127 *Publications Étrangères au Canada* v. *DMNRCE* (1978), C.Gaz. 1978.I.5375 (T.B. Apps. 1306, 1320). See also *Cartanna International Sales Inc.* v. *DMNRCE* (1986), 11 T.B.R. 52, 11 C.E.R. 1 (T.B. App. 2122); *British Columbia Automobile Association* v. *DMNRCE* (1986), 11 T.B.R. 545, 13 C.E.R. 69 (T.B. App. 2464).

128 *Musicstop Ltd.* v. *DMNRCE* (1986), 11 T.B.R. 356, 12 C.E.R. 97 (T.B. App. 2490). See also: *Cockshutt Plow Co.* v. *DMNRCE* (1951), 1 T.B.R. 63 (T.B. App. 252). For HS decisions, see *Research Products/Blankenship of Canada Ltd.* v. *DMNRCE* (1992), 5 T.C.T. 1080 (C.I.T.T. AP-90-174); *Dumex Medical Surgical Products Ltd.* v. *DMNRCE* (1992), 5 T.C.T. 1297 (C.I.T.T. AP-91-132).

129 *Colgate-Palmolive-Peet Co.* v. *DMNRCE* (1950), 1 T.B.R. 34 (T.B. App. 214). See also, concerning the presumed purpose for imported goods: *McAinsh & Co.* v. *DMNRCE* (1958), 2 T.B.R. 169 (T.B. App. 487); *B. L. Marks Sales Co.* v. *DMNRCE* (1986), 11 T.B.R. 216, 11 C.E.R. 314 (T.B. App. 2199), aff'd (1987), 14 C.E.R. 56 (F.C.A.). Under the HS, see *Outils Royal Tools Corp.* v. *DMNRCE,* [1993] C.I.T.T. No. 108 (QL) (AP-92-151).

130 *Ponsen's Trading Co.* v. *DMNRCE* (1956), 1 T.B.R. 262 (T.B. App. 391); *Weil Dental Supplies Ltd.* v. *DMNRCE* (1973), C.Gaz. 1973.I.3049 (T.B. Apps. 1038, 1044); *J. R. Macdonald* v. *DMNRCE* (1980), 7 T.B.R. 156, 2 C.E.R. 228 (T.B. App.1493).

131 *C. Itoh & Co. (Canada)* v. *DMNRCE* (1979), 6 T.B.R. 847, 1 C.E.R. 187 (T.B. Apps. 1308 etc.); *H. T. Griffin Inc.* v. *DMNRCE* (1984), 9 T.B.R. 305, 7 C.E.R. 25 (T.B. App. 2118).

132 *General Mills Canada Ltd.* v. *DMNRCE* (1979), 6 T.B.R. 876, 1 C.E.R. 206 (T.B. Apps. 1407, 1411). See also *I.D. Foods Corp.* v. *DMNRCE* (1986), 11 T.B.R. 559, 13 C.E.R. 90 (T.B. App. 2526); *General Mills Canada Inc.* v. *DMNRCE* (1987), 12 T.B.R. 256, 14 C.E.R. 209 (T.B. Apps. 2457 etc.), aff'd (1988), 18 C.E.R. 161 (F.C.A.).

Eo nomine items that involved naming by function or purpose were to be distinguished from true end use items. The difference was illustrated in an early Tariff Board reference concerning an item for "articles of glass . . . designed to be cut or mounted." Departmental practice had been to admit under this item any glassware that the importer certified would be upgraded by cutting to at least 25 per cent of the value. This practice would have been appropriate in the application of an end use item, but it was rejected by the Tariff Board for the item in question:

> We find it impossible to overlook the fact that the word "designed" is there; and we can conclude only that, in incorporating the word in the tariff item, the legislators knew what they had in mind in creating this particular classification and in wording it as they did. We cannot agree that "designed" relates to a concept or an intention existing in the mind of the *importer*; but, rather, that it relates to a concept and a deliberate intention in the mind of the original manufacturer of the article of glass as to its ultimate use, which intention must be embodied or expressed in the article of glass as imported.[133]

Classification can take account of context without following actual end use. In *Margo Corporation*, for example, the Board rejected the appellant's argument that imported paper was "beer mat or coaster board" without checking the actual end use of the goods. The paper was of the appropriate thickness, but because it did not have the absorbency required for the purpose, it could not be classified under that item.[134] In the *Harold T. Griffin* appeal, the imported goods, dehydrated green pepper, were classified as vegetables rather than as spices because they lacked pungency and colour and thus were "eaten more as a vegetable . . . than as a spice."[135] And in *Akhurst Machinery*, the Board rejected the Department's arguments that an item for "machinists' precision tools" was an end use item. Relying on trade usage, the Board decided that this was an *eo nomine* item describing the small tools that machinists would normally be

133 *Reference . . . re Administration of Tariff Item 326e* (1954), 1 T.B.R. 192 at 193 (T.B. App. 322). See also *Terochem Laboratories Ltd.* v. *DMNRCE* (1986), 11 T.B.R. 223, 11 C.E.R. 319 (T.B. App. 2401); *Western Medi-Aid Products Ltd.* v. *DMNRCE* (1986), 11 T.B.R. 229, 11 C.E.R. 326 (T.B. Apps. 2357 etc.); *EEV Canada Ltd.* v. *DMNRCE* (1991), 4 T.C.T. 3339 (C.I.T.T. App. 2372).

134 *Margo Corp.* v. *DMNRCE* (1984), 9 T.B.R. 206, 6 C.E.R. 240 (T.B. App. 2064).

135 *Harold T. Griffin Inc.* v. *DMNRCE* (1984), 9 T.B.R. 305 at 307, 7 C.E.R. 25 (T.B. App. 2118). See also *Redi Garlic Distributors Inc.* v. *DMNRCE* (1984), 9 T.B.R. 385, 8 C.E.R. 126 (T.B. App. 2141); *Aliments Tousain Inc.* v. *DMNRCE* (1985), 10 T.B.R. 134, 9 C.E.R. 94 (T.B. Apps. 2135, 2150), rev'd (1988), 16 C.E.R. 351 (F.C.A.), reheard (1988), 18 C.E.R. 185 (T.B. App. 2135).

expected to supply themselves. It therefore did not cover the imported readout equipment, even though that equipment would later be attached to instruments to be used by machinists.[136] Classification can depend on the use and purpose of imported goods without requiring a system to monitor end use of particular imports.[137]

The purpose had to apply to the goods in their condition as imported, without further processing. In the *Carruthers* appeal, for example, imported toys could not be classified as diagnostic medical instruments, since they had not yet been equipped with remote control devices for use in the importer's practice of pediatric ophthalmology.[138] Although there was no doubt about intended end use, that in itself was not sufficient.

This does not say that the goods need to be in their final form. In *Weil Dental*, the imported containers were dental instruments even though they would still have to be shaped before actual use, since they were nevertheless committed to that purpose by the time of importation.[139]

To say that purpose is a fundamental consideration in naming is not to say that it is the only consideration. The fact that goods have the same use and can be substituted for each other does not of itself mean that they will be classified under the same item. Photographic tongs, for example, are not film processors even though they may fulfil the same function as processors.[140] And gamma ray equipment is not X-ray apparatus even though it serves the same purpose.[141]

---

136 *Akhurst Machinery Ltd.* v. *DMNRCE* (1987), 12 T.B.R. 181, 14 C.E.R. 98 (T.B. App. 2630); *MTI Canada Ltd.* v. *DMNRCE* (1988), 13 T.B.R. 154, 16 C.E.R. 109 (T.B. App. 2776).

137 In *Atlas Asbestos Co.* v. *DMNRCE* (1961), 2 T.B.R. 186 (T.B. App. 498). In the absence of other evidence, the Board had to look to actual use of the imported goods to see if they were "strength testing machines."

138 *Carruthers* v. *DMNRCE* (1987), 12 T.B.R. 242, 14 C.E.R. 193 (T.B. App. 2551). See also *Cargill Grain Co.* v. *DMNRCE* (1978), C.Gaz. 1978.I.3954 (T.B. App. 1299); *Mitel Corp.* v. *DMNRCE* (1985), 10 T.B.R. 90, 9 C.E.R. 49 (T.B. App. 2159).

139 *Weil Dental Supplies Ltd.* v. *DMNRCE* (1967), 4 T.B.R. 41 (T.B. App. 856). For a decision under the Harmonized System, see *Dumex Medical Surgical Products Ltd.* v. *DMNRCE* (1992), 5 T.C.T. 1297 (C.I.T.T. AP-91-132).

140 *Kindermann (Canada) Ltd.* v. *DMNRCE* (1962), 2 T.B.R. 310 (T.B. App. 614).

141 *Aries Inspection Services Ltd.* v. *DMNRCE* (1980), 7 T.B.R. 18, 2 C.E.R. 25 (T.B. App. 1446). See also *P. C. O'Driscoll Ltd.* v. *DMNRCE* (1964), 3 T.B.R. 189 (T.B. App. 748); *Ascor of Canada Ltd.* v. *DMNRCE* (1965), 3 T.B.R. 273 (T.B. App. 798); *Carl Zeiss Canada Ltd.* v. *DMNRCE* (1967), 4 T.B.R. 31 (T.B. App. 849);

Even when some functions overlap, such as the decorative function fulfilled by both bedspreads and comforters that was at issue in the *Imperial Feather* appeal, distinctions can still be made as they were in that decision based on other characteristics and additional purposes.[142]

Use was acknowledged to have a fundamental place in classification in earlier versions of the Customs Act. Section 58, which was repealed in 1950, provided for classification when no item applied specifically:

> On each and every non-enumerated article which bears a similitude, either in material or quality, or the use to which it may be applied, to any enumerated article chargeable with duty, the same rate of duty shall be payable which is charged on the enumerated article which it most resembles in any of the particulars before mentioned.[143]

Function was also considered directly when the Board and the courts had to construe the notion of similarity in an item for "lard compound and similar substances." In the *Frito-Lay* appeal, the Board found goods not to be similar substances because of differences in "crystal structure, solidity, colour and translucency, as well as function."[144] In the *Hunt Foods* appeal, however, the Exchequer Court found that the goods in issue qualified as similar substances because of similarities in "function, use, appearance, melting point, hardness, solidity at various temperatures, stability, flavour, odour and colour."[145] The thesis argued in this section is not that use determines everything, but that it is a fundamental

---

Tri-Hawk International Traders Ltd. v. *DMNRCE* (1977), C.Gaz. 1978.I.837 (T.B. App. 1213); *G. B. Fermentation Industries Inc.* v. *DMNRCE* (1981), 7 T.B.R. 303, 3 C.E.R. 87 (T.B. App. 1591); *Squibb Canada Inc.* v. *DMNRCE* (1986), 11 T.B.R. 488, 12 C.E.R. 255 (T.B. App. 2261).

142 According to the Board, the comforters were intended to provide warmth, were smaller than bedspreads, and were quilted in a different fashion: *Imperial Feather Corp. (Toronto)* v. *DMNRCE* (1982), 8 T.B.R. 80, 4 C.E.R. 43 (T.B. Apps. 1668, 1709).

143 R.S.C. 1927, c. 42, s. 58 (repealed S.C. 1950, c. 13, s. 4). See *Canada Packers Ltd.* v. *DMNRCE* (1951), 1 T.B.R. 45 (T.B. App. 236).

144 *Frito-Lay Canada Ltd.* v. *DMNRCE* (1978), 6 T.B.R. 634 at 652 (T.B. Apps. 1241, 1264, 1272), aff'd (1980), [1981] 1 F.C. 177, 2 C.E.R. 143 (F.C.A.).

145 *Hunt Foods Export Corp. of Canada* v. *DMNRCE*, [1970] Ex. C.R. 828, 4 T.B.R. 333 at 342-43 (Ex. Ct.), rev'g (1969), 4 T.B.R. 328 (T.B. Apps. 907, etc.). See also Tariff Board, *Reference* 154: Edible Oil Products, Sept. 30, 1978; *Consumers Foodcraft Corp.* v. *DMNRCE* (1955), 1 T.B.R. 237 (T.B. App. 343); *Les Entreprises Mair Fried Enrg.* v. *DMNRCE* (1978), C.Gaz. 1979.I.3048 (T.B. App. 1220).

factor that should be considered. Naming that ignores context as extrinsic to goods will be artificial. Application should receive direct acknowledgment in the theory of classification.

The participatory approach to classification appeared in decisions on the long-standing tariff item permitting free entry or reduced duty for agricultural implements and agricultural machinery. The Board decided in an early appeal that this meant that the "major if not sole use" should be in agriculture,[146] and that statistical evidence could be accepted on this point.[147] Goods could then be classified as agricultural even though there was no guarantee that any particular imports would actually be employed in agriculture.[148] Application could be considered without turning the item into an end use one. If the goods had other significant uses — particularly if those uses were identified in product advertising — then they would not be classified under the item.[149]

The use in question had to be "recognizably" agricultural.[150] Such use was not limited to things employed directly in tilling the soil, but could extend to ancillary goods such as disc sharpeners[151] and seed-cleaning machinery.[152] Household use was excluded,[153] but the concept was otherwise fairly widely interpreted, covering seed-mixing machinery brought to farms by dealers,[154] potato storage machinery used by farmers and dealers,[155] and a greenhouse

---

[146] *Superior Separator Co. of Canada* v. *DMNRCE* (1952), 1 T.B.R. 94 at 95 (T.B. App. 273).

[147] *Franklin Serum Co. of Canada* v. *DMNRCE* (1953), 1 T.B.R. 95 (T.B. Apps. 274, 275, 276). See also *ETF Tools* v. *DMNRCE* (1961), 2 T.B.R. 315 (T.B. App. 623).

[148] *Cockshutt Plow Co.* v. *DMNRCE* (1951), 1 T.B.R. 63 (T.B. App. 252). See also *General Bearing Service Inc.* v. *DMNRCE* (1986), 11 T.B.R. 150, 11 C.E.R. 122 (T.B. App. 2349).

[149] *D. T. Gillespie* v. *DMNRCE* (1969), 4 T.B.R. 389 (T.B. App. 914); *Massot Nurseries Ltd.* v. *DMNRCE, supra* note 107. For particular goods, other tariff items might also provide more specific descriptions: *Zukiwski* v. *DMNRCE* (1987), 12 T.B.R. 581, 15 C.E.R. 217 (T.B. App. 2819); *Ripley's Farm* v. *DMNRCE* (1988), 13 T.B.R. 280, 16 C.E.R. 153 (T.B. App. 2681).

[150] *W. L. Ballentine Co.* v. *DMNRCE* (1951), 1 T.B.R. 46 at 47 (T.B. App. 237).

[151] *R.* v. *Specialties Distributors Ltd.*, [1954] Ex. C.R. 535.

[152] *R. W. Nelson Seed Farms* v. *DMNRCE* (1987), 12 T.B.R. 566, 15 C.E.R. 206 (T.B. App. 2693).

[153] *Mercury Tool & Stamping Ltd.* v. *DMNRCE* (1962), 2 T.B.R. 328 (T.B. App. 696).

[154] *Dubeau* v. *DMNRCE* (1959), 2 T.B.R. 198 (T.B. App. 506).

[155] *Alta-Fresh Produce Ltd.* v. *DMNRCE* (1968), 4 T.B.R. 145 (T.B. App. 873).

sprinkler system.[156] In all of these, context was taken into account without necessarily requiring the item to be treated as an end-use one.[157]

Tariff classification can consider the application of goods in context without requiring customs authorities to trace the use of each import. In the U.S. tariff before the Harmonized System was implemented, descriptions such as "agricultural implements," "household utensils," and "all medicinal preparations" were viewed as implied-use provisions. Goods were classified according to the chief use of goods of that class or kind nation-wide. Testimony concerning this chief use could come from importers or from others knowledgeable in the trade.[158] Tariff classification does not have to take place at one moment of inspection artificially isolated from all knowledge of what will happen to the goods after importation. If the description of physical characteristics is specific, there may be no need for further inquiry; however, it should not be assumed that the function and purpose of goods must be ignored.

The Canadian International Trade Tribunal decided in 1989 that an imported ship was a "pleasure boat" rather than a commercial

---

156 *WER Holdings Inc.* v. *DMNRCE* (1986), 11 T.B.R. 306, 12 C.E.R. 37 (T.B. App. 2393). See further *Tutt* v. *DMNRCE* (1991), 4 T.C.T. 3098 (C.I.T.T. App. 2975). In *Major Irrigation (1974) Ltd.* v. *DMNRCE* (1982), 8 T.B.R. 446, 5 C.E.R. 93 (T.B. App. 1830), machinery for off-farm highway transport of agricultural produce was excluded; in that decision, the Board seems to have been reading in qualifications from another part of the same tariff item that listed certain goods *eo nomine* and required that they be "for use on the farm for farm purposes only."

157 The goods still had to qualify as machinery or as implements. In several appeals, the Board determined that agricultural implements were things like hoes and rakes used in active work. These were to be distinguished from apparatus and other equipment such as milking stalls, fencing, and specialized flooring, which did not qualify because they were only used passively. See *Babson Bros. Co. (Canada)* v. *DMNRCE* (1950), 1 T.B.R. 31 (T.B. App. 208); *Delage* v. *DMNRCE* (1964), 3 T.B.R. 197 (T.B. App. 757); *F. Lawson and Sons Ltd.* v. *DMNRCE* (1965), 3 T.B.R. 277 (T.B. App. 802); *Sheep Producers Association of Nova Scotia* v. *DMNRCE* (1979), 6 T.B.R. 785, 1 C.E.R. 94 (T.B. App. 1379); *Riverside Colony Ltd.* v. *DMNRCE* (1985), 10 T.B.R. 258, 10 C.E.R. 129 (T.B. App. 2327); *J. P. Soubry Distribution Representation Ltd.* v. *DMNRCE* (1986), 11 T.B.R. 448, 12 C.E.R. 181 (T.B. App. 2442); *Beekeepers' Supply Co.* v. *DMNRCE* (1987), 12 T.B.R. 209, 14 C.E.R. 149 (T.B. App. 2533); *Schmidt* v. *DMNRCE* (1987), 12 T.B.R. 218, 14 C.E.R. 143 (T.B. App. 2601); *Nova Aqua Sea Ltd.* v. *DMNRCE* (1990), 3 T.C.T. 2233 (C.I.T.T. App. 3027).

158 Ruth F. Sturm, *Customs Law and Administration*, 490-99 (2d ed., New York: American Importers Association, 1980).

vessel, because the importer's intention to use the boat in the sport fishing business was treated as irrelevant. It was also irrelevant that the importer had received an excise tax exemption based on the intended use. The issue was debatable, because the boat required some additional work to qualify as a commercial passenger vessel under domestic regulations. Nevertheless, the Tribunal's rejection of all consideration of use was unnecessary, and also probably contrary to the later decision of the Federal Court of Appeal in the *John Deere* appeal concerning power lawn mowers.[159] The customs tariff, of course, could have referred specifically to the excise tax provisions. Even in the absence of such a reference, there was no need to assume that intended use was irrelevant.[160] Naming that ignores use as extrinsic to goods is likely to be artificial.

F   PURPOSIVE INTERPRETATION

Economic factors occasionally influenced an *eo nomine* classification,[161] but the Tariff Board generally avoided looking to economic results or a presumed legislative intent to favour particular industries or sectors. Indeed, the reported decisions rarely contain any indication of what the actual rates were for the items in question.[162]

[159] *John Deere Ltd.* v. *DMNRCE* (1990), 3 T.C.T. 5097 (F.C.A.), aff'g. (1988), 13 T.B.R. 33, 16 C.E.R. 22 (T.B. Apps. 2247 etc.).

[160] *Sealand of the Pacific Ltd.* v. *DMNRCE* (1989), 2 T.C.T. 1149 (C.I.T.T. App. 3042). Even based on the physical characteristics of the vessel, it may have been possible to argue for a commercial context. The ship was 133 feet long. It had two lounges (one with a fireplace), full kitchen service, television and sound equipment, deck areas with barbecue and jacuzzi, and 17 staterooms with private washrooms.

[161] In *Cataphote Corp. of Canada* v. *DMNRCE* (1962), 2 T.B.R. 259 (T.B. App. 572), the dissenting member of the Tariff Board declined to find that the imported goods were "broken glass or cullet" since they had been finely ground to a common size and were much more expensive than ordinary waste glass or cullet. While the majority acknowledged the price difference, they found that it was not enough to move the goods to the Department's chosen tariff item, "manufactures of glass." Concerning economic factors and end use items, see *Alex L. Clark Ltd.* v. *DMNRCE* (1967), 4 T.B.R. 53 (T.B. App. 860).

[162] In *Dentists' Supply Co. of New York* v. *DMNRCE* (1960), 2 T.B.R. 87 (Ex. Ct.), the Exchequer Court mentioned that the difference in the appeal was between 0 per cent and 20 per cent (at 88). Rates were also mentioned by the Exchequer Court or Federal Court of Appeal in *Metropolitan Life Insurance Co.* v. *DMNRCE*, [1966] Ex. C.R. 1112, 3 T.B.R. 216; *Central Electric Wire Ltd.* v. *DMNRCE* (1967), 3 T.B.R. 296 (Ex. Ct.); *DMNRCE* v. *GTE Sylvania Canada Ltd.* (1985), 10 C.E.R. 200, 64 N.R. 322 (F.C.A.). In *C. J. Rush Ltd.* v. *DMNRCE*

In the *Freedman* appeal, the Board refused to consider differences in tariff rates, which it called "purely fortuitous."[163] In the *Tractor Reference*, the Board brushed aside a mention in the Deputy Minister's reference letter that clear guidelines could assist in the establishment of a domestic manufacturing industry:

> [T]he fact that there is or is not Canadian production of a particular type of machine is a circumstance irrelevant to the determination of whether or not the machine is a tractor within the meaning of the tariff item; it is a circumstance which can neither narrow nor broaden the meaning of the word "tractor" nor can it properly be taken into account when the construction of the item is in issue before the Board on an appeal. If Parliament seeks to exclude additional types of tractors from the item, it will, presumably, pass legislation in clear words to that effect.[164]

This rejection of the purposive approach was quite in line with the Supreme Court's choice of literal interpretation in the *Pfizer* appeal, in which the Court reversed the decisions below and produced a resulting tariff protection that the Federal Court of Appeal had characterized as "improbable":

> [T]he only protection afforded to the manufacturer in Canada of chlortetracycline and its salts would be against the importation of the salts of tetracycline. Not only would there be no protection against the importation of oxytetracycline or its salts but there would be no protection against the importation of chlortetracycline or its salts.[165]

It has been argued above that the Supreme Court's rejection of trade meaning in *Pfizer* was unnecessarily strong. The rejection of narrow purposive interpretation is, however, in accordance with the thesis of this paper. The participatory model of interpretation looks to the commercial use of goods, not to the economic policy of any particular government at any particular time. If the Harmonized

---

(1979), 6 T.B.R. 902, 1 C.E.R. 231 (T.B. App. 1422), the Tariff Board rejected the appellant's argument, which was based on the tariff structure and on the idea that higher tariff rates indicated a greater degree of manufacturing.

163 *J. Freedman & Son Ltd.* v. *DMNRCE* (1954), 1 T.B.R. 172 (T.B. App. 314), aff'd (*sub nom Canadian Horticultural Council* v. *Freedman*) (1954), 1 T.B.R. 174 (Ex. Ct.). For further rejections of attempted purposive arguments, see *Quaker Oats Co. of Canada* v. *DMNRCE* (1984), 9 T.B.R. 276, 8 C.E.R. 1 (T.B. App. 2115); *Benoit Belanger* v. *DMNRCE* (1984), 9 T.B.R. 295, 7 C.E.R. 18 (T.B. App. 2102).

164 *Reference re . . . Internal Combustion Tractor[s]* (1966), 3 T.B.R. 259 at 261 (T.B. App. 795).

165 *Pfizer Co.* v. *DMNRCE*, [1973] F.C. 3, 5 T.B.R. 236 at 238 (F.C.A.), rev'd (1975), [1977] 1 S.C.R. 456, 5 T.B.R. 257.

System is to be accepted on a world-wide basis, then its interpretation cannot favour the customs or economic policy of any one country or group of countries. Purposive interpretation that is this narrow is out of place in the Harmonized System. International interpretation of an HS heading or subheading should not depend on whether there was a manufacturer of chlortetracycline in Canada at any given time.

This is not to say that meaning is to be viewed in an artificial light, detached completely from the circumstances in which communication normally takes place. Such an extreme approach would call into question the ordinary leeway for understanding that is inherent in language. Rejection of the narrow purposive approach does not imply a rejection of more general, teleological interpretation. It will not undermine the goals of the Harmonized System to assume that its headings and subheadings were intended to have some useful effect and to interpret them in this light. In *Simplicity Patterns*, for example, the Tariff Board interpreted a tariff exemption for catalogues that related exclusively to products or services of countries entitled to the British preferential tariff. The Board ruled that the catalogue in question was not disqualified because it contained a Canadian address for ordering. The patterns themselves were clearly products of the United Kingdom. To disqualify the catalogue because of the address would, according to the Board, render the item useless and destroy the purpose of the tariff exemption.[166] Narrow purposive interpretation should be viewed with suspicion in the Harmonized System, but a general teleological approach is not objectionable.

Tariff Board decisions were very rarely purposive in the narrow sense, but in one the Board perhaps went over the line. In the *Supreme Plating* appeal, the Board decided that the prohibition against the import of "used or secondhand" automobiles did not apply to a vehicle that the owner had purchased through a dealer in Canada and used briefly in Europe before importation. The Board reasoned that the item did not cover an automobile still owned by the original purchaser, especially since the intervening use was

166 *Simplicity Patterns Ltd.* v. *DMNRCE* (1980), 7 T.B.R. 214, 2 C.E.R. 315 (T.B. App. 1508), aff'd (1981), 3 C.E.R. 344 (F.C.A.). See also *Sargent-Welch Scientific of Canada Ltd.* v. *DMNRCE* (1988), 13 T.B.R. 118, 16 C.E.R. 73 (T.B. App. 2813); *AKA Music Import Distribution* v. *DMNRCE* (1988), 13 T.B.R. 122, 16 C.E.R. 87 (T.B. App. 2883). Under the Harmonized System, see *National Geographic Society* v. *DMNRCE*, [1993] C.I.T.T. No. 121 (QL) (AP-92-194). From the European Court of Justice, see *Hamlin Electronics GmbH* v. *Hauptzollamt Darmstadt*, Case C-338/90, [1992] Rec. I-2333.

minimal. This import did not threaten the market for secondhand vehicles in Canada.[167] This decision may be acceptable as an interpretation of the meaning of "used or secondhand" as applied to automobiles. It may also be acceptable as applying to any market anywhere for secondhand vehicles. When, however, interpretation looks to the circumstances of a particular domestic market in a manner that the institutions of the Customs Co-operation Council could not be expected to follow, then the approach is too narrow and should be rejected.

By about the middle of this century, legal philosophy in North America, following the realists, was already somewhat receptive to the idea that judges have leeway in their interpretations. The formalist view that judges should simply find existing meanings in rules or in the words of a statute had declined in popularity. There was a tendency to recognize the purposive approach to statutory interpretation, with judges interpreting according to the general intentions of democratic institutions.[168] The current interest in interpretation theory has directed increased attention to the assumptions of the judges themselves, as well as to the assumptions in the statutory texts.[169]

The defence of formalism often involves the naming of concrete objects:

The manufacture of a five-pronged implement for manual digging results in a fork even if the manufacturer, unfamiliar with the English language, insists that he intended to make and has made a spade.[170]

167 *Supreme Plating Ltd.* v. *DMNRCE* (1985), 10 T.B.R. 205, 9 C.E.R. 255 (T.B. App. 2220). Classification appeals should be distinguished from the Tribunal's inquiry function: Canadian International Trade Tribunal Act, R.S.C. 1985 (4th Supp.), c. 47, ss. 18, 19. On appeals, the Tribunal is not asked to recommend changes to tariff items: *Canadian Thermos Products Inc.* v. *DMNRCE*, [1993] C.I.T.T. No. 4 (QL) (AP-92-015); *Gasparotto/Panontin Construction Ltd.* v. *DMNRCE*, [1993] C.I.T.T. No. 75 (QL) (AP-91-152).

168 John Willis, "Statute Interpretation in a Nutshell," 16 Can. Bar Rev. 1 (1938).

169 For two recent reviews of the field, see Rosemary J. Coombe, "'Same As It Ever Was': Rethinking the Politics of Legal Interpretation," 34 McGill L.J. 603 (1989); William N. Eskridge Jr., "Gadamer/Statutory Interpretation," 90 Colum. L.R. 609 (1990).

170 Templeman J. in *Street* v. *Mountford*, [1985] A.C. 809 at 819, cited in J. W. Harris, "Unger's Critique of Formalism in Legal Reasoning: Hero, Hercules and Humdrum," 52 Mod. L. Rev. 42 at 60 (1989). It may be noted that this example, in fact, involves an element of participatory interpretation, since it mentions use of the fork for digging. The example does not follow a pure observation model.

Rejecting the observation model implies rejection of formalism. It does not, however, require acceptance of narrow purposive interpretation as the only alternative. Customs tariff statutes will reflect legislative policy to protect and promote certain domestic industries. A customs tariff law that implements the Harmonized System, however, is also part of an international arrangement. The Customs Co-operation Council could not be expected to base its interpretation decisions on policies in favour of particular domestic industries in member countries. The same approach should be taken when the Harmonized System is interpreted in national judicial and administrative decisions.

IV HARMONIZED SYSTEM RULES

General Rule 1 for the interpretation of the Harmonized System gives priority to the headings and legal notes for any doubts concerning classification of particular goods. Should difficulties arise, the explanatory notes or classification opinions may help to resolve the problem. Although these last two sources are not binding within the HS, it is expected that most countries will try to follow them in their classification decisions. When the headings and legal notes apply, they determine the relevant factors for interpretation.[171] The factors can relate to physical features, reflecting the observation model of classification.[172] The participatory approach is also evident in the drafting of some provisions, such as note 3 to section XVI, which provides that composite machines are to be classified according to their principal function.[173] General Rule 1 states what would probably be obvious in any case — that interpretation starts with the headings and legal notes.

General Rule 2 contains two parts that are not closely linked to each other and could easily stand alone. The first, Rule 2(a), states that goods will be treated as a complete article even where they are presented unfinished or unassembled. As long as the unfinished or

---

171 *Esden Ltd.* v. *DMNRCE* (1992), 5 T.C.T. 1078 (C.I.T.T. AP-90-006); *York Barbell Co.* v. *DMNRCE* (1992), 5 T.C.T. 1150 (C.I.T.T. AP-91-131); *Udisco Ltd.* v. *DMNRCE*, [1992] C.I.T.T. No. 121 (QL) (AP-91-269); *Black & Decker Canada Inc.* v. *DMNRCE*, [1992] C.I.T.T. No. 143 (QL) (AP-90-192); *Canadian Thermos Products Inc.* v. *DMNRCE*, [1993] C.I.T.T. No. 4 (QL) (AP-92-015); *Bionaire Inc.* v. *DMNRCE*, [1993] C.I.T.T. No. 83 (QL) (AP-92-110).

172 *Pollard Banknote Ltd.* v. *DMNRCE* (1990), 4 T.C.T. 3108 (C.I.T.T., AP-89-279).

173 *Royal Telecom Inc.* v. *DMNRCE* (1991), 4 T.C.T. 3175 (C.I.T.T. AP-90-027); *R. G. Dobbin Sales Ltd.* v. *DMNRCE*, [1993] C.I.T.T. No. 25 (QL) (AP-92-032).

incomplete goods have the "essential character" of the complete article, they will be considered complete. Explanatory note II clarifies this somewhat by saying that the rule would cover blanks not specified in another heading so long as they were committed for processing into the complete article.[174] The rule verges on a question of customs technique, making sure that goods cannot be imported at lower rates for parts or raw materials when the processing after importation is not significant.[175]

Rule 2(b) provides that a reference to a material or substance includes a reference to that material or substance in mixture or combination with other materials or substances. Goods that consist of more than one material or substance are to be classified according to Rule 3. This is not what it looks like at first glance, an immediate detour to Rule 3 for any headings that refer to goods of a given material or substance. The reference to constituent elements is not infinitely elastic, so that goods could be of a named substance even if that substance constituted an insignificant percentage of the goods' composition. Rule 1 is still paramount and the descriptions in the headings apply.[176] Goods do not have to consist entirely of one named element, so long as they meet the description. Past this point, they could be considered to be of more than one substance and thus subject to Rule 3.

The interesting question about Rule 2(b) is why it is in a position of such importance — that is, the first theoretical approach to try when the terms of the headings and legal notes are insufficient. It is even prior to Rule 3(a), the principle of greater specificity, the one principle that should be fundamental to the entire classification exercise. Rule 2(b) illustrates the strong pull of the observation

---

174 See *Dumex Medical Surgical Products Ltd.* v. *DMNRCE* (1992), 5 T.C.T. 1297 (C.I.T.T. AP-91-132); *Diamant Boart Truco Ltd.* v. *DMNRCE* (1992), 5 T.C.T. 1315 (C.I.T.T., AP-90-166). In the law of the European Union, see *Herbert Fleischer Import-Export* v. *Hauptzollamt Flensburg*, Case 49/73, [1973] Rec. 1199; *Directeur général des douanes et des droits indirects* v. *Powerex-Europe*, Case C-66/89, [1990] E.C.R. I-1959.

175 Concerning unassembled goods, see *Bradley* v. *DMNRCE* (1990), 3 T.C.T. 2188 (C.I.T.T. AP-89-228); *Procedair Industries Inc.* v. *DMNRCE*, [1993] C.I.T.T. No. 87 (QL) (AP-92-152). In the law of the European Union, see *IMCO — J. Michaelis GmbH & Co.* v. *Oberfinanzdirektion Berlin*, Case 165/78, [1979] E.C.R. 1837.

176 See Patrick L. Kelley and Ivo Onkelinx, *EEC Customs Law: Legislation, Case Law and Explanatory Text on the Customs System of the European Economic Community*, T-66, T-67 (Oxford: ESC Publishing, 1986 (4th Supp., 1991)).

model in tariff matters. Classification is thought to depend on physical fact. If difficulty arises, it is assumed that the best description will be one that refers to goods by material composition. It is as if the crucial fact about a wooden table is that it is made of wood, and not that it fulfils certain functions.[177]

If goods might potentially be covered by two or more headings, Rule 3 contains three sections to be applied in order. Rule 3(a) sets out the principle of greater specificity.[178] Rule 3(b) refers to the material or component that gives goods their essential character. If these two sub-rules fail to provide a solution, Rule 3(c) opts for the heading that occurs last in numerical order. The second sentence of Rule 3(a) negates the principle of greater specificity whenever headings refer to part only of the materials or components of goods or to part only of the items in a set.[179] It was added during the drafting of the Harmonized System, drawn from a previous CCCN explanatory note.[180] In these situations, Rule 3(a) does not apply and goods are judged under Rule 3(b) as if they consisted entirely of the substance or component that gives them their essential character. The assumed importance of material composition is again evidence of the power of the observation model. It should be

---

[177] In the European Union, see *E.I. Du Pont de Nemours Inc.* v. *Commissioners of Customs and Excise*, Case 234/81, [1982] E.C.R. 3515, in which imitation marble building material was classified as an article of plastic rather than an artificial stone, despite the fact that plastic was only 33 per cent of its composition. Rule 2(b) was used to expand the reference to material composition. Even if Rule 3(a) had been used, the Court would have found the description of articles that had the properties of building stone less specific than the description by material composition.

[178] For a literal interpretation of specificity, see *Éditions Panini du Canada Ltée* v. *DMNRCE*, [1993] C.I.T.T. No. 38 (QL) (AP-92-018); *Praher Canada Products Ltd.* v. *DMNRCE*, [1993] C.I.T.T. No. 99 (QL) (AP-92-112). The question should not be which tariff item covers the smallest class of goods, but rather which item is the most specific description of the imports in question.

[179] It should be noted that "goods put up in sets for retail sale" could have a fairly wide application, as the Explanatory Notes indicate. In previous case law of the European Union, the phrase has been held to apply to composite machinery if the components are not all included in the "functional unit" according to the Notes to Section 16. See *Metro International Kommanditgesellschaft* v. *Oberfinanzdirektion München*, Case 60/83, [1984] E.C.R. 671; *Hauptzollamt Hannover* v. *Telefunken Fernseh und Rundfunk GmbH*, Case 163/84, [1985] E.C.R. 3299.

[180] See *Baupla GmbH* v. *Oberfinanzdirektion Köln*, Case 28/75, [1975] E.C.R. 989.

noted, however, that participatory interpretation is often present in decisions concerning the "essential character" of goods.[181] In decisions of the European Court of Justice, naming has been done by both function and purpose. In *Farr*, Case 130/82, for example, air filters were classified according to the filtering material, since that function was their essential character.[182] In *Kaffee-Contor*, Case 192/82, the essential character of jewellery boxes was the varnished paper covering that made them suitable for their purpose.[183] And in *Elba*, Case 205/80, the essential character of decorations with flashing lights was their use as articles for entertainment.[184]

Rule 4 is the residual rule that applies when there are no headings that describe the goods directly. Goods are then to be classified under the heading for goods to which they are most akin.[185] According to the European Court of Justice, similarity could depend on several factors. In *Bollmann*, Case 40/69, it related to the physical characteristics, use, and value of the goods.[186] In *Luma*, Case 38/76, however, the Court confirmed the primacy of the observation model and descriptions by composition. Goods could not be classified by analogy under Rule 4 if they could be described by composi-

---

181 *Pigmalion Services* v. *DMNRCE* (1992), 5 T.C.T. 1247 (C.I.T.T. AP-90-138); *Sandvik Rock Tools* v. *DMNRCE* (1992), 5 T.C.T. 1292 (C.I.T.T. AP-91-110, AP-91-138); *Oriental Trading (MTL) Ltd.* v. *DMNRCE* (1992), 5 T.C.T. 1363 (C.I.T.T. AP-91-081, AP-91-223); *Weil Co.* v. *DMNRCE*, [1993] C.I.T.T. No. 64 (QL) (AP-92-096). See Explanatory Note 7 to Rule 3(b), which states that "the role of a constituent material in relation to the use of goods" may be a factor in determining essential character.

182 *Naamloze vennootschap Farr Co.* v. *Belgian State*, Case 130/82, [1983] E.C.R. 327. A contrary example is *Gustav Schickedanz KV* v. *Oberfinanzdirektion Frankfurt am Main*, Case 298/82, [1984] E.C.R. 1829, in which the leather supports on running shoes were less "essential" than the textile fabric despite their more important function.

183 *Kaffee-Contor Bremen GmbH & Co. KG* v. *Hauptzollamt Bremen-Nord*, Case 192/82, [1983] E.C.R. 1769. See also *Sportex GmbH & Co.* v. *Oberfinanzdirektion Hamburg*, Case 253/87, [1988] E.C.R. 3351.

184 *ELBA Elektroapparate- und Maschinenbau Walter Goettmann KG* v. *Hauptzollamt Berlin-Packhof*, Case 205/80, [1981] E.C.R. 2097.

185 *IEC-Holden Inc.* v. *DMNRCE* (1992), 5 T.C.T. 1187 (C.I.T.T. AP-91-150); *John Martens Co.* v. *DMNRCE*, [1993] C.I.T.T. No. 69 (QL) (AP-92-022).

186 *Hauptzollamt Hamburg-Oberelbe* v. *Firma Paul G. Bollmann*, Case 40/69, [1970] Rec. 69 ("Turkey Tails"). The function of the goods was significant in *Telefunken Fernseh und Rundfunk GmbH* v. *Oberfinanzdirektion München*, Case 223/84, [1985] E.C.R. 3335.

tion in some other heading.[187] Rule 4 is only residual. Priority goes to other headings, even other headings expanded by Rule 2(b). The first four rules are very similar to the rules of the previous CCCN, and refer only to headings at the four-digit level. Rule 6 applies the same system to the subheadings and subheading notes up to six digits. Canadian Rule 1 applies the same principles to tariff items up to the eight-digit level, along with any related supplementary notes. For statistical purposes, the same principles apply to the ten-digit classification numbers under Canadian Rule 3, which is not part of the tariff legislation. The rules are not specifically made applicable to interpretation of the concessionary provisions in other Schedules to the *Customs Tariff*. These usually refer to the headings, subheadings, and tariff items of Schedule I, however; the rules will apply at least to that extent.[188]

The major criticism of these rules for interpretation is that they give too much emphasis to the material composition of goods, reflecting the influence of the observation model for classification. Goods are to be judged by physical characteristics present at the time of importation. Any other factors are thought to be extrinsic, subjective, and unreliable. Numerous decisions of the European Court of Justice emphasize that classification must be objective and verifiable.[189] Imported jeans in *Lampe*, Case 222/85, for example,

---

[187] *Industriemetall LUMA GmbH* v. *Hauptzollamt Duisberg*, Case 38/76, [1976] E.C.R. 2027.

[188] Canadian Rule 2 confirms that international terms take precedence in those instances where the tariff contains the Canadian term in parenthesis after the international term. This Canadianization of the tariff occurred after recommendations from the Tariff Board concerning the difficulty of understanding an HS-based tariff that referred to things like "crane lorries" (mobile cranes) and "gear boxes" (transmissions). See Tariff Board, *Reference No. 163, Canada's Customs Tariff According to the Harmonized System*, Vol. 1, Chapters 1-24 (1985) at 15 and Vol. 2, Part 1, Chapters 25-46 (1985) at 15; Revenue Canada, Customs and Excise, *Submission to the Tariff Board, Reference No. 163: Canada's Customs Tariff According to the Harmonized System*, July 29, 1986, at 7.

[189] See *Günther Henck* v. *Hauptzollamt Emden*, Case 36/71, [1972] Rec. 187; *Past & Co. KG* v. *Hauptzollamt Freiburg*, Case 128/73, [1973] E.C.R. 1277; *Hauptzollamt Bielefeld* v. *Offene Handelsgesellschaft in Firma H.C. König*, Case 185/73, [1974] E.C.R. 607; *Belgian State* v. *Vandertaelen*, Case 53/75, [1975] E.C.R. 1647; *Carstens Keramik & Firma August Hoff* v. *Oberfinanzdirektion Frankfurt am Main*, Cases 98 & 99/75, [1976] E.C.R. 241; *Industriemetall LUMA GmbH* v. *Hauptzollamt Duisberg*, Case 38/76, [1976] E.C.R. 2027; *Carlsen Verlag GmbH* v. *Oberfinanzdirektion Köln*, Case 62/77, [1977] E.C.R. 2343; *Westfälischer Kunstverein* v. *Hauptzollamt Münster*, Case 23/77, [1977] E.C.R. 1985; *Firma*

were men's garments because they fastened left over right, despite arguments from the importer that women wore this style as well. The Court reasoned that:

the intended use of goods, which is not an inherent quality of the goods, cannot be used as an objective criterion for the purposes of its Common Customs Tariff classification at the time of importation since it is impossible at that time to determine the actual use to which the goods will be put.[190]

Interpretation was quite literal, so that a bonded fibre was classified as a fabric despite its use as a floor covering,[191] and a pocket calculator with a simple programming language was classified as a data-processing machine despite its intended use for basic calculating. The requirements of legal certainty and simple checks for customs clearance meant that the definition for data-processing machines had to be applied. Any updating to take account of

---

Hako-Schuh Dietrich Bahner v. *Hauptzollamt Frankfurt am Main-Ost*, Case 54/79, [1980] E.C.R. 311; *Hauptzollamt Hamburg-Jonas* v. *Ludwig Wünsche & Co.*, Case 145/81, [1982] E.C.R. 2493; *Almadent Dental-Handels-und Vertriebsgesellschaft mbH* v. *Hauptzollamt Mainz*, Case 237/81, [1982] E.C.R. 2981; *Hans Dinter GmbH* v. *Hauptzollamt Köln-Deutz*, Case 175/82, [1983] E.C.R. 969; *Thomasdünger GmbH* v. *Oberfinanzdirektion Frankfurt am Main*, Case 166/84, [1985] E.C.R. 3001; *Directeur général des douanes et droits indirects* v. *Artimport*, Case 42/86, [1987] E.C.R. 4817; *Weber* v. *Milchwerke Paderborn-Rimbeck e.G.*, Case 40/88, [1989] E.C.R. 1395; *Ministère public* v. *Rispal*, Case 164/88, [1989] E.C.R. 2041; *Raab* v. *Hauptzollamt Berlin-Packhof*, Case C-1/89, [1989] E.C.R. 4423; *Farfalla Flemming und Partner* v. *Hauptzollamt München-West*, Case C-228/89, [1990] E.C.R. I-3387; *Gebr. Vismans Nederland BV* v. *Inspecteur der Invoerrechten en Accijnzen*, Case C-265/89, [1990] E.C.R. I-3411; *Ministère public* v. *Tomatis*, Case C-384/89, [1991] E.C.R. I-127; *Ludwig Post GmbH* v. *Oberfinanzdirektion München*, Case C-120/90, [1991] E.C.R. I-2391. Treatment that "cannot be seen with the naked eye" meant just that in *Howe & Bainbridge BV* v. *Oberfinanzdirektion Frankfurt am Main*, Case 317/81, [1982] E.C.R. 3257. See further *NV Koninklijke Lassiefabrieken* v. *Hoofdproduktschap voor Akker-bouwprodukten*, Case 80/72, [1973] Rec. 635. Verifiability by taste was also acceptable: *Gijs van de Kolk-Douane Expéditeur BV* v. *Inspecteur der Invoerrechten en Accijnzen*, Case C-233/88, [1990] E.C.R. I-265.

190 *Hauptzollamt Osnabrück* v. *Kleiderwerke Hela Lampe GmbH & Co. KG*, Case 222/85, [1986] E.C.R. 2449 at 2456.

191 *3M Deutschland GmbH* v. *Oberfinanzdirektion Frankfurt am Main*, Case 92/83, [1984] E.C.R. 1587. For other cases that similarly reject use as a criterion, see *Dr. Ritter GmbH & Co.* v. *Oberfinanzdirektion Hamburg*, Case 114/80, [1981] E.C.R. 895; *Handelsonderneming J.Mikx BV* v. *Minister van Economische Zaken*, Case 90/85, [1986] E.C.R. 1695; *WeserGold GmbH & Co. KG* v. *Oberfinanzdirektion München*, Case C-219/89, [1991] E.C.R. I-1895; *Parma Handelsgesellschaft mbH* v. *Hauptzollamt Bad Reichenhall*, Case C-246/90, [1992] Rec. I-3467.

technological developments was to be done through amendments to the tariff and not through judicial interpretation.[192] The requirement of objective certainty at the time of importation was so overwhelming that it was seen as exceptional to rely on certificates of origin to distinguish reindeer meat as either from domestic animals or from wild game, since there was no physical difference in the goods as imported.[193]

In the European Union, the strong emphasis on the observation model may be due to the fact that goods can clear customs in one member state of the Union even when they are destined for use in another member state. The administrative problems of customs unions can be solved through other co-operative measures, however, and do not require that interpretation take place in an artificial setting isolated from all knowledge of ordinary commerce. Participatory interpretation has also been present for questions relating to the "essential character" of goods and in other situations.[194] It would be worthwhile to examine previous decisions in the European Union and in other jurisdictions around the world with experience in applying the CCCN to determine whether the emphasis on material composition in the general rules for interpretation is still appropriate.

V INTERPRETATION AND THE HARMONIZED SYSTEM

The Harmonized System is a more detailed, modern nomenclature than the CCCN. A major goal of the updating project was to provide a system that would be adaptable for the various classifications to which goods were subject in international trade. A study by

192 *Casio Computer Co. GmbH Deutschland* v. *Oberfinanzdirektion München*, Case 234/87, [1989] E.C.R. 63. See also: *Analog Devices GmbH* v. *Hauptzollamt München-Mitte*, Case 122/80, [1981] E.C.R. 2781; *Gerlach & Co. BV* v. *Inspecteur der Invoerrechten en Accijnzen*, Case C-43/89, [1990] E.C.R. I-3219.

193 *Otto Witt KG* v. *Hauptzollamt Hamburg-Ericus*, Case 149/73, [1973] Rec. 1587. See D. Lasok and W. Cairns, *The Customs Law of the European Economic Community* 64 (Deventer, The Netherlands: Kluwer, 1983).

194 A participatory approach was used to determine similarity in *Nederlandsch Bevrachtingskantoor BV* v. *Inspecteur der Invoerrechten en Accijnzen, Amsterdam*, Case 37/82, [1982] E.C.R. 3481. On machines for measuring or checking, see *International Container et Transport (ICT)* v. *Direction générale des douanes et droits indirects de Roissy*, Case 19/88, [1989] E.C.R. 577; *Shimadzu Europa GmbH* v. *Oberfinanzdirektion Berlin*, Case C-218/89, [1990] E.C.R. I-4391. In Canadian case law, see *Outils Royal Tools Corp.* v. *DMNRCE*, [1993] C.I.T.T. No. 108 (QL) (AP-92-151).

the CCC Secretariat in 1970 indicated that goods in an international transaction might be coded in a number of different ways for import and export formalities, statistics, and modes of transport. This diversity of codes increased relevant administrative costs (to as much as 10 per cent of the value of goods), made statistics unreliable, and discouraged the use of electronic data processing.[195] After initial exploratory work, the Harmonized System Study Group reported in 1973 that development of the new system was feasible. The Study Group suggested that it should be based on the Brussels Tariff Nomenclature and the Standard International Trade Classification (SITC Rev.2, the UN statistical nomenclature), but should also take account of a variety of other customs, statistical and transport codes.[196] While the Study Group concentrated its attention on international classifications, the report also hints at wider objectives. The new system was expected to benefit private commercial interests. Those involved substantially in international trade would be likely to add the HS codes to their internal data systems to quote in invoice and shipping information. There might also be a possibility of linking HS codes to national production statistics.[197] At its most ambitious, this could be a universal commodity code capable of describing goods in all contexts, available for use as a basic six-digit number to which other digits could be added for details of

---

195 General Secretariat, Customs Co-operation Council, *Development of a Commodity Description and Coding System for Use in International Trade,* Doc. 17.210, Dec. 4, 1970, paras. 21-23.

196 The suggested codes were: (1) *Customs nomenclatures* (Brussels Tariff Nomenclature, Tariff Nomenclature for the Latin American Free Trade Association (NABALALC), Customs tariff of Canada, Customs tariff of the United States, Customs tariff of Japan); (2) *Statistical nomenclatures* (Standard International Trade Classification (SITC, Rev.2), Nomenclature of Goods for the External Trade Statistics of the Community and Statistics of Trade between Member States (NIMEXE), Import Commodity Classification (Canada), Export Commodity Classification (Canada), Schedule B (Export, United States)); (3) *Transport nomenclatures* (Standard Commodity Nomenclature (NUM) of the International Union of Railways (UIC), Worldwide Air Cargo Commodity Classification (WACCC), Freight Tariff of the Association of West India Trans-Atlantic Steamship Lines (WIFT), Standard Transportation Commodity Code (STCC)); (4) *Other classifications* (Standard Foreign Trade Classification (SFTC) of the Council for Mutual Economic Assistance). See Harmonized System Study Group, *Report to the Customs Co-operation Council of the Study Group for the Development of a Harmonized Commodity Description and Coding System for International Trade,* Doc. 19.513, Mar. 28, 1973 (hereinafter "HS Study Group, *Report*"), Annex C.

197 HS Study Group, *Report,* paras. 23, 42, 45.

purchase, sale, inventory, finance, product standards, government regulation, taxation, and specific characteristics such as colour and size, etc. With the use of computers, many other details could be coded, while the HS number would serve as a multipurpose identification tag for everyone involved.[198]

It is not clear that the Harmonized System as it developed is truly a different sort of nomenclature from the previous CCCN. The Study Group that reported to Council in 1973 thought that the HS would simply be a recommendation within the CCCN and not a completely new convention.[199] It was not until February 1983, just a few months before the signing of the Convention, that the Harmonized System Committee finally settled in favour of that form.[200] A recommendation would have been less disruptive but it would also have been optional and therefore less effective. The use of a convention signals a clear choice in favour of a combined multipurpose nomenclature, rather than the previous CCCN tariff nomenclature with optional statistical digits. The choice of a multipurpose nomenclature is also reflected in Article 3 of the Convention, which makes the HS obligatory for both tariffs and the reporting of trade statistics. As well, the preamble lists several intended objectives, including the correlation of trade and production statistics, use of the HS in freight tariffs and transport statistics, and general use in commercial coding systems to the greatest extent possible.

[198] See J. H. Hoguet, Director of CCC Nomenclature, "The Case for an International Goods Nomenclature," mimeograph, April 1976, at 17: "An instrument which began as a Customs nomenclature (1955), grew into a Customs and statistical Nomenclature (1960-1980), and will eventually evolve into a 'Harmonized System' (1980 onwards) represents a progressive response to the development of various needs which, though not entirely new, are becoming ever more important in such areas as taxation, market research, investment, planning, etc."

[199] HS Study Group, *Report*, para. 20.

[200] Summary Record, 30th Session of the Harmonized System Committee and Working Party, Feb. 7-15, 1983, Doc. 29.850, Mar. 10, 1983; Summary Record, 27th Session of the Harmonized System Committee and Working Party, Feb. 8-26, 1982, Doc. 28.400, Apr. 8, 1982; Summary Record, 26th Session of the Harmonized System Committee and Working Party, Oct. 5-23, 1981, Doc. 28.000, Nov. 25, 1981; Summary Record, 21st Session of the Harmonized System Committee and Working Party, May 19-June 6, 1980, Doc. 26.320, July 18, 1980. See United States International Trade Commission, *Interim Report on the Harmonized Commodity Description and Coding System*, Publication No. 1106, November 1980, at 11-12.

The Study Group in 1973 took a fairly strict approach and recommended that the system should exclude the following criteria "which do not serve to define the commodity itself":

(a) distinctions made to provide for tariff rate charges directly related to specific dates;
(b) the origin of goods, by country or supplier;
(c) the destination of goods, by country or user;
(d) packaging or handling characteristics such as "fragile," "toxic," "dangerous," etc.[201]

Concerning the end use of goods, the Group noted that it might be possible to classify according to the main use, but only if this were "directly related to the technological characteristics of the commodity."[202] In a report in 1975, the United States International Trade Commission had a similar view of criteria that should be used for an international commodity code. The code was to be suitable for import and export regulation, for trade and production statistics, and for transport documents. One of the criteria identified by the International Trade Commission was that the code should be capable of uniform application. This implied that:

[t]o the extent practicable, articles should be properly classifiable within the system by reference to their intrinsic characteristics, without reliance upon extrinsic factors such as subsequent or intended use or the process of manufacture.[203]

It has been argued throughout this paper that the observation model does not work in this way. To the extent that uniformity is attainable, it comes from shared understandings that consider as many of the relevant viewpoints as possible.[204] It is these shared understandings from commercial practice and the use of goods in application are most likely to provide generally accepted interpretations. Especially if the Harmonized System is to fulfil its promise as a multipurpose commodity code, classification theory should concentrate less on "What is this made of?" and more on "What is this for?"

---

201 HS Study Group, *Report*, para. 22.

202 *Ibid.*, Annex D, para. 9.

203 United States International Trade Commission, *Concepts and Principles Which Should Underlie the Formulation of an International Commodity Code*, 94th Congress, 1st Session, House Document No. 94-175, June 1975 at 8.

204 See George Lakoff, *Women, Fire and Dangerous Things: What Categories Reveal about the Mind*, 264, 301 (Chicago: University of Chicago Press, 1987): "Acknowledging alternative conceptual schemes does not abandon objectivity; on the contrary, it makes objectivity possible."

For the Harmonized System, authoritative interpretation at this point is likely to be done by customs officials, either in national administrations or acting through the Customs Co-operation Council. Interpretation of the HS will clearly require standards that are sufficiently precise and uniform for legal application to particular imports. Customs officers' concern with individual instances of classification will be quite appropriate. It may be questioned, however, whether the observation model as expressed by the CCC and the emphasis on physical features of goods reflect current procedures. More and more, customs clearances are done through electronic exchanges of data with large importers or brokers, after or even before goods cross the border.[205] The standard instance no longer needs to be the wooden wagon pulling up to the customs house, with clearance done through on-the-spot inspection. Electronic clearances can take place at a time when fairly complete information is available on surrounding transactions. Particularly for the products of manufacturing and high technology, use can be more significant than material composition.

The appropriate model for tariff classification should take account of the commercial context. In addition, if the HS is to serve as a multipurpose code, the assumptions of private commercial actors should be considered. Customs officials are by training somewhat mercantilist, required in their enforcement role to think of importing as a vaguely suspicious activity. It may be sensible to de-emphasize their perspective in order to develop a commodity code that will facilitate commercial exchange.

The focus on the assumptions of decision-makers raises general questions about the influence of power and whether all relevant voices are heard. At the international level, this can be seen as a question of whether the interests of developing countries are adequately reflected, in the choice of goods to be classified and in the ongoing administration of the system. It would be unfortunate if the Harmonized System served only the interests of the developed world when customs duties are proportionately more important as a source of revenue for governments of developing countries. UNCTAD and several developing countries participated in the elaboration of the HS. Many developing countries have become contract-

---

205 The Customs Co-operation Council is active in encouraging this development: see its *Annual Report 1989-90*, Bulletin No. 35 at 19. See also Revenue Canada, Customs and Excise, *Customs 2000: A Blueprint for the Future*, undated (1989-90); Revenue Canada, Customs and Excise, *Customs Commercial System: General Information on the Customs Commercial System*, 1986.

ing parties. The Harmonized System is about commodities in international trade and the major trading countries will have an important say in decisions. From the beginning, however, the Customs Cooperation Council has attempted to ensure that the interests of developing countries are recognized.[206] The Council has undertaken extensive programmes of technical assistance and training for application of the HS. As well, the Council has assisted a number of developing countries with the work of tariff transposition to the new system.[207]

It has been argued throughout this study that interpretation of the Harmonized System should be based on a participatory model that reflects the perspectives of users, rather than on an observation model that concentrates on the material features of goods. For the naming of natural kinds, physical characteristics may be paramount. Manufactured goods, however, reflect human design and can be most reliably identified through interpretation that considers that design. A wooden table is more like a metal table than it is like a wooden chair. Interpretation should concentrate on factors with overall, global relevance. These could involve material composition. As well, they should involve the use of goods, including both their function and their suitability for the particular purpose. The emphasis on physical characteristics in the HS general rules for interpretation risks creating a classification system that is at odds with commercial practice.

In the Harmonized System, words alone are used as a basis for international law that is to apply in the domestic systems of differing societies in a number of contexts. The possibility of consensus in interpretation depends on looking to what is shared. Both for national decisions and for decisions from the Customs Co-operation Council, interpretation should be as open as possible to the interests of all potential users of the Harmonized System, including private businesses, non-governmental organizations, and governments from all parts of the globe.

---

206 HS Study Group, *Report*, paras. 13-15.

207 Customs Co-operation Council, *Annual Report 1985-86*, Bulletin No. 31 at 13-14; Customs Co-operation Council, *Annual Report 1986-87*, Bulletin No. 32 at 12; Customs Co-operation Council, *Annual Report 1987-88*, Bulletin No. 33 at 11-12; Customs Co-operation Council, *Annual Report 1988-89*, Bulletin No. 34 at 13-14; Customs Co-operation Council, *Annual Report 1989-90*, Bulletin No. 35 at 14-15; A. Musa, "Technical Assistance for Developing Countries Implementing the Harmonized System," in Customs Co-operation Council, *Implementing the Harmonized System: A Management Perspective* 9 (1986).

Sommaire

Interprétation et désignation: l'intégration du Système harmonisé
au droit canadien relatif au tarif douanier

*Le 1er janvier 1988, le Canada a remplacé son tarif douanier par le
Système harmonisé de désignation et de codification des marchandises, une
convention internationale généralement acceptée par les nations commer-
çantes du monde entier. Dans cet article, l'auteur examine les approches
interprétatives adoptées par les tribunaux canadiens en matière de classification tarifaire, avant et après la mise en œuvre du nouveau système, et fait
allusion aux décisions de la Cour européenne de justice. Les Règles générales
pour l'interprétation du nouveau système mettent l'accent sur les caractéristi-
ques physiques des marchandises, y compris leur assemblage et leur composition. Selon les Règles, les interprètes devraient rejeter les facteurs extrinsèques
et se concentrer sur les qualités des marchandises, telles que perçues par un
observateur objectif.*

*L'auteur critique ce modèle d'observation pour l'interprétation et propose à
la place un modèle plus participatif qui tient compte des perspectives des
usagers d'un tarif douanier. Cette approche accorde une plus grande attention à l'utilisation des marchandises, ainsi qu'à leur fonction et au fait
qu'elles soient appropriées au but projeté. L'auteur soutient qu'il est futile de
chercher la certitude et l'uniformité en ce qui concerne les objets concrets,
puisque l'ensemble de la langue reflète les buts et la culture de la personne.
On devrait plutôt avoir pour but d'atteindre un consensus en tenant compte
des perspectives du plus grand nombre d'interprètes possible, y compris les
entreprises, les organisations internationales et les gouvernements du monde
entier.*

Truth, Tradition, and Confrontation:
A Theory of International Human Rights

JOHN F. G. HANNAFORD*

INTRODUCTION

FOR THE INTERNATIONAL LAWYER, the pressures of cultural difference emerge in the documents of human rights. Consider, for instance, this passage from the report of the regional meeting for Asia (the "Bangkok Declaration") of April 1, 1993:

> While human rights are universal in nature, they must be considered in the context of a dynamic and evolving process of international norm-setting, bearing in mind the significance of national and regional particularities and various historical, cultural and religious backgrounds.[1]

A milder form of this language is found in the subsequent documents and report of the World Conference on Human Rights:

> While the significance of national and regional particularities and various historical backgrounds must be borne in mind, it is the duty of states, regardless of their political, economic and cultural systems, to promote and protect all human rights and fundamental freedoms.[2]

Such statements are, of course, accompanied by declared adherence to the universality of human rights, but they represent a core

---

B.A.(Hons.) (Queen's), M.Sc.(Econ.) (London School of Economics), LL.B. (University of Toronto). I wish to thank the following for their assistance and encouragement: Professors Craig Scott and Brian Langille of the University of Toronto, Faculty of Law; Douglas Harris; Frederick and Grace Hannaford; and, of course, my wife, Anne Lawson.

---

1 World Conference on Human Rights, *Regional Meeting for Asia*, UN Doc. A/CONF.157/ASRM/7 (1993).

2 *Report of the Drafting Committee to the World Conference on Human Rights*, UN Doc. A/CONF.157/DC/1/Add.1 (1993).

of dissent concerning human rights and the generality of their application. The expression of this dissent in international law is softened through diplomatic language, yet it is closely related to the more strident philosophical doctrine of cultural relativism. And, from the vantage point of this philosophy, a profound critique of international human rights law is mounted; the contours of this critique are visible in the passages cited above.

In the world of the relativist, the very idea of international or transcending norms is without moral content. Norms, the relativist says, inhere only to the cultures that developed them. The proponents of human rights, on this view, have no moral authority to judge others. Relativists make an argument of the following kind: for too long western civilization has been obsessed with finding concrete and objective truths. Yet no consensus has formed around the various offerings. This is so precisely because there have never been truths to be found. Therefore, we should recognize that there is no truth beyond ourselves and the institutions we create; and, in admitting this, we should recognize the limitations of our convictions.

If these conclusions are correct, the very idea of an international human right is fundamentally misguided.[3] And, to a certain extent, I think this is right. In the following pages I want to show how the objectivist[4] notion of international human rights — a view that these rights represent certain objective truths of human existence — is incorrect. Put briefly, I see truth as immanent in human relations; so conceived, the idea of truth makes no sense outside the context of human society. But I do not accept the relativist's conclu-

---

[3] See Alison Rentlen, "The Unanswered Challenge of Relativism and the Consequences for Human Rights," 7 Hum. Rts. Q. 514 (1984) and Fernando Teson, "Human Rights and Cultural Relativism," 25 Va. J. of Int'l L. 869 (1985).

[4] The distinction between "objectivism" and "universalism" is this: where the objectivist conceives of truths beyond human experience, the universalist may deny that such truths exist, yet assert that there are "universal" truths that are inter-subjectively applicable to all of humanity. The objectivist understands the world according to what Richard Bernstein has described as the "distinction between the subject and the object [where] what is 'out there' is presumed to be independent of us, and knowledge is achieved when a subject correctly mirrors or represents objective reality": Richard J. Bernstein, *Beyond Objectivism and Relativism: Science, Hermeneutics, and Praxis,* 9 (Philadelphia: University of Pennsylvania Press, 1988). The universalist, on the other hand, does not necessarily make this distinction, but instead insists only that the assertion pertain to all humans. It is the viewpoint of objectivism that I will question in this paper.

sion that, because of this, the concept of truth has no meaning. That truths inhere in societies makes them no less valid or *communicable*, I will argue. Through the vehicle of communication, assessment is possible. And through the nexus of communication and assessment, the relativist critique of international human rights can be answered: we *can* use these rights as the basis of a cross-cultural conversation.

THE HISTORICAL IMPETUS BEHIND OBJECTIVISM

In the aftermath of the Second World War and the horrors of the German concentration camps, the call for international human rights resonated powerfully in western minds.[5] The spectre of Auschwitz, Birkenau, Bergen-Belsen, Dachau, and the myriad other extermination sites was a chilling reminder of society gone awry. Nazi death camps had operated entirely within the *legal* authority of the German state — a state at the very heart of western civilization.[6] Indeed, the leaders of National Socialism believed themselves to be agents of justice and civilization. As Hitler had said:

[S]hould the Government act shamefully, the law is in no position to prevent it. . . . If the Government of a State is composed of indifferent individuals, the Body Judicial can do nothing to correct the mistakes of the legislators; but when the reins are in the hands of an honest and capable legislator, the law can support him wholeheartedly in his task of strengthening the bonds of the national community, and of thus laying

5 Louis Sohn has noted that, before 1945, "a state's own citizens were almost completely at its mercy, and international law had little to say about mistreatment of persons by their own government": Sohn, "The New International Law: Protection of the Rights of Individuals Rather than States," 32 Am. U.L. Rev. 1 at 9 (1992).
   It should also be noted that the exponents of human rights acting after the Second World War built upon the long-lived tradition that natural law was the arbiter of domestic law. As J. A. Andrews has written, "within the philosophical heritage [of international human rights] is contained the thought that some rights of man are so fundamental that they are reflected in a higher order which is above the authority and responsibility of the lawmaker, be he prince, governor or a democratic legislature": *International Protection of Human Rights*, 5 (New York: Facts on File Inc., 1987).

6 As Ian Kershaw has indicated, the planning of the "Final Solution" at the Wansee Conference, Jan. 20, 1942, and during the preceding month involved the very highest levels of the German state. "[I]t is clear that not only the SS leadership but also the Foreign Office, the Ministry for the Occupied Eastern Territories and the Chancellory of the Fuhrer were in the picture": *The Nazi Dictatorship*, 103 (London: Edward Arnold, 1985). See also Christopher Browning, *The Final Solution and the German Foreign Office* (New York: Macmillan, 1978).

the ideal foundation on which a healthy and dignified constitution can be built.[7]

To this end, such statutes as the *Law for the Prevention of Progeny of the Genetically Unhealthy* (1933), the *Law for the Protection of German Blood and Honour* (1935), and the *Law for the Treatment of Community Aliens* (1944) were created — developments that to many appeared the legislation of evil.[8] The world was thus confronted with hitherto inconceivable horrors, promulgated in the name of the law.

This was the impetus behind the wide recognition, or perhaps the creation, of international human rights after the Second World War. Informed in part by a natural rights theory of justice, the aim of the *Universal Declaration of Rights and Freedoms*, the *International Covenant on Civil and Political Rights*, the *International Covenant on Economic, Social and Cultural Rights*, and the various other specific[9] and regional[10] human rights conventions was to stand above the laws of individual states and prevent the recurrence of the sort of atrocities that were committed by Germany. The drafters of these instruments felt that only an appeal to transcendent and objective rights held by humans as humans could deter similar horrors. In this, the philosophical tradition of natural law played a crucial role. As Jerome Shestack states:

Natural rights theory makes an important contribution to human rights. It affords an appeal from the realities of naked power to a higher

---

[7] Hugh Trevor Roper (ed.), *Hitler's Table-Talk*, 643 (Oxford: Oxford University Press, 1988).

[8] The official aim of the *Community Alien Law* was the denial of all social services to those of "deficiency of mind or character." As the explanatory text stated: "The National Socialist view of welfare is that it can only be granted to national comrades who both need it and are worthy of it. In the case of community aliens who are only a burden on the national community welfare is not necessary." Cited in Jeremy Noakes, "Social Outcasts in the Third Reich" in Richard Bessel (ed.), *Life in the Third Reich*, 92 (Oxford: Oxford University Press, 1987).

[9] See e.g., *Convention on the Prevention and Punishment of the Crime of Genocide*, 78 UNTS 277 (1948); *Convention Against Torture and Other Cruel, Inhuman or Degrading Treatment or Punishment*, adopted by the General Assembly as an annex to resolution 39/46, UN GAOR, 39th Sess., 708 Plen. Mtg., UN Doc. A/39/708 (1984), text found at GAOR Supp. 51 at 197, UN Doc. E/CN.4/1984/72 (1984). In 1987 the *Convention* came into force. See also *International Convention on the Elimination of All Forms of Racial Discrimination*, 660 UNTS 195 (1966).

[10] See the *European Convention for the Protection of Human Rights and Fundamental Freedoms*, 213 UNTS 221 (1948); *American Convention on Human Rights*, OASTS No. 36 (1969); *African Charter on Human and People's Rights*, reprinted in 21 ILM 59 (1981).

authority which is asserted for the protection of human rights. It identifies with human freedom and equality from which other human rights easily flow. And it provides properties of dependability, security, and support for a human rights system both domestically and internationally.[11]

This yearning for internationality and transcendent morality is at the heart of the objectivist approach to international human rights. In this spirit, international lawyers created a series of documents that bear the impress of natural law and universal rights. The preamble of the *Universal Declaration* is unambiguous on this point when it states that "recognition of the inherent dignity and of the equal and inalienable rights of all members of the human family is the foundation of freedom, justice and peace in the world."

THE CRITIQUE OF OBJECTIVISM

Nevertheless, the foregoing developments beg a crucial question: what if these rights are *not* objective; what then becomes of international human rights law? This is a question that cannot be avoided. Is the law of human rights not, after all, a reflection of western values and thus a moral code without meaning in the rest of the world?[12]

These questions go to the philosophical axioms of international human rights law. If a general critique of objectivism can succeed, then the basis of this law disappears. The critique of objective human rights must therefore begin with a critique of objectivism. The argument in the following pages moves away from the objectivist theory of international human rights. Instead of positing these rights as objectively verifiable truths of human existence, this argument situates the idea of truth at the level of human communication and experience. In so doing, it will explore avenues that may seem to lead far from international law. The following sections first review the objectivist faith in neutral rationality as the identifier of truth — a faith that was manifest in the work of René Descartes; second, they assess the idea of an objective, external, or internal truth. This foray will ultimately lead back to international human

11 Shestack, "The Jurisprudence of Human Rights," in Theodor Meron (ed.), *Human Rights in International Law: Law and Policy Issues*, 78 (Oxford: Oxford University Press, 1984).

12 For further discussion of this point, see Philip Alston, "The Universal Declaration at 35: Western and Passé or Alive and Universal," 30 Int'l Com. of Jur. Rev. 60 (1983), and Jack Donnelly, "Human Rights and Human Dignity: An Analytic Critique of Non-Western Conceptions of Human Rights," 76 Am. Pol. Sci. Rev. 303 (1986).

rights law; for, if there is neither a neutral rationality nor an objective truth to be found, then the idea of objective human rights cannot be upheld, and an alternative must be considered.

NEUTRAL RATIONALITY: THE CARTESIAN EXEMPLAR

To such thinkers as René Descartes, rationality was the only means by which true knowledge could be achieved. The Cartesian method, which is often still the pedagogical starting point of philosophy, is the exemplar of this belief. Crudely put, Descartes believed that all knowledge could, through rational contemplation, be grounded to an Archimedean point, or unassailable central foundation: either God or the cognito. Once this point was identified, it would form the basis of all objective knowledge. As Charles Taylor has explained:

[F]or Descartes the whole point of the reflexive turn [was] to achieve a quite self-sufficient certainty. What I get in the cognito, and in each successive step in the chain of clear and distinct perceptions, is just this kind of certainty, which I can generate for myself by following the right method.[13]

In Descartes' view, something was knowledge only if it could be verified through a rational deduction from the Archimedean point. In describing his own project, Descartes said:

I was convinced that I must once for all seriously undertake to rid myself of all the opinions which I had formerly accepted and commence to build anew from the foundation, if I wanted to establish any firm and permanent structure in the sciences.[14]

The sole arbiter of validity, in the Cartesian world, was reason. Implicit in the Cartesian method and in the traditions that followed is a conception of reason standing outside history — that is, outside the contingencies of human experience. Reason is thus conceived as a neutral means of discovering and assessing truth.

Rationality, however, can be described in a different way. Where the objectivists place reason outside history, in my view exactly the opposite is correct. In order to clarify this proposition, I must first distinguish the terms "logic" and "rationality." While it may be

13 Charles Taylor, *Sources of the Self: The Making of the Modern Identity*, 86 (Cambridge, Mass.: Harvard University Press, 1989).

14 Descartes, *Meditations*, Vol. 1 of *Philosophical Works of Descartes*, 144, trans. Elizabeth S. Haldane and G. R. T. Ross (Cambridge: Cambridge University Press, 1969).

true that the laws of logic — those laws isolated by Aristotle — are component parts of any definition of rationality, rationality must extend beyond this core. Rationality, in other words, brings more to a problem than just the rules of logic. But what else does it involve? Rationality also rests on a series of propositions or axioms from which inferences may be drawn, but which in themselves defy logical verification. To be rational is therefore to use logic to make extrapolations from recognized propositions.

Using the example of Descartes might make this clearer. While we cannot be certain, as Richard Bernstein notes, whether Descartes' Archimedean point was God or the *cognito*,[15] the fact remains that neither one of these is subject to "rational" confirmation. They are tautologies of the following order: X is so because it is inconceivable that it could be otherwise. In other words, the axioms upon which the Cartesian edifice of rationality stands cannot independently be verified as "rational." And if these truths resist rational verification, they fail Descartes' test for "knowledge." Thus, the foundation of the Cartesian objective theory of truth can be understood as a belief, or, to use Descartes' terms, an "opinion" rather than an externally verified truth.[16]

By redescribing the Cartesian project in this manner, we invert its self-perception: the truths that the Enlightenment claimed to have discovered are the truths that it assumed. Enlightenment thinkers supposed that at the end of their search for knowledge they would find a self-evident standard that would be true in itself. But the standards that they found, rather than being objectively true, were reflections of the dreams and desires of an era — that is, contingencies rather than certainties.

Descartes was searching, after all, for a form of enlightenment that was very closely tied to the intellectual and social preoccupations of his time.[17] Fear of uncertainty and meaninglessness in God's terrestrial kingdom informed Cartesian philosophy: if truth could not be confirmed, there was no truth at all. Faith was not

---

[15] *Ibid.*, 16.

[16] I offer this, rather bluntly, as an illustration of the contingency of Descartes' own thought. For much more subtle and comprehensive assessments of Descartes' work in the light of its intellectual context, see Taylor, *supra* note 13 and MacIntyre, *infra*, note 17.

[17] Alisdair MacIntyre has suggested this point when he described Descartes as "a late follower of the Augustinian tradition as well as someone who attempted to refound philosophy de novo": *Whose Justice, Which Rationality*, 358 (London: Duckworth's, 1988).

enough and Descartes' methods were means of addressing some of its deficiencies. We can thus conceive of Cartesian theory as a means of quelling some of the concerns of the era and a method of buttressing some of its most closely held beliefs. Far from arriving at a truth outside history, Descartes gave voice to a series of truths that inhered contingently to his circumstance.

So what are the alternatives to the Cartesian project? How else can we conceive of rationality? Instead of trying to place rationality outside history, I want to argue that reason is a facet of the traditions that spawned it. Just as Descartes' axioms reflect a quest for certainty about God and His world and a belief that systemic reflection will arrive at truth, so do all theories of rationality associate with a given set of concerns. Rationality is infused with the intentions of its use, and those intentions are shaped by the society and circumstance of the user. So conceived, rationality may be understood as a tool, or a means of addressing one's environment, rather than a method of reflecting truth. Alisdair MacIntyre has argued that the claim to neutral rationality will always fail because it "illegitimately ignores the inescapably historical, socially context-bound character which any substantive set of principles of rationality, whether theoretical or practical, is bound to have."[18] Cast in this light, we see the vanity in the Enlightenment conviction that reason could provide objective certainty.

EXTERNAL TRUTH

Just as the Cartesian account of rationality was flawed because of the contingency of reason, so also was its faith in an external truth. Two motifs recur in the Enlightenment story: rationality was the path of the right, and truth, pristine and inviolable, was the end of the journey — the reward for virtuous passage. This telling of the story places truth at a definable point of discovery. But, just as I have questioned the validity of a neutral theory of rationality, I will now examine the idea of autonomous truth. Rather than arguing that truths exist "out there," to borrow Richard Rorty's phrase,[19] I want to argue that truths are features or products of communal experience. Thus, to stretch Rorty's metaphor, truths are found and make sense only "in here." The sources of truth, I will argue, are the contingencies of our experience.

18 *Ibid.*, 4.

19 Richard Rorty, *Contingency, Irony and Solidarity*, 5 (Cambridge: Cambridge University Press, 1989).

Consider the following assertion: a thing may not be true in and of itself; rather, its truth value must be inherent in its expression. It is meaningless to state that a rock is true. However, we might *say* something *about* that rock that is true.

Truth cannot be out there — cannot exist independently of the human mind — because sentences cannot so exist or be out there. The world is out there, but descriptions of the world are not. Only descriptions of the world can be true or false. The world on its own — unaided by the describing activities of human beings — cannot.[20]

Is this necessarily so? Accepting what I have already said, it may be correct that truth is a property of language, but this says nothing about a common source of truth outside language. The truth value of the statement "the rock is pink" may inhere in the mode of expression, but this does not deny the fact that the rock itself *really is* pink. The words I have used appear to correspond to the thing I have described — thus I may be tempted to conclude that my statement is true.

But this correspondence approach to truth will only take us so far.[21] The rock may indeed be pink, but how do I assess the truth-value of a statement like "a quest for the good is the highest goal of humanity"? Is this true? If your answer is yes, on what basis can you support your claim? Unlike the example of the rock, there is no "hard reality" external to the mode of expression that can confirm or deny its veracity. There is no "hard" or "external" standard to which the statement may or may not correspond. A correspondence theory of truth will therefore tell us very little about the truth or falsity of the "quest for the good."[22]

The fact that there is no identifiable form against which we can measure the truth-value of "the quest for the good" does not mean that we cannot assess the truth of this statement. All that we know is that there is no objective standard; but I don't view this as an end to the argument. Correspondence theory — posited as a defence of objective truth — may be wrong, but this does not mean that we cannot make sense of truth. In my view, the meaning and the truth of a statement can be determined from the broader vocabulary or language used. That is to say, the standard against which the statement is measured is a property of the language I have spoken.

---

20 *Ibid.*, 5.

21 For a good overview and critique of the correspondence theory of truth, see Davidson, "The Structure and Content of Truth," 87(6) J. Phil. 279 (1990).

22 Richard Rorty discusses this limitation in some detail in *supra* note 19.

If we return to the original example, this idea may become more clear. I say that the rock is pink. My statement is true if our shared vocabulary leads us both to the conclusion that the rock is pink. In other words, the rock is not pink in any sort of abstract sense; its pinkness was not there for us to find. Instead, the description of pinkness and its accompanying truth-value arise only in the vocabulary we are using and the metaphors that give it structure. Language is not a medium through which truth is conveyed; it is instead the place where truth is found.

This point has been forcefully made by the American philosopher Donald Davidson.[23] Davidson contends that traditional theories of epistemology have been misguided by virtue of their monological axioms.[24] Put another way, epistemology has been understood as simply the interaction of an individual with his or her environment. Davidson contends this is fundamentally misconceived. The process of accumulating and classifying knowledge is, he suggests, primarily social. Davidson argues that that an individual does not simply know the world by virtue of his or her singular experience. Rather, he argues that epistemology must be externalized from the self and positioned at the nexus of the self and others. The process of arriving at knowledge involves a triangulation between the object and at least two observers — perhaps a learner and a teacher.

The learner is responding to two things: the external situation and the responses of the teacher. All these relations are causal. Thus the essential triangle is formed which makes communication about shared objects and events possible.[25]

Davidson is suggesting that mere reflection does not arrive at knowledge and therefore that the Cartesian project is misconceived. Knowledge, says Davidson, is a product of interaction and shared perception.

---

[23] Donald Davidson, "Epistemology Externalized," unpublished lecture delivered at the University of Toronto, November 14, 1992.

[24] See also Davidson, "Reply to Burge," 85 J. Phil. 664 (1988).

[25] *Supra* note 23. It should be noted that Davidson distances himself from theories he refers to as "social externalism": see Tyler Burge, "Individualism and the Mental" in Peter French, et al. (eds.), *Midwest Studies in Philosophy*, Vol. 4 (Minnesota: University of Minnesota Press, 1979). Davidson's position is not that society simply informs us of the world about us, but rather that there is a causal interrelation between social, external, and individual factors that allows us to have perceptual knowledge.

This conception of epistemology places knowledge in the shared space of human experience rather than in the abstract realm of the "internal self." By redescribing the acquisition of knowledge in this way, Davidson redefines epistemology in profoundly social terms. And in so doing he places the very idea of knowledge at the point in time and place of the triangulation, rather than attempting to transcend that point through a theory of reflection. At the level of basic knowledge, the contingencies of history, society, and culture shape our perceptions of the world about us. It is within the thicket of language, society, and culture that we find our most basic truths.

INTERNAL TRUTHS

The idea of a truth-constitutive vocabulary shifts our attention away from abstract truths either beyond us or within us. Not only are universal truths rendered meaningless, but the manner in which we understand ourselves is redefined. Enlightenment thought posited an essential human nature that unites us all as humans. As Christopher Berry has written:

Confronted by the . . . extensive evidence of the diversity of human life the thinkers of the Enlightenment did not embrace relativism but sought universal constants. They sought common principles to be found in all societies and in terms of which all societies could be judged. Human nature served conspicuously as one of these universals.[26]

Axiomatic to the idea of common humanity was the notion that there is an essence to being human — an essence that transcends cultural or linguistic boundaries.

It seems to me that, like the fallacy of external truths, this too must be false. Our self-descriptions are as bound to modes of expression as our dealings with the outside world. The very idea of the self is a construct of language and is dependent upon language for its significance.[27] The way that we understand ourselves and give expression to this understanding is immersed in the language that we speak. Recall that Davidson's externalized epistemology placed truths on a dialogical as opposed to monological plane. So too can

26 Christopher Berry, *Human Nature*, 65 (London: Macmillan, 1986).

27 Alasdair MacIntyre has argued that, in fact, the idea of a self was developed as a means of dealing with the historical contingencies of emerging modernity. It is therefore of no more use to speak of the "self" or of the "inherent nature of the individual" than it is to speak of "justice." Indeed, they are different sides of the same coin. MacIntyre, *After Virtue: A Study of Moral Theory*, 61 (London: Duckworth's, 1981).

we conceive the expression and understanding of truths about
ourselves — about what we mean when we say who or what we are
and why we do what we do. It is association with others that provides
us with the measure of the self. Thus, just as there are no truths to
be found "out there" beyond our language-constituted reality,
there are no internal truths forming a human nature that transcends language.

This shift from the Enlightenment conception of objective
truths to the theory of truth that I have posited involves a move
away from truths grounded in universality towards truths conceived in language and linguistic tradition.[28] And this is a crucial
transformation. It means, quite simply, that the Enlightenment
project has failed, and indeed was bound to fail precisely because
it was dependent upon untenable bases. Language is a product of
social, cultural, and historical dimensions. Barbara Herrnstein
Smith puts it this way:

> The "meaning," in the sense of "force," "functions," and apparent
> "claims," of *all* judgements and justifications and, indeed, of *all state-*
> *ments or "expressions"* are conditional, contingent, and variable. To be
> sure, the ranges of variability tend to become relatively stabilized within
> some verbal community, but this is the emergent effect of the interactive
> practices of members of the community themselves and not the product
> of some essential/residual semantic force inhering in verbal *forms.*[29]

Language, in this sense, is what we use to denote the product of
incremental shifts in expression, at any given time, allowing the
user relatively better means of dealing with his environment.[30] In

28 For the purpose of this article, the terms "tradition" and "culture" may appear
interchangeably.

29 Emphasis in the original. See Barbara Herrnstein Smith, *Contingencies of Value:*
Alternative Perspectives for Critical Theory, 90 (Cambridge, Mass.: Harvard University Press, 1988).

30 Donald Davidson has argued that the very word "language" is deceptive
because it suggests a monolithic *thing* that can be learned and completely
understood. In Davidson's view, language is better conceived as a fluid series of
theories that are ever-adapting to their changing environs:
    [A]n interpreter has, at any moment of a speech transaction, what I persist
    in calling a theory. (I call it a theory, as remarked before, only because a
    description of the interpreter's competence requires a recursive account.)
    I assume that the interpreter's theory has been adjusted to the evidence so
    far available to him: knowledge of the character, dress, role, sex of the
    speaker and whatever else has been gained by observing the speaker's
    behaviour, linguistic or otherwise. As the speaker speaks his piece the

short, languages are contingencies. And as such the truths that they nurture must as well be contingent.[31]

So now the path has led us back to the law of international human rights. I have argued thus far that the premises upon which objectivism depends — the neutrality of rationality and the externality of truth — crumble in a world where both truths and reason are contingent upon circumstance. If I am correct in this, the search for a natural, objective, law is futile. And the effect of this on international human rights may be profound.[32] What becomes of human rights if they are stripped of their "objectivity"? Do they simply fade away as so many good intentions? For the relativist, the answer is clear: if there are no transcendent truths, then there are no truths whatsoever. Claims to transcendent human rights, says the relativist, are therefore meaningless.

As I indicated at the start of this essay, on one level I want to say that this is correct. But I must be careful not to accept too much. The idea that there are no objective truths, or at least that no sense can be made of objective truths, does not necessarily mean that the idea of truth is completely devoid of content. To my mind, a contingent truth is a truth nonetheless. The argument I have been following up to this point is not a denial of truth *per se*, but a denial of objectivity. The difference is critical, I think, because it allows us to move truth from the abstract world of forms and

---

interpreter alters his theory, entering hypotheses about new names, altering interpretation of familiar predicates, and revising part interpretations of particular utterances in the light of new evidence.
See "A Nice Derangement of Epitaphs" in Ernest LePore (ed.), *Truth and Interpretation: Perspectives on the Philosophy of Donald Davidson*, 441 (Oxford: Blackwell, 1986).

31 For a thorough discussion of language and international politics from the perspective of structuralist and post-structuralist theory, see Mark Hoffman, "Critical Theory and the Inter-paradigm Debate," in Hugh C. Dyer (ed.), *The Study of International Relations: The State of the Art* (London: Macmillan, 1989) and Pauline Rosenau, "Once Again into the Fray: International Relations Confronts the Humanities," 19(1) Millennium: J. Internat'l Stud. 83 (1990).

32 Note the discussion of what Hayward R. Alker, Jr., echoing Robert Keohane, has called the "reflective tradition" in international studies. This tradition, suggests Alker, employs a "contextual and historicist conception of rationality" in approaching questions of international relations and understands language as a "constitutive force" in world politics: "Rescuing 'Reason' from the 'Rationalists': Reading Vico, Marx and Weber as Reflective Institutionalists," 19(2) Millennium: J. of Int'l Stud. 178-79 (1990).

situate it instead in the traditions that have developed around human experience.[33]

THE CARTESIAN ANXIETY:
THE OBJECTIVIST/RELATIVIST DICHOTOMY

Rather than simply choosing between the objectivist and the relativist, I wish to deny the terms of their debate. The very choice between these two approaches belies a shared notion of truth — a notion to which I do not subscribe. For the relativist is as much a victim of Enlightenment thinking as the objectivist; both are products of what Richard Bernstein has called the Cartesian anxiety. Descartes approached philosophy in search of stability. He, and the philosophers who followed him, sought objectively verifiable truths precisely because they feared the alternative — a world devoid of truth. "[A]t the heart of the objectivist's vision, and what makes sense of his or her passion, is the belief that there are or must be some fixed permanent constraints to which we can appeal and which are secure and stable."[34] The Cartesian anxiety involves living with this conundrum: either there are objectively verifiable truths, or there are no truths. Objectivism claims that truths may be objectively identified, whereas relativism denies the same and concludes that there are no truths. When their debate is expressed this way we can begin to understand relativism as the complement of objectivism. Both accept the same reasoning; both accept the same choice. And both claim to occupy the same space.

Bernstein addresses this issue by denying the common premise:

It is important to emphasise that I am not primarily concerned with taking sides on this grand Either/Or or with assessing the strengths and weaknesses of the varieties of objectivism and relativism. On the contrary,

[33] It might be asked why I continue to use the word "truth" when it implies the sort of objectivism against which my paper has been directed. While I accept that there is a certain ambiguity of usage, I must say that the intention of this article is, in part, to denude "truth" of the objective heritage I believe it has outlived. It is also the case, I think, that no ready replacement for the term is apparent. As Herrnstein Smith has noted, despite its compromised theoretical value, "the term 'truth' itself continues to be reinforced by its numerous — and it must be emphasised here, irreducibly various — idiomatic and technical uses. Indeed the term appears to be irreplaceable and indeed priceless: for its rhetorical power in political discourse alone — and there is perhaps no other kind of discourse — would seem to be too great to risk losing or even compromising": *supra* note 29, at 95.

[34] *Supra* note 4, at 19.

I view this dichotomy as misleading and distortive. It is itself parasitic upon an acceptance of the Cartesian persuasion that needs to be questioned, exposed, and overcome.[35]

We need to look beyond the terms of the debate that Descartes and others have set for us and find our truths elsewhere.

TRUTH, UNDERSTANDING, AND RESPONSE

The depiction of relativism in the preceding pages involves two components. The first is unambiguously descriptive: there are no objective truths. The second might be either descriptive or normative: that either we *cannot* or *should not* extend our truths to others. I have already accepted the first element as accurate, but I take issue with either of the possible interpretations of the second. And it is this second component of the relativist's view that is most relevant to international human rights, since it relates precisely to the extension of these norms beyond the boundaries of a given tradition.

RELATIVISM AS DESCRIPTION

Consider first the *descriptive* possibility of the assertion that we cannot extend our truths beyond ourselves. The argument might be restated in this manner: we cannot apply our truths to a situation outside our cultural background because we cannot *understand* this extrinsic situation.[36] When cast in these terms, the proposition fails, I think, at a basic level. If we conceive of ourselves as products of a given tradition, little sense can be made of the claim that we will recognise the limits of our understanding in the manner supposed by this assertion. In other words, the question one must ask of relativism is: how would we know when we have reached beyond our cultural limits?

The answer cannot be that we can go only so far as our *understanding* allows. This is so for two reasons. First, if something may be

---

35 *Supra* note 4, at 19.

36 I should note that there is a further possibility to this point, and that is that our understanding of truth will not apply to matters beyond the contact of our society and thus beyond our moral horizons. In more concrete terms, this would mean that our notions of truth would be inapplicable to a hypothetical society with which we have had no contact of any sort. I leave this issue aside because it is irrelevant to my present project. If we had no contact whatsoever with this hypothetical society we would not be confronted with any potential human rights concerns. And as such the limits of our truths would never arise.

understood one way in a certain tradition and another way in a second, then understanding forms no limit whatsoever to either tradition's sense of truth.[37] Both *understand* the situation; they simply understand it differently. Second, questions of understanding and misunderstanding in this context presuppose some basic degree of commonality between two traditions. We must know something about the situation and how it is perceived by others in order to find that we do not understand their perception. Were this not so, we would not realize that we had misunderstood, because we would never perceive our error. If our misunderstanding can be recognized, then there is some possibility of understanding, and the line drawn around our conceptions of truth becomes decidedly obscure. Both understanding and misunderstanding, in this way, imply some "pre-understanding," or at least some potential understanding.

A similar argument has been made in a slightly different context by Donald Davidson with reference to what he calls "conceptual schemes." Although addressing himself to "conceptual relativists" — those who assert that "[r]eality itself is relative to a scheme: what counts as real in one system may not in another"[38] — Davidson's comments are equally relevant to the present discussion. The sharp, irreducible barriers to understanding described by some[39] as existing between schemes make no sense on their own terms:

The dominant metaphor of conceptual relativism, that of differing points of view, seems to betray an underlying paradox. Different points of view make sense, but only if there is a common co-ordinate system on which to

[37] Hermeneuticists emphasize the circularity to understanding — a circularity that would allow the same phenomena to be understood in separate ways. As Martin Heidegger wrote:"Any interpretation which is to contribute understanding, must already have understood what is to be interpreted": *Being and Time*, H152, trans. John Macquarrie (Oxford: Blackwell, 1962). Understanding, in this sense, operates within the confines of a tradition. And it is this tradition that provides the means of pre-understanding a given situation or thing. J. E. Malpas has explained in "Analysis and Hermeneutics," 25(2) Philosophy and Rhetoric 93 at 97 (1992): "understanding is characterised by its pre-understanding, its foresight into the concepts that it seeks to understand."

[38] "On the Very Idea of a Conceptual Scheme" in Donald Davidson, (ed.), *Inquiries into Truth and Interpretation*, 183 (Oxford: Oxford University Press, 1984).

[39] Davidson identifies the philosopher of science, Thomas Kuhn, in this regard: *ibid.*, 184. Kuhn has been associated with a brand of "scientific relativism."

plot them; yet the existence of a common system belies the claim of dramatic incomparability.[40]

In other words, the very idea of understanding and misunderstanding tears down the walls between traditions that have been built up by the relativists; and as such, understanding does nothing to demarcate the limits of a given conception of truth. For these reasons, there is little to commend the descriptive possibility of relativism whereby truths are limited only to our fields of understanding. By extension, there is conceptual difficulty with the relativist's implied view of "tradition."[41] Our truths apply only to us, the relativist claims; but who are we? And at what point do "we" become "them"? I will divide my comments on this point into three: first, that the possibility of dialogue between traditions brings into question the descriptive possibilities of relativism; second, that there are significant overlaps between traditions that obscure the borders between them; and third, that our conceptions of solidarity may extend beyond the borders of our traditions, however defined.

As to the first point, the relativist's assertion that we should stake our moral claims only within the borders of our own tradition suggests that such borders are clearly definable. In my view, the relativist's understanding of "tradition" is unduly elegant. The term "tradition" is not a demarcation of something exclusive and static, but is instead a means of grouping certain like ideas and standards; standards that have developed and refined through a history of contrast with other modes of thought and action. This process of change is not necessarily "rational" — in the sense that ideas are eschewed only when refuted — but it is dialectical or interactive. As Alisdair MacIntyre explains:

How and under what conditions [traditions] can be . . . resolved is something only to be understood after a prior understanding of the nature of such traditions has been achieved. From the standpoint of

---

40 *Supra* note 38, at 184.

41 It may appear that I am putting words in the mouth of the relativist in this regard. Relativism, after all, need not be confined to "traditions" — it was I who described truths in this fashion. I accept that this is the case, but argue that the relativist must attach to some form of division, whether it be ideology or tradition, for his or her claim to make sense. Were this not the case there would be no need for contrast — a thing being relative to one unit rather than the other. I therefore use tradition as a shorthand for the necessary units in relativism.

traditions of rational enquiry the problem of diversity is not abolished, but it is transformed in a way that renders it amenable to solution.[42]

To illuminate this idea we need only think of the way theories originating in one tradition have been translated and incorporated into another. There are numerous examples of this conceptual cohabitation. Vladimir Lenin's thought, for instance, owed a considerable ideological debt to liberal doctrine. Specifically, it was the British liberal thinker L. T. Hobhouse[43] who first developed the economic theory of imperialism that became the cornerstone of Marxist-Leninist international relations. This intellectual debt is impossible to understand if traditions form closed systems.

I mention this only to illustrate the way in which traditions interact and change through contact. In Donald Davidson's view, it is inconceivable for two recognizable conceptual schemes to be truly incommensurable.[44] Language, as Davidson understands it, is not static but instead involves a series of passing theories that adjust to the circumstances of the speaker and the interpreter.[45] Communication between any two schemes will always be possible, says Davidson, by virtue of this linguistic malleability and the potential convergence of language theories.

In order . . . for communication to succeed, a systematic method of interpretation must be shared. . . . The sharing comes to this: the interpreter uses his theory to understand the speaker; the speaker uses the same (or an equivalent) theory to guide his speech. For the speaker,

[42] *Supra* note 17, at 10.

[43] *Liberalism* (Oxford: Oxford University Press, 1911).

[44] The *Fontana Dictionary of Modern Thought* defines this concept as follows: "Two theories or sets of beliefs are held to be incommensurable if there is no means of interpreting or understanding one in terms of the other or of comparing them." Similarly, the *Concise Oxford Dictionary* defines incommensurable as "having no common measure . . . irrational . . . not worthy to be measured with."

[45] Theories are "passing," in this sense, as opposed to static. Davidson has provocatively suggested that in fact there is no such thing as "language" in anything more than a fleeting sense: "[W]e might try to say in what a person's ability to interpret or speak to one another person consists: it is the ability that permits him to construct a correct, that is, convergent, passing theory for speech transactions with that person. . . . This characterisation of linguistic ability is so nearly circular that it cannot be wrong: it comes to saying that the ability to communicate by speech consists in the ability to make oneself understood. . . . There are no rules for arriving at passing theories, no rules in any strict sense, as opposed to rough maxims and methodological generalities." *Supra* note 30, at 445-46.

it is a theory about how the interpreter will interpret him. Obviously this principle does not demand *that speaker and interpreter speak the same language.*[46]

I will discuss this theory of communication again in the coming pages, but for our present purposes what is significant is the specific repudiation of incommensurability as a descriptive limit to any tradition (and hence to any tradition's truths).

The second concern I have with the relativist conception of tradition relates to some concrete observations concerning the communication between traditions in the context of our contemporary world. In this age of telecommunications, travel, and commerce, the mixing and remixing of ideas and beliefs has become part of the modern experience. Traditions continue to function but they do not do so alone in the rarefied air of their past and present. Instead, they develop in conjunction with other traditions. No one tradition may claim absolute hegemony over any facet of human experience.[47] Traditions, both in the abstract and in fact, converse and reconfigure rather than colliding. If I am right in this description, then the idea that the truths of a given tradition are limited to that tradition becomes opaque. Why should this be if truths are communicable and have been communicated in the past? On descriptive grounds, relativism cannot answer this question.

The third, and final, issue arising out of my assertion that relativism is descriptively impoverished concerns our feelings of human solidarity. If we are to understand relativism as descriptively limiting our morals to the locality of our tradition, we should wonder whether we, as humans, feel some sense of solidarity with those beyond our tradition — perhaps with humanity at large. And if we do, does this not bring into question the value of a description that cannot accommodate this solidarity?

---

46 *Ibid.*, 438 [emphasis added].

47 Rorty has recently discussed the way in which we understand ourselves in terms of a wider group. As he says: "When we want to emphasise what binds epochs and cultures together, we mention things like birth and death, paternal power and maternal love, the cycle of seasons and the imperatives of survival, incest taboos and the starry heavens above": "Interpreting across Boundaries," 39(3) *Philosophy East and West* 332 (1989). In short, the factors that join us and inform us of our place in the world are hardly static concepts, developed through a rigorous "rule-making" procedure. Instead, as Rorty's passage implies, those things that place us in the world and in society — those traditions that join to nurture our selves — may amount to a loose grouping of custom and belief.

Definitions of the "we" — in the sense of solidarity as opposed to cultural demarcation — are by no means clear. Limits may be drawn around those with whom we have personal contact, but if this is our limit then solidarity must be felt with only the smallest of numbers; after all, "what man knows ten thousand faces?" Richard Rorty has discussed at some length the idea of communal solidarity in a world without moral foundations. His conclusions, in my view, are remarkably unsatisfactory. When we speak of the moral "we," Rorty suggests, we cannot mean "humanity as a whole"; instead we can only conceive of ourselves as part of such smaller units as "fellow Catholics" or "comrades in the movement."

> I want to deny that "one of us human beings" (as opposed to animals, vegetables, and machines) can have the same sort of force as any of the previous examples. I claim that the force of "us" is, typically, contrastive in the sense that it contrasts with a "they" which is also made up of human beings — the wrong sort of human beings.[48]

In my view, there is good reason to wonder why solidarity should be so limited. If indeed no man knows ten thousand faces, why should Rorty's wider circles — fellow Catholics or fellow travellers — achieve any solidarity at all? That they do suggests that the limits of our personal experience do not necessarily demarcate the limits of our sense of solidarity, for we no more know all Catholics than we know our fellow North Americans. And if this is so, why should we believe that solidarity must stop shy of "humanity"?

Recent empirical studies have thrown into question the limits that Rorty has imposed on our understanding of the "we." In their 1990 article concerning the motivations of altruism, Monroe, Barton, and Klingemann interviewed a group of Europeans who had rescued and protected Jews during the Second World War. Contrary to Rorty's assertions, the study revealed that the common motivator was a sense of membership in "humanity," rather than allegiance to smaller units or other forms of attachment. "All of our rescuers explained their actions using phrases such as the following: 'You help whoever you can when you are asked.' . . . 'You help people because you are human and you see that there is a need. . . . There are things in this life you have to do and you do it. . . .'"[49] This study suggests that our personal experience of community does not limit

---

[48] *Supra* note 19, at 190.

[49] Kristen R. Monroe, Michael C. Barton, and Ute Klingemann, "Altruism and the Theory of Rational Action: Rescuers of Jews in Nazi Europe," 101 Ethics 103 at 118 (1980).

our sense of responsibility to a wider whole — a whole extending perhaps to the limits of humanity. In the contemporary world, there are indications that our feelings of solidarity have spread to wider and wider numbers of people. Vojin Dimitrijevic observed in 1980:

Recent historical experience, the growing level of interdependence, the "shrinking of the world," the improvement of communications, etc., have changed the reactions of average persons. They are truly concerned with the fate of distant fellow human beings. It is an empirically verifiable moral reaction, witnessing to a kind of "territorial" expansion of the ethical sphere of contemporary men and women.[50]

I take from these studies a sense of dissatisfaction with the descriptive possibilities of relativism. These feelings of solidarity with humanity as a whole — feelings denied by relativists and by Rorty — seem to be empirically verified in the contemporary world. How can relativism accommodate this sentiment? In a descriptive theory that understands truths to be limited only to narrow traditions, the mere fact that there are significant numbers among us who feel a solidarity with groups outside our traditions and outside our direct personal experiences suggests that we can conceive of truths expanding beyond ourselves. And if this is so, then I conclude that the descriptive possibilities of relativism are themselves highly limited.

RELATIVISM AS PRESCRIPTION

I noted above that there are two possible interpretations of the claim that our truths are limited to the confines of our traditions. The first was the descriptive assertion tested in the preceding pages and found wanting. The second is a normative interpretation: because our notions of truth are derived from our traditions, we *ought* not to impose them on others.[51] If we understand relativism in this manner, the limitation of our truths is not a matter of fact, so much as it is a matter of moral imperative. Yet in my view this understanding of relativism is as unsatisfactory as the descriptive interpretation set out above.

My argument is this: if there are no objective truths, then there is no *necessity* that another's ideas of right and wrong should be respected. Relativism as a normative theory appears to suggest that

50 V. Dimitrijevic, "The Place of Helsinki on the Long Road to Human Rights," 13 Vand. J. of Transnat'l L. at 253 (1980).

51 I leave this definition open-ended so as to give this theory its widest application.

we ought to limit our understanding of truth only to ourselves because this follows from a recognition that there are no objective truths. To my mind, this conflates the initial assertion of relativism — that there is no objective truth — with the terms of one version of *liberalism* — that we should be tolerant of others' views. And in this way relativism incorporates into itself a normative element derived from a contingent tradition.

The separation of potential descriptive and normative facets of relativism is crucial, I think, to understanding the limitations of relative theory. The very idea of relativism is that morality or normativity is specific only to a circumstance or set of circumstances. It is difficult to imagine how this vision of morality can accommodate a theory of universal tolerance. If morality is applicable only to one specific tradition, why should we suppose that all other traditions *should* be tolerant of their neighbours? If a tradition proved intolerant, would not moral condemnation be itself an application of morality outside the confines of our moral boundaries and therefore contrary to the normative element of relativism?

It makes nonsense of relativism to claim that it posits any sort of objective moral imperative, for to do so is to suggest a moral theory that transcends all boundaries. And this claim is itself a repudiation of relativism. A normative claim of this sort is at once paradoxical and self-refuting. This analysis leads me to conclude that the relativistic assertion that our truths should be limited only to our own moral communities lacks force — either descriptively or normatively.

THE ALTERNATIVE RESPONSE

So here is the conundrum: objectivist theories of international human rights are untenable because of their reliance on objective truth; and relativism is likewise indefensible as a theory of truth, and hence a critique of international human rights law. Where, then, do we go from here? What are the possibilities for international human rights both in theory and in practice?

In order to approach either the theoretical or practical aspect of this inquiry, I must first describe the scheme through which these ideas will be developed. Inter-traditional issues of human rights will only arise where there has been a confrontation between the individual or group who conceives of a right as "true" and the perpetrator of the perceived wrong.[52] Confrontation in this sense need not mean physical or visual contact. It could involve little more than an awareness of a certain state of affairs on the part of the human rights advocate. What is crucial, however, is knowledge of the situation. Once this condition is satisfied, the issue of response arises.

How do we respond to what we believe is an improper situation, given that there are no objective truths? I have already discussed the relativist's answer to this question and illustrated why it is not helpful. The alternative, I think, is this: once we have knowledge of a situation, it has entered our moral horizons and we will begin to understand the matter in our own way. We cannot do otherwise.

Davidson's theory of communication, noted earlier, is equally applicable here. We respond to situations of discourse with the pre-existing theory of communication that has hitherto served us. In the context of a human rights concern we would respond to a situation of torture, for instance, with initial horror — provided that the situation amounts to torture as we understand it and that torture is something that appals us. The beliefs that we carry with us would lead to this response and as such there is no question of it being "appropriate" in any sort of normative sense. We react because we understand that a wrong is being committed.

The next obvious question is how we should act on the basis of this reaction. And it is here, I think, that we can begin to make sense of human rights norms as means of addressing what we conceive to be wrong. To proceed from this point I must make several assumptions. First, I must assume that I feel some moral compulsion to act in the defence of the victim, or in the vindication of his or her rights. If this is not the case, then my debate with the perpetrator will never begin. Second, I must assume that there is a difference between the way I understand the act in question and the way it is conceived by the perpetrator. Third, for the narrow purposes of this paper I will assume that the response that I feel is appropriate takes the form of a debate, rather than an act of aggression. I recognize that this may appear highly stylized, but the central intention of this article has been to understand how a debate about values may take place between cultures and traditions, and to understand international human rights accordingly. Within the confines of this project, I believe that my final supposition is

52 I use the term "wrong" advisedly in this context, for I do not wish directly to discuss the question of moral culpability in this paper.

warranted, for without this assumption I would be thrust into a discussion far wider than was intended at the outset.

Bearing these assumptions in mind, my response must be undertaken with a view to changing the perpetrator's chosen course of action — to stopping the torture, as I understand it, or to preventing further events of this kind in the future. As I have already noted, there is no reason for me to suppose that I "misunderstand" what is going on. If the actions in question amount to torture according to my truths, then (barring a mistake in my understanding within this set of beliefs) I am correct. But this recognition does not assist the victim. My firm conviction in the rightness of my understanding may do little more than steel my resolve to act.

In the first half of this paper I argued that truths are not objective but rather derive from shared experience and the interactions of community. This being the case, the perpetrator is unlikely to be swayed by the depth of my convictions precisely because he has not been privy to this same development. Indeed, as I assumed at the outset of this discussion, he may believe (perhaps with equal conviction) in the rightness of his actions. In order to influence the way the perpetrator acts, I must first understand why he is acting "offensively." Short of physically preventing his further action, this is the only way I can begin to shape an argument that might change his behaviour. The quest is therefore to understand the way that truths develop in the tradition that bore the torturer.

Can such an understanding ever be reached? Languages, rather than being static and whole, are better understood as fluid "theories" or bodies of rules adaptable to changing circumstances. In this sense, or rather by virtue of this understanding of language, what at first appear to be irreconcilable manners of expression may coalesce through convergent theory. As Richard Bernstein asserts:

> There are always points of overlap and criss-crossing, even if there is not perfect commensuration. We must not succumb to "the myth of the framework." Our linguistic horizons are always open. This is what enables comparison, and even sometimes "fusion of horizons."[53]

Incommensurability, in this way, begins to fade into obscurity. The basis of the misunderstanding — or nonunderstanding — may disappear as communication proceeds.

This is what Charles Taylor has referred to as the development of a language of "perspicuous contrast." In his view, cultures may be

[53] Bernstein, *The New Constellation*, 65 (Cambridge: Polity Press, 1991).

understood through an immersion into the common pool of understanding that defines their tradition.

[M]y claim amounts to this: that the explicit formulation of what I
understand when I understand you requires my grasping the desirability
characterizations that you yourself clairvoyantly use, or else those which
you would use if you had arrived at a more reflective formulation of your
loves, hates, aspirations, admirabilia, etc.[54]

Taylor posits that it is only through this approach that an understanding of the subject culture may be derived and, by extension, a
theory to explain the behaviour of that culture may be developed.

It is crucial to Taylor's thesis, and to mine as well, that this theory is
not dependent on a neutral language. Instead, Taylor conceives of
this inquiry as a form of communication, much in the way Davidson
understands the word. Rather than depending on a transcendent
language, neutral to both the student and the subject culture, Taylor
posits that a language might develop through the interaction of these
two cultures; a language of "perspicuous contrast."

This would be a language in which we could formulate both their way of
life and ours as alternative possibilities in relation to some human constants at work in both. It would be a language in which the possible human
variations would be so formulated that both our form of life and theirs
could be perspicuously described as alternative such variations. Such a
language of contrast might show their language of understanding to be
distorted or inadequate in some respects, or it might show ours to be so.[55]

Through immersion into the tradition of the perpetrator, we may
understand, to some extent, the way that the perpetrator's actions
are conceived of in his or her tradition. Only then may we begin to
assess these actions and form arguments designed to alter the
perpetrator's conduct, provided we remain convinced that the conduct must change.

Three points follow from this contention. First, as Taylor indicates and Davidson implies, our own conceptions of the world may
change through this process of communication. Just as we will
assess the perceptions of the subject culture, so too will we scruti-
nize our own understandings; for the act of immersion will force us
to confront the way we view life and the world around us. This is
consistent with the view of tradition-constitutive truth espoused
earlier in this essay. Traditions change and develop new under-

---

54 Taylor, "Understanding and Ethnocentricity," in *Philosophy and the Human Science:
Philosophical Papers*, vol. 2, 119 (Cambridge: Cambridge University Press, 1985).

55 *Supra* note 54, at 125.

standings of truth through pressure from both inside and outside their domains. Through seeking to understand a certain situation in the way it is understood by another culture, our own truths may be changed to accommodate a view hitherto unrealized but now accepted as correct.

Consider the potential modes of argument. It is quite possible, for instance, that the perpetrator is violating norms accepted in his own culture. It may therefore be possible to form a persuasive argument in terms consistent with his own understanding of truth. Abdullahi Ahmed An-Na'im has noted this sort of possibility in his discussion of some of the "extremes" of Islamic criminal law — the Shari'a. "Islamic religious texts emphasize extreme caution in inflicting any criminal punishment," An-Na'im says. "The Prophet said that if there is any doubt (shubha), the Qu'anic punishments should not be imposed."[56] Using these threads, woven together with other arguments conceivable within Islamic culture and analogous cultures, An-Na'im argues that changes might be brought about in the scope of the Shari'a's application.[57]

I also want to argue that it is equally possible to introduce previously foreign concepts into the pantheon of truths accepted in the perpetrator's tradition. Our own conception of truth may influence the behaviour of the perpetrator or his culture when they are interpreted into terms of comparison. Putting this another way, the confrontation between the two traditions in the form of Taylor's "language of perspicuous contrast" may arrive at a shifting conception of truth and a form of argument never before possible in the perpetrator's tradition.

It is, of course, imaginable (and indeed likely) that the perpetrator will not be swayed by argument made in these terms or any

[56] Abdullahi Ahmed An-Na'im (ed.), *Human Rights in Cross Cultural Perspectives: A Quest for Consensus*, 36 (Philadelphia: University of Pennsylvania Press, 1989).

[57] An-Na'im's own conclusions are somewhat vague on the wider issue of cultural relativism. After fashioning the arguments set out above, and emphasizing the importance of "cross-cultural approaches," whereby concepts may be borrowed from other cultures such as Judaism, An-Na'im concludes that, in the final analysis, "the interpretation and practical application of the protection against cruel, inhuman or degrading treatment or punishment in the context of a particular society should be determined by the moral standards of that society" [*ibid.*, 37]. While I find An-Na'im's analysis of Islamic culture compelling, I am unable to accept his conclusions. The theory of communication I have presented in this paper would render this conclusion meaningless by conceiving of the standards of society in a fluid manner and thus obscuring what is meant by the "final analysis."

other. Yet the strategy of change need not be directed entirely at the perpetrator. Instead the arguments may be put to a wider group or to another group within the tradition in question. The approach may be to fashion arguments so as to foster further arguments made by new voices. Or, conversely, one might try to bring external pressures to bear on the perpetrator and his tradition. The conversation need not, therefore, be between the self-styled vindicator of human rights and the person considered to be a violator; it may instead involve a number of conversations at a number of levels that may ultimately isolate the perpetrator and gradually render that person's perceptions of truth obsolete.

The changes in Eastern Europe provide an example of this sort of multifaceted conversation involving voices both outside and inside the indigenous traditions. William H. Luers, former American ambassador to Czechoslovakia, has described the manner in which change came about in Czech society. Influenced by the terms of the *Final Act of the Conference on Security and Co-Operation Europe*[58] (*Final Act*) and the human rights movements in other Eastern European countries, the Czech "revolutionaries" developed a language of human rights tailored to their social setting. Vaclav Havel, says Luers, came to espouse a vision wherein "human rights [were] not something granted as a political reward or withheld as a punishment, but [were] what allow[ed] individuals to flourish in a free society."[59] In this way, the general terms of the *Final Act* were melded with a social ideology familiar to Czech society and resulted in a revision of the Czech state.[60]

Rather than simply appealing to "self-evident" truths, as the objectivist might have us do, I suggest that the focus of human rights discourse should instead shift to an inquiry into *legitimate* argumentation in the terms of tradition-constituted truth. For only where arguments resonate with legitimacy will they influence behaviour. "Legitimacy," says Thomas Franck, "is the standard by which the community measures rules' capacity to obligate."[61] The

---

58 Reprinted in 14 ILM 1292 (1975).

59 William H. Luers, "Czechoslovakia: Road to Revolution," 69(2) Foreign Affairs 88 (1990).

60 V. Dimitrijevic appeared to anticipate part of this effect when in 1980 he wrote: "Constant reminders by the public abroad and at home threaten a nation's prestige, which is in itself an element of power to be neglected at one's own peril": *supra* note 50, at 273.

61 Thomas M. Franck, *The Power of Legitimacy Among Nations*, 206 (Oxford: Oxford University Press, 1990).

quest for legitimacy may rely on the extant truths of a target culture or may involve truths that have been translated from one tradition to another. In either case, the principal thrust of any human rights argument across cultural boundaries must rest on terms that are legitimate in the target culture.[62]

Case Study: The Definition of Torture

The implications for international human rights law of the theoretical discussion above may be illustrated through the example of a single legal concept. Of the myriad human rights now protected in international law, one of the most commonly noted is torture. Torture is, after all, the paradigm case of human rights abuse. Nevertheless, a consideration of the legal definition of torture, and the attendant effects of this definition, quickly shows some of the complications of an objective conception of human rights, while at the same time providing an example of the practical potential for such concepts.

To what are we referring when we speak of "torture"? Article 1 of the *United Nations Convention against Torture and Other Cruel, Inhuman or Degrading Treatment or Punishment*[63] (hereinafter the *Torture Convention*) defines the term in the following way:

[62] Philip Alston has put this idea into stark relief in his discussion of his campaign to have the United States act upon the International Covenant on Economic, Social and Cultural Rights. The major hurdle to this, says Alston, has been "[T]he extent to which [the ICESCR] seems to be viewed with suspicion by many Americans who tend to think of it less as an international treaty seeking to promote the satisfaction of basic material needs than as a 'Covenant on Uneconomic, Socialist and Collective Rights.' Only by facing that reality and by taking it as a starting point for an open . . . public debate, is there any real prospect of securing the broad based support and momentum without which the Senate is unlikely ever to act": "U.S. Ratification of the Covenant on Economic, Social and Cultural Rights: The Need for an Entirely New Strategy," 84(2) AJIL 365 at 366 (1990). In other words, the failure to seek a means of presenting the Convention in terms legitimate to the American public has led to its being ignored in the United States.

[63] As of Dec. 31, 1991, the following states had ratified the Torture Convention: Afghanistan, Algeria, Argentina, Belarus, Belize, Brazil, Bulgaria, Cameroon, Canada, Chile, China, Colombia, Cyprus, Czechoslovakia, Denmark, Ecuador, Egypt, Estonia, Finland, France, Germany, Greece, Guatemala, Guinea, Guyana, Hungary, Israel, Italy, Jordan, Libyan Arab Jamahiriya, Liechtenstein, Lithuania, Luxembourg, Malta, Mexico, Monaco, Nepal, Netherlands, New Zealand, Norway, Panama, Paraguay, Peru, Philippines, Poland, Portugal, Romania, Russia, Senegal, Somalia, Spain, Sweden, Switzerland, Togo, Tunisia, Turkey, Uganda, Ukraine, United Kingdom and Northern Ireland, Uruguay,

"[T]orture" means any act by which severe pain or suffering whether physical or mental is intentionally inflicted on a person for such purposes as obtaining from him or a third person a confession, punishing him for an act he or a third person has committed or is suspected of having committed, or intimidating or coercing him or a third person, or for any reason based on discrimination of any kind, when such pain or suffering is inflicted by or at the instigation of or with the consent or acquiescence of a public official or other person acting in an official capacity. It does not include pain or suffering arising from, inherent in or incidental to lawful sanctions.

For the purposes of international law concerning torture, this is the authoritative statement. Its terms have been borrowed in large part from the 1975 *Declaration on the Protection of All Persons from Being Subject to Torture and Other Cruel, Inhuman or Degrading Treatment or Punishment,*[64] passed by the United Nations General Assembly to give some content to the prohibitions against torture found in so many United Nations instruments. Further, a very similar definition has been incorporated into the *Inter-American Convention to Prevent and Punish Torture.*[65] Thus, Article 1 of the *Torture Convention,* with its emphasis on pain,[66] state action[67] or acquies-

---

Uruguay, Venezuela, Yemen, Yugoslavia. It should also be noted that these states have signed but not ratified the *Convention*: Belgium, Bolivia, Costa Rica, Cuba, Dominican Republic, Gabon, Gambia, Iceland, Indonesia, Morocco, Nicaragua, Nigeria, Sierra Leone, Sudan, United States of America (*Human Rights: Status of International Instruments as of 31 December 1991* (New York: United Nations Publications, 1992)).

64 30 UN GAOR, Supp. 34, UN Doc. A/1034 (1975). The one significant difference between the *Declaration*'s definition and that contained in the *Convention* is the former's reference to "international standards" when referring to the use of lawful sanctions by states. I will discuss this at greater length in the coming pages.

65 Signed Dec. 9, 1985, Cartagena, Colombia.

66 Maxime E. Tardu has criticized the definition for what he refers to as the "pain-centred concept of torture, flowing from the medieval Inquisition." Tardu indicates that this understanding of torture fails to address the use of mind-control techniques that cause the surrender of the individual without any pain. That the Convention does not endorse this wider definition may demonstrate, once again, a reluctance to stray too far from the core concern with painful, degrading treatment: "The United Nations Convention against Torture and Other Cruel, Inhuman, or Degrading Treatment," 56 Nordic J. Int'l L. 303 at 304 (1987).

67 The drafters were here reflecting the law of state responsibility as it had developed to this date. The responsibility of governments for their acquiescence to actions carried out by private or semi-private actors had been

cence, and coercion, is a starting point for any discussion of torture under international law.

Yet what does this definition really tell us? The key concepts within Article 1 are ultimately indeterminate in their content. For instance, the list of purposes that will transform an action into torture includes intimidation or coercion. The definition of these concepts will depend on the perspective of the definer. Presumably all legal systems rely, to some degree, on intimidation or coercion.[68] For the threat of imprisonment to be meaningful, prison must be less pleasant than the outside world. This is so because the threat of prison is intended, in part, to coerce or intimidate those inclined to commit crimes to fight their inclinations. Is imprisonment torture? The answer, I think, is not to be found in Article 1 of the *Torture Convention*. Nor, indeed, could we expect it to be. No general normative statement can encompass every possible situation within its ambit.

---

firmed by the Inter-American Court of Human Rights in the *Valasquez Rodriguez Case* (1988), 9/2-3 HRLJ 212. In this case, the court found that the government of Honduras was responsible for the disappearance and subsequent murder of Manfredo Valasquez: "The evidence showed a complete inability of the procedures of the state of Honduras, which was theoretically adequate to ensure the investigation of the disappearance of Manfredo Valasquez "(*ibid.*, para. 178). For further commentary on this decision, see Thomas Buergenthal, "Inter-American Court of Human Rights: Judgement in *Valasquez Martinez Case* (Forced Disappearance and Death of Individual in Honduras)," ILM 291 (1989). For a more general discussion of state responsibility for human rights, see F. V. Garcia-Amador, "Violations of Human Rights and International Responsibility," [1956] 2 YBILC 199, reproduced in L. B. Sohn and T. Buergenthal, *International Protection of Human Rights*, 124-35 (New York: Bobbs-Merrill Co., 1973); M. Forde, "Non-Governmental Interferences with Human Rights," (1985) BYBIL 253 at 260.

68 It should be noted that the *Torture Convention* adds, as a rider to the definition set out above: "[Torture] does not include pain or suffering arising only from, inherent in, or incidental to lawful sanction." This was, perhaps predictably, a controversial provision. Amnesty International, for instance, lamented that "the exclusion of 'lawful sanctions' from the prohibition opens a potentially serious loophole for governments": *Torture in the Eighties*, 14 (London: Amnesty International Publications, 1984). Similarly, the United States felt that the qualification itself required qualification. They proposed the following form: "Torture does not include pain or suffering arising only from, inherent in or incidental to sanctions lawfully imposed; but does include sanctions imposed under colour of law but in flagrant disregard of accepted international standards" (UN Doc CHR/XXXV/10). This suggestion failed to gain the support of sufficient delegates at the negotiations and did not appear in the following revised draft.

This, on first blush, may appear to play into the relativist critique. If these words cannot be defined so as to apply across cultural borders, then what use are they? Perceived offenders may plead cultural differences, and succeed because the definition has no objective content. Consider the example of female circumcision. In some cultures, the genitals of young women are routinely altered in a painful ceremony:

> The term "female circumcision" may include any of the following: circumcision, the least severe operation, in which only the prepuce or hood of the clitoris is removed; excision, in which the clitoris and all or part of the labia minora are removed without closing the vulva; and infibulation, the most severe operation in which the clitoris, labia minora, and all or most of the medial part of the labia minora are removed.[69]

The ages of the females affected vary from region to region. In some cases women are circumcised on the eve of their wedding, whereas in other places, the practice involves very young girls. Governments in the relevant regions generally acquiesce to this practice. In Kenya, for instance, President Daniel Arap Moi has repeatedly condemned female circumcision but has, as yet, done nothing to prevent it.[70] Some countries have explicitly embraced the practice as a manifestation of their culture. When this issue was discussed in the UN Sub-Commission for the Prevention of Discrimination and the Protection of Minorities, the representative of Senegal, Sambacor Konate, condemned the suggestion that female circumcision might be a denial of human rights. This suggestion, he said, "lacked the necessary respect for cultural differences and the identity of the African world."[71]

Is female circumcision torture? For some the answer is clear. This initiation rite is a classic means of coercing women into subservience by means of pain. Yet for others, female circumcision is a time-honoured rite of passage; an expression of culture, not an act of torture. When confronted with this debate, the relativist will conclude that neither side can prevail. Certainly the definition in the *Torture Convention* will settle nothing. In it are elements that can

---

[69] Kay Boulware-Miller, "Female Circumcision: Challenges to the Practice as a Human Rights Violation," 8 Harv. Women's L.J. 155 at 156 (1985).

[70] *Ibid.,* 159.

[71] *Summary Record of the 19th Meeting* at 2, cited in Katherine Brennan, "The Influence of Cultural Relativism on International Human Rights: Female Circumcision as a Case Study," 7 L. & Inequality 367 at 385, note 87 (1989).

work to the benefit of either side. The opponent of female circumcision can point to the pain, but the proponent may reply that no discrimination, intimidation, or coercion is involved. But even this exchange relies on a common understanding of words like pain, discrimination, or coercion. As I have indicated, the relativist might not even concede this common understanding, and would instead argue that the words and norms in Article 1 have meaning and application only in the limited context of western society; a debate of the sort envisaged above could thus never get beyond this basic fact.

This view fails to take into account a crucial aspect of the *Torture Convention.* Like most multilateral agreements, this treaty was negotiated by a wide range of delegates representing a wide range of cultures. Each contributed to the shaping of the definition found in Article 1, and by subsequently ratifying the convention, states have agreed to abide by the terms they helped to define. Indeed, even if states signed the convention after it had been negotiated, they did so after reaching some understanding of the meaning attached to the text by the other parties. These facts suggest that there was at least some agreement on the wording of the text of Article 1; these words had similar meaning for all parties.

Through the discussion of the concept of torture, and particularly the definition to be included in the *Torture Convention,* states assured themselves that they were all speaking the same language — attaching the same meaning to the same words. There is no mystery to this process, nor is it distinct to international relations. The framing of any contract or agreement — whether legal or otherwise — will involve a mutual assessment by the parties: are they getting what they think they are getting? While there may be no absolute certainty that a common understanding has been reached, an agreement at least signifies a strong impression on the part of those involved that they understand each other *and agree.*

I am not suggesting that all parties left the table with an identical view of the agreement they had reached. There is, I should say, a role for "constructive ambiguity" in defining certain terms during negotiations; such ambiguity may be used to placate diverging views while preserving key areas of agreement. However, this ambiguity usually occupies the periphery of a treaty — it does not go to the core objectives. It seems clear, for instance, that all parties to the *Torture Convention* understood that they had created an instrument preventing torture; it also appears that the concept of torture had *some* meaning for all the cultures involved; they would hardly have prohibited something they did not understand.

This degree of commonality does not, of course, decide the characterization of female circumcision. No agreement anticipates every circumstance in which it might apply. Agreements over a text should therefore not be expected to amount to a common understanding of how that text may govern unforeseen situations. There will always be situations in which different interpretations can prevail, regardless of initial interpretive agreement. The resolution of these debates will not be determined by the objective meaning of the words in the provision, because these words *have no objective meaning*. Neither will these debates be settled by a reference to "a meeting of the minds" over the terms of the text; these agreements, as I have said, do not anticipate every vicissitude of life. Instead, a resolution will rely on the manner of argumentation and on the advocacy skills of the interlocutors. Both sides of the debate will attempt to shape their arguments so as to account for past and present interpretations of the words at issue, while at the same time drawing in new interpretative approaches that will have legitimacy in the relevant context.

Arguments concerning female circumcision may, for instance, follow this course: those who defend it may say that circumcision is not the product of coercion by governments or anyone else; it is instead a voluntary act of young women coming of age in their cultures. Women in societies that promote this activity submit so as to identify themselves as African women. It is, in other words, a means of participating in their culture; a matter of social connection. Nor indeed is this a tradition without rationale. Circumcision, say its proponents, promotes the health and appearance of women.

It is . . . believed that a woman's genitalia, if left uncut, will produce offensive discharges: an uncut woman is considered polluted and unclean. Another reason given under the rubric of health is that circumcision increases the fertility of women and that it has other healing powers. Finally, in some cultures, the clitoris is considered poisonous or evil and therefore must be removed.[72]

In short, those who support female circumcision allege that it is not torture for the purposes of the *Torture Convention*. Women voluntarily submit to circumcision, and they do so for many good rea-

---

[72] Valerie Oosterveld, "Refugee Status for Female Circumcision Fugitives: Building a Canadian Precedent," 51 U. T. Fac. L. Rev. 278 at 283 (1993).

sons. This is not a place where international human rights should intervene.

The opponents of female circumcision, predictably, take a different approach. Questions of voluntariness, they say, mean very little in a world of enormous social pressure. In some cultures uncut women are considered to be good only as prostitutes; indeed their sexual appetites are thought to know no bounds.[73] In such an environment, women are effectively coerced into allowing the mutilation of their genitals. Furthermore, the real rationale behind female circumcision, say those who would like to see it end, is the domination of women by men. Circumcision "is the most effective means to keep the girls' virginity intact."[74] It is also an effective way of curbing sexual desire, and thus reducing the risk of adultery.

So, say the opponents of circumcision, this is not a voluntary act. It is instead the product of coercion, imposed with discriminatory intent. That the operation is painful seems beyond doubt. And the governments involved have done next to nothing to prevent this harm from occurring. Thus, the opponents conclude that this practice qualifies as torture under Article 1 of the *Torture Convention*.[75]

I will not attempt to settle this debate here. Instead, I use it only to illustrate the manner in which debates over human rights may proceed. Based on the analysis I have provided above, there is no objective meaning to torture that will allow us to say with certainty what actions will contravene the *Torture Convention*. But neither is there reason to suggest that no common understanding can be reached. Christine Hodge, a United Nations employee working in Chad, has recounted the story of her exposure to female circumcision; it is a story that nicely illustrates my point. Although at first a rabid opponent of the practice, through debate with participants she arrived at a position that she would never have imagined. After attending a modified circumcision ceremony, where the clitoris was "nicked" rather than being removed, Hodge made the following comment:

I still think female circumcision is barbaric, but in attending the ceremony — something I once thought I would never do — I showed my support for what I hope is an interim solution. Through my empathy and

[73] H. Lightfoot-Klein, *Prisoners of Ritual: An Odyssey into Female Genital Circumcision in Africa*, 39 (New York: Harrington Press, 1989).

[74] B. Harden, "Female Circumcision: A Norm in Africa," *International Herald Tribune*, July 29, 1985, 1, as cited in Oosterveld, *supra* note 72, at 281.

[75] See, e.g., the reasoning espoused by Oosterveld, *supra*, note 72 at 296 and 297.

by continuing to work for the abolition of circumcision, I am helping more than I ever did when I passed judgment on something I did not understand.[76]

In order to be legitimate — in order to command adherence — common understandings will have to consider the idiosyncracies of the cultures involved. And in reaching a legitimate resolution of their differences, cultures may ultimately change the way they have conceived of a given activity. This is the process of conversation; a process through which the definition of concepts such as torture will evolve through ongoing confrontation and debate.

CONCLUSIONS

I have proposed, in the preceding pages, an alternative conception of human rights: a theory that moves away from both objectivism and relativism. The effect of this shift in aspect is, I think, a move away from strict legalism in human rights language.[77] The approach to human rights documents that seeks to parse out the "real content of the right" or the "objective meaning of the words" misconceives the flexibility of the concepts we describe as rights and posits a neutrally verifiable interpretation of the text. The words of Paul Sieghart illustrate this approach:

Only a detailed study of the treaty texts themselves will show that they have in fact been drafted with all the legal precision necessary to apply them to real situations, and that their restriction and limitation clauses outline clear and sufficient boundaries for all those rights and freedoms for which that is necessary in order to ensure the orderly conduct of human society.[78]

This sort of ossification of human rights through a theory that conceives of rights as fixed standards, is, in my view, precisely the sort of reasoning we should seek to avoid. Human rights instruments should instead be conceived as rough guidelines — starting

76 "Throwing Away the Circumcision Knife," *[Toronto] Globe and Mail,* Jan. 15, 1994, D2.

77 To this end, it should be noted that the use of "rights language" itself may be inappropriate or ineffective depending on the sort of circumstances within which one operates. I use the term "human right" in this context as an expression of the way we in the west conceive of the body of interests protected under this concept, rather than using it to connote transcending norms.

78 Paul Sieghart, *The International Law of Human Rights,* 19 (Oxford: Oxford University Press, 1983).

points for conversation[79] — rather than definitive explanations of the "rights of humanity."[80]

At the same time, the vision of international human rights espoused in this article should increase the number of ways we might react to perceived violations. Human rights instruments and organs are only two venues through which the vindication of rights may take place. Equally valid may be other methods of discourse that will be rhetorically forceful in a given target tradition.[81] It is crucial therefore to employ what John Lukacs has called "functional rhetoric" in the enunciation of human rights claims.[82] In other words, these rhetorical approaches must be tailored to the context of the violation and may be combined with other strategies so as to alter the behaviour of the perpetrator. What is important, I think, is a shift away from strict legalism towards a more creative cast of mind.[83] The defender of human rights must move through the fluid pool of available arguments rather than appealing to a higher reason in an effort to make his or her claim.

[79] This process of conversation has been explicitly recognized by some of those most intimately involved with the vindication of human rights. Guatemalan human rights advocate Rigoberta Menchu said, after winning the Nobel Peace Prize: "For 11 years, I've been going through the hallways and corridors of the United Nations, to one meeting after another. We ourselves have found it extremely difficult to accept that we have to *negotiate* human rights — but we have done it": Graham Fraser "Nobel Peace Prize opens doors for Rigoberta Menchu," *[Toronto] Globe and Mail*, Nov. 13, 1992, A5 [emphasis added].

[80] I do not suggest that "legal rhetoric" is at all times ineffective. There may be venues in which the best argument should be presented in a legal mode of discourse. My point is simply that this use of legalism as a means of ascertaining "objective" meaning is misconceived and may be counterproductive to the vindication of human rights.

[81] For a detailed discussion of the development of strategy when confronted with multiple perpetrators and multiple abuses of human rights, see David Weissbrodt, "Strategies for Selecting and Pursuing International Human Rights Matters," in Hurst Hannum (ed.), *Guide to International Human Rights Practice*, 20 (Philadelphia: University of Pennsylvania Press, 1984).

[82] "The End of the Twentieth Century: Historical Reflections on a Misunderstood Epoch," *Harper's Magazine*, January 1993, 54.

[83] A fairly recent example of this sort of creativity is the distribution by the human rights group "Lawyers Committee for Human Rights under Law" of videotaping equipment to natives of the Amazon rain forest (among other groups worldwide) so that they might document through images the abuses meted out to them by their government. The effect of this strategy has yet to be fully realized, but it may serve to isolate Brazil and indeed change the way in which other Brazilians conceive of the native situation in their country. Furthermore,

by permitting the perceived victims of abuse the chance to document their experience in this way, an opportunity has been created to widen the conversation to an audience far beyond the borders of Brazil. This widening of the discourse may entail a persuasive mode of argument and therefore combine with internal pressures to change the behaviour of the Brazilian state: Colum Lynch, "Recording Repression: The Video Is Mightier Than the Sword," *[Toronto] Globe and Mail*, Nov. 14, 1992, D3. Manuela Carneiro de Cunha has also discussed the plight of the Brazilian Indians and has noted their increasing participation in human rights discourse. The Yanomami Indians, she says, "have entered the cross-cultural dialogue, stating the global significance of their own specific history." This sort of dialogue forces the values we understand as correct to change so as to accommodate new voices and new ideas. Cunha concludes that our experience indicates "how relative and historically based our own values are": "Custom Is Not a Thing, It Is a Path: Reflection on the Brazilian Indian Case," in An-Na'im (ed.), *supra* note 56, at 293-94].

Sommaire

Vérité, tradition, et confrontation: une théorie des droits de la personne sur le plan international

Le relativisme culturel fait une critique des droits de la personne sur le plan international qui peut être accablante. S'il est pris au sérieux, ce type de relativisme nie la légitimité des normes qui transcendent les frontières culturelles. Cependant, les tentatives visant à trouver une explication logique aux droits de la personne et faisant appel à des valeurs morales objectives sont également problématiques, car les idées que nous nous faisons du monde sont formées par les différents aspects de notre expérience. L'auteur soutient que le débat entre l'objectivisme et le relativisme se méprend sur les possibilités des droits de la personne. Les différences culturelles ne dressent pas d'obstacles à la compréhension et à la communication. Bien que ces droits ne soient pas objectifs, l'auteur affirme qu'ils pourraient être transmis d'une culture à l'autre et constituer le fondement d'un débat moral. Il se pourrait que ces droits ne tranchent pas le débat, mais ils peuvent amorcer un dialogue qui pourrait finalement introduire dans la culture des deux parties de nouveaux moyens permettant de comprendre les intérêts humains.

Teaching, Research, and the Dissemination of International Law in China: The Contribution of Wang Tieya

ZHAOJIE LI*

INTRODUCTION

THE PUBLICATION OF *Wang Tieya Wenxuan (Selected Essays of Wang Tieya)* has presented Professor Wang Tieya with a very special gift, not only in honour of his eightieth birthday but also to commemorate his prominent, sustained, and outstanding contributions to the development of international law in China. Wang Tieya is highly regarded both in China and abroad as a remarkable and dedicated academician.

Wang Tieya's career in international law dates back to 1931 when he studied international law at the National Qinghua University. Since then, his exemplary service to international law in China has been lifelong and multi-dimensional, characterized by his love for his teaching and for his students. To quote Professor R. St. J. Macdonald, Wang is

the longest serving full-time teacher of international law in recent Chinese history, probably in all of Chinese history; he is a builder of libraries and institutions; he is a builder of international relationships and exchanges. . . .[1]

---

* SJD candidate, University of Toronto; Correspondent Research Fellow, International Law Institute, Peking University, China.

---

[1] R. St. J. Macdonald, "Wang Tieya: Persevering in Adversity and Shaping the Future of Public International Law in China," in R. St. J. Macdonald (ed.), *Essays in Honour of Wang Tieya*, 21 (Dordrecht: Martinus Nijhoff, 1994).

Indeed, since 1940, Wang "has been at the centre of every major advance in the teaching and research of public international law in China,"[2] and the number of students of international law whom he has personally tutored and brought up has topped the record in Chinese history. In spite of his age, he still enthusiastically offers guidance and assistance to students, and even teaches in the classrooms. He ardently hopes that younger generations of Chinese scholars of international law will soon carry on the undertakings pioneered by him and others and continue to contribute to the development of the science of international law.

The publication of this book is also a significant event that is worth celebrating in the international legal community at large. Historically, modern international law was exclusive to states of European background. It was only introduced into China in a systemic manner when the expanding western powers forced open China's door in the mid-nineteenth century. Although Chinese scholars and officials soon came to recognize that international law was useful for China's participation in international relations, it was the rise of Chinese nationalism around the beginning of this century that transformed this understanding. Serious efforts were made to bring international law into full play in the nation-wide struggle to shake off the yoke of foreign domination in China and to win China a respected place as a sovereign equal in the family of nations. In order to have international law — this "exotic Western plant" — take root in Chinese cultural soil, from the 1920s on many Chinese scholars committed themselves to developing this foreign body of legal learning into an academic discipline through diligence in teaching, writing, and translation.

Wang Tieya is one of the most distinguished of the scholars who devoted themselves to this great undertaking. The earliest article collected for this book dates back to 1932. Given that the history of teaching and studying international law as an academic discipline in China commenced only in the mid 1920s, this book is an excellent reflection of the inspiration and aspirations of Chinese international legal scholars over more than half a century. Indeed, without their tireless efforts, international law could not have gained ground in China.

As a result of the profound changes in the international community since the end of the Second World War, classical international law based on the European state system is being transformed

2 *Ibid.*, 22.

into a universal, international legal system that applies to all nations in the world. In the process of this transformation, the extent to which contemporary international law can really be said to be universal in character depends largely on China's attitudes towards international law. The majority of the articles collected in this book were written by Wang after 1949, and particularly over the past fourteen years. They represent Chinese contributions to the literature of international law in the world at large. For scholars who are serious about China's attitude towards international law, these writings offer "the teachings of the most highly qualified publicists" of China, from which one may discern the response of China's academic world to various international legal issues.

The writings collected in this book were written by the author over the past six decades. In the foreword, Duanmu Zheng, Wang's former student and currently Vice-President of the Supreme People's Court of the People's Republic of China, points out that this book manifests only a small part of what Wang has done during his sixty years of academic pursuits. Since most international law materials and documents are not available in Chinese, Wang has devoted a great deal of his energy to compiling reference materials in Chinese and translating foreign works on international law into Chinese to provide Chinese students and scholars with materials with which they may pursue their studies. His *A Complete Collection Of Sino-Foreign Treaties and Agreements, 1698-1949* is an indication of his tremendous success in this respect. The completeness of this monumental work surpassed all previous efforts, whether published in Chinese or in a foreign language, and whether by private or by official entities. Another major landmark in his career is the translation into Chinese, in collaboration with the late Professor Chen Tiqiang (T. C. Chen), of the eighth edition of *Oppenheim's International Law* revised by Lauterpacht. *Oppenheim* is still the most reprinted and distributed translated foreign work on international law in China.

WANG TIEYA: THE PERSON

Before proceeding with a discussion of the book, a few words should be said in tribute to the author. This collection of Wang's writings spans a period of sixty years. In the light of what has happened to Wang during those years, one can only conclude that these works are the result of determination and perseverance in the face of almost insurmountable adversity. As Macdonald later wrote, for over sixty years Wang's life has been closely intertwined with the social upheavals that have, throughout this century, transformed China from a semi-feudal and semi-colonial society into an independent republic and major world power. That transformation has not been easy, and the hardship that has marked the growth of China has also marked Wang personally. Wang has endured the ravages of war and all kinds of domestic political turmoil. He himself was victimized in the two long calamitous periods of internal ideological purges (1957-64 and 1966-76), of which the last one, namely the ten-year "Great Cultural Revolution," brought the entire nation to the verge of collapse. Yet, in spite of inconceivable suffering that might have deterred many — perhaps most — others, Wang has adhered to his commitment to the ideals of scholarship, to the interests of his students, and to the high aspiration of developing the science of international law in China.[3] Thus, these writings not only embody sixty years of toil, they reflect a personal character and integrity, a will power, and a sense of responsibility that is worthy of emulation by those of us of today's generation who are Chinese scholars.

WANG TIEYA: THE SCHOLAR

Wang Tieya Wenxuan records the author's major contributions to and his extraordinary scholarship in teaching, research, and the study of international law in China. Both will exert lasting influence over the development of international law in China. Throughout his career in international law, Wang has continually stressed the importance of the distinction between writings of a political nature and academic writing. For him, as meaningful and important as the former may be, they can be but time-specific commentaries, and therefore are of primary value for propaganda and other political purposes. The latter, however, are characterized by original views and perspectives that result from scientific research and studies, and thus they are conducive to clarifying norms, principles, and rules of international law. The two cannot, and should not, be equated with each other. It is for this reason that this volume collects only those of Wang's writings that have academic significance.

While paying great attention to the distinction between academic and political writing, Wang also takes into account the practical

3 *Ibid.*

significance of any topic chosen for academic research, although he does not believe that such topics should necessarily be confined to issues that are immediately and directly related to contemporary international affairs. According to Wang, scientific studies in international law must be able both to address the practical needs of today and to answer questions that may arise in the future. This point of view has been reflected throughout the writings collected in this book. For example, from 1932 when his first article, "Interpretation of the Most Favoured Nation Clause," was published in Qinghua Review, down to 1948, the eve of the founding of the People's Republic of China, most of Wang's writings focused on issues related to the abolition of the unequal treaty regime imposed upon China by foreign imperialist powers. Studying the law of treaties was not just Wang's personal interest. Abolishing the unequal treaties had become the primary task confronting China's foreign relations in the thirty-year period from the end of the First World War, and teaching and research in international law in China during this period generally centred around this subject. In this regard, Wang's academic contribution mirrored the academic orientation of that time.

Wang's teaching and research in international law are characterized by an emphasis on the interaction between international law and international relations. To him, international law is not only a branch of legal science; it is also an offspring of international relations. While governing principles and rules are indispensable for maintaining harmony in relations among states, progress in international law is equally dependent on the development of international relations. Thus, just as domestic lawyers need to study political theory, international lawyers must conduct their inquiry into the nature, substance, and development of international law in the light of contemporary international relations. In other words, since international law is formed by states because of the necessity to regulate their relations, its normative relevance to world affairs can be fully understood only by examining the way the actors of international relations see it rather than the way scholars understand or re-imagine it. However, it is equally important to bear in mind that international law provides legal principles and rules that bind states in the form of rights and obligations. Thus, any inquiry into a specific international legal issue must take the legal nature of international law — that is, its binding force upon the states concerned — as the starting point. For over sixty years, Wang has

194   *Annuaire canadien de Droit international 1993*

followed this interdisciplinary approach in his academic pursuits in China. Most of the writing collected for this book bears the imprint of such a nexus between international law and international relations.

WANG TIEYA WENXUAN: THE BOOK

OVERVIEW

This volume includes thirty-six articles from Wang's many writings over the past sixty years. All of them were selected by Wang himself, and they are arranged in six groups. They cover a wide range of topics on public international law. Although the author does not designate a subheading for each group, the following subjects are dealt with: the contemporary development of international law; basic issues of international law; research, study, and teaching of international law in China; specific issues of international law in theory and practice; specific issues of the law of treaties; and specific issues of the law of war.[4] Most of Wang's writings from the past fourteen years are arranged in the first three groups: they are regarded as the cream of his writings. The last three groups primarily contain articles written before 1949. Although most of the issues that they address no longer exist today, these articles are still of great value to scholars as references on the international legal issues in China's foreign relations at that time, and the response to them from the then Chinese international law community. Due to the limitations of space, this review will cover primarily the six articles in the first three groups that, this writer considers, have had the greatest influence on teaching, research, and the study of international law in China and best represent the author's academic attainments and contributions.

GROUP ONE: THE CONTEMPORARY DEVELOPMENT OF
INTERNATIONAL LAW

The articles in this first group were written between 1980 and 1988. All of them focus on the contemporary development of international law. Given the long isolation of the Chinese international legal community from the outside world and the complete disruption of teaching, research, and study in international law during the 1966-76 domestic political calamity, Chinese publica-

[4] For the English title of each article, see the advertisement in 87 Am. J. Int'l L. (1993).

tions on international law up to the 1970s basically followed traditional approaches both in scope and in dimension. Thus, when the Chinese interest in international law was revitalized in the late 1970s, Chinese scholars desperately needed to learn about recent developments in international law.

In writing "The Current Trend in International Law"[5] in early 1980, Wang became the first in China to address this need. Pinning his thesis on the relationship between international law and international relations, he observed that the fundamental changes in post-war international relations — characterized by the rise of newly independent states, the expansion of international organizations, changes in the international economic order, and the rapid advance of science and technology — have brought about profound changes in both the scope and dimension of the international legal system. This development in post-war international relations has resulted in such new ramifications as the law of international organizations, international economic law, international development law, new chapters of the law of the sea, the international law of outer space, and international environmental law. Some traditional principles and rules have been altered or rescinded while others have been reaffirmed and given renewed emphasis. A particular example given by Wang is that the obsolete principles and rules that justified imperialism and colonialism have been discarded and replaced by principles of self-determination and sovereign equality among all nations. He notes particularly that, within the changing scope and dimensions of the present international legal system, efforts to establish principles and rules for a new international economic order and the impact of a scientific and technological revolution have gained greater salience. Issues like the development of Third World nations and the protection of the global environment have posed increasingly serious challenges for the whole international community. Contemporary international law must be developed to meet these challenges.

Based on this analysis, Wang concludes that contemporary international law is in a dynamic state — a state of transition from a Eurocentric system to a truly universal system that applies to all nations in the world. Being the first of its kind as a Chinese response to the development of contemporary international law, this article provides Chinese scholars with significant guidance for their research and for the study of international law. Since most of

5 *Selected Essays of Wang Tieya*, 1-26.

its points are still valid today, the article has been listed as required reading for Chinese students of international law.

Subsequently, Wang published a series of articles inquiring into the development of contemporary international law. In "The Third World and International Law,"[6] written in 1982, he discusses specifically the impact of the rise of Third World nations upon the development of international law. He draws attention to the fact that the rise of Third World nations has resulted in the expansion of the subjects of international law, and consequently has brought all non-European nations into the realm of the international legal system. Facing such a fundamental change, a number of western commentators have lamented the destruction of the basis on which international law was originally founded, depicting international law as in crisis. Wang criticizes such unwarranted pessimism, arguing that, as an offspring of international relations, contemporary international law must adapt itself to the changed and still changing circumstances of a new era; in this sense, what is really in crisis is only that part of international law that cannot keep pace with the reality of today's world, not the international legal system as a whole. However, Wang does not agree that the expanding scope and dimension of contemporary international law will lead this legal system eventually to become "world law" as advocated by some western commentators. In his view, the international community should, and will still in the foreseeable future, be organized on the basis of sovereign equality and independence. Therefore, the idea of "world law" based on the notion of "world government," although it sounds appealing, is nothing but an impractical illusion.

Wang devotes close attention in this article to the attitude of Third World nations towards international law. Indeed, since much of international law predates the independence of Third World nations, and was therefore formed without their participation, there is a fundamental concern in the international legal community: will the Third World accept the binding force of international law? Wang observes that the attitude of Third World nations towards this question is not an all-or-nothing view. While they have every reason to repudiate those principles and rules of traditional international law that were established to protect the interests of imperialism and colonialism, Third World nations do respect the principles and rules that govern international relations on the basis

6 *Ibid.*, 27-59.

of equality and independence among sovereign nations. States cannot be created in a vacuum, and their existence requires them to enter into relations with each other. Therefore, it is in their interest to follow principles and rules regulating these relations.

In fact, instead of denying the binding effect of international law, all of the newly independent nations have unquestionably accepted the bulk of the international legal system. Moreover, as they constitute a majority of the states of the international community, their active participation in the process of making international law has exerted a great impact on its progressive development. Their prominent role has been demonstrated in particular through their initiation of support for many of the United Nations resolutions that have had a significant bearing on the development of international law. In addition, Wang notes the Third World's multi-dimensional contributions to the development of contemporary international law in the areas of recognition of states and governments, state responsibility, territorial regimes, abolition of unequal treaties, and the law of armed conflict.

Also worthy of note are Third World nations' attitudes towards the judicial settlement of international disputes. Wang attributes their reluctance to resort to the International Court of Justice for the settlement of disputes to cultural traditions on the one hand, and to the pro-western composition of the Court on the other. However, Wang observes that this does not mean that Third World nations completely refuse to accept the jurisdiction of the Court, and some of them have had their disputes settled there.

As to the impact of the Third World upon the development of international law, what is most striking to Wang is the extraordinary emphasis that Third World nations have placed on the principles of self-determination and sovereign independence and equality. Since they have a common history of suffering from western imperialism and colonialism, Third World nations share a common interest in protecting their hard-won independence and territorial integrity. They prize these principles as powerful legal weapons in their defence against foreign intervention and aggression. Furthermore, the Third World does not insist on adherence to static principles. Instead, the principles of self-determination and sovereign independence and equality have evolved and been expanded and enriched through the addition of economic and cultural dimensions. Through Third World nations' unceasing efforts in this regard, the notion that peoples and nations have permanent sovereignty over their own natural resources has been universally recognized. Significantly, since China is also a Third World nation, most of Wang's observations in this respect can be equally applied to the study of China's attitude towards international law.

In the next article, which he wrote in 1986, "The United Nations and International Law,"[7] Wang addresses the significance of the United Nations for the development of international law. To this end, he first examines the nature of the Charter of the United Nations. While viewing the Charter as a multilateral treaty, *stricto sensu*, the unprecedented universal acceptance of the binding force of the Charter convinces Wang that the substance of this document constitutes part of universal international law. Beyond that, however, conceptualizing the juridical quality of the Charter within the framework of the international legal system seems to create a problem for Wang.

On the one hand, in view of the obligation imposed on non-member states by Article 2(6) to observe the principles of the Charter and the overriding effect of Charter obligations in respect of both prior or subsequent treaty obligations as provided by Article 103 — both provisions constituting departures from well-established rules of treaty law — Wang agrees that the Charter has a character superior to that of an ordinary multilateral treaty. On the other hand, he seems to be uncomfortable with the idea that the Charter is a kind of "constitution" for the international community. Almost reluctantly he seems to be in favour of treating the Charter as a kind of "higher law," contending nevertheless that such an approach, helpful as it is in explaining the legal effect of the Charter, does not in fact bring to light its real essence. He is more inclined to investigate the issue from the perspective of the special nature and the extraordinary functions that characterize the United Nations.

On the basis of this approach, Wang concludes that the Charter should be regarded as a multilateral treaty *sui generis*, and it is this special nature of the Charter that has had significant and profound implications for the development of international law. Taking into account the time at which this article was written, Wang's conclusions are not exceptional. Indeed, few if any socialist international legal theorists at that time were in favour of the constitutional approach to the Charter advocated by western commentators. Their concern was that this approach might lead to an incorrect under-

[7] *Ibid.*, 60-82.

standing of the nature of the Charter, since in their view "the international community composed of sovereign states cannot, and should not, have a constitution in the sense that a sovereign state does." Within this context, the *sui generis* approach seems to be a better way to overcome the conceptual difficulty. Be that as it may, Wang appreciated the value of the constitutional approach to the extent that it could offer some analogical guidance to the inquiry into this issue. He noted that the purposes and principles of the Charter were formulated to deal with the basic issues of international relations, thus "there is no doubt whatever that they have constituted the fundamental principles of contemporary international law."

In fact, if Wang recognizes the principles of the Charter as the fundamental principles of the entire international legal system, there should be no substantial distance between him and those who ascribe certain concepts of constitutional law to the Charter. Instead of being seen as advocating the notion of "world government," the constitutional approach to the Charter should be understood as meaning that Charter-based principles are endowed with an overriding effect in respect of the international community as a whole. By analogy to a constitution of a state, these overriding principles constitute the starting point for the entire international legal order — they must be complied with as rights and obligations *erga omnes*. They can qualify the effect of other rules of international law, and no derogation from them should be permissible.

Wang also provides insight into the role of the United Nations in the codification and progressive development of international law. He regards highly the work of the International Law Commission. In his opinion, even if some of its draft documents do not finally turn into conventions, they still have considerable authority, parallel to or even on a higher plane than "the teachings of the most highly qualified publicists" of various nations. Wang also reviews the important role of the United Nations in sponsoring the formulation of many important law-making treaties. Wang is particularly interested in resolutions adopted by the General Assembly of the United Nations that express principles of international law. He notes that today many important international legal issues cannot be fully discussed and decided without referring to these resolutions. Indeed, given their increasing number, their important content and wide-ranging coverage, and the way in which they are adopted (some by unanimous vote and some by consensus), these resolutions are playing a significant role in the development of international law. Under the United Nations Charter, however, these resolutions are by and large recommendations, thus not legally binding upon states that vote for them except when addressed to certain internal matters of the organization. This gives rise to an interesting and widely debated question: how do these resolutions promote the development of international law if they are not binding on states?

Wang seeks answers to this question by examining the legal significance of these resolutions. He observes that some General Assembly resolutions are designated as "declarations," purporting thereby to indicate what constitute legal rights and obligations. In this respect, they take on a "treaty-like" status. Sometimes even the term "shall" is used, rendering the stated rights and obligations more imperative. Since these types of resolutions express the agreement of states on what the law should be, in Wang's view their contents, *mutatis mutandis*, are capable of becoming treaty provisions. Thus, these resolutions lay down the basis for subsequent law-making conventions. The General Assembly has simply accelerated this process.

Wang further notes that certain other Assembly resolutions elaborate upon general principles and rules that are found in the Charter. In his view, to the extent that such resolutions evidence agreement as to the meaning of the Charter, they constitute an authentic interpretation of its provisions, particularly when adopted by unanimous vote. The most obvious effect of these resolutions on the development of international law, in Wang's view, is their evidential value in the formation of customary international law. In Wang's opinion, in the light of intensified international transactions and highly advanced communications technologies, the traditional requirement of repeated state practice over a considerable period of time has proved unnecessary for the emergence of a new customary rule. In these circumstances, if an Assembly resolution is intended to express principles and rules of international law, and it does so with legal formality and in terms that underscore that member states truly mean what the resolution says, it is difficult to argue that governments that vote for the resolution are not aware of its legal significance. Although a resolution does not have the binding force of a treaty, voting for it reflects at least the official intent of governments to approve the legal norms embodied in it, and this intent is precisely what the concept of *opinio juris* relates to.

Thus, even if the length of time is short or state practice is inconclusive, the statement of legal norms in a resolution may be sufficient to form the *opinio juris* that constitutes a necessary element of customary international law. A resolution adopted by member states unanimously or by consensus constitutes persuasive evidence of the *opinio juris communis*. Wang's observations in this regard are clearly well founded.

Given that there are two limbs to customary international law — *opinio juris* and state practice — Wang's thesis would be more complete if he had provided further reflections on the significance of state practice before and after the adoption of a resolution. If a resolution is persuasive evidence of customary international law, what can be said about state practice that is significantly inconsistent with the principles and rules declared in the resolution? Can we say that a deviating state violates international law? In Wang's view, the question whether General Assembly resolutions can constitute an independent source of international law is still pending, to be answered in the light of future developments. Whatever legal effect is to be ascribed to them, Wang considers that the authority of General Assembly resolutions is definitely higher than "judicial decisions and the teachings of the most highly qualified publicists." According to Wang, if Article 38(1) of the Statute of the International Court of Justice were to be redrafted today, the legal effect of General Assembly resolutions would be taken into account. In any event, as presently drafted, Article 38(1) does not purport to enumerate all sources of international law and hence is broad enough to cover such resolutions.

In another major article in this group, "On the Concept of the Common Heritage of Mankind,"[8] written in 1984, Wang discusses in depth the legal merits of the "common heritage" concept. In a comprehensive review of the concept's historical development, he explains that "common heritage" was the legal response to the exploitation of the resources of the deep seabed beyond the limits of national jurisdiction. Due to its great importance for the development of the international law of the sea, the concept was at the core of the entire Third United Nations Conference on the Law of the Sea.

The legal issues concerning the exploitation of the resources of the deep seabed beyond the limits of national jurisdiction did not arise until mining the seabed became technically possible in the

8 *Ibid.*, 83-117.

1960s. At that time, the central questions were who should own the deep seabed, and on what legal basis should its resources be exploited? The major part of this article goes on to address these questions. In doing so, Wang inquires into traditional legal doctrines that may apply to the new situation. He starts by analysing the proposition that the resources of the deep seabed should be treated as *res nullius*, concluding that, with regard to the legal status of the deep seabed, the proposition of *res nullius* cannot find support either historically or in current state practice. He disagrees with those who advocate that the deep seabed should be treated as *res communis*, arguing that while this concept is consistent with the resources of the seabed being public property over which no individual nation can claim ownership, it does allow an individual nation to mine the resources and to reap the benefits for itself. Wang argues that the special nature of the resources of the seabed does not justify such individualist exploitation and enjoyment. Since *res communis* is unable to address the special nature of the resources of the seabed, Wang rejects the principle of the freedom of the seas, which itself is based essentially on the concept of *res communis*, as an appropriate legal basis for the exploitation of the resources of the deep seabed.

In this regard, Wang criticizes in particular the position of the United States, which accepts the analogy of deep seabed mining to the freedom of fishing on the high seas. He considers the United States position, which purports to separate the legal status of the deep seabed from the right to exploit its resources, as far-fetched. Unlike the living resources of the high seas, the mineral resources of the deep seabed are non-reproductive; after being mined, the seabed becomes a wasteland. Moreover, unlike fisheries, mineral resources are linked to particular areas of the seabed; without exclusive ownership of a specific area, a mining activity by one party may not be immune from interference by another would-be miner, unless one accepts "first come, first served" as the established legal basis for exploiting the resources of the deep seabed. For Wang, however, such a doctrine provides theoretical support to the technologically advanced and financially adequate nations in their race for the wealth of the deep seabed — a kind of neo-colonialism applied to the frontier of deep seabed mining.

In the light of these reflections, it is clear that Wang rejects the applicability of traditional doctrines to determining the legal status of the resources of the deep seabed because of their inability to address the circumstances specific to that area. However, this does not mean that the exploitation of deep seabed resources must operate in a vacuum. According to Wang, as soon as seabed mining becomes possible, new principles and rules of international law will quickly emerge to regulate the newly developed situation. Since 1967, when the concept of the common heritage of mankind was put forward as the governing principle for the international regime of the deep seabed, this concept has been reiterated and affirmed by resolutions of both the General Assembly and other United Nations agencies. This convinces Wang that the concept of the common heritage of mankind has gained universal recognition and acceptance.

Based on his theory that certain kinds of resolutions adopted by the General Assembly are able to express the *opinio juris communis*, Wang believes that General Assembly Resolution 2749 (XXV 1970), which solemnly declares that "[T]he seabed and ocean floor, and the subsoils thereof, beyond the limits of national jurisdiction, as well as the resources of the area, are the common heritage of mankind," has evidenced the establishment of this concept as the legal basis for the newborn legal regime for the exploitation of the resources of the "area." The signing of the 1982 United Nations Convention on the Law of the Sea by 117 states at Montego Bay further reinforces this belief. Developing this line of thought, Wang regards the concept of the common heritage of mankind as a truly legal concept containing specific principles and rules.

Although opinions vary among commentators as to what these principles and rules are and how they should be understood and implemented, some common ground has been established. The principles and rules declared by Resolution 2749 and later affirmed by the 1982 Law of the Sea Convention reflect the general understanding of what the major legal principles and rules based on the concept of the common heritage of mankind should be. Wang observes that these principles and rules have never met with open opposition, and that some of the more important, such as the principles of non-appropriation, peaceful purposes, and benefit of mankind, have been recognized and accepted by all, or by an overwhelming majority of states. Thus, even if one may claim *pacta non obligant nisi gentes inter quas initia*, these principles still have gained their binding effect from customary international law.

Wang makes special mention of China's attitude towards the concept of the common heritage of mankind. He remarks that, after the restoration of China to its lawful seat in the United Nations, China was able to participate fully throughout the nine-year conference and negotiations in formulating the Law of the Sea Convention, and the concept of the common heritage of mankind has been the most basic tenet of China's position on the seabed and ocean floor beyond the limits of national jurisdiction. China has not only accepted this concept, but has also given its constant support to it.

Whatever merit the concept of the common heritage of mankind may have, its impact on the development of the international regime for the deep seabed is beyond dispute. In this regard, Wang notes that consensus has been reached in respect of at least two principles: first, the benefits reaped from the exploitation of the resources of the deep seabed must go to mankind as a whole and, second, an international authority must be set up to administer the exploitation of deep seabed resources. Wang concludes that the advent of the concept of the common heritage of mankind has brought a profound change to the law of the sea. Its impact, however, does not stop there. This concept has also been applied to outer-space law, and moreover, has appeared in discussions about legal regimes such as the Antarctic. This reveals a basic or generic element in the concept. Although it is too early to assess the impact of the "common heritage" concept on the entire landscape of international law, its extension beyond the law of the sea proves that it has a vitality worthy of international lawyers' attention. Since Wang wrote this article shortly after the 1982 Convention on the Law of the Sea was opened for signature, he no doubt felt that the time was not yet ripe for him to speculate on the legal implications of the concept.

In fact, since Wang wrote this article, no substantial progress has been made in implementing the "common heritage" concept. One stumbling block has been the concern that equitable distribution of the benefits of deep seabed resources under the suggested international authority could lead to economic inefficiency and undermine incentives to apply state-of-the-art technology to seabed mining. This argument is typically made by technologically advanced nations. It is incumbent on international lawyers to address these issues. Wang's analysis focuses primarily on the legal merits of the concept of the common heritage of mankind without much mention of the social, political, and economic foundations that sustain the concept. Ultimately, however, the difference of views on the concept of the common heritage of mankind lies in different perceptions of international political and economic relations. If these relations are perceived in terms of interstate solidarity rather than as a zero-sum game, then the concept of the common heritage of mankind becomes the logical expression of the legal status of the resources beyond the limits of national jurisdiction.

GROUP TWO: BASIC ISSUES OF INTERNATIONAL LAW

The leading article in this second group of Wang's writings is "An Introduction to International Law."[9] This article is, in fact, Wang's contribution to the introductory part of China's national uniform textbook on international law[10] of which Wang is the chief editor. Similar to standard textbooks used in most other countries, this introductory part of the Chinese textbook discusses all of the basic issues of international law, including the nature of international law, its legal basis and history, the sources of international law, codification, and the relationship between international law and domestic law. In principle, Wang's writing in this area displays no major differences from the writings of scholars from outside China. Nevertheless, Wang's article and the articles in the textbook contributed by other Chinese scholars reflect by and large how international law was understood and taught in the then Chinese international law community. In this regard, there are several points worthy of this reviewer's comments.

First, unlike some western authors, in analysing the specific nature of international law Wang rejects the attempt to seek "world law" based on "world government" as the means to strengthen the effectiveness of international law. He argues that such an attempt denies the sovereignty of states, which is pivotal to the present-day international legal system. Thus, in his view, "world law" and "world government" are unwarranted in both theory and practice. Continuing this line of thought, Wang does not agree that individuals should be subjects of international law. He writes that if individuals were to become subjects of international law, the very foundation on which the international legal system has been built would be destroyed and international law would be changed into "world law." Wang's position on this issue represents the prevailing view of China's international law community. According to Chinese inter-

9 *Ibid.*, 176-224.

10 This textbook, which was published in 1981, was the first of its kind since 1949.

national law theory, the subjects of international law are only those that the legal system recognizes as capable of playing a direct role in the legal system and that it can directly address. Certainly, international law in general does not recognize that individuals are capable of bearing the rights and duties under the legal system even if they may benefit from it. It is this view that basically shapes the Chinese attitude towards the international protection of human rights.

In his quest for the true legal basis for international law, Wang writes: "[w]hile states are subject to the binding force of international law, they are also the makers of international law. Therefore, the basis for the legal effect of international law can only be attributed to states themselves, that is, the will of states." Wang further explains that such will is not the arbitrary will of a single state, nor does it refer to the "common will" of states, but rather agreement between the wills of various states.

It is of central importance in a standard textbook to present international law as it is, and, in this sense, the will of states is indeed a decisive and most direct factor in shaping the legal basis of international law. In a scholarly presentation, however, it is preferable to assess the relevance of the will of states through an understanding of the forces that nurture that will — history, culture, philosophy, politics, and economics. These are the factors from which the entire landscape of international law has been formed, and they continue to shape the complicated structure of this legal system. An analysis of these factors makes clear to students that today's international law is a product of the historical development of human civilization, which has embraced both subjective and objective elements. What is being achieved today is built on the lessons of history and will continue to provide guidance into the future. In this context, an unbiased appreciation should be given to the various schools of international legal thinking that have been formed around the issue of the basis for the binding nature of international law, and that have exerted different degrees of influence on the legal behaviour of states, their law-making processes, and their law-abiding habits.

Unfortunately, in this regard Wang's treatment of the binding nature of international law is not satisfactory. He categorically criticizes various western theories while neglecting their positive elements — for instance, the role of value judgments in evaluating national motivations. This article may not, however, reflect Wang's real position. In both earlier and later writings, Wang examines various international legal issues without forgetting the central objective of seeking international justice. In his "Nationalist Perception of International Law,"[11] published in 1936, he writes that, in the light of the spirit of nationalism, the balance between national freedom and equality and mutual assistance among nations should constitute the source of the binding nature of the rules of international law. In his "International Law in China: Historical and Contemporary Perspectives,"[12] which he presented as his lecture at the Hague Academy of International Law in 1990, he concluded that the present task of international lawyers "is to take account of different histories and cultures of various countries and to find out principles of law and justice which are common to all."

Another issue related to the legal basis of international law is its class character. This issue has been heatedly debated by Chinese scholars since the 1950s. Historically, it was brought to the Chinese international law community as a result of the introduction to China of the Soviet theory of international law in the early 1950s. Based on a dogmatic application of a Marxist definition of law to international law, this theory advocates that the essence of international law, like that of other laws, rests on its class character. Given its long influence in the Chinese international law community, it is not surprising that this theory is reflected in this standard textbook. Thus, Wang writes, because law in general has its class character, international law as a branch of law in general is no exception. Since the basis for the legal effect of international law is the will of states, which is the will of the ruling class of those states, international law will reflect that class character. Wang does not, however, elaborate upon this theory. Instead, he stresses that, because of the absence of a ruling class in the international community, the class character of international law does not reflect the will of a single ruling class but rather the agreement of the ruling classes of various states. This low-key reflection seems to indicate Wang's scepticism of the validity of the class theory of international law. As he later explains in "Some Problems Concerning the Textbook of International Law,"[13] what has been reflected in this textbook in this regard is not the result of recent research and studies, and he is not sure that this question can be discussed scientifically in the second edition of the textbook. In any event, the ascription of a class

---

[11] *Selected Essays of Wang Tieya*, 435-47.

[12] *Ibid.*, 273-410.

[13] *Ibid.*, 249-57.

character to international law in this textbook should primarily be viewed as the imprint of Soviet theory on international law in China.

In this reviewer's opinion, whether or not such a theory exists as a dominant force in a domestic legal system, to ascribe a "class character" theory to international law is far-fetched and self-contradictory. The concept of class refers to a specific group of people who are in the same or similar economic status in a given society. Class character in this context is understood to be substantially exclusive and nonreconcilable. If one admits the absence of a ruling class in the international community and regards international law as representing the agreement of the ruling classes of various states, then what is its class character, and how can the class character of a specific ruling class be identified? Can we pinpoint the class character of the principle of sovereign equality and independence, which has existed since the genesis of modern international law and has been recognized by every state in the world, whether feudal, bourgeois, or socialist?

Because nation states make up the component elements of the international community today and in the foreseeable future, a state is subject to a certain rule of international law not because this rule represents its class character, but rather because the observance of such a rule is required by its national interest in the international community. Therefore, even if the basis for the legal effect of international law is attributed to the will of states, the motivation of such will has never been, and will not be, dominated by the class character of each state. This observation is demonstrated and will continue to be demonstrated by prevailing state practice: states of different class characters can co-exist very well if they respect and observe the established principles and rules of international law in their mutual relations. Nevertheless, even between states of the same class character, derogation from the established principles and rules of international law will lead to a deterioration in their mutual relations.

Wang's analysis of the relationship between international law and municipal law does not follow the traditional debate between monism and dualism. His is a dialectical line of inquiry. Accepting that municipal law is enacted by states and international law is formulated through the participation of states, Wang focuses on the interrelationship between the two legal systems rather than on their conflicts. According to him, the two systems interact and supplement each other. Without domestic rules, many international obligations cannot be performed; on the other hand, if domestic rules are enacted that are contrary to international obligations and infringe on the rights and interests of other states, then state responsibility is incurred. Therefore, when states enact domestic laws, they should take into account their obligations under international law. Similarly, before states enter into international obligations they should take care to bring their domestic law into line with those international obligations. In a later article, "A Few Issues of International Law,"[14] Wang maintains that mutual interaction between the two legal systems includes the adoption of each other's legal concepts.

GROUP THREE: INTERNATIONAL LAW IN CHINA

Wang's writings in this third group encompass a far-reaching subject. Among the four articles, three address China's attitude towards international law from a historical perspective. The most important article in this category is "International Law in China: Historical and Contemporary Perspectives,"[15] which in substance is the Chinese version of Wang's lecture at the Hague Academy of International Law in 1990. In the history of the Hague Academy, Wang is the first, and only, Chinese scholar to have presented a lecture on public international law. To him, this lecture marks the peak of his entire academic career in international law.

The lecture is divided into five parts: international law in ancient China (722-221 B.C.); international law in modern China (1839-1949); China and the "Five Principles of Peaceful Coexistence"; China's attitudes towards the concept of sovereignty; and China's attitude towards the law of treaties. Through these five chapters, Wang hopes to shed light on the impact of Chinese history and culture on its attitude towards international law, the subject to which he has drawn particular attention in recent years. As he remarks in "International Law in Transition,"[16] as a universal international legal system, international law must represent the various forms of culture and legal systems that exist in the family of nations, and must reflect the contributions made by these various forms of culture and legal systems to the progressive development of international law.

14 *Ibid.*, 225-48.
15 *Ibid.*, 273-415.
16 *Ibid.*, 22-26.

In the first chapter, Wang provides answers to a long-debated question: was there international law in ancient China? In his view, if *ubi societas ibi jus* is the starting point, some fragmentary practices and usages similar to modern rules of international law can be traced back to the period of "Spring and Autumn and the Warring States" in China. After a brief review of these practices and usages, such as sending diplomatic envoys, convening intervassal conferences, and concluding treaties, Wang concludes that they did not develop into international law in its modern sense. The social circumstances that gave rise to these practices and usages were not characterized by interstate relations based on the concept of sovereign equality and independence. Wang remarks that, until China's door was forced open by western powers, the prevailing image of the world in China was that China was the centre of the world. Thus, the starting point of the Chinese perspective on world order was that of a universal state based on China's cultural superiority, which permitted it to assimilate neighbouring nations. As a result, relations between China and its neighbours were built on Confucian norms of domestic bonds of father and son, husband and wife, and king and subject, instead of on the concept of sovereign equality and independence. The typical embodiment of this sinocentric world order was the tribute system that governed transactions between China and its peripheral countries. This explains why modern international law based on the concept of sovereign equality and independence was completely foreign to China. Thus, when the first encounter between China and modern European powers took place, it was extremely difficult for the Chinese to understand the western multistate system, and conflicts caused by differences in cultural backgrounds were inevitable.

In the second chapter, Wang discusses Chinese reactions to the introduction of western international law. He reviews three historical events that are particularly important in this regard. The first was the conclusion of the Treaty of Nerchinsk between China and Russia in 1689, under which "international practices of that time were scrupulously followed." Wang maintains that, although the influence of western international law was strong, it does not mean that China had accepted it as a legal system for interstate relations. The second event was the first Opium War (1840-42). Before the war broke out, Commissioner Lin Zexu of the Qing dynasty ordered the translation of Vattel's *Le Droit des Gens* in an attempt to use it as an instrument in his suppression of opium consumption and trade.

The translation, however, turned out to be impossible to understand. Wang remarks that western international law was not systematically introduced into China until the country was forced open as a result of western imperialist expansion and invasion, which eventually destroyed the Sinocentric conception of world order. In 1864, William A. P. Martin, an American missionary and Sinologist, as well as an interpreter to the American Ministers to China, finished his translation of Henry Wheaton's *Elements of International Law*, and three hundred copies were distributed for use by Chinese officials. The first successful application of international law was to an incident in which a Prussian man-of-war seized three Danish merchant ships as war prizes within Chinese internal waters. This incident convinced Chinese officials that international law was useful for preventing diplomatic conflict from turning into something more serious. Therefore, the Qing government approved the publication and distribution of Martin's translation.

Although the introduction of western international law into China was regarded as a great event in the Far East (Japan first learned western international law through Martin's translation), its effect upon Chinese foreign relations of the time was very limited. On the one hand, the Chinese did not trust this foreign legal learning, which was regarded as incompatible with Chinese "institutions and systems." At most it was perceived only as one of the methods for circumscribing the "craftiest consuls." On the other hand, international law was then considered to apply exclusively to relations among "civilized" nations with European or Christian backgrounds. Since China was not regarded as a "civilized" nation by the West, western nations never intended to apply international law in its full sense to their relations with China. Replacing the Sinocentric view of world order was the unequal treaty regime that had been imposed upon China by foreign powers instead of a regime of equal relations based on international law.

After a succinct review of the origin, scope, and nature of the unequal treaty regime, which from 1842 on inflicted tremendous humiliation and suffering on China for about one hundred years, Wang remarks that of the factors that have influenced China's attitude towards the western classical international law, the unequal treaty regime is of decisive importance. The western powers first subdued China by force, and then placed China under this regime. All relations with China were conducted pursuant to these treaties, and the major role of international law was to guarantee their implementation. Moreover, without the support of military, political, and economic power, efforts to invoke international law to defend China's interests simply made the situation worse. At that time, there was no alternative available to China other than accepting the status quo under the unequal treaty regime. Wang observes that this unfortunate historical reality has had a decisive influence upon China's perception of international law. Wang quotes the words of a Chinese diplomat of the late nineteenth century, "[i]nternational law is . . . reasonable but unreliable. If there is right without might, the right will not prevail." These words, according to Wang, typically represent the then-prevailing attitude of China towards international law. In fact, as the rest of Wang's lecture attests, this historical legacy still plays a role today in determining China's attitude towards international law.

While Wang has no doubt identified the major factor for the shaping and development of China's attitude toward international law, if the issue is examined within a historical and cultural context there are other important factors. For example, the differing perceptions between China and the West of the function of law as a means of social regulation also help to explain why the Chinese were dubious of the value of western concepts of international law.

The following three chapters of Wang's Hague lecture focus on contemporary Chinese attitudes towards international law. In discussing such an important subject, Wang does not attempt to give a full account of China's practice in international law, or to analyse specific issues in this regard. Rather, he examines some basic issues of international law that have a permanent and pervasive effect upon China's international legal behaviour. For this purpose, he selects three topics: the "Five Principles of Peaceful Coexistence," the concept of state sovereignty, and the rule of *pacta sunt servanda*. Perhaps, in his mind, an understanding of these three topics can best assist an understanding of contemporary Chinese perspectives on international law.

The "Five Principles of Peaceful Coexistence" (mutual respect for sovereignty and territorial integrity, mutual non-aggression, non-interference in each other's internal affairs, equality and mutual benefit, and peaceful coexistence) represent, according to Wang, China's most significant contribution to the development of international law. After chronicling their origin and development, he points out that the significance of the "Five Principles" for international law must be understood within the context of the need for overriding principles to re-establish the international legal order in the post-war period. Wang observes that the formal declaration of the "Five Principles" by China, India, and Burma in 1955 reflects their efforts to meet such a need.

Given the universal recognition of these principles and the nature of the issues that they purport to address, Wang concludes that the "Five Principles of Peaceful Coexistence" constitute fundamental principles of international law. In this regard, Wang lodges his objections to attempts to discredit the principles, arguing that their merits go beyond a mere duplication of the principles enshrined in the United Nations Charter. He points out that these principles were developed as a systematic and integral whole, emphasizing mutuality among nations. Further, they were designed to achieve distributive justice in the international community by linking juridical equality with mutual economic benefit, and to address the relations between states with different social and political systems. Considering their unique characteristics, Wang suggests that the "Five Principles" are complementary to the principles reaffirmed in the United Nations Charter.

Wang's reflection on the concept of fundamental principles of international law is also worthy of note. He is of the opinion that every legal system must contain certain ultimate principles that impose obligations *erga omnes* upon all subjects of the system and from which all other subordinate principles and rules derive their legal effect. His use of China's General Principles of Civil Law as an example to justify the necessity for such fundamental principles seems to imply that the necessity for having these "ultimate principles" in the international community is in conformity with a common legal conviction and the experience of human civilization at large.

Wang observes that the principle of state sovereignty is regarded by China as the cornerstone of the entire system of international law, and that strict adherence to the inviolability of state sovereignty is central to China's foreign policy thinking. He explains that this attitude is conditioned primarily by two factors. First, China's experience of dismemberment, oppression, and humiliation, verging on subjugation and extinction, at the hands of foreign imperialism for about a century has forced the Chinese to realize the vital importance of the principle of state sovereignty in international relations. To China, sovereignty is really a hard-won prize in the struggle to shake off the yoke of foreign domination in the form of the unequal treaty regime; to transform the country from a dynastic, semi-feudal regime into a strong republic; to achieve national respect, independence, and equality in the family of nations; and to protect itself from foreign expansion and aggression. This traumatic history lesson has convinced the Chinese that the principle of state sovereignty serves as the cornerstone on which international relations can be established and on which rights and obligations under international law can prevail.

The second factor emerges from the hard realities of international life. Up to now, the international community has been composed of sovereign states that are legally independent of each other. State practice has always endorsed the principle of sovereignty, and even the major powers often refer to it in the conduct of their foreign relations. This indicates that the principle of sovereignty possesses certain inherent values on which the system of international law depends. In Wang's opinion, although the sovereignty principle is one of the most controversial concepts in international law, it does not involve any threat to peace or any obstacle to the development and dignity of states, nor does it involve any contravention of juridical logic or any contradiction with the realities of life.

On the other hand, what must be opposed, in Wang's view, is the doctrine of *absolute* sovereignty. In this regard, Wang advises that China has never claimed absolute sovereignty in its international practice; on the contrary, it has always placed emphasis on states showing mutual respect for each other's sovereignty. China's practice in regard to the rule *pacta sunt servanda* reveals that state sovereignty is subject to the limitation of treaty obligations. Such an attitude towards the principle of sovereignty explains China's constant rejection of the notion of "world law" and "world government." In Wang's opinion, the debates held at the United Nations indicate that China has no enthusiasm for any attempt to strengthen the organization in a way that might lead towards world government.

Wang's observation that the principle of state sovereignty constitutes the *leitmotif* of the contemporary Chinese approach towards international law is absolutely correct. It is submitted, however, that Wang's thesis would be more insightful if he could associate this phenomenon with more profound cultural values. In this regard, it might be suggested that traditional perceptions of the central role of the state in the development of Chinese civilization and in the maintenance of China's territorial integrity and cultural unity should also be taken into account when considering Chinese approaches to international law. Also, Wang's reflections on the principle of state sovereignty are primarily based on international relations of the Cold War era. Given the time of his lecture, Wang did not have the opportunity to ponder the implications of the drastic changes in the post-Cold War international community where questions concerning the relationship between state sovereignty and such matters as global interdependence, human rights, and the role of international organizations have become increasingly prominent. At present, the role of the principle of state sovereignty in the quest for a new world order has become a focal point for debate, and the Chinese approach to state sovereignty will have a significant bearing on the progress of that debate.

In considering how the principle of *pacta sunt servanda* is applied by China, Wang points out that the faithful performance of treaty-based obligations is a basic tenet of China's attitude towards international law. Given the time-honoured conviction in Chinese culture that no sovereign entity can survive without keeping its promises, Wang believes that such an attitude is reflected in the traditional Chinese value that promises should be kept in good faith.

Wang divides this topic into two parts, *pacta* and *servanda*, discussing China's practice in regard to each. Wang observes that the scope of what are included as treaties under the official treaty series of the People's Republic of China is very broad. It includes not only the instruments that are titled as "treaties" or "agreements" but also those that come under other appellations, such as joint communiqués, declarations, and announcements. Wang speculates that this practice seems to be based on a notion that, in addition to formal treaties and agreements, official documents that express consensual commitments and are signed or approved by high authorities of states should also be regarded as a category of international treaties with binding force. Nevertheless, Wang's own words indicate some reservation and an acknowledgment of the problem posed by his speculation. It is generally agreed that a mere consensual commitment expressed between subjects of international law is not in itself sufficient to constitute an instrument as a treaty. The commitment must be a legal as opposed to a political or moral commitment. It must create, alter, or terminate rights and obligations or establish relations that are governed by international law. Sometimes, however, it is not easy to determine whether an instrument, whether called a joint declaration, communiqué, or announcement, contains such a legal commitment, particularly when it does not contain precisely defined obligations or includes merely a statement of policy or intention. Wang feels uncomfortable with the term "non-binding agreement" as used by some authors to characterize this type of instrument, arguing that the lack of precision or the political nature of an instrument should not prevent it from having legally binding force. Neither does he completely agree with the suggestion that in deciding the legally binding effect of an instrument the intention of the parties should be the controlling factor, warning that very often such intention is not easy to find. In Wang's opinion, both theory and practice have left many questions to be answered.

In respect of the performance of treaty obligations, Wang provides insight into the Chinese practice in relation to the effect of treaties in municipal law. Under China's legal system, treaties and statutes appear to have equal legal force, because the power to enact statutes and the power to conclude treaties both rest with the same national legislative body, namely, the standing committee of the National People's Congress, and both statutes and treaties have to be proclaimed by the president of the People's Republic of China in order to have legal effect. Wang also notes that, as a general rule, when a treaty to which China is a contracting party enters into force on the international plane, it automatically becomes part of China's domestic law, and, if there is a conflict between a treaty and a national statute, the former always overrides the latter.

Wang's conclusions in this regard are based on the relevant statutory provisions rather than on China's constitution, which is silent on this issue. Accordingly, in Wang's view these statutory provisions are not of a constitutional nature. The constitution of the People's Republic of China does make a distinction between treaties and agreements but, since there is no practice on the matter, Wang provides no opinion on the implications of this distinction.

Perhaps for the same reason, Wang does not discuss another issue of practical importance; namely, how treaties are directly applied by the Chinese courts. However, with the rapid growth of China's treaty relations with other nations and with international organizations, the effect of treaties in China's legal system is an issue that is becoming increasingly prominent. To guarantee the proper performance of its treaty obligations, China must establish general principles and rules that will govern the effect of treaties within its legal system. In this regard, the article "Conflicts Between Treaties and

Municipal Law,"[17] which Wang wrote about fifty years ago, deserves attention. In this article, Wang argues that the most powerful guarantee for the sanctity of international law is to accord full superiority to treaties in a domestic legal system, and that the most effective way to do this is to entrench definite provisions in the constitution. His viewpoint remains valid today.

China's practice in performing its treaty obligations is linked to its attitude towards unequal treaties. In addressing this issue, Wang succinctly describes the legal grounds invoked by China for abolishing the unequal treaties that were imposed upon it by foreign imperialism. Following Articles 52 and 53 of the Vienna Convention on the Law of Treaties, Wang considers that, since unequal treaties are always characterized by the imposition of grossly unequal obligations on a weaker state by a stronger one through the use or threat of force, they violate not only the law of treaties but also the principle of sovereign equality. The abolition of these treaties therefore constitutes a lawful exception to the *pacta sunt servanda* rule. For China, as Wang notes, unequal treaties are in principle null and void *ab initio*.

Nevertheless, in dealing with certain types of unequal treaties, particularly those involving boundaries with its neighbours, the Chinese government has adopted a flexible approach. While considering these treaties null and void in principle, China is always willing to settle the boundary problems posed by them through negotiations. Pending settlement, the position of China is that the status quo established by these treaties should be maintained. According to Wang, another rule of international law that China has applied to abolish unequal treaties is that of *rebus sic stantibus*. He agrees that the founding of the People's Republic of China in 1949 brought to an end the conditions that existed at the time of the conclusion of the unequal treaties, thus justifying the abrogation of these treaties on the ground of *rebus sic stantibus*. However, as Wang notes, the Chinese government is very cautious about invoking this rule in order to terminate or revise its treaty obligations. He finds only two cases that may be considered as examples of the rule being applied. This indicates that, for the People's Republic of China, *rebus sic stantibus* as a complementary rule to *pacta sunt servanda* is to be applied only in exceptional cases.

In his conclusion, Wang is optimistic about the future of international law in China. As he points out, soon after the founding of the

17 *Ibid.*, 551-77.

People's Republic of China, which brought to an end a history of humiliation and oppression and allowed China to regain its sovereignty in the family of nations, China realized that international law was both useful and necessary. In the end, he notes, the practice of China demonstrates that differences in history and culture have not created an unbridgeable gap between western and non-western nations in relation to their attitudes towards international law. On the contrary, if international lawyers keep in mind the need to establish an effective universal international legal system, these differences can be well accommodated, and more fruitful results will ensue.

All in all, *Wang Tieya Wenxuan* is a comprehensive collection of Wang's writings over the past six decades. These writings are unique in providing the author's profound insights into many important international legal issues, both contemporary and historical. No comparable international legal publication in China covers such a lengthy time span or touches upon so many important issues. That alone makes this book extraordinarily valuable.

Sommaire

Enseignement, recherche, et diffusion du droit international en Chine: la contribution de Wang Tieya

L'auteur fait une recension de l'ouvrage intitulé Wang Tieya Wenxuan *(Essais choisis de Wang Tieya écrits en chinois). Wang Tieya est le plus ancien professeur de droit international à temps complet dans l'histoire récente de la Chine. Il est considéré, aussi bien en Chine que sur la scène internationale, comme un universitaire remarquable et consciencieux. Cet ouvrage rassemble trente-six des nombreux articles que Wang a écrits pendant les soixante dernières années. Ces articles, qui sont répartis en six groupes, embrassent un grand nombre de sujets d'actualité dans le domaine du droit international, dont le droit de la guerre, le droit des traités, l'attitude de la Chine envers le droit international, l'enseignement et la recherche en droit international, les théories et les pratiques fondamentales et le développement actuel du droit international. L'article le plus ancien remonte à 1932 et le texte le plus important est la conférence prononcée par Wang devant l'Académie de droit international de La Haye. Ensemble, ces articles résument bien l'étude et la pratique du droit international en Chine pendant les soixante dernières années, et ils reflètent, par conséquent, la contribution remarquable que Wang a apportée à l'avancement du droit international en Chine.*

Notes and Comments /
Notes et commentaires

Rereading *Trail Smelter**

INTRODUCTION

THE FIRST VOLUME OF this *Yearbook* contained an article entitled "The Trail Smelter Dispute"[1] by John Read, one of Canada's most distinguished international lawyers and former member of the International Court of Justice. Read drew on his own experience on the Canadian side of the dispute, which involved residents of Washington state who claimed to have suffered damage from the operation of a lead smelter in Trail, British Columbia, to illuminate various aspects of its eventual resolution through international arbitration.[2] Thirty years after the publication of Read's piece, and more than fifty years after the Arbitral Tribunal's final decision, *Trail Smelter* has come to occupy a prominent but somewhat mysterious position in the legal canon. While it is one of the best known and most frequently cited international decisions, and is regarded by many scholars as the fountainhead of modern international

---

* The author would like to thank Dr. Charles Bourne for his helpful comments on an earlier version of this note.

---

1 J. Read, "The Trail Smelter Dispute," 1 Can. Y.B. Int'l L. 213 (1963).

2 *Trail Smelter Arbitration* (*United States* v. *Canada*), 3 R.I.A.A. 1905 (includes *Convention for Settlement of Difficulties Arising from Operation of Smelter at Trail, B.C.* and the two decisions of the Arbitral Tribunal). Decision of Apr. 16, 1938: (1939) 33 AJIL 182. Decision of Mar. 11, 1941: (1941) 35 AJIL 684. All further references are to the AJIL.

220   *The Canadian Yearbook of International Law 1993*

environmental law,[3] it is more an object of reverence than a subject of analysis. All too often it is invoked as authority by scholars who pause only long enough to mention its name and the principle to which it is said to lend support before moving on. While the potential dangers involved in overstating either the scope of application or overall significance of the Arbitral Tribunal's decisions have been noted on numerous occasions,[4] there has been less emphasis on the equally important concern that these passing references constitute reductionist accounts of a highly complex set of circumstances, and as such represent a series of lost opportunities to learn the lessons of *Trail Smelter.*

The numerous warnings about the misuse of *Trail Smelter* tend to focus on its invocation, along with the *Corfu Channel* case[5] and the *Lake Lanoux Arbitration,*[6] as support for the existence of customary duties to avoid causing transboundary environmental damage and to make reparation for such damage should it occur. The applicable principle, referred to as the *sic utere tuo* standard (from the Latin maxim *sic utere tuo ut alienum non laedas*: use your own property so as not to harm that of another), has been characterized as a description of "the other face of the coin of sovereignty"[7] and can be seen as the fundamental building block of a system of international environmental protection.

3 Writing in 1971, one scholar went so far as to say, "Every discussion of the general international law relating to pollution starts, and must end, with a mention of the Trail Smelter Arbitration": A. P. Rubin, "Pollution by Analogy: The Trail Smelter Arbitration," 50 Oregon L. Rev. 259 (1971). Though international environmental law has obviously undergone tremendous development since that time, *Trail Smelter* remains a landmark. A recent treatise on international environmental law asserts that "the arbitral judgment . . . in the Trail Smelter case is considered as having laid out the foundations of international environmental law, at least regarding transfrontier pollution." A. Kiss and D. Shelton, *International Environmental Law,* 107 (London: Graham & Trotman, 1991).

4 See especially Rubin, *ibid.*

5 *U.K.* v. *Albania* (1949), ICJ Rep. 4.

6 *Spain* v. *France,* 12 R.I.A.A. 285 at 303 (text of Tribunal's decision in French); (1957) 24 Int'l L. Rep. 101; (1959) 53 AJIL 156. All further references are to the AJIL.

7 R. Q. Quentin-Baxter, "Preliminary Report on International Liability for Injurious Consequences Arising out of Acts not Prohibited by International Law," UN Doc. A/CN.4/334 and Add. 1 and 2, 2:1 *Yearbook of the International Law Commission 1980,* 247 at 258 (New York: 1982).

The three decisions make up a rather disjointed trilogy, having little in common with one another. *Trail Smelter* is the only one of the three that lies squarely in the environmental area. The two decisions rendered by the Arbitral Tribunal in 1938 and 1941 jointly represent the first (and only) time that an international Tribunal has addressed the question of transboundary environmental damage. One statement in the 1941 decision has come to be regarded as the classic articulation of the *sic utere tuo* standard as applicable to such damage:

[U]nder the principles of international law . . . no State has the right to use or permit the use of its territory in such a manner as to cause injury by fumes in or to the territory of another or the properties or persons therein, when the case is of serious consequence and the injury is established by clear and convincing evidence.[8]

Corfu Channel has no direct applicability to environmental damage; it involved a claim by the United Kingdom against Albania for damage from mines suffered by a British ship while in transit through the channel, an international strait falling within Albanian territorial waters. Its significance stems from the fact that it is the only decision of the International Court of Justice among the three decisions usually cited. The Court appeared to invoke a version of the *sic utere tuo* principle when it referred to "every State's obligation not to allow knowingly its territory to be used for acts contrary to the rights of other States."[9] The most recent decision is the 1959 *Lac Lanoux Arbitration*, involving a claim by Spain that a French proposal to divert the waters of Lake Lanoux required Spanish consent, since it would affect the flow of a river originating in that lake and running into Spanish territory. While ruling that the consent of Spain was not required under relevant treaty provisions or general principles of international law, the Tribunal indicated that, had the dispute involved an argument that the river would be polluted, Spain might have claimed that her rights under the applicable treaty had been impaired.[10] This remark again has been interpreted along the lines of *sic utere tuo*.

While *Trail Smelter* and the other decisions are almost invariably cited in the literature dealing specifically with liability for environmental damage, they are usually accompanied by a caveat regarding

[8] 1941 decision, *supra* note 2, at 716.

[9] *Corfu Channel*, *supra* note 5, at 22-23.

[10] *Lake Lanoux*, *supra* note 6, at 160.

their limited usefulness as support for a general liability standard applicable to environmental damage in particular. The problems associated with using these cases as support for such a standard are well documented. For one thing, each of these variations on the *sic utere tuo* theme has clear limitations, as even a cursory reading of the circumscribed statements of principle reveals.[11] What is even more problematic is that *Trail Smelter*, the only decision that is directly on point in terms of environmental damage, has limited "precedential value" because of the unique circumstances that surround both the decision to submit the dispute to arbitration and

---

[11] The *Trail Smelter* formulation of the principle, for example, includes the requirements that the case be of "serious consequence" and that the injury be "established by clear and convincing evidence"; not every case of transboundary environmental damage will give rise to liability on the part of the state under whose jurisdiction the allegedly harmful activity occurred. While the definition of "serious consequence" is open to question, it is clear that at the very least there is a *de minimus* requirement. Rubin criticizes *Trail Smelter* for precisely this reason; he argues that the acceptance of the *Trail Smelter* formulation in the context of air pollution has led to some degree of certainty in these matters that "favors the polluter in continuing his polluting activities to continue as long as they do not cause 'damage' in the sense of direct injury measurable in money terms to the industrial or agricultural production of a second state": *supra* note 3, at 272. In *Corfu Channel*, the ICJ's use of the term "knowingly" ties the obligation to the state's knowledge of the activity alleged to be contrary to the rights of other states; it should also be borne in mind that the facts of the case involved injury suffered by a British ship within the Albanian territorial sea. Moreover, the reference to the "rights of other states" indicates that an affected state must show that more than a mere "interest" has been impaired. The reference made in passing by the Tribunal in *Lake Lanoux* to a potential Spanish claim if impairment of water quality were at issue is too brief to give any indication of the scope of the principle being invoked, but the remark must be read in light of the fact that the decision involved rights under a treaty and the importance accorded by the Tribunal to balancing the interests of states. In particular, it must be read in the light of statements such as those in which the Tribunal notes that it has not found either in the Treaty or in customary international law "any rule that prohibits one State, acting to safeguard its legitimate interests, to put itself in a situation that would permit it in effect, in violation of its international pledges, to injure a neighboring State even seriously": *Lake Lanoux, supra* note 6, at 163. It is also questionable whether the Tribual would have made its offhand remark about water quality under customary international law, in the absence of a clear treaty regime purporting to regulate the interests of the two states involved. Whatever the Tribunal may have meant by its oblique reference to Spain's possible cause for complaint, its decision cannot be taken as authority for a broadly defined notion of international liability, any more than the decisions in *Trail Smelter* or *Corfu Channel* can.

the decision of the Tribunal.[12] Scholars have repeatedly pointed out that the significance of these decisions has been exaggerated,[13] and that they should be approached with a certain degree of scepticism. Regarding *Trail Smelter,* for example, one writer notes:

Such heavy reliance on a single precedent breeds overstatement as analysts attempt to reinterpret the case to fit various hypothetical circumstances and new cases. Frequently, the precedent can be applied only by raising it to a level of abstraction far beyond the range of its logic.[14]

12 In particular, two factors must be taken into account. First, and most importantly, this was a case in which liability was not even at issue, because the Convention setting up the Arbitral Tribunal involved an acknowledgment of Canadian liability. In fact, as one writer points out, "it was the agreement of the parties as to Canadian liability for 'damages' that is the great precedent of the case, not the decision of the tribunal itself": Rubin, *supra* note 3, at 264. In his 1963 article, Read gives an account of how the Canadian "admission" of liability was intended to get around some of the obstacles that international law places on the bringing of international claims. Read, *supra* note 1, at 222-23. Second, the Tribunal was directed to apply United States law both to the question of whether damage had occurred and to the measure of compensation payable by Canada. Read indicates that U.S. law was chosen because of concern on the part of the Canadian negotiators that "the Tribunal might be impressed by the law of nuisance as set forth in precedents binding on Canadian courts. Those precedents were unfavourable to industrial enterprise, and, if applied, might be disastrous to the Smelter and to the economy of an important part of British Columbia. On the other hand, the decisions in the courts of the United States, including the Supreme Court cases, were much more evenly balanced in their effect on industrial and agricultural enterprise": *ibid.,* 227. While the Tribunal itself asserted that the requirements arising under the law of the United States were "in conformity with the general rules of international law" (1941 decision, *supra* note 2, at 713), this part of the decision has been criticized. See, e.g., Rubin at 267. As ultimately resolved between the two states, then, the application of "the principles of international law" was subject to clear limitations; even if international law did operate on the basis of precedent, this decision would be of very narrow applicability.

13 See, e.g., P. W. Birnie and A. E. Boyle, *International Law and the Environment,* 145 (Oxford: Clarendon Press, 1992); C. B. Bourne, "The International Law Commission's Draft Articles on the Law of International Watercourses: Principles and Planned Measures," 3 Colo. J. Int'l Envtl. L. & Pol'y 65 at 84-88 (1992). As one scholar aptly put it, *Trail Smelter* "has become accepted — and, to a certain extent, mythologized — as a landmark case in international law": D. Munton, "Dependence and Interdependence in Transboundary Environmental Relations," 36:1 Int'l J. 139 at 140 (1980-81). This characterization may apply equally to the other decisions.

14 Rubin, *supra* note 3, at 259.

Whatever the formal status of the *sic utere tuo* principle within the international legal system, it is clear that *Trail Smelter* and the other two decisions usually cited as support for a general liability standard applicable to transboundary environmental damage fall well short of the mark. However, this has not prevented the widespread misrepresentation of these decisions as providing support for such a standard, particularly in general discussions of international environmental law in which liability is not the focus.[15] The reasons for this are unclear, though it may be that the perception that a *sic utere tuo* standard is indispensable to international environmental law makes scholars particularly eager to find support for it, and that judicial and arbitral decisions provide a convenient reference point. Frequently, the brief statements of principle or allusions referred to above are extracted from the decisions and lumped together; the fact that the principles as articulated in these decisions are subject to clear limitations is often downplayed or omitted. Any detailed discussion of the cases themselves or the unique circumstances out of which they emerge is rare, and the possibility that the decision-maker's articulation of a principle might be tailored to the circumstances in which a dispute arose appears to be overlooked. What is unfortunate about this approach is that a separation of abstract statements of principle from the context in which they were articulated runs the risk of creating a fundamentally inaccurate impression of these decisions, as can be illustrated by a consideration of *Trail Smelter*.

The circumstances surrounding the dispute are well known but are nonetheless worth recalling. The dispute revolved around the zinc and lead smelter operated at Trail, British Columbia, by the Consolidated Mining and Smelting Company of Canada (Cominco). Since acquiring the smelter in 1906, Cominco had built it up into what the Tribunal described as "one of the best and largest equipped smelting plants on this continent."[16] In 1925, and again in 1927, improvements to existing infrastructure resulted in greatly increased output both of zinc and lead ores and of the sulphur dioxide fumes that were their by-product. The first formal complaint concerning damage caused across the border in Stevens County, Washington, was made in 1926.[17] After initial attempts to

---

15 See, e.g., Kiss and Shelton, *supra* note 3, at 107-108.

16 1938 decision, *supra* note 2, at 189-90.

17 *Ibid.*, 190. Cominco had already had to deal with complaints from Canadian farmers, but had dealt with these through the purchase of easements. See D. H.

deal with the matter through direct negotiation between Cominco and the complainants, it was taken up through diplomatic channels by the United States in June 1927. In December that same year, the United States government proposed that the situation be referred to the International Joint Commission. An agreement to involve the Commission was not reached until August 1928. The Commission issued a series of recommendations in 1931, including one to the effect that the quantum of damages be set at $350,000. The United States government was dissatisfied with the recommendations, considering the assessment of damages in particular to be too low, and began to press for the dispute to be submitted to arbitration.

After significant diplomatic manoeuvering, a mixed Arbitral Tribunal was constituted under a Convention signed at Ottawa on April 15, 1935. Among its provisions was Article 1, which provided that a sum of $350,000 would be paid by Canada to the United States as compensation for damage that had occurred before January 1, 1932, in accordance with the International Joint Commission's recommendation. Article 3 of the Convention provided that the Tribunal was to decide the following questions:

(1) Whether damage caused by the Trail Smelter in the State of Washington has occurred since the first day of January, 1932, and, if so, what indemnity should be paid therefor?
(2) In the event of the answer to the first part of the preceding question being in the affirmative, whether the Trail Smelter should be required to refrain from causing damage in the State of Washington in the future and, if so, to what extent?
(3) In the light of the answer to the preceding question, what measures or regime, if any, should be adopted or maintained by the Trail Smelter?
(4) What indemnity or compensation, if any, should be paid on account of any decision or decisions rendered by the Tribunal pursuant to the next two preceding questions?

The first (preliminary) decision of the Tribunal was rendered on April 16, 1938.[18] The Tribunal gave a final answer to the first

---

Dinwoodie, "The politics of international pollution control: the Trail Smelter case," 1980-81 Int'l J. 219 at 220 (1980-81).

18 As constituted under the 1935 Convention, the Tribunal was called upon to render its final decision within three months of the conclusion of the proceedings. It does not seem to have taken the members of the Tribunal long to decide that to render a decision within that period of time would be problematic if not impossible; in the event, the governments were notified that "unless the time limit should be extended, the Tribunal would be forced to give a

question and gave temporary decisions to the second and third question, with a final decision on these two questions as well as to the fourth question to be rendered within three months of October 1, 1940. The second and final decision of the Tribunal, rendered on March 11, 1941, contains the passage for which the arbitration has become famous.

While there has been a great deal of discussion regarding the merits of the *Trail Smelter* decision, the discussion tends to focus on this single celebrated (or denigrated) passage. The crucial question, which is seldom considered, is the extent to which the circumstances of the case may have influenced the Tribunal's approach, and how this is reflected in its decisions. It is clear that the Tribunal itself treated the surrounding circumstances as being of importance.[19] The 1938 decision began with a description of the topography, climatic conditions, and economic history of the region, thus providing a context for both the dispute and their findings.[20] Although the Tribunal did not indicate what weight was given to these circumstances in its decision, it made the following statement:

In all the consideration which the Tribunal has given to the problems presented to it, and in all the conclusions which it has reached, it has been guided by that primary purpose of the Convention expressed in the words of Article IV, that the Tribunal "shall give consideration to the desire of the high contracting parties to reach a solution just to all parties concerned," and further expressed in the opening paragraph of the Convention as to the "desirability and necessity of effecting a permanent settlement" of the controversy.[21]

Clearly, in attempting to reach a "just" solution, and one that would represent a permanent settlement of the dispute, the Tribunal was guided by considerations that required taking these

---

permanent decision on April 2, 1938, on the basis of data which it considered inadequate and unsatisfactory": 1938 decision, *ibid.*, 184.

[19] It is worth bearing in mind that before hearing arguments by counsel in Ottawa from Oct. 12-19, 1937, the Tribunal did a substantial amount of background preparation. The members conducted inspections both of the area alleged to have been damaged and of the smelter site: *ibid.*, 183. "Sessions for the reception and consideration of such evidence, oral and documentary, as was presented by the Governments or by interested parties, as provided in Article VIII," were held not only in Ottawa and Washington D.C. but also in Spokane," Washington: *ibid.*

[20] Much of this background information is reproduced in the 1941 decision, *supra* note 2, at 688-96.

[21] 1938 decision, *supra* note 2, at 184.

circumstances into account. An analysis of the decision reveals at least four factors that were of crucial importance, not only in the decision on the part of the Canadian and United States governments to submit the dispute to arbitration in the first place but also in the approach taken by the Tribunal. These factors are described below.

Proof of damage and identification of its cause: The importance of there being a clearly identified source of damage as well as clearly established harm is reflected in the Tribunal's language limiting the generality of the *sic utere tuo* standard: that is, that the case be "of serious consequence" and the injury be "established by clear and convincing evidence." From the outset, because of the relative lack of industrial development in the border region, it seemed clear that the source of the alleged damage was the smelter. Originally, however, the question of whether damage had in fact occurred was disputed. The scientists involved in the deliberations of the International Joint Commission split in their findings. While the U.S. experts found evidence of widespread damage resulting from the sulphur dioxide fumigations, the scientists brought in by the Canadian government and Cominco, as well as two scientists employed by the Commission, found the damage to be quite limited.[22] No such uncertainty troubled the Tribunal. Its starting point was that "damage occurred in the State of Washington, resulting from the sulphur dioxide emitted from the Trail Smelter" from 1925 at least until the end of 1931,[23] in accordance with the Commission's finding as formalized in the 1935 Convention. The first question before the Tribunal was limited to whether damage had occurred since the beginning of 1932. Thus, there was no room for doubt that the smelter at Trail was the cause of damage, and given that the smelter's operations had not undergone substantial changes between 1931 and 1932, it was not difficult for the Tribunal to reach the conclusion that compensable damage had occurred.

Perception of importance of interests at stake on both sides of the border: Both states involved perceived significant interests as being involved in the dispute. The economic importance of the smelter appears to

---

22 Dinwoodie, *supra* note 17, asserts that the Commission was "stymied by contradictory expert opinion" (at 226). He notes that these experts blamed the failure of the region's agricultural economy on "a variety of causes unrelated to the Trail emissions: earlier smelter operations at Northport, forest fires, insect infestations, inadequate soil composition, and poor farming practices" (at 226-27).

23 1938 decision, *supra* note 2, at 190.

have been an important factor in the willingness of the Canadian government to become involved and to attempt to ensure that the outcome would not shut down the operation. The smelter constituted the economic backbone of the economy of Trail and the surrounding region, and Cominco was the largest employer in the area, paying taxes in the range of one million dollars per year.[24] On the other side of the border, the perception of the interests at stake was equally clear. While the land allegedly damaged by the fumes was hardly among the most fertile in the state, it was the basis of the livelihood of the inhabitants of Stevens County, a predominantly agricultural area.[25] Concern regarding the smelter's activities triggered an early example of environmental activism, involving the formation of a group called the "Citizen's Protective Association," which initially lobbied fiercely to have the matter taken up by the United States government and later continued to express its concern directly and through the Washington State representative in Congress.[26]

Reciprocity of risk: The element of reciprocity of risk, on the other hand, seems to explain the initial unwillingness of the United States to pursue the matter, given the heavy industrialization on the U.S. side of the border further east and its accompanying concern that a dangerous precedent could be set.[27] In its decision, the Tribunal acknowledged that as between the two states the risk of transboundary damage from industrial sources was reciprocal, and that each had an interest in seeing a decision that would take into consideration the need to balance competing interests. The Tribunal stated:

As between the two countries involved, each has an equal interest that if a nuisance is proved, the indemnity to damaged parties for proven damage

[24] Dinwoodie, *supra* note 17, at 219.

[25] There were indications that it was in fact unproductive. For this reason, Cominco's view during the early stages of the dispute was that the whole affair constituted "an attempt at holdup by farmers in a nearly hopeless section who have come to think that they can get much more out of farming this rich corporation across the boundary than from farming their farms, and who are endeavoring to use the Governments at Washington and Ottawa to threaten a complete cessation of operations and thus force extravagant indemnity": *ibid.*, 222, note 5.

[26] *Ibid.*, 221.

[27] Regarding the question of why there was not an insistence on the "absolute cessation" of damage, Read notes, "[t]he acceptance of the principle of absolute cessation of damage might have shut down the Trail Smelter; but it would also have brought Detroit, Buffalo and Niagara Falls to an untimely end": *supra* note 1, at 224-25.

shall be just and adequate and each also has an equal interest that unproven or unwarranted claims shall not be allowed. *For, while the United States' interests may now be claimed to be injured by the operations of a Canadian corporation, it is equally possible that at some time in the future Canadian interests might be claimed to be injured by an American corporation.* As has well been said, "It would not be to the advantage of the two countries concerned that industrial effort should be prevented by exaggerating the interests of the agricultural community. Equally, it would not be to the advantage of the countries that the agricultural community should be oppressed to advance the interest of industry."[28]

The fact that the damage suffered could easily have been on the Canadian side and might be so at some point in the future may well have accounted for the Tribunal's willingness to phrase its decision so as to impose liability on Canada outside the terms of the 1935 Convention.

Broader bilateral relations between the states: By the time the dispute was submitted to arbitration, the United States and Canada had an established history of co-operation on matters that had an "environmental" aspect to them. This relationship is most clearly illustrated by the operation of the International Joint Commission which, as noted above, had been the body initially entrusted with the Trail Smelter dispute. Established pursuant to the Boundary Waters Treaty of 1909, the Commission was empowered to deal with issues arising from the common boundary. However, the existence of mechanisms for co-operation should not obscure the fact that the relative imbalance of power between the two countries also had an influence; the decision to submit the dispute to arbitration appears to have been at least partly the result of overt pressure brought to bear on the Canadian government by the government of the United States.[29]

While the four factors identified above could be characterized as political/economic/social factors that have little to do with the legal aspects of the decision, they are crucial to an understanding of that decision. In fact, the legal analysis in *Trail Smelter* is difficult to understand when separated from its political, social, and economic context. If one ignores the enormous complexities surrounding the dispute, it is easy to dismiss the principle articulated by the Tribunal as a "lax rule" at worst,[30] a ringing but hollow statement at best. It is

28 1941 decision, *supra* note 2, at 685 (emphasis added).

29 See the description of the circumstances leading up to the 1935 Convention in Dinwoodie, *supra* note 17, at 227-33.

30 As it is described by Rubin, *supra* note 3, at 275.

therefore unfortunate that these complexities are rarely explored in the legal literature in which the decision makes occasional brief appearances accompanied by *Corfu Channel* and *Lake Lanoux*. What is perhaps most puzzling about the use of these decisions as support for a general liability standard, apart from being problematic for all the reasons summarized above, is that it is essentially unproductive. The ritual invocation of principles that enjoy only dubious status as "customary norms" has little practical use; states are unlikely to accept such hazy concepts as a guide to their behaviour. Nor does it have conceptual value, for it does nothing to clarify the theoretical basis of a general liability standard.

Given that the way these decisions have been used has been less than enlightening, one possible response is to acknowledge openly that there are no international cases "on point" in the environmental area, regard those decisions that have hitherto been misused as irrelevant and unimportant, and concentrate on more promising sources of law such as treaties. Many scholars have taken this approach, interpreting the factors that undermine *Trail Smelter* as "precedent" as grounds for downplaying the importance of the decision.[31] Alternatively, the legal significance of Trail Smelter can be trivialized by focussing solely on the political process leading up to the decision to establish the Arbitral Tribunal. In a 1971 article, D. H. Dinwoodie characterized the dispute and its resolution as being dominated by "the quest for political and economic advantage."[32] Having read his fascinating account of the unique political and historical circumstances surrounding the dispute, and the manoeuvering that both the Canadian and U.S. governments went through during the fourteen years leading up to the Tribunal's decision in 1941, one might conclude, as Dinwoodie appears to, that the resolution of these types of disputes is simply a matter of

---

[31] Writing in the early 1970s, Ian Brownlie referred to the "overworked Trail Smelter arbitration, which is actually a rather modest contribution to the jurisprudence — as it was bound to be in view of the restricted terms of reference with which the Tribunal worked": "A Survey of International Customary Rules of Environmental Protection" in L. A. Teclaff and A. E. Utton (eds.), *International Environmental Law* 1 at 2 (New York: Praeger Publishers, 1974). See also G. Handl, "Balancing of Interests and International Liability for the Pollution of International Watercourses: Customary Principles of Law Revisited," 3 Can. Y.B. Int'l L. 156 at 167-8 (1975), in which *Trail Smelter* is referred to as a "much cited, and with regard to its international legal relevance also often overestimated, decision."

[32] Dinwoodie, *supra* note 17, at 234.

power politics between governments more interested in meeting short-term political goals than in discovering long-term solutions to environmental problems.[33] Either way, *Trail Smelter* dwindles into insignificance, an object of little more than historical interest.

To take this approach is misguided. The fact remains that an arbitral decision exists. Decisions are important for more reasons than the obvious appeal that they hold for those with legal training; they represent something more than the mechanical application of rules to a set of facts.[34] Fitzmaurice, in arguing that it is a mistake to place judicial decisions in the same category as the writings of publicists, as "subsidiary means for the determination of rules of law," once asserted that a decision based on a concrete set of circumstances inevitably carries a different kind of weight (either with other decision-makers or with states) than an abstract statement of principle formulated by a scholar.[35] Decision-makers have had to grapple with complex problems and are not able simply to ignore this complexity in formulating their response thereto. If Fitzmaurice is correct, it is ironic that the common use of *Trail Smelter* and the other decisions reduces them to simplistic and abstract statements of principle, thereby discarding that which makes them valuable in the first place.

The alternative to abandonment is to use the available cases quite differently, by analysing how relevant principles were articulated in

33 Dinwoodie states, "[p]olitical and economic influences in both countries heightened the bitterness of this air pollution controversy, prolonged it for a decade, and eventually determined the diplomatic agreement providing for settlement": *ibid.*, 219.

34 For a discussion of the formal status of international judicial and arbitral decisions as sources of international law, see G. G. Fitzmaurice, "Some Problems Regarding the Formal Sources of International Law," in *Symbolae Verzijl*, 153 at 168-73 (The Hague: Martinus Nijhoff, 1958); M. Sorensen, "Les Precedents Judiciares" in *Les Sources du Droit International*, c. 7 (Copenhagen: Einar Munksgaard, 1946). This issue has not received a great deal of attention from scholars during the past three decades. Most are content to cite Art. 38(1)(d) of the statute of the ICJ, according to which judicial decisions constitute "subsidiary means for the determination of rules of law" rather than being considered sources of international law in themselves (this is made subject to Art. 59, which provides that a decision of the Court has binding force only as between the parties to the matter and in respect of that particular case). It is widely acknowledged that the decisions of the ICJ and its predecessor in particular, and those of other international judicial and arbitral bodies to a lesser degree, have significant persuasive value. See, e.g., S. Rosenne, *Practice and Methods of International Law*, 91-92 (London: Oceana Publications, 1984).

35 Fitzmaurice, *ibid.*, 172.

the light of the decision as a whole and of its surrounding circumstances. To begin, the crucial importance of the context of these disputes must be recognized. It is necessary first to distinguish both the factors that lead states to resort to judicial or quasi-judicial dispute settlement mechanisms, and the factors that are taken into account by the decision-maker in resolving the dispute. As *Trail Smelter* illustrates, the two sets of factors are often intertwined. Such an approach would take into account the fact that "the quest for political and economic advantage" plays a major, if not predominant, role in disputes of this kind, but that other factors come into play as well. There is still a significant legal dimension, which is better understood in the light of these other considerations. Analysed in this way, *Trail Smelter* would remain a landmark, although its usefulness is not so much as a "case," but as a "case study," providing a framework for the analysis of interstate disputes with environmental dimensions. The factors mentioned above only begin to scratch the surface of the *Trail Smelter* decisions. Aspects of the dispute that could fruitfully be studied include the early example of valuation of environmental damage and the use of scientific experts.[36]

A "contextualized" analysis is both more accurate and more useful than the standard invocation of abstract principles. While confirming that a case like *Trail Smelter* offers only a shaky precedent even for closely analogous situations and certainly does not provide a general standard that applies broadly in all circumstances, such an analysis fully captures the complexity of the deci-

[36] The Tribunal had to tread carefully in its treatment of the damage described by the expert witnesses. The Tribunal notes that "the number of experiments was still too limited to warrant in all cases so positive conclusions as witnesses were inclined to draw from them" (1938 decision, *supra* note 2, at 194), and goes on to state (at 195): "[a]s is usual in this type of case, though the poor condition of the trees was not controverted, experts were in disagreement as to the cause — witnesses for the United States generally finding the principal cause of injury to be sulphur dioxide fumigations, and witnesses for Canada generally attributing the injury principally to ravages of insects, diseases, winter and summer droughts, unwise methods of logging, and forest and ground fires." The Tribunal adds diplomatically, "[i]t is possible that each side laid somewhat too great emphasis on the causes for which it contended": *ibid.* It goes on to point out that while it had the highest regard for the honesty and sincerity of the witnesses, these may very well have been influenced by the position of the governments that had hired them. As those familiar with current attempts to grapple with the question of environmental damage are all too well aware, the comments of the Tribunal are of more than historic interest.

sion. Moreover, by providing an example of an analytical approach to the legal resolution of interstate environmental disputes, a contextualized reading of the Tribunal's decision represents a potential foundation for a more general analytical framework; whether one agrees with the Tribunal's decision is irrelevant. A "decontextualized" invocation of abstract principles, on the other hand, perpetuates the notion that international environmental law has developed in a virtual vacuum and is made up of little more than narrow conventional regimes and vague principles. This is inaccurate and misleading, and ignores the rich body of material that does, in fact, exist. Perhaps more than any other part of the international legal system, the norms applicable to environmental protection are significantly influenced by historical, economic, and political factors, and must be understood in that context.

An approach that takes into account the overall context of a particular case does not require the abandonment of law in favour of economics, history, or international relations, although it may draw on the work of scholars in all of these fields to provide insight into the kind of factors discussed above. What is being advocated here is legal analysis that incorporates these insights, not merely in order to ride the current wave favouring interdisciplinary or multidisciplinary research, but in order to improve and enrich the legal analysis itself. An international judicial or arbitral decision need not be reduced to its historical, economic, and political context; neither ought it to be entirely abstracted therefrom. There is a middle ground between those who would reduce cases to their facts, and those who would uproot general statements of principle without any regard for the context within which they were articulated. For those who would explore that middle ground, *Trail Smelter* and the other decisions continue to provide a rich vein to be tapped, one that is worthy of serious attention and analysis.

KARIN MICKELSON
Faculty of Law, University of British Columbia

Sommaire

Une relecture de l'*Affaire de la fonderie de Trail*

L'Affaire de la fonderie de Trail *est la décision de droit international la mieux connue et la plus souvent citée. Elle est aussi une source importante du droit international de l'environnement, mais elle fait rarement l'objet d'une analyse approfondie. Outre les préoccupations exprimées par les universitaires au sujet du mauvais emploi qu'on peut faire de l'Affaire de la fonderie de Trail lorsqu'on l'invoque comme précédent, les comptes rendus qui font abstraction des circonstances de l'affaire ratent l'occasion d'utiliser les décisions arbitrales d'une façon plus significative. On comprend mieux les aspects juridiques de la décision lorsqu'on tient compte de facteurs spécifiques tels que ceux relatifs à la preuve du préjudice et à l'établissement de sa cause, à la perception de l'importance des intérêts en jeu des deux côtés de la frontière, à la réciprocité des risques et à l'ensemble des relations bilatérales des États concernés. Une analyse de l'Affaire de la fonderie de Trail qui prend en considération le contexte est à la fois plus exacte et plus utile que l'invocation usuelle de principes abstraits, car elle saisit la complexité de la décision et peut constituer le fondement d'un cadre analytique plus général.*

Proof Beyond a Reasonable Doubt?: Collecting Evidence for the International Criminal Tribunal for the Former Yugoslavia

INTRODUCTION

IN MAY 1993 the United Nations Security Council established the first "international criminal court" since Nuremberg, an international tribunal for the prosecution of persons responsible for serious violations of international humanitarian law in the territory of the former Yugoslavia since 1991 (the "International Criminal Tribunal").[1] Although the Tribunal's jurisdiction is restricted temporally, geographically, and in terms of the offences over which it has jurisdiction, its existence marks a dramatic step forward for the international community.[2] Having overcome many obstacles to establish the International Criminal Tribunal, the international community must now deal with the practical legal issues arising from the operation of such an institution. One of the most important of those issues is what evidentiary standards the Tribunal will apply.

That question was faced by a small group of Canadian military lawyers and military police investigators who, in the spring and

---

* Director, International Law, Department of National Defence, Canada.

---

1 SC Res. 827 (1993) 25 May 1993, UN Doc. S/250593. The Tribunal has since established its official title to be the "International Criminal Tribunal for the Former Yugoslavia."

2 The International Law Commission has been working on the development of a draft Code of Offences against the Peace and Security of Mankind since 1948, and an integral part of that process has been consideration of the establishment of an international criminal court. A detailed review of the history and current status of these initiatives can be found in the *Report of the International Law Commission on the Work of its Forty-Fourth Session, 4 May-24 July 1992*, GAOR 47th Sess., Supp. No. 10, UN Doc. A/47/10.

summer of 1993, were working in the territory of the former Yugoslavia conducting on-site investigations into allegations of war crimes and other violations of international humanitarian law for the United Nations. The "Canadian War Crimes Investigation Team" was collecting evidence before the evidentiary standards of the International Criminal Tribunal had been developed. The team had to analyse existing sources and produce its own procedures for collecting evidence with the goal of maximizing the admissibility of that evidence before a court which, when the team began its activities, did not yet exist.[3] This note will outline the considerations taken into account by the team in undertaking its task and describe three of its missions to the territory of the former Yugoslavia. By the time of publication, the International Criminal Tribunal should have promulgated its own rules of evidence and procedure pursuant to Article 15 of its statute.[4]

BACKGROUND

In the summer of 1992 reports of war-related atrocities from the territory of the former Yugoslavia, in particular Bosnia, were noted with growing concern by the Security Council. In October 1992 in response to the alarming number of reports of such atrocities and the difficulties inherent in determining their validity, the Security Council established a "Commission of Experts" to advise the Secretary-General on substantiated allegations of violations of the Geneva Conventions and other international humanitarian law in the territory of the former Yugoslavia. This Commission of

---

[3] The Canadian War Crimes Investigation Team was a joint activity of the (then) Department of External Affairs and International Trade Canada and the Department of National Defence. The offer to the Commission was made through the initiative of the Office of the Legal Adviser of the Department of External Affairs, Mr. Barry Mawhinney, whose staff provided support throughout this project. For a number of reasons, including the hazards of the military situation in which the investigations were to be conducted, all members of the Canadian War Crimes Investigation Team were military personnel. The team itself consisted of seven people, three lawyers and four military police investigators. At different times throughout its existence the following persons served as members: Lieutenant Colonel Kim Carter, Lieutenant Colonel Dominic McAlea, Major Luc Boutin, Major Bert Herfst, Major Joe Holland, Major Pat Olson, and Major Andrew van Veen (all members of the Office of the Judge Advocate General) and Captain Serge Réné, Warrant Officer Steve Murray-Ford, Sergeant Jean-Luc Lamothe, Petty Officer Jocelyn Ross, Sergeant Ray Roy, and Master-Corporal Tammy McComb (all members of the Security Branch).

[4] The statute of the court can be found annexed to SC Res. 827, *supra* note 1.

Experts, which consisted of a full-time chair and four part-time commissioners,[5] included a Canadian lawyer, Commander William Fenrick.[6]

In December 1992 the Government of Canada offered a team of Canadian military lawyers and military police investigators to assist the Commission of Experts in conducting any on-site investigations. In January 1993 the Commission of Experts accepted that offer and the Canadian War Crimes Investigation Team began, on an as-required basis, to work for the Commission of Experts. At that time, the establishment of an international criminal tribunal was under active discussion, although no statute had been developed,[7] and it was not entirely clear what the precise role of the team would be. Discussions with the Commission's Rapporteur for On-Site Investigations led to two decisions: that strict legal/investigatory standards would be observed at all times, and that a primary goal of the team was to ensure that evidence would be collected in a manner calculated to enhance admissibility before a court, national or international.

Those decisions in retrospect may have seemed anything but revolutionary; however, that was not necessarily the case. Although at that time many allegations of violations of international humanitarian law were being made and information was being collected by many groups, the required analysis and selection necessary to determine that material collected was actually potentially admissible

---

5 The Commission of Experts was established on Oct. 6, 1992, by SC Res. 780 (1992). The original members of the Commission were Professor Frits Kalshoven (first chair, who retired from the Commission in August 1993); Professor Torkel Upsahl (second chair, who died in September 1993); Professor Cherif Bassiouni (third chair); Judge Kéba Mbaye; Commander William Fenrick; and since October 1993 Judge Hanne-Sophie Greve and Professor Christine Cleiren.

6 Commander Fenrick, a Canadian Forces legal officer, served as rapporteur for legal issues and also rapporteur for on-site investigations for the Commission.

7 In February 1993 at least three proposals for an international tribunal, which included draft statutes, were submitted to the Secretary-General. These were: the French Committee of Jurists proposal submitted as an annex to a letter from the Permanent Representative of France to the United Nations addressed to the Secretary-General, UN Doc. S/25266, Feb. 10, 1993; an Italian proposal submitted as an annex to a letter from the Permanent Representative of Italy to the United Nations addressed to the Secretary-General, UN Doc. S/25300, Feb. 17, 1993; and the proposal of the Conference on Security and Cooperation in Europe ("Corell-Turk-Thune proposal") submitted in their report to the Secretary-General, UN Doc. S/25307, Feb. 18, 1993.

evidence was often not being done.[8] It was these two decisions and the procedures developed to implement them which were critical to the team's usefulness in the seven missions in which it participated.[9]

There were two factors that had to be taken into account in developing standards that would enhance the admissibility of evidence: legal norms, and the situation in the territory of the former Yugoslavia. Although legal research and analysis could establish what legal norms a national or international court might follow, only experience in conducting on-site investigations would establish if these standards could be met in the circumstances. The next section will deal with the considerations taken into account in the development of legal norms or standards, and the following section will deal with the actual experience of the team in its on-site investigations.

DEVELOPMENT OF EVIDENTIARY STANDARDS

NUREMBERG AND TOKYO INTERNATIONAL MILITARY TRIBUNALS

The trials of major Axis political and military leaders after the Second World War at Nuremberg and Tokyo on charges of war crimes, crimes against humanity, and crimes against peace was probably the first source at which any future international tribunal, established to try similar offences, would look. There were, however,

---

[8] For a variety of reasons many groups collecting allegations and information may not wish to impose the more rigorous requirements of evidentiary admissibility upon this material. The allegations and information may be collected for political, sociological, and humanitarian (i.e., victim support) reasons. All these may be valid reasons but such allegations and information may not be "translatable" into evidence. For example, an allegation of rape may be used for humanitarian or political reasons even if the perpetrator or perpetrators cannot be identified. Such information, however, would be less useful in terms of a criminal prosecution except, potentially, if the military affiliation of the perpetrators of a number of rapes could be established, leading to the possibility of charges using the doctrine of command responsibility against more senior military commanders. It was the experience of the author that there was, to some degree, an emphasis on the number of allegations or "cases" which could be pointed to rather than on the quality of the information relating to a particular incident. The team quickly began to distinguish between allegations, the sub-category of reliable information, and a further sub-category of potentially admissible evidence.

[9] The Canadian War Crimes Investigation Team worked on three projects in Sarajevo, and on projects in Dubrovnik, Medac, Ovcara, and Packrac Poljana in Croatia.

significant differences between those situations and the current situation in the territory of the former Yugoslavia. The Nuremberg and Tokyo trials were conducted after the termination of hostilities by, essentially, the unconditional surrender of the defendants to the prosecutors. The prosecuting allied powers — France, the Soviet Union, the United Kingdom, and the United States — had the evidence and to some degree the witnesses, and most certainly had the defendants all firmly within their control.[10] The prosecutors benefitted not only from "the Teutonic penchant for meticulous record keeping. . . ."[11] but also from "the scope and significant detail of captured documents . . . numerous documents from the highest level of the Reich government."[12] The prosecution at Nuremberg was very much a document-based prosecution, but the quality, quantity, and nature of those documents was overwhelming.[13] There was no indication that there existed a parallel "Balkan penchant for meticulous record keeping," nor did it appear that a prosecution based on self-generated, irrefutable, incriminating documentation was likely. In addition to these practical differences, the evidentiary rules at Nuremberg also appeared directly to encourage a prosecution that relied more on documentary evidence than on witnesses.

The rules of evidence were embodied in Article 19 of the Charter of the International Military Tribunal which stated:

> The Tribunal shall not be bound by technical rules of evidence. It shall adopt and apply to the greatest possible extent expeditious and non-technical procedures, and shall admit any evidence which it deems to have probative value.[14]

This article was specifically designed to be less technical than rules of evidence applicable to courts of ordinary criminal jurisdiction within states, particularly common law states which, combined with the abundance of documentation, led at Nuremberg to the "document-

---

10 Probably the best and certainly the most recent discussion of the Nuremberg prosecutions can be found in Telford Taylor's *The Anatomy of the Nuremberg Trials* (New York: Alfred A. Knopf, 1992).

11 *Ibid.*, 57.

12 Bradley F. Smith, *Reaching Judgement at Nuremberg* 82 (New York: Basic Books, 1977).

13 *Supra* note 10, at 169-73.

14 *Ibid.*, 651.

heavy" prosecution.[15] This heavy reliance on documentation, although ultimately successful, had its drawbacks in the courtroom presentation, described as follows: "after the first American documentary rush, the shock value of paper evidence had simply worn off. . . . [A]fter the first weeks only living witnesses could occasionally break through the haze and bring the courtroom back to life. . . ."[16]

The Nuremberg precedent was also of limited use because of the role of the defence. At any current war crimes trials it was believed the defence would be given full disclosure and adequate time to prepare. It is highly debatable whether that was the case at Nuremberg, where the defence counsel have been described as "the auxiliaries of the damned. . . ."[17]

The Nuremberg and Tokyo trials, the Canadian team decided, would thus be of limited value. Not only were the circumstances surrounding the trials quite different, but so also was the available evidence and the acceptability of certain evidentiary rules and practices.

EICHMANN TRIAL

A more recent and potentially more procedurally relevant war crimes trial was conducted in Israel in 1960 — the Adolf Eichmann trial. As this trial was successfully prosecuted in a common law system, its more technical evidentiary approach would, the Canadian team felt, be useful.[18]

The majority of evidence at the Eichmann trial, even though much documentation was introduced, was oral testimony of either eye-witnesses or authoritative expert witnesses.[19] Many of the eye-witnesses had actually seen and spoken to the accused and could reliably identify him in court.[20] The prosecution discovered, however, that because of the traumatic nature of the events they had undergone, many potential witnesses had to be carefully

[15] *Supra* note 12, at 87.

[16] *Ibid.*, 88.

[17] *Ibid.*, 83.

[18] A detailed examination of the trial, from the prosecutorial viewpoint, can be found in Gabriel Hausner's *Justice in Jerusalem* (New York: Harper Row, 1966).

[19] *Ibid.*, 326.

[20] *Ibid.*, 327.

selected because of the potential for emotional bias.[21] Indeed, certain witnesses were not called because of their particular biases for or against certain people other than the accused, such as alleged collaborators, which undermined their general credibility. The difficulties faced by the Eichmann prosecutor, Gideon Hausner, seemed similar to the problems that would be faced by any prosecutor in an emotionally charged war crimes trial; therefore his approach to overcoming those problems appeared to the Canadian team to be relevant.

In the Eichmann case, the prosecution adopted a "spotlight of evidence" approach. Aware that in order to prove that the accused had committed the crimes alleged it was also necessary to prove the broader circumstances in which the particular offences occurred, the prosecution consequently had to introduce large numbers of documents but did so as an integral part of the oral testimony.[22] In the first month of trial, fifty prosecution witnesses and 800 documents were introduced.[23] These included hundreds of documents personally signed by Eichmann.[24] Although some affidavit evidence was admitted, it was mainly of an expert nature such as an affidavit from a professor who had done a study for the German courts on the possibility of obtaining a discharge from the SS to avoid "emotionally nervous duties."[25] The introduction of documentary evidence at the Eichmann trial faced more rigorous admissibility standards than those applied at Nuremberg. Eichmann's in-custody statements to Israeli investigators — seventy-six tapes transcribed into six volumes — were held admissible, while his statements given in a less formal, setting to a journalist were not.[26] The demands of admissibility proved in some situations, however, to be beneficial; a report that had not been admitted at Nuremberg, as a result of further investigation into its origin, was admitted in the Eichmann trial.[27]

Although the ready availability of reliable and useful documentary evidence was, in the team's view, something it did not expect to be able to rely upon, the more demanding procedures and eviden-

21 *Ibid.*, 341.
22 *Ibid.*, 329.
23 *Ibid.*, 334.
24 *Ibid.*, 336.
25 *Ibid.*, 337.
26 *Ibid.*, 325.
27 *Ibid.*, 346.

tiary standards of the Eichmann trial, providing a greater protection for the rights of the accused, were a more useful guide to the standards to be currently observed in the collection of evidence of war crimes. The guidance derived from the Eichmann trial was that the prosecution must be able to establish that any statements were given knowingly and voluntarily. This meant that any media interviews or similar material would have to be carefully reviewed before being relied upon. Also many witnesses, even after a number of years, could still be so emotionally involved with the situation and demonstrably biased that their credibility might be questioned. Finally, if people exercising command responsibility are to be tried, solid expert witnesses should be found to establish the historical context, and the overall political and military situation which surrounded the charges they face.

INTERNATIONAL COVENANT ON CIVIL AND POLITICAL RIGHTS

It seemed reasonable to the Canadian team that, as a leading international convention on the protection of legal rights, the provisions of the International Covenant on Civil and Political Rights[28] would, at a minimum, be observed by any international tribunal. The protections under the Convention that could affect how evidence should be collected were:

(1) no one shall be subjected to . . . cruel, inhuman or degrading treatment (Article 7);

(2) all accused persons shall be entitled to trial within a reasonable time or to release. It shall not be the general rule that persons awaiting trial shall be held in custody (Article 9);

(3) in the determination of a criminal charge the accused is entitled to a fair and public hearing by an independent and impartial tribunal established by law (Article 14);

(4) everyone charged with a criminal offence shall be presumed innocent until proven guilty according to law (Article 14);

(5) everyone so charged shall be informed promptly and in detail of the charge against him or her (Article 14);

(6) everyone so charged has the right to be present for the trial, to have legal assistance of his or her choosing and without payment if he or she does not have sufficient funds, and to have adequate time and facilities to prepare a defence (Article 14);

[28] Can. T.S. 1976 No. 47.

(7) everyone so charged has a right to examine witnesses against him or her and to obtain the attendance of witnesses on his or her behalf on the same basis (Article 14); and

(8) everyone so charged has the right not to be compelled to testify against himself or herself or to confess guilt (Article 14).

In light of these provisions of the International Covenant on Civil and Political Rights, the Canadian team drew the following conclusions:

(1) that to be admissible statements would have to be voluntary;

(2) that charges should not be laid until investigations were complete since there was entitlement both to a trial within a reasonable time and detailed information on the charge being faced;

(3) that there would be no trials in absentia;

(4) that subject to the usual security and necessary protection of victims, witnesses, and the public, hearings would be open;

(5) that there would be a full and active defence which would be in a position to challenge the admissibility of evidence;

(6) that oral testimony would be the predominant form of evidence presented, with documentary evidence being introduced through witnesses; and

(7) any flexibility regarding the admissibility of evidence would work equally effectively for the defence as well as the prosecution.

WAR CRIMES TRIAL EXPERIENCE IN CANADA

Current war crimes trials under the Criminal Code of Canada highlighted procedural and evidentiary processes similar to the Eichmann trial. The most useful lesson that could perhaps be drawn from the experience was that having to go back forty-five or fifty years to authenticate documents and find credible, reliable witnesses could be an almost overwhelming task. In addition to such technical difficulties, these trials emphasized the temporal and cultural gaps in knowledge and understanding which the prosecution had to overcome when trying accused in a society far removed from the one in which the offences were committed.

The primary lesson drawn from this source was that evidence must be collected and preserved as soon as possible in its most reliable form to maximize its usefulness regardless of when and where the trial actually takes place. This was highlighted by the

Ontario Court of Appeal decision in the *Finta* case.[29] The *Finta* appeal dealt with several evidentiary issues, which although presented in the guise of hearsay exceptions do in fact have a broader relevance to the issue of when and who should collect evidence and how it can best be preserved. In *Finta*, evidence described as "crucial" to the defence was only available in the form of judicial or quasi-judicial statements given in 1947 by a person who was now dead.[30] By virtue of his position in the brickyard camp of which Mr. Finta was alleged to have been the commandant, the witness, Mr. Imre Dallos, could provide testimony about Mr. Finta's actual role. As Mr. Dallos was a Jewish victim of the oppression going on in Hungary at that time, it was presumed that if he did have any interest it would be adverse to Mr. Finta.[31] Mr. Dallos had provided two official statements to Hungarian officials in 1947. The first was a formal deposition to Hungarian state police in which he had been reminded of his obligation to state the truth to the best of his knowledge and conscience.[32] The second statement had been made in May 1947, in the form of a deposition, before a court, the "People's Tribunal" trying Mr. Finta in absentia for war crimes.[33]

The Ontario Court of Appeal held that the two statements by Mr. Dallos were admissible because they met the general principles of reliability and necessity.[34] The indicia of reliability were that the statements were made on a solemn occasion similar to a court, by a person adverse in interest to the party presenting the evidence who had peculiar means of knowledge (i.e., position and access) and who distinguished generally in his statements between personal knowledge and information obtained from other parties.[35] The fact that the statements were officially recorded and preserved also supported their admissibility.[36]

An analysis of the *Finta* case led the Canadian team to the conclusion that by obtaining formal statements in at least a quasi-judicial form and keeping complete, and as far as possible "offi-

[29] *R. v. Finta*, [1992] 73 C.C.C.(3d) 65 (Ont. C.A.).

[30] *Ibid.*, 98.

[31] *Ibid.*, 98, 203.

[32] *Ibid.*, 193.

[33] *Ibid.*

[34] *Ibid.*, 198.

[35] *Ibid.*, 200.

[36] *Ibid.*

cial," records of those statements, admissibility, even if the witness died or was otherwise unavailable, was greatly enhanced.

PROPOSALS FOR AN INTERNATIONAL CRIMINAL TRIBUNAL

The appendix to the report of the International Law Commission on the work of its forty-fourth session, dealing with the question of an international criminal code and an international criminal court,[37] contains a summary of the major proposals on this subject from the 1926 International Law Association Draft Statute of the International Penal Court to the 1990 Committee of Experts on International Criminal Policy Revised Draft Statute for the Creation of an International Criminal Court (Eighth United Nations Congress on the Prevention of Crime and the Treatment of Offenders). In addition, Part B of that report reviewed in detail the discussion of the establishment of an international criminal court held during the Commission's forty-second, forty-third, and forty-fourth sessions.[38] Much of this discussion focused on the desirability and feasibility of establishing such a court; however, some comments were made regarding procedural requirements.

The ILC's Working Group on International Criminal Jurisdiction took the position that the essential minimum standards of due process for proceedings before such a tribunal are found in the International Covenant on Civil and Political Rights; that there would be no in absentia trials; that national law, particularly in the area of defences, may have some applicability; and that, preferably, an independent prosecutor should be responsible for the investigation, collection, and production at trial of all necessary evidence.[39] The lack of focus on the specifics of procedure meant that little new information was derived from this source though it did confirm some of the conclusions already drawn.

An independent initiative, considered by the Canadian team, was the draft statute for an international tribunal prepared by Professor Cherif Bassiouni.[40] This document was designed to provide for an all-encompassing international criminal court. As with other proposals, however, the actual rules of evidence were left for the inter-

[37] *Supra* note 2, at 199.

[38] *Ibid.*, 148-198.

[39] *Ibid.*, 174-187.

[40] M. Cherif Bassiouni, *Draft Statute International Tribunal*, 2nd ed. (1993) 10 Nouvelles Études Pénales 1.

national tribunal to write. Two sections were of some use. Article 22 contained a subsection on the assistance of counsel which stated that anyone suspected, charged, or being tried before the tribunal should have the right to have competent legal counsel of his or her own choosing at all stages of the proceedings; that such representation should be paid for by the tribunal if the accused was financially unable to do so, and that counsel should have the right to be present at all stages of the proceedings. Another subsection entitled "Evidentiary Questions" provided:

All procedures and methods of securing evidence shall be in accordance with internationally guaranteed human rights, the standards of justice set forth in the Statute, and in the Rules of the Tribunal.

(a) the admissibility of evidence in all proceedings must take into account the lawfulness of the process by which the evidence was obtained, the integrity of the judicial system, the rights of the defense, the interests of the victim, and the interests of the world community.

(b) Evidence obtained directly or indirectly, by illegal means which constitute a gross violation of internationally protected human rights under rules of the Tribunal, shall be inadmissible in court proceedings.

(c) An accused person shall be afforded the opportunity to challenge evidence produced by the prosecution and to present evidence in defense of the charges.

(d) An accused person has the right to be present at all judicial proceedings and to confront and examine the witnesses against him/her.

(e) Counsel for the accused shall be provided with all incriminating evidence available to the prosecution as well as all exculpatory evidence as soon as possible but no later than at the conclusion of the investigation or before adjudication and in reasonable time to prepare the defense.[41]

Although desirable, it seemed unlikely that defence counsel would be available and participating throughout the entire process due to the novelty of the procedure, the geographic diversity of the investigation locations, and the likelihood that a number of accused would decline to participate until actually apprehended and in the custody of the tribunal. This did, however, again highlight that collection of evidence would have to be scrupulously correct and fully respect the rights of the person accused. The proposed restrictions on the admissibility of illegally obtained evidence were ones that the team felt it could live with, but they

41 *Ibid.*, 66, 67.

reminded it that the sources of evidence presented would have to be thoroughly checked to ensure that in the collection of such evidence those sources had observed the relevant evidentiary standards.

INTERNATIONAL TRIBUNALS

A brief review of two existing tribunals was conducted by the Canadian team to see if their procedures could provide any useful guidance. These were the European Court of Justice and the Inter-American Court.[42] It was found that from a strictly evidentiary point of view such tribunals were of little assistance. They are mainly mechanisms for protecting human rights, not courts determining whether an individual is or is not guilty of a specific criminal offence.[43] Although petitions may be received from individuals as well as from governments, judgments are issued and decisions are binding against states.[44] Indeed, the procedures of the European Court of Justice and its Commission were not really set up to deal with a process that is founded on potentially contradictory oral testimony. They are far more efficient in a situation where the facts are clear and it is the law on which they are required to rule.[45] The Inter-American Court faces the same difficulties. Given the different aims and structure of these tribunals it was felt that although their decisions might well be potentially useful substantively, they could not provide a useful procedural model.

PROPOSALS FOR TRIBUNALS APPLICABLE SPECIFICALLY TO THE FORMER YUGOSLAVIA

In February 1993 three proposals were submitted to the United Nations urging the establishment of an international criminal tribunal to try persons accused of committing war crimes and other violations of international humanitarian law in Yugoslavia and including, in varying degrees of detail, draft statutes for such a tribunal.

42 These were selected on the basis that, if they proved useful models, materials about them would be readily available.

43 For a brief summary of the jurisdiction and procedures of these courts, see William A. Schabas, *International Human Rights Law and the Canadian Charter: A Manual for the Practitioner* (Toronto: Carswell, 1991).

44 *Ibid.*, 55.

45 Conversation with Professor Torkel Upsahl, September 1993.

The first such proposal was from France.[46] In January 1992 the French Minister of Foreign Affairs M. Roland Dumas commissioned a committee of French jurists to study the possibility of establishing a judicial mechanism to prosecute those responsible for atrocities while the conflict in the former territory of Yugoslavia was ongoing.[47] The Committee completed its report without including a comprehensive proposal for a statute.[48] The report did, however, include an outline of the provisions which the jurists believed such a statute should contain and the principles which they believed should guide the tribunal in its task.[49]

This proposal again provides no specific direction as to what evidence would be admissible. In the general principles it outlines the Committee provides that the statute of the tribunal should include, with the appropriate drafting changes, the provision on criminal procedure found in paragraphs 2 and 3 of Article 14 of the International Covenant on Civil and Political Rights.[50] It goes on to say that the rules of procedure of the tribunal should ensure respect for basic human rights and accord with the general principles of law of criminal procedure.[51] The report does outline the types of investigatory methods envisioned as necessary in seeking evidence both against and for the accused. These include questioning the accused, questioning victims and witnesses, and character checks and visits to the scene.[52]

The second proposal was from Italy, prepared by a commission of Italian jurists chaired by the Italian Minister of Justice, and consisted of a draft statute for a tribunal to try persons charged with committing war crimes or crimes against humanity in the territory of the former Yugoslavia.[53] Again there is little that would provide guidance in the collection of evidence. Article 11 provides that the tribunal itself shall decide on its own rules (presumably including the rules of evidence), after hearing the submission of the prosecutor. Those rules are to be based on the rights guaranteed by the

[46] *Supra* note 7.
[47] *Ibid.*, 5, 6.
[48] *Ibid.*, 7.
[49] *Ibid.*
[50] *Ibid.*, 33.
[51] *Ibid.*, 33, 67.
[52] *Ibid.*, 29.
[53] *Supra* note 7.

International Covenant on Civil and Political Rights. The proposal also emphasized the requirement to ensure that victims and witnesses are protected against intimidation and pressure.[54]

The paragraph which was of most interest to those involved in the collection of evidence was Article 11, paragraph 1 (h), which stated that every person charged with a crime has the right, "not to have any evidence acquired unlawfully, whether directly or indirectly, used against him."[55] Unfortunately, again no further elaboration on this point was offered.

The third proposal was submitted by Sweden on behalf of the Chairman-in-Office of the Conference on Security and Cooperation in Europe (CSCE).[56] This draft was prepared by the rapporteurs under the CSCE Moscow Human Dimension Mechanism to Bosnia and Herzegovina and Croatia, Ambassador Corell, Mr. Turk and Ms. Thune. This proposal was the most detailed of the three, perhaps because the authors had already spent some time investigating reports of atrocities occurring in Bosnia and Croatia.[57] Section 8.3 of the proposal concentrated on collection of information. The rapporteurs recommended that a committee of experts immediately be convened to propose the necessary rules for the collection of information on suspected war criminals. Although the term "information" was used, rather than "evidence," the authors of the report were careful to point out that there was a difference between collecting information generally and collecting it within the framework of a criminal investigation.[58] Although the rapporteurs make several useful suggestions regarding the collection of information and evidence, such as the need for a central, competent authority to which all such material could be forwarded and the importance of investigations being conducted at an early stage, there were no specific guidelines on what evidence would or would not be admissible.[59] This is not surprising since the proposal suggested that with respect to those charged with war crimes relating to incidents in the territory of the former Yugoslavia, the administration of justice should be based on the application of the Penal Code

---

[54] *Ibid.*, 6, 7, and 14.

[55] *Ibid.*, 7.

[56] *Supra* note 7.

[57] *Ibid.*, 10.

[58] *Ibid.*, 62.

[59] *Ibid.*, 59-61.

of the former Socialist Federal Republic of Yugoslavia.[60] Article 31 of the draft statute also provided that the accused will be guaranteed, without discrimination, the rights in the International Covenant on Civil and Political Rights, as well as the European Convention on Human Rights.[61]

INTERIM REPORT OF THE COMMISSION OF EXPERTS

Contemporaneously with the three proposals for the establishment of an international tribunal, the Interim Report of the Commission of Experts was filed.[62] Although this report was not concerned directly with the establishment of an international tribunal, it did mention that such action would "be consistent with the direction of its work."[63] It also outlined some of the problems it foresaw in the collection of the evidence necessary to substantiate the allegations it was receiving:

Tangible evidence of these violations must, however, be secured in the form of testimonies, written statements, identification of victims, pathological/forensic reports, films, photographs and maps of location and other forms of corroborating evidence. The Commission is aware of the difficulties which may arise in this context: evidence may be destroyed either wilfully or as a result of weather conditions and the victims and witnesses may be either difficult to locate or reluctant to supply information due to intimidation and fear of reprisals.[64]

This highlighted for the team the twin necessities of collecting evidence as soon as possible and of preserving it in its most reliable form.

PERSONAL EXPERIENCE

Among the various other sources drawn upon in order to develop the team's procedures for collecting evidence, the most significant was the personal experience of team members. It was concluded that if the team observed Canadian evidentiary standards then it was likely that any international or other national standard could be

[60] *Ibid.*, 53.

[61] *Ibid.*, 182.

[62] Annex 1 to a letter dated 9 February 1993 from the Secretary-General addressed to the President of the Security Council, United Nations Document S/25274 10 February 1993.

[63] *Ibid.*, 20.

[64] *Ibid.*, 12.

met. Of course, there would have to be some modifications. There was no intention to refer to the rights guaranteed under the Canadian Charter of Rights and Freedoms. Moreover, as the team had no authority or power to arrest or detain, it was highly unlikely that team members would in a position to advise anyone of the right to retain and instruct counsel. A suspect would be advised that any statement was voluntary but could be used as evidence at subsequent proceedings, although there would be some intentional vagueness about the forum in which those proceedings might take place. In addition, some time was spent in refreshing team members' expertise in interviewing victims, particularly victims of rape. Finally, material dealing specifically with potential evidentiary difficulties which might be encountered in the territory of the former Yugoslavia was examined.[65]

STATUTE OF THE TRIBUNAL

On February 22, 1993, the Security Council decided, in resolution 808, that an international criminal tribunal was to be established to try persons accused of serious violations of international humanitarian law in the territory of the former Yugoslavia since January 1991.[66] On May 3, 1993, pursuant to the direction of the Security Council, the Secretary-General reported on the establishment of such a tribunal.[67] In addition to a detailed discussion of the legal basis for the establishment of the International Criminal Tribunal, by decision of the Security Council on the basis of its

65 This material was obtained from a variety of sources. An article by Payam Akavan, a Canadian who had worked for the Corell-Turc-Thune Commission, provided insight into the potential reaction of local authorities to a foreign war crimes investigation: "Punishing War Crimes in the Former Yugoslavia: A Critical Juncture for the New World Order," (1993) 15 Hum. Rts. Q. 31. A conference hosted by the International Centre for Criminal Law Reform and Criminal Justice Policy held in Vancouver from 22 to 26 March 1993, provided access to a number of proposals relating to evidence collection, such as a document entitled "Toward Principles for the International Prosecution of Sexual Atrocities, with Particular Reference to Genocide in Croatia and Bosnia-Herzegovina" distributed by Professor Catharine MacKinnon of the University of Michigan outlining special protective measures for victims of sexual assault, and a discussion paper on pre-trial and trial processes by Christopher A. Amerasinge, Q.C., Senior General Counsel, Crimes Against Humanity and War Crimes Section, Department of Justice, Canada.

66 UN Doc. S/25357 Feb. 22, 1993.

67 Report of the Secretary-General pursuant to paragraph 2 of United Nations Security Council Resolution 808 (1993), UN Doc. S/25704 May 3, 1993.

Chapter VII authority to take measures to maintain or restore international peace and security following a determination of a threat to or breach of the peace or and act of aggression, the report included a draft statute for the Tribunal.[68] This draft statute was adopted by the Security Council on 25 May 1993.[69]

Article 15 of the Statute of the International Criminal Tribunal provided that:

The judges of the International Tribunal shall adopt rules of procedure and evidence for the conduct of the pre-trial phase of the proceedings, trials and appeals, the admission of evidence, the protection of victims and witnesses and other appropriate matters.[70]

The provision was not elaborated upon in the accompanying report of the Secretary-General.[71] Again it was necessary to look at other parts of the statute to find guidance on evidentiary standards.

Part V of the Statute, relating to trial and post-trial proceedings, outlined a number of requirements which provided the skeleton of a procedural code.[72] An analysis of these provisions led the team to few new conclusions. The requirement to have a prima facie case before the indictment is preferred (Article 18(4)) and the possibility of the discovery of a new and potentially decisive fact leading to judicial review of a conviction (Article 26) re-emphasized the need for a comprehensive investigation. The right to examine or have examined witnesses against the accused (Article 21(4)) and to obtain witnesses on the accused's behalf on the same basis as those against the accused confirmed that oral testimony would be of vital importance and any flexibility, such as permitting commission evidence or video testimony from another location, could be used equally well by the defence as the prosecution. An area where new conclusions could be drawn was in regard to the protection of witnesses and victims (Article 22). Clearly the International Criminal Tribunal was prepared to be quite innovative in this regard, which could mean that certain witnesses who were reluctant to testify under normal conditions might now be able to do so if their identities could be protected.

---

[68] *Ibid.*, 7.
[69] *Supra* note 1, at 2.
[70] *Supra* note 67, at 42.
[71] *Ibid.*, 21.
[72] *Ibid.*, 43-47.

EXPERIENCE IN THE TERRITORY OF THE FORMER YUGOSLAVIA

As any prosecutor knows, a great deal can be learned through research and analysis, but nothing can replace experience. That was true in the present situation, where the on-site investigations refined and sharpened the team's conclusions. Although it is not possible to reveal results, the evidentiary lessons learned from the investigations can be discussed.[73]

THE FIRST MISSION

The first visit of the team to the territory of the former Yugoslavia was primarily a reconnaissance trip. An old military saying, ignored at peril, is that time spent on "recce" is seldom wasted. This saying proved very true as the two team members who participated learned invaluable lessons about the reality of collecting evidence on war crimes allegations in the territory of the former Yugoslavia.[74]

The team's task on this mission was to do an analysis of what would be required to complete the first project that the Commission of Experts had asked the team to work on, that is, an investigation into the deaths of persons found in a mass grave site in Ovcara, near Vukovar in the eastern part of Croatia. This was clearly a complex project and in addition to the two Canadian team members, the Commission's Special Rapporteur for On-Site Investigations and two members of Physicians for Human Rights, a group who were to provide the forensic/medical expertise during the proposed exhumation, also participated in the reconnaissance trip.[75]

The trip took place in early March 1993. Its main purpose was to assess the requirements of the large project which the Commission

73 The terms of the co-operative services agreement between the Government of Canada and the United Nations under which the services of the Canadian War Crimes Investigation Team were provided prohibits the disclosure of such information without the permission of the United Nations. As certain investigations were still outstanding at the time of writing, such permission could not be granted.

74 The two members were the author and Captain Serge Réné.

75 Physicians for Human Rights is a United States based non-governmental organization which has extensive experience in the exhumation and identification of the bodies of victims of human rights abuses. Their most notable work to date in identifying the bodies of a number of people who "disappeared" during the period of military dictatorship in Argentina. More recently they have been involved in substantiating human rights abuses during the Anfal campaign in Iraqi Kurdistan.

of Experts had asked the team to undertake. A secondary purpose was to do preliminary work on the investigation by interviewing some witnesses to the circumstances surrounding the disappearance of approximately 250 patients from the hospital in Vukovar in November 1991. There was some reason to believe that those who "disappeared" might be connected with the 200-230 bodies estimated to be in the mass grave approximately ten kilometres away.

On arrival in Zagreb the team met with the Vukovar "municipal council in exile" and was provided with the names of a number of potential witnesses. Originally there had been some concern that witnesses would be inaccessible or unwilling to speak. In fact, in Zagreb the reverse proved true and the greatest concern was not the unavailability of witnesses, but how to assess their credibility. To some degree this was because in this particular situation the persons who had disappeared were almost all Croatians. The majority of other Croatians who had lived in the Vukovar area had apparently left when it became part of the self-designated Republic of Serbian Kryenia. Many had moved to Zagreb and had kept in touch through the "municipal government in exile." Although there was no reason to be suspicious, the fact that witnesses were being provided by "the authorities" reinforced the team's commitment to seeking, wherever practicable, independent corroboration of testimonial evidence, particularly physical evidence which could be independently analysed.

The team interviewed several witnesses and learned a number of lessons. As expected, some witnesses were still so emotionally traumatized by their experiences that the reliability of their recollections would be subject to challenge. On the other hand there were other witnesses, typically younger people with presumably more resilience, who proved to be comprehensive, precise, and relatively non-emotional in their interviews. They were the kind of witnesses a prosecutor would be confident in putting on the stand to testify.

Although the process of conducting interviews through translators is slow and laborious, it became clear that in most cases two or three interviews of each witness would be desirable. In the first instance, this was necessary in order to understand the context. The prosecutors of Second World War war crimes found it necessary to "educate" themselves, the judge, and the jury about historical and political circumstances in order to understand how atrocities could and did happen. The Canadian team, too, had to allow witnesses to provide useful, even if not entirely relevant, information. When talking to witnesses who have undergone traumatic experiences, it is simply not possible to draw them directly to a point and ask them to tell you only about that point. It may be of no relevance to the case that a particular individual was killed, but both as a basic courtesy as well as necessary precursor it would be necessary to listen to this in a first interview. Thus, a second, more structured interview was often necessary.

A third interview was also a definite possibility if a formal, "sworn" statement was desirable in order to maximize admissibility of a statement where a witness would subsequently be unavailable to testify. Video-recorded, formal, "sworn" testimony would be as reliable a standard as the team would be able to achieve. Some concern was expressed about the potential for contradiction if multiple interviews were recorded; however, the team believed that this was significantly less than the disadvantage from not collecting and preserving the evidence in its most reliable form.

The initial interviews also highlighted the need for competent, impartial and strong interpreters as the average interview took three to four hours. To enhance the formality of the statements being taken, inquiries were made with local judicial authorities as to how the statements of witnesses "under oath" were obtained in Croatia. According to the Assistant Minister of Foreign Affairs, an oath was not always required, but a judge had to warn a witness before testifying that he or she must tell the truth, and must provide all the information he or she had about the offence, and that failure to do this was a criminal offence.[76] The team therefore offered witnesses the opportunity to provide "sworn" testimony using a formulation which closely resembled that provided for in Croatian criminal law.

It was clearly established during this initial trip that potential witnesses faced imminent threats of death in many cases. These threats made interviewing very difficult since the presence of members of the team conducting interviews would be generally known to neighbours and local authorities, some of whom might well be implicated as perpetrators. As a result, it was suggested that initial contacts should be made through less obvious means using already existing, independent organizations. Although such threats were not a concern when interviewing people in Zagreb who had

[76] This information was provided in a letter from Dr. Ivan Simonovic, Assistant Minister of Foreign Affairs, dated Mar. 10, 1993.

information regarding the disappearance of the Croatians from the Vukovar hospital, it was a problem in the case of people still in the Vukovar area. It was felt that the process of taking formal "sworn" videoed statements, which it could be argued would be admissible if the witness was subsequently unavailable due to death or other serious injury, might reduce any rationale for carrying out death threats. However, on the basis of the information that it received and its own observations, the team was not always convinced that a "rationale" guided behaviour in such cases.

After conducting the initial interviews in Zagreb, the team proceeded to the Daruvar area in the United Nations Protected Area West. Although reports had been received about three alleged mass grave sites located in the Packrac Poljana area, a decision was made not to visit them during this phase of the trip in order to avoid alerting local authorities to the team's knowledge of these reports. The preservation of any evidence at the sites was dependent upon it not being apparent that the team knew about them, and given the prevalence of such reports, it was not possible for the United Nations to mount a twenty-four-hour-a-day guard over all such sites.

The issue of "local authorities" was confronted by the team in a rather direct fashion while in the Vukovar area. The area was effectively controlled by the authorities of the self-designated Republic of Serbian Kryenia. Although the team had been encouraged in Zagreb to investigate fully and actively in the Vukovar area, local authorities appeared unmoved by the enthusiasms of Zagreb, which wielded no practical authority in the area. It was necessary to approach these authorities directly to seek their independent concurrence to any activities proposed. During this trip the team's intention was only to visit the site to record its location on film and video in order to assist in providing potentially independent corroboration of statements that had been recorded in Zagreb and to assess the logistic requirements of the proposed exhumation. The team was introduced to the local military commander, who, after protracted discussions, approved the visit to the mass grave site. He provided the services of the local Minister of Propaganda and made his consent conditional on that of the local municipal council, which eventually also approved the visit.

In the company of local United Nations civil and police authorities, the team proceeded to the mass grave site. However, on departure from the site the team encountered representatives of the local police/militia force who apparently had not been informed that permission had been given for the visit and filming. This force insisted that everyone accompany them to the local police station where the group was detained for several hours until the local police/militia decided that they too granted their permission for the visit to the site. The experience highlighted the very practical difficulties that were going to be faced in trying to conduct an investigation without the authority to compel co-operation.

On its return from the reconnaissance trip the team was in an excellent position to develop certain standard operating procedures relating to the questioning of witnesses and also a series of general principles relating to the collection of evidence. Those brief and simple rules, based on both the background research and analysis and the experiences of the reconnaissance trip, were encapsulated as follows:

(1) The collection of evidence will be based strictly on legal considerations.

(2) All evidence that appears relevant will be collected.

(3) Responsibility for offences will be followed as far up the chain of command as the evidence leads.

(4) The presumption of innocence is always applicable.

(5) Evidence will be collected in accordance with the rights guaranteed in relevant international instruments such as the International Covenant on Civil and Political Rights.

(6) Evidence will be preserved in its most reliable form.

(7) Whenever practicable statements will be obtained in the form of depositions, orally, on videotape, and in writing.

(8) Independent analysis of physical and documentary evidence will be sought.

(9) Whenever practicable independent corroboration of testimonial evidence will be sought.

(10) Procedures in accordance with, or similar to, national provisions will be used whenever practicable.

THE SECOND MISSION

The team's second mission, in July 1993, was to Sarajevo to work on three projects for the Commission of Experts. The first was a trial project on the mass rape issue, the second an in-depth investigation of a particular shelling incident, and the third a general military-legal analysis of the battle of Sarajevo. This mission, which was conducted under even more challenging and restrictive conditions, confirmed much of the previous experience.

Although welcomed by the Bosnian government, the team discovered that despite good will a certain basic level of mobility and freedom was required to collect useful evidence. While in Sarajevo, the team at all times travelled in United Nations armoured personnel carriers in accordance with United Nations safety directives. This meant that each investigation took far longer than it would under normal circumstances.

The two military policewomen on the team, both of whom had experience in dealing with victims of rape in Canada, worked exclusively on the rape project, which was one of the primary reasons for dispatching the team to Sarajevo. In a visit to Sarajevo in April 1993, the Commission of Experts had asked about the number of women who had been raped in Bosnia during the conflict. Although the total number provided was much higher, the Bosnian War Crimes Commission stated it had eighty-nine files dealing specifically with cases of rape.

An initial difficulty was in obtaining the files, due in part to the severe travel restrictions imposed on people in Sarajevo, but also because of a lack of understanding on the part of the Bosnians that the team actually wanted to see files, and not just extrapolate numbers or listen to and record second-hand anecdotal accounts. Other "commissions" that had visited Sarajevo had apparently had not wanted actually to see the files. Eventually 105 files were provided, although they seemed to have rather slim contents. Since the material was in Bosnian, and in the difficult conditions of Sarajevo translation took time, the team chose to collect and copy material without waiting to have it translated so that relevance could be determined.

The team then used the four interpreters provided by the United Nations as translators to begin translating the files. After some discussion a standard translation terminology was developed and these terms were recorded to assist future prosecutors in deciding whether or not they felt comfortable relying on these translations. The priority for translation was based on information obtained from the Bosnian War Crimes Commission on which victims they could identify as still being in Sarajevo and who would be willing to be interviewed by the team. The Bosnian War Crimes Commission believed that there were fifteen victims still in Sarajevo, but could not say at that time how many were willing to be interviewed.

Before leaving Canada the team had developed a simple data base for organizing any material that might be received.[77] The files received from the Bosnian War Crimes Commission had already been entered in their own database which identified 113 incidents, 126 victims, 73 witnesses, and 252 suspects. As it was translated the material was entered in the Canadian team's database. A first review of the files indicated that approximately 80 of the 105 obtained did relate to allegations of rape. However, the files consisted of varying types of documentation. At worst they comprised only a newspaper article or a copy of an official government statement; at best they contained copies of handwritten statements by victims. It quickly became clear that the files did not contain sufficient evidence to support prima facie cases.

The team also attempted to obtain interviews with the handful of victims identified as still being in Sarajevo. Unfortunately, due to difficulties with shelling, the victims' unwillingness to be transported in United Nations vehicles, shortages of gasoline for any other vehicles, and time constraints, it did not prove possible to conduct those interviews. Local contacts with the Kosevo hospital and the Chief of Obstetrics and Gynecology did prove useful, however, in arranging an interview with a young rape victim whose case was not already in the files. This interview, conducted with the consent of the victim and her doctor and through an interpreter raised certain other practical difficulties. The victim stated that she had been raped by a group of Serbian soldiers in her mother's presence, as had her mother been raped in her presence. When asked what she meant by the term "rape," she became both very emotional and confused. This reaction highlighted the problems that will be faced by a prosecutor in getting such victims to testify in a manner consistent with their own cultural norms but sufficient to establish the essential elements of an offence. The team's view was that, if culturally acceptable, anatomically correct dolls would be a useful tool in future interviews. As a result of the lessons learned during the rape investigation, the team was able to provide substantial input into the production of a set of guidelines for the conduct of inquiries and interviews for the Commission of Experts.

The project to prepare a legal/military study of the battle of Sarajevo understandably did not rely predominantly on local resources. From an evidentiary point of view perhaps the most

---

77 This database was developed for the team by Lieutenant-Colonel Jim Rycroft of the Office of the Judge Advocate General.

valuable lesson was the importance of establishing command responsibility and the strong likelihood that this could be done. Applied to the two other investigations, this meant that even if, in cases of rape or shelling, the individual perpetrator could not be identified, under certain circumstances the responsibility of a particular commander for those actions could be established and that commander could be identified. In the case of the rape investigation, this procedure led to the grouping of allegations by time and location in an attempt to determine whether a correlation with particular military or para-military organizations could be proven.

THE THIRD MISSION

The final mission of the Canadian War Crimes Investigation Team took place in October and November 1993. The main projects were the exhumation stage of the investigations into the deaths of persons buried at mass grave sites in Ovcara and Packrac Poljana. The team was to provide the legal/investigatory support during that phase. The project was very ambitious, involving in addition to the six members of the Canadian team, approximately twenty members of Physicians for Human Rights and fifty members of a Dutch engineering unit who provided the necessary logistical and technical support. All these personnel operated under the authority of the Commission's Rapporteur for On-Site Investigations, who had spent considerable time in the preceding months obtaining national, and the always important local, authority to conduct the exhumations.

The project at Ovcara was the largest and had the aim of exhuming all the bodies found there and conducting autopsies on a number of them to determine conclusively their manner of death. Unfortunately, the "local authorities' consent" issue precluded this action. Although written permission and promises of co-operation had been obtained from what appeared to be the appropriate authorities in Knin, the capital of the self-designated Serbian Republic of Kryenia, who had themselves spoken with their local, "subordinate" authorities, the local authorities again took matters into their own hands. Within twenty-four hours of the group arriving at the site and before any exhumation had actually commenced, local authorities indicated that the project did not have their consent and that they would take "all necessary means" to prevent it. Consultation with local United Nations authorities made it clear that it was at best impractical to try and continue in the face of such opposition, and at worst it was very dangerous. The decision was made to postpone the exhumation. The site at Ovcara today remains under United Nations guard but no exhumation has yet been commenced.

The second project, at Packrac Poljana, was much more successful from the team's perspective. On the basis of a very brief and circumspect investigation by United Nations Civilian Police in the area it was determined that there was a strong possibility that a mass grave site was located in a farmer's field along a tree line paralleling a road. Estimates of the numbers buried there ranged up to 1700 people. The victims were alleged to be ethnic Serbs who were victims of the Croatian majority in the area. The intention at Packrac was to do a preliminary excavation in order to determine the scale of the site.

Two team members, together with representatives of Physicians for Human Rights and the Dutch support unit, which included the Dutch War Graves Registration Unit, began preliminary work with the consent of the local authorities. It soon became apparent that a number of large filled-in trenches, which had originally been suspected to be mass graves, did not in fact contain any bodies. After painstaking and careful sample excavations across two of the trenches no bodies were found, nor was there anything to suggest that the trenches had been used to bury anything. Concurrently several smaller grave sites containing multiple bodies were discovered by the head of the Dutch War Graves Registration Unit in another part of the field. The efforts of the Physicians for Human Rights then concentrated on these graves and eventually nineteen bodies were exhumed.

The lack of bodies in the other twenty-three trenches created its own evidentiary issue — how can it be proved that in fact no bodies are buried where people suspect that they are buried — particularly when local lore and legend has already identified a site as containing the bodies of thousands of martyrs to a cause? This was an important consideration since one of the purposes of collecting evidence is to establish what did not happen as well as what did. The on-site leader of the team, Major Pat Olson, decided that he would have to take the necessary steps to establish a negative — what was not buried in those trenches. To do this he created an international ad hoc verification team consisting of himself, a member of the Dutch War Graves Registration Unit, an American and Argentinian member of Physicians for Human Rights, and an officer from the

Jordanian troops guarding the site. He then had a total of seventy-six holes excavated in the trenches. The ad hoc verification team then checked each hole to establish that no bodies were or had been buried there. Once this was established, and after the excavations had been videoed, they were then filled. This procedure proved to be useful not only to satisfy the standards the team had established but also to respond to a letter, received several months after the investigation, accusing the project of being biased, having failed to find the 1700 bodies buried in that location.

The final project in which the Canadian team became involved was Medac. This involvement was not planned but occurred because of the timing of the team's mission and the unexpected early termination of the Ovcara project. Medac is in United Nations Protected Area South in Croatia and in September 1993 had been in the path of a Croatian push to regain an area under Kryenian Serb control. As a result of military activities a number of civilians were killed and villages were destroyed. The closest United Nations unit, a Canadian one, conducted an investigation into the incident within a very short time of its occurrence and in addition to identifying witnesses made extensive photographic and video records of what had happened. Two members of the team, a lawyer and a military police investigator, liaised with the Canadian unit and obtained all the information in their possession. In addition, the two team members conducted their own investigation. As a result of the early and comprehensive independent record made by the Canadian unit, the ability to interview witnesses in a timely fashion, the availability of independent witnesses to some events, and the non-interference in the investigation by local authorities, a very satisfactory report was produced, identifying exactly what violations of international humanitarian law had occurred, who was responsible, and most importantly what could be proven by evidence likely to be admissible before the International Criminal Tribunal.

CONCLUSION

The missions conducted by the Canadian War Crimes Investigation Team, in particular the three projects in Sarajevo, were a valuable test of whether any investigations could be conducted under "combat" conditions, and whether the evidence produced would meet the standards for admissibility which the team believed an international tribunal would apply. The answer to both was a cautious yes — cautious because the desired results would require the dedication of far more resources than were available and for a far longer period of time — but it was a definite yes. The evidence collected by the team will be reviewed and turned over to the prosecutor for the International Criminal Tribunal. It is hoped that, due to the initial legal analysis and the procedures applied during collection, most of what has been collected will be admissible.

KIM CARTER
Department of National Defence, Canada

Sommaire

La récherche de la preuve pour le Tribunal international chargé de juger les crimes de guerre commis sur la territoire de l'ex-Yougoslavie: peut-on établir la preuve hors de tout doute raisonnable?

Cet article examine les règles de preuve qui ont été élaborées par la Commission d'enquête canadienne sur les crimes de guerre. Cette Commission se composait de juristes de l'armée et d'enquêteurs de la police militaire. En 1993, elle effectua une série d'enquêtes sur place pour le compte des Nations Unies, relativement aux crimes de guerre commis sur le territoire de l'ex-Yougoslavie. Afin de maximiser l'admissibilité de la preuve recueillie devant le Tribunal international chargé de juger les crimes de guerre à La Haye, la Commission a dû, en l'absence de normes clairement applicables, élaborer ses propres règles de preuve en s'appuyant sur une analyse juridique de documents pertinents ainsi que sur ses expériences en territoire ex-Yougoslave.

The St. Pierre and Miquelon
Maritime Boundary Case and the
Relevance of Ancient Treaties

INTRODUCTION

THE DECISION OF JUNE 10, 1992, of the Court of Arbitration in the case concerning the delimitation of the maritime areas between Canada and France off the coasts of St. Pierre and Miquelon and Newfoundland is of particular interest from the standpoint of the Court's rejection of one of the equitable factors raised by Canada and argued extensively by both countries. This factor concerns the restrictions or stipulations contained in the eighteenth century treaties of cession governing the status of St. Pierre and Miquelon.

Canada argued that these restrictions created a special legal regime that had to be taken into account by the Court in reaching an equitable solution to the maritime boundary delimitation. Conversely, France argued that the treaties were extinguished and, even if they were still in force, had no bearing on the delimitation. While the majority of the Court (Jimenez de Arechaga, Arangio-Ruiz, and Schachter) did not decide that the restrictions were no longer in force, it concluded that they were ineffective because of the "contemporary law of the sea" and "the legal rights of France under contemporary international law." There is little indication in the

* Although the writer was a legal adviser to the arbitration team representing Canada, this note was written in his personal capacity and does not necessarily represent the views of the Canadian government. The author expresses appreciation for the views of Professor Luigi Condorelli, Director, Public International Law, Faculty of Law, University of Geneva, on an earlier version of this paper. Professor Condorelli, one of Canada's Counsel in the arbitration, made the main ancient treaty arguments for Canada during the oral proceedings. The assistance of M. E. J. Cooper on technical aspects of the Court's decision is also gratefully acknowledged.

Court's reasoning of the rather extensive Canadian and French arguments in both the written and oral pleadings. Of the two dissenting judges only Judge Gotlieb attached significance to the ancient treaties.[1] Judge Weil, although agreeing with the majority decision on "many points,"[2] does not mention them specifically.

Since the continuing relevancy of the restrictions has been raised periodically over the past two centuries, first by Great Britain in discussions with the French and in this century in the Canadian parliament, and is of more than historic interest to many Canadians, especially in Atlantic Canada, a fuller account of these arguments, made for the first time to any court, may be useful.[3]

First, it might be noted that Canada had maintained during the arbitration that St. Pierre and Miquelon was entitled to a maritime belt of twelve nautical miles in the seaward area in dispute where the boundary had not been delimited under the 1972 Canada-France fishing agreement.[4] Apart from a claim to the continental shelf beyond 200 miles, the French claim based on equidistance comprised 14,773 square nautical miles (including the twelve-mile territorial sea and the area allocated under the 1972 delimitation). The Court accepted the calculation of its geographical expert that the size of the area relevant for checking the results of the delimitation, as identified by the Court, was approximately 63,000 square nautical miles. It awarded 59,434 square nautical miles to Canada and 3,617 square nautical miles to St. Pierre and Miquelon, and considered that these allocations met the requirements of the test of proportionality as an aspect of equity. Thus, France received an

---

[1] Decision of the Court of Arbitration of June 10, 1992; dissenting opinion, para. 60.

[2] Dissenting opinion, para. 1.

[3] France argued that international tribunals had demonstrated reluctance to consider the historical aspects of a dispute, citing the *Minquiers and Ecrehos* case, [1953] ICJ Rep. 47, and the *Western Sahara* case, [1975] ICJ Rep. 12, in support of this thesis. Canada pointed out that both of these cases demonstrated the contrary.

[4] Agreement between Canada and France on their Mutual Fishing Relations, Mar. 27, 1972, Can. T.S. 1979, No. 37, Art. 8 and annex. The boundary established in 1972 between the coast of St. Pierre and Miquelon and the mainland coast of Newfoundland (a distance of approximately nine nautical miles) was a compromise between the French "mid-channel line" and the strict equidistance line proposed by Canada. The "mid-channel line" can be traced to the "middle of the channel" fishery limit specified in the British and French Declarations accompanying the Treaty of Versailles, Sept. 3, 1783. See Canadian Memorial, paras. 253-57.

exclusive economic zone twelve miles in width on the seaward side of the islands beyond its twelve-mile territorial sea, and a corridor of exclusive economic zone 10.5 nautical miles in width running a distance of some 200 nautical miles south from the islands.[5]

ORIGIN OF THE RESTRICTIONS

While the conquest of Canada by the British was confirmed by the Treaty of Paris of 1763, the French had insisted on at least a landing place for their fishing fleets. Accordingly, Article 6 of the Treaty provided:

The King of Great Britain cedes the Islands of St. Pierre and Miquelon, in full right to His Most Christian Majesty, to serve as a shelter to the French fishermen: and His said Most Christian Majesty engages not to fortify the said Islands; to erect no buildings upon them, but merely for the convenience of the fishery; and to keep upon them a guard of fifty men only for the police.[6]

In 1778 France joined in support of the American War of Independence and that year the islands were captured by a British fleet. They were restored to France by Article 4 of the Treaty of Versailles of 1783:

His Majesty the King of Great Britain is maintained in His Right to the Island of Newfoundland, and the adjacent Islands, as the whole were assured to Him by the Thirteenth Article of the Treaty of Utrecht; excepting the islands of St. Pierre and Miquelon, which are ceded in full right, by the present Treaty, to His Most Christian Majesty.[7]

On the same day that the Treaty was signed, "Declarations" containing the restrictions were exchanged on behalf of the two Sovereigns. The British Declaration stated:

The King of Great Britain, in ceding the Islands of St. Pierre and Miquelon to France, regards them as ceded for the purpose of serving as a real shelter to the French fishermen, and in full confidence that these possessions will not become an object of jealousy between the two nations[.]

5 The general implications of the decision are discussed in Hornby and Hughes, "L'affaire de la délimitation maritime Canada/France," 30 Can. Y.B. Int'l L. 3-41 (1992).

6 Treaty of Paris, Feb. 10, 1763, Art. 6.

7 Treaty of Versailles, Sept. 3, 1783. The Treaty of Utrecht, Mar. 31/Apr. 11, 1713, had provided in Art. 13 that "[t]he island called Newfoundland, with the adjacent islands, shall from this time forward belong of right wholly to Britain . . . ." St. Pierre and Miquelon fell within the description of "adjacent islands."

The French Counter-Declaration stated:

The King of Great Britain undoubtedly places too much confidence in the uprightness of His Majesty's intentions, not to rely upon His constant attention to prevent the Islands of St. Pierre and Miquelon from becoming an object of jealousy between the two nations.

Obviously the islands have developed far beyond the stage of a "shelter," and the restriction on their becoming an "object of jealousy" would be looked at quite differently in some respects today. These changes were recognized in the Canadian Memorial's observation that "[t]he issues today are not what they were in past centuries. . . ."[8] Nevertheless, the question was one of degree. The French claim to a vast area off the small islands, if upheld, could in Canada's view have rendered the stipulations meaningless for all practical purposes. Thus, Canada argued that the French claim was incompatible with the original grant:

First, with respect to the fisheries, the spirit of the original grant is wholly at odds with the idea that any portion of the offshore banks of North America would become the exclusive or privileged domain of the French fleet to the prejudice of Great Britain and its successors. Secondly, with respect to all other matters, it was a cession for the sole purpose of serving as a "shelter" for French fishermen, and the nature of the grant therefore excludes any claim of the comprehensive character implied by the modern regimes of the continental shelf and the exclusive economic zone.[9]

Moreover, the "object of jealousy" provision was, in Canada's view, of an evolving nature (the same could be said of the shelter provision):

It constitutes a recognition, through a conventional norm of continuing legal relevance, that the anomalous and unique situation of the islands constitutes a "special circumstance" which must not be permitted to jeopardize the vital interests of the coastal state . . . the breadth and generality of the concept allows its practical impact to evolve in order to extend to new issues as they develop over the years. But the basic principle remains constant: the "special situation" of these islands, as it was put in the 1972 Fisheries Agreement, must never become a threat to the fundamental interests of the coastal state. . . .[10]

---

8 Canadian Memorial, para. 435.

9 *Ibid.*, para 438. It is of interest that Art. 2 of the 1972 Fisheries Agreement provided for reciprocal fishing rights for the nationals of both Canada and France in the event of a modification of their territorial sea and fishing zones. Canada argued that it was envisaged that the French extension would not exceed 12 miles.

10 *Canadian Counter-Memorial,* paras. 537-38.

ARGUMENTS OF THE PARTIES

Canada argued that an equitable solution should be based, in part, on the following reasoning. From the standpoint of maritime boundary delimitation, equity would be applied differently in the case of islands depending on whether they were independent or dependent.[11] According to this view, equity countenances a greater extension of the maritime belt of independent islands than of distant islands that are dependencies of a mainland state. Such a differentiation is recognized on the basis that an island state requires for its security a larger exclusive maritime area than a small fragment clearly detached from the territory of its home state. This position is all the more so when the fragment of the state is nestled against the metropolitan territory of another state. This approach was seen to be particularly applicable to St. Pierre and Miquelon, whose special status provided a specific treaty foundation for this equitable criterion. The result would be to reduce substantially the extensive maritime belt of jurisdiction claimed by France.

France provided a somewhat contradictory historical and legal analysis in support of the contention that the ancient treaties had been extinguished. It is not proposed to discuss the various aspects of these arguments exhaustively, but only to provide the main lines of the French argument.[12]

France asserted that the restrictions had been terminated when that country joined the United States in the war against Great Britain in 1778, and by the outbreak of war in 1793, and had not been renewed by the Treaty of Amiens, 1802, and the two treaties of Paris of 1814 and 1815. All of these treaties were concluded following wars between France and Great Britain during which the islands were captured by British forces.[13] In France's view, this had the effect of extinguishing the 1783 Treaty of Versailles, since the doctrine of the British government at the time was that it "knows of

---

11 See generally Canadian Memorial, para. 304 et seq.

12 Discussion of the treaties is to be found in: Canadian Memorial, paras. 216-34, 430-38; Canadian Counter-Memorial, paras. 164-69, 182, 533-38; Transcript of the 1991 Hearing: Aug. 1, 308-53; Aug. 6, 503-15; Aug. 7, 654-79; Aug. 13, 985-88; Aug. 14, 1070-84; Aug. 19, 1168-79. France has declined to make its written pleadings public. The oral hearings were open to the public.

13 They were captured by a British fleet in 1793, restored to France in 1802 (Arts. 3 and 15 of the Treaty of Amiens), reoccupied by the British on the reopening of hostilities, and restored by the treaties of Paris of May 30, 1815 (Art. 8) and Nov. 20, 1815 (Art. 11).

no exception to the rule that all treaties are put to an end by a subsequent war between the same parties."[14] France contended, therefore, that the 1783 Treaty could have been revived only by an express stipulation.

France contended also that the restitution of the colonies was made on a different basis from that of the fisheries: that is, Great Britain restored, as stipulated in Article 8 of the 1814 Treaty, the "colonies which were possessed by France on the 1st of January 1792." Moreover, according to France, the 1783 Treaty was not renewed, since it was not specifically mentioned. What the Treaty accomplished was to delink French sovereignty and fishing rights while restoring only the latter. The final result, in France's view, was the unconditional restoration of French sovereignty over St. Pierre and Miquelon, with the restrictions losing all significance.

In support of this reasoning, France pointed to a discontinuity in the juridical regimes relating to the fisheries treaties. In its view, the regimes that prevailed during the period 1713-1783 (Treaty of Utrecht to the Treaty of Versailles) and that were restored in 1814 were replaced by the 1904 and 1972 treaties. As for the restrictions, their objective was limited to the fishery on the "French Shore," which had nothing to do with the boundary delimitation.

In response, it was first of all essential for Canada to set the record straight regarding Lord Bathurst's note to John Quincy Adams, an extract from which is quoted in the French Counter-Memorial as to the effect of war on treaties. J. B. Moore has pointed out, after referring to the same note:

Nevertheless, his lordship in the same note declared: "The Treaty of 1783, like many others contained provisions of different characters — some in their own nature revocable, and others of a temporary character." And it may be assumed that if the treaty had been composed wholly of provisions deemed by his lordship to be of the former character, there would have been no controversy between him and Mr. Adams.[15]

The French also relied on the nineteenth century opinions of the British law officers of the Crown in support of the extinction of the 1783 Treaty. In fact, the three opinions cited were those of a single law officer, Sir John Dodson, and did not concern St. Pierre and

---

[14] British note of Oct. 30, 1815, quoted in A. D. McNair, *Law of Treaties*, 699 (1961). The note was addressed by Lord Bathurst to John Quincy Adams, the United States representative in London.

[15] J. B. Moore, *A Digest of International Law*, vol. 5, 383 (1906).

Miquelon but different provisions of that Treaty.[16] Other opinions reported in McNair — before and after the Dodson opinions — were all to the contrary and were not discussed in France's pleadings. In 1818, the Queen's Advocate, Christopher Robinson, gave such an opinion.[17] In 1856, the law officers (Harding, Cockburn, and Bethell) and again in 1872 (Coleridge, Jessel, and Travers Twiss) considered that Article 4 of the 1783 Treaty, which ceded the islands to France "en toute propriété," created property rights that could not be exercised to the prejudice of Great Britain. The 1872 opinion stated:

That we are of opinion, having regard to the terms of the British Declaration of the 3rd September, 1783, that the French Counter-Declaration of the same day . . . is equivalent to a pledge or engagement on the part of the French Government to use the islands of St. Pierre and Miquelon for the purpose for which they were ceded, and to prevent them from becoming an object of jealousy between the two nations, and that it would be a breach of such engagement for the French Government to dispose of those islands to a third Power if Great Britain objected to it.[18]

Canada pointed out that the effect of war on treaties was more complicated than stated in the French Counter-Memorial. For example, in the leading case of *Society for the Propagation of the Gospel in Foreign Parts* v. *New Haven and Wheeler*,[19] the Supreme Court of the United States had rejected the argument that certain stipulations in Article 9 of the Treaty of 1794 between the United States and Great Britain (the Jay Treaty) had not survived the war, in view of Article 28, which provided that the first ten articles were permanent. It held, therefore, that British citizens continued to enjoy the right to hold and enjoy real property in the United States. In 1830, the Court of Chancery in Great Britain reached a similar result regarding Article 9 of the 1794 Treaty in *Sutton* v. *Sutton*.[20]

The jurisprudence as reflected in *Society* and *Sutton* accords with the view of Clive Parry, the editor of the highly respected *Consolidated Treaty Series*, who comments as follows on the 1783 Treaty:

The French text and English Translation of this, the definitive Treaty of Versailles, are here taken from Jenkinson, Treaties, Vol. III, P.334, the text

16 The opinions are reprinted in McNair, *supra* note 14, at 523-26.

17 *Ibid.*, 523.

18 *Ibid.*, 450-51.

19 (1823), 21 U.S. 464. Extracted in M. O. Hudson, *Cases on International Law*, 910 (2nd ed., 1936).

20 (1830), 1 Russ. and My. 666.

including, in particular, the Declaration and Counter-Declaration, respecting the North Atlantic Fisheries, etc. which along with arts 4,5 and 6, were renewed by the Treaty of 30 May 1814. The Treaty, which was ratified by Great Britain on 18 September 1783, is printed in many other places. . . .[21]

Canada argued also that the treaties of Amiens (1802) and of Paris (1814 and 1815) restored to France the fishery off Canada's Atlantic coast as it had existed in 1792. The restrictions in the ancient treaties were therefore not impaired by these subsequent treaties. Moreover, they were not affected by the 1904 Convention Respecting Newfoundland and West and Central Africa.[22] Its purpose was to resolve issues relating to the fishery provisions of the eighteenth century treaties, particularly privileges to catch fish and to dry them in certain parts of the coast of Newfoundland known as the "French Shore" or "Treaty Shore."

The Agreement between Canada and France on their Mutual Fishing Relations,[23] which came into force on March 27, 1972, superseded all previous treaty provisions relating to fishing by French nationals off the Atlantic coast of Canada.[24] In return, for renunciation of these privileges, France was provided with continued fishing access in Canadian waters as well as rights in what became, in 1977, Canada's extended 200-mile fishing zone. No mention was made of the restrictions in the ancient treaties. It was Canada's position throughout the arbitration that the 1972 Agreement was concerned only with fishery matters and with the delimitation of the maritime boundary between Newfoundland and St. Pierre and Miquelon as provided in Article 8.

INTERPRETATION OF THE RESTRICTIONS IN LATER PRACTICE

As might be expected, the arguments of both Canada and France were often interwoven with historical (and sometimes political) factors. For example, Canada pointed out that the "object of jealousy" provision was first invoked in 1785 when the Governor of

[21] Art. 4 ceded St. Pierre and Miquelon to France, Art. 5 adjusted the limits of the "French Shore," and Art. 6 confirmed the French fishery in the Gulf of St. Lawrence in conformity with Art. 5 of the Treaty of Paris, 1763: *Consolidated Treaty Series*, ed. and annotated by Clive Parry, vol. 48 (1781-83), 487 (1969).

[22] Convention Respecting Newfoundland and West and Central Africa, London, Apr. 8, 1904, ratified Dec. 8, 1904: Brit. T.S. 1905, No. 5.

[23] *Supra* note 4.

[24] Art. 1.

Newfoundland indicated that he planned to revoke the authorization that he had given in 1783 to the inhabitants of St. Pierre and Miquelon to cut wood on Newfoundland to meet their needs.[25] On learning of this, the French Minister of Marine de Castries wrote to Foreign Minister Vergennes with a view to obtaining his intervention with the British.

Some seventy years later, the restrictions were in the minds of the British authorities when there was concern about fortifications being built on the islands. The undertaking not to fortify was specified in the 1763 Treaty of Paris, but was dropped in the Declarations accompanying the 1783 Treaty of Versailles. Nevertheless, the Law Officers of the Crown in an opinion of July 26, 1856, were of the view that France was required "to abstain from so fortifying the islands as that they shall not become an object of jealousy between the two nations." Subsequently, after the Governor of Newfoundland had made an inspection and report concerning the fortifications, the law officers advised that:

these fortifications do not amount to any infraction of the treaties existing between this Country and France, or present any just cause of complaint on the part of Her Majesty's Government.[26]

In 1894 the British expressed concern about fishermen from St. Pierre and Miquelon carrying on small boat fishing on the "Treaty Shore" of Newfoundland. Before taking the matter up with the French, an opinion was sought from the British international jurist W. Hall. In his view:

St. Pierre and Miquelon were, however, only ceded to the French for a narrow and strictly-defined purpose, which, to my mind, is wholly inconsistent with the use which it is now intended to make of them . . . they were to serve as a purely temporary shelter . . . the word is incapable of bearing the interpretation that the islands are to be treated as a Colony, with fishery interests of its own, with fishery Regulations different from

25 Charles de la Morandière, *Histoire de la pêche française de la morue dans l'amérique septentrionale*, vol. II, 81 (1962). It is significant that, in spite of extensive efforts by Canadian researchers, no evidence was found that might have brought the survival of the restrictions into question. This research included access to originals or copies of original documents in the British, Canadian, and French archives. In addition, contemporary accounts of the negotiations concerning the ancient treaties and numerous scholarly works were examined. A substantial collection of this documentation is to be found in the annexes to the written pleadings or filed separately with the Court. These documents are referred to in the Canadian Counter-Memorial.

26 McNair, *supra* note 14, at 491.

those of the fishermen of France, with an independent share in the privileges of the "French Shore."[27]

The French Minister of Foreign Affairs, G. Hanotaux, in a response dated July 31, 1894 stated:

It seems to us the effect of these texts, subject to the formally-stated exceptions, is that France is free to exercise, in respect of these islands all the attributes of sovereignty included in a cession "in full right" ("en toute propriété").[28]

Hall had been consulted further on the Hanotaux letter:

Cession "en toute propriété" conveys full rights of sovereignty within the territory ceded. . . . In the instances of St. Pierre and Miquelon, it is not to be questioned that France owns all sovereign powers within the territory, except in so far as they are limited by the engagement that the islands shall not become an "objet de jalousie."

He added that the restrictions upon the use of the islands were such as to make them a shelter ("abri") in the narrowest sense of the word.[29]

The term "object of jealousy" was not defined in the 1783 Declarations and doubt as to its exact meaning has never been resolved. Nevertheless, this ambiguity did not deter Great Britain from taking up matters of concern with France. Thus, in 1907 the Colonial Office wrote to the Foreign Office that closer links seemed to be developing between St. Pierre and Miquelon and the United States. It urged that, in any discussions with France, Great Britain should make clear that any transfer to a foreign power without British consent would be "a virtual infringement of the Treaty obligations of France to this country." It was also suggested that the word "retrocession" should be used instead of "cession" as more consistent with the nature of the British claim to reversion of

[27] Memorandum by W. Hall received Mar. 12, 1894 (London: Public Record Office), Foreign Office 414, Confidential Prints, North America, vol. 123, 91-92. A copy is available in the National Archives of Canada, Ottawa, Microfilm No. B-2407. Also reproduced in Canadian Memorial, para. 230.

[28] Canadian Memorial, para. 231.

[29] Canadian Memorial, para. 231. See memorandum by W. Hall received Aug. 18, 1894 (London: Public Record Office), Foreign Office 414, Confidential Prints, North America, vol. 124, 13-14. A copy is available in the National Archives of Canada, Ottawa, Microfilm No. B-2407. It is reprinted in the annexes to the Canadian Memorial, Vol. II, Annex N-18.

ownership of the islands.[30] The matter was taken up with the French ambassador, who responded with a strict interpretation but did not deny that the Treaty was still in force:

France considered herself completely at liberty to deal with the islands as she pleased, in the event of her wishing to part with them, as no restriction was imposed on her liberty of action by the terms of cession.[31]

In support of the thesis that the ancient treaties were extinct, France relied on statements by a number of senior Canadian officials made before and after the conclusion of the 1972 Fisheries Agreement. One of these statements was made by the head of the Canadian delegation during negotiations with French officials in July 1964. The negotiations concerned only the fisheries provisions of the earlier treaties, and there is no indication in the Canadian minutes that the stipulations affecting St. Pierre and Miquelon were discussed.[32] The minutes do confirm that one issue was whether the French continued to enjoy a right to fish in the Gulf of St. Lawrence under Article 6 of the 1783 Treaty.[33]

France also asserted that, when the negotiations that led to the 1972 Fisheries Agreement commenced in 1971, Canada's view, as confirmed by the response of Prime Minister Trudeau to a question in the House of Commons on April 26, 1972, was that the ancient treaties were no longer in force:

It is hard to have a unique opinion on the Treaty of Paris of 1763. Various results flowed from it for various parts of the country. I can only say that it is an historic fact, that we in Quebec are prepared to live with it and I hope that you in Newfoundland are also prepared to live with it.[34]

---

30 Canadian Counter-Memorial, para. 168. H. Bertram Cox to the Foreign Office, Jan. 17, 1907 (London: Public Record Office), Colonial Office 880, vol. 19, 28. A copy is available in National Archives of Canada, Ottawa, Microfilm No. B-3955.

31 Transcript of the Hearing, Aug. 7, 1991, 669.

32 Law of the Sea Talks with France, Second Round, Paris, July 20-21, 1964, annex 42 to the Canadian Memorial submitted to the Arbitral Tribunal in "Dispute Concerning Filleting within the Gulf of St. Lawrence," Arbitral Tribunal Established by Agreement of Oct. 23, 1985. The decision of the Tribunal, of July 17, 1986, is known as the La Bretagne Award.

33 The La Bretagne Tribunal accepted the Canadian minutes of the 1964 and 1971 meetings. There seems to be no French record of the meetings: La Bretagne Award, para. 57.

34 H.C. *Debates*, Apr. 26, 1972, at 1646-47.

It is difficult to conclude from this ambiguous reply that the Prime Minister was expressing the view that the 1763 Treaty was extinct. Rather he was saying that it was "an historic fact." It is of interest that Prime Minister Bennett was explicit in responding to a question in the House of Commons on April 30, 1931, concerning press reports that St. Pierre and Miquelon might be acquired by the United States. He stated:

The government of Canada has no knowledge of the matter to which the honourable gentleman has directed attention. Doubtless he is aware that under the treaty by which these islands were relinquished to France there are provisions as to the uses to which they may be put and as to the buildings which may be erected thereon.[35]

THE DISPOSITION OF THE ANCIENT TREATIES ARGUMENT

The Court's discussion of the restrictions is remarkably brief.[36] After referring to the cessionary Article 4 and the restrictions contained in the declarations accompanying the 1783 Treaty of Versailles, the Court stated in paragraph 55:

In the Court's view, even assuming that these stipulations are still in force, they cannot reasonably be construed as limiting the rights of France to maritime areas under the contemporary law of the sea. The reference to the islands as a "real shelter" for French fishermen has not been construed by Great Britain, or by Canada in later years, as limiting the right of Saint Pierre and Miquelon to be a base for fishing activities by its inhabitants. The stipulation that the islands will not become "an object of jealousy" between the Parties cannot plausibly be interpreted to mean that the legal rights of France under contemporary international law must be denied because of "jealousy."

Thus the Court did not decide that the restrictions were no longer in force. Instead of pursuing that doubtful path, the Court bypassed it by a convenient judicial mechanism: that is, it concluded that, "even assuming that these stipulations are still in force" they were ineffective because of the "contemporary law of the sea" and "the legal rights of France under contemporary international law."

35 H.C. *Debates*, Apr. 30, 1931, at 1122. This reminder of the restrictions was no doubt reassuring to the Canadian public. Little more than a generation later, the continental shelf issue would come to the fore, to be followed a few years later by the maritime boundary crisis. Ultimately the unprecedented strains in Canada-France relations emphasized the need for rationalized management of the cod fishery and made arbitration of the maritime boundary inevitable.

36 Decision of the Arbitral Tribunal, June 10, 1992, paras. 53-55.

From the standpoint of Canada-France relations the approach adopted by the Court — insofar as resolution of the central issue was concerned — was astute. The settlement of the boundary and the consequent elimination of French overfishing was imperative if those relations were to be stabilized. Experience had shown this beyond doubt during the period of excessive overfishing in the 1980s.[37] Fortunately France accepted the Court's decision, which was far more favourable to Canada than to France.[38]

At the same time it is interesting to note that, although it was based on other equitable criteria, in practical terms the Court's decision to establish a twelve-mile exclusive economic zone and a corridor for St. Pierre and Miquelon did not exceed in total what might have been within the reasonable expectations of Canada if the ancient treaties argument had been given specific weight in the decision. Is it possible, therefore, that the arguments exerted some unconscious influence on the mind of the Court in its consideration of concepts of equity and justice?

Canada's ability to manage the fishery would have been considerably diminished if it had lost control over a substantially larger area of the disputed zone. This is shown by the depletion of the stocks within Canada's fishery zone by foreign overfishing on the nose and tail of the Grand Banks beyond Canada's 200-mile fishing zone. At the same time, the award of an access corridor to St. Pierre and Miquelon removed France's apprehensions that Canada was seeking to regulate shipping through its fishery zone. In sum, the Court

37 In Judge Weil's view: "Any conflict between Canada and France is particularly lamentable and I welcome the fact that this Court should have seen fit to contribute to put French-Canadian relations back on the road to friendship and co-operation": dissenting opinion, para. 52.

38 The dissatisfaction of the inhabitants of St. Pierre and Miquelon with the decision was underlined in January 1993 by the sending of two fishing vessels to fish illegally in Canadian waters. The vessels with politicians and journalists on board were quickly seized by Canadian fishing patrol officers and taken to St. John's. The demonstration was mounted to protest the sharp cut in Canadian fishery quotas given to St. Pierre and Miquelon pursuant to the 1972 Canada-France Fisheries Agreement. The quota reductions were necessitated by the decline in fish stocks (cod) that has been experienced in recent years off Canada's Atlantic coast. See *Ottawa Citizen*, Jan. 8, 9, 15, and 16, 1993. This decline led to the announcement by Fisheries Minister Ross Reid in late August 1993 of closure of most of what remained of the cod fishery following the closure in 1992 of cod fishing off eastern Newfoundland and quota cuts imposed to save fish stocks devastated by overfishing and climate change. It was estimated that the two closures would cost the jobs of 42,000 people: *Ottawa Citizen*, Sept. 1, 1993.

did what it could to resolve basic points of serious conflict between the parties.

The only inkling as to the precise reasoning for the rejection of the ancient treaties argument is to be found in the last two sentences of paragraph 55 quoted above. But Canada had readily conceded in its pleading that it, as well as Great Britain in later years, had not construed the 1783 stipulation of a "real shelter" for French fishermen as limiting the right of St. Pierre and Miquelon to be a base for fishing activities by its inhabitants. Nor did Canada argue that the "object of jealousy" provision should be construed to deny France its legal rights under contemporary international law. Canada's essential argument was that any determination of the maritime boundary that ignored or minimized the restrictions would not produce an equitable result.[39] In other words, while the Canadian position was that St. Pierre and Miquelon was entitled to a twelve-mile maritime zone, the Court could, of course, decide the boundary, but an equitable result necessitated taking the restrictions into account.

The 1982 Law of the Sea Convention seems to contain no provision that would have prevented the Court from taking such an approach. Article 311(2) provides:

This convention shall not alter the rights and obligations of States Parties which arise from other agreements compatible with this Convention and which do not affect the enjoyment by other States Parties of their rights or the performance of their obligations under this Convention.

The restrictions would not affect the enjoyment by other states of their rights or the performance of their obligations under the Convention. Moreover, there are numerous delimitation agreements between states, including those involving islands, in which variations in the distances specified in the Convention have been effected, and which are fully compatible with its principles.[40] While those agreements are, of course, distinguishable from the ancient treaties involving St. Pierre and Miquelon, there would seem to be

---

39 In the *Tunisia-Libya Continental Shelf* case, [1982] ICJ Rep. 18, Judge Jimenez de Arechaga stated in a separate opinion (para. 24): "Equity here is nothing other than the taking into account of a complex of historical and geographical circumstances the consideration of which does not diminish justice but, on the contrary, enriches it." See also Jimenez de Arechaga, "The Conception of Equity in Maritime Delimitation," in *International Law at the Time of its Codification, Essays in Honour of Roberto Ago* (Milan: Guiffre, 1987).

40 Canadian Memorial, paras. 324-47.

no reason why a state could not commit itself to refrain from claiming extensive areas of the sea off its coasts. The Canadian position was consistent with this reasoning.

THE IMPLICATIONS OF THE ANCIENT TREATIES ARGUMENT FOR FUTURE MARITIME BOUNDARY DELIMITATIONS

The Court's disposal of the ancient treaties argument may be useful in future arbitrations in clarifying to some extent the exact nature of some of the considerations that qualify as "relevant circumstances." Canada had categorized the unique situation of the islands as a "special circumstance" and a "relevant circumstance," but the Court did not make use of such terminology.[41] In fact there is a great deal of uncertainty as to the components of a special, or relevant, circumstance. Thus in the *Tunisia-Libya* case, the Court noted that Tunisia's definition of "relevant circumstances" was less restrictive than Libya's since, "in appropriate cases economic and historical particularities as well as geological and geographical factors may be included as relevant circumstances."[42] In accepting the Tunisian submission, the Court considered geographical factors and historical and political circumstances, including the location of the land frontier, and a *modus vivendi* that had been approved by the colonial powers for sponge fishing. The significance of the Court's approach has been emphasized by Jimenez de Arechaga:

[I]t is not true that equity comes into play only after applying equidistance in order to correct its results. There is no such succession in time and the process must be a simultaneous one. All the relevant circumstances are to be considered and balanced: they are to be thrown together into the crucible and their interaction will yield the correct equitable solution of each individual case.[43]

As a result, to conclude, as the Court did, that the restrictions in the ancient treaties had been overtaken for purposes of maritime boundary delimitation by the contemporary law of the sea and by international law entailed their exclusion from the "crucible" of determining both relevant circumstances and an equitable result.

---

41 Judge Gotlieb used the word "relevant" in referring to St. Pierre and Miquelon: dissenting opinion, para. 60.

42 *Tunisia-Libya* case, *supra* note 39, at 76-77.

43 See essay by Jimenez de Arechaga, *supra* note 39, at 232.

280 The Canadian Yearbook of International Law 1993

THE IMPLICATIONS FOR CANADA-FRANCE RELATIONS

At the same time, the decision leaves virtually intact the basic position of Canada — that is, that the restrictions in the ancient treaties have never been extinguished. This is significant, since the Canadian public perception of the restrictions is so embedded that it will not easily be dislodged and could come to the fore in various future contexts. For example, Canada's relations with France have occasionally been strained by visits of French warships to the islands, sometimes on the eve of negotiations aimed at the resolution of the boundary issue.[44]

It is possible also that the stipulations might again be revived if proposals should arise, as they have in the past, that involve a change of status for the islands. It seems clear that the inhabitants are not in favour of some form of integration with Canada. Nor does independence hold attraction, given the lack of economic resources other than the fishery and tourism. Proposals for annexation by a third state would excite concern, as happened earlier this century when there were indications that the United States might be interested in acquiring the islands. While such a development is unlikely, it cannot be permanently foreclosed. In such an event, the restrictions in the ancient treaties could be a factor in the discussions that would inevitably take place between Canada and France, and that would undoubtedly be facilitated by the extensive documentation compiled during the arbitration.

CHARLES V. COLE*
of the New Brunswick and Ontario Bars

---

[44] Canada's concern about a naval presence is reflected in Art. 7 of the 1972 Canada-France Fisheries Agreement, which provides that "[t]he French patrol vessel which usually accompanies the French fishing fleet may continue to exercise its functions of assistance in the Gulf of St. Lawrence."

Sommaire

L'affaire de la délimitation des espaces maritimes au large de Saint-
Pierre-et-Miquelon et la pertinence des anciens traités

*Devant le Tribunal d'arbitrage chargé de procéder à la délimitation des
espaces maritimes entre le Canada et la France, on a présenté des arguments
approfondis concernant les restrictions qui ont été imposées par le traité de
Paris de 1763 et le traité de Versailles de 1783 à la cession des îles St-Pierre-
et-Miquelon à la France par la Grande-Bretagne. Le Canada a soutenu que
le Tribunal devait tenir compte du régime juridique spécial qui avait été créé
s'il voulait parvenir à un résultat équitable. Le Canada a affirmé que seules
les dispositions des traités portant sur la pêche avaient été remplacées et que,
bien qu'on considérerait très différemment aujourd'hui, à certains égards, le
fait que ces îles avaient été cédées afin de servir d'abri pour les pêcheurs
français et le fait que la France avait l'obligation d'éviter qu'elles ne
deviennent un objet de jalousie entre les deux nations, ces faits n'étaient pas
sans rapport avec le différend. De son côté, la France a soutenu que les traités
étaient expirés et que même s'ils étaient en vigueur ils n'avaient aucun effet
sur la délimitation. De manière significative, le Tribunal n'a pas déclaré
qu'ils n'étaient plus en vigueur, mais a statué qu'ils étaient sans effet en
raison "du droit la mer contemporain" et des "droits que le droit international contemporain reconnaît à la France." Dans ce commentaire, l'auteur
analyse la décision qui, bien que manifestement fondée sur d'autres critères
équitables, a accordé au Canada une aussi grande partie de l'espace maritime en litige que ce à quoi on se serait attendu si le Tribunal avait donné
effet aux restrictions. En outre, l'auteur commente brièvement les conséquences de la décision sur les relations entre la France et le Canada.*

The United Nations Decade of International Law: A Canadian Perspective

INTRODUCTION

THE UNITED NATIONS DECADE OF International Law was born out of the recognition by member states of the United Nations that international law has a critical role to play in the shaping of the changing world order. Coinciding with the ninetieth anniversary of the 1899 Hague Peace Conference, and with its final days marking the one-hundredth anniversary, the Decade also serves as a reminder of the disappointments of that Peace Conference, the 1907 Hague Peace Conference, and subsequent efforts to engender respect for international law.[1] The Decade arrives at a time when the role and structure of the United Nations is being re-evaluated, and during a period when Canada is living in the aftermath of constitutional deliberations, probing how, if at all, its internal structure might be arranged to cope with domestic demands and the constraints of an increasingly interdependent international order. The scope of material within the ambit of the Decade of International Law is potentially enormous, and the challenges for Canada and the international law community within Canada immense.

Within this note, the authors briefly chronicle the progress of the United Nations Decade of International Law[2] at the global level and

---

[1] Jason Reiskind, then Deputy Director, Legal Operations, External Affairs and International Trade Canada, address at the Faculty of Law, University of Toronto, Apr. 5, 1990.

[2] For an earlier and more expansive introduction to the Decade generally, see R. St. J. Macdonald, "The United Nations Decade of International Law," 28 Can. Y.B. Int'l L. 417 (1990); Jeremy Thomas, "The United Nations Decade of International Law — Insights into an Asian Perspective of International Law," 14 Dalhousie L.J. 266 (1991); and Brian Ruhe and Bruce Torrie, "The United Nations Decade of International Law 1990-1999," 48 The Advocate 757 (1990); and Special Issue, 3 Leiden J. Int'l L. (1990).

examine the results of a continuing enterprise they initiated in 1991 that was aimed at the development of a Canadian perspective on the Decade. The rudimentary framework and many substantive elements of a Canadian perspective have already emerged from this endeavour and constitute an important popular contribution to the Decade. These ideas, as well as the official Canadian response, are documented and assessed within the context of current and changing international approaches to the Decade. The authors hope by means of this record to provoke and encourage further thought about the Decade and a Canadian contribution to it.

THE UNITED NATIONS DEBATE ON THE DECADE

On November 17, 1989, the forty-fifth session of the United Nations General Assembly declared the period 1990-99 the United Nations Decade of International Law.[3] Resolution 44/23, adopted by consensus, outlined four purposes for the Decade:

(1) The promotion of the acceptance of and respect for the principles of international law;

(2) The promotion of means and methods for the peaceful settlement of disputes between states, including resort to and full respect for the International Court of Justice;

(3) The encouragement of the progressive development of international law and its codification; and

(4) The encouragement of the teaching, study, dissemination, and wider appreciation of international law.

The resolution also proposed that the possibility of convening a third international peace conference at the end of the Decade be discussed. Resolution 44/23 was both the culmination of efforts by states of the non-aligned movement, and the springboard for work by the United Nations and the international community.

Pursuant to Resolution 44/23, Budislav Vukas of the former Yugoslavia was appointed chairman of a working group on the United Nations Decade of International Law. The working group was to canvass member states and appropriate international and non-governmental organizations in order to develop a program for the Decade that would be generally acceptable to those involved.

---

[3] See G/A Res. 44/23, UN G.A. Official Records, 44th Session, Supp. No. 49, UN Doc. A/44/49 (1989).

The Vukas Report[4] was presented to the Sixth (Legal) Committee of the General Assembly and debated between November 13 and November 15, 1990. Delegates expressed strongest support for the proposals surrounding the peaceful settlement of disputes and the encouragement of the teaching, study, and dissemination of international law. The other proposals received relatively little attention. The reception for the report was generally favourable, with many states expressing an interest in actively participating in the program.

In 1992, the Sixth Committee reconvened the working group under the chairmanship of Alfonso Maria Dastis of Spain to consider the report of the Secretary General on the Decade,[5] to discuss the implementation of activities for the first term (1990-92), and to exchange views on the nature of the program for the next two-year term.[6] The report of the working group was the foundation for the debates of the Sixth Committee in November 1992[7] that led to the adoption of draft resolution A/C.6/47/L.16. Those debates and the documents examined therein provide an insight into the likely shape of the Decade over the next few years, and into the development of the Decade's activities to this point. Within this broader context, the Canadian perspectives explored below may be more clearly assessed.

Before we consider the substance of the debates, however, a brief review of the critical documents may be helpful. The report of the Secretary-General was prompted by the invitation of the General Assembly on December 9, 1991, in Resolution 46/53 to all states, international organizations, and institutions to provide, update, or supplement information on activities undertaken to implement the programme for the Decade outlined in the annex to General Assembly Resolution 45/40, adopted on November 28, 1990. The Secretary-General was asked to submit a progress report on the basis of the information submitted, and to supplement it with "new information on the activities of the United Nations relevant to the progressive development of international law and its codification"[8]

---

4 UN Doc. A/C.6/45/L.5 (1990).

5 Aug. 26, 1992, UN Doc. A/47/384 (1992) and also A/47/384/Add.1, Sept. 23, 1992.

6 See the 10 November 1992 Report of the Working Group, at UN Doc. A/C.6/47/L.12 (1992).

7 See Summary Records of the sessions at UN Docs. A/C.6/47/ SR.34-37.

8 UN Doc. A/47/384 (1992) at 5.

over the previous year. The report presents an exhaustive summary of the activities undertaken by United Nations agencies, member states, and other international and national governmental and non-governmental organizations, grouping the submissions under the general headings of the four principles articulated by the General Assembly for the Decade in Resolution 44/23.

Of particular note is the summary of states' suggestions for the Sixth Committee's consideration that concern the progressive development of international law and its codification.[9] This summary includes the proposal by Australia that the topic of "the environment in times of armed conflict" be examined and further developed in the framework of the Decade, and the proposal by Iran that a week-long congress on public international law be held during the next term of the Decade to "take some practical measures to uphold the aims of the Decade."[10] Both topic areas attracted significant attention and comment during the November 1992 debates.

The report of the working group, upon which the Sixth Committee debates centred, was the product of fourteen meetings between September 28 and November 6, 1992. The report concluded that the nature of the program for the next two-year term "should be kept in general terms along the lines of the 1990-92 programme with necessary adjustments."[11] The focal points for discussion evidenced in the report include:

(1) the difficulties in encouraging acceptance of the compulsory jurisdiction of the International Court of Justice;

(2) the potential for wider use of the Permanent Court of Arbitration for the settlement of disputes between states as well as between states and international organizations;

(3) the suggestion that international law concerning the fight against organized crime and international terrorism was "ripe

---

9 *Ibid.*, 18-20. It is also interesting to note that none of the replies received by the Secretary-General touched on any suggestions for consideration by the Special Committee on the Charter of the United Nations and on the Strengthening of the Role of the Organization: *ibid*, 20, para. 56. See also Virginia Morris and M. Christiane Bouloyannis, "The Work of the Sixth Committee at the Forty-Seventh Session of the UN General Assembly," 87 AJIL 306 at 311 (1993) for a brief review of the history of the Special Committee and most recent responses to its work.

10 *Supra* note 8, at 19.

11 UN Doc. A/C.6/47/L.12 at 2.

for progressive development and codification" through the establishment of an international criminal court; and

(4) the suitability of international environmental protection and further development of humanitarian law as topics for particularized effort during the Decade.

The report also declared that the working group considered the section of the program of activities for the Decade devoted to the "encouragement of the teaching, study, dissemination and wider appreciation of international law" to be "particularly important": "There was a widespread view that the popularization of international law was at the heart of the United Nations Decade of International Law and that the activities relating to it should be encouraged."[12]

The working group also emphasized the importance of teaching international law at all levels of education, and the suggestion was made that "a comprehensive international law course be elaborated under the auspices of the United Nations, with the participation of eminent specialists in various fields of international law."[13] Various delegations also made reference to a number of round-table discussions that had been organized on the initiative of a group of members of the Sixth Committee, in co-operation with non-governmental organizations such as the American Society of International Law and the World Federalist movement. "The view was expressed that such meetings, which provided the opportunity for an interesting exchange of views, should be continued in the same informal manner which had ensured their success."[14]

Finally, the working group canvassed organizational aspects of the Decade. The establishment of national committees to implement the program for the Decade was seen as a "useful means of coordinating activities at the national level." However, the suggestion that non-governmental organizations might establish a committee on the Decade that would include members of the Sixth Committee, the International Law Commission, the United Nations Secretariat, and judges of the International Court of Justice was met with "serious doubts." In contrast, the idea of a five-day congress on public international law attracted widespread support and detailed scrutiny.

[12] *Ibid.*, 5.

[13] *Ibid.*

[14] *Ibid.*, 6.

It was suggested that the conference could be linked both to the Decade and to the fiftieth anniversary of the United Nations, but that sufficient time for proper preparation was essential. Funding would have to be met through existing resources as well as through voluntary funds. Further aspects of the organizational dimensions of the conference are canvassed in the debates noted below, but it is significant that the congress appears in the report to be the potential big-ticket, attention-grabbing event for the Decade; in this light, the report also notes that reservations were expressed even in the working group as to whether such a congress "could address all the issues before the Decade in a responsible, non-politicized manner."[15]

In introducing the report of the working group, Alfonso Maria Dastis noted that the annex to the report contained the program for the activities for 1993-94, a program very similar to that of the first term. He commented that the similarity was "due firstly to the delicate balance with which the program for the first term had fixed the goals to be achieved in each one of the objectives of the Decade. Secondly, the program for the first term, because of its very nature, could not have been completed in two years."[16]

The deliberations reviewed the intense level of activity and interest at state and sub-state levels in the work of the Decade, with particular focus on the efforts to educate about and popularize international law. The representative of the Republic of Korea aptly summarized the views of many when he stated that

generating public support for national integration into the global legal framework would promote greater acceptance of and respect for international law. Such support could be developed most effectively through the encouragement of the teaching, study, dissemination and wider appreciation of international law, which is a fundamental component of the Decade.[17]

The other topics receiving the most attention and discussion included the proposal for an international congress on public international law, and the further development of international environmental law, particularly during times of armed conflict. These areas, and other undercurrents in the debate, are summarized below.

15 *Ibid.*, 7.

16 UN Doc. A/C.6/47/SR.34 at 2.

17 Statement by Mr. Jong Moo Choi, Delegate of the Republic of Korea, to the Sixth Committee of the Forty-Seventh Session of the General Assembly on Agenda Item 128: Press Release, Permanent Mission of the Republic of Korea to the United Nations, New York, Nov. 16, 1992.

The representative from Iran, Saeid Mirazaee Yengejeh, noted a significant difference from the program for the first term of the Decade. Where the first term had focused primarily on seeking the views of governments and international organizations on how best to achieve the goals of the Decade, the new program allocated a specific activity to the Sixth Committee itself — the drafting of a preliminary operational plan for a congress on public international law in 1994 or 1995. The representative noted that the proposal had enjoyed broad support in the working group "partly because it was felt that the program of activities for the Decade should not be limited to the Member States of the United Nations, but should also involve relevant institutions, scholars and interested individuals in every country, in order to promote the objectives of the Decade throughout the world."[18] He commented further on the importance of such a conference both for the success of the Decade and for the United Nations more generally:

The proposed congress, if held, would be the first of its kind in the history of the United Nations, and in our opinion, it would serve a variety of purposes: it would stress promotion of the acceptance of and respect for the principles of international law; it would assess the achievements of and prospects for the future progressive development of international law and its codification; and, it would contribute immensely to the study, dissemination and teaching of international law. Ways and means of promoting the peaceful settlement of disputes between states, including strengthening of the role of the International Court of Justice, would also be discussed at the proposed congress. . . . [O]f the five working days [proposed for the congress], the first four should each be devoted to one of the four purposes of the Decade, and the fifth should focus on an evaluation of the results achieved thus far, as well as on consideration of activities for the second half of the decade and prospects for the next century.[19]

The proposal for such a congress met with the interest and general approval of many speakers, including the representatives from the Nordic countries, Mexico, the Republic of Korea, the European Community, Cuba, Malta, Malaysia, and Singapore. The delegate from China, Liao Jincheng, stated that his government "particularly noted" the proposal, and was "prepared to consult

18 Statement by Mr. Saeid Mirazee Yengejeh, Representative of the Islamic Republic of Iran before the Sixth Committee, New York: Press Release from the Permanent Mission to the United Nations of the Islamic Republic of Iran, Nov. 13, 1992.

19 *Ibid.*, 3.

with other interested delegations on that proposal." The representative from Sweden, speaking on behalf of the Nordic countries, noted that the idea of a congress was worthwhile, but suggested that rather than devoting one day to each of the different topics of the Decade, focused seminars and workshops for participants with special interests would serve better to achieve practical results.

The representative from the United Kingdom, speaking on behalf of the European Community and its member states, was more cautious in his enthusiasm for the congress, and looked forward to considering the matter in more detail at the next session of the General Assembly. The Japanese delegate, Chusei Yamada, was more blunt: before a final decision was made as to whether such a congress should be convened, "further definition and clarification needed to be sought on its purpose, agenda and participants."[20] Teunis Halff, representative of the Netherlands, commented that careful planning is necessary "in order not to end up with having a congress for the sake of having a congress."[21]

The congress has the potential to be a focal point for the activities and profile of the Decade, but the decision as to whether indeed it will be held is yet to be made, and the scope of its activities remains largely undefined.

Birgit Kofler, the representative from Austria, highlighted the environment as an area ripe for development and focus in the activities of the Decade. She stated that, in considering the promotion of procedures for the peaceful settlement of disputes, special emphasis should be placed on those areas in which differences between states are most likely to occur in the future. She continued:

One of these areas is the environmental field. Recent years have already witnessed a sharp increase of environmental conflicts [*sic*]. Such conflicts, some with potentially explosive political implications, have brought into sharp focus the urgent need for specific measures for their prevention and settlement. Let me in this context also refer to the "Agenda 21" adopted by the United Nations Conference on Environment and Development which states in Chapter 39: "In the area of avoidance and settlement of disputes, States should further study and consider methods to broaden and make more effective the range of techniques available at

20 Statement by the representative of Japan, Chusei Yamada, to the Sixth Committee, Nov. 13, 1992; Press Release, Permanent Mission of Japan to the United Nations, Nov. 13, 1992, at 5.

21 "Statement by the Representative of the Kingdom of the Netherlands, Mr. Teunis Halff, in the Sixth Committee": Press Release, Permanent Mission of the Kingdom of the Netherlands to the United Nations, New York, Nov. 16, 1992.

present, taking into account, among others, relevant experience under existing international agreements, instruments and institutions and, where appropriate, their implementing mechanisms such as modalities for dispute avoidance and settlement."[22]

Austria also stressed the importance it attached to the protection of the environment in armed conflicts, an area "which truly merits in-depth study with a view to further developing the respective international norms."[23]

The delegate from Greece picked up the environmental theme in his statement, stressing that the "sustained efforts of specialists were needed more than ever before; lawyers, whose role in the field had for various reasons been rather modest, should be invited to offer their best and most imaginative contribution."[24] Canada, Australia, and New Zealand, in a joint statement, pointed to concrete achievements in the field as signs of progress; these included the opening for signature of the Convention on Biological Diversity and the United Nations Framework Convention on Climate Change, both of which had emerged from the United Nations Conference on Environment and Development held in 1992 in Brazil.[25] The three also noted that they were participating in the debate on the protection of the environment in times of armed conflict and "hoped that it would constitute a vibrant element of the work of the Decade."[26]

General reflections on the activities of the Decade and its potential also reveal the ambitions for and potential limitations of the Decade's remaining eight years. For many, the central problem was not the need for new international law but rather for effective means by which existing law might be implemented. The representative from Singapore identified two aspects to this problem. First, he noted, ignorance of existing rules and principles constituted the

22 Statement by Ms. Birgit Kofler on Agenda Item 129: United Nations Decade of International Law, New York: Press Release of the Permanent Mission of Austria to the United Nations, Nov. 13, 1992.

23 *Ibid.*

24 UN Doc. A/C.6/47/SR.36 at 4.

25 Cyprus also welcomed the signing of these two conventions. See Statement by the Permanent Representative of the Republic of Cyprus, Ambassador A. J. Jacovides, on Agenda Item 128: United Nations Decade of International Law in the Sixth Committee of the 47th Session of the General Assembly of the United Nations: Press Release, Permanent Mission of the Republic of Cyprus to the United Nations, Nov. 16, 1992.

26 UN Doc. A/C.6/47/SR.36 at 7-8.

main obstacle to their implementation. There was an "imbalance" between the supply of international legal expertise and the supply of destructive weapons, "which might partly explain the propensity among countries in the South to resort to military solutions to their disputes instead of seeking legal redress. The Decade provide[s] a rare opportunity to correct that imbalance."[27] He suggested that some of the activities of the Decade should be geared towards improving the flow of what he termed "legal technology" through bilateral or multilateral arrangements, including scholarships or other financial assistance for study, and internships with government departments in developed countries. Second, and closely related to the first aspect, there was a need to "market" international law to policy-makers, "particularly leaders in the socio-economic and political sectors who influenced the shaping of national policies."[28] The delegate from the Russian Federation similarly noted that "newly independent States could benefit from cooperation with the United Nations in matters relating to international law, in particular the question of acceding to basic international and regional instruments, and ensuring compatibility between domestic legislation and international obligations."[29]

Other political considerations were a subtext to the deliberations. The Malaysian delegate, for example, noted that not much progress had been achieved in promoting wider acceptance of existing multilateral treaties:

primarily because of the failure to acknowledge that those treaties did not fully take into consideration the interests of all States, since most of them had been drawn up and concluded when the majority of States were under the yoke of colonialism. With the emergence of a new spirit of international understanding and cooperation, all parties concerned must pay urgent attention to those treaties with a view to making appropriate adjustments in order to reflect in a more balanced way the interests of all parties.[30]

The Indian delegate stated bluntly that the "cause of peace and peaceful settlement of disputes could not be adequately served

27 UN Doc. A/C.6/47/SR.36 at 12.

28 *Ibid.* See also the statement of the Nigerian representative, who "agreed that assistance and technical advice should be provided to developing countries to facilitate their participation in the process of multilateral treaty-making": UN Doc. A/C.6/47/SR.36 at 10.

29 UN Doc. A/C.6/47/SR.34 at 7.

30 *Ibid.* at 5.

unless the present world order was structurally modified and fundamental decisions were taken on vital issues repeatedly highlighted by the Non-Aligned Movement."[31] The Cuban delegate suggested that, since the United Nations had also designated the 1990s as the International Decade for the Eradication of Colonialism, the Decade of International Law "should provide a suitable context for the elimination of the remaining vestiges of colonialism in the world."[32] The Pakistani delegate looked to expand the scope of the Decade's activities to include the "resolution of international economic problems, particularly of the developing countries, through such measures as reduction in interest rates, increase in development assistance, curbs on protectionist policies and trade barriers, technology transfer to developing countries" and the like.[33] The delegate from Indonesia also looked to the Decade as a "useful instrument to reiterate faith in the utility of international law" and implored a focus on the "objectives enunciated by the non-aligned countries for a new international economic order, a new international information and communication order and for the democratisation of international relations as a whole."[34]

These remarks evince the expectations and tensions threading through the deliberations. The likely obstacles that such challenges pose to the work of the Decade should not be underestimated. Canada's response to the Decade is tempered by the need to address these tensions, and Canada's activities throughout the Decade will of necessity be constrained by this international environment.

In 1990, the official Canadian reaction to the Decade was positive yet conservative. The response centred around the promotion of respect for international law, the encouragement of improved implementation of treaties, and work on the development of means

---

31 UN Doc. A/C.6/47/SR.34 at 12.

32 UN Doc. A/C.6/47/SR.36 at 9.

33 Statement of Justice Akhtar Ali Kazi, Pakistan Delegate at the Sixth Committee of the Forty-Seventh United Nations General Assembly on Agenda Item 128: United Nations Decade of International Law: Press Release, Pakistan Permanent Mission to the United Nations, New York, Nov. 16, 1992.

34 Statement by Mr. Sadewo Joedo Before the Sixth Committee on Agenda Item 128: United Nations Decade of International Law: Press Release, Permanent Mission of the Republic of Indonesia to the United Nations, New York, Nov. 16, 1992.

and methods for the peaceful settlement of disputes.[35] The Canadian position was reasonably consistent with the initial recommendations of other member states. The delegations expressed common concerns, but emphasized themes and aspects of those concerns differently. For example, while Canada focused on states and their negligent application of present international law, Japan,[36] Singapore,[37] and Sweden[38] stepped inside the nation state and put much more emphasis on the need to educate the populace in order to generate the political will that will in turn force governments to live up to their international obligations. Canada's approach was very traditional, working state to state, "contracting" for the betterment of humankind. Other nations believe that for progress to be made, a new approach must be found — one that compensates for, or at least takes into account, the inequalities of the international system.

At the 1992 meetings of the Sixth Committee, the Canadian statement was consistent with this earlier position. Canada delivered a joint statement with Australia and New Zealand,[39] emphasizing the need to ensure a practical focus for programs for the rest of the Decade. Howard Strauss, Canadian representative to the meetings, noted that the three states "welcomed the development of international legal rules relating to environmental protection, international humanitarian law and human rights" and saw "the improved implementation of current international legal norms and more frequent recourse to existing international organs and mech-

---

[35] Address by Jason Reiskind, Deputy Director, Legal Operations Division, External Affairs and International Trade Canada, at the University of Toronto, Apr. 5, 1990; address by Ambassador Phillippe Kirsch, at the Faculty of Law, University of Sherbrooke, Feb. 22, 1991. See also Serge April, Director General, Legal Affairs Bureau, External Affairs and International Trade Canada, Statement to the Sixth Committee of the 45th Session of the UN General Assembly: Press Release, Permanent Mission of Canada to the United Nations, New York, Nov. 14, 1990. See also note 2, *supra*.

[36] Statement of Masahiro Fukukawa, representative of Japan, to the Sixth Committee of the 45th Session of the General Assembly: Press Release, Nov. 14, 1990.

[37] Statement by T. Jasudasen, representative of Singapore, speaking to the Sixth Committee of the 45th Session of the General Assembly: Press Release, Nov. 13, 1990.

[38] Statement by Ambassador Jan Eliasson, Permanent Representative of Sweden to the United Nations, to the Sixth Committee of the 45th Session of the General Assembly: Press Release, Nov. 14, 1990.

[39] See UN Doc. A/C.6/47/SR.36 at 6.

anisms" as a priority for the Decade. Other specific suggestions included support for the Secretary-General's call[40] for universal acceptance of the compulsory jurisdiction of the International Court of Justice; increased and expanded resort to requests for advisory opinions of the Court; the development of an effective regime to deal with problems related to conservation and management of fisheries resources; and further development of measures relating to the law of non-navigational uses of international watercourses and international liability for injurious consequences arising out of acts not prohibited by international law. With regard to Part 4 of the program for the Decade (teaching, study, dissemination and wider appreciation of international law), the statement noted that:

[o]ver the previous two years, Canadian universities had organized a series of meetings aimed at advancing the objectives of the Decade. During the XXI Annual Conference of the Canadian Council of International Law . . . a round-table discussion on the Decade had taken place. Efforts were under way to integrate the teaching of the principles of international law into university courses dealing with related subjects. There had also been efforts to advance the teaching of basic international legal principles at the secondary level.[41]

The emphasis in the November 1992 Canadian statement is thus on the pragmatic and the concrete, in line with earlier Canadian responses.

In sum, then, the ideas and initiatives brought forward by the Canadian government have been reserved, but they have nonetheless provided a springboard to further discussion. In at least one respect, as noted in the 1992 statement, they have served as a catalyst for action.

Our initiative, the United Nations Decade Project, draws on the expertise of the Department of Foreign Affairs, the Bar, and academic and student communities for participants in what have so far been open and educational sessions on the Decade and on Canada's place in international law. To date, seven round-table discussions have taken place. In co-operation with students, professors, and international law societies, the University of Toronto, the University of Western Ontario, Queen's University, the University of

---

40 "An Agenda for Peace," Report of the Secretary-General pursuant to the statement adopted by the Summit Meeting of the Security Council on Jan. 31, 1992, UNSC Doc. S/24111, June 17, 1992. Also UN Doc. A/47/277-S/47111 (1992).

41 UN Doc. A/C.6/47/SR. 36 at 8.

Saskatchewan, Dalhousie University, and the University of Windsor have in turn hosted a round-table discussion, attracting participants from coast to coast. The seventh round-table discussion took place at the 1992 Annual Conference of the Canadian Council on International Law.[42]

The format of the round-table sessions has been relatively simple, with introductions and a keynote address being followed by responses from the academic community and the Bar. The floor has then been opened for comments, insights, and debate, guided by a moderator. The aim is not to produce any resolution or one position at the end of the day; instead, our hope has been that each session would promote further thought and discussion on the United Nations Decade and the development of a broader Canadian perspective on it. The insights emerging from the sessions can be loosely grouped under the four purposes for the Decade as outlined in the Vukas Report, plus one additional category — the role of Canada during the Decade. Each round-table discussion had its own character, reflecting the diverse experiences and expertise of the participants and the host region.

CANADIAN PERSPECTIVES ON THE UN DECADE

ACCEPTANCE OF AND RESPECT FOR THE PRINCIPLES OF
INTERNATIONAL LAW

International law is often viewed as "that which the evil ignore and the righteous refuse to enforce."[43] However, before one can enforce international law, it must be accepted that it has the power to bind international actors. Professor Jean-Guy Quennville of the Department of Political Science at St. Thomas More College at the University of Saskatchewan[44] summarized the thoughts of many in noting that law emerges from relationships between people. Regimes are implemented that guide those relations. But, he queried, are those regimes binding because they are the accepted order and therefore have coercive power, or because they have emerged from international society and are therefore credible? Participants at each of the round-table sessions noted that, in order to successfully

---

[42] See Tamra Hopkins and Paul Paton, "Developing a Canadian Perspective on the United Nations Decade of International Law: A Round-Table Discussion," 21 Can. Council Int'l L. Proc. 205 (1992).

[43] Professor Dawn Russell, Faculty of Law, Dalhousie University, Feb. 27, 1992.

[44] Feb. 21, 1992.

encourage the acceptance of and respect for the principles of international law, international law must be credible and legitimate for those it seeks to bind.

Retired ambassador Arthur Andrew[45] was more critical in his analysis of the difficulty inherent in implementing international law. He postulated that international law is not in fact a legal system that needs to be implemented, but rather simply a "means for bolstering a political cause." He commented:

[W]hat we are talking about does not meet the standard of law, almost any standard of law you want to apply. There is no legislature, there is no police force and there is no court that has compulsory jurisdiction and there is no jail.

Behind the facade of the state, there is an international political process, not an international legal process. There was the view that "the legal system inside a country works, if it works at all, because the community has confidence in it."[46] True implementation of a system of international law is not possible because there is no like-minded community to support the system. Professor Hugh Kindred of Dalhousie University mused, "I sometimes have wondered just how much community of interest there is between me as a common law lawyer looking outwards from a western culture, and someone from an arid state who has grown up and believes in the legal culture of the sharer." Like many others, he doubted that there are sufficient "points of contact" to support an international legal system.

Whether international law can respond to the varied demands of the international community was the focus of much discussion. There was a view that the present bias of international law towards the European concept of state-centred relations undermines its credibility and effectiveness,[47] particularly since the traditional concept of international law cannot help groups that are not organized states.[48] Until it is clear whether and how new, non-state actors can participate, and what constraints are on that participation, any discussion focusing on the improvement of international law lacks the necessary means of broad implementation.

45 Dalhousie University, Feb. 27, 1992.

46 Professor Hugh Kindred, Faculty of Law, Dalhousie University, Feb. 27, 1992.

47 William McAinsh, a student at the College of Law at the University of Saskatchewan, University of Saskatchewan, Feb. 21, 1992.

48 Edward Stanek, Chief Librarian at the College of Law at the University of Saskatchewan, University of Saskatchewan, Feb. 21, 1992.

Further, international law is presently limited by the degree to which states wish to develop, implement, and enforce it. There are states that have no desire to participate in the "global community" because that community is viewed only as a limitation upon their actions. There are also states that simply cannot carry out their international obligations because of their internal difficulties. Both of these bring into focus the difficulty of reconciling national sovereignty and the need for an effective method of enforcing international law.[49] One of the greatest barriers to effective United Nations action is the continuing cry of "state sovereignty" and the principle of non-interference in the domestic affairs of a member state. Dismantling that barrier poses one of the many challenges for international law during the Decade.

It was suggested that, as we re-evaluate the basis of international law, we should "see the government of a country as not the top of the hierarchy but one little summit in a much more complex system — one that is partly hierarchical, going upwards, but also partly horizontal."[50] The object would not be to get rid of the state itself, but to develop a more comprehensive system permitting diverse centres of authority. In this way, legitimacy could be given to an increased range of international actors. Permitting non-governmental organizations (NGOs) to accept greater responsibility in the international arena could permit issues to be approached on a sectoral, rather than territorial, basis.[51] And, as retired ambassador Alan Beesley[52] noted, participation through NGOs is a way in which "we the people" might have access to international decision-making processes. Further, focusing on the individual in the international arena, and defining that individual by his or her interaction with others rather than by the individual's connection with a piece of geography, permits more meaningful and responsive international interaction.[53]

While increasing the range of participation in international law can enhance its credibility and legitimacy, and therefore hopefully enhance respect for and acceptance of international law, many

---

[49] Professor Greg Dickinson, Faculty of Education, University of Western Ontario, Oct. 8, 1991.

[50] Professor Kindred, Dalhousie University, Feb. 27, 1992.

[51] Bakes Mitchell, a student at Dalhousie Law School, Dalhousie University, Feb. 27, 1992.

[52] Queen's University, Nov. 7, 1991.

[53] Professor Isabel Anderson of the Department of Economics at the University of Saskatchewan, University of Saskatchewan, Feb. 21, 1992.

believe that this shift is not sufficient. It was argued that the Decade provides the opportunity to completely re-craft the international system. Professor K. Venkata Raman of the Faculty of Law at Queen's University[54] criticized the limited scope envisioned for the United Nations and the Decade:

Part of the problem lies in the disproportionately narrow emphasis peace and security issues have generally received within the United Nations system and the relative nonchalance with which issues touching upon "human welfare" are treated in general in the deliberations at the international level. The United Nations Charter underscores the importance not only of preventing breaches of peace and acts of aggression, but also of promoting social development and human welfare. These are two complementary and inter-related goals.

Similarly, others have maintained that, considering the myriad international organizations and committees that are already competently addressing the issue of improving international law, the only justification for the Decade could be that it is to provide "an opportunity to see how radically the system can be altered." People have been challenged to "come up with something new and creative. If we don't, we're going to turn the United Nations Decade of International Law into the United Nations Decade for More of the Same."[55] Because international law is not presently able to address all the problems of the international community and because new problems will continue to emerge throughout the Decade, many agreed that the continual re-evaluation of international law should be an ongoing purpose for the Decade.[56]

On the other hand, a strong contrary opinion has questioned the wisdom of using the Decade only to develop "the law of humanity worldwide."[57] The concern was that widening the field and opening it up to all possible actors would result in a divergence of interest and a dearth of solutions. The positive and practical contribution we could make to bettering international society by codifying, clarifying, and improving the accessibility of existing international law could easily be lost if the scope of the Decade became too broad.

54 University of Toronto, Apr. 5, 1991.

55 *Ibid.*

56 Joseph Bradford of the Queen's University International Law Society, Canadian Council on International Law, Annual Conference, Oct. 16, 1992; Professor R. G. Williamson of the Department of Anthropology and Archaeology at the University of Saskatchewan, University of Saskatchewan, Feb. 21, 1992; and Professor Williamson, University of Saskatchewan, Feb. 21, 1992.

57 William Hearn, Cassels, Brock and Blackwell, University of Toronto, Apr. 5, 1991.

There is great concern that the Decade make and be seen to make a discernible difference. Much of the debate at the United Nations is remote and abstract.[58] The layers of bureaucratic endeavour give the average citizen the perception of non-involvement. While we may feel morally obligated to participate in the Decade of International Law, it is very easy to abrogate responsibility for involvement to the Canadian government — after all, Canada has consistently supported the United Nations and its projects, so we know that the Decade would not pass unnoticed. Its impact, however, would be diminished.

Instead, there should be two levels of participation in the Decade: one through governments and the other through interactions between individuals in the international community. While we should spend a good part of the Decade discussing the principles and the basis of international law, the important work for the Decade lies in addressing and resolving issues that touch individual Canadians as they interact with the international community.[59] A first step towards this goal can be made by integrating international law into the domestic system. Professor Bill Graham of the Faculty of Law at the University of Toronto[60] noted that "the impact of international law must be felt on the individual level." Individuals must, he stated, have access to it before their governments and their courts. In this way, international law would, and should, become relevant to ordinary people, engaging their interest. This could engender a national understanding from which an international structure might be crafted and, in turn, give public international law an enhanced meaning for, and impact on, society.

As a first and fundamental step, the Canadian government must be convinced to bring its legislation into line with its international obligations. Because there is a lack of continuity between those individuals who negotiate international agreements and those who are responsible for implementing them, the resolve to follow through and implement international obligations must come from the citizenry at large.[61] H. Scott Fairley,[62] 1992-93 President of the Canadian Council of International Law, noted that Canada should

58 Professor Isabel Anderson, University of Saskatchewan, Feb. 21, 1992.

59 *Ibid.*

60 University of Toronto, Apr. 5, 1991.

61 Professor Sharon Williams, Osgoode Hall Law School, University of Toronto, Apr. 5, 1991.

62 University of Toronto, Apr. 5, 1991.

honour its international obligations not only as a matter of principle, but also because its failure to do so could change the status of international law. Effective domestic implementation is therefore critical. Further, as part of its duty to implement its international obligations effectively, Canada must also be encouraged to adopt a consistent approach to "sensational breaches of international law."[63] Enhancing the public's perception of international law was considered to be an important focus for the Decade, and it is these events that attract public attention. If the public sees the law failing or being applied inconsistently in these situations, there will be a great deal of scepticism about its usefulness.

Professor Gerald Fridman of the Faculty of Law at the University of Western Ontario noted that there are two aspects to international law: the "everyday stuff" that functions efficiently and which everyone takes for granted, and the "pathological" aspects of international law — those that remain constantly unresolved.[64] To date, the public perception of international law has focused on its pathological side. The task at hand is to make people aware of the broad areas of consensus and successful implementation. This, by itself, can promote respect for international law.

PROMOTION OF THE PEACEFUL SETTLEMENT OF DISPUTES

The need to develop the means to settle international disputes peacefully was identified as the most pressing goal for the Decade. Participants recommended increased resort to the International Court of Justice and to regional or sectoral dispute resolution mechanisms. In particular, the compulsory jurisdiction of the Court should be recognized, standing should be opened up, and the Court's decisions should be binding.[65] It was suggested that the Court could increase its profile by sitting on a rotating basis in every continent.[66] Further, each region or sectoral interest should establish its own system of problem management that would reflect the values and aims of those subject to it. Increased resort should be had to bodies like the International Atomic Energy Agency, the Conference on Security and Co-operation of Europe, the Organiza-

63 Professor Dawn Russell, Dalhousie University, Feb. 27, 1992.

64 University of Western Ontario, Oct. 8, 1991.

65 Marina Drell, an LL.M. candidate at Dalhousie University, Professor Donald Fleming, Faculty of Law, University of New Brunswick, Professor Russell, and Professor Kindred, Dalhousie University, Feb. 27, 1992.

66 Professor K. Venkata Raman, Queen's University, Nov. 7, 1991.

tion of American States, and others.[67] The establishment of a universal court for human rights and an international criminal court were encouraged.[68] Participants stressed the need for new means and methods of peacekeeping, conciliation, mediation, and fact finding on an international level beyond these agencies, but no specific alternatives emerged. Ambassador Beesley[69] recommended that non-intervention be reassessed as an appropriate instrument in the international legal arsenal. He commented that permitting apparent injustice in the name of non-interference in the internal affairs of a state poses serious questions for international law and raises a barrier to its credibility. Finally, Rear-Admiral Fred Crickard[70] warned that, when faced with "powerful transgressions of international law by states armed to the teeth," these dispute resolution mechanisms will likely prove insufficient.

DEVELOPMENT AND CODIFICATION OF INTERNATIONAL LAW

The third objective of the Decade is to encourage the progressive development of international law and its codification. There was general consensus that it would be useful to codify existing international law. To this end, it was suggested that the United Nations should undertake an effort to consolidate the law and/or codify the law as it now stands.[71] A list of topical areas could be devised, and experts in each area could be assigned to present reports on a codification of that area. Synthesizing the concepts of international law into written documents would be a very useful learning process, and could be a first step in promoting accessibility for those not familiar with or sceptical of the subject.[72]

There was a fear, nevertheless, that codification produces too rigid a system.[73] Since the United Nations and most of the countries that comprise it are very young, they should be given the

---

[67] Aldo Chircop, Professor of Maritime Law at Dalhousie University, Rod Berger, Patterson, Kitz in Halifax, Dalhousie University, Feb. 27, 1992; Ambassador Alan Beesley, Queen's University, Nov. 7, 1991.

[68] Professor John Humphrey, Canadian Council on International Law, Annual Conference, Oct. 16, 1992; Ambassador Beesley, Queen's University, Nov. 7, 1991.

[69] Queen's University, Nov. 7, 1991.

[70] Dalhousie University, Feb. 27, 1992.

[71] Professor Lakshman Marasinghe, University of Windsor, Mar. 9, 1992.

[72] H. Scott Fairley, University of Toronto, Apr. 5, 1991.

[73] Hamoody Hassan, Cohen, Delanghe, Highley, Vogel and Dawson, London, Ontario, University of Western Ontario, Oct. 8, 1991.

chance to formulate their own internal codes before effort is expended trying to establish a more overarching international code. A more manageable goal might be to focus on reform and codification of one or two specific areas of international law.[74] Many agreed that there is a pressing need to develop and codify international environmental law since a United Nations sponsored initiative in this area would be the most effective and perhaps only effective means of success.

Finally, at Dalhousie University,[75] attention centred around concrete suggestions for modifying the structure of the United Nations. Ideas included changes to the Security Council and the General Assembly, and Charter amendments. At the very least, it was felt that the membership of the Security Council should be modified to reflect the changes in the world since 1945. Many believed that both the veto power and the Security Council itself should be abolished. It was suggested that the practice and procedures of the General Assembly be reviewed in order to address issues raised by the debate over the Assembly's usefulness.[76] With respect to the Charter, Professor Fleming remarked, "[a]s Canadians now recognize too well, no constitution can claim perfection nor remain relevant to contemporary need without undergoing periodic review and change."[77] He suggested the following steps or areas of focus for change in the United Nations Charter:

(1) define the "use of force";

(2) add provisions that will outline when a state is justified in intervening in another state's affairs for "humanitarian purposes";

(3) establish the International Court of Justice as the authoritative interpreter of the Charter;

(4) define the United Nations' "peacekeeping" role.

---

74 Brian Rose, Stikeman, Elliott (Toronto), Queen's University, Nov. 7, 1991.

75 Feb. 27, 1992.

76 Professor Fleming noted that many developed states believe that the bias of General Assembly resolutions, which are passed by the most numerous but weakest constituency, discredit the work of the General Assembly. Others counter that the General Assembly mirrors the true state of global opinion. The strong anti-western sentiment reflects the frustration that the majority of states face when attempting to obtain an effective voice in the international community: Dalhousie University, Feb. 27, 1992.

77 Professor Fleming, Dalhousie University, Feb. 27, 1992

However, Ambassador Andrew cautioned against amending the Charter. He maintained that "changing constitutions should come after the event, not before the event. You should in effect have something that is working and then try to write the rules to describe how it works, rather than try to set up an ideal government."

TEACHING, STUDY, AND THE WIDER DISSEMINATION OF
INTERNATIONAL LAW

This topic engendered the greatest debate, yet generated the greatest consensus. Elizabeth Cheung, of the International Law Society at the University of Western Ontario,[78] clearly articulated the importance of education to the success of the Decade. She emphasized that education is the first step towards attaining the goals set for the Decade. Before states, organizations, corporations, or individuals will accept or respect international law, they must have knowledge of and understand it. The need to generate support within the academic community was considered paramount, given the considerable influence of those who continue to "dismiss international law in sneering terms."[79]

Canadians are increasingly aware of international forces at work in their lives. The task is not to alert Canadians to the importance of international law, but rather to help them understand the force that is becoming more and more prevalent in their lives.[80] The key will be to present this information in a form that is accessible and to an audience to which it is useful. First, before presenting any particular vision of international law, we must acknowledge the theoretical decisions we have made that underpin that vision.[81] Second, education must be interactive and facilitated by access to meaningful participation in the process of developing, implementing, and enforcing international law.[82] Third, we must expand the target audience, reaching individuals earlier on in the education process

[78] University of Western Ontario, Oct. 8. 1991.

[79] Professor Gerald Morris, University of Toronto, Apr. 5, 1991.

[80] Professor Fleming, Dalhousie University, Feb. 27, 1992.

[81] Charlotte Chiba, graduate student at the University of Ottawa, Canadian Council on International Law, Annual Conference, Oct. 16, 1992.

[82] Megan Aston, doctoral candidate at the Ontario Institute for Studies in Education, recommended in a supplementary paper following the Toronto round table that the application of "critical pedagogy" may be particularly useful in this context.

— as early as primary school.[83] One group that was specifically targeted for educational efforts was the media. The media have a tremendous influence over popular perceptions and understandings and are therefore an obvious conduit for the popularization of international legal issues and concerns. However, efforts must be made to package international law in a form that is accessible, relevant, and understandable to the media in the light of the time and other constraints under which they operate.[84]

Further, an interdisciplinary approach to the teaching of international law at law schools was recommended. International legal issues should be incorporated into each of the core courses to give a true picture of the increasing interconnectedness of domestic and international legal issues.[85] The private bar, academia, and the Canadian government were urged to contribute to education in international law throughout the Decade and beyond,[86] since

[83] Professor John Gamble, Penn State University, Canadian Council on International Law, Annual Conference, Oct. 16, 1992; Professor Donald Buckingham, Faculty of Law at the University of Western Ontario, University of Toronto, Apr. 5, 1991; Earl Mullen, teacher at Catholic Central Secondary School in London, Ontario, University of Western Ontario, Oct. 8, 1991; Hamoody Hassan, University of Western Ontario, Oct. 8, 1991; and Jane Bolden, freelance legal researcher, Queen's University, Nov. 7, 1991.

[84] Kurt Leavins, program director for radio station C95 Saskatoon, University of Saskatchewan, Feb. 21, 1992.

[85] Peter Morawsky, student at the Faculty of Law at the University of Western Ontario, Oct. 8, 1991; Andrew Pinto, student at the Faculty of Law at the University of Windsor, Mar. 9, 1992; Professor Buckingham, University of Western Ontario, Oct. 8, 1991; Professor William Schabas of the Université du Québec à Montréal, Canadian Council on International Law, Annual Conference, Oct. 16, 1992.

[86] William Hearn, an associate with the law firm of Cassels, Brock and Blackwell, advocated a number of initiatives. In his view, co-operation between the practising bar and academia should be encouraged so as to create fellowships for students interested in international law. Hearn suggested that a good model is the International Business and Trade Law program of the Faculty of Law at the University of Toronto and the Osgoode Hall Law School of York University, a program where the student spends half of a summer work period working with a law firm and the other half doing research for a law professor in an international law area, the cost of which is paid for by the law firm. Lawyers should help themselves by getting more involved in organizations like the Canadian Institute of International Affairs and the Canadian Institute for Strategic Studies. Governments could assist in the promotion of international law and the education of practitioners by creating a Canadian-sponsored international legal aid network. Hearn suggested that this bold, if expensive, undertaking would help those in developing countries gain

success in achieving the aims set out in this fourth purpose for the Decade can have an impact that reaches beyond its scope to support the Decade's other purposes. As Professor Fleming noted:

The heightened awareness of international law in Canada has created a demand for more knowledge about, and new approaches to, the subject. Meeting those educational needs will encourage a larger — and hopefully more effective — lobby to provoke the Canadian governments and judiciary to implement our international legal responsibilities into our domestic laws (something they have long hesitated to do). Further, a more broadly-based segment of the population with a greater understanding of, and appreciation for, the international legal system cannot help but force our leaders to increase their commitments and contributions to the ongoing development and improvement of international law.[87]

CANADA'S ROLE IN THE DECADE

A number of concrete recommendations for action during the Decade have already been canvassed under the discussion of the purposes for the Decade. In addition to these recommendations, participants commented on the unique contribution that Canada might be able to make to the Decade. Judge Ronald St. John Macdonald of the European Court for Human Rights and Senior Scholar in Residence at the Faculty of Law at the University of Toronto[88] recommended that Canada constitute a national committee[89] on the Decade that would develop and implement Canada's program for the Decade. This program should tackle manageable issues and exploit the expertise of its different regions to develop a constructive approach to the Decade. Many noted[90] that Canada has particular expertise in the areas of the environment (specifically Arctic pollution and resource exploitation), human rights, the self-determination of indigenous peoples, terrorism, the drug trade, and the peace-

---

access to Canadian expertise and in turn give Canadian lawyers greater opportunities in international law areas. More generally, he recommended that governments and those in private practice should co-operate in "cross-fertilization" systematically, not simply on an ad hoc basis. Further, the federal government should consider strongly qualified private practitioners for international appointments.

87 Dalhousie University, Feb. 24, 1992.

88 University of Western Ontario, Oct. 8, 1991.

89 A number of states have already constituted such national committees, including Mexico, Romania, and Hungary.

90 For example, Professor Williamson, University of Saskatchewan, Feb. 21, 1992, and Jason Reiskind, University of Western Ontario, Oct. 8, 1991.

ful settlement of disputes. Canada should build from its experience in these areas to make a significant contribution to the Decade.

There was, however, criticism of these premises. First, how persuasive is Canada's leadership in the international arena? One participant cautioned that "if Canada can't even organize its own constitution, how can we expect our opinions to be respected when we put forward plans to organize the international arena? We must be able to reconcile the groups within Canada and *then* we can bring our expertise to bear on the international arena. Canada's role for the moment may be to teach by example."[91] Second, while small tasks may be "do-able," they will not capture the imagination of the public and enlist the support necessary for a successful program.[92]

In response, George Cotsaris of the Canadian Consulate in Detroit[93] suggested that the Decade borrow from another United Nations agency's slogan and have "thinking globally, acting locally" as its focus. He noted that this may be a way to combine the best of both the concern for concrete achievement and the desire to capture the imagination of Canadians.

Finally, Ambassador Vernon Turner, then on leave from the Department of External Affairs and a Distinguished Visitor at the Centre for International Studies at the University of Toronto,[94] focused his remarks on the possibility of convening a third international peace conference. He suggested that Canada come out fully in support of the conference, and that this be done sooner rather than later. He advocated this position for five reasons:

(1) if a full commitment is made to the peace conference, international law will gain a higher profile at the political level and greater status within the government system;

(2) this commitment will increase the pressure on all governments to bring their legislation into line with their international obligations;

(3) it will force the larger global governmental community, the non-legal professionals, to focus on international law as something that forms part of the framework within which they must operate;

91 Professor Gerald Fridman, University of Western Ontario, Oct. 8, 1991.

92 University of Windsor, Mar. 9, 1992.

93 University of Windsor, Mar. 9, 1992.

94 University of Toronto, Apr. 5, 1991. Ambassador Turner was speaking in a personal capacity at the session.

(4) it will force Canada to develop its own ideas and approach as it assumes a leadership role in the conference; and

(5) it will strengthen the position of the Legal Branch within the Department of External Affairs.

CHALLENGES FOR CANADA AND THE DECADE: AN ASSESSMENT

The range of ideas and dreams articulated for the Decade are diverse. With each expansion of the Decade's purview, new and divergent aims are put forward. The risk for Canada and the international community is: "that the Decade's substance [could] either be the object of a political quarrel among countries with diverging preferences, or that it would have to be formulated in such general terms in order to ensure general acceptance that would make it practically meaningless."[95] In considering the Decade and Canada's participation against the backdrop of the 1992 debates and the round table discussions, the related question of how broadly the international community wishes to engage in law reform over what is only a ten-year period arises. Resolution 44/23 specifically emphasizes two functions or aims for the Decade: the improvement of means and attitudes for the peaceful settlement of disputes, and the promotion of international law through education. Any attempt at law reform must proceed incrementally within a coherent conceptual framework, particularly when it is to take place over such a brief period.[96] To achieve consensus that can lead to action, the Canadian effort must start small, on solid ground. We have found that solid ground in the area of education.

The dissemination of the principles and purposes of international law is something that has captured the attention of participants in each round-table session. For the Decade to have some recognizable form, there must be a clear outline of defined activities. Educational efforts lend themselves to this sort of organization and they also accommodate a simple measure of progress. These efforts will enable the Decade to take on form and demonstrate tangible substance. Education, which works from the ground up, will give law a solid base that includes people's ideas and will be

95 Statement by Dr. Erkki Kourula, representative of Finland to the Sixth Committee of the 45th Session of the General Assembly on Nov. 14, 1990: Press Release, Nov. 14, 1990.

96 This will be true at least in its initial phase. Perhaps one of the tasks will be to map out a timetable for any reform envisaged for the period beyond the Decade.

more meaningful to them than ideologies imposed from above. This approach will encourage domestic interest and participation in the international legal arena.

Educational efforts are possible and needed at all levels. With creativity and sensitivity, there is a role for greater involvement of the Departments of Foreign Affairs and Justice, practitioners, and academics in the development of curricula and texts, in issuing up-to-date information about international law activities, in providing speakers to classrooms, and in training teachers.

A re-evaluation of the way international law is presented in Canadian law schools is critical. Domestic law courses must not be taught in a vacuum, in total ignorance or denial of the impact of international law on domestic law and vice versa. More courses in public international law do not appear to be the answer, since only those already interested will continue to take them. Instead, efforts should be directed to increasing the relevance and general understanding of international law for those who will likely not encounter it again in a significant way in their professional careers. Exploration of this topic is an area ripe for future discussion.

The education of the media has been noted by many as an important undertaking for the Decade. Domestic coverage of international law issues has been noted as weak or non-existent, and the assumption is made that this is the result of a lack of understanding amongst those who report the news. However, lengthy bulletins of the sort presented by Foreign Affairs that document recent developments in international law and academic treatises are simply too unwieldy for those writing to deadline. Further, the bulletins and articles are presumably not written for general consumption. These issues must be addressed if the media are to convey an accurate and much needed understanding of international law to the public.

Other debates have emerged: the need for more international law versus a focus on existing law; whether to devote resources to greater codification of international legal rules; the utility or likelihood of increased recourse to the International Court of Justice; and whether the process of law reform in the international law sphere should be incremental or radical. Concern has also been expressed that the Decade is ripe for co-option into other agendas or programs, and the legitimacy of process has been questioned. As the November 1992 meetings of the Sixth Committee reinforce, these debates are far from over. The Decade may have served its purpose by ensuring that attention has been drawn to these issues; to resolve them in a ten-year period is perhaps wildly unrealistic.

Before these issues may be approached, however, we find it essential that the question of the shape of the international order be revisited within a legal context. The role of the nation state in an increasingly interdependent world is arguably in flux, and the place that the nation state is assigned will be the key to understanding the role of a legal framework for an international society; that in turn will affect the strategy and likely success of the domestic implementation of international legal regimes. Canada, in the continuing grip of agonizing debates about the shape of the internal organization of the country and the role of federalism in an internal union, should be particularly aware of the international implications of domestic decisions, constitutional and otherwise. The constraints imposed by international society on those internal choices should also be recognized. The challenges for Canada during this Decade are considerable.

Meeting these challenges seems to require some new organization or revitalization of the international legal community in Canada. The danger is that the momentum from the early interest in the Decade will be lost. The goal of such organizational efforts can be a structure within which wider domestic consultation and meaningful contribution by both the international legal community and the general public are encouraged. This cannot but help what has been noted as a credibility problem. Canada has much expertise that can and should be drawn upon: the environment, aboriginal peoples, remote sensing, peacekeeping, human rights, electoral process, and administration are all issues or areas likely to be important in international law during the Decade and beyond. In these areas, Canadian experience and knowledge should allow us to be at the forefront in shaping the international legal order. Canada has traditionally had a strong voice at the United Nations, and should be raising it even more forcefully during this period. Canada's internal difficulties should not hamper this contribution. The round-table sessions view the fact that Canada does not have her constitutional house in order as a negative point; we view it optimistically as presenting an opportunity for greater understanding of the relevance and functioning of international law. Canada's continuing constitutional debates will, of necessity, cover issues such as succession, treaty-making, and self-determination. There may be great strength under adverse conditions; this, we would suggest, may emerge as a theme for the Decade and for international law in a hostile world.

While normally one would consider defining the scope of a project before attempting to fulfil that project, the opposite approach may be needed for the Decade. As the "easy" tasks are tackled, momentum can build. As concrete, positive results become available, faith in the success of the Decade will provide it with the strength to withstand queries as to the Decade's possible scope. Tangible results will prevent the Decade for International Law from becoming yet another abstract, academic pursuit. The areas noted above constitute the areas in which we believe tangible results may be achieved.

TAMRA HOPKINS
Stikeman, Elliott, Toronto

PAUL D. PATON
Davies, Ward, and Beck, Toronto

Sommaire

La Décennie des Nations Unies pour le droit international: une perspective canadienne

Dans cet article, les auteurs décrivent brièvement les progrès de la Décennie des Nations Unies pour le droit international dans le monde entier. Ensuite, ils passent en revue les résultats d'une entreprise continue lancée par les auteurs en 1991 et visant à élaborer une perspective canadienne de la Décennie. Les auteurs commentent la diversité des idées qu'on a exprimées et des rêves qu'on a faits à propos de la Décennie. Mais ils préviennent que, bien qu'une telle diversité soit nécessaire pour la discussion, il faut adopter un thème plus précis si l'on veut faire des progrès perceptibles dans l'accomplissement des objectifs de la Décennie. En outre, ils discutent des chances de succès de la Décennie sur le plan international, étant donné les désaccords idéologiques déjà exprimés. Les auteurs recommandent que le programme canadien pour la Décennie soit axé sur l'information. En diffusant les principes et les objectifs du droit international, on peut attirer l'attention d'un grand nombre de personnes qui désirent participer à la Décennie. Un programme d'information à grande échelle portant sur le droit international fera mieux comprendre la Décennie aux Canadiens et Canadiennes et, par conséquent, il les incitera à s'intéresser et à participer aussi bien à la Décennie qu'aux débats de droit international. En faisant des progrès dans le domaine de l'information en droit international, on pourrait obtenir des résultats tangibles pour la Décennie et éviter qu'elle ne soit condamnée comme étant encore une autre étude théorique et abstraite.

Chronique de Droit international économique en 1992 / Digest of International Economic Law in 1992

I Commerce

préparé par

MARTIN ST-AMANT*

E N 1992, L'ACTION JURIDIQUE DU Canada en matière de commerce international se sera manifestée par la poursuite effective de la mise en oeuvre de l'Accord de libre-échange Canada-États-Unis. Dans l'attente des résultats des négociations commerciales de l'Uruguay Round, les conflits et activités impliquant le Canada dans le cadre du GATT furent également en cette année relativement nombreux.

I CONFLITS ET ACTIVITÉS DANS LE CADRE DU GATT

Tout comme pour l'année précédente, les litiges à l'égard de la bière et des boissons alcooliques occupèrent en cette année 1992, une place prépondérante dans l'action du Canada au GATT. Premièrement, celui-ci ne s'est pas opposé, conformément à son engagement pris en 1991, à l'adoption par le Conseil du GATT du rapport du Groupe spécial chargé d'étudier les pratiques canadiennes d'importation, de distribution et de vente de bière.[1] Le Conseil adopta donc le rapport le 18 février.[2] Du fait que la distribution

---

* Avocat, Leduc Lebel (Montréal); candidat au Doctorat en droit commercial international (Université de Paris I-Panthéon-Sorbonne).

---

[1] Voir le texte du rapport du Groupe spécial dans le document du GATT: DS17/R (1991). Au sujet de ce rapport, voir par ailleurs M. ST-AMANT, "Chronique de droit international économique," (1992) 30 *ACDI*, 337.

[2] GATT: C/M/254 (1992).

et la vente de boissons alcooliques sont des prérogatives exclusives des provinces, des négociations intensives eurent lieu, par la suite, entre le gouvernement fédéral et les gouvernements provinciaux pour mettre en oeuvre le rapport du Groupe spécial.[3] Le Canada a ainsi, aux termes de l'entente intervenue avec les provinces, présenté au secrétariat du GATT, un rapport visant à donner suite aux recommandations du Groupe spécial et ce, dans le délai imparte, soit au plus tard le 31 mars 1995.[4] Puis, compte tenu de la déception des États-Unis concernant le rapport du Canada et des possibilités réelles de mesures de représailles à son encontre, des négociations bilatérales furent engagées entre les deux pays.[5] Un accord de principe, prévoyant que les bières importées bénéficieront d'un accès amélioré au Canada après une période de transition révisée s'étendant jusqu'au 30 septembre 1993, fut dans ce cadre annoncé par le Canada et les États-Unis, le 25 avril.[6] Toutefois, les deux pays ayant été incapables de formaliser cet accord de principe,[7] les États-Unis décidaient le 23 juillet d'imposer unilatéralement des mesures de représailles à l'encontre du Canada, prenant la forme d'un droit

[3] Voir à ce sujet "Beer Brawl" dans le *Journal of Commerce*, 23 mars 1992, p. 4.

[4] Voir Ministre de l'Industrie, des Sciences et de la Technologie et ministre du Commerce extérieur, *Communiqué de presse*, no 62, 3 mars 1992. Ce rapport énumère, province par province, les mesures devant permettre au Canada de respecter ses obligations internationales aux termes de l'Accord général. Ces mesures visent notamment à garantir le traitement national aux bières importées en ce qui concerne la taille des emballages, les majorations, l'accès aux points de vente au détail et la livraison depuis les entrepôts jusqu'aux points de vente. Les provinces s'engagent en outre à ce que la fixation des prix tienne compte de la décision du Groupe spécial voulant que les prix minimums ne soient pas fixés en fonction du prix des bières d'origine locale.

[5] Les critiques des États-Unis portaient entre autres sur l'établissement des prix minimums dans certaines provinces et sur la trop longue période de transition. Voir à cet égard, 16 *Int'l Trade Rep.* (BNA) 694 (1992).

[6] Voir Office of the United States Trade Representative, *Press Release*, no 92-25, 25 avril 1992. Voir également D. FAGAN, "Beer Agreement Heads Off Threat of Trade War," dans le *Globe and Mail*, 27 avril 1992, p. B-1.

[7] Les États-Unis contestaient le système de fixation des prix de l'Ontario, lequel comportait des frais de service supplémentaires ne s'appliquant qu'à la bière importée ainsi que le prélèvement environnemental perçu par cette province uniquement sur les canettes de bière et non sur les bouteilles. Les pratiques d'entreposage, pratiques imposées par les monopoles provinciaux de l'Ontario et du Québec, s'assimilaient également, selon les États-Unis, à des mesures incompatibles avec le principe du traitement national. Voir à ce sujet, D. FAGAN, "U.S. Rejects Canada's Offer to Resolve Beer Dispute," dans le *Globe and Mail*, 15 juillet 1992, p. B-2.

ad valorem de 50% sur les bières exportées par la province de l'Ontario.[8] Le même jour, le Canada répliquait lui aussi avec un droit *ad valorem* de 50% sur certaines importations de bières américaines destinées au marché ontarien.[9] Les États-Unis ont par ailleurs demandé lors de la réunion du Conseil du GATT du 14 juillet d'entériner leurs mesures de représailles, refusant tout nouvel arbitrage,[10] alors que le Canada proposait un examen accéléré des éléments litigieux, conformément aux procédures de règlement des différends prévues par le projet d'Acte final de l'Uruguay Round, tout en soutenant que la demande des États-Unis était injustifiée.[11]

D'autre part, le Groupe spécial chargé d'examiner certaines pratiques américaines de commercialisation de la bière, du vin et du cidre a, le 16 mars, présenté son rapport aux Parties Contractantes.[12] Le Groupe, à cet égard, a confirmé le bien-fondé de la plainte canadienne. Il a conclu que la plupart des 75 dispositions fédérales et des 44 dispositions des États portées à son attention étaient contraires aux règles de l'Accord général et plus particulièrement à l'article III:2.[13] Le rapport du Groupe spécial, lequel

8 Voir Office of the United States Trade Representative, *Press Release*, no 92-45, 23 juillet 1992.

9 Voir Ministre de l'Industrie, des Sciences et de la Technologie et ministre du Commerce extérieur, *Communiqué de presse*, no 157, 24 juillet 1992.

10 Voir *Focus, Bulletin d'information du GATT*, no 91, 1992, p. 2.

11 *Ibid.* Le Canada, à cette occasion, affirmait que les provinces avaient fait de réels efforts pour en venir à un règlement négocié avec les États-Unis et ce, en effectuant d'importants changements à leurs méthodes de commercialisation de la bière. En outre, il a soutenu que les États-Unis n'ayant pas notifié à l'avance leur demande, le Conseil n'était pas justifié d'autoriser des mesures de représailles.

12 Voir le texte du rapport du Groupe spécial dans le document du GATT: DS 23/R (1992). Voir également à propos de ce litige M. ST-AMANT, *loc. cit. supra* note 1, p. 338.

13 Il s'agissait notamment en l'espèce des dispositions concernant les crédits d'impôt ou les remboursements de taxes pour les producteurs locaux; des pratiques de distribution empêchant les produits importés d'être livrés directement aux points de ventes; des restrictions concernant le transport des produits importés; des licences plus onéreuses pour les fournisseurs étrangers; des prix maxima pour la vente des produits importés aux grossistes locaux et des pratiques d'inscription au catalogue et de radiation. Le Groupe spécial s'est également prononcé à l'effet que l'obligation pour les fournisseurs étrangers d'utiliser les services de grossistes locaux n'était pas protégée par le protocole d'application provisoire et que les États-Unis ne bénéficiaient pas de la responsabilité limitée au titre de l'article XXIV:12, eu égard au manque de preuve sur l'incapacité du gouvernement fédéral d'abroger les dispositions des États.

recommandait aux États-Unis de rendre ses mesures fédérales et d'État conformes à l'Accord général, fut adopté par le Conseil, le 19 juin.[14] Les États-Unis émirent toutefois certaines réserves sur la relation entre le gouvernement fédéral et les États, lesquelles selon eux soulevaient des problèmes relevant du droit constitutionnel américain.[15] Des consultations se sont en outre engagées entre les deux pays pour examiner les dispositions que les États-Unis envisageaient de prendre pour donner effet aux recommandations du Groupe spécial. Aucun accord n'a cependant pu intervenir entre les deux pays à ce sujet en 1992.

Par ailleurs, le 26 mars, le Comité des subventions et des droits compensateurs adopta pour la première fois depuis que le Code sur les subventions est entré en vigueur en 1980, un rapport d'un Groupe spécial. Il s'agissait en l'occurence du rapport sur les droits compensateurs appliqués par le Canada aux importations de maïs en grains en provenance des États-Unis.[16] Le Groupe concluait sans équivoque que la détermination du Tribunal canadien des importations contrevenait aux prescriptions énoncées à l'article 6 du Code sur les subventions car le Tribunal n'avait pas, sur la base d'éléments de preuve positifs, déterminé que le préjudice des producteurs canadiens de maïs en grains était causé par les importations de maïs en grains subventionné originaire des États-Unis.[17] Le Groupe spécial recommandait donc que le Comité demande au Canada d'instituer son droit compensateur en conformité avec les obligations insérées dans le Code sur les subventions.[18]

---

[14] GATT: C/M/320 (1992).

[15] Voir *Focus, Bulletin d'information du GATT*, no 91, 1992, p. 4.

[16] Voir le texte du rapport du Groupe spécial dans le document du GATT: SCM/140 (1992).

[17] Le Groupe spécial plus précisément était appelé à se prononcer à savoir si la détermination du Tribunal se fondait sur un examen objectif (a) du volume des importations subventionnées de maïs en grains originaire des États-Unis et de leurs effets sur les prix des produits similaires au Canada et (b) des répercussions de ces importations sur les producteurs canadiens du produit similaire.

[18] Soulignons que le Canada avait cependant dès le 15 janvier cessé de prélever des droits compensateurs sur les importations de maïs en grains américain en vertu de la clause d'extinction automatique contenue dans sa législation sur les droits compensateurs. Voir *Maïs-grain subventionné, sous toutes ses formes, à l'exception du maïs de semence du maïs sucré et du maïs à éclater, originaires ou exportés des États-Unis d'Amérique*, expiration no LE-91-003, 15 janvier 1992.

D'autres événements survenus dans le cadre du GATT auront retenu notre attention en 1992. Soulignons d'abord que le Comité des pratiques antidumping accéda à la requête des États-Unis visant à établir un Groupe spécial en vertu de l'Accord relatif à la mise en oeuvre de l'article VI de l'Accord général et ce, pour examiner l'application par le Canada des droits antidumping à l'égard de la bière d'origine américaine.[19] Par ailleurs, le Groupe spécial chargé d'examiner les prétentions canadiennes à l'égard de la décision des États-Unis d'ouvrir une enquête sur le magnésium en provenance du Canada, aura suspendu ses travaux à la demande des deux pays et ce, jusqu'au moment où sera prononcée la décision finale du Département du commerce concernant la procédure de révision pour changement de circonstances. Mentionnons finalement que le secrétariat du GATT a publié au cours de l'année son second rapport sur les politiques commerciales du Canada.[20] Le secrétariat reconnaissait plus particulièrement que le Canada depuis les années 80 avait mis en oeuvre des réformes visant à rationaliser son régime réglementaire et à ouvrir les marchés protégés à la concurrence. Des préoccupations auront toutefois encore été exprimées sur différents sujets tels l'existence de crêtes tarifaires sur les textiles, les vêtements et les chaussures de même que les limitations des avantages du Tarif de préférence général pour les fournisseurs de ces produits, l'application de régimes restrictifs notamment sur la volaille et les produits laitiers, ainsi que la mise en oeuvre par les provinces de politiques de soutien incluant des pratiques de commercialisation et de passation de marchés discriminatoires de la part des monopoles d'État.

---

[19] GATT: ADP/90 (1992). Les États-Unis étaient particulièrement préoccupés par la décision du Tribunal canadien du commerce extérieur de conclure à l'existence d'un préjudice à une branche de production régionale, en l'occurrence celle de la Colombie-britannique, sans qu'une concentration d'importations faisant l'objet d'un dumping dans cette province, critère essentiel pour la détermination d'un marché régional au sens du Code antidumping, n'ait été prouvée. Voir à cet égard la décision du Tribunal *La bière originaire ou exportée des États-Unis d'Amérique*, enquête no NQ-91-002, 2 octobre 1991.

[20] Voir le rapport préparé par le Secrétariat du GATT à titre d'information pour les Parties contractantes, dans le document du GATT: C/RM/S/25A (1992). Ce rapport fera l'objet prochainement d'une publication du Secrétariat à l'intention de la population. Rappelons que les politiques commerciales des Parties contractantes sont examinées régulièrement en vertu du Mécanisme d'examen des politiques commerciales institué lors de l'examen à mi-parcours de l'Uruguay Round.

II   MISE EN OEUVRE DE L'ACCORD DE LIBRE-ÉCHANGE CANADA-ÉTATS-UNIS

La quatrième année de mise en oeuvre de l'Accord de libre-échange Canada-États-Unis[21] aura tel que prévu permis aux deux pays d'améliorer les conditions d'accès à leurs marchés respectifs tout en leur assurant des relations commerciales bilatérales plus sûres et prévisibles. Les échanges bilatéraux sont passés de 244 milliards de dollars en 1988 à 256,8 milliards de dollars en 1991, soit une augmentation de 12,8 milliards de dollars, et ce, malgré la récession qui a sévi au Canada et aux États-Unis pendant cette période.[22] Alors que le 17 décembre, les deux pays concluaient les négociations avec le Mexique, par la signature de l'Accord de libre-échange Nord-Américain,[23] il est maintenant approprié de décrire comment s'est traduite en 1992 la mise en oeuvre législative et jurisprudentielle de l'Accord de libre-échange Canada-États-Unis.

A   MISE EN OEUVRE LÉGISLATIVE

Outre la quatrième réduction progressive des droits de douanes, laquelle s'est effectuée conformément à l'Accord de libre-échange,[24] il y a lieu de mentionner que le 5 septembre, le Gouvernement du Canada publiait dans la Gazette du Canada la liste des propositions en vue de l'élimination accélérée des droits de

[21] *Accord de libre-échange entre le Gouvernement du Canada et le Gouvernement des États-Unis d'Amérique*, signé le 2 janvier 1988, en vigueur le 1er janvier 1989, reproduit dans (1988) 27 ILM 281 (ci-après dénommé l'Accord de libre-échange).

[22] Voir Ministre de l'Industrie, des Sciences et de la Technologie et ministre du commerce extérieur, *Communiqué de presse*, no 118, 9 juin 1992.

[23] Cet Accord, qui doit entrer en vigueur le 1er janvier 1994 après ratification par les trois pays, sera étudié dans une prochaine chronique.

[24] Tel que le dispose l'Accord, une quatrième réduction tarifaire de 20% et de 10% s'est opérée le 1er janvier 1992 sur les catégories d'échelonnement B et C respectivement. *Accord de libre-échange, supra*, note 21, art. 401 (2)(b) et 401 (2)(c). Soulignons également la réduction de l'écart de majoration des prix du vin supérieur, qui le 1er janvier 1992 ne devait plus dépasser 30% de l'écart de base entre l'écart de majoration appliqué par les autorités en 1987 et l'écart des frais de service réels. *Id.*, art. 803 (2)(d), de même que l'élimination graduelle des restrictions à l'importation des automobiles d'occasion, autorisant l'admission en franchise dès 1992 de ces dernières, si elles sont vieilles de deux ans et plus. *Id.*, art. 1003 (d). D'autre part, les redevances pour opérations douanières qui s'appliquent aux importations en provenance du Canada ont été comme prévu réduites et elles représentent ainsi maintenant 40% des redevances par ailleurs applicables. *Id.*, art. 403 (3)(c).

douanes.[25] Cette troisième et dernière série de consultations publiques pour devancer l'échéance prévue pour l'abolition des droits de douanes ne porte cependant que sur les produits pour lesquels l'élimination des droits se devait d'être effective après une période de 10 ans. La date limite pour soumettre des commentaires à l'égard de ces propositions fut fixée au 2 novembre afin que les changements aux listes tarifaires puissent s'opérer au printemps 1993.[26] Par ailleurs, suite à une entente intervenue entre les deux pays sur des normes de rendement compatibles à l'égard du contreplaqué, les droits de douanes applicables sur ce produit seront dès le 1er janvier 1993 réduits de moitié et le seront par la suite progressivement chaque année conformément à l'Accord de libre-échange.[27] Dans le secteur de l'agriculture, les deux pays sont d'autre part arrivés à une entente modifiant la méthodologie à appliquer pour le calcul du niveau de soutien pour l'orge.[28] Puisque, suite à l'application de cette méthode de calcul, le niveau de soutien accordé par le Canada à l'égard de ce produit, s'avérait inférieur à celui des États-Unis, le Canada conformément à l'article 705 de l'Accord de libre-échange, a pu continuer à exiger des licences d'importation pour l'orge américain.[29] Par ailleurs, au titre de la disposition relative au "retour aux droits antérieurs" pour les

25 *Invitation à commenter les demandes d'élimination accélérée des droits de douane en vertu de l'Accord de libre-échange*, (1992) Gaz. Can. I 3023. Près de 280 demandes portant sur 400 positions tarifaires ont à cet égard été présentées à la date limite de la réception des demandes du secteur privé, date fixée au 17 janvier. Rappelons par ailleurs que l'Accord de libre-échange, en vertu de l'article 401 (5), prévoit l'élimination anticipée des droits, sous réserve de l'accord des deux pays.

26 Gouvernement du Canada, *Communiqué de presse*, no 179, 3 septembre 1992.

27 Voir Ministre de l'industrie, des Sciences et de la Technologie et ministre du Commerce extérieur, *Communiqué de presse*, no 243, 22 décembre 1992. Pour les produits connexes tels que les panneaux de grandes particules et les panneaux de particules, les droits seront complètement abolis dès le 1er janvier 1993. On se rappellera que les deux pays avaient, au moment de l'entrée en vigueur de l'Accord de libre-échange, suspendu les réductions de droits de douanes à l'égard du contreplaqué et des produits connexes. Voir M. ST-AMANT, "Chronique de droit économique international," (1990) 28 *ACDI*, 442.

28 Voir *Échange de Lettres constituant un Accord entre le gouvernement du Canada et le gouvernement des États-Unis d'Amérique modifiant l'appendice 2 de l'Annexe 705.4 de l'Accord de libre-échange*, (1992) R.T. Can., no 25.

29 Le Canada a cependant été obligé, au titre de l'article 705 de l'Accord, de continuer à ne pas imposer de licences d'importation à l'égard du blé ou des produits du blé. Sur cette disposition de l'Accord, voir par ailleurs, M. ST-AMANT, "Chronique de droit économique international," (1991) 29 *ACDI*, 424.

fruits et légumes frais, énoncée à l'article 702 de l'Accord de libre-échange, le Canada a imposé à la lumière de l'accroissement des importations en provenance des États-Unis, un droit temporaire additionnel sur les importations de laitues pommées à l'état frais ou réfrigérées, les choux à l'état frais ou réfrigérés et les pêches à l'état frais.[30] Soulignons, en outre qu'une entente administrative est intervenue entre Agriculture Canada et le Département américain de l'agriculture sur l'inspection des viandes et de la volaille.[31] En ce qui concerne le chapitre de l'Accord de libre-échange sur l'autorisation de séjour temporaire pour gens d'affaires, les deux gouvernements se sont entendus pour faciliter cette autorisation sur une base de réciprocité en élargissant la liste des personnes admissibles à l'entrée temporaire et en modifiant à certains égards les exigences minimales en terme d'études pour certaines professions.[32] Soulignons en dernier lieu, l'adoption par les deux pays de nouvelles règles de procédures pour les Groupes spéciaux binationaux institués en vertu de l'article 1904 de l'Accord de libre-échange[33] et le

[30] Voir *Arrêté visant le droit temporaire imposé sur les laitues pommées à l'état frais ou réfrigérées*, (1992) 126 Gaz. Can. II 3058; *Arrêté visant le droit temporaire imposé sur les laitues pommées à l'état frais ou réfrigérées*, arrêté no 2, Gaz. Can. II 3085; *Arrêté visant le droit temporaire imposé sur les choux à l'état frais ou réfrigérés*, Gaz. Can. II 3087; *Arrêté visant le droit temporaire imposé sur les pêches à l'état frais*, Gaz. Can. II 3513. Cette disposition de l'Accord repose sur des critères relatifs au prix à l'importation et à la superficie des terres en culture dans le pays importateur. Les droits rétablis ne doivent pas dépasser les taux NPF en vigueur antérieurement à l'Accord ou, s'ils sont moins élevés, les taux en vigueur au moment où le droit temporaire est institué.

[31] "Entente Canada-US sur l'inspection des viandes" dans *Le devoir*, 15 juin 1992, p. 4. Cette entente réduira les coûts pour les exportateurs et les importateurs. Les cargaisons qui seront sélectionnées pour inspection ne seront plus en effet bloquées à la frontière mais pourront être examinées à l'un des bureaux d'inspection existant aux États-Unis ou au Canada. Vu la similitude des procédures d'inspection, les deux pays avaient d'ailleurs tenté depuis l'entrée en vigueur de l'Accord de libre-échange, d'assouplir les mesures de quarantaine et d'inspection à la frontière.

[32] Voir *Échange de Notes entre le gouvernement du Canada et le gouvernement des États-Unis d'Amérique modifiant les appendices 1 et 2 de l'annexe 1502.1 de l'Accord de libre-échange (avec Appendices)*, entrée en vigueur le 4 août 1992. Pour la mise en oeuvre en droit canadien, voir *Autorisation de séjour temporaire pour gens d'affaires*, (1992) Gaz. Can. I 2571.

[33] Pour la mise en oeuvre de ces règles en droit canadien, voir *Règles de procédure des Groupes spéciaux binationaux formés en vertu de l'article 1904*, (1992) Gaz. Can. I 1621.

dépôt du rapport final du Comité sélect de l'automobile sur la capacité concurrentielle de l'industrie.[34]

B   MISE EN OEUVRE JURISPRUDENTIELLE

Les deux principaux mécanismes de règlement des différends prévus par l'Accord de libre-échange ont comme les années précédentes, fonctionné adéquatement. Ils auront encore permis aux exportateurs canadiens d'affronter la concurrence sur le marché américain dans des conditions plus prévisibles et plus équitables. Dans le cadre du chapitre 18, outre les consultations bilatérales engagées au titre de l'article 1804 concernant les problèmes liés à l'application des règles d'origine soulevées par la vérification des automobiles Honda[35] et l'accréditation de certains organismes de certification,[36] on peut souligner les demandes par le Canada et les États-Unis de création de Groupes d'experts en ce qui concerne respectivement les livraisons de lait UHT à Porto Rico,[37] et le blé dur.[38] Un seul Groupe d'experts aura cependant rendu une décision en 1992. Ce Groupe, institué à la demande du Canada pour examiner le traitement des intérêts comme coût direct d'assemblage dans l'interprétation des règles d'origine, aura jugé, dans une décision unanime, que tous les paiements d'intérêts sur quelque dette que ce soit contractée pour financer l'acquisition de matériel

34 Voir *Competitiveness of the North American Automotive Industry, Report of the U.S.-Canada Automotive Select Panel*, juin 1992. Le Comité concluait que la compétivité de l'industrie automobile en Amérique du Nord avait décliné significativement pendant les deux dernières décennies et que les probabilités d'un nouveau déclin se devaient d'être prises au sérieux. Le Comité pour endiguer ce déclin a donc défini neuf catégories de facteurs pouvant améliorer la capacité concurrentielle de l'industrie. Le Comité recommandait en outre qu'un programme stratégique soit adopté en considérant certaines initiatives que pourraient prendre le secteur privé et le secteur public.

35 Cette demande de consultation présentée par le Canada fait suite à une décision des douanes américaines d'imposer un droit de douane de 2.5% sur chaque automobile produite par cette compagnie et importée aux États-Unis. Selon le service douanier des États-Unis, le contenu canado-américain s'avérait insuffisant pour répondre à la norme de 50% prévue par l'Accord de libre-échange. Voir à ce sujet 10 *Int'l Trade Rep.* (BNA)384 (1992).

36 Cette demande de consultation originait des États-Unis et visait à l'accréditation de certains organismes américains par le Canada.

37 *Dans l'affaire de la réglementation de Porto Rico sur l'importation, la distribution et la vente de lait U.H.T. du Québec*, Dossier USA-93-1807-01.

38 *Dans l'affaire de l'interprétation et de l'application par le Canada de l'article 701.3 relativement au blé dur*, Dossier CDA-92-1807-01.

d'usine ou de biens immeubles pouvaient être inclus dans le coût direct du traitement ou de montage dont il est question à l'article 304 de l'Accord de libre-échange.[39] En outre, le Groupe a constaté que l'interprétation administrative des États-Unis relativement à ces frais d'intérêts s'avérait incompatible avec les dispositions de l'Accord de libre-échange. De l'avis du Groupe, ce ne sont donc pas, comme le prétendaient les États-Unis, exclusivement les intérêts hypothécaires qui constitueraient des dépenses admissibles dans le calcul de la teneur régionale aux termes de l'Accord. Quant au mécanisme particulier de règlement des différends en matière de droits antidumping et compensateurs, les décisions des Groupes spéciaux binationaux formés au terme du chapitre 19 de l'Accord de libre-échange auront été moins nombreuses que par les années passées. Trois des quatre décisions nationales examinées par les Groupes spéciaux concernent au demeurant des décisions du Département du commerce des États-Unis relativement à l'examen administratif des ordonnances d'impositions des droits. Les ordonnances contestées portent ainsi sur la décision après renvoi à l'égard des pièces de rechange pour les épandeuses automotrices de revêtements bitumineux du Canada,[40] sur le quatrième examen administratif de l'ordonnance d'imposition des droits compensateurs à l'égard des porcs vivants du Canada,[41] et sur le cinquième

---

[39] *Traitement des intérêts selon le chapitre 3*, Dossier USA-92-1807-01.

[40] *Pièces de rechange pour les épandeuses automotrices de revêtement bitumineux du Canada*, Dossier USA-90-1904-01. Il s'agissait premièrement dans ce dossier de déterminer si la décision du Département du commerce à l'égard du calcul de la marge de dumping était, selon les critères d'examen prévus par le droit américain, appuyée par une preuve substantielle au dossier ou conforme au droit. A cet égard, les corrections d'erreurs administratives, les rectifications de la marge de dumping ainsi que l'inclusion des ventes prétendument d'origines non canadiennes furent des sujets examinés. La seconde question en litige était de savoir si la décision du Département du commerce d'utiliser les meilleurs renseignements disponibles quant au solde des ventes effectuées aux États-Unis et son choix comme meilleurs renseignements disponibles de la marge de dumping issue de l'enquête initiale, s'avéraient justifiées par une preuve substantielle au dossier ou autrement conforme au droit américain. Le Groupe spécial confirmait en partie et renvoyait en partie la décision du Département.

[41] *Porcs vivants en provenance du Canada*, Dossier USA-91-1904-03. Les plaignants contestent sept des neuf programmes jugés compensables par le Département du commerce, c'est-à-dire conférant des subventions donnant lieu à compensation. Les questions à décider, eu égard aux critères d'examen prévus par le droit américain, portaient entre autres sur la norme juridique à appliquer pour conclure à la spécificité de facto d'un programme, sur le principe de l'autorité

examen administratif quant à ce même produit.[42] L'unique décision canadienne portée devant un Groupe spécial concerne la décision définitive de dumping rendue par le sous-ministre du Revenu national pour les Douanes et l'Accise dans l'affaire de la bière.[43]

---

de la chose jugée, sur l'exclusion de certains produits de l'ordonnance, sur le calcul des subventions et la question des avantages économiques et finalement sur l'interprétation de la Section 771 A (upstream subsidy). Le Groupe spécial confirmait en partie et renvoyait en partie la décision du Département.

42 *Dans l'affaire des porcs vivants,* Dossier USA-91-1904-04. Les plaignants contestent ici, cinq des seize programmes jugés compensables par le Département du commerce. La plupart des questions à examiner étaient semblables à celles du quatrième examen administratif. Le Groupe spécial confirmait en partie et renvoyait en partie la décision du Département.

43 *Dans l'affaire de: La bière originaire des États-Unis d'Amérique et provenant de G. Heileman Brewing Company Inc., Pabst Brewing Company and the Stroh Brewery Company, ou exportée par ces sociétés, pour utilisation ou consommation dans la province de la Colombie-Britannique,* Dossier CDA-91-1904-01. Parmi les questions portées à l'étude du Groupe spécial figurait, le sens de l'expression "marchandises similaires," laquelle est définie dans la Loi sur les mesures spéciales d'importation, et les déterminations de la valeur normale et du prix à l'exportation. Le Groupe spécial confirmait en partie et renvoyait en partie la décision de Revenu Canada.

II Le Canada et le système monétaire international en 1992

préparé par

BERNARD COLAS*

I L Y A DIX ANS DÉJÀ que la crise de la dette des pays en développe- ment a débuté. Le Mexique, dont la décision de suspendre ses remboursements avait déclenché la crise, s'est vu en 1992 radier par le Canada de la liste des pays désignés[1] et a retrouvé accès, dans une certaine mesure, aux marchés internationaux des capitaux. Pour les banques commerciales canadiennes, cette crise apparaît structurellement terminée car l'endettement des pays en dévelop- pement ne représente plus une menace systémique au système bancaire international et parce qu'elles ont réduit leurs créances à l'égard de certains pays fortement endettés. Toutefois pour de nombreux pays à faible revenu ou à revenu intermédiaire, notam- ment en Afrique, l'endettement porte toujours de pénibles conséquences.[2]

Outre la Conférence des Nations unies sur l'environnement et le développement (Rio, juin 1992) au cours de laquelle le Canada a promis d'augmenter à 0,7 pour cent du PNB la part d'aide

---

* Avocat au Barreau du Québec, Consultant auprès de l'Organisation de coopéra- tion et de développement économiques, Vice-président à la recherche de la Société de droit international économique. Les opinions exprimées n'engagent que leur auteur.

---

1 Le Canada a décidé de ne plus exiger l'établissement de provisions pour les prêts consentis au Mexique et d'autres risques liés à ce pays. Voir Banque du Canada, *Rapport annuel du gouverneur au Ministre des finances et relevé de comptes pour l'année 1992*, p. 11.

2 Banque mondiale, *World Debt Tables 1992-1993* (1993), pp. 58-59.

publique au développement d'ici l'an 2000[3] alors qu'elle atteignait
0,46 pour cent,[4] l'année 1992 ne brille pas d'événements particulièrement spectaculaires; au niveau interne, le gouvernement fédéral s'attache à réduire le déficit budgétaire[5] et à proposer une
nouvelle réforme constitutionnelle. Au niveau international, la
situation des républiques de l'ex-URSS dont la production a dimi-
nué de 20% en 1992 retient l'attention du Canada (partie I) de
même que les efforts d'harmonisation des règles des marchés financiers et l'intensification de la coopération des autorités de contrôle
du système bancaire et financier (partie II).

I   INSTITUTIONS FINANCIÈRES INTERNATIONALES

L'action du Canada pour venir en aide aux pays de l'ex-URSS est
coordonnée sur le plan bilatéral par son Groupe de travail sur
l'Europe centrale et l'Europe de l'est. Au niveau multilatéral, le
Canada participe au Groupe des vingt-quatre[6] et à plusieurs institutions financières internationales.

En 1992, le Canada, avec ses partenaires du Groupe des sept,[7] a
soutenu l'adhésion des nouvelles républiques issues du démantèle-
ment de l'ex-URSS au Fonds monétaire international (FMI),[8] à la
Banque mondiale[9] et à la Banque européenne pour la reconstruction et le développement (BERD). Cette participation leur donne
droit d'obtenir de ces institutions une assistance financière et technique destinée à contribuer au développement de leur économie et
à faciliter leur passage à l'économie de marché. Le tableau ci-
dessous permet d'apprécier la rapidité avec laquelle les institutions

---

[3] Déclaration du ministre de l'Environnement, Jean Charest, rapportée par
André Noël, "Ottawa portera à 4,7 milliards son aide aux pays pauvres," *La
presse*, 9 juin 1992. D'autres pays tels la France et l'Allemagne ont également
souscrit à un tel objectif.

[4] OCDE, *Ressources financières mises à la disposition des pays en développement en 1992 et
tendances récentes*, SG/PRESS(93)41.

[5] Le Canada a adopté des mesures destinées à réduire le déficit budgétaire. *Loi
instituant des plafonds pour les dépenses publiques*, Chap. 19, sanctionnée le 18 juin
1992.

[6] Composé des vingt-quatre pays Membres de l'Organisation de coopération et de
développement économiques (OCDE).

[7] Déclaration de Munich, 1992.

[8] "Canada Makes IMF Plea," *Financial Post*, 25 janvier 1992.

[9] La BIRD, comme le FMI, a porté en 1992 le nombre des administrateurs de 22 à
24. *Rapport annuel de la Banque mondiale 1993* (1993), p. 19.

financières internationales ont accueilli ces nouveaux Etats; situation qui confirme pour la première fois la vocation universelle des institutions de Bretton Woods (FMI et BIRD).

L'élargissement du champ d'intervention des institutions financières internationales a opéré une pression sur leurs ressources. En 1992, le FMI a mis en oeuvre la décision, approuvée en 1990 à l'occasion de la 9ème révision générale, d'augmenter les quotes-parts. Cet accroissement des ressources, entré en vigueur le 11 novembre 1992, porte la taille du Fonds à 144,8 milliards DTS, soit une progression de 50% et met le FMI en mesure d'appuyer les programmes d'ajustement de la balance des paiements dans les Etats de l'ex-URSS et dans les pays en développement. Cette augmentation permet aussi au FMI de financer ses activités de prêts sans avoir à emprunter de ressources à ses membres.[10] Au sein du Groupe de la Banque mondiale, le Conseil des gouverneurs de la SFI a approuvé une augmentation de capital de 1 milliard USD le 4 mai 1992, ce qui a fait passer le capital de la SFI de 1,3 milliard à 2,3 milliards USD.[11] Le Canada peut souscrire jusqu'à 35 366 nouvelles actions de la SFI, évaluées à 35,4 millions USD. Les actions devraient être libérées au cours des cinq prochaines années. Enfin, l'accord sur la dixième reconstitution des ressources de l'Agence internationale de développement (IDA),[12] conclu en décembre 1992, porte le capital à environ 13 milliards DTS (18 milliards USD) et lui assure des ressources pour trois années (jusqu'au 30 juin 1996) débutant en juillet 1993.[13] La part du Canada représente 4% de la reconstitution; il fournira 519,91 millions DTS (829 millions CAD) sur une période de huit ans.

Au niveau européen, le Canada a effectué le 27 mai 1992 un deuxième versement de 23,8 millions USD au capital social de la

---

[10] Les Accords généraux d'emprunts, reconduits par les pays du G-10, n'ont pas été utilisés par le FMI en 1992. Par ailleurs, le ministre des Finances Don Mazankowski, président du G-10, soutenait la proposition de créer un Fonds de stabilisation du rouble avec l'aide des Accords généraux d'emprunts. Notes pour une allocution du ministre des Finances l'Honorable Don Mazankowski au Comité intérimaire du Fonds monétaire international (FMI), *Ministère des Finances information*, no. 92-037, Ottawa, 27 avril 1992.

[11] *Rapport annuel de la Banque mondiale 1993* (1993), pp. 116-17.

[12] L'IDA accorde actuellement des crédits pour 35 à 40 ans sans intérêt, moyennant des frais de service de 0,75% et une franchise de remboursement du principal de dix ans.

[13] *Op. cit.*, note 11, p. 65.

Banque européenne pour la reconstruction et le développement (BERD)[14] et a créé dans le cadre de la BERD le 24 janvier 1992 le Fonds canadien de coopération technique (FCCT) doté d'un million de dollars CAD.[15] La dissolution de l'ex-URSS et de l'ex-Yougoslavie a soulevé des questions de succession aux quotes-parts. Par exemple, les gouverneurs de la BERD et du FMI ont décidé que les actions détenues par l'ex-URSS et par l'ex-Yougoslavie seraient partagées entre les États qui lui ont succédé.[16]

L'assistance accordée par ces institutions est fréquemment liée à l'adoption de programmes comportant une forte composante de réformes structurelles. Le Canada est d'avis que ces réformes ont contribué au succès de la stratégie de la dette dont la conclusion des accords de rééchelonnement du Club de Paris[17] dépend.[18] Le Canada, membre du Comité d'aide au développement (CAD) de

---

[14] Le Canada s'est engagé à verser 30% du capital souscrit de 340 millions d'écus, représentant 3,44% du capital souscrit total, sur cinq ans. Le premier versement de 23 807 004 USD a été effectué en 1991. À la suite d'une décision du 25 novembre 1991 relative à l'encaissement des billets futurs, seule la somme de 3,9 millions USD a été encaissée représentant le tiers du versement sous forme de billets. *Rapport sur les opérations réalisées en vertu de la Loi sur l'Accord portant création de la Banque européenne pour la reconstruction et le développement 1992* (1993), Ottawa, pp. 14-15.

[15] Ce fonds a pour principal objectif de retenir les services de Canadiens comme experts-conseils pour fournir à la BERD des services d'aide technique, de formation et de consultation. Il est géré avec le concours du Groupe de travail du Canada sur l'Europe central et l'Europe de l'est. Deux projets totalisant 460 000 CAD ont été financés par le Fonds en 1992. *Op. cit.*, note 14, pp. 14-15.

[16] *Rapport annuel 1992 de la Banque européenne pour la reconstruction et le développement* (1993), pp. 8.

[17] Le Club de Paris est le nom donné aux réunions ad hoc de gouvernements créanciers qui, depuis 1956, conviennent, le cas échéant, de renégocier la dette contractée envers les créanciers publics ou garantie par ces derniers. En 1992, 12 pays qui entreprennent des programmes d'ajustement avec le FMI ont bénéficié des "conditions de Toronto élargies" pour une somme consolidée globale de 2,5 milliards USD. *Op. cit.*, note 2, pp. 58-59.

[18] Le ministre des Finances l'Honorable Don Mazankowski a affirmé au Comité intérimaire du FMI que "les succès obtenus au cours des dernières années confirment la justesse de la stratégie de la dette internationale, qui a lié l'aide financière de la communauté internationale à la mise en oeuvre d'une réforme économique solide. . . ." De plus, selon le ministre "les pays d'Afrique qui ont instauré des programmes d'ajustement structurel affichent une croissance deux fois plus élevée que les pays qui n'ont pas adopté de tels programmes . . . ," *op. cit.*, note 10.

l'Organisation de coopération et de développement économiques (OCDE),[19] se fait fréquemment l'avocat d'une amélioration de l'efficacité des conditions d'assistance.

Par exemple, le Canada a continué d'encourager la Banque mondiale à promouvoir des stratégies d'aide par pays plus complètes. Ces stratégies établissent le cadre dans lequel s'inscrivent les interventions financières de la Banque mondiale dans un pays donné. Elles définissent les principales questions et défis économiques ainsi que les domaines dans lesquels l'aide de la Banque est la plus nécessaire. Plus précisément, le Canada a insisté en 1992 pour que soient détaillés certains points comme les efforts du pays en matière de bonne administration (y compris en ce qui concerne l'importance relative des dépenses militaires), la mise en oeuvre des projets, l'engagement de réduire la pauvreté, ainsi que la protection et l'amélioration de l'environnement. Au cours des négociations relatives à la reconstitution de l'IDA, le Canada a obtenu que l'Agence augmente sa part des investissements consacrés au secteur social et à la lutte contre la pauvreté. Il a également souligné la nécessité pour l'IDA de renforcer le rôle des femmes dans le développement et la planification démographique car les investissements engagés dans ce domaine sont essentiels à l'efficacité des programmes d'allègement de la pauvreté.[20]

II Coopération des autorités de contrôle bancaires et financières

L'entrée en vigueur le 1er juin 1992 au Canada des lois sur les institutions financières[21] et l'adoption de nombreux textes réglementaires élargissent le pouvoir des banques et soumettent notam-

---

19 L'OCDE a publié en 1992 "les principes du Comité d'aide au développement (CAD) pour une aide efficace" dont les lignes d'action et les conseils de mise en oeuvre sont le fruit d'une coopération et d'une concertation étroites entre les organismes d'aide des Membres du CAD d'une part et la Banque mondiale, le Fonds monétaire international (FMI) et le Programme des Nations Unies pour le développement (PNUD) d'autre part.

20 *Rapport sur les opérations effectuées en vertu de la Loi sur les accords de Bretton Woods et des accords connexes 1992* (1993), Ottawa, pp. 41-43.

21 *Loi sur les sociétés de fiducie et de prêt, loi sur les banques, loi sur les sociétés d'assurances* et *loi sur les associations coopératives de crédit* sanctionnées le 13 décembre 1991, S.C. 1991, c. 45 à 48. Décrets fixant la date d'entrée en vigueur de ces lois, adoptés le 7 mai 1992, C.P. 1992-926 à 1992-929, dans: *Gazette du Canada Partie II*, vol. 126, no. 11.

ment les institutions financières non bancaires à de nouvelles règles.[22]

L'harmonisation des règles régissant le secteur bancaire et financier intervient également au niveau international par l'entremise de comités qui tiennent leurs réunions à la Banque des règlements internationaux (BRI) et des organismes de contrôle des marchés financiers membres de l'Organisation internationale des commissions de valeur (OICV).

A   BANQUE DES RÈGLEMENTS INTERNATIONAUX (BRI)

À la suite de l'expérience acquise dans la surveillance d'établissements de crédits internationaux connaissant des problèmes sérieux, comme la Banque de crédit et commerce international (BCCI),[23] le Comité de Bâle sur le contrôle bancaire, avec l'approbation des gouverneurs des banques centrales des pays du Groupe des Dix,[24] a rendu public le 6 juillet 1992 des normes minimales relatives à la surveillance des groupes bancaires internationaux et de leurs établissements à l'étranger. Ces normes minimales, adoptées et appliquées par le Canada,[25] reformulent certains principes exposés dans le Concordat de Bâle[26] et dans son Supplément.

Les quatre normes, formulées en termes généraux, sont destinées à accroître les garanties qu'aucune banque internationale ne pourra opérer à l'avenir sans être assujettie à un contrôle consolidé efficace. Celles-ci doivent être appliquées par les autorités de contrôle lorsqu'elles évaluent leurs relations avec leurs homologues dans d'autres pays. Il incombe notamment à l'autorité du pays d'accueil, dans le ressort de laquelle une banque ou un groupe bancaire cherche à s'implanter, de déterminer si l'autorité de contrôle du pays d'origine de l'établissement en question possède les capacités de surveillance requises pour appliquer les normes minimales suivantes:

---

[22] Lire, par exemple, les textes réglementaires DORS/92-272 à DORS/92-285 et DORS/92-295 à DORS/92-331 dans *Gazette du Canada Partie II* (1992), Vol. 126, no 12.

[23] Voir chronique 1991.

[24] Le G-10 est composé de l'Allemagne, de la Belgique, du Canada, des États-Unis, de la France, de l'Italie, du Japon, des Pays-Bas, du Royaume-Uni, de la Suède et de la Suisse.

[25] *Rapport annuel 1992 du Bureau du surintendant des institutions financières* (1992), pp. 15.

[26] Concordat de Bâle révisé en 1983 et Supplément au Concordat adopté en 1990. Voir Chroniques 1988 et 1990.

(1) Tous les groupes bancaires internationaux et toutes les banques internationales devraient être contrôlés par une autorité du pays d'origine apte à mener à bien la surveillance consolidée.

(2) La création d'un établissement bancaire à l'étranger devrait recevoir l'assentiment préalable de l'autorité de contrôle du pays d'accueil ainsi que de celle(s) du pays d'origine de la banque et, le cas échéant, du groupe bancaire.

(3) Les autorités de contrôle du pays d'origine devraient avoir le pouvoir d'obtenir des informations auprès des établissements à l'étranger des banques ou groupes bancaires sous leur responsabilité.

(4) Si l'autorité du pays d'accueil juge qu'une des normes minimales précédentes n'est pas respectée à sa satisfaction, elle pourrait imposer les restrictions qu'elle estime nécessaires pour satisfaire à ses exigences prudentielles dans le cadre de ces normes minimales, y compris interdire la création d'établissements bancaires.

Le Comité passera en revue, dans le cadre de son examen régulier de contrôle des banques internationales, l'expérience acquise par ses membres en ce qui concerne la mise en oeuvre de ces normes, en vue de déterminer les améliorations ultérieures nécessaires.

Cet effort d'harmonisation s'est également poursuivi en matière de fonds propres. Le Comité de Bâle sur le contrôle bancaire a examiné la possibilité d'intégrer à l'accord de 1988 sur les fonds propres les risques du marché issus des activités commerciales des banques. Les délibérations de ce Comité ont été coordonnées avec les travaux du Groupe technique de l'Organisation internationale des commissions de valeurs (OICV).

B ORGANISATION INTERNATIONALE DES COMMISSIONS DE VALEURS (OICV)

L'OICV,[27] dont le siège et le Secrétariat général permanent sont à Montréal,[28] regroupe l'ensemble des organismes de contrôle des marchés de valeurs développés de même qu'un grand nombre d'organismes de réglementation des marchés de valeurs en voie d'émergence. En 1992, elle compte environ 63 membres réguliers, répartis dans une soixantaine de pays, parmi lesquels l'Ontario Securities Commission et la Commission des valeurs mobilières du

27 Jean-Pierre CRISTEL, "L'Organisation internationale des commissions de valeurs et la coopération internationale en matière de valeurs mobilières," dans *Développements récents en droit des valeurs mobilières 1992*, Service de la formation permanente du Barreau du Québec (1992), Montréal, pp. 93-129.

28 *Loi concernant l'Organisation internationale des commissions de valeurs*, L.Q. 1987, Chap. 143, sanctionnée le 1 décembre 1987.

Québec.[29] La British Columbia Securities Commission participe à titre de membre associé.

Le Comité des présidents de l'OICV, réuni à Londres en juin 1992, a entériné les principes établis par le Groupe technique relatifs à la surveillance des conglomérats financiers.[30] Ces principes sont destinés à servir de guide à l'évaluation des risques des conglomérats financiers, au développement de règles nationales et à la coopération internationale.

Inspirés par l'approche arrêtée par les autorités bancaires, ces principes privilégient l'évaluation globale des risques au sein d'un conglomérat et la coopération entre autorités de contrôle. Ainsi, le premier principe recommande de compléter la surveillance individuelle d'une entité particulière réglementée d'un conglomérat, dont les difficultés présentent un risque de contagion, par une évaluation des risques du groupe dans son ensemble. Les second et troisième principes précisent que les liens de financement et de capital entre entités d'un même groupe doivent faire l'objet de contrôles appropriés et que les risques intra-groupes doivent faire l'objet d'un contrôle particulier et, si nécessaire, certaines limites à ces risques doivent être posées pour les entités réglementées du groupe.

La structure, l'actionnariat et les équipes dirigeantes sont abordés aux principes quatre à six. Ainsi, les autorités de contrôle doivent faire en sorte que la structure financière et décisionnelle d'un conglomérat financier leur soit aisément compréhensible afin qu'elle ne soit pas un obstacle à une surveillance appropriée. Elles doivent également s'efforcer d'identifier les actionnaires susceptibles d'avoir une influence sur l'activité des entités réglementées du groupe, et de s'assurer que ceux-ci offrent toutes les garanties d'honorabilité. Enfin, les autorités de contrôle doivent s'assurer que les dirigeants qui exercent, directement ou indirectement, un contrôle sur une entité réglementée du conglomérat le font dans le respect des normes réglementaires.

En vertu du septième principe, les autorités de contrôle devraient s'efforcer dans la mesure du possible de coopérer de manière à améliorer la surveillance d'un conglomérat. Si plusieurs autorités de contrôle sont responsables de diverses composantes du conglomérat, l'une d'entre elles devrait être désignée comme responsable de l'évaluation des risques du groupe dans son ensemble, sans pour autant

---

29 *Annual Report 1992 of the International Organization of Securities Commissions* (1992), Montréal, pp. 23-28.

30 OICV, *Principles for the supervision of financial conglomerates*, octobre 1992, 34 p.

interférer sur les contrôles particuliers. Enfin, les autorités de contrôle devraient, en vertu du huitième principe, prendre en compte les travaux des auditeurs externes dans la mesure où ils contribuent à une meilleure surveillance du conglomérat dans son ensemble.

Les membres ont également approuvé lors de la conférence de Londres des recommandations relatives au blanchiment de l'argent.[31] Elles faisaient suite aux voeux exprimés par les membres du Groupe d'action financière sur le blanchiment de capitaux, réunis au sein de l'OCDE, d'appliquer les mesures contre le blanchiment de capitaux plus largement dans le secteur financier non bancaire.[32]

Enfin, la Commission des valeurs mobilières du Québec,[33] l'Ontario Securities Commission et la British Columbia Securities Commission (BCSC) ont complété leur réseau d'accords bilatéraux de coopération et d'échanges d'information avec notamment leur homologue français, la Commission des opérations de bourse. Inspirés du modèle d'accord de coopération établi au sein de l'OICV, ces accords visent à la fois le marché des valeurs mobilières et les marchés à terme. Ils prévoient notamment que les signataires joindront leurs efforts pour assurer une action efficace contre les manipulations de marché, les opérations d'initié, le non respect des règles relatives à l'information des actionnaires, les manquements des professionnels à leurs obligations et plus généralement contre tout abus ou activité frauduleuse susceptible de porter préjudice aux investisseurs ou de porter atteinte à la sécurité du marché. Les signataires s'accorderont mutuellement assistance pour se communiquer les informations utiles, recueillir des témoignages et obtenir des documents.[34]

En conclusion, l'universalisation des institutions financières internationales combinée à l'harmonisation des règles régissant les marchés bancaires et financiers créent les conditions propices à la globalisation des marchés.

[31] *Op. cit.*, note 29, p. 8.

[32] Par ailleurs, le Canada a aidé en 1992 à l'établissement d'un groupe de travail sur le blanchiment des fonds dans la région des Caraïbes. Ministre des Finances, *Communiqué*, 92-052.

[33] Des accords de coopération avec des organismes de contrôle du Royaume Uni, des Pays Bas, de l'Italie, de Hong Kong, de la Pologne et de la Roumanie ont été élaborés. Par ailleurs, la Commission a signé une entente concernant la création du Conseil des autorités de réglementation des valeurs mobilières des Amériques (Council of Securities Regulators of the Americas).

[34] *Commission des opérations de bourse 1992*: Rapport au Président de la République (1992), Paris, pp. 248-49.

III   Investissement

préparé par
PIERRE RATELLE*

I   ACTIONS UNILATÉRALES

A   MISE EN OEUVRE DE L'ACCORD DE LIBRE-ÉCHANGE CANADA-ÉTATS-UNIS

COMME LE PRÉVOIT L'ACCORD de libre-échange Canada-États-Unis (ALÉ), la *Loi sur investissement Canada* ("LIC") a été modifiée, le 1er janvier 1992, pour une quatrième année consécutive en faveur des investisseurs américains.

Le seuil d'examen par l'agence Investissement Canada de l'acquisition directe d'une entreprise canadienne par un Américain passe de 100 millions à 150 millions de dollars;[1] ce qui représente un seuil 30 fois plus élevé que celui auquel sont soumis les autres investisseurs étrangers.[2] Quant à l'acquisition indirecte d'une entreprise canadienne par un Américain, elle ne sera plus soumise dorénavant à un examen de la part d'Investissement Canada;[3] tandis que les autres investisseurs étrangers demeurent, quant à eux, toujours assujettis au seuil d'examen de 50 millions de dollars.[4]

---

* Avocat au Barreau de Montréal, Chargé de cours à l'Université du Québec à Montréal, Docteur en droit de l'Université de Paris I, DEA de droit international économique de l'Université de Paris I, DEA de droit international public de l'Université de Paris II, LL.B. de l'Université Laval.

1 Voir *Loi de mise en oeuvre de l'Accord de libre-échange entre le Gouvernement du Canada et le Gouvernement des États-Unis d'Amérique*, S.C. 1988, c. 65, Annexe 1607.3, art. 2 § (i) (d).

2 Voir *LIC*, S.C. 1985, c. 20, art. 14.

3 *Supra* note 1, art. 2 § (ii) (d).

4 *Supra* note 2, art. 15.

B   BUDGET FÉDÉRAL FAVORABLE AUX INVESTISSEMENTS
    ÉTRANGERS

Au mois de février 1992, le gouvernement fédéral a présenté à la Chambre des communes un budget qui comprenait des propositions de réforme de l'impôt visant à garantir que le régime fiscal des sociétés au Canada demeure concurrentiel par rapport aux régimes fiscaux en vigueur à l'échelle internationale, en particulier aux États-Unis.[5]

Parmi les propositions visant "à favoriser les initiatives et les investissements productifs," on peut mentionner: (1) La hausse de la déduction pour amortissement du matériel de fabrication et de transformation;[6] (2) La réduction du taux d'imposition des bénéfices de fabrication et de transformation;[7] (3) La réduction de la retenue fiscale sur les dividendes directs;[8] (4) L'amélioration des mesures fiscales concernant la recherche et le développement (R.-D.).[9]

C   NOUVELLE POLITIQUE DANS LE SECTEUR ÉNERGÉTIQUE
    CONCERNANT LA PROPRIÉTÉ ÉTRANGÈRE

À la suite de son budget de février 1992, le gouvernement fédéral a décidé, le mois suivant, d'abandonner sa politique sur les acquisitions pétrolières et gazières, qui interdisait la vente à des investisseurs étrangers de sociétés pétrolières et gazières canadiennes en bonne situation financière.[10]

L'abandon de cette politique ne signifie toutefois pas l'élimination du rôle du gouvernement dans ce domaine. En effet, les

[5] Voir DEPARTMENT OF FINANCE OF CANADA, *The Budget 1992, Tabled in the House of Commons by the Honourable Don Mazankowski, Minister of Finance, February 25, 1992*, Ottawa, Department of Finance of Canada, 1992, 170 p.

[6] Le gouvernement fédéral propose de porter le taux d'amortissement de 25% à 30% *Id.*, pp. 149-50.

[7] Le taux passerait de 23% à 22% à compter du 1er janvier 1993, et diminuerait d'un autre point le 1er janvier 1994. *Id.*, pp. 150-51.

[8] Le gouvernement fédéral est disposé à négocier une entente de réciprocité avec ses partenaires commerciaux, afin de ramener à 5% cette retenue fiscale. *Id.*, pp. 151-54.

[9] Le budget comprend un engagement visant à accroître le crédit d'impôt en R.-D. d'environ 230 millions de dollars au cours des cinq prochaines années. *Id.*, pp. 154-56.

[10] Voir "Ottawa assouplit les règles d'investissement pour les étrangers dans le secteur énergétique," dans *Le Devoir*, 26 mars 1992, p. A5.

acquisitions directes d'entreprises canadiennes de plus de cinq millions de dollars et les acquisitions indirectes d'entreprises canadiennes de plus de 50 millions de dollars par des investisseurs étrangers, seront soumises à un examen d'Investissement Canada, qui les évaluera selon le critère prévu par la LIC, soit celui de "l'avantage net pour le Canada."[11]

D'autre part, la LIC sera modifiée de manière à ce que les investissements américains dans le secteur pétrolier et gazier soient assujettis aux même seuils d'examen que ceux qui s'appliquent aux autres secteurs de l'économie aux termes de l'ALÉ. Ainsi, le seuil d'examen pour l'acquisition directe d'une entreprise canadienne par un investisseur américain sera de 150 millions de dollars; tandis qu'une acquisition indirecte ne sera soumise à aucun examen.[12]

II ACTIONS BILATÉRALES ET MULTILATÉRALES

A CONVENTION SUR LA PROMOTION ET LA PROTECTION DES INVESTISSEMENTS

Le 9 mars 1992, la convention de promotion et la protection des investissements (CPPI), conclue deux ans plus tôt avec la Tchécoslovaquie, est entrée en vigueur.[13] Le Canada peut maintenant compter sur un réseau de six CPPI.[14]

Le contenu de la CPPI avec la Tchécoslovaquie est semblable à celui des CPPI antérieures.[15] On y trouve une définition des termes "investissement,"[16] "investisseur,"[17] "revenus"[18] et "territoire."[19]

---

11 *Supra* note 2, art. 21.

12 Voir R. BUSHNELL, "Nouvelle politique sur les acquisitions pétrolières et gazières," dans *Investir au Canada*, vol. 5, no. 4, printemps 1992, p. 9.

13 Voir *Accord entre le gouvernement du Canada et le gouvernement de la République fédérale tchèque et slovaque sur l'encouragement et la protection des investissements*, [1992] R.T. Can., no 10.

14 Les autres CPPI ont été conclues avec l'ex-URSS, la Hongrie, la Pologne, l'Uruguay et l'Argentine.

15 Au sujet de ces CPPI, voir P. RATELLE, "Investissement," (1992) 30 *ACDI* 337; (1991) 29 *ACDI* 446-47; (1990) 28 *ACDI* 453-54.

16 *Supra* note 13, art. I § (a).

17 *Id.*, art. I § (b).

18 *Id.*, art. I § (c).

19 *Id.*, art. I § (d).

Des règles concernant l'admission,[20] le traitement,[21] la protection,[22] le transfert des fonds,[23] la subrogation[24] et le règlement des différends[25] sont également prévues.

B CONVENTIONS FISCALES

Le réseau canadien de conventions fiscales (CF), qui en compte une soixantaine, s'est encore accru en 1992 avec la conclusion de trois CF avec, dans l'ordre chronologique, la Hongrie,[26] le Zimbabwe[27] et le Nigéria.[28] De plus, trois CF sont entrées en vigueur durant l'année, soit deux avec le Mexique[29] et une avec la Tchécoslovaquie.[30] Les principes et règles qui sont contenus dans ces CF sont similaires aux CF antérieures, lesquelles ont pour modèles originels ceux de l'OCDE.[31]

[20] *Id.*, art. II.

[21] *Id.*, art. art. III § (2), (3) et (4).

[22] *Id.*, art. III § (4) et VI.

[23] *Id.*, art. VII.

[24] *Id.*, art. VIII.

[25] *Id.*, art. IX.

[26] Voir *Convention entre le gouvernement du Canada et le gouvernement de la République de Hongrie en vue d'éviter les doubles impositions et de prévenir l'évasion fiscale en matière d'impôts sur le revenu et la fortune*, signée à Budapest, le 15 avril 1992.

[27] Voir *Convention entre le gouvernement du Canada et le gouvernement de la République du Zimbabwe en vue d'éviter les doubles impositions et de prévenir l'évasion fiscale en matière d'impôts sur le revenu et la fortune et sur les gains en capital*, signée à Harare, le 16 avril 1992.

[28] Voir *Convention entre le gouvernement du Canada et le gouvernement de la République fédérale du Nigéria en vue d'éviter les doubles impositions et de prévenir l'évasion fiscale en matière d'impôts sur le revenu et sur les gains en capital*, signée à Abuja, le 4 août 1992.

[29] Voir *Convention entre le gouvernement du Canada et le gouvernement des États-Unis Mexicains sur l'échange de renseignements en matière fiscale*, [1992] R.T. Can., no 13; *Convention entre le gouvernement du Canada et le gouvernement des États-Unis Mexicains en vue d'éviter les doubles impositions et de prévenir l'évasion fiscale en matière d'impôts sur le revenu (avec Protocole)*, [1992] R.T. Can., no 15.

[30] Voir *Convention entre le gouvernement du Canada et le gouvernement de la République fédérative tchèque et slovaque en vue d'éviter les doubles impositions et de prévenir l'évasion fiscale en matière d'impôts sur le revenu et sur la fortune*, [1992] R.T. Can., no 16.

[31] Le texte de ces modèles de conventions est reproduit dans OCDE, *Modèle de convention de double imposition concernant le revenu et la fortune* (septembre 1977), 226 p.; *Modèle de convention de double imposition concernant les successions et les donations* (mai 1983), 152 p.

C SIGNATURE DE L'ACCORD DE LIBRE-ÉCHANGE NORD-AMÉRICAIN

À la fin de 1992, le Premier ministre canadien, Brian Mulroney, le Président américain, Georges Bush, et le Président mexicain, Carlos Salinas de Gortari, ont signé l'Accord de libre-échange nord-américain (ALÉNA).[32] Il est prévu qu'il entrera en vigueur le 1er janvier 1994, après avoir été examiné et approuvé par la Chambre des communes du Canada, le Congrès américain et le Sénat du Mexique.[33]

L'ALÉNA contient un chapitre sur l'investissement qui s'applique aux investisseurs d'un pays de l'ALÉNA et à leurs investissements et, en ce qui concerne les prescriptions de résultats et les mesures environnementales, à tous les investissements étrangers effectués sur le territoire d'un pays de l'ALÉNA et ce, peu importe leur origine.[34] Quant aux investissements dans le secteur des services financiers, ils sont couverts par un autre chapitre de l'ALÉNA.[35]

Dans l'ALÉNA, les trois pays ont convenu d'accorder aux investisseurs qui originent de la zone de libre-échange nord-américaine le meilleur traitement possible entre le traitement national et le traitement de la nation la plus favorisée.[36] Il est prévu que le traitement national doit aussi être appliqué par les États ou les provinces de chaque pays.[37]

L'ALÉNA interdit aux trois pays signataires de recourir à plusieurs types de prescriptions de résultats contre un investisseur d'un pays signataire, qui envisage d'effectuer un investissement dans un autre pays de l'ALÉNA.[38] Le recours à certains types de prescriptions de résultats est cependant permis sous certaines conditions.[39]

L'ALÉNA prévoit que les mesures gouvernementales qui sont en vigueur, mais qui ne sont pas conformes à l'Accord, et que les trois

[32] Voir J. DION, "L'ALÉNA signé ce matin," dans *Le Devoir*, 17 décembre 1992, p. A5.

[33] Voir ALÉNA, art. 2203. Le texte de l'Accord est reproduit dans *Accord de libre-échange nord-américain entre le Gouvernement du Canada, le Gouvernement des États-Unis d'Amérique et le Gouvernement des États-Unis du Mexique*, Ottawa, Ministre des Approvisionnements et Services Canada, 1992, pagination multiple.

[34] *Id.*, c. 11.

[35] *Id.*, c. 14.

[36] *Id.*, art. 1102-4.

[37] *Id.*, art. 1102 § 2 et 3.

[38] *Id.*, art. 1106 § 1-3.

[39] *Id.*, art. 1106 § 4-6 et 1107.

TABLEAU 1

Adhésion des Républiques de l'ex-URSS et des États baltes
aux institutions financières internationales en 1992

1992	FMI	BIRD	BERD
Arménie	28 mai	16 septembre	27 novembre
Azerbaïdjan	18 septembre	18 septembre	25 septembre
Bélarus	10 juillet	10 juillet	10 juin
Estonie	26 mai	23 juin	28 février
Géorgie	5 mai	7 août	4 septembre
Kazakhstan	15 juillet	23 juillet*	27 juillet
Kirghizistan	8 mai	18 septembre*	5 juin
Lettonie	19 mai	11 août*	18 mars
Lituanie	29 avril	6 juillet	5 mars
Moldova	12 août	12 août	5 mai
Ouzbékistan	21 septembre	21 septembre*	30 avril
Russie	1 juin	16 juin	9 avril
Tadjikistan			16 octobre
Turkménistan	22 septembre	22 septembre	1 juin
Ukraine	3 septembre	3 septembre	13 août

* Adhésion à l'Agence internationale de développement (IDA).

pays désirent maintenir, devront être inscrites dans l'annexe I de
l'Accord, le 1er janvier 1994, afin qu'elles ne soient pas touchées
par l'application de certains articles du chapitre sur l'investissement.[40] Les États et les provinces jouiront toutefois d'un délai de
deux ans pour ajouter à cette annexe les mesures non conformes
qu'ils désirent conserver.[41] Les administrations locales ne sont pas
concernées par cette exigence, puisque l'ALÉNA les en exempte
expressément.[42]

De plus, les secteurs, sous-secteurs ou activités que le gouvernement fédéral désire soustraire de l'application de certains articles
du chapitre sur l'investissement, sont inscrits à l'annexe II de
l'Accord. Il est à souligner que non seulement des mesures existantes non conformes, mais aussi toute nouvelle mesure également

[40] *Id.*, art. 1108.
[41] *Ibid.*
[42] *Ibid.*

non conforme ou plus restrictive, pourront être incluses à cette annexe.[43]

En ce qui concerne les transferts résultant d'investissements effectués par un investisseur d'un autre pays de l'ALÉNA, chaque pays s'engage à ce que ces transferts soient libres de toutes contraintes, en particulier en ce qui concerne les bénéfices, les dividendes, les gains en capital ou produits de la vente partielle ou totale de l'investissement, et que ces transferts puissent être faits dans une devise librement utilisable, au taux de change courant.[44]

Les expropriations et les indemnités visant à réduire l'impact négatif de l'expropriation pour l'investisseur étranger sont encadrées par des règles claires. L'ALÉNA n'autorise que les expropriations ou les nationalisations qui sont faites par un pays dans le strict intérêt public et de façon non discriminatoire.[45] Il faut également que l'investisseur étranger exproprié reçoive une indemnité équivalant à la juste valeur marchande de l'investissement exproprié.[46]

Une clause de l'ALÉNA traite de la protection de l'environnement. Il y est précisé que les pays signataires ne doivent pas déroger ni renoncer à des mesures nationales relatives à la santé, à la sécurité ou à l'environnement dans le but d'encourager l'établissement, l'acquisition, l'expansion ou le maintien sur leur territoire d'un investissement effectué par un investisseur d'un pays de l'ALÉNA ou d'un pays non partie à l'Accord.[47]

Enfin, l'ALÉNA met en place un mécanisme de règlement des différends spécial pour l'investissement qui est distinct du mécanisme général de règlement des différends qui est prévu par l'Accord. Tout investisseur d'un pays de l'ALÉNA, qui estime avoir subi un préjudice à la suite d'une action posée par le gouvernement d'un autre pays de l'ALÉNA où il avait l'intention d'investir, pourra soumettre son cas à l'arbitrage.[48] L'investisseur peut choisir principalement entre deux procédures d'arbitrage: la procédure de la Convention CIRDI (Centre international pour le règlement des différends relatifs aux investissements),[49] et les Règles d'arbitrage

[43] *Id.*, Annexe II, art. 1.

[44] *Id.*, art. 1109.

[45] *Id.*, art. 1110 § 1.

[46] *Id.*, art. 1110 § 2.

[47] *Id.*, art. 1114.

[48] *Id.*, art. 1116-7.

[49] *Id.*, art. 1120 § 1 (a).

de la CNUDCI (Commission des Nations Unies pour le droit commercial international).[50] Si le différend met en présence deux pays et a trait à l'application ou à l'interprétation de l'ALÉNA, il faudra alors se référer au mécanisme général de règlement des différends qui est prévu au chapitre 20 de l'Accord.[51]

[50] *Id.*, art. 1120 § 1 (c).

[51] *Id.*, art. 1115 et 2004.

Canadian Practice in International Law / La pratique canadienne en matière de droit international public

At the Department of External Affairs in 1992-93 / Au ministère des Affaires extérieures en 1992-93

compiled by / préparé par
BARRY MAWHINNEY*

DIPLOMATIC AND CONSULAR RELATIONS

The Right to Consular Assistance

IN AN *amicus curiae* brief filed in the United States District Court for the Eastern District of Texas in support of the appeal of Mr. Stanley Faulder, a Canadian citizen who was convicted of murder in Texas in 1977 and sentenced to death, the Canadian government stated:

The issue in this brief relates to the treatment of a Canadian citizen in the United States and the failure of the Government of the United States to fulfil the terms of the Vienna Convention on Consular Relations. The Government of Canada places a high priority on the right of Canadian

---

* Barry Mawhinney, Legal Adviser, Department of Foreign Affairs, Ottawa. The extracts from official correspondence contained in this survey have been made available by courtesy of the Department of Foreign Affairs. Material appearing in the House of Commons debates is not included. Some of the correspondence from which extracts are given was provided for the general guidance of the inquirer in relation to specific facts which are often not described in full in the extracts contained in this compilation. The statements of law and practice should not necessarily be regarded as a definitive statement by the Department of Foreign Affairs of that law or practice.

citizens arrested abroad to be informed of their right to meet with a Canadian consul and receive assistance from the consul. The failure to inform Mr. Faulder of his right to see a Canadian consul deprived him of the right to assistance from his government, a right that is recognized by the community of nations and is codified in an international convention to which more than 125 countries, including the United States of America, are parties. . . .

The right of consuls to assist their nationals has been affirmed by the practice of states and the works of many writers on international law. The United States has long recognized the right of consular access and assistance, even before the Vienna Convention on Consular Relations came into force on March 17, 1967. The Vienna Convention codified the rules relating to consular relations. The Convention is binding on both countries. It provides in Article 36:

(1) With a view to facilitating the exercise of consular functions relating to nationals of the sending State:

(a) consular officers shall be free to communicate with nationals of the sending State and to have access to them. Nationals of the sending State shall have the same freedom with respect to communication with and access to consular officers of the sending State;

(b) if he so requests, the competent authorities of the receiving State shall, without delay, inform the consular post of the sending State if, within its consular district, a national of that State is arrested or committed to prison or to custody pending trial or is detained in any other manner. . . . *The said authorities shall inform the person concerned without delay of his rights under this sub-paragraph.* [Emphasis added.]

This Article of the Vienna Convention on Consular Relations codifies one of the cardinal principles of international law. It states unequivocally that there is a requirement that the officials of an arresting state inform a foreign prisoner of his right to see his consul. The importance of this provision has been stressed by both the United States and Canada. . . .

The failure of the "competent authorities" of the United States to carry out their obligations under Article 36(1)(b) of the Vienna Convention on Consular Relations to inform Mr. Faulder of his right to have the appropriate Canadian consular post informed of his arrest and detention amounted to a breach of the Convention and a breach of obligations of the United States Government to the Canadian Government thereunder. It is submitted that this breach of the Convention deprived Mr. Faulder of a right under international law that may have prejudiced his ability to receive a fair trial and sentencing hearing. The Government of Canada urges the Court to take this into consideration in making its decision on Mr. Faulder's application.

HUMAN RIGHTS

Minority Rights

In a memorandum dated February 9, 1993, the Legal Bureau wrote:

A range of international legal instruments, and the treaty bodies they create, protect certain minority rights. The International Covenant on Civil and Political Rights, with its complaint mechanism under the *Optional Protocol* could be a primary focus for strengthening international juridical protection of minority rights. Other international instruments and treaty bodies which may be a useful focus for initiatives include the International Convention on the Elimination of All Forms of Racial Discrimination (CERD), the Convention relating to the Status of Stateless Persons, and the Convention on the Elimination of All Forms of Discrimination Against Women (CEDAW). The recently adopted Declaration on the Rights of Minorities, although not legally binding, could also provide standards by which state respect for minority rights may be measured. . . .

The International Covenant on Civil and Political Rights contains a number of provisions which protect minority rights, (1) either as specific rights accorded to members of certain protected minorities, or (2) as an element or manifestation of individuals' rights.

i. *Specific Rights of Minorities Recognized in the Covenant*

The specific rights accorded to minorities are set out in Article 27, which protects the rights of "ethnic, religious or linguistic minorities to enjoy their own culture, to profess and practice their own religion, or to use their own language." In addition, minorities are protected by other collective rights in the Covenant — for instance the right to be free from national, racial or religious hatred that constitutes incitement to discrimination, hostility or violence. As well, in its General Comments on the guarantee of equality in Article 26 of the ICCPR, the Human Rights Committee has stated that special measures to assist disadvantaged groups may be required: "[i]n a State where the general conditions of a certain part of the population prevent or impair their enjoyment of human rights, the State should take specific action to correct these conditions."

ii. *Collective Rights in Individual Rights*

The classic *individual* rights and freedoms contained in most international human rights instruments possess a "collective rights" element as well. For example, while freedom of association is granted to individuals, it is largely meaningless unless exercised in association with others for political, religious, social or economic purposes. Similarly, freedom of religion in effect permits religious groups to practice their faith, by virtue of the entitlement of individual members to practice together. . . .

The Optional Protocol to the ICCPR grants a right of petition to the Human Rights Committee to *individuals* who claim that their Covenant rights have been violated. Individual members of minorities may use the petition mechanism to vindicate denial of their collective rights. In fact, a large number of communications before the UN Human Rights Committee involving Canada have involved some form of collective or communal rights. The Committee is currently considering a communication alleging that Quebec's Bill 178 violates the guarantees of freedom of expression, equality and the rights of minorities in the ICCPR. Other petitions have involved allegations of violations of equality rights and Article 27 cultural rights by the federal Indian Act, and allegations by the Society of Friends (Quakers) of violations of their Article 18 rights by the Income Tax Act. The Human Rights Committee has been willing to receive petitions brought by individuals on behalf of the minority group to which they belong. In 1991, the Committee considered a complaint against Canada lodged on behalf of the "Mikmaq people as a whole," alleging a violation of Article 25, the right to participate in the conduct of public affairs. . . .

The Declaration on the Rights of Minorities reaffirms many of the rights already set out in the ICCPR. It requires that States protect the existence of the national or ethnic, cultural, religious and linguistic identity of minorities within their territories, and reaffirms the rights of persons belonging to those minorities to enjoy their own culture, religion, and language. The Declaration also reaffirms the rights of political participation, association, and equal treatment, and reiterates the right, set out in general comments of the Human Rights Committee, to special measures to assist disadvantaged groups. The rights set forth in the Declaration are to be exercised both individually and in community with other members of their group.

Rights of Women

On February 11, 1993, the Legal Bureau wrote:

The right to gender equality appears in all of the major international human rights instruments — Article 3 of the Universal Declaration and Article 2 of the Covenants on Civil and Political Rights and on Social, Economic and Cultural Rights, as well as the various regional human rights conventions.

Violations of other inherent rights, such as the right to liberty and security of the person and the right to be free from inhuman or degrading treatment, can also disproportionately affect women. . . .

The primary UN Convention which addresses women's human rights is the Convention on the Elimination of Discrimination against Women, which was adopted by the UN in 1979 and which Canada ratified in 1982. The CEDAW Convention amplifies the legal content of the general prohibition of sex discrimination and includes a range of State duties such as measures to modify social and cultural patterns, affirmative action programs, education, etc.

Under the CEDAW Convention, States party are required to report on their progress in implementing the Convention one year after ratification and every four years after that. Canada's third report to the CEDAW Committee has been submitted and should be examined in 1994 or 1995. At last year's Commission on the Status of Women, Canada successfully called for an extension of the CEDAW Committee's meeting time to address the backlog of reports. . . .

Under the 1951 Geneva Convention on Refugees, a refugee is any person who has a "well-founded fear of persecution for reasons of race, religion, nationality, membership in a particular social group or political opinion." Gender is conspicuously absent from the definition of Convention refugee. In 1985, the High Commission for Refugees adopted a resolution that "women asylum-seekers who face harsh or inhumane treatment due to their having transgressed the social mores of the society in which they live may be considered as a 'particular social group' within the meaning of the present Geneva Convention definition of refugee." Canada supported this resolution.

INTERNATIONAL ECONOMIC LAW

Extraterritorial Application of U.S. Law

In an *amicus curiae* brief filed in the Supreme Court of the United States on November 19, 1992 in the case of *Hartford Fire Insurance Co., et al.* v. *State of California, et al.*, the Government of Canada wrote:

Established United States law follows and applies international law. . . . No comity balancing analysis is required. Absent a clearly expressed intent to the contrary, U.S. law follows customary international law in that a state should not apply its economic law to regulate conduct by persons located in a foreign territory where doing so directly conflicts with and undermines the law of the foreign territorial sovereign. This principle is established in international law, is the law of the United States, and has been consistently applied by this Court in several cases involving statutes with jurisdictional clauses analogous to that of the Sherman Act. The Sherman Act, as amended, and 100 years of Supreme Court decisions interpreting it, express no intent to depart from this principle. Repudiating it here would be an unwarranted departure from an unbroken tradition of jurisprudence in the Supreme Court of the United States and in other major states. Following this tradition preserves the extraterritorial application of U.S. antitrust law, or the effects doctrine generally, except where to do so is to undercut the ability of another sovereign state to regulate conduct in its own territory.

GATT and Article 22 of the Convention on Biological Diversity

On August 7, 1992, the Legal Bureau wrote:

Examination of the relationship between the GATT and the Convention on Biological Diversity (CBD) involves, on the one hand, consideration of the compatibility of the substantive rights and obligations of the two treaties and, on the other hand, consideration of which forum or fora could assess that compatibility.

In exceptional circumstances the (CBD) *might* lend itself to a state arguing that compliance with obligations under the GATT would pose a serious damage or threat to biological diversity in that state's territory and that a right or obligation under the CBD took precedence over a right or obligation under the GATT. For instance, a state might seek to rely on the CBD to justify a restriction on importation or exportation that would contravene the GATT. Even if one assumes that the application of GATT disciplines could be incompatible with rights or obligations under the CBD, in the final analysis a GATT contracting party cannot be compelled to remove a GATT-inconsistent measure. It can only be "required" to pay (through the suspension of concessions or other obligations) for maintenance of the measure. Consequently, we are of the view that the exercise of rights and obligations under the GATT (i.e., the pursuit of GATT remedies) would never in law *cause* a serious damage or threat to biological diversity. That said, given the potential diversity and complexity of situations involving trade measures and biological diversity, it is impossible to be certain that a dispute settlement body constituted under the CBD would share our assessment of the substantive compatibility of the GATT and the CBD and arrive at the same conclusion. (paras. 5-18)

In our view, Article 22 of the CBD does not diminish Canada's access to GATT dispute settlement. Legally a GATT panel is entitled to hear a GATT dispute even if one of the contracting parties involved in the dispute claims that the CBD takes precedence over the GATT. Conversely, contracting parties to the GATT could not preclude a dispute settlement forum seized under the CBD from considering whether the exercise of rights and obligations under the GATT would cause a serious damage or threat to biological diversity. However, in our view the faint possibility that dispute settlement under the CBD might address the compatibility of rights and obligations arising under the GATT and the CBD does not warrant an interpretative statement about the relationship between the GATT and the CBD.

"Laws, Regulations or Requirements" under GATT

In a memorandum dated October 22, 1993, the Legal Bureau wrote:

The GATT, as a treaty, generally applies to its parties. Furthermore, Article III appears to only apply to GATT parties. The phrase "laws, regulations or requirements" in Article III.4 appears to refer only to government action; private firm discrimination does not appear to violate Article III.4 (Jackson, at p. 289). . . .

There are few cases defining the scope of the phrase "laws, regulations or requirements." However, in at least one case, an action by a private body was considered to be a "requirement" within the scope of Article III.4 of the GATT.

In *Canada: Administration of the Foreign Investment Review Act* (BISD 30S/140), the Panel was asked to review the process whereby an investor sought approval by the Canadian Government to acquire or establish a business in Canada. The Panel, at p. 158, concluded that written undertakings given by potential investors to purchase Canadian origin goods in preference to imported goods

> once . . . accepted, became part of the conditions under which the investment proposals were approved, in which case compliance could be legally enforced. The Panel therefore found that the word "requirements" as used in Article III.4 could be considered a proper description of existing undertakings.

The issue of whether a voluntary measure could be a government prohibition or restriction was discussed at length in *Trade in Semiconductors* (BISD 35S/116). In this case, the Panel considered whether voluntary measures by Japanese semiconductor manufacturers not to sell semiconductors at prices below company-specific costs violated Article XI.1 of GATT. The Panel stated that two criteria must be met for a voluntary measure to be considered a government measure: sufficient incentives or disincentives existed for non-mandatory measures to take effect and the operation of the measures was essentially dependent on Government action or intervention. The Panel concluded, at p. 155, that

> if these two criteria were met, the measures would be operating in a manner equivalent to mandatory requirements such that the difference between the measures and mandatory requirements was only one of form and not of substance, and that there could be therefore no doubt that they fell within the range of measures covered by Article XI.1.

We would note that, although this case dealt with a different provision of the GATT, this line of argument is likely applicable to cases involving alleged violations of Article III.4.

Thus, it appears that an action of a private entity may become a "requirement" within the meaning of Article III.4 of the GATT.

In order to violate Article III.4, a law, regulation or requirement must provide less favourable treatment to imported goods with respect to their internal sale, offering for sale, purchase, transportation, distribution or use. . . .

However, recent cases suggest that Article III.4 should be given a more expansive reading to ensure the effective equality of opportunities for imported products as well as precluding any adverse modification of conditions of competition.

In *Italian Discrimination Against Imported Agricultural Machinery* (BISD 7S/60), the Panel considered whether provisions granting special credit facilities to some categories of farmers for the purchase of agricultural machinery were inconsistent with Italy's obligations under Article III of the GATT. The Panel stated, at p. 64, that Article III.4 was intended to cover "not only the laws and regulations which directly governed the conditions of sale or purchase but also any laws or regulations which might adversely modify the conditions of competition between the domestic and imported products on the internal market."

As well, in *Section 337 of the Tariff Act of 1930* (BISD 36S/345), the Panel stated, at p. 386, that

> The words "treatment no less favourable" in paragraph 4 call for *effective equality of opportunities for imported products in respect of the offering for sale purchase*, transportation, distribution or use of products. This clearly sets a minimum permissible standard as a basis. [Emphasis added.]

Finally, in *Measures Affecting Alcoholic and Malt Beverages* (DS23/R dated 16 March 1992) the Panel stated, at p. 81, that "the inconsistency with Article III.4 stems from the denial to the imported products of competitive opportunities accorded to the domestic like products."

Limits on the National Security Interest under GATT

On February 10, 1993, the Legal Bureau wrote:

To date, there have been only two Panel decisions dealing with the [Government Procurement] Code; unfortunately, Article VIII.1 of the Code was not raised in either case. However, GATT Article XXI, which is similar to Article VIII.1 of the Code, has been considered by GATT Panels.

GATT Article XXI provides for a general exception to all GATT obligations and states, in part, that

> Nothing in this Agreement shall be construed . . . to prevent any contracting party from taking . . . in time of war or other emergency in international relations . . . any action which it considers necessary for the protection of its essential security interests.

Jackson, in *The World Trading System: Law and Policy of International Economic Relations*, reviewed GATT Article XXI and concluded, at p. 204, that this provision was "so broad, self-judging, and ambiguous that it obviously can be abused. . . . In general, the GATT approach to Article XXI is to defer almost completely to the judgment of an invoking contracting party."

However, a recent GATT Panel decision, *United States: Trade Measures Affecting Nicaragua* (L/6053, dated October 13, 1986), suggests that GATT Article XXI may not necessarily be as broad as suggested by Jackson. Although the Panel's terms of reference were extremely narrow as the United States would not agree to the Panel reviewing its decision to invoke Article XXI, and the Panel report was never adopted due to objections from the United States, we suggest that the Panel's consideration of the U.S. embargo of Nicaragua may shed some light on how a future GATT panel could approach this matter. The Panel concluded, at p. 18, that:

> the General Agreement protected each contracting party's essential security interests through Article XXI and that the General Agreement's purpose was therefore not to make contracting parties forego their essential security interests for the sake of these aims. However the Panel considered that the GATT could not achieve its basic aims unless each contracting Party, whenever it made use of its rights under Article XXI, carefully weighed its security needs against the need to maintain stable trade relations.

The Panel noted further, at p. 18, that:

> If it were accepted that the interpretation of Article XXI was reserved entirely to the contracting party invoking it, how could the contracting parties ensure that this general exception to all obligations under the General Agreement is not invoked excessively or for purposes other than those set out in this provision?

Given this line of reasoning, and in a case where a Panel's terms of reference included reviewing a Party's claim that its actions were necessary under Article VIII.1 of the Code, that Party's invocation of "national security interests" could be subject to the Panel's scrutiny.

MFN and Dispute Settlement in the NAFTA, GATS, and FIPAS

In a letter of April 26, 1993, the Legal Bureau wrote:

[The question is] . . . whether the MFN provisions of the GATS (General Agreement on Trade and Services) or the NAFTA might enable the countries party to those agreements to claim the benefits of the dispute settlement provisions of Canada's FIPAs (Foreign Investment Protection Agreements). You noted in this connection that during negotiation of the NAFTA it had been agreed that the NAFTA dispute settlement mechanism could not be used to settle disputes under other agreements. The NAFTA and the FIPA both have provisions for investor-state (NAFTA Ch. 11) and state-to-state (NAFTA Ch. 20) dispute settlement.

The GATS contains an exception to its MFN obligations for free trade areas, thus exempting the NAFTA. FIPAs will also contain an MFN exception for free trade agreements, and therefore they too will ensure that the NAFTA dispute settlement mechanism will not apply to disputes arising under FIPAs. However, the GATS contains no such exception for FIPAs.

The MFN provision of the NAFTA would entitle our NAFTA partners to any treatment accorded pursuant to a FIPA which is more favourable than the treatment accorded by the NAFTA. In our opinion the FIPA will not provide more favourable treatment than the NAFTA in any respect, and certainly would not do so in respect of dispute settlement.

National Treatment under GATT and FTA

On January 15, 1993, the Legal Bureau wrote:

The GATT distinguishes between the obligation on a Party to accord national treatment to the products of another Party *imported* into the territory of the other Party (Article III) and the obligations on a Party not to institute or maintain quantitative restrictions (other than duties, taxes or other charges) on the *importation* of products from another Party (Article XI). Although there are refinements, the Article III obligation is generally applicable to "internal measures" that discriminate against products that have entered the territory of a Party, whereas the Article XI obligation applies to "border restrictions" that apply to restrict importation.

An Article XI prohibition or restriction must be instituted on the *importation* of a product, rather than on goods already in the domestic commerce of the importing country. As noted in Canada in *Administration of the Foreign Investment Review Act* (BISD 30S/140), the General Agreement "distinguishes between measures affecting the 'importation' of products, which are regulated in Article XI:1, and those affecting 'imported products', which are dealt with in Article III."

Article III is incorporated into the FTA pursuant to Article 501; Article XI is incorporated into the FTA under Article 407. . . .

Recent GATT cases suggest that Article III should be given an expansive reading to ensure the effective equality of opportunities for imported products as well as to preclude any adverse modification of conditions of competition.

In *Italian Discrimination Against Imported Agricultural Machinery* (BISD 7S/60), the Panel considered whether provisions granting special credit facilities to some categories of farmers for the purchase of agricultural machinery were inconsistent with Italy's obligations under Article III of the GATT. The Panel stated, at p. 64, that Article III.4 was intended to cover "not only the laws and regulations which directly governed the conditions of sale or purchase but also any laws or regulations which might adversely modify the conditions of competition between the domestic and imported products on the internal market."

As well, in *Section 337 of the Tariff Act of 1930* (BISD 36S/345), the Panel stated, at p. 386, that

> The words "treatment no less favourable" in paragraph 4 call for *effective equality of* opportunities for imported products in *respect of the offering for sale*, purchase, transportation, distribution of *use of products*. This clearly sets a minimum permissible standard as a basis. [Emphasis added.]

Finally, in *Measures Affecting Alcoholic and Malt Beverages* (DS23/R dated March 16, 1992), the Panel stated, at p. 81, that "the inconsistency with Article III.4 stems from the denial to the imported products of competitive opportunities accorded to the domestic like product. . . ."

GATT and FTA panels have concluded that Article XI is to be interpreted liberally and broadly so as to have its intended effect: see, for example, *Lobsters from Canada* (May 21, 1990), para. 8.2.4 and *Japan: Trade in Semiconductors* (BISD 35S/116) at p. 154.

In *EEC: Programme of Minimum Import Prices Licences and Surety Deposits for Certain Processed Fruits and Vegetables* (BISD 25S/68), the Panel considered whether an EEC regulation prohibiting the importation of tomato concentrate at below a certain price was a restriction within Article XI on the importation of goods. The Panel concluded, at p. 99, that "the minimum import price system, as enforced by the additional security, was a restriction 'other than duties, taxes or other charges' within the meaning of Article XI.1."

In *Canada — Import. Distribution and Sale of Alcoholic Drinks by Canadian Provincial Marketing Agencies* (BISD 35S/37), the Panel concluded, at p. 90, that provincial measures and practices concerning the granting of listings of imported products by provincial marketing agencies and the availability of points of sale and sales outlets discriminated against imported alcohol and were restrictions contrary to Article XI of the GATT.

INTERNATIONAL ORGANIZATIONS

Legal Effect of OECD Decisions, Recommendations, etc.

In a recent opinion the Legal Bureau wrote:

Formally, only OECD *decisions* are binding. A decision must normally be taken by consensus, i.e., if one Member state opposes, it cannot pass, unless all the Member states agree otherwise beforehand. If one or more Member states *abstain* (as opposed to voting no), the decision can still bind those Member states who concur with it.

The OECD recognizes the federal/state/constitutional complexities of several of its Member states and provides that no decisions shall be binding on a Member state until it has complied with the requirements of its own constitutional procedures. Other Member states may agree, in the meantime, that the decision shall apply provisionally to them.

Unlike the case of treaties or other binding international agreements, there is no process of initialling leading to signature and then to ratification with OECD decisions. Once a decision is agreed to by all Member states, subject to the "constitutional procedures" referred to above, it is binding.

There is no provision for dealing with non-compliance by Member states, e.g., sanctions or other means of redress.

Resolutions are decisions on internal OECD matters concerning the work of the Organization, e.g., budgets, personnel and other administrative matters.

In contrast, OECD *recommendations* are not binding on Member states. Rather, Member states may provide for their implementation if they consider it opportune. Normally, however, a Member state would not agree to a recommendation unless it had the intention to comply with it.

While decisions and recommendations are specifically referred to in the OECD Convention, *guidelines* are not. As such, guidelines could have an even lesser status, from an international legal point of view, than a recommendation. Guidelines, however, could be included as an integral part of a recommendation and thereby take on the recommendation's legal status or could, based on their specific wording, attain a higher legal status similar to a recommendation.

In the case at hand, it seems clear from the following excerpts from the Draft Report to the Meeting of the Council at Ministerial level that the Guidelines are not intended to be binding. They are seen as the *first stage* in a process leading to final recommendations which "governments *should* follow to improve the compatibility of trade and environmental policies." The "exercise" of identifying, describing and understanding of factors at the interface between trade and environment policies is said to be *not yet completed*. "All . . . problems, differences of view and options *have not yet been fully explored.* . . ." "Further . . . analysis . . . will be required *before final recommendations* can be made. Finally, the Guidelines are described as being intended to "*guide* governments in the conduct of the further stages of the work programme."

INTERNATIONAL TRIBUNALS

Burden of Proof

In a recent memorandum the Legal Bureau wrote:

(a)   General Principle

It is Canada's submission that the burden of proof in this case rests with the United States, because it is the Party alleging non-compliance with a treaty obligation. Canada's position as to where the burden lies is consistent with the fundamental principle of law expressed in the Latin maxim *actori incumbit probatio* — or, the burden of proof rests with the claimant. The principle is also stated in the following terms: *ei qui affirmat non ei qui neqat incumbit probatio* — *onus of proof* is on him who affirms, and not on him who denies.

(b)   International Practice

This time-honoured principle of law has been accepted in international procedure as well. A review of the practice in the last century of international tribunals, international claims commissions, the Permanent Court of International Justice and the International Court of Justice supports this proposition. It is also confirmed in a recent publication entitled *General Principles of Law as Applied by International Courts and Tribunals,* which concludes that:

> there is in substance no disagreement among international tribunals on the general principle that the burden of proof is on the claimant, *i.e.* the plaintiff must prove his contention under penalty of having his case refused. *Actore non probante reus absolvitur.* [Emphasis in original.]

There is clear authority to apply the general rule on burden of proof to a case where a State had claimed non-compliance with a treaty on the part of its treaty partner. J. L. Simpson and Hazel Fox note in their study on *International Arbitration* that "where the claim is for the performance of an alleged obligation under a treaty, the burden is upon the claimant to establish the existence and extent of the obligation."

Canada and the United States have both relied on this general principle in previous dispute-settlement proceedings under Chapter 18 of the Free Trade Agreement. The Final Report of the Panel in the *Lobsters from Canada* case refers to the United States argument that Canada, as the moving party in the dispute, had the burden of proving that the 1989 amendment was inconsistent with Article 407 of the FTA. In the *Salmon and Herring* case, the submissions of both parties contended that the burden of proof in that case fell on the United States, because it was the party alleging the treaty violation.

(c)   Allegations of Treaty Violations: A High Standard of
      Proof Is Applied

Leading publicists in international law have written about the high standard of proof imposed on a claimant making an allegation that a State is in violation of its treaty obligations. The burden is particularly heavy, because in international law there is a presumption that States act in accordance with the law, and allegations tending to call into question the compliance of a State with its international obligations are very serious.

(d) Exceptions to the General Rule on Burden of Proof

International law recognizes certain situations where the general rule that the burden of proof rests on the complaining party will not apply. For example, in certain disputes it may be that the classical distinction between plaintiff and defendant is inapplicable, such as in a case where both parties have long standing rival claims to the same territory. In such circumstances, the court must decide the case by weighing the relative evidence put forward by each party, and neither one of them will bear the *prima facie* burden of proof. This is the approach followed by the International Court of Justice in the *Minquiers and Ecrehos* case, where the Court said as follows:

> Having regard to the position of the parties, both claiming sovereignty over the same territory . . . the Court is of the opinion that each Party has to prove its alleged title and the facts upon which it relies. . . .

It has also been suggested in the literature that the burden of proof rule may be inoperable in instances where it is impossible to ascertain which party is the claimant and which is the defendant. The theory is that the distinction may not be apparent when the international proceedings are the result of an agreement between the parties to adjudicate certain issues. Or, the distinction between claimant and defendant could be blurred when parties follow the method of simultaneous presentation of written pleadings and evidence. There is support and criticism for these arguments among international law scholars. In any event, courts have been able, in practice, to identify the claimant and defendant in cases before them, even *when* similar factors such as those referred to were present. It is submitted that this case presents no difficulty in this regard. It is clear that the United States is the claimant, and that Canada is the defendant.

There is also support in international practice for relaxing the rigours of the burden of proof requirements in circumstances where it would be extremely difficult for the claimant to obtain the evidence necessary to furnish direct proof of facts it has alleged. . . .

This could arise, for example, if a claimant State is unable to obtain the necessary evidence because it is in the control of the opposing State. The International Court of Justice has stated that in such circumstances "such a State should be allowed a more liberal recourse to inferences of fact and circumstantial evidence."

LAW OF THE SEA

Conférence des Nations Unies sur les stocks chevauchants et les stocks de poissons grands migrateurs

Le 9 mars 1993 l'Ambassadeur du Canada près les Communautés européennes écrivait au Commissaire européen aux Pêches:

Comme vous le savez, le Canada s'est fermement engagé en faveur de la convocation d'une conférence des Nations Unies sur les stocks chevauchants et les stocks de poissons grands migrateurs, d'abord à la Conférence des Nations Unies sur l'Environnement et le Développement puis à la dernière session de l'Assemblée générale. . . .

Aux termes de la résolution 47/192 de l'Assemblée générale, la Conférence des Nations Unies a essentiellement pour mandat de "formuler des recommandations appropriées" au sujet "des moyens d'améliorer la coopération entre les Etats dans le domaine de la pêche" afin de faire face aux "problèmes liés à la préservation et à la gestion" des stocks chevauchants et des stocks de poissons grands migrateurs et ainsi favoriser l'"utilisation durable et (la) conservation des ressources biologiques marines en haute mer."

Cette résolution précise en outre que la Conférence devra "promouvoir l'application efficace des dispositions de la Convention des Nations Unies sur le droit de la mer" relatives aux stocks susmentionnés, que ses travaux et ses résultats "devront être pleinement conformes aux dispositions" de cette Convention, en particulier en ce qui concerne les droits et obligations des Etats côtiers et des Etats pratiquant la pêche en haute mer, et que les Etats devront appliquer intégralement les dispositions relatives à la pêche hauturière de ladite Convention en ce qui concerne ces mêmes stocks. Il s'agit en somme de convenir des moyens d'assurer le contrôle de la pêche en haute mer, conformément aux dispositions pertinentes de la Convention sur le droit de la mer.

Parmi ces dispositions, le paragraphe 2 de l'article 63 de la Convention stipule que l'Etat côtier et les Etats qui exploitent des stocks chevauchants dans un secteur de la haute mer adjacent à sa zone économique exclusive "s'efforcent . . . de s'entendre" sur les mesures de conservation applicables à ces stocks en haute mer. En ce qui concerne les stocks de poissons grands migrateurs, l'article 64 prévoit que l'Etat côtier et les autres Etats qui exploitent ces stocks "coopèrent" afin d'assurer leur conservation et de promouvoir leur exploitation optimale, tant dans la zone économique exclusive qu'en haute mer.

La Convention ne précise pas le contenu de ces obligations de "s'efforcer de s'entendre" et de "coopérer" et elle ne prévoit à leur égard ni limite de temps, ni règles permettant le règlement efficace des différends dans l'éventualité où les Etats intéressés ne parviennent pas à s'entendre ou à coopérer efficacement. Ces lacunes sont en partie responsables des graves problèmes que posent aujourd'hui la préservation et la gestion des stocks chevauchants et des stocks de poissons grands migrateurs en haute mer, problèmes dont la convocation de la Conférence des Nations Unies illustre la reconnaissance par la communauté internationale.

Comme l'a déclaré l'honorable John C. Crosbie, ministre des Pêches et des Océans du Canada, à la Réunion de St. John's [de pays d'optique commune sur la pêche en haute mer],

> le cadre légal international ne pourra autoriser la conservation et la gestion efficaces des ressources en haute mer que lorsque seront acceptés des principes et des mesures destinés à donner un effet concret aux obligations juridiques des Etats de coopérer entre eux à cette fin.

C'est l'acceptation par la communauté internationale de tels principes et mesures que recherchera le Canada dans le cadre de la Conférence des Nations Unies qui, je le rappelle, a précisément pour mandat de "promouvoir l'application efficace" des dispositions pertinentes de la Convention.

Les principes et mesures autour desquels le Canada souhaite favoriser l'émergence d'un consensus international portent notamment sur la gestion et la conservation des stocks chevauchants et des stocks de poissons grands migrateurs en haute mer, la surveillance et le contrôle de l'exploitation de ces stocks et le règlement des différends. Il s'agit donc de donner pleinement effet aux dispositions de la Convention et non pas de remettre en cause les fondements du régime juridique qu'elle a établi, en particulier l'établissement à 200 milles marins de l'étendue maximale de la zone économique exclusive.

C'est parce qu'elles privilégient l'approche multilatérale que mes autorités ont tant milité pour la convocation de la Conférence des Nations Unies. Elles ne ménageront donc pas leurs efforts pour que celle-ci élabore un régime efficace de conservation et de gestion des stocks chevauchants et des stocks de poissons grands migrateurs, qui fonctionne réellement en pratique. Elles attachent du prix à la coopération de la Communauté européenne dans cette entreprise et c'est pourquoi elles tiennent à dissiper tout malentendu sur leurs objectifs.

TREATIES

Authentication of Texts

In a memorandum dated October 7, 1992, the Legal Bureau wrote:

This memorandum . . . concerns . . . procedures other than initialling that might be adopted to authenticate the definitive text of an agreement . . . once negotiations have been completed.

Once negotiation of the [treaty] has been concluded, the resulting text will need to be authenticated. By "authentication" of the text is meant an act or procedure which identifies and certifies the text as the correct, definitive and authentic text of the treaty. . . . A variety of devices is available. . . . initialling a negotiated text can be used as a device for authentication, but initialling could be a cumbersome device in a multilateral negotiation involving approximately fifty countries.

Signature could also serve to authenticate the final text of [a treaty]. However, given the provision for provisional application currently found in article [in this case], signature would not be an appropriate device for authentication of the negotiated text. Participating countries will want to carefully examine the final negotiated text before proceeding with signature (and thereby provisional application). Moreover, it is envisaged in [this text] that it will be authentic in six languages. . . . Although the other authentic language versions do not need to be prepared before a final text . . . can be authenticated, as each authentic text . . . will be equally authoritative, there must be an opportunity between the close of negotiation . . . and the opening of the Agreement for signature to prepare the other language versions and to ensure their conformity with the negotiated text. The requirement for comparison of the text in the various languages also rules out use of signature ad referendum as a device for authentication.

A "final act" or other analogous concluding document would be the most appropriate device to establish the authentic and definitive text. . . . A final act or other concluding document could be signed or initialled by delegations, or more conveniently, it could be adopted under the authority of the Chairman of Working Group or the Chairman of Conference.

Declarations

On May 12, 1993, the Legal Bureau wrote:

The Vienna Convention on the Law of Treaties does not provide for the altering or withdrawal of declarations. In fact, the Treaty does not provide for declarations at all. Canadian practice in entering declarations has been to use the same procedure as when entering reservations. Notice is given to the depositary of the treaty, who passes the information on to member states.

Canada also treats declarations as similar to reservations in that it will object to unacceptable declarations made by other states. Declarations are often used to make statements that are just as important as those made by reservations. In this regard, there is little to distinguish between the two.

These similarities suggest that the procedure for altering or withdrawing declarations should be the same as that used for reservations. This involves the giving of written notice of the intended change, as outlined in the Vienna Convention at Article 23, Paragraph 4.

A search of our files revealed no instance where Canada actually changed a declaration. As a matter of internal procedure, the entering of a declaration requires an authorization by the Governor-General-in-Council (called an Order-in-Council). Thus, any change to that declaration would also require an Order-in-Council. . . .

Some suggestions for procedure follow from the above discussion. Since declarations are made in the same manner as are reservations, it can be argued that the procedure for making changes should also be the same. Moreover, this has the benefit of clarity and simplicity.

Initialling of Texts of Treaties

On September 17, 1992, the Legal Bureau wrote:

For most delegations to the Plenary, the *Vienna Convention on the Law of Treaties* (VC) will provide the starting point for any discussion of initialling. Article 10 of the *Vienna Convention on the Law of Treaties* envisages the use of initialling to establish the authentic and definitive text of a treaty. However, initialling can have either much less or much more substantial significance. On the one hand, initialling may be used "to authenticate a text *at a certain stage* of the negotiations, pending further consideration by the governments concerned. In this usage, initialling would not establish the authentic and definitive text of the treaty, but rather would identify an interim text that negotiators had agreed to submit for review and consideration in their respective countries. On the other hand, Article 12 of the VC provides that when the negotiating states so agree, the initialling of a treaty can be an expression of consent to be bound by the treaty. In the absence of a clear understanding that initialling is intended as an interim measure in the negotiation pending consideration of a particular text by governments, the act of initialling, particularly at the ministerial level, would probably be taken at a minimum to mark the end of negotiation of the substance of the agreement; subsequent editorial modifications might be possible. However, initialling also could be understood to establish the authentic and definitive text to be signed.

What domestic authority would be required for Canadian representatives to initial a text? Unless the states involved in the negotiation of a treaty agree that initialling will express consent to be bound (VC, Article 12(2)) or be equivalent to the procedural act of signature, a representative who initials a text destined to become a treaty does not commit his country to sign, let alone be bound, by the treaty. Consequently, in Canadian practice, order-in-council authority is not required to initial a text. Whether or not a Canadian representative can initial a negotiating text depends essentially on political judgement rather than on formal legal authority. The representative's mandate and instructions would determine whether or not it would be appropriate to initial the text. Where initialling is used as a negotiating device to settle a particular text without prejudice to future negotiations on that text, the representative probably requires no particular authorization. However, where the effect of initialling is to establish the authentic and definitive text, the representative would have to be confident that the text was fully within his negotiating mandate or that the appropriate ministers had assented, implicitly or expressly, to initialling in the knowledge that the text probably would not meet the Canadian objectives set for the negotiator.

Parliamentary Declarations in 1992-93 / Déclarations parlementaires en 1992-93

compiled by / préparé par
MAUREEN IRISH*

A. RESOLUTIONS / RÉSOLUTIONS

L'hon. Barbara McDougall (secrétaire d'État aux Affaires extérieures) propose: Que la Chambre réaffirme son appui a toutes les résolutions pertinentes du Conseil de sécurité des Nations Unies concernant la situation actuelle en Somalie, ainsi qu'à la participation canadienne à l'effort multinational visant à créer aussitôt que possible un climat sûr pour les opérations d'aide humanitaire en Somalie.

(House of Commons Debates, December 7, 1992, p. 14771)
(Débats de la Chambre des Communes, le 7 décembre 1992, p. 14771)

Le président suppléant (M. DeBlois): ... Plaît-il à la Chambre d'adopter cette motion?
Des voix: D'accord.
Le président suppléant (M. DeBlois): Je déclare la motion adoptée.

(House of Commons Debates, December 8, 1992, p. 14865)
(Débats de la Chambre des Communes, le 8 décembre 1992, p. 14865)

B. GOVERNMENT STATEMENTS / DÉCLARATIONS GOUVERNMENTALES

1. Human Rights/Les droits de la personne

(a) Bosnia-Hercegovina — La Bosnie-Herzégovine

Ms. Dawn Black (New Westminster-Burnaby): ... I rise to ask the Canadian government to show international leadership to close the rape-death camps of Bosnia-Hercegovina.

---

* Faculty of Law, University of Windsor; Johnston Visitor, Faculty of Law, University of Manitoba (Fall 1993).

At least 20,000 women and little girls have been interned and gang raped. Many have died. Babies born of this violence and hatred are being abandoned. . . .

My . . . colleagues and I have risen in the House and have written letters to the ministers asking Canada to target humanitarian aid to the survivors of the rape camps.

Following our interventions, $250,000 was specifically targeted to aid the rape survivors. However, that really is just a drop in the bucket. . . .

I want to point out that rape is a crime of war and oppression around the world that Somalian, Peruvian, East Timorese women and women from every continent have experienced. In every war against races, religions and ethnicities, there is also within it a separate war against women. . . .

Mme Suzanne Duplessis (secrétaire parlementaire de la ministre des Relations extérieures et ministre d'État (Affaires indiennes et Nord canadien)): . . . L'une des atteintes parmi les plus pernicieuses et parmi les moins reconnues contre les droits de la personne est la violence envers les femmes. Et l'exemple le plus répugnant est certainement le viol systématique des femmes qui a actuellement cours sur le territoire de l'ex-Yougoslavie, particulièrement en Bosnie-Herzégovine. De façon non équivoque, le gouvernement canadien a condamné à maintes reprises ces actes barbares et dégradants. De telles actions dans le but de terroriser des populations civiles constituent des manquements graves aux droits humanitaires.

Le gouvernement s'est engagé à ce que les responsables de ces violations soient jugés. C'est pour cela que nous sommes en faveur d'un tribunal *ad hoc* international chargé de juger ces crimes. Face à ces violations, nous avons réagi de façon concrète, en octroyant par l'intermédiaire du Haut-Commissariat pour les réfugiés une aide de 250 000$ pour les victimes de viol en Bosnie-Herzégovine. Nous avons également mis sur pied un Centre d'information chargé de recevoir du public canadien des témoignages relativement à ces crimes. Nous sommes en train d'étudier activement quelles autres formes d'aide nous pourrions apporter aux victimes.

Lors de la Session des commissions des droits de l'homme à Genève, le Canada entend jouer un rôle de leadership et demandera de nouveau à la Communauté internationale de faire cesser ces violations. Ces viols constituent une violation de la Convention de Genève et des protocoles additionels.

Nous comprenons que la Commission d'experts chargée par l'ONU d'enquêter sur les allégations de crimes de guerre dans l'ex-Yougoslavie va faire enquête sur ces viols systématiques, car ceci fait parti de son mandat. . . .

La violence envers les femmes en Bosnie-Herzégovine ne constitue pas une action isolée, bien au contraire, dans un phénomène plus global que l'on retrouve dans toutes les sociétés. Afin de réagir contre la violence dont sont victimes les femmes, le Canada a pris un rôle de leadership à la Commission de la condition de la femme à Vienne dans l'élaboration d'une déclaration contre la violence à l'égard des femmes. . . .

(House of Commons Debates, February 8, 1993, pp. 15595-960)
(Débats de la Chambre des Communes, le 8 février 1993, pp. 15595-96)

(b) Refugees/Les réfugiées

Mr. Joe Fontana (London East): . . . What will the minister and this government do to end the gender discrimination of refugees. . . .
   Hon. Bernard Valcourt (Minister of Employment and Immigration): Mr. Speaker, the hon. member will be pleased to know that today, the chairperson of the Immigration and Refugee Board, Madame Mwani, has issued guidelines on gender-based persecution.
   Members of the board will now assess the particular circumstances which have given rise to the claimant's fear of persecution. They will also assess the conditions in the country of origin before entering their decision.
   These guidelines are intended to ensure a thorough and sensitive method in this difficult and complex matter. They will promote consistency across Canada and coherence in those decisions rendered on refugee claimants.

(House of Commons Debates, March 9, 1993, pp. 16725-26) (Débats de la Chambre de Communes, le 9 mars 1993, pp. 16725-26)

Hon. Warren Allmand (Notre-Dame-de-Grâce): . . . On March 9, the chairperson of the Immigration and Refugee Board issued instructions to the Immigration and Refugee Board members that they should interpret the definition of refugee to consider gender persecution. She said on that occasion that these instructions were not binding and that the gender persecution was not to be a ground of refugee status in itself but must be linked to one of the existing grounds such as race or religion and so on.
   It is for these reasons I asked the minister on March 15 to go one step further to make gender a distinct ground for refugee status and make it binding by putting it in the law. The minister answered on that day that he could not do it because it would go beyond the international convention on refugees. To that I say that the convention is only a floor, not a ceiling. Nothing prevents Canada from having a larger, more generous definition of a refugee, but we cannot do less than the convention we have signed. . . .
   Mr. Ross Belsher (Parliamentary Secretary to Minister of Fisheries and Oceans and Minister for the Atlantic Canada Opportunities Agency): . . . I want to tell the hon. member that the guidelines on gender based persecutions issued by the chairperson of the Immigration and Refugee Board on March 9 are intended to promote consistency in decisions of refugee claims. They are consistent with the interpretation of the definition of a refugee convention proposed in the 1985 resolution of the executive committee of the United Nations High Commission for Refugees which Canada supported. This allows decision makers to consider women refugee claimants as members of a social group.
   These guidelines were the first issued pursuant to the authority of the chairperson contained in recent amendments to the Immigration Act, Bill C-86. There is no reason to believe these non-binding guidelines that

364   *The Canadian Yearbook of International Law 1993*

respect the independence of decision makers and that were developed in a consultative process will be less effective in promoting consistency than binding direction on the interpretation of the convention definition.

Persecution against a woman based on any one of the five grounds delineated in the refugee convention can result in that woman being recognized as a refugee. If the persecution is solely the consequence of the fact that the individual is a woman or is directed against a particular subgroup of women, the claim can be accepted on the basis that she is a member of a particular social group. The process of evaluation of a refugee claim would not be any easier if the definition of a convention refugee were amended either within Canada or internationally to include gender.

(House of Commons Debates, April 20, 1993, pp. 18208-9)

(Débats de la Chambre des Communes, le 20 avril 1993, pp. 18208-9)

2. Peacekeeping/Le maintien de la paix

(a) Somalia — La Somalie

Hon. Barbara McDougall (Secretary of State for External Affairs): After the overthrow of former dictator Mohammed Siad Barre in 1991, Somalia has degenerated swiftly into violent and brutal anarchy. Tens of thousands of innocent men, women and children have been victimized. The absence of civil order has created a vicious circle of violence, counter-violence, terror and counter-terror, pillaging and senseless killing. . . .

As things stand today, Somalia is a country only in name. Warlords who are more preoccupied with their hunger for power than the hunger of their people have created untold death and suffering in Somalia. . . .

Le Canada a solidement appuyé l'intervention de l'ONU en Somalie. . . .

Lorsque le Conseil de sécurité a approuvé le déploiement de quatre bataillons d'infanterie dans les régions entourant Mogadiscio, le Canada a été l'un des premiers pays à répondre à la demande du secrétaire général.

Le Canada a joué un rôle de chef de file dans les efforts humanitaires internationaux pour fournir des vivres et des médicaments au peuple somalien. Nous avons envoyé trois avions militaires chargés de denrées et d'autres fournitures; nous avons fourni près de 22 millions de dollars en secours humanitaires à la Somalie et aux refugiés somaliens dans les pays voisins. . . .

As relief supplies began to arrive in Somalia, they were increasingly the object of theft and attack by armed bandits. It became dangerous, in fact impossible, to guarantee delivery of supplies to those most in need, though supplies did reach some people. Thousands of others were left to starve, cut off from supplies.

Faced with this situation, the United Nations approved the deployment of a peacekeeping mission known as UNOSOM. Its mandate was to protect the delivery of food and other humanitarian assistance, to promote national reconciliation and contribute to internal security and order. . . .

Le Canada n'a jamais changé de position sur cette question. En plus d'affecter 750 militaires à l'ONUSOM, nous avons maintes fois inciter l'ONU à adopter une approche de la situation en Somalie qui englobe la sécurité, les secours humanitaires et le règlement politique du conflit.

Sadly, over the past several weeks it became clear that humanitarian operations in southern and central Somalia could not overcome the problems of obstruction, looting and extortion by heavily armed bandits. The United Nations was unable to secure the concurrence of Somali factors for the deployment of peacekeepers in key areas of the country where the fighting is going on. . . .

Dans une . . . lettre qu'il adressait le 29 novembre au président du Conseil de sécurité, le secrétaire général priait le Conseil d'envisager de toute urgence un certain nombre d'options pour venir à bout de la situation. . . .

Le secrétaire général en venait à la conclusion que des mesures plus énergétiques devaient être prises de toute urgence.

Une . . . option soumise au Conseil de sécurité par le secrétaire général et recommandé par ce dernier, était le recours à l'action coercitive, tel que prévu au chapitre VII de la Charte des Nations Unies. Cette proposition a reçu l'approbation unanime du Conseil de sécurité jeudi dernier. . . .

Last Friday, my cabinet colleagues and I had to review our original decision in light of recent developments. After full consultation with the Secretary General, we agreed to participate in the enforcement mission.

We did so because we concluded that only such a mission as this can effectively put an end to the rule of warlords. Only such a mission can restore sufficient order that the hungry can be fed, the sick can have medicine and the injured can have treatment.

Only such a mission can create the kind of environment necessary so that work can begin toward a peaceful, negotiated settlement of the internal political conflict and toward the reconstruction of this nation by the Somalis themselves.

(House of Commons Debates, December 7, 1992, pp. 14772-73)
(Débats de la Chambre des Communs, le 7 décembre 1992, pp. 14772-73)

Mr. Ross Reid (Parliamentary Secretary to Minister of Indian Affairs and Northern Development): Canada cannot be everywhere all the time. That I think is clearly understood in a number of ways by national defence.

For instance, in Somalia, while we are part of the enforcement action, we have made it clear to the United Nations that we are not going to be able to be part of the subsequent UNOSOM II process. These are decisions one has to make.

(House of Commons Debates, February 25, 1993, p. 16508)
(Débats de la Chambre des Communes, le 25 février 1993, p. 16508)

(b)   Bosnia-Hercegovina — La Bosnie-Herzégovine

Hon. Barbara MacDougall (Secretary of State for External Affairs): Mr. Speaker, I think it is clear to all of us that the tragic war in the former Yugoslavia is unparalleled in terms of its complexity and of the political, economic and ethnic forces involved. It continues to severely challenge the international community and we continue to search for effective ways of responding to this enormous humanitarian crisis. . . .

Canadians continue to demonstrate their solidarity and their compassion for those who have been forced into these terrible situations and who are suffering all forms of human degradation. . . .

To channel this humanitarian assistance we have chosen to utilize international relief organizations. We have disbursed over $25 million through the United Nations and other organizations. . . .

En décembre 1992, et de nouveau vendredi dernier, j'ai annoncé l'octroi d'une subvention expressément destinée aux victimes de violence sexuelle. Les Canadiens ont été choqués par le viol et l'agression sexuelle des femmes et des enfants dans cette guerre. Nous devons sans plus attendre venir en aide aux victimes de ces crimes répugnants.

La ministre chargée de la condition féminine et moi-même avons indiqué vendredi que le Canada fournirait un montant additionel de 1,5 million dollars pour répondre à ces besoins. . . .

Today, I am pleased to announce a further contribution of $9.5 million in response to the ongoing international appeals. . . .

As this House knows, the Canadian forces are present on the ground in Bosnia as part of the UN Protection Force. Our troops, a battalion of the Royal Canadian Regiment, have already begun the task of ensuring safe delivery of humanitarian assistance in eastern Bosnia, an area of great need. Our forces have also brought large quantities of food and medical supplies by air to Sarajevo during more than 354 missions.

(House of Commons Debates, March 8, 1993, pp. 16620-21)
(Débats de la Chambre des Communes, le 8 mars 1993, pp. 16620-21)

Mr. Steve Butland (Sault Ste. Marie): Given the fact that economic sanctions are now in place and some type of military intervention is imminent, will the minister indicate to Canadians if she is prepared to commit futher Canadian support to any military escalation that might occur?

Hon. Barbara McDougall (Secretary of State for External Affairs): . . . The sanctions indeed go into effect at midnight tonight. This is something that Canada has been advocating for a long time, including the sanctions and their enforcement on the Danube as well as the Adriatic. We are very pleased that this action is being taken.

It is not inevitable that there will be an escalation. I want to underline that. In the question there was an implication that this was automatically coming. Obviously we are all concerned about that.

(House of Commons Debates, April 26, 1992, p. 18451)
(Débats de la Chambre des Communes, le 26 avril 1993, p. 18451)

Hon. Barbara McDougall (Secretary of State for External Affairs): Throughout the many years during which Canada has been sending peace-keepers abroad . . . successive governments have had to face the question of risk and of the role which Canada believes it should play in the world. In so doing we have developed guidelines that are weighed carefully before a decision is made to respond to a clear and precise request from the United Nations to send Canadian troops to a trouble spot.

There has to be a threat to international peace and security. That is the first determinant. Major parties to the conflict must accept the peace-keeping mission and accept Canadian participation in it. The operation has to be linked to an agreement by the parties to work toward a political settlement. The operation must be accountable to a political authority, such as the UN Security Council. The operation must have a clear and realistic mandate and it must have a sound logistic and financial basis. Those are the tests we put forward before any of our troops are sent on any peacekeeping mission.

Ces lignes directrices ont guidé notre gouvernement lorsqu'il a décidé d'envoyer des troupes de maintien de la paix, particulièrement en Croatie, en Bosnie et en Somalie.

Nos soldats de la paix assument aujourd'hui de nouvelles tâches, notamment d'ordre humanitaire, ce qui est particulièrement évident en Bosnie et en Somalie. À d'autres occasions, par exemple au Cambodge, il coopèrent avec des observateurs de l'action civile, des organismes de secours humanitaire, des policiers et bien d'autres organismes, pour soulager la souffrance et préparer la reconstruction de sociétés désintégrées. . . .

Les Nations Unies avaient la responsabilité d'un effectif de 10 000 soldats de la paix il y a six ans, et en dirige près de 50 000 aujourd'hui. Ce chiffre pourrait bientôt doubler. Il est donc crucial pour le Canada de veiller à ce que l'ONU soit mieux équipée pour les tâches que lui assignent ses États membres. . . .

Nous réclamions une salle de situation qui demeure en alerte 24 heures par jour et sept jours par semaine. Nous avons étés entendus, et les Nations Unies sont à mettre sur pied sur l'installation en question. . . .

We joined UNPROFOR in Croatia to help monitor a ceasefire and to prevent massive bloodshed. The international community's efforts there, and I want to underline this for the House, have met with success. . . .

UNPROFOR I, with Canadian participation, has saved countless lives in Croatia and Canadians are proud to share this success.

Canada joined UNPROFOR II in Bosnia for a compelling human-itarian mission: to escort convoys of food and medicine, and to protect refugees from attack. Again this has saved thousands of lives but has tragically not resolved the conflict. . . .

I want to reassure Canadians particularly about Srebrenica, a place where all the world is focused at the moment. On April 6 the Security Council decided to establish a UN presence and a "safe area" there to avoid a mass slaughter of some 30,000 beseiged Bosnian Muslims.

UNPROFOR decided to send a company of Canadians and brokered a demilitarization agreement between Serbs and Muslims. The mission, I want to point out very proudly, is a major barrier to further tragedy in that town.

While it is not without risks, we have examined thoroughly the safety of our troops. We are satisfied by our consultations with the United Nations and with key colleagues such as the United Kingdom and France that have offered their support and assistance if necessary.

I want to clarify the mission because, despite mistaken assertions that our 194 soldiers are there to defend thousands of unarmed Muslims against thousands of well armed Serbs, this is not the case. This is a peacekeeping situation where UN peacekeepers are asked to monitor an agreement signed by both parties. It is not their mandate to become a party to open warfare.

There is some kind of mythology that soldiers in peacekeeping missions are not well equipped. They are not well enough equipped to resist a major attack, but they are better equipped than the public has been led to believe by the sceptics opposite.

The soldiers can defend themselves and they can protect villages against rogue elements. They are trained to do so and they are equipped to do so. Should there be a massive onslaught, of which there is no indication as we speak, the peacekeepers would be backed up or they would be pulled out.

(House of Commons Debates, April 29, 1993, pp. 18688-90)
(Débats de la Chambre des Communes, le 29 avril 1993, pp. 18688-90)

M. Charles A. Langlois (secrétaire parlementaire du leader du gouvernement à la Chambre des communes et du ministre de la Défense nationale): L'automne dernier, le Canada, avec 1 p. 100 de la population mondiale, représentait 10 p. 100 des soldats du maintien de la paix des Nations Unies répartis à travers le monde.

Il est également bon de noter que bien que la Force régulière subisse actuellement une réduction de ses effectifs, l'accroissement correspondant du nombre de réservistes et l'intégration de ceux-ci au sein de la Force totale permet aux Forces canadiennes de continuer à soutenir toutes les opérations en cours.

Je sais que l'honorable député se soucie . . . du nombre de réservistes présentement affectés aux missions de paix. Récemment, un de ses collègues disait à la Chambre que 50 p. 100 des troupes de remplacement en Yougoslavie allaient être composées de réservistes. La situation est plutôt qu'une fois la rotation complétée, près du quart de nos troupes dans les Balkans seront composées de réservistes, et non pas 50 p. 100.

(House of Commons Debates, May 6, 1993, pp. 19082-83)
(Débats de la Chambre des Communes, le 6 mai 1993, pp. 19082-83)

Hon. Lloyd Axworthy (Winnipeg South Centre): This past weekend the foreign ministers from the United States, Great Britain, France and Spain met in Washington to discuss the notion of a safe haven policy which clearly has major implications for Canadian troops. . . .

With all this consultation and discussion, what is the Canadian position? Do we or do we not support a safe haven policy?

Hon. Barbara McDougall (Secretary of State for External Affairs): The Canadian position on safe havens is very clear. We regard them as useful on a temporary basis but not as a permanent solution. Therefore we have some questions about the implementation which I have raised with my international colleagues. As I say, in the Washington proposal there are a number of proposals that we endorse and have indeed led other countries on.

On the safe havens issue, I and the government do not want to see this as a permanent solution for Bosnia. We do not want the Bosnian Serbs keeping territory they gained by force.

In the meantime a useful purpose can be served if lives can be saved as they were by Canadians in Srebrenica and if the wounded can by treated and there can be room for negotiation to a more permanent solution.

(House of Commons Debates, May 26, 1993, pp. 19822-23)
(Débats de la Chambre des Communes, le 26 mai 1993, pp. 19822-23)

Hon. Lloyd Axworthy (Winnipeg South Centre): . . . There is a new UN resolution presently being looked at by the Security Council today and to be voted on tomorrow which proposes:

That the UN would take necessary measures including the use of force to stop attacks against all civilians. . . . Does Canada support this resolution?

Right Hon. Brian Mulroney (Prime Minister): Madam Speaker, yes, we support the resolution which is presently being debated before the Security Council.

Hon. Lloyd Axworthy (Winnipeg South Centre): . . . Does the Prime Minister agree that it would be very important that before we authorized Canadian UN peacekeeping troops to use force that it be approved by the Canadian people through their Parliament?

Right Hon. Brian Mulroney (Prime Minister): . . . We have some 2,500 peacekeepers on the ground now. Their protection and their safety is the prime concern of the Government of Canada. If there is going to be a change in their assignment or if the United Nations or any member thereof is going to undertake unilateral action that could compromise the well-being of those Canadians and other peacekeepers, we obviously want this to go to the Security Council for a new resolution.

The only matter in which there can be a change in our position is if it is blessed by the Security Council of the United Nations.

My hon. friend's position is not unreasonable. If we have the opportunity and if it moves along, I would be happy to consult both him and all members of the House in regard to any changes because the well-being of our troops there plus the effectiveness of Canada's contribution is always enhanced with the benefit of parliamentary consultation and debate.

(House of Commons Debates, June 3, 1993, p. 20323)
(Débats de la Chambre des Communes, le 3 juin 1993, p. 20323)

Hon. Lloyd Axworthy (Winnipeg South Centre): This weekend the Prime Minister is quoted as saying that he is prepared to support the UN resolution setting up safe havens in Bosnia and is prepared to send more Canadian troops to that area. . . .

I want to ask the external affairs minister if Canada is prepared to send more troops on the UN resolution that was passed this weekend? Are we going to change the mandate of the troops that are there so they can defend civilians and will we be re-equipping those troops so that they can meet this risky and new assignment?

Hon. Barbara McDougall (Secretary of State for External Affairs): . . . We are providing some 20 per cent of the forces that are on the ground in Bosnia. If there are additional forces we can put in, I think we all recognize that it would not be a large number. There might be some infill. There might be some logistics. There might be the potential of people to provide air cover or ships and so on. What we are doing is trying to come up with a way of co-operating with the resolution on safe havens to the extent we can.

On the other part of the hon. member's question, the implementation and the change in mandate is something that is being looked at by the Secretary-General and he will be reporting back to the Security Council . . . In the meantime he will be consulting with troop-contributing countries, not just there but some who may not yet be there. . . .

Hon. Lloyd Axworthy (Winnipeg South Centre): Considering the serious implications of this decision . . . does the government intend to live up to the commitment made last Thursday by the Prime Minister to have a full, open examination by Parliament of the new mandate . . . ?

Hon. Barbara McDougall (Secretary of State for External Affairs): Madam Speaker, as yet there is no new mandate or any plan for implementation. That is why I am suggesting that after further discussions by the Secretary-General and my discussions with my colleagues would be a more appropriate time to answer the hon. member's question and perhaps have a further parliamentary discussion.

We have always said that if there was a change we would be happy to have some form of parliamentary discussion, whether in committee, in the House or a full debate.

(House of Commons Debates, June 7, 1993, pp. 20460-61)
(Débats de la Chambre des Communes, le 7 juin 1993, pp. 20460-61)

(c)   Cyprus — Chypre

Hon. Mary Collins (Associate Minister of National Defence and Minister Responsible for the Status of Women): . . . After extensive consultations with the United Nations, Greece, Turkey, as well as Greek and Turkish Cypriots, the government has informed the Secretary General of the United Nations that Canada will withdraw its troops from Cyprus beginning June of 1993, the withdrawal to be completed by September. . . .

After 28 years of service in Cyprus, after 28 years of watching both sides in the dispute being either unable or unwilling to negotiate a political solution, after 28 years of significant expenditures to maintain troops and equipment in that region without any measurable progress, it was time to face facts and come to certain conclusions.

Our experience in Cyprus has taught us many lessons.

One of the most important is that parties in a dispute must understand that there are limits to the duration of any peacekeeping operation. Peacekeeping must never be considered as an end in itself or as a substitute for political leadership, negotiation and honourable compromise. The basis for any peacekeeping operation has always been an agreement by the parties involved to work toward a political settlement. Whether or not Canadian troops remain in Cyprus, Greek and Turkish Cypriots bear the ultimate responsibility for resolving the dispute.

It appears that instead of taking advantage of the peace and order which the UN mission has afforded, some political leaders have used the presence of UN forces to avoid making the compromises required to ensure peaceful coexistence. At a time when there are increasing demands for peacekeeping around the world, we must ensure that we establish our priorities carefully and manage our resources and contributions effectively.

(House of Commons Debates, December 11, 1992, pp. 15108-9) (Débats de la Chambre des Communes, le 11 décembre 1992, pp. 15108-9)

3.   Diplomatic Relations/Les relations diplomatiques

Mr. Svend J. Robinson (Burnaby — Kingsway): Mr. Speaker, I rise to pursue a question . . . concerning the tragic plight of two Canadians, Christine Lamont and David Spencer.

I am sure that members of this House are well aware of the fact that Christine and David were victims of a harsh and quite unfair Brazilian justice system which resulted in sentences of 28 years of imprisonment for each of them. . . .

M. Jean-Guy Guilbault (secrétaire parlementaire du ministre des Approvisionnements et Services): . . . On ne peut présumer que si le Canada demandait l'expulsion de Christine Lamont et de David Spencer, celle-ci serait accordée automatiquement. Bien que le président brésilien ait le pouvoir d'accorder l'expulsion, on nous a fait savoir qu'il existe une distinction claire entre le pouvoir tel qu'il est établi dans la constitution brésilienne et la pratique selon laquelle il est exercé.

On nous dit qu'en principe, l'expulsion ne serait pas accordée pendant que les appels sont en cours ou avant que le prisonnier reconnu coupable ait purgé sa peine.

On nous a dit également que le gouvernement brésilien n'accepterait pas l'expulsion dans ces circonstances, car cela équivaudrait à une ingérance injustifiée du pouvoir dans les affaires du judiciaire et serait discriminatoire envers les autres prévenus qui ne seraient pas libérés ou expulsés.

Le secrétaire d'État aux Affaires extérieures a exprimé, à de nombreuses occasions, sa préoccupation concernant la sévérité des peines reçues par Mme Lamont et M. Spencer, et ces peines et les condamnations comme telles font l'objet d'un appel auprès des tribunaux brésiliens. . . .

Les efforts de l'ambassade pour accélérer la ratification du Traité sur le transfèrement des délinquants entre le Canada et le Brésil signé le 15 juillet dernier ont également donné des résultats. Le Traité permettrait à Mme Lamont et M. Spencer de purger le reste de leurs peines dans des installations canadiennes où ils seraient assujettis aux lois canadiennes sur la mise en liberté conditionnelle.

(House of Commons Debates, March 11, 1993, pp. 16893-95)
(Débats de la Chambre des Communes, le 11 mars 1993, pp. 16893-95)

Mr. Stan Wilbee (Delta): Two weeks ago, a home was levelled in Managua by an explosion of a stash of missiles. Investigators of the blast found a stash of documents and fake IDs. . . .

Could the minister tell us what she believes to be the significance and the reality of this information?

Hon. Barbara McDougall (Secretary of State for External Affairs): Madam Speaker, late last week we learned of the article in the Managua newspaper *Barricada* which featured photographs of Christine Lamont's ID cards. The article itself described documents that were found with a large arms cache that was discovered recently in Managua.

The newspaper claimed that the documents concerned plans to kidnap a number of prominent Latin American business and political leaders. At the same time Nicaraguan authorities informed our ambassador that there were 306 foreign passports found with the arms cache, including three Canadian passports. They asked Canada to verify the authenticity of the Canadian passports. The passport office has confirmed the authenticity of two passports issued to Christine Lamont in Ottawa in November and December 1988 and one passport issued to David Spencer at the same time. One of the passports had been altered.

I want to say that this development does not affect our approach to the Lamont-Spencer case. We will continue to be governed by our respect for due process and fairness to all Canadians imprisoned abroad. We will continue to press Brazil to ratify as quickly as possible the transfer of offenders treaty which would allow Miss Lamont and Mr. Spencer to return to Canada to serve their sentences.

That treaty has passed the lower house of the Brazilian congress and is now under consideration in the senate. I also want to assure all hon. members that while we are proceeding with that process, we will provide all possible consular services to Miss Lamont and Mr. Spencer and monitor prison conditions as we do for others who find themselves in this situation abroad.

(House of Commons Debates, June 16, 1993, p. 20902)

(Débats de la Chambre des Communes, le 16 juin 1993, p. 20902)

4.   Law of the Sea/Le droit de la mer

Mr. Francis G. LeBlanc (Cape Breton Highlands — Canso): Mr. Speaker, I would like to return to a question I asked on May 11 concerning an extraordinary meeting of the fisheries commission of NAFO, the Northwest Atlantic Fisheries Organization, to deal with blatant overfishing by the European Community, principally by Spain and Portugal, on the nose and tail of the Grand Banks. . . .

In July the minister imposed a domestic moratorium on the Newfoundland northern cod fishery, putting over 20,000 Canadians out of the fishery, some for the length of the moratorium and many others forever. . . .

Some hope arose from the September NAFO meeting when the European Community made a solemn promise to follow NAFO quotas in 1993. . . .

At the same time the EC scuttled Canada's attempt to change the objectors clause, the very loophole through which EC overfishers have jumped for years. . . .

Mr. John A. MacDougall (Parliamentary Secretary to Minister of Energy, Mines and Resources): . . . At Canada's request, the fisheries commission of the North Atlantic Fisheries Organization, NAFO, met in a special session at Dartmouth, Nova Scotia, last May to discuss Canada's proposals to improve surveillance and control of the NAFO regulatory area outside Canada's 200-mile limit.

New measures developed by the special session were reviewed and adopted at the annual meeting of NAFO in September. All NAFO members, including the EC, have agreed to put them in place. . . .

The measures adopted in September include a pilot project for an observer program of the NAFO area. . . . Beginning in January 1993, observers will be placed on vessels outside 200 miles during 10 per cent of the fishing days.

Important new measures were . . . adopted to eliminate fishing for undersized fish. Minimum mesh sizes and minimum landing sizes were established. A one net rule was adopted whereby vessels would not be permitted to have nets on board with mesh smaller than the minimum size. These measures will apply to all ground-fish fisheries in the area which will help considerably to reduce catches of juvenile fish. In addition, the adoption of minimum landing sizes will make it illegal for undersized fish to be sold to the EC and other markets.

(House of Commons Debates, November 26, 1992, pp. 14140-41)
(Débats de la Chambre des Communes, le 26 novembre 1992, pp. 14140-41)

Mr. Ross Belsher (Parliamentary Secretary to Minister of Fisheries and Oceans and Minister for the Atlantic Canada Opportunities Agency): . . . The comprehensive agreement with the European Community which was reached in December 1992 has the potential to go a long way toward ending the calamity of overfishing outside the 200 mile limit. . . .

Central to this is that the EC will now, as it did until 1986, accept and abide by NAFO quotas and other conservation and management decisions. . . .

Let me review briefly the elements of the agreement. The EC and Canada agreed to comply with all of NAFO's conservation and management decisions, including quotas, and the EC will ensure that catches by its fleets do not exceed NAFO quotas. By way of comparison, from 1986 to 1992 the EC set for itself unilateral quotas higher than those set for it by NAFO. EC catches exceeded most NAFO quotas and in some cases the EC's higher unilateral quotas.

Canada and the EC will work together to end fishing by non-NAFO fleets. These fleets, largely comprising Korean and reflagged EC vessels, have become an increasingly serious threat to resources outside 200 miles.

Canada and the EC will work together to revitalize NAFO through joint proposals to add a dispute settlement mechanism to avoid abuse of the objection procedure.

Canada will set a total allowable catch (TAC) for northern (2J-3KL) cod once the present moratorium ends, based on advice from Canadian and international scientists. Scientific advice indicates that on average 5 per cent of the biomass is outside 200 miles. Canada and the EC will propose that NAFO make allocations of 2J-3KL cod equal to 5 per cent of the total allowable catch. Canada will retain 95 per cent of the TAC.

As the EC will now be co-operating with Canada in conservation of fisheries resources outside 200 miles, as soon as both parties have given formal approval Canada will provide access to ports and any surplus allocations and permit commercial arrangements.

If problems arise from the agreement there will be consultations to seek to resolve them. Either Canada or the EC can terminate the agreement on 60 days notice.

Now we have a forum. In June 1992 the UN Conference on Environment and Development called for a high seas fisheries conference. In late 1992 the UN General Assembly created the conference. Canada is no longer alone. We have more than 50 states with us to deliver a powerful ecological message against high seas overfishing.

(House of Commons Debates, February 11, 1993, pp. 15814-16)
(Débats de la Chambre des Communes, le 11 fevrier 1993, pp. 15814-16)

Mr. Ross Belsher (Parliamentary Secretary to Minister of Fisheries and Oceans and Minister for the Atlantic Canada Opportunities Agency): . . . The issue of ratification of the United Nations Convention on the Law of the Sea, commonly referred to as UNCLOS, has been reviewed exhaustively. . . .

Ratification of UNCLOS at this time would do nothing in terms of practical results to resolve the overfishing issue. However slowly, significant progress is being made. Overfishing on the high seas is increasingly recognized as an international environmental issue.

In terms of control of fisheries resources, Canada already benefits from one of the most significant provisions of UNCLOS. That is the creation of the 200-mile exclusive economic zone, since this now forms part of customary international law. Indeed the foreign overfishing problem is related to fishing beyond the 200-mile limit so Canada would not enhance its control over this problem whether or not it ratifies the UNCLOS.

Further, it is widely known that the long-standing difficulties within the international community with regard to the UNCLOS ratification concern not the control of fisheries resources but the seabed mining provisions. All industrialized countries except Ireland have serious concerns in this regard. Ratification by Canada at this time could well commit the Canadian treasury to disproportionate financial obligations to the UN authority responsible for the exploitation of deep seabed resources.

(House of Commons Debates, March 9, 1993, p. 16749)
(Débats de la Chambre des Communes, le 9 mars 1993, p. 16749)

5. Environmental Law/Le droit de l'environnement

Ms. Lynn Hunter (Saanich — Gulf Islands): . . . In Washington in the past two days the U.S. trade representative's office said it was this government, the Canadian government, that seriously hampered environmental provisions in the NAFTA, such as section 104 regarding the Basel Convention on Hazardous Waste. . . .

Hon. Jean J. Charest (Minister of the Environment): Mr. Speaker, Canada and our government, I think it was in November, signed and ratified the Basel convention, which is an international convention. Furthermore, we have bilateral agreements with the United States on the issue of transboundary transportation of waste, both hazardous and non-hazardous. We are now looking at a system by which we will have a notification for even non-hazardous waste between both countries.

(House of Commons Debates, March 17, 1993, pp. 17114-15)
(Débats de la Chambre des Communes, le 17 mars 1993, pp. 17114-15)

Mrs. Marlene Catterall (Ottawa West): . . . Yesterday environmental groups gave the Minister of the Environment failing grades for breaking the environmental promises made at the earth summit just one year ago. It is a miserable record: no sign of the law to guarantee the safety of

Canadian drinking water, no legislation to prohibit the wholesale export of Canadian water, no national plan to freeze greenhouse gas emissions, no action plan to protect old growth forests and constant cuts to green plan funds.

Hon. Mary Collins (Minister of Western Economic Diversification and Minister of State (Environment) and Minister Responsible for the Status of Women): . . . The report the Sierra Club provided was interesting. I actually felt that it really had not done its homework. I do not think it attended the meeting on Monday when our Canadian ambassador for environment and sustainable development, Mr. Campeau, brought out the report card on what we have done on the UNCED follow-up.

We have met our commitments. We are the first industrialized country to ratify the climate change convention and biodiversity convention. We are already implementing both of those and we are developing national plans. We have been the leader in the development of the United Nations Conference on High Seas Fisheries, a very critical component.

(House of Commons Debates, June 2, 1993, pp. 20208-9)
(Debats de la Chambre des Communes, le 2 juin 1993, pp. 20208-9)

6. *International trade/Le commerce exterieur*

(a) *North American Free Trade Agreement — L'accord de libre-echange nord-americain*

Mr. Lee Clark (Parliamentary Secretary to Minister of the Environment): . . . In August of this year after more than a year of negotiations, Canada, the United States and Mexico agreed to the North American free trade agreement, which we generally call NAFTA, providing a new set of rules to govern investment and to govern more than what would be $300 billion in annual three-way trade. . . .

NAFTA is the first trade agreement to recognize the principles of sustainable development and environmental protection. The preamble in NAFTA explicitly identifies the promotion of sustainable development and environmental protection and enforcement as fundamental goals of the agreement. . . .

NAFTA protects trade provisions of a number of key international environmental agreements. The trade obligations under CITES, the Montreal Protocol, the Basel Convention, and any other future agreements agreed to by all three countries will take precedence over NAFTA.

Again, NAFTA affirms the right of each country to choose the level of protection in the environment that it considers appropriate to its own circumstances and according to its own priorities. Furthermore, it affirms the right of each country to adopt standards to secure such protection.

This agreement provides that no NAFTA country should lower its environmental standards to attract investment. This is a far-reaching provision. It can be found in no other trade agreement.

NAFTA provides for a more environmentally sensitive dispute resolution process. For example, the responding party in a trade dispute involving either one of these international environmental agreements or a measure taken to protect its environment has the right to have the dispute considered exclusively in NAFTA, which among other things provides input from environmental experts and puts the burden of proof on the complaining party.

(House of Commons Debates, December 1, 1992, pp. 14366-67) (Débats de la Chambre des Communes, le 1 décembre 1992, pp. 14366-67)

Hon. Michael Wilson (Minister of Industry, Science and Technology and Minister of International Trade): . . . The bill before us today, when passed by Parliament, will affirm Canada's foresight in negotiating the North American free trade agreement. When the agreement goes into force next January with the approval of all three countries, the North American free trade agreement will provide Canadians with a strengthened base from which to tackle the rugged terrain of the global marketplace.

La levée des barrières commerciales entre le Canada et le Mexique, combinée à l'ouverture des marchés obtenus grâce à l'Accord de libre échange entre le Canada et les États-Unis, donnera accès à un marché dynamique à 360 millions de consommateurs.

Plus que jamais auparavant, l'ALÉNA ouvrira le marché mexicain aux Canadiens. Les barrières tarifaires, les licences d'importation, les restrictions à l'investissement, les prescriptions relatives à l'équilibre de la balance commerciale, ainsi que d'autres obstacles auxquels se heurtent les exportateurs canadiens de produits et de services, seront supprimés.

Le Mexique jouit déjà d'un accès relativement facile au marché canadien. En fait, à l'heure actuelle, près de 80 p. 100 des marchandises mexicaines entrent au Canada en franchise, et nous avons donc, à toutes fins pratiques, un libre-échange à sens unique. . . .

Nous avons renforcé le système de règlement des différends commerciaux. Nous avons clarifié les règles d'origine et les avons rendues plus prévisibles. Autrement dit, les différends concernant le contenu exclusivement nord-américain des véhicules Honda fabriqués au Canada seront désormais chose du passé.

Les disciplines que renferme l'Accord serviront à garantir que les normes ne sont pas utilisées comme mesures de protectionnisme déguisées. . . .

We also strengthened energy provisions through the NAFTA and obtained stronger disciplines on U.S. regulators from interfering with freely negotiated contracts between Canadian exporters and U.S. buyers.

We negotiated a very attractive government procurement deal and for the first time suppliers of Canadian building materials will have competitive access to U.S. and Mexican government construction contracts. . . .

We entered the negotiations intent on making improvements to the FTA and I think it is clear that we have done that. . . .

Canada had a choice when it entered the negotiations. We could have stood back and let the United States and Mexico sign a deal by themselves. . . .

However, such an agreement would have given a tremendous advantage to the United States. The U.S. would have been the only country with barrier-free access to all of North America. Under those circumstances the decision for investors wanting to gain access to the entire North American market would have been obvious: locate in the United States.

Instead we made the right decision and that was to become a full partner of the wider North American market. . . .

Canada is committed to pursuing additional environmental and labour accords in trilateral discussions with Mexico and the United States. That was our objective in February 1992 when we first put forward Canadian proposals in this regard. We welcome the initiative the Clinton administration has taken in bringing these proposals back to the table because they will lead to strengthened environmental co-operation among our three countries and an open dialogue about the work place in the new North American market.

(House of Commons Debates, March 25, 1993, pp. 17548-49-50, 17553)
(Débats de la Chambre des Communes, le 25 mars 1993, pp. 17548-49-50, 17553)

(b)   Patents/Les brevets

Mrs. Dorothy Dobbie (Parliamentary Secretary to Minister of Consumer and Corporate Affairs and Minister of State (Agriculture)): We are dealing with Bill C-91 in the House today which is an act to amend the Patent Protection Act.

I want to begin by going right back to the beginning and asking what is a compulsory licence. A lot of people must be scratching their heads and asking what does compulsory licence mean. If you have a patent does that not give you some protection against infringement on that patent for x number of years? Is that not something everybody would just take for granted? That is what a patent means, is it not?

That is what a patent means in most countries and that is what a patent will mean in Canada after the passage of Bill C-91. Currently, much to my dismay when I came here and learned of this, a patent can be infringed by a special system set up by the Liberal government that provides for something called compulsory licensing. Those words mean we give someone the special privilege to copy a drug while it is still under patent protection.

This bill removes this artificial and damaging provision that has been inserted into our Canadian intellectual property rights. It creates an atmosphere of fairness and a level playing field.

(House of Commons Debates, December 10, 1992, pp. 15029-30)
(Débats de la Chambre des Communes, le 10 décembre 1992, pp. 15029-30)

Mr. David Dingwall (Cape Breton — East Richmond): Madam Speaker, I am seeking a clarification from the minister. I ask this sincerely with regard to whether or not the minister believes there is a conflict between the wording of the Dunkel report on GATT and the proposed NAFTA agreement, particularly as it relates to intellectual property.

It is my understanding that Article VI on pharmaceuticals of Annex 1001.2a, Chapter 10, pages 10 to 55 of NAFTA the text reads: "Until January 1, 2002, this chapter shall not apply to the procurement by the Secretaria and the Secretaria de Marina of drugs that are not currently patented in Mexico or whose Mexican patents have expired." Then there is another sentence and this is where I need clarification. It says: "Nothing in this paragraph shall prejudice rights under Chapter 17 (intellectual property)." Am I right to conclude that under the NAFTA agreement, the Mexican pharmaceutical industry will have a transition period of eight years under NAFTA, which is not the case under GATT?

Hon. Michael Wilson (Ministry of Industry, Science and Technology and Minister for International Trade): Madam Speaker, my hon. friend would have been able to get a better answer had he given me some notice of this question. . . .

Mrs. Dorothy Dobbie (Parliamentary Secretary to Minister of Consumer and Corporate Affairs and Minister of State (Agriculture)): . . . There have been a lot of charges from the opposition that we are making this bill retroactive and that somehow that is unfair or unusual. I wonder if the minister could tell us why the effective date is December 20, 1991.

Mr. Wilson (Etobicoke Centre): Madam Speaker, the importance of that date is to provide some certainty in the marketplace. If we had not established a date when the new provisions take hold, there would be chaos in the marketplace. Neither the generic companies nor the patent medicine companies would know where they stood with regard to new investments that either one of them might want to make because of the cash flows from drugs that are currently under development now would be quite up in the air as to who would get access to that cash flow. . . .

It was a grandfathering of compulsory licences that were already given. That was done in the interests of the generic companies. By picking that specific date in compliance with the Dunkel proposal, we guard against the market distortions that clearly would have been there if we had said that we are going to wait and establish a date sometime in future.

(House of Commons Debates, December 10, 1992, p. 15023)
(Débats de la Chambre des Communes, le 10 décembre 1992, p. 15023)

7. Aid and Development/*L'aide et le développement*

Hon. David MacDonald (Rosedale): . . . A year ago at this time the Government of Canada led by the Prime Minister participated in the earth summit and in particular signed two very important treaties pointed in the direction of achieving international co-operation. . . .

One important commitment was to achieve the target of .7 per cent of ODA by the year 2000. This has since been ratified by two parliamentary committees this year. However, the estimates of the department have suggested that we will only eventually achieve the target of .7 per cent. . . .

L'hon. Monique Vézina (ministre des Relations extérieres et ministre d'État (Troisième âge)): Madame la Présidente, je n'étais pas au Sommet de Rio, mais je sais pertinemment bien que ni le premier ministre, ni le ministre de l'Environnement n'ont pris l'engagement de respecter le .7 p. 100 lors de discours officiels. Pour des raisons que nous connaissons tous ici en cette Chambre, nous avons dû réduire le rythme de croissance de l'ACDI et l'objectif du .7 p. 100 est un objectif que nous maintenons à long terme.

Je peux toutefois donner la confirmation de l'intention qu'a le gouvernement, par le biais de l'ACDI, de respecter les engagements qui ont été pris lors de cet Sommet. Cela étant dit, je peux aussi rappeler que le Canada demeure toujours en deuxième position des pays donateurs au niveau du G-7. Donc, l'ACDI respecte et soutient le suivi du Sommet de Rio, coordonne la contribution de 25 millions de dollars et applique l'initiative de conversion de la dette d'APD pour utilisation au niveau environmental, ce qui représente 145 millions de dollars.

(House of Commons Debates, June 9, 1993, pp. 20590-91)
(Débats de la Chambre des Communes, le 9 juin 1993, pp. 20590-91)

Treaty Action Taken by Canada in 1992 / Mesures prises par le Canada en matière de traités en 1992

compiled by / préparé par
CÉLINE BLAIS*

* Treaty Registrar, Legal Advisory Division, Department of Foreign Affairs/ Greffier des Traités, Directions des consultations juridiques, Ministère des Affaires étrangères.

I: BILATERAL

Antigua and Barbuda
Agreement on Social Security between the Government of Canada and the Government of Antigua and Barbuda (with Administrative Arrangement). Ottawa, September 2, 1992.

Australia
Protocol amending the Reciprocal Agreement on Social Security between the Government of Canada and the Government of Australia. Ottawa, October 11, 1990. *Entered into force* January 1, 1992. CTS 1992/17.

Brazil
Treaty on Transfer of Offenders between the Government of Canada and the Government of the Federative Republic of Brazil. Brasilia, July 15, 1992.

Chile
Agreement between the Government of Canada and the Government of the Republic of Chile for the Avoidance of Double Taxation of Income from the Operation of Ships and Aircraft. Santiago, July 30, 1992.

Czechoslovakia
Agreement between the Government of Canada and the Government of the Czech and Slovak Federal Republic for the Promotion and Protection of Investments. Prague, November 15, 1990. *Entered into force* March 9, 1992. CTS 1992/10.

Convention between the Government of Canada and the Government of the Czech and Slovak Federal Republic for the Avoidance of Double Taxation and the Prevention of Fiscal Evasion with Respect to Taxes on Income and on Capital. Prague, August 30, 1990. *Entered into force* July 22, 1992. CTS 1992/16.

Finland
Agreement between the Government of Canada and the Government of Finland for Air Services between and beyond their Respective Territories. Ottawa, May 16, 1977. *Entered into force* November 7, 1977. CTS 1977/32. *Superseded* by the Air Agreement signed May 28, 1990. *Terminated* February 21, 1992.

Exchange of Notes between the Government of Canada and the Government of Finland extending for an Indefinite Period the Air Agreement between Canada and Finland signed on May 16, 1977. Ottawa, May 16, 1986. *Entered into force* May 16, 1986. CTS 1986/11. *Superseded* by the Air Agreement signed May 28, 1990. *Terminated* February 21, 1992.

Agreement between the Government of Canada and the Government of Finland for Air Services between and beyond their Respective Territories (with Annexes). Helsinki, May 28, 1990. *Entered into force* February 21, 1992. CTS 1992/4. Applied provisionally from the date of signature.

Convention between the Government of Canada and the Government of Finland for the Avoidance of Double Taxation and the Prevention of Fiscal Evasion with Respect to Taxes on Income. Helsinki, May 28, 1990. *Entered into force* August 20, 1992. CTS 1992/30.

France

Exchange of Notes between the Government of Canada and the Government of the Republic of France constituting an Agreement further amending the Agreement on Television Relations of July 11, 1983. Ottawa, September 8, 1992. *Entered into force* September 8, 1992. CTS 1992/27. *Notes signed* April 11, 1991, and September 8, 1992.

Exchange of Notes between the Government of Canada and the Government of the Republic of France constituting an Agreement further amending the Agreement concerning the Promotion of Co-produced Cinematographic Projects of July 11, 1983. Ottawa, September 8, 1992. *Entered into force* September 8, 1992. CTS 1992/29. *Notes signed* April 11, 1991, and September 8, 1992.

Exchange of Notes constituting an Agreement between the Government of Canada and the Government of the Republic of France further amending the Agreement concerning Cinematographic Relations of May 30, 1983. Ottawa, September 8, 1992. *Entered into force* September 8, 1992. CTS 1992/26. *Notes signed* April 11, 1991, and September 8, 1992.

Exchange of Notes between the Government of Canada and the Government of the Republic of France constituting an Agreement amending the Agreement concerning the Promotion of Film and Video Co-Production Projects in the Field of Animation of January 10, 1985. Ottawa, September 8, 1992. *Entered into force* September 8, 1992. CTS 1992/28. *Notes signed* April 11, 1991, and September 8, 1992.

Gabon

General Agreement on Development Co-operation between the Government of Canada and the Government of the Gabonese Republic. Montreal, June 8, 1992. *Entered into force* June 8, 1992. CTS 1992/14.

Germany

Exchange of Notes between the Government of Canada and the Government of the Federal Republic of Germany constituting an Agreement on the Training of German Armed Forces in Canada. Brussels, December 10, 1992. *Entered into force* December 10, 1992. CTS 1992/22.

Hungary

Agreement between the Government of Canada and the Government of the Republic of Hungary concerning the Guarantee of a Loan. Budapest, October 6, 1992. *Entered into force* October 6, 1992. CTS 1992/24.

Convention between the Government of Canada and the Government of the Republic of Hungary for the Avoidance of Double Taxation and the Prevention of Fiscal Evasion with Respect to Taxes on Income and on Capital. Budapest, April 15, 1992.

ICAO

Agreement between the Government of Canada and the International Civil

Aviation Organization regarding the Headquarters of the International Civil Aviation Organization (with Exchange of Notes). Montreal, April 14, 1951. *Entered into force* May 1, 1951. CTS 1951/7. *Terminated* February 20, 1992.

Headquarters Agreement between the Government of Canada and the International Civil Aviation Organization. Calgary and Montreal, October 4 and October 9, 1990. *Entered into force* February 20, 1992. CTS 1992/7.

Ireland
Agreement on Social Security between the Government of Canada and the Government of Ireland. Ottawa, November 29, 1990. *Entered into force* January 1, 1992. CTS 1992/6.

Luxembourg
Protocol to the Convention on Social Security between the Government of Canada and the Government of Luxembourg. Ottawa, February 6, 1992.

Malta
Agreement on Social Security between the Government of Canada and the Government of the Republic of Malta. Toronto, April 4, 1991. *Entered into force* March 1, 1992. CTS 1992/5.

Mexico
Convention between the Government of Canada and the Government of the United Mexican States for the Exchange of Information with Respect to Taxes. Mexico, March 16, 1990. *Entered into force* April 27, 1992. CTS 1992/13.

Convention between the Government of Canada and the Government of the United Mexican States for the Avoidance of Double Taxation and the Prevention of Fiscal Evasion with Respect to Taxes on Income. Ottawa, April 8, 1991. *Entered into force* May 11, 1992. CTS 1992/15.

Netherlands
Treaty between the Government of Canada and the Government of the Kingdom of the Netherlands on

Mutual Assistance in Criminal Matters. The Hague, May 1, 1991. *Entered into force* May 1, 1992. CTS 1992/9.

Nigeria
Agreement between the Government of Canada and the Government of the Federal Republic of Nigeria for the Avoidance of Double Taxation and the Prevention of Fiscal Evasion with Respect to Taxes on Income and Capital Gains (with Protocol). Abuja, August 4, 1992.

Norway
Exchange of Notes between the Government of Canada and the Government of Norway constituting an Agreement regarding a Transfer of Canadian-Obligated Uranium to Norway. Oslo, March 18, 1992. *Entered into force* March 18, 1992. CTS 1992/31.

Romania
Agreement between the Government of Canada and the Government of Romania on Cinematographic Relations (with Rules of Procedure). Bucharest, January 23, 1992. *Applied provisionally* on the date of its signature.

Russia
Agreement between the Government of Canada and the Government of the Russian Federation on Cooperation in the Arctic and the North (with Annex). Ottawa, June 19, 1992. *Entered into force* June 19, 1992. CTS 1992/18.

Protocol between the Government of Canada and the Government of the Russian Federation concerning Questions Relating to Credits for Deliveries of Capital Goods and Services to the Russian Federation from Canada. Ottawa, April 28, 1992. *Entered into force* April 28, 1992. CTS 1992/12.

Protocol between the Government of Canada and the Government of the Russian Federation concerning Questions Relating to Credits for Deliveries of Agricultural Products and Foodstuffs to the Russian Federation from Canada. Ottawa, April 28, 1992. *Entered into force* April 28, 1992. CTS 1992/11.

Agreement between the Government of Canada and the Government of the Russian Federation on Trade and Commerce. Ottawa, June 19, 1992. *Entered into force* December 29, 1992. CTS 1992/21. *Superseded*, as between Canada and the Russian Federation, the Canada-USSR Agreement of February 29, 1956.

Treaty on Concord and Cooperation between the Government of Canada and the Government of the Russian Federation. Ottawa, June 19, 1992. Agreement between the Government of Canada and the Government of the Russian Federation on the Supply of Grain. Ottawa, February 1, 1992. *Entered into force* February 1, 1992. CTS 1992/35.

Singapore
Air Transport Agreement between the Government of Canada and the Government of the Republic of Singapore. Singapore, June 14, 1984. *Denounced* with effect from August 16, 1992.

Sri Lanka
General Agreement on Development between the Government of Canada and the Government of the Democratic Socialist Republic of Sri Lanka (with Annexes). Colombo, October 28, 1992.

St. Kitts and Nevis
Agreement on Social Security between the Government of Canada and the Government of the Federation of St. Kitts and Nevis (with Administrative Arrangement). Ottawa, August 17, 1992.

United Kingdom
Exchange of Notes constituting an Agreement to amend the Treaty between the Government of Canada and the Government of the United Kingdom of Great Britain and Northern Ireland on Mutual Legal Assistance in Criminal Matters (Drug Trafficking), done at Ottawa on June 22, 1988. London, March 26, 1992.

United States of America
Exchange of Notes between the Government of Canada and the Govern-

ment of the United States of America constituting an Agreement further amending the Agreement concerning the Application of Tolls on the St. Lawrence Seaway (with Memorandum of Agreement). Washington, June 30, 1992. *Entered into force* June 30, 1992. CTS 1992/20. *Notes signed* June 15 and June 30, 1992.

Exchange of Notes between the Government of Canada and the Government of the United States of America amending Annex 1502.1, Schedules 1 and 2 of the Free Trade Agreement (with Appendices). Washington, August 4, 1992. *Entered into force* August 4, 1992. CTS 1992/32.

Exchange of Letters constituting an Agreement between the Government of Canada and the Government of the United States of America to amend Schedule 2 of Annex 705.4 of the Free Trade Agreement. Washington, May 14, 1992. *Entered into force* May 14, 1992. CTS 1992/25.

Exchange of Notes between the Government of Canada and the Government of the United States of America constituting an Agreement to amend the Agreement concerning the Transboundary Movement of Hazardous Waste signed on October 28, 1986. Washington, November 25, 1992. *Entered into force* November 25, 1992. CTS 1992/23. *Notes signed* November 4 and 25, 1992.

Exchange of Notes constituting an Agreement between the Government of Canada and the Government of the United States of America for cooperation in connection with the CANEX-2 payload on a space shuttle flight (with Attachment). Ottawa, October 14, 1992. *Entered into force* October 14, 1992. CTS 1992/34. *Notes signed* August 4 and October 14, 1992. *In force* October 14, 1992, *with effect* as of March 31, 1992.

USSR
Trade Agreement between the Government of Canada and the Government of

the Union of Soviet Socialist Republics and Protocols of Extension. Ottawa, February 29, 1956. *Entered into force* May 26, 1956. CTS 1956/1. *Terminated* December 29, 1992 as between Canada and the Russian Federation upon the entry into force of the Canada-Russia Agreement of June 19, 1992.

Zimbabwe
Agreement between the Government of Canada and the Government of the Republic of Zimbabwe for the Avoidance of Double Taxation and the Prevention of Fiscal Evasion with Respect to Taxes on Income, Capital and Capital Gains. Harare, April 16, 1992.

II: MULTILATERAL

Agriculture
International Convention for the Protection of New Varieties of Plants as Revised at Geneva on November 10, 1972, on October 23, 1978, and on March 19, 1991. Geneva, December 2, 1961. *Signed* by Canada March 9, 1992.

Aviation
Protocol Relating to an Amendment to Article 56 of the Convention on International Civil Aviation. Montreal, October 6, 1989. *Ratified* by Canada September 14, 1992.

Commerce
North American Free Trade Agreement between the Government of Canada, the Government of the United Mexican States and the United States of America. Ottawa, December 17, 1992. *Signed* by Canada December 17, 1992. (Signed at Ottawa December 11 and 17, at Mexico December 14 and 17, and at Washington December 8 and 17, 1992).

Conservation
Convention for the Conservation of Anadromous Stocks in the North Pacific (with Annex). Ottawa, September 20, 1991. *Signed* by Canada February 11, 1992. *Ratified* by Canada November 6, 1992.

Copper
Terms of Reference of the International Copper Study Group (with Annex). Geneva, February 24, 1989. *Acceded to* by Canada June 19, 1992. *Entered into force* for Canada June 19, 1992. CTS 1992/33.

Defence
Treaty on Open Skies. Helsinki, March 24, 1992. *Signed* by Canada March 24, 1992. *Ratified* by Canada July 21, 1992.

Disarmament
Treaty on Conventional Forces in Europe (with Protocols). Paris, November 19, 1990. *Signed* by Canada November 19, 1990. *Ratified* by Canada November 22, 1991. *Entered into force* for Canada November 9, 1992. CTS 1992/37.

Environment
Basel Convention on the Control of Transboundary Movements of Hazardous Wastes and their Disposal. Basel, March 22, 1989. *Signed* by Canada March 22, 1989. *Ratified* by Canada August 28, 1992. *Entered into force* for Canada November 26, 1992. CTS 1992/19.

Convention on the Transboundary Effects of Industrial Accidents (with Annexes). Helsinki, March 17, 1992. *Signed* by Canada March 17, 1992.

United Nations Framework Convention on Climate Change. New York, May 9, 1992. *Signed* by Canada June 12, 1992. *Ratified* by Canada December 4, 1992.

Convention on Biological Diversity. Rio de Janeiro, June 5, 1992. *Signed* by Canada June 11, 1992. *Ratified* by Canada December 4, 1992.

Finance
Agreement for the Administration of the Multilateral Investment Fund. Washington, February 11, 1992. *Signed* by Canada February 11, 1992.

Agreement Establishing the Multilateral Investment Fund. Washington, February 11, 1992. *Signed* by Canada February 11, 1992.

386   Annuaire canadien de Droit international 1993

Fisheries

Protocol to the International Convention on the Conservation of Atlantic Tunas. Paris, July 10, 1984. *Signed* by Canada September 10, 1984. *Ratified* by Canada February 3, 1992.

Human Rights

Convention on the Rights of the Child. New York, November 20, 1989. *Signed* by Canada May 28, 1990. *Ratified* by Canada December 13, 1991. *Entered into force* for Canada January 12, 1992. CTS 1992/3. Reservations and Statement of Understanding deposited by Canada at the time of ratification.

Industrial Development

Constitution of the United Nations Industrial Development Organization. Vienna, April 8, 1979. *Signed* by Canada August 31, 1982. *Ratified* by Canada September 20, 1983. *Entered into force* for Canada June 21, 1985. CTS 1985/46. *Denounced* by Canada December 3, 1992 with effect December 31, 1993.

Law

United Nations Convention on Contracts for the International Sale of Goods. Vienna, April 11, 1980. *Acceded to* by Canada April 23, 1991. *Entered into force* for Canada May 1, 1992. CTS 1992/2. *Declarations* deposited by Canada at the time of accession.

Convention on the Law Applicable to Trusts and on their Recognition. The Hague, July 1, 1985. *Signed* by Canada October 11, 1988. *Ratified* by Canada October 20, 1992. *Declarations and Reservation* deposited by Canada at the time of ratification.

Marine Science

Convention for a North Pacific Marine Science Organization (PICES). Ottawa, December 12, 1990. *Signed* by Canada October 22, 1991. *Ratified* by Canada October 22, 1991. *Entered into force* for Canada March 24, 1992. CTS 1992/8.

Navigation

Protocol, as amended, relating to the 1973 International Convention for the Prevention of Pollution from Ships (MARPOL 73/78). London, February 17, 1978. *Acceded to* by Canada November 16, 1992. *Declarations* deposited by Canada at the time of accession.

Telecommunications

Constitution and Convention of the International Telecommunication Union. Geneva, December 22, 1992. *Signed* by Canada December 22, 1992. *Declaration* made by Canada at the time of signature. (Part of the Final Acts of the Additional Plenipotentiary Conference (APP-92) of the International Telecommunication Union (ITU)).

Optional Protocol on the Compulsory Settlement of Disputes Relating to the Constitution of the ITU, to the Convention of the ITU and to the Administrative Regulations, Nice, 1992. Geneva, December 22, 1992. *Signed* by Canada December 22, 1992. Declaration made by Canada at the time of signature. (Part of the Final Acts of the Additional Plenipotentiary Conference (APP-92) of the International Telecommunication Union (ITU).

Partial Revision of the Radio Regulations and the Appendices thereto. Malaga-Torremolinos, March 3, 1992. *Signed* by Canada March 3, 1992. Declaration made at the time of signature (Part of the Final Acts of the World Administrative Radio Conference for Dealing with Certain Parts of the Spectrum (WARC-92).

Textiles

Protocol Maintaining in Force the Arrangement Regarding International Trade in Textiles. Geneva, December 9, 1992. *Signed* by Canada December 21, 1992.

United Nations

Resolutions adopted by the United Nations Security Council acting under Chapter VII of the Charter of the United Nations on different subjects related to the situation in Iraq, Liberia, Somalia and the former Yugoslavia, as well as on international terrorism (Libya). New York, beginning January

8, 1992. *Entered into force* for Canada when passed by the Security Council. CTS 1992/36.

I: BILATÉRAUX

Allemagne
Échange de Notes entre le gouvernement du Canada et le gouvernement de la République fédérale d'Allemagne constituant un Accord relatif à l'entraînement au Canada d'unités des Forces armées allemandes au Canada. Bruxelles le 10 décembre 1992. *En vigueur* le 10 décembre 1992. RTC 1992/22.

Antigua et Barbuda
Accord sur la sécurité sociale entre le gouvernement du Canada et le gouvernement d'Antigua et Barbuda (avec Arrangement administratif). Ottawa, le 2 septembre 1992.

Australie
Protocole modifiant l'Accord réciproque de sécurité sociale entre le gouvernement du Canada et le gouvernement de l'Australie. Ottawa, le 11 octobre 1990. *En vigueur* le 1er janvier 1992. RTC 1992/17.

Brésil
Traité sur le transfèrement des délinquants entre le gouvernement du Canada et le gouvernement de la République fédérative du Brésil. Brasilia, le 15 juillet 1992.

Chili
Accord entre le gouvernement du Canada et le gouvernement de la République du Chili tendant à éviter la double imposition sur les revenus provenant de l'exploitation des transports maritime et aérien. Santiago, le 30 juillet 1992.

États-Unis d'Amérique
Échange de Notes entre le gouvernement du Canada et le gouvernement des États-Unis d'Amérique modifiant les appendices 1 et 2 le l'Annexe 1502.1 de l'Accord de libre-échange (avec Appendices). Washington, le 4 août 1992. *En vigueur* le 4 août 1992. RTC 1992/32.

Échange de Lettres constituant un Accord entre le gouvernement du Canada et le gouvernement des États-Unis d'Amérique modifiant l'appendice 2 de l'Annexe 705.4 de l'Accord de libre-échange. Washington, le 14 mai 1992. *En vigueur* le 14 mai 1992. RTC 1992/25.

Échange de Notes entre le gouvernement du Canada et le gouvernement des États-Unis d'Amérique constituant un Accord modifiant l'Accord concernant l'application des taux de péage sur la Voie maritime du Saint-Laurent (avec Memorandum d'Accord). Washington, le 30 juin 1992. *En vigueur* le 30 juin 1992. RTC 1992/20. Notes *signées* les 15 et 30 juin 1992.

Échange de Notes entre le gouvernement du Canada et le gouvernement des États-Unis d'Amérique constituant un Accord modifiant l'Accord concernant les déplacements transfrontaliers de déchets dangereux signé le 28 octobre 1986. Washington, le 25 novembre 1992. En vigueur le 25 novembre 1992. RTC 1992/23. Notes *signées* les 4 et 25 novembre 1992.

Échange de Notes constituant un Accord entre le gouvernement du Canada et le gouvernement des États-Unis d'Amérique relatif aux activités entourant l'exploitation de la charge utile CANEX-2 à bord de la navette spatiale en orbite (avec Annexe). Ottawa, le 14 octobre 1992. *En vigueur* le 14 octobre 1992. RTC 1992/34. Notes *signées* le 4 août et le 14 octobre 1992. *En vigueur* le 14 octobre 1992 avec effet à compter du 31 mars 1992.

Finlande
Accord entre le gouvernement du Canada et le gouvernement de la Finlande relatif aux services aériens entre leurs territoires respectifs et au-delà de ceux-ci. Ottawa, le 16 mai 1977. *En vigueur* le 7 novembre 1977. RTC 1977/32. *Remplacé par l'Accord signé*

le 28 mai 1990. *Terminé* le 21 février 1992.

Échange de Notes entre le gouvernement du Canada et le gouvernement de la Finlande prolongeant pour une période indéfinie l'Accord aérien entre le Canada et la Finlande signé le 16 mai 1977. Ottawa, le 16 mai 1986. *En vigueur* le 16 mai 1986. RTC 1986/11. *Remplacé* par l'Accord signé le 28 mai 1990. *Terminé* le 21 février 1992.

Accord entre le gouvernement du Canada et le gouvernement de la Finlande concernant le transport aérien entre leurs territoires respectifs et audelà (avec Annexes). Helsinki, le 28 mai 1990. *En vigueur* le 21 février 1992. RTC 1992/4. *Appliqué provisoirement* à compter de la date de signature.

Convention entre le gouvernement du Canada et le gouvernement de la Finlande en vue d'éviter les doubles impositions et de prévenir l'évasion fiscale en matière d'impôts sur le revenu. Helsinki, le 28 mai 1990. *En vigueur* le 20 août 1992. RTC 1992/30.

France
Échange de Notes entre le gouvernement du Canada et le gouvernment de la République française constituant un Accord modifiant davantage l'Accord sur les relations dans le domaine de la télévision du 11 juillet 1983. Ottawa, le 8 septembre 1992. *En vigueur* le 8 septembre 1992. RTC 1992/27. Notes *signées* les 11 avril 1991 et 8 septembre 1992.

Échange de Notes entre le gouvernement du Canada et le gouvernement de la République française constituant un Accord modifiant davantage l'Accord relatif à la promotion de projets de coproduction cinématographique du 11 juillet 1983. Ottawa, le 8 septembre 1992. *En vigueur* le 8 septembre 1992. RTC 1992/29. Notes *signées* les 11 avril 1991 et 8 septembre 1992.

Échange de Notes entre le gouvernement du Canada et le gouvernement de la République française constituant un Accord modifiant l'Accord relatif à la promotion de projets de coproduction cinématographique ou audiovisuelle dans le domaine de l'animation du 10 janvier 1985. Ottawa, le 8 septembre 1992. *En vigueur* le 8 septembre 1992. RTC 1992/28. Notes *signées* les 11 avril 1991 et 8 septembre 1992.

Échange de Notes entre le gouvernement du Canada et le gouvernement de la République française constituant un Accord modifiant l'Accord sur les relations cinématographiques du 30 mai 1983. Ottawa, le 8 septembre 1992. *En vigueur* le 8 septembre 1992. RTC 1992/26. Notes *signées* les 11 avril 1991 et 8 septembre 1992.

Gabon
Accord général sur la coopération au développement entre le gouvernement du Canada et le gouvernement de la République gabonaise. Montréal, le 8 juin 1992. *En vigueur* le 8 juin 1992. RTC 1992/14.

Hongrie
Accord entre le gouvernement du Canada et le gouvernement de la République de la Hongrie concernant un garantie d'emprunt. Budapest, le 6 octobre 1992. *En vigueur* le 6 octobre 1992. RTC 1992/24.

Convention entre le gouvernement du Canada et le gouvernement de la République de la Hongrie en vue d'éviter les doubles impositions et de prévenir l'évasion fiscale en matière d'impôts sur le revenu et sur la fortune. Budapest, le 15 avril 1992.

Irlande
Accord sur la sécurité sociale entre le gouvernement du Canada et le gouvernement de l'Irlande. Ottawa, le 29 novembre 1990. *En vigueur* le 1er janvier 1992. RTC 1992/6.

Luxembourg
Avenant à la Convention sur la sécurité sociale entre le gouvernement du Canada et le gouvernement de Luxembourg. Ottawa, le 6 février 1992.

Malte

Accord sur la sécurité sociale entre le gouvernement du Canada et le gouvernement de la République de Malte. Toronto, le 4 avril 1991. *En vigueur* le 1er mars 1992. RTC 1992/5.

Mexique

Convention entre le gouvernement du Canada et le gouvernement des États-Unis Mexicains sur l'échange de renseignements en matière fiscale. Mexico, le 16 mars 1990. *En vigueur* le 27 avril 1992. RTC 1992/13.

Convention entre le gouvernement du Canada et le gouvernement des États-Unis Mexicains en vue d'éviter les doubles impositions et de prévenir l'évasion fiscale en matière d'impôts sur le revenu. Ottawa, le 8 avril 1991. *En vigueur* le 11 mai 1992. RTC 1992/15.

Nigéria

Accord entre le gouvernement du Canada et le gouvernement de la République du Nigéria en vue d'éviter les doubles impositions et de prévenir l'évasion fiscale en matière d'impôts sur le revenu et sur les gains en capital (avec Protocole). Abuja, le 4 août 1992.

Norvège

Échange de Notes entre le gouvernement du Canada et le gouvernement de la Norvège constituant un Accord relatif à un transfert à la Norvège d'uranium faisant l'objet d'une obligation envers le Canada. Oslo, le 18 mars 1992. *En vigueur* le 18 mars 1992. RTC 1992/31.

OACI

Accord de siège entre le gouvernement du Canada et l'Organisation de l'aviation civile internationale. Calgary et Montréal, les 4 et 9 octobre 1990. *En vigueur* le 20 février 1992. RTC 1992/7.

Accord entre le gouvernement du Canada et l'Organisation de l'Aviation civile internationale relatif au siège de l'Organisation de l'aviation civile internationale (avec Échange de Notes). Montréal, le 14 avril 1951. *En vigueur*

le 1er mai 1951. RTC 1951/7. *Terminé* le 20 février 1992.

Pays-Bas Traité d'entraide judiciaire en matière pénale entre le gouvernement du Canada et le gouvernement du Royaume des Pays-Bas. La Haye, le 1er mai 1991. *En vigueur* le 1er mai 1992. RTC 1992/9.

Roumanie

Accord entre le gouvernement du Canada et le gouvernement de la Roumanie sur les relations cinématographiques (avec Règles de Procédure). Bucarest, le 23 janvier 1992. *Appliqué* à titre provisoire dès sa signature.

Royaume-Uni

Échange de Notes constituant un Accord modifiant le Traité d'entraide en matière pénale (trafic de drogue) entre le gouvernement du Canada et le gouvernement du Royaume-Uni de la Grande Bretagne et d'Irlande du Nord fait à Ottawa le 22 juin 1988. Londres, le 26 mars 1992.

Russie

Accord entre le gouvernement du Canada et le gouvernement de la Fédération de Russie sur la coopération dans l'Arctique et le Nord (avec Annexe). Ottawa, le 19 juin 1992. *En vigueur* le 19 juin 1992. RTC 1992/18.

Accord entre le gouvernement du Canada et le gouvernement de la Fédération de Russie concernant la fourniture de céréales. Ottawa, le 1er février 1992. *En vigueur* le 1er février 1992. RTC 1992/35.

Protocole entre le gouvernement du Canada et le gouvernement de la Fédération de Russie concernant les questions relatives aux crédits consentis pour la fourniture, à partir du Canada, de produits agricoles et de denrées alimentaires à la Fédération de Russie. Ottawa, le 28 avril 1992. *En vigueur* le 28 avril 1992. RTC 1992/11.

Accord de commerce entre le gouvernement du Canada et le gouvernement de la Fédération de Russie. Ottawa, le 19 juin 1992. *En vigueur* le 29 décembre 1992. RTC 1992/21. À remplacer entre le Canada et la Russie l'Accord canado-soviétique du 29 février 1956.

Protocole entre le gouvernement du Canada et le gouvernement de la Fédération de Russie concernant les questions relatives aux crédits consentis pour la fourniture, à partir du Canada, de services et de biens de production à la Fédération de Russie. Ottawa, le 28 avril 1992. *En vigueur* le 28 avril 1992. RTC 1992/12.

Traité d'entente et de coopération entre le gouvernement du Canada et le gouvernement de la Fédération de Russie. Ottawa, le 19 juin 1992.

Saint-Kitts-et-Nevis
Accord de sécurité sociale entre le gouvernement du Canada et le gouvernement de la Fédération de Saint-Kitts-et-Nevis (avec Arrangement administratif). Ottawa, le 17 août 1992.

Singapour
Accord sur le transport aérien entre le gouvernement du Canada et le gouvernement de la République de Singapour. Singapour, le 14 juin 1984. *Dénonciation* avec effet à compter du 16 août 1992.

Sri Lanka
Accord général sur la coopération au développement entre le gouvernement du Canada et le gouvernement de la République socialiste démocratique de Sri Lanka (avec Annexes). Colombo, le 28 octobre 1992.

Tchécoslovaquie
Convention entre le gouvernement du Canada et le gouvernement de la République fédérative Tchèque et Slovaque en vue d'éviter les doubles impositions et de prévenir l'évasion fiscale en matière d'impôts sur le revenu et sur la fortune. Prague, le 30 août 1990. *En vigueur* le 22 juillet 1992. RTC 1992/16.

Accord entre le gouvernement du Canada et le gouvernement de la République fédérale Tchèque et Slovaque sur l'encouragement et la protection des investissements. Prague, le 15 novembre 1990. *En vigueur* le 9 mars 1992. RTC 1992/10.

URSS
Accord commercial entre le gouvernement de l'Union des Républiques socialistes soviétiques et Protocoles de prorogation. Ottawa, le 29 février 1956. *En vigueur* le 26 mai 1956. RTC 1956/1. *Terminé* le 29 décembre 1992 entre le Canada et la Fédération de Russie au moment de l'entrée en vigueur de l'Accord canada-russie du 19 juin 1992.

Zimbabwe
Accord entre le gouvernement du Canada et le gouvernement de la République du Zimbabwe en vue d'éviter les doubles impositions et de prévenir l'évasion fiscale en matière d'impôts sur le revenu, sur la fortune et sur les gains en capital. Harare, le 16 avril 1992.

II: TRAITÉS MULTILATÉRAUX

Agriculture
Convention internationale pour la protection des obtentions végétales du 2 décembre 1961, revisée le 10 novembre 1972, le 23 octobre 1978 et le 4 mars 1991. Genève, le 2 décembre 1961. *Signée* par le Canada le 9 mars 1992.

Aviation
Protocole portant amendement de l'Article 56 de la Convention relative à l'aviation civile internationale. Montréal, le 6 octobre 1989. *Ratifié* par le Canada le 14 septembre 1992.

Commerce
Accord de libre-échange nord-américain entre le gouvernement du Canada, le gouvernement des États-Unis Mexicains et le gouvernement des États-Unis d'Amérique. Ottawa, le 17 décembre 1992. *Signé* par le Canada le 17 décembre 1992. Signé à Ottawa les 11 et 17 décembre, à Mexico les 14 et 17 décembre et à Washington les 8 et 17 décembre 1992.

Conservation

Convention concernant la conservation des espèces anadromes dans l'océan Pacifique Nord (avec Annexe). Ottawa, le 20 septembre 1991. *Signée* par le Canada le 11 février 1992. *Ratifié* par le Canada le 6 novembre 1992.

Cuivre

Statuts du Groupe d'étude international du cuivre (avec Annexe). Genève, le 24 février 1989. *Adhésion* du Canada le 19 juin 1992. *En vigueur* pour le Canada le 19 juin 1992. RTC 1992/33.

Défense

Traité sur le régime «Ciel Ouvert». Helsinki, le 24 mars 1992. *Signé* par le Canada le 24 mars 1992. *Ratifié* par le Canada le 21 juillet 1992.

Désarmement

Traité sur les forces armées conventionelles en Europe (avec Protocoles). Paris, le 19 novembre 1990. *Signé* par le Canada le 19 novembre 1990. *Ratifié* par le Canada le 22 novembre 1991. *En vigueur* pour le Canada le 9 novembre 1992. RTC 1992/37.

Développement industriel

Acte constitutif de l'Organisation des Nations Unies pour le développement industriel. Vienne, le 8 avril 1979. *Signé* par le Canada le 31 août 1982. *Ratifié* par le Canada le 20 septembre 1983. *En vigueur* pour le Canada le 21 juin 1985. RTC 1985/46. *Dénonciation* par le Canada le 3 décembre 1992 avec effet à compter du 31 décembre 1993.

Droit

Convention relative à la loi applicable au trust et à sa reconnaissance. La Haye, le 1er juillet 1985. *Signée* par le Canada le 11 octobre, 1988. *Ratifiée* par le Canada le 20 octobre 1992. *Déclarations et réserve* déposées par le Canada au moment de la ratification.

Convention des Nations Unies sur les contrats de vente internationale de marchandises. Vienne, le 11 avril 1980. *Adhésion* par le Canada le 23 avril 1991. *En vigueur* pour le Canada le 1er mai 1992. RTC 1992/2. *Déclarations* déposées par le Canada au moment de l'adhésion.

Droits de la personne

Convention relative aux droits de l'enfant. New York, le 20 novembre 1989. *Signée* par le Canada le 28 mai 1990. *Ratifiée* par le Canada le 13 décembre 1991. *En vigueur* pour le Canada le 12 janvier 1992. RTC 1992/3. *Réserves et déclaration d'intépretation* déposées par le Canada au moment de la ratification.

Environnement

Convention de Bâle sur le contrôle des mouvements transfrontières de déchets dangereux et de leur élimination. Bâle, le 22 mars 1989. *Signée* par le Canada le 22 mars 1989. *Ratifiée* par le Canada le 28 août 1992. *En vigueur* pour le Canada le 26 novembre 1992. RTC 1992/19.

Convention sur les effets transfrontières des accidents industriels (avec Annexes). Helsinki, le 17 mars 1992. *Signée* par le Canada le 17 mars 1992. Convention-cadre des Nations Unies sur les changements climatiques. New York, le 9 mai 1992. *Signée* par le Canada le 12 juin 1992. *Ratifiée* par le Canada le 4 décembre 1992.

Convention sur la diversité biologique. Rio de Janeiro, le 5 juin 1992. *Signée* par le Canada le 11 juin 1992. *Ratifiée* par le Canada le 4 décembre 1992.

Finance

Accord relatif à l'administration du Fonds multilatéral d'investissement. Washington, le 11 février 1992. *Signé* par le Canada le 11 février 1992.

Accord constitutif du Fonds multilatéral d'investissement. Washington, le 11 février 1992. *Signé* par le Canada le 11 février 1992.

Nations Unies

Résolutions adoptées par le Conseil de Sécurité des Nations Unies, agissant en vertu du chapitre VII de la Chartre des Nations Unies sur divers sujets relatifs à la situation en Iraq, au Libéria, en Somalie, en ex-Yougoslavie, ainsi que sur le terrorisme international (Libye). New York, à compter du 8 janvier 1992. *En vigueur* pour le Canada à la date d'adoption. RTC 1992/36.

Navigation
Protocole de 1978, tel que modifié, relatif à la Convention internationale de 1973 pour la prévention de la pollution sur les navires (MARPOL 73/78). Londres, le 17 février 1978. *Adhésion* du Canada le 16 novembre 1992. *Déclarations* déposées par le Canada au moment de l'adhésion.

Pêche
Protocole à la Convention internationale pour la conservation des thonidés de l'Atlantique. Paris, le 10 juillet 1984. *Signé* par le Canada le 10 septembre 1984. *Ratifié* par le Canada le 3 février 1992.

Sciences Marines
Convention portant création d'une organisation pour les sciences marines dans le Pacifique Nord (PICES). Ottawa, le 12 décembre 1990. *Signée* par le Canada le 22 octobre 1991. *Ratifiée* par le Canada le 22 octobre 1991. *En vigueur* pour le Canada le 24 mars 1992. RTC 1992/8.

Télécommunications
Constitution et Convention de l'Union internationale des télécommunications (UIT). Genève, le 22 décembre 1992. *Signées* par le Canada le 22 décembre 1992. *Déclaration* faite au moment de la signature. (Partie composante des

Actes finals de la Conférence de plénipotentiaires additionelle (APP-92) de l'Union internationale des télécommunications (UIT)).

Protocole facultatif concernant le règlement obligatoire des différends relatifs à la Constitution de l'Union internationale des télécommunications, à la Convention de l'Union internationale des télécommunications et aux Règlements administratifs, Nice, 1992. Genève, le 22 décembre 1992. *Signé* par le Canada le 22 décembre 1992. *Déclaration* faite au moment de la signature. (Partie composante des Actes finals de la Conférence de plénipotentiaires additionelle (APP-92) de l'Union internationale des télécommunications (UIT)).

Révision partielle du Règlement des radiocommunications et des appendices au dit Règlement. Malaga-Torremolinos, le 3 mars 1992. *Signée* par le Canada le 3 mars 1992. *Déclaration* faite au moment de la signature (Partie composante des Actes finals de la Conférence administrative mondiale des radiocommunications chargée d'étudier les attributions de fréquences dans certaines parties du spectre (WARC-92)).

Textiles
Protocole portant maintien en vigueur de l'Arrangement concernant le commerce international des textiles. Genève, le 9 décembre 1992. *Signé* par le Canada le 21 décembre 1992.

Canadian Cases in International Law in 1992-93 / La jurisprudence canadienne en matière de droit international en 1992-93

compiled by / préparé par

JOOST BLOM*

I. PUBLIC INTERNATIONAL LAW/DROIT INTERNATIONAL PUBLIC

Human Rights — war crimes and crimes against humanity

Rudolph v. *Canada*, [1992] 2 F.C. 653. Federal Court of Appeal.

A removal order was made against the applicant, a national and resident of Germany, on the ground that section 19(1)(*j*) of the Immigration Act, R.S.C. 1985, c. I-2 (as am. by R.S.C. 1985 (3rd Supp.), c. 30, section 3), prohibited his admission into Canada. That provision refers to persons who there are reasonable grounds to believe have committed an act or omission outside Canada that constituted a war crime or a crime against humanity within the meaing of section 7(3.76) of the Criminal Code, R.S.C. 1985, c. C-46 (as am. by R.S.C. 1985 (3rd Supp.), c. 30, section 1). The Criminal Code definitions of "war crime" and "crime against humanity" require, *inter alia*, that the act or omission, at the time and place of its commission, constitutes a contravention of customary international law or conventional international law. The applicant had admittedly called for, made use of, and directed forced labour by allied civilians and prisoners of war in the Mittelwerk V-2 rocket plant in 1943-45.

The Federal Court of Appeal noted that customary and conventional international laws were incorporated by reference into Canadian law, not only by section 7(3.76) of the Criminal Code, but also by section 11(*g*) of the Canadian Charter of Rights and Freedoms (Constitution Act, 1982, Schedule B, Part I). (That paragraph gives

---

* Faculty of Law, University of British Columbia.

any person charged with an offence the right "not to be found guilty on account of any act or omission unless, at the time of the act or omission, it constituted an offence under Canadian or international law or was criminal according to the general principles of law recognized by the community of nations.") Although there was no express prohibition in conventional international law before 1945 against employing prisoners in the manufacture of munitions, such a prohibition was readily inferred from the Hague Convention of 1907 on the Laws and Customs of War on Land, Articles 6 (prisoners' labour to have no connection with the operation of the war), 23 (nationals of hostile country not to be compelled to take part in operations of war directed against their own country), and 52 (inhabitants of occupied countries not to be forced to take part in military operations against their own country). The applicant's conduct fell within these provisions by necessary implication. As for customary international law, the use of slave labour was expressly included in the definitions of "war crimes" and "crimes against humanity" in Article 6 of the London Agreement of 1945 establishing the Charter of the International Military Tribunal. These definitions were recognized by the Tribunal itself as declaratory of customary international law. Moreover, by resolution of December 11, 1946, the United Nations General Assembly had affirmed the principles of international law "recognized by" the Charter of the tribunal. It would not be possible to find stronger evidence of the content of customary international law at the relevant period.

Seas — application of criminal law

R. v. Blanco (1991), 97 Nfld. & P.E.I. R. 86. Newfoundland Supreme Court, Trial Division.

Cameron, J. held in this case that two foreign nationals could not be charged with obstructing a protection officer in Canadian fisheries waters, because the alleged offences had occurred outside Canadian fisheries waters as defined by the Coastal Fisheries Protection Act, R.S.C. 1985, c. C-33, and the Territorial Sea and Fishing Zones Act, R.S.C. 1985, c. T-8. There was no indication that the Criminal Code provision in question was intended to apply outside those waters. The doctrine of hot pursuit was said to apply because, it was alleged, the vessel in question had been boarded by the protection officers within Canadian waters. This argument failed, since hot pursuit would be relevant only if there was an offence committed within the jurisdiction of Canada; the doctrine could not be used to give jurisdiction over an offence that was committed on the high seas outside Canadian fisheries waters.

Treaties — effect on domestic law

Note. See *R.* v. *Vincent* (1993), 12 O.R. (3d) 427 (C.A.), which held that a native Indian charged with smuggling cigarettes could not invoke a provision of the Jay Treaty of 1794, between Great Britain and the United States, as giving her the right to bring commercial goods into Canada free of duty. Like any other treaty it conferred rights only on the nations party to it, not on individuals.

II. CONFLICT OF LAWS/DROIT INTERNATIONAL PRIVÉ

A. *Jurisdiction/Compétence des tribunaux*

1. *Common law and federal*

(a) *Jurisdiction* in personam

Attornment to the jurisdiction of the local forum

Note. In *Edgar* v. *Ronald* (1993), 78 B.C.L.R. (2d) 299 (S.C.), it was held to be too late for a defendant to argue that the court should decline jurisdiction, because, as well as entering an appearance, she had been negotiating a settlement with the plaintiff for a considerable time, so that the limitation period in the alternative forum, Alberta, had now run.

Service ex juris — *grounds* — *proceeding in respect of the administration of a deceased person*

Note. See *Kraus* v. *Cookson* (1992), [1993] 2 W.W.R. 67, 13 C.P.C. (3d) 126 (Sask. C.A.), which held that certain claims made by the beneficiaries of an estate to set aside transactions made by the testator during his lifetime were not a proceeding "in respect of the administration of a deceased person" who died domiciled in Saskatchewan, and so did not qualify for service *ex juris* without leave.

Service ex juris — *grounds* — *tort committed within the province*

Quest Vitamin Supplies Ltd. v. *Hassam* (1992), 79 B.C.L.R. (2d) 85. British Columbia Supreme Court.

The plaintiff company sued its own directors, as well as an individual acting as agent of a United Kingdom company (Quest UK) in which the plaintiff had shares, for unlawfully conspiring to injure it by persuading it to settle, on unfavourable terms, litigation pending in England between it and Farmoza, a Liechtenstein-based entity to which it had agreed to sell its Quest UK shares. Quest UK, its agent, and Farmoza were served *ex juris* and now sought a declaration that the court had no jurisdiction or, alternatively, should decline jurisdiction. Boyd, J. held that the conspiracy claim was a claim "founded on a tort committed in British Columbia." Although some of the events had taken place in England, the thrust of the claim related to a conspiracy with respect to the negotiation of the settlement; all the relevant communications between the defendants were said to have occurred in Vancouver, and all of the transactions in relation to the plaintiff's business that were the subject of the action had taken place in Vancouver. To the extent that the plaintiff had suffered harm, it had probably been suffered in British Columbia; the impugned agreement had been made there, payment was received there, and the losses arising from performing the agreement were incurred there. An exclusive choice of an English forum in the share purchase agreement with Farmoza was irrelevant because, even as against Farmoza, the claims did not arise under the agreement but out of the alleged conspiracy to injure the plaintiff through the agreement. The plaintiff had also satisfied the onus on it to show that British Columbia was the *forum conveniens.* If the court declined jurisdiction, the plaintiff would have to mount litigation in three or possibly four jurisdictions. The assertion of jurisdiction by a British Columbia court in this case had a sufficient basis to be reasonably fair and just by national and international standards.

Declining jurisdiction — agreed choice of another forum

Ash v. *Corporation of Lloyd's* (1992), 9 O.R. (3d) 755, 7 C.P.C. (3d) 364. Ontario Court of Appeal

The plaintiffs, Canadian-resident underwriting members of Lloyd's, brought an action in Ontario against that corporation, seeking a declaration that their contracts with it were void for fraud. They also brought actions against seven banks, four of them Canadian chartered banks, claiming interlocutory injunctions against them to refrain from paying Lloyd's on letters of credit issued by the banks on the instructions of one or more of the plaintiffs. The Court of Appeal affirmed the motions judge's decision to stay the action against Lloyd's. Each of the plaintiffs' agreements with

Lloyd's contained an exclusive choice of an English forum. So did each agreement of the plaintiffs with a number of different members' agents, and the trust agreements that each plaintiff had entered into. Even without those clauses the litigation had an overwhelming affinity with England, where the agreements were to be performed and where the wrongful acts complained of had allegedly taken place. It was no answer to say that fraud vitiated the agreed choice of forum. It would be anomalous and detrimental to international commerce if a plaintiff, just by alleging fraud, could neutralize a choice of jurisdiction clause.

The Court of Appeal reversed the motions judge's decision not to stay the actions against the Canadian chartered banks, and affirmed his stay of the actions against the other banks. All of the banks were amenable to English proceedings, and an Ontario order against them was unnecessary to achieve the objective of the interlocutory injunctions because an injunction against Lloyd's would do as well. Once it was determined that the action against Lloyd's should be pursued in England, there was nothing of substance to pursue in Ontario. There was no claim against the banks that would form the basis for a determination at trial. An interlocutory injunction granted in Ontario would effectively be interlocutory until a trial in England. Interlocutory orders for English trials should be made in England.

Note. An exclusive choice of jurisdiction clause was refused effect in *Northern Sales Ltd.* v. *Saskatchewan Wheat Pool* (1992), 78 Man. R. (2d) 200 (C.A.), mainly because giving effect to it would have split the litigation between courts in two provinces.

Declining jurisdiction — forum non conveniens — *defendant served in the jurisdiction*

P.W.A. Corp. v. *Gemini Group Automated Distribution Systems Inc.* (1992), 98 D.L.R. (4th) 277, [1993] 3 W.W.R. 67. Alberta Queen's Bench.

The plaintiff, an Alberta company that owned Canadian Airlines International, brought an action in Alberta for a declaration that Gemini, the general partner in a limited partnership formed under Ontario law to operate an airline reservations system, was insolvent. Under the partnership agreement, this was grounds for the dissolution of the partnership. The other limited partners besides the plaintiff were Air Canada and Covia. Gemini and Air Canada were served in Alberta; Covia was served *ex juris* in Ontario. Covia sought to have the service *ex juris* set aside, and the other two defendants sought to have the proceedings stayed, all arguing *forum non conveniens*. Virtue, J. granted the stay. The burden was on all the defendants to show that there was another available forum that was clearly and distinctly more suitable, and they had done so. Ontario was the forum that was more convenient and appropriate for the pursuit of the action and for securing the ends of justice. The plaintiff chose to leave Alberta to do business through an Ontario limited partnership. The problem of the insolvency of that business should be resolved in the Ontario courts, especially in light of the fact that under the relevant agreements the parties had agreed to be governed by the laws of Ontario and had irrevocably attorned to the non-exclusive jurisdiction of the Ontario courts. In the context of the agreements, this meant that the parties attorned to the jurisdiction of those courts except in matters where some extraordinary condition or reason would require that the matter be determined elsewhere.

Note. Proceedings against a defendant served in the province were stayed in *Novatel Communications Ltd.* v. *Ericsson G.E. Mobile Communications Can. Inc.* (1993), 9 Alta. L.R. (3d) 141 (Q.B.) (action by Alberta company for commission said to be owing on sales by Ontario-based telephone equipment supplier to Ontario-based cellular telephone company; jurisdiction declined in favour of Ontario, mainly because the witnesses and documentary evidence were largely there); *Osmosis Waste Systems Ltd.* v. *Guardian Ins. Co. of Canada* (1993), 12 O.R. (3d) 786, 17 C.C.L.I. (2d) 162 (Gen. Div.) (Ontario company suing casualty insurer on policy issued in British Columbia in respect of a loss by theft suffered in British Columbia; jurisdiction declined in favour of British Columbia); *Sterling Software Int'l (Canada) Inc.* v. *Software Recording Corp.* (1993), 12 O.R. (3d) 694, 47 C.P.R. (3d) 420 (Gen. Div.) (Ontario software licensee suing Texas software manufacturer for breach of contract and breaches of Canadian trade-mark legislation; jurisdiction declined pending outcome of Texas litigation brought by the Texas company against the Ontario company in respect of the same major factual issue); *Owen* v. *Tinmouth* (1992), 116 N.S.R. (2d) 245 (T.D.) (action against disability insurer by Prince Edward Island resident injured in an accident in Nova Scotia but insured under a policy issued in Prince Edward Island and governed by that province's law; jurisdiction declined in favour of Prince Edward Island); and *Tomlinson* v. *Turner* (1991), 99 Nfld. &

P.E.I. R. 288 (P.E.I. T.D.) (Saskatchewan residents suing Prince Edward Island residents in respect of injuries suffered in a road accident in Quebec; jurisdiction declined in favour of Quebec).

A stay of proceedings against a defendant served in the province was refused in *Hunt* v. *T & N plc.*, [1993] 1 W.W.R. 354, 72 B.C.L.R. (2d) 14 (S.C.) (action against asbestos producer not stayed because alternative forum was in the United States, and it was unclear whether, as the defendant said, the plaintiff would be able to claim there against a trust fund set up by order of a bankruptcy court); *Zurich Indemnity Co. of Canada* v. *Reemark Lincoln's Hill Project Ltd.* (1992), 73 B.C.L.R. (2d) 234 (S.C.) (Ontario lender's foreclosure action in respect of land in B.C. not stayed, despite borrower's having begun a breach of contract action in Ontario relating to the same transaction; a stay would prejudice the lender's security); and *Amarualik* v. *Barker* (1992), 8 C.P.C. (3d) 46 (N.W.T. C.A.) (action by Native resident of Northwest Territories against sixteen defendants, all but two resident elsewhere, in respect of medical negligence; no compelling reason for a stay as far as evidence and witnesses were concerned, and special emphasis given to broader public interest in affording local access to justice to indigenous residents of the Northwest Territories).

Declining jurisdiction — forum non conveniens — *defendant served ex juris*

Note. Jurisdiction over a defendant served *ex juris* was declined in *Plug-In Storage Systems Inc.* v. *Dasco Data Products Ltd.* (1993), 48 C.P.R. (3d) 15 (F.C.T.D.) (service *ex juris* set aside in action against U.S. corporation for patent and trade-mark infringement, because plaintiff had to show arguable claims based on wrongdoing in Canada, not just make bare allegations); *Frymer* v. *Brettschneider* (1992), 10 O.R. (3d) 157, 9 C.P.C. (3d) 264 (Gen. Div.) (action by Ontario resident to set aside various agreements made in Florida with her relatives, expressly governed by Florida law and dealing with the administration in Florida of a trust that was part of her father's estate; jurisdiction declined in favour of Florida); and *Wilson* v. *Moyes* (1993), 13 O.R. (3d) 202 (Gen. Div.) (Ontario-resident victims of Florida automobile accident suing Scottish-resident driver and Florida car rental companies as owners of the vehicle; jurisdiction declined in favour of Florida).

Courts refused to decline jurisdiction over a defendant served *ex juris* in *Witham* v. *Liftair Int'l (1985) Ltd.* (1992), 114 N.S.R. (2d)

43 (T.D.) (Nova Scotia resident brought wrongful dismissal action against Alberta corporation that had employed him in Yemen; insufficient reasons shown to disturb plaintiff's choice of forum); *Monahan (Guardian ad litem of)* v. *Trahan* (1992), 117 N.S.R. (2d) 393, 13 C.P.C. (3d) 52 (N.S.T.D.) (Nova Scotia-resident hydroplane racer suing defendant residents of Ontario and Quebec in respect of injuries suffered in a racing accident in Quebec; Nova Scotia held to be *forum conveniens* because all the evidence as to quantum of damage was there and because the plaintiff could not afford to sue in Quebec); *Upper Lakes Shipping Ltd.* v. *Foster Yeoman Ltd.* (1992), 12 C.P.C. (3d) 31 (Ont. Gen. Div. (M.C.)) (Alberta company suing British company for breach of a contract that was arguably made in Ontario, for the supply of two ships to be built in Japan; defendant failed to discharge onus of showing that England was clearly the better forum); *Standard Trust Co.* v. *Ginnell*, discussed below in part D., 1., (a); and *Dickhoff* v. *Armadale Communications Ltd.* (1992), 103 Sask. R. 307 (Q.B.) (jurisdiction taken in libel action by Saskatchewan businessman against Ontario newspapers that circulated in Saskatchewan, mainly because the plaintiff's business activities and reputation were centred in the province).

Defendant served ex juris — lis alibi pendens

May v. *Greenwood* (1992), 96 D.L.R. (4th) 581, 11 O.R. (3d) 42. Ontario Court of Appeal.

The plaintiffs, husband and wife, were injured in an accident in Manitoba on a cabin cruiser. In July 1987 they commenced an action in Manitoba against the defendant, the owner and operator of the boat. In December 1987 they commenced a second action against the defendant in Ontario. This action included claims under section 61 of the Family Law Act, now R.S.O. 1990, c. F.2, for the damage that the couple's children and the husband's mother suffered as a result of the plaintiffs' injuries. No equivalent claims existed under Manitoba law. Before discoveries in the Manitoba action, the defendant's solicitors wrote to the plaintiffs' solicitors stating that if discoveries proceeded, the defendant would treat that as an election to proceed in Manitoba rather than in Ontario. There was no reply from the plaintiffs. Discoveries were held in the Manitoba action. The plaintiffs took no step in the Ontario action except to amend their pleadings. The defendant applied for a stay of the Ontario proceedings. Steele, J. refused the stay, primarily on the ground that it might deprive the plaintiffs of their claims under the Family Law Act. He did, however, impose on the plaintiffs the condition that they not continue with the Manitoba action and that the Manitoba proceedings and discoveries were to be incorporated into the Ontario action with necessary amendments.

The Ontario Court of Appeal reversed his decision. Manitoba and Ontario were both convenient places to try the action. It would be difficult to enforce the conditions the judge had imposed regarding the Manitoba proceedings. The plaintiffs had proceeded first in Manitoba and were now, four years later, seeking to litigate in Ontario. They had not shown the existence of a legitimate advantage in Ontario, let alone that such an advantage outweighed the desirability of letting the Manitoba action proceed. The stay should be granted pending the outcome of the Manitoba action. If the Family Law Act claims were not dealt with in Manitoba, those claims alone could subsequently proceed in Ontario.

Note. The relationship between the issue of *forum conveniens* and the plaintiff's legitimate advantage in the local forum was discussed by the Supreme Court of Canada in *Amchem Products Inc.* v. *British Columbia (Workers' Compensation Board)*, noted below under (e) of this part.

(b) *Actions Relating to Property*

Gillespie v. *Grant*, [1992] 6 W.W.R. 599, 4 Alta. L.R. (3d) 122. Alberta Supreme Court.

The issue in this case was the proper forum for probate and testator's family maintenance proceedings in respect of the will of a man whose family and most of whose business interests were in Alberta but who in recent years had lived most of the time with his lover in British Columbia. The estate consisted of a single immovable property in Alberta and movable property in both Alberta and British Columbia. The executors of the estate applied to the Alberta Surrogate Court for directions, including a declaration that the testator died domiciled in Alberta. Two disinherited children of the testator sought to stay the probate proceedings in Alberta on the ground of *forum non conveniens*, relying in part on the fact that probate and testator's family maintenance proceedings were under way in British Columbia. Mason, Surr. Ct. J. refused the stay. The parties were agreed that the courts of either province had jurisdiction in the probate of the estate. The question of domicile was governed by Alberta law. It was to the advantage of both provinces' courts to have that question decided first, because jurisdiction in a testator's family maintenance application depended on the testator's last domicile having been in the province, and the law governing the issues of capacity and undue influence also depended on domicile. Although, given the nature of the issues and the evidence, either province's court was an appropriate and suitable forum for that determination, the proceedings were much further advanced in Alberta, which made it the *forum conveniens*.

(c)   *Matrimonial Actions*

Divorce — transfer of proceedings to another province

   Note. In *Ruyter* v. *Samson* (1992), 99 D.L.R. (4th) 552, 44 R.F.L. (3d) 35 (Ont. Gen. Div.), a wife's application for the transfer of divorce proceedings from Quebec to Ontario, made under section 6(1) of the Divorce Act, R.S.C. 1985, c. 3 (2nd Supp.), was dismissed. The application should have been made to the court in which the proceedings were commenced. Even if that were not so, the ground for transfer to Ontario, that the children were most substantially connected with the province, could not be relied upon when the husband's consent to the children's removal to Ontario was conditional on the wife's undertaking to continue their education in French, an undertaking that she had broken.

Divorce — jurisdiction to vary corollary order

   Note. See *Lavoie* v. *Yawrenko* (1992), 74 B.C.L.R. (2d) 321 (C.A.) (jurisdiction taken under section 5(1)(a) of the Divorce Act, R.S.C. 1985, c. 3 (2nd Supp.) to vary support order made corollary to divorce by Alberta court).

(d)   *Infants and Children*

Child abduction — Hague Convention

   Note. See *Zimmerman* v. *Zimmerman* (1992), 42 R.F.L. (3d) 264 (B.C.S.C.) (children not wrongfully detained by their mother in Germany, because the petitioner father had agreed to their moving back there, albeit with the hope, which did not materialize, that he himself would return there as well).

Custody — jurisdiction

   Note. See *Hodgins* v. *Hodgins* (1992), 104 Sask. R. 211 (Q.B.) (no jurisdiction in custody under section 15(1) of the Children's Law

Act, S.S. 1990-91, c. C-8.1, because the children were not habitually resident in the province and none of the exceptions to that jurisdictional requirement applied).

Custody — enforcement of extraprovincial order

G. (P.A.) v. G. (K.A.) (1992), 96 D.L.R. (4th) 731 (*sub nom.* *Gillespie v. Gillespie*), 10 O.R. (3d) 641. Ontario Court of Appeal.

The parents, the father originally from the United States and the mother from Canada, lived in New Zealand from their marriage in 1985. After their separation in 1990 the parties engaged in litigation about custody, the outcome of which, in August 1991, was that the mother was awarded custody and the father, unsupervised access. In January 1992 the mother moved with the children from Nelson, where all the parties had been living, to Dunedin, some 800 km away. The father immediately brought an application in Family Court in Nelson seeking custody, an order enforcing his access, and an order to restrain the mother from moving the children from Nelson. The parents agreed at the end of January that the father should have five days' access in March and a week in May 1992. As a result of the judge's commitments, the hearing of the father's application was adjourned from its scheduled date of March 19, 1992 to June 11, 1992. In early April the father learned that the mother and children had left Dunedin and, later, that they had moved to Ontario, where the wife's parents lived.

On June 12, 1992, lawyers acting for the father applied to the Ontario Court for an order for the return of the children to New Zealand. At the same time, the father's application for custody, which had been commenced in January, was heard in Nelson. The mother had filed a defence and, in March, had given evidence in Family Court in Dunedin to be used in the Nelson proceedings. On the basis of the father's oral testimony, the evidence given in March by the mother, and the files of the previous litigation between the parties, the court in Nelson made an order on June 11, 1992, granting custody to the father, reserving access to the mother to be exercised in New Zealand. This custody order was placed before the Ontario Court in support of the father's application for return of the children to New Zealand.

The Ontario Court, General Division, made an order granting custody to the mother. The judge placed no weight on the New Zealand custody order because, she said, it was not a determination on the merits, it was made as a punishment to the mother for removing the children (this was based on critical comments made by the New Zealand judge about the mother's conduct), and it did not reflect the best interests of the children. The Court of Appeal reversed her decision and ordered that the children be returned to New Zealand in recognition of the custody order made by the court in Nelson.

The recognition of an extraprovincial custody order was required, except in five defined sets of circumstances, by section 41 of the Children's Law Reform Act, R.S.O. 1990, c. C.12. None of the exceptions applied. In particular, it could not be said that the mother had not been given an opportunity to be heard in the New Zealand proceedings (section 41(1)(b)). When she left the country the mother had agreed that the father should have access in May; she knew that the proceeding in which the father sought custody was still pending; and through her lawyers she knew that this had been adjourned until June. On those facts, the mother had had an opportunity to be heard but deliberately chose not to avail herself of the opportunity to be personally present at the hearing.

Section 42(1), which allows an Ontario court to supersede the extraprovincial order if there has been a "material change in circumstances that affects or is likely to affect the best interests of the child," was also inapplicable. A party who had relocated a child in the face of pending custody proceedings could not rely on the relocation as a material change in circumstances. To do so would defeat one of the principal objects of the legislation, namely "to discourage the abduction of children as an alternative to the determination of custody rights by due process" (section 19(c)).

It appeared that the Ontario judge had declined to recognize the New Zealand order because she did not agree with it. That approach was not consistent with the statutory requirements. In addition, contrary to certain findings by the judge, the decision in New Zealand was a determination on the merits, based on a primary regard for the welfare of the children, and decided on substantially more complete evidence than had been available to the trial judge in Ontario. The mother was directed to return the children to Nelson within four weeks. The father had agreed not to enforce the New Zealand order for seven days following the children's arrival in New Zealand.

Note. Extraprovincial custody orders were given effect under the Extra-Provincial Custody Orders Act, R.S.A. 1980, c. E-17, in *Koffler v. Hruby* (1992), 40 R.F.L. (3d) 369 (Alta. Q.B.) (refusal to vary), and *Vielle* v. *Vielle* (1992), 41 R.F.L. (3d) 316 (Alta. Prov. Ct.) (enforcement).

(e) *Injunction Against Prosecution of an Action in Another Jurisdiction*

Amchem Products Inc. v. *British Columbia*, [1993] 1 S.C.R. 897, 102 D.L.R. (4th) 96. Supreme Court of Canada.

The claimants, 194 individuals, began an action in Texas District Court against 33 corporate defendants ("the companies"), asbestos manufacturers, most of whom were incorporated somewhere in the United States, the remainder including a Quebec and a United Kingdom corporation. All but 40 of the claimants had received benefits from the British Columbia Workers' Compensation Board for injury to their health from exposure to asbestos. They alleged that the companies, with the possible exception of the Quebec and United Kingdom companies, had engaged in tortious conduct in the United States relating to the manufacture and marketing of asbestos products. The claimants' injuries were said to have been suffered through exposure to asbestos in various jurisdictions, including the United States, five Canadian provinces, and Europe, although the companies maintained that virtually all of the plaintiffs' damages were suffered in British Columbia. The claimants' causes of action included negligence and conspiracy. None of the companies had any connection with British Columbia and none was incorporated in Texas, but most carried on business in Texas in some form, and it was on that ground that the Texas court rejected their arguments against jurisdiction. A further attempt by the companies to have the actions stayed on the ground of *forum non conveniens* was rejected without reasons, after the claimants had argued that the doctrine had no application because it had been abolished in Texas by statute.

In November 1989, a month before the trial was to begin in Texas, the companies applied to the Supreme Court of British Columbia for a permanent injunction restraining the claimants from continuing their actions in Texas, on the basis that British Columbia was the natural forum to litigate the issue whether the companies were liable to the claimants. They also sought an interlocutory injunction against the claimants' taking any step in Texas to obtain an order enjoining the companies from prosecuting their British Columbia action. The interlocutory injunction was granted *ex parte* for two weeks until argument on it could be heard. The day before the hearing, the claimants who were not resident in British Columbia (and so not bound by the *ex parte* injunction) obtained an *ex parte* injunction in Texas against the companies' obtaining similar injunctions in Canada against them. Partly because, in his view, the Texas court in making this order had shown a disregard for the issue of *forum non conveniens*, Esson C.J.S.C. granted the interlocutory injunction that the companies sought. The British Columbia Court of Appeal (as noted in 29 *Canadian Yearbook of International Law* 549 (1991)) affirmed his decision. It thought that the Texas court's claim to jurisdiction was somewhat tenuous, and that British Columbia was clearly the natural forum for the action. And, like the judge below, it attached importance to the absence of the doctrine of *forum non conveniens* from the Texas courts. It therefore concluded that the claimants' recourse to the Texas courts would be oppressive or vexatious as against the companies. In applying that test, the court followed *Société Nationale Industrielle Aérospatiale* v. *Lee*, [1987] A.C. 181, [1987] 3 All E.R. 510 (P.C.).

The unanimous decision of the Supreme Court of Canada was given by Sopinka, J. He agreed, in broad terms, that the *Aérospatiale* case should be followed, but held that the courts below had come to the wrong conclusion on the facts. Anti-suit injunctions were like stays of proceedings, in that both were means to ensure that litigation took place in the most appropriate forum, but, unlike stays of proceedings, an anti-suit injunction was a direct breach of comity among courts. It was justified only where a foreign court itself did not respect comity.

As a general rule the domestic court should not entertain an application for an injunction if there is no foreign proceeding pending. It was also preferable that the decision of the foreign court not be pre-empted until a proceeding had been launched in that court and the applicant for an injunction in the domestic court had sought from the foreign court a stay or other termination of the foreign proceedings and failed. If that occurred, the domestic court should proceed to entertain the application for the injunction, but only if it was alleged to be the most appropriate forum.

In reviewing the Canadian doctrine of *forum non conveniens* (the first time the Supreme Court has done so), Sopinka, J. accepted the English jurisprudence culminating in *Spiliada Maritime Corp.* v. *Cansulex Ltd.*, [1987] A.C. 460 (H.L.). In Canada as in England, *forum non conveniens* is no longer confined by the notion of abuse of process, and is now based squarely on the test of what is the appropriate forum for the litigation. The law on this point was remarkably uniform in all the common law jurisdictions. Each jurisdiction applied principles designed to identify the most appropriate forum for the litigation based on factors that connect the litigation and the parties to the competing fora. Regard for comity suggested that, if a foreign court has assumed jurisdiction in circumstances consistent with these principles, that should be an important factor militating against granting an injunction.

The first question was therefore whether there was another forum that was clearly more appropriate than the foreign court in which the plaintiff had brought the action. If, applying the principles relating to *forum non conveniens*, the foreign court could reasonably have concluded that there was no alternative forum that was clearly more appropriate, the domestic court should respect that decision and the application for the injunction should be dismissed. Where there was a genuine disagreement between the courts of Canada and those of another country, the courts of Canada should not arrogate to themselves the decision for both jurisdictions. It did not matter whether the foreign court actually applied the principles of *forum non conveniens*; the question was whether its taking jurisdiction was consistent with those principles.

In this case, the choice of a forum in Texas was consistent with the Canadian concept of *forum non conveniens*. No other forum was clearly more appropriate. In particular, it could not be said that British Columbia was more appropriate. The companies had no connection with the province, and the acts that were the foundation for the claims took place outside British Columbia and in the United States. If some weight was given to the choice of forum by the claimants in the absence of related litigation pending elsewhere, the decision of the Texas court could be recognized having regard to the principles of comity. In these circumstances the factor especially relied upon by Esson, C.J.S.C. and the Court of Appeal, that the Texas court had no doctrine of *forum non conveniens*, was beside the point. Moreover, the courts of Texas were bound by the due process standards of section 1 of the Fourteenth Amendment to the United States Constitution. This had been interpreted as requiring certain minimum contacts with the forum so that the maintenance of the suit did not offend traditional notions of fair play and substantial justice. The companies had conceded that their being present, or at least carrying on business, in Texas met the due process test. The application of this constitutional requirement was consistent with Canadian rules of private international law relating to *forum non conveniens.*

In any event, the application also failed at the second step in the analysis, relating to the considerations that were peculiar to anti-suit injunctions. While he agreed that the principles outlined in the *Aérospatiale* case should be the foundation for the test applied in Canada, Sopinka, J. deprecated the use of the terms "oppressive" and "vexatious" because, he thought, they had never been satisfactorily defined. The question was simply whether the injunction was necessary to prevent a serious injustice to the defendant by depriving it of some personal or juridical advantage that was available in the domestic forum. Conversely, the injunction should be denied if it would be unjust to deprive the plaintiff of some personal or juridical advantage that was available in the foreign forum. The loss of a personal or juridical advantage by one party or the other was not necessarily the only potential cause of injustice in this context, but it would be by far the most frequent.

In this case, the companies had not established that continuation of the proceedings would deprive them of a legitimate juridical advantage of which it would be unjust to deprive them by proceeding in Texas. The companies had raised two principal factors. These were, first, the right to claim over against the Workers' Compensation Board and a British Columbia asbestos producer that was not being sued in Texas, and, secondly, the presence of some other actions in British Columbia by other plaintiffs against some of the defendants. Neither of these suggested advantages had much substance in the actual circumstances. Moreover, they were not advantages that the companies could reasonably have expected to have, based on their previous connection to British Columbia.

Note 1. Given that anti-suit injunctions are a relatively rare phenomenon, and likely to be even rarer after this decision, the principal significance of the *Amchem* case is in what the Supreme Court said about *forum non conveniens,* a doctrine that is in daily use. The approval of the line of English cases that reformulated the concept was anticipated by many lower court decisions. However, in two respects the Supreme Court went beyond the position the House of Lords has taken.

First, it disagreed with the treatment, in *Spiliada* and the English cases that preceded it, of a legitimate personal or juridical advantage on the part of the plaintiff. According to the English cases, if the plaintiff can show that he or she would enjoy a legitimate advantage in the local forum, that may justify the court in allowing an action before it to continue, despite the local forum's being in other respects less appropriate than the alternative forum. Sopinka, J. thought there was no reason in principle why the loss of legitimate advantage should be treated as a separate and distinct second question. It should simply be weighed together with other factors in identifying the appropriate forum. The court should consider the advantages that either party would enjoy in either forum. The weight to be attached to such advantages depended on whether the connections that the party and the litigation had with that forum gave the party a legitimate claim to the advantages of that forum. The party would have a legitimate claim to them if he or she could reasonably have expected, based on all the circumstances, that in the event of litigation he or she would have had access to them.

The other respect in which the Supreme Court's view of *forum non conveniens* differed from that of the English courts had to do with burden of proof. The English cases maintain a firm distinction between cases of service in the jurisdiction, where, to obtain a stay, the defendant must clearly show that there is a more appropriate forum elsewhere, and cases of service *ex juris*, where, to obtain leave for such service, the plaintiff must show that England is clearly and distinctly more appropriate than any alternative forum. Sopinka, J. downplayed this distinction because the place of service (as distinct from the defendant's genuine residence) had relatively little bearing on the appropriateness of a forum. In addition, the trend in Canada was away from requiring leave for service *ex juris*, a procedural factor that had a lot to do with the English court's insistence on treating such service differently from service in the jurisdiction. The general rule in Canada was that the defendant had clearly to establish the existence of a more appropriate forum to displace the forum selected by the plaintiff, subject only, in a service *ex juris* case, to any applicable rule of court that placed the onus on the plaintiff to justify his or her choice of forum.

The last proviso would presumably apply in the two provinces (Alberta and Newfoundland) that retain the leave requirement for service *ex juris*, which has always been taken to require the plaintiff to show affirmatively that the local forum is more appropriate than the alternative. Less clear is whether the proviso applies in the other provinces, which have all dispensed with the leave requirement in the great majority of cases. Sopinka, J.'s comments imply that this removes the historical rationale for having a different

burden of proof in service *ex juris* cases. But the British Columbia
Court of Appeal has held that even where, under that province's
rules of court, service *ex juris* may be effected without leave, it is for
the plaintiff, once the defendant raises the issue, to show that the
province is clearly the appropriate forum (*Bushell* v. *T & N plc*
(1992), 92 D.L.R. (4th) 288 (B.C.C.A.), noted in 30 *Canadian
Yearbook of International Law* 408 (1992)).

Note 2. It is clear from the *Amchem* decision that, no matter how
hard the foreign proceedings may be on the defendant, a court
cannot grant an injunction against the plaintiff's conduct of those
proceedings unless the foreign court can be shown to be *forum non
conveniens*. This means that another recent decision, *Paterson* v.
Hamilton (1992), 7 Alta. L.R. (3d) 335 (C.A.), affirming (*sub nom.
Southern Hills Invts. Ltd.* v. *Hamilton*) (1991), 83 Alta. L.R. (2d) 368
(Q.B.), is probably not good law. There the Alberta courts held that a
party should be enjoined from pursuing contempt proceedings in
the United States on a federal court judgment. The contempt proceedings were aimed at stopping an Alberta action in respect of the
same subject matter. The basis for the injunction was that the American proceedings were oppressive in denying the other party access to
the Alberta court, which was a natural forum. There was no finding,
however, that the United States court was not a natural forum. On
the contrary, it was described as an alternative natural forum. In these
circumstances, the injunction granted by the Alberta court would
seem to be inconsistent with comity as defined by the *Amchem* case. It
could be argued that the use of the American court in effect to
prevent a lawsuit in Alberta, also a natural forum, was itself contrary
to comity and so opened up the possibility of taking reprisals in the
Alberta court. *Amchem* does not offer a great deal of room for such an
argument. This is especially so since the Texas proceedings, which
the Supreme Court refused to enjoin, included measures taken by
the claimants to prevent the companies from litigating in Canada.

2. *Québec*

(a)   *Lieu de l'introduction de l'action*

Biens situes au Québec

Brunet c. *Chrysler Canada Ltd.*, [1992] R.J.Q. 2276, [1992] A.J.D.Q.
860, No. 2441. Cour Supérieure du Québec.

Le demandeur, vendeur et exportateur de pièces d'auto, a poursuivi les défenderesses en dommages à la suite de leur défaut de se

conformer à une décision du Tribunal de la concurrence leur ordonnant de continuer à lui vendre des pièces. La défenderesse Chrysler Corp., au moyen d'une exception déclinatoire, allégua que la Cour supérieure n'était pas compétente pour entendre le litige aux motifs que son siège social était situé au Michigan, qu'elle n'avait pas de domicile ou de place d'affaires au Québec, qu'elle n'y possédait aucune bien, que l'action était basée sur un contrat et que tout la cause d'action n'avait pas pris naissance dans le district de Montréal. Le demandeur répliqua que cette compagnie possédait des biens au Québec, en l'occurrence des marques de commerce, des brevets d'invention, des dessins industriels, des comptes-clients de divers distributeurs, ainsi que, à l'occasion, des biens en transit dans le port de Montréal.

La Cour a accueilli l'exception déclinatoire. L'article 68 C.P., qui permet d'assigner un étranger devant le tribunal du lieu où il a des biens, est motivé par la possibilité d'exécuter le jugement dans la province. Il s'applique aux biens incorporels comme les marques de commerce et les brevets d'invention, mais le seul élément, en l'espèce, pouvant donner compétence aux tribunaux du Québec était que le registre de ces biens était situé à Hull, au Québec. Cet élément à lui seul n'était pas suffisant. Par ailleurs, la preuve ne montrait l'existence au Québec ni des comptes-clients, ni des conteneurs en transit, appartenant à la défenderesse Chrysler. De toute façon, des biens simplement en transit n'étaient pas suffisants pour donner compétence à la Cour supérieure; ils n'avaient pas été saisis avant jugement et ne seraient pas disponibles lorsque de demandeur obtiendrait un jugement déclaratoire.

(b) *Requête pour jugement déclaratoire* — lis alibi pendens — *article 462 C.P.*

Simcoe & Erie Gen. Ins. Co. v. Lavalin Inc. (1993), 54 Q.A.C. 44. Cour d'appel du Québec.

Bell Lavalin, an Alaska subsidiary of Lavalin Inc., was the engineer and prime contractor on a project to construct gas storage tanks and related installations in Alaska. A subcontractor brought an action against Bell Lavalin and Lavalin Inc. in Alaska and obtained judgment against Bell Lavalin only, the damages being in excess of $6.5 million. Both sides appealed. Simcoe & Erie had issued a liability insurance policy to Lavalin Inc. that covered both it and its subsidiaries. Simcoe & Erie began an action in Superior Court for the District of Montreal seeking a declaration that it was not liable to indemnify Lavalin Inc. or Bell Lavalin in respect of the damages payable under the Alaska judgment. In Alaska, the court-appointed receiver of Bell Lavalin commenced proceedings against Simcoe & Erie claiming $7.2 million in damages and other relief in respect of its failure to perform its obligations under the insurance policy. The receiver moved, by way of declinatory exception and exception to dismiss, to contest the jurisdiction of the Superior Court for the District of Montreal to hear the insurers' motion for declaratory judgment. Meyer, J. maintained the declinatory exception and dismissed the motion for declaratory judgment.

The Court of Appeal affirmed the dismissal of the motion. The Superior Court had jurisdiction to hear the action, both on the basis that the contract that gave rise to the action was made in Quebec (article 68(3) C.C.P.), and on the basis of the domicile in Quebec of the respondent insured Lavalin Inc. (article 68(1) C.C.P.). However, the court had a discretion to decline jurisdiction on either of two grounds.

One was analogous to *lis alibi pendens*. The strict doctrine did not apply where the proceedings pending elsewhere were outside Canada, but a "kind of *lis pendens*" could be invoked to justify a refusal to exercise jurisdiction, where a declaratory judgment was sought for the purpose of avoiding the exercise of jurisdiction by a competent foreign court. According to article 69 C.C.P., a court of the country where the insured is domiciled has jurisdiction in an action against the insurer. Since there was no evidence of the law of Alaska on this point, it could be presumed to be the same, so that the Alaskan court was competent in the action and a "kind of *lis pendens*" therefore applied to the insurer's attempt to avoid its jurisdiction by means of a Quebec declaratory judgment.

The other ground for declining jurisdiction was that found in article 462 C.C.P.: namely, the court's discretion to refuse a declaratory judgment when it "will not put an end to the uncertainty or controversy which gave rise to the action." A declaratory judgment in Quebec would not resolve the issues in the Alaskan proceedings, which were properly brought there by the insured and involved substantially the same questions as it was sought to litigate in Quebec. It was therefore entirely reasonable for the judge to exercise his discretion under article 462 C.C.P.

The receiver could not rely on *forum non conveniens* as a ground for declining jurisdiction, since that doctrine had no application in

Quebec, at least in purely civil matters (*Aberman* v. *Solomon*, [1986] R.D.J. 385 (Que. C.A.) (noted in 25 *Canadian Yearbook of International Law* 507 (1987)); *80890 Canada Ltd.* v. *Frank B. Hall Co.*, [1986] R.D.J. 544 (Que. C.A.)).

(c) *Demande en matière familiale — article 70 C.P.*

L.H.T. c. *D.T.T.* (1991), 50 Q.A.C. 314. Cour d'appel du Québec.

L'appelante se pourvut contre un jugement de la Cour supérieure qui a rejeté sa requête pour l'obtention d'une pension alimentaire dirigée contre son père en conformité des articles 813.3 et 813.8 C.P. La Cour d'appel accueillit l'appel. Les dispositions du Code civil relatives à l'obligation alimentaire obligent tous ceux qui se trouvent dans la province, même ceux qui n'y sont domiciliés. Mais ceux qui ne se trouvent pas dans la province ne sont pas tenus si la loi de leur domicile ne connaît pas une telle obligation. Le rapport d'un expert sur la loi du Nouveau-Brunswick montrait qu'il existait un cas où des aliments sont réclamables par des enfants majeurs, soit celui où le père a assumé une obligation plus étendue envers leur éducation ou s'il a assumé une telle responsabilité envers eux, ce que prétendait l'appelante. En matière d'une requête en moyen déclinatoire *ratione materiae*, s'il existe un doute quant au droit d'une partie de faire valoir le mérite de sa demande au fond, ce doute doit être interprété en sa faveur et il doit lui être permis de faire sa preuve.

(d) *Divorce*

Transfert d'un dossier

Note. Veuillez voir *Droit de la famille — 1657*, [1992] R.J.Q. 2238, [1992] A.J.D.Q. 279, No. 28 (C.S.) (requête de la défenderesse pour renvoi d'une action en divorce devant un tribunal ontarien rejetée parce que les liens avec Ontario étaient moins importants que ceux avec Québec).

B. *Procedure/Procédure*

Common law and federal

Remedies — claims for losses in foreign currency — conversion date

Note. See *Costello* v. *Blakeson*, [1993] 2 W.W.R. 562, 74 B.C.L.R. (2d) 3 (S.C.) (special damages and cost of future care in personal injury action calculated in United States dollars and converted into Canadian currency at the exchange rate on the date of judgment); and *Kiat* v. *Ng* (1992), 128 N.B.R. (2d) 374 (Q.B.) (promissory note in Singapore dollars converted into Canadian currency at the exchange rate on the date the note was due; none of the more recent authority, allowing later dates to be chosen, cited).

C. Foreign judgments/jugements étrangers

1. Common law and federal

(a) Conditions for enforcement by action or registration

Judgment — Nature of

Note. See *Days Inns of America Franchising Inc.* v. *Khimani* (1992), 11 C.P.C. (3d) 74 (Ont. Gen. Div.) (judgment for costs enforced).

Jurisdiction of original court — sufficient connection with the foreign jurisdiction

Note. The consequences of *Morguard Investments Ltd.* v. *De Savoye*, [1990] 3 S.C.R. 1077, 76 D.L.R. (4th) 256 (noted in 29 *Canadian Yearbook of International Law* 556 (1991)) are working their way through the lower courts. The *Morguard* case established that a default judgment from another province should be recognized, notwithstanding that the defendant was not served in that province and did not submit to its courts' jurisdiction, if the litigation was otherwise sufficiently connected with that province. The sufficiency of the connection is to be judged in accordance with comity, seen by the Supreme Court as the practical need to enable the movement of goods, skills, and wealth across jurisdictional boundaries in accordance with the requirements of order and fairness. In *Amopharm Inc.* v. *Harris Computer Corp.* (1992), 93 D.L.R. (4th) 524, 10 O.R. (3d) 27 (C.A.), a Quebec judgment in favour of a Quebec buyer against an Ontario seller of computer equipment was held enforceable in Ontario under the new rule. The creditor could avail itself of the *Morguard* decision, although the Supreme Court's judgment came down after the case on appeal — the enforcement action in Ontario — was decided at trial. Another Quebec default judgment was enforced pursuant to the *Morguard* principle in *87313 Canada Inc.* v. *Neeshat Oriental Carpet Ltd.* (1992), 11 C.P.C. (3d) 7 (Ont. Gen. Div.).

As noted in 30 *Canadian Yearbook of International Law* 415 (1992), in connection with *Federal Deposit Ins. Corp.* v. *Vanstone* (1992), 88 D.L.R. (4th) 448 (B.C.S.C.), this expansion of the rules for recognizing extraprovincial judgments has been extended in a series of first-instance decisions to judgments from outside Canada.

The pre-*Morguard* criteria for jurisdiction are still reflected in the uniform reciprocal enforcement of judgments legislation in all the provinces except Quebec. These statutes provide an alternative procedure for enforcing foreign judgments but do not affect the right to sue on the judgment at common law. Thus, as *Morguard* itself held, a default judgment that meets the Supreme Court's test is enforceable by an action at common law, even though it cannot be registered under the uniform reciprocal enforcement of judgments statute. See also, to this effect, *Acme Video Inc.* v. *Hedges* (1993), 12 O.R. (3d) 160*n*. Two provinces, New Brunswick and Saskatchewan, long ago adopted a second uniform Act codifying the traditional common law rules for recognition and enforcement of foreign judgments. It has now been held in both provinces that this Act was intended to supplant the common law, with the result that in those provinces the courts cannot have recourse to the new, wider recognition rule in the *Morguard* case: *844903 Ontario Ltd.* v. *Vander Pluijm* (1992), 130 N.B.R. (2d) 361, 12 C.P.C. (3d) 71 (Q.B.); *Cardinal Couriers Ltd.* v. *Noyes* (1993), 101 D.L.R. (4th) 712, [1993] 5 W.W.R. 704 (Sask. C.A.).

In *P.C.H. Inc.* v. *Fedyk* (1992), 11 C.P.C. (3d) 77 (Ont. Gen. Div.), the court dismissed an action on a default judgment from Nevada on the basis of the pre-*Morguard* rules as to jurisdiction, without referring to *Morguard.*

(b)   *Enforcement by registration under reciprocal enforcement of judgments legislation*

Note. Because, as noted immediately above, the uniform reciprocal enforcement of judgments legislation reflects the pre-*Morguard* criteria for the recognition or enforcement of an extraprovincial judgment, jurisdiction based on service *ex juris* is insufficient by itself for the registration of a judgment. There must be submission, either during the proceedings (see *Draglund* v. *McCutcheon* (1992), 106 Sask. R. 262 (Q.B.)), or by agreement between the parties before the litigation (see *Cardel Leasing Ltd.* v. *Jewett* (1992), 127 N.B.R. (2d) 21 (Q.B.)).

(c)   *Enforcement by registration under reciprocal enforcement of maintenance orders legislation*

Note. See *Bryant* v. *Petkau* (1992), 78 Man. R. (2d) 109 (C.A.) (provisional child maintenance order made against natural father by court in Ontario; finding of paternity held not to be part of the provisional order, but the Manitoba court could confirm the order if, on the evidence, it agreed with that finding). The operation of the confirmation procedure was also considered in *Stephens* v. *Stephens* (1992), 95 D.L.R. (4th) 321 (Alta. Q.B.) (sufficiency of proof of provisional order), and *Larson* v. *Larson* (1992), 106 Sask. R. 257 (Q.B.) (the confirming court free to disagree with provisional order on the basis of the evidence presented). The choice of law aspects of the confirmation system were considered in *Thibeault* v. *Green* (1991), 7 O.R. (3d) 437 (Prov. Div.). The judge decided that, although section 6 of the Reciprocal Enforcement of Support Orders Act, R.S.O. 1990, c. R.7, requires a confirming court to give effect to defences under the law of the originating jurisdiction that are pleaded and proved, this did not preclude giving effect to a defence under the *lex fori* if the facts giving rise to it took place in the forum province. The issue was the extent to which a person, by cohabitation with the parent of a child, became liable to support that child. The cohabitation in question had been in Ontario, and the judge held that, even if the respondent had been liable (which the court held he was not) for child support under the laws of British Columbia, where the provisional order had been made, the judge would have refused to confirm the order because the respondent was not liable under the law of Ontario, where the cohabitation had taken place.

(d)   *Defences to enforcement or registration*

Proceedings contrary to natural justice

Note. The argument that extraprovincial legal proceedings were contrary to natural justice has hardly ever succeeded, and never within Canada. It failed again in *Servotech Ltée* v. *Hayward Burry Ltd.* (1992), 98 Nfld. & P.E.I. R. 112 (Nfld. T.D.). The judgment debtor's contention that it had been prevented from making a proper defence, because the proceedings of the Quebec court had been in French, was an unacceptable objection within Canada and was unsupported by the facts.

D.   *Choice of law (including status of persons)/conflits de lois*
     (y compris statut personnel)

1.   *Common law and federal*

(a)   *Contract*

Express agreement as to choice of law — formation

Canastrand Industries Ltd. v. *The Lara S.*, [1993] 2 F.C. 553, 60 F.T.R.
1. Federal Court Trial Division.

The owners of a cargo of baler twine that was shipped from Brazil
to Canada on board the defendant vessel brought an action in
respect of damage to the cargo. The booking note that had been
issued on behalf of the charterers on March 11, 1988 was on the
Conline form. It provided that the Hague Rules as enacted in the
country of shipment should apply to the contract. When no such
enactment was in force in the country of shipment (as was the case
here), the corresponding legislation of the country of destination
(that is, Canada) should apply. The bills of lading issued when the
goods were received on board stipulated that they should have
effect subject to the provisions of the Carriage of Goods by Sea Act
of the United States and to the terms of the charterers' long form
bill of lading. The long form stated that unless it was otherwise
expressly provided, the contract evidenced by the bill of lading was
to be construed and governed by U.S. law. Reed, J. accepted that the
booking note and the bills of lading represented in substance a
single contract. She held that, as between the contradictory choice
of law clauses in the two documents, the one in the long form bill of
lading should prevail. The bills of lading were issued after the
booking note. It could not be said that the use of a short form
incorporating the long form by reference had given insufficient
notice of the choice of law. The short form included an express
reference to the United States statute, which impliedly included the
jurisprudence on the application of that Act. The short form thus
gave notice that United States law was to apply. (In the result, the
law of the United States was held not to have been proved, and
Canadian law was therefore applied to the issues.)

Implied agreement as to choice of law

Standard Trust Co. v. *Ginnell* (1992), 96 D.L.R. (4th) 693, [1993] 2
W.W.R. 201. Saskatchewan Queen's Bench.

The developer of a 144-unit condominium project in Saskatoon, Saskatchewan, defaulted on a mortgage and 120 units were sold by judicial sale to the mortgagee, Standard Trust. The beneficial owners of the units were individual investors who had executed guarantees for any shortfall on the mortgage in respect of their units. Standard Trust brought an action in Saskatchewan on these guarantees. Thirty-nine defendants who had been served *ex juris* argued that they were not subject to the court's jurisdiction. Barclay, J. upheld the validity of the service on the basis of Queen's Bench Rule 31(1)(*f*), which authorizes service *ex juris* in an action in respect of a contract where, *inter alia*, "(*iii*) the contract provides that it is to be governed by . . . the law of Saskatchewan." The guarantees lacked an express choice of law clause, but they contained an acknowledgment by the guarantor that he or she was aware of the provisions of the Land Contracts (Actions) Act, R.S.S. 1978, c. L-3, and the Limitation of Civil Rights Act, R.S.S. 1978, c. L-16. This reference to Saskatchewan legislation showed that the parties intended that Saskatchewan law should govern the guarantees.

The defendants had not shown that there was a more convenient forum than Saskatchewan. The onus was on them to do so. The property foreclosed upon was situated in the province, the breach of contract might have occurred there, the damages might have been suffered there, and Standard Trust should not be forced to conduct actions in several jurisdictions where the chosen forum exhibited a real and substantial connection between the damages suffered and the jurisdiction.

(b)   *Corporations — law applicable to takeover transaction*

Note. Although it is not strictly a case on choice of law, *Québec* v. *Ontario (Securities Commission)* (1992), 97 D.L.R. (4th) 144 (Ont. C.A.) (leave to appeal refused May 27, 1993 (S.C.C.)), is of interest. It upheld the application of section 91 of the Securities Act, R.S.O. 1980, c. 466, to the province of Quebec, which had bought a controlling interest in ACL, a federally incorporated asbestos producer, from its United States parent company. The relevant section imposed an obligation on Quebec to make a follow-up offer to holders of the publicly traded shares of ACL. The basis for applying the statute was that ACL's shares were traded on the Toronto Stock Exchange. Those who took advantage of Ontario's capital markets were properly subject to the Ontario laws that regulated those markets. Defences based on constitutional arguments (extraterritorial application of Ontario law, sovereign immunity of Quebec) were rejected. Compare *Bennett* v. *British Columbia (Securities Commission)* (1992), 94 D.L.R. (4th) 339 (B.C.C.A.), which held that the British Columbia legislation on insider trading offences applied to conduct that had taken place in the province, although the trades were actually carried out, through Ontario brokers, on the Toronto Stock Exchange.

(c) *Tort*

Tort outside the province

Williams v. *Osei-Twum* (1992), 99 D.L.R. (4th) 147, 11 O.R. (3d) 737. Ontario Court of Appeal.

The plaintiffs, a husband, wife, and two children, resident in Ontario, drove in their Ontario-licensed and insured vehicle into Quebec, where they were injured in a collision with a Quebec-licensed and insured rental car driven by the defendant, who was resident in Ontario. On a case stated for the opinion of the court, Matlow, J. decided that the plaintiffs' claims failed because no civil action lay according to the law of Quebec. All delictual claims in respect of automobile accidents were abolished by the Automobile Insurance Act, S.Q. 1977, c. 68, and replaced by a scheme of no-fault insurance. By agreement between the insurance authorities of Quebec and Ontario, an Ontario resident who is injured in an accident in Quebec has the right, under the applicable Ontario insurance policy, to claim no-fault benefits the same as those provided by Quebec law. The plaintiffs had applied for and received those benefits. It was not open to the plaintiffs to rely on *McLean* v. *Pettigrew*, [1945] S.C.R. 62. If that case applied, their tort claims could be decided according to Ontario law, subject only to the requirement that the defendant's act or omission be wrongful, either civilly or criminally, under the law of Quebec. The Ontario Court of Appeal, in *Grimes* v. *Cloutier* (1989), 61 D.L.R. (4th) 505, and *Prefontaine Estate* v. *Frizzle* (1990), 65 D.L.R. (4th) 275, had distinguished *McLean* v. *Pettigrew* on the ground that in *McLean* both parties were from the forum province, not from the province where the accident occurred, whereas in the cases before the Court of Appeal either the plaintiff or the defendant was resident in Quebec, where the accident occurred. Under those circumstances the Court of Appeal thought that the Quebec rule barring civil liability should be given effect, since the local resident would have had no reasonable expectation that any delictual law other than the law of Quebec would apply. Matlow, J. reasoned that the defendant in this case, driving a Quebec rental car on the highway in Quebec, would likewise have had no reasonable expectation that the law of Ontario would decide his civil liability.

The Court of Appeal reversed the decision of Matlow, J. The correct interpretation of *Grimes* v. *Cloutier* and the other Court of Appeal cases was that their distinction of *McLean* v. *Pettigrew* had been based solely on either the plaintiff or the defendant's being a resident of the province in which the accident occurred. *McLean* v. *Pettigrew* continued to apply where both plaintiff and defendant were from the province of the forum. It was therefore immaterial that the defendant's car was registered and insured in Quebec. Both parties were resident in Ontario, and its law applied to the parties' rights in tort to the exclusion of the civil law of Quebec.

Note 1. This case demonstrates how the series of Ontario cases beginning with *Grimes* v. *Cloutier* have mitigated the arbitrariness of the rule in *McLean* v. *Pettigrew* (itself based on *Phillips* v. *Eyre* (1870), L.R. 6 Q.B. 1 (Exch. Ch.)) by a distinction that is hardly less arbitrary. The practical result is that, as far as an Ontario court is concerned, an Ontario resident who is injured in Quebec has no action in tort against a negligent Quebec resident, but does have an action against a negligent Ontario resident — even one, as this case shows, who was driving a car licensed and insured in Quebec. (The *McLean* v. *Pettigrew* requirement that the defendant's conduct be "not justified" by Quebec law is usually easily satisfied by showing the commission of a traffic offence.) Conversely, an Ontario driver who causes an accident in Quebec will not be liable in tort to a victim whose home is in Quebec, but will be liable to one whose home is in Ontario. This mechanical approach cannot be regarded as a rational solution to the problem.

There is something to be said for the idea that Ontario tort law applies, to the exclusion of the Quebec law of delict, as between two parties who travel together from Ontario into Quebec. (That is especially so where the issue can be seen as having to do with the passenger-driver relationship itself, such as the driver's legal responsibility for the safety of a gratuitous passenger, which was the issue in *McLean* v. *Pettigrew*.) There is much less to be said for excluding the Quebec law of delict where, as here, there is no pre-existing relationship between the two Ontario parties and it is pure happenstance that the plaintiff was resident in the same province as the defendant. A factor that is rationally unconnected to anything the defendant has done, or could know, is an odd choice to play the critical role in deciding whether the defendant should be liable. (But, admittedly, the House of Lords has done exactly what the Court of Appeal did: see *Chaplin* v. *Boys* (1970), [1971] A.C. 356.)

The whole area of choice of law in tort is ripe for reconsideration by the Supreme Court of Canada, and this is probably forthcoming. Two cases were under appeal to the Supreme Court at the time of writing: *Tolofson* v. *Jensen* (1992), 89 D.L.R. (4th) 129, [1992] 3 W.W.R. 743 (B.C.C.A.) (noted in 30 *Canadian Yearbook of International Law* 422 (1992)) (leave to appeal granted October 1, 1992 (S.C.C.)), and *Lucas* v. *Gagnon* (1992), 99 D.L.R. (4th) 125, 15 C.C.L.T. (2d) 41 (Ont. C.A.) (leave to appeal granted May 27, 1993 (S.C.C.)). Both involved actions between two family members who lived in the forum province, the one having been injured as passenger while the other was driving. In both cases the courts applied *McLean* v. *Pettigrew*: that is, they applied the tort law of the forum province to the exclusion of the tort law of the province in which the accident occurred. The latter province's law was relevant only to establish the threshold requirement of "wrongfulness." In both cases it was regarded as immaterial that a claim was also being made against the driver of another car who lived in the province in which the accident occurred and who, on that account, could rely on defences in that province's tort law.

Note 2. In *Banco do Brasil S.A.* v. *The Alexandros G. Tsavliris*, [1992] 3 F.C. 735 (C.A.), charterers of a vessel brought actions for intimidation and inducing breach of contract against a Brazilian bank for its threat to have the vessel arrested at the Panama Canal to enforce its mortgage security on the vessel. The charterers claimed losses owing to their having been forced to divert the vessel around Cape Horn. The *lex loci delicti* for the alleged torts was assumed to be English law, since the bank's English solicitors had done the acts in question. However, the actions failed because the conduct of the bank was not actionable under the *lex fori*, Canadian law.

(d) *Property*

Movables — tangible — inter vivos *transfer — personal property security legislation*

Note. The registration provisions with respect to security interests in property brought into the province were considered in *Re*

Donaghy (Bankrupt) (1992), 132 A.R. 155 (Q.B.); *Holland* v. *Chrysler Credit Canada Ltd.* (1992), 5 Alta L.R. (3d) 258, 4 P.P.S.A.C. (2d) 250 (Q.B. (M.C.)); and *McLean (Bankrupt)* v. *General Motors Acceptance Corp.* (1992), 101 Sask. R. 178 (Q.B.).

Matrimonial property

Note. In *Duyvewaardt* v. *Barber* (1992), 71 B.C.L.R. (2d) 396, 43 R.F.L. (3d) 139 (C.A.), the question was whether a husband and wife resident in British Columbia, who had made a marriage contract when they married in Belgium in 1923, had validly taken their house in British Columbia out of the community regime that the agreement created. Although the agreement was immutable by Belgian law, which governed it, the court accepted expert testimony that Belgian law would regard as effective a modification of the agreement that was made in a foreign country where the parties were domiciled. The court therefore applied British Columbia law to determine the validity and interpretation of the agreement to transfer the house.

(e) *Husband and wife*

Marriage — formal validity

Note. See *Re Lin* (1992), 99 D.L.R. (4th) 280 (Alta. Q.B.), which held invalid a traditional Chinese marriage ceremony celebrated in Alberta between a recent immigrant from the People's Republic of China and a resident of Canada. No grounds existed for holding the marriage exempt from the requirements of the marriage law of Alberta.

2. *Québec*

(a) *Contrats*

Contrats spéciaux — jeu

Note. Veuillez voir *Condado Plaza Hotel & Casino* c. *Lee,* [1992] A.J.D.Q. 159, No 444 (C.Q.) (contrat signé au Québec reconnaissant une dette de jeu contractée à Puerto Rico, où le jeu est légal; selon le contrat, les lois du Québec s'appliquaient; action en réclamation de la dette rejetée).

(b) *Mari et femme*

Divorce — homologation du jugement

Note. Veuillez voir *Droit de la famille — 1537*, [1992] R.D.F. 171; [1992] A.J.D.Q. 479, No 1488 (C.S.) (requête en homologation d'un jugement de divorce prononcée en Floride rejetée; l'exemplification d'un jugement qui sert simplement à établir l'état ou la qualité d'une personne serait inutile).

(c) *Enfants*

Adoption — reconnaissance d'un jugement étranger

Note. Veuillez voir *Droit de la famille — 1561*, [1992] A.J.D.Q. 273, No 817 (C.Q.) (adoption prononcée aux Philippines sans une approbation préalable du projet d'adoption; adoption reconnue selon l'art. 15 de la Loi concernant l'adoption et modifiant le Code civil du Québec, le Code de procédure civile et la Loi sur la protection de la jeunesse (L.Q. 1990, c. 29); les deux critères selon lesquels le Tribunal peut exercer sa discretion de reconnaître l'adoption, c'est-à-dire des motifs sérieux et l'intérêt de l'enfant, étaient satisfaits). Dans *Droit de famille — 1597*, [1992] R.J.Q. 1711; [1992] A.J.D.Q. 275, No 818 (C.Q.), et *Droit de famille — 1665*, [1992] R.D.F. 636, [1992] A.J.D.Q. 274, No 819 (C.Q.), le Tribunal a refusé de reconnaître des adoptions étrangères, au motif que la preuve ne montrait pas qu'elles sont prononcées judiciairement.

Book Reviews / Recensions de livres

Law, Policy, and International Justice: Essays in Honour of Maxwell Cohen. Edited by William Kaplan and Donald McRae. Foreword by the Rt. Hon. Brian Dickson. Montreal and Kingston: McGill-Queen's University Press, 1993. Pp. xvi, 503. ISBN 0-7735-1114-8.

Maxwell Cohen is one of the seminal minds of Canadian law in the twentieth century. It is no criticism of this volume to remark that it does not quite equal its subject. It does not capture, for instance, what one contributor, Oscar Schachter, refers to as "his wit, learning, and exuberance" (p. 6), to say nothing of his exceptional talent for phrase-making. I well remember his quick-as-a-flash quip on seeing me (another former law dean) about 1970: "We're just a couple of old has-deans." There is also no recognition of the contribution of his devoted wife Isle to his scholarly success, in roles ranging from typist and receptionist, to intellectual sounding board, to social sparkplug.

But this is not a real criticism of this work, because it does all that any book, especially a learned tome by nearly a score of first-rank intellectuals, could do. The distinguished contributors survey topics in four different fields that reflect Cohen's principal interests: *international affairs* (scholar in international law, Canadian chair of the International Joint Commission, ad hoc judge of the International Court of Justice, and a Canadian founder of the International Law Association); *public law* (chair of the Special Committee on Hate Propaganda and intellectual contributor to the Canadian Bill of Rights, the Canadian Charter of Rights and Freedoms, and official bilingualism in Canada); *legal history* (studies on the history of habeas corpus); and *legal education* (Director of the Institute of Air and Space Law 1961-65 and Dean of Law at McGill 1964-69, originator of McGill's national law program with a four-year integrated B.C.L./LL.B., and theorist of Canadian legal education).

About a third of the contributors have been connected with the common law school at the University of Ottawa (to which Cohen has been affiliated in retirement), and two of them, Professor William Kaplan and Dean Donald McRae, acted as editors. Their own contributions are on the Report of the Special Committee on Hate Propaganda and on international dispute settlement under the Free Trade Agreement respectively.

Two of the contributing scholars are non-Canadian and write in the international section: Shabtai Rosenne, a former Israeli diplomat, on the agent in litigation in the International Court of Justice, and Oscar Schachter, the Hamilton Fish Professor Emeritus at Columbia, on legal aspects of the 1991 Gulf War and its aftermath. Others who write on international law are Professors Donat Pharand and Anne F. Bayefsky of the University of Ottawa, on the case for an arctic regional council and international human rights law in Canadian courts respectively, and Professor Dale Gibson, Bowker Professor of Law at the University of Alberta, on Canadian-American extradition before 1890.

Other contributors on public law are Annemieke Holthuis of the Department of Justice on Cohen's perspective on human rights in Canada; Professor Irwin Cotler of McGill on the right to protection against group-vilifying speech; Professor William W. Black of the University of British Columbia (formerly director of the Human Rights Centre at Ottawa) on positive obligations under the Charter; and Professor Julius Grey of McGill and the Montreal Bar on bilingualism in Canada.

Legal history makes up the shortest part of the book, with fine contributions from Louis A. Knafla on the writ of *habeas corpus* in early modern England and Dean Robert J. Sharpe of the University of Toronto on a particular *habeas corpus* case, that of the man who escaped from Devil's Island.

Part Four on legal education makes for a strong finish with contributions by Professor Roderick A. Macdonald of McGill on Cohen's role in McGill's national law program, Professor Edward McWhinney of Simon Fraser (and recently elected Member of Parliament) on Cohen's role in anglophone Quebec in the "Quiet Revolution," Professor John P. S. McLaren of the University of Victoria on Cohen's views on legal education, Justice David C. McDonald of the Alberta Court of Queen's Bench and first president of the Canadian Institute for the Administration of Justice on the latter's role in judicial education, and Justice William Stevenson, formerly of the Supreme Court, on the founding of the Canadian Judicial Centre.

The book includes a useful eleven-page Cohen bibliography compiled by Annemieke Holthuis, and commences with a short, graceful foreword written by the Rt. Hon. Brian Dickson, recently retired Chief Justice of Canada.

With such an array of brilliant contributions, it is impossible to describe the contents of the collection in any reasonable compass. It is, however, worth quoting Irwin Cotler's overview of Cohen's work (p. 275):

> Just as [Myers] MacDougal, together with Harold Lasswell, founded the policy-oriented school of jurisprudence, so did Maxwell Cohen impart a "Gestalt" view of law and society, with society itself as the lawyer's client. For Professor, Dean, Judge, Mᶜ Cohen, law was not only a technical body of rules, but articulated the values that men and women should seek to live by; law was not only an agency of social control, but an organizing principle for the reconfiguration of society — with respect for human dignity at its core.

This to me is a reasonable summation of Cohen's life work.

Personally, I found of special interest Professor Schachter's analysis of the new world order after the invasion of Kuwait, Professor Bayefsky's account of the reception of international human rights law in Canadian courts, and Professor Kaplan's accurate account of the proceedings and aftermath of the Special Committee on Hate Propaganda, on which I had the privilege of associating with chairman Cohen. The whole collection, however, maintains a uniform level of excellence, and bears reading both by specialists and by neophytes.

This volume is, in sum, a worthy tribute by recognized experts to a life of excellence in thought, achievement, and inspiration that has been devoted to internationalism, constitutionalism, and legal scholarship with a distinctively Canadian stamp that has permanently enriched our collective life as a nation.

HON. MARK R. MACGUIGAN, P.C.
Federal Court of Appeal

An International Law Miscellany. By Shabtai Rosenne. Dordrecht: Martinus Nijhoff, 1993. Pp. xxii, 843. (U.S.$308) ISBN 0-7923-1742-4.

Had Shabtai Rosenne not been an Israeli, and thus a victim of Arab state antagonism, it is very likely that he would have been elected to the International Court of Justice. This collection of some of his writings is indicative of the width of his interests and the depth of his knowledge. His decision to include only those works written between 1957 and 1991 means that some of his more specialist writing on the law of prize, published in some of the early post-war volumes of the *British Yearbook*, and indicative of his early interest in the law of the sea, have not been included. His decision to include some of the pieces that he originally wrote in Hebrew, covering such issues as "The United Nations and Israel's War of Independence," that would not otherwise be available to the generality of scholars in the field, does to some extent make up for this lacuna, although it is perhaps to be regretted that he has not included such papers as his useful analysis of "Israel's Armistice Agreements with the Arab States," written in 1951, or his piece on the *Eichmann* case, "6,000,000 Accusers." In view of current discussions under the auspices of the Red Cross relating to the possible selection of a single emblem, inclusion of his paper on "The Red Cross, Red Crescent, Red Lion and Sun, and the Red Shield of David" might well have been useful in clarifying the issues involved.

The twenty-seven papers in Rosenne's *International Law Miscellany* are divided into four groups: the International Court and international litigation (9), the law of treaties and the sources of law (9), the law of the sea (2), and Jewish and Israeli matters (7). There are also two obituaries, one devoted to "Sir Hersch Lauterpacht's Concept of the Task of the International Judge," and the other to the work of Jacob Robinson, a great legal fighter for Jewish causes and described by Rosenne as "scholar, polyglot, diplomat, historian, jurist and above all Jew, a powerful advocate whose word was heard in the highest councils . . . an advocate of righteousness to plead against the witness of transgression" (p. 843), a tribute that may easily be applied to Rosenne himself.

The bulk of the material relating to the Court consists of a reprint of Rosenne's monograph, *The Time Factor in the Jurisdiction of the International Court of Justice*, published in 1960. To this he has added an afterword (pp. 87-109) in which he discusses the various ways states have sought to evade "surprise acceptances of the jurisdiction for a specific dispute through an appropriate provision in their own acceptance of jurisdiction" (p. 87). He also looks at the impact of those cases in which proceedings are initiated on the merits simultaneously with a plea for provisional measures of protection (p. 91), as well as those in which an "unwilling respondent refused to have any part in the proceedings . . . adding to the difficulties of jurisdiction and admissibility" (p. 92). The *Nicaragua* case has been cited for innumerable issues since it was rendered, but Rosenne emphasizes certain jurisdictional aspects of the decision, such as the importance of the discussion of the effect of reciprocity on behalf of the defendant when the plaintiff's acceptance of jurisdiction has been unconditional, enabling (so the United States claimed) the defendant to amend its own declaration at pleasure (p. 99). The amended version of this monograph is of sufficient interest for a reader to press Rosenne to update his monumental work, *The Law and Practice of the International Court*, which appeared some thirty years ago.

From the point of view of treaty-making, perhaps one of the most significant developments in recent years has been the participation of non-governmental organizations, and probably the most significant instance of this participation has been the invitation to national liberation movements to attend the Geneva Diplomatic Conference on Humanitarian Law in Armed Conflicts 1974-77. Not only did these movements participate, but arrangements were made for them to sign the final text and to accede. The significance of this development for the law of treaties has been assessed by Rosenne in his paper "Participation in the Geneva Conventions (1864-1949) and the Additional Protocols of 1977." While he has some reservations as to the value of Article 1(4) of Protocol I, he states that:

> [t]aking a broad view of international law today . . . one cannot avoid the impression that it is still too closely tied to the inherited nineteenth century concepts which saw only the independent State as the "subject" (and "object") of international law, and that the realities of international life do not fit into that tidy mould. The problem of the correct place in the international legal system of entities which are not independent States, be they governmental organizations, non-governmental organizations, movements of national liberation . . . or even individuals with an international role cannot be resolved satisfactorily so long as it is approached in a highly emotional and highly political context [as were Art. 1(4) and the other relevant provisions of the protocol], with little time and patience for legal technicalities. It is doubtful if a single or unitary or generalized solution is really feasible" (p. 439).

Perhaps each instance must be settled on its own merits, paying due attention to the content of the proposed treaty.

Of equal interest is Rosenne's paper "International Law As It Stands at the End of the Twentieth Century," based to some extent on his experience as a member of the International Law Commission. Making a point that has become of increasing significance in recent years, he reminds us that:

international law is tension-centred. At the same time, and paradoxically, when the tensions grow too strong . . . the conduct-regulating role of international law will be temporarily eclipsed until the political evolution turns attention again towards the control or reduction of international tension. . . . That is why I find a positive development in the shape of certain trends of international thinking from the field of dispute settlement to that of dispute prevention (p. 458).

Little need be said of the two papers on the law of the sea, other than to draw attention to Rosenne's comment that:

the new law of the sea, intended to be universal in time and in space, is hardly reconcilable with the law as expounded by Grotius, and which was in principle found to be adequate for its purposes by the audience for which it was intended. The purposes have changed. The audience has changed. . . . [However,] I like to think that . . . Grotius would have derived satisfaction from the attempts to produce a universally accepted comprehensive standard of conduct for States on the sea, which is what the . . . Convention in its entirety aims at doing. While I hesitate to think he would have approved everything that appears in that instrument, I have no doubt that, experienced diplomat that he was and well versed in the art of parliamentarianism, he would have given his blessing to the spirit of compromise, of seeking consensus, of give and take, which alone has made it possible for this remarkable instrument to come into existence (pp. 492-93).

Perhaps the most interesting and useful paper of those on Jewish and Israeli matters is the first devoted to "The Influence of Judaism on the Development of International Law." Rosenne points out that while modern international law is "essentially a product of the civilization of Western Europe" (p. 512), reflecting the influence "of the ancient Mediterranean world, the heritage of Rome, Athens and Jerusalem," other regions and peoples have been faced with similar international issues and have, in many cases, developed their own system of "international law," not necessarily regarded as of universal application (*ibid.*).

Some of the classical writers have referred to the influence of the Old Testament, but their studies do not for the main part seem to have been based on the Hebrew text, nor have they been acquainted with the writings of the Rabbinic commentators — Selden appears to have been the main exception. There is as yet, however, no carefully researched work devoted to the Judaic influence on international law — how many modern lawyers know of the inclusion by Maimonides in his *Code* of a section devoted to the "Laws of Kings and their Wars"? This paper in the *Miscellany* should serve to encourage some graduate student, who would need to be well acquainted with Rabbinic and *halachic* (religious) law in all its aspects, to follow the path blazed by Rosenne and fill this lacuna in the doctrine and history of international law.

Rosenne suggests that when Jews were permitted by European rulers and the Ottoman empire to live under their own legal system, relations between them and their Christian neighbours may have been governed by some form of "international" law. He goes on to suggest that:

[t]he intensive Jewish diplomatic activities that have taken place since 1919 [with the creation of the Palestine mandate] mean that there certainly exists sufficient material to permit a start to be made in describing what other countries call "State practice" which could form the basis for a more empiric distillation of the philosophy and practice of international law developed by Jewish nationalism and which, in some respects at least, may be influencing the practice of the State of Israel (p. 533).

The final section of this fascinating paper "concerns the elements of international law that exist within the framework of the Jewish legal system, the *halacha* itself. This is not international law in the modern sense, but prescriptions on how, in the view of Jewish law, the Jewish polity should handle its external affairs" (p. 533), a matter that is also to be found in Islam and the Koran.

Rosenne points out that the biblical approach to the *jus ad bellum* lies in distinguishing between war as a religious duty (*mitzva*), as a war of national existence and self-defence, and optional war, with different legal rules and consequences. This distinction might be compared to the later theory of just and unjust war (pp. 534-55). In both, there appears to have been application of what today would be called principles of international humanitarian law.

In post-biblical times, there seems to have been a difference in the approach of the religious from the non-religious teachings, with emphasis in the former on observance of the rules of *halacha*, with the king declaring an optional war only after a decision of the Great Sanhedrin of 71, and the Talmud defining optional war, calling attention to the difference between the wars of Joshua and those of territorial expansion waged by David (p. 539). Maimonides includes a war of self-defence among religious duties, and in his *Laws Concerning Kings and Their Wars* he obligates the king always to be accompanied by a Scroll of the Law. In the *Laws* we also find rules relating to peace as well as the conduct of war and the limitations thereon (p. 541). Despite the references to religious and optional war, most of the great Jewish thinkers were aware of the inherent immorality of war and in the *Mishna* the Jews are enjoined "Be of the disciples of Aaron, loving peace and pursuing peace, loving mankind and bringing them nigh to the Law" (p. 545).

That point of view found its most sublime expression in the great vision of the Prophets of Israel, the lodestar of the Jewish people and indeed of the whole world: "and they shall beat their swords into plowshares and their spears into pruning hooks; Nation shall not lift up sword against nation, neither shall they learn war any more" (p. 545).

As to the law of treaties, these, like private contract, were reinforced by oath, "as indeed was customary to the end of the seventeenth century" (p. 538). Such treaties as were entered into between the semi-independent Judea and Rome were in the form of a Senatus-Consultum appearing as an agreed minute of diplomatic discussion (p. 540).

Reference has already been made to Rosenne's interest in the law of the sea. Perhaps this is not to be wondered at in view of the fact that the Talmud already lays down rules for the delimitation of the maritime frontier of islands in the Mediterranean, while in the Book of Numbers there is to be found an early reference to the right of innocent passage, though over land (pp. 542-43).

Underlying the whole of Jewish law in its relation to the individual, to the state, and to the world is recognition of the overriding significance of morality. This principle applies to the whole world, for, as Maimonides pointed out:

a State whose failings are in excess of its virtues is at once doomed to extinction as it is written: "Because the cry of Sodom and Gemorrah is great, and because their sin is very great." Similarly the whole world. If its failings exceed its virtues it is immediately condemned to destruction. (p. 547)

Problems have frequently arisen when recently decolonized states argue that they are not bound by this or that traditional rule of international law; however, Rosenne, indicating his fundamental belief in the rule of law, maintains that:

the theory of law, if properly used, could adapt the law in a way which would be politically acceptable. . . . [T]he law has a consolidating role to play. Its task is to ensure a well integrated international society in which the conflicting rights and interests of its different components are carefully reconciled. The far-reaching claims once made for the law as the universal panacea must be resisted, but by the same token so must the legal nihilism of revolutionary concepts be equally firmly opposed. I am not one for excessive caution and conservatism in our world of constant change, but I do insist that legal evolution should be the deliberate product of careful and thorough study of all the elements, and that the decision should be reached *en toute connaissance de cause*. That is the discipline of our science. That is what the law, all law, including international law has to contribute to international cooperation. *(pp. 465-68)*

Given this avowal of the importance of the law, and in the light of the varied fascinating materials to be found in *An International Law Miscellany*, one is inclined to ask of Shabtai Rosenne when we may expect his general textbook on international law.

L. C. GREEN
University of Alberta, Edmonton

The Abolition of the Death Penalty in International Law. By William A. Schabas. Cambridge: Grotius Publications, 1991. Pp. xxxii, 384 including index and tables. (U.S.$96) ISBN 1-85701-012-4.

The Abolition of the Death Penalty in International Law was presented in 1992 by Professor William A. Schabas of the University of Quebec at Montreal for the Doctor of Laws degree (LL.D.) at the University of Montreal. I am delighted that it has quickly been made available to a wider audience. The work is of a consistently high standard. The research is imaginative and meticulously done. The writing is clear and elegant. Unlike many doctoral dissertations, the work was publishable in book form with very little change.

No one had ever tried before to synthesize in any careful and coherent way the work that has been done since the Second World War at the regional and global levels moving towards the abolition of the death penalty as a legal standard. Schabas does just that, and he does it well.

He begins with an elegant tour of the historical landscape that demonstrates how the abolitionist movement as an aspect of public international law is very much a creature of the post-war period. He then discusses carefully the drafting by the United Nations of the capital punishment provisions of the Universal Declaration of Human Rights and the International Covenant on Civil and Political Rights. He examines the significant resolutions and reports of the United Nations since 1959 that have contributed to the creation of an international customary rule working towards abolition. Particularly well done in this section is his discussion of the Safeguards Guaranteeing Protection of the Rights of those Facing the

Death Penalty adopted by the Economic and Social Council in 1984 and the follow-up 1989 resolution on the "Implementation" of the Safeguards. Neither of these significant documents, developed under the aegis of the now defunct United Nations Committee on Crime Prevention and Control, had previously received the detailed consideration that they receive here. With careful attention to the drafting process, Mr. Schabas neatly places them in context with the various treaty instruments. He then discusses the drafting of the Second Optional Protocol to the Covenant on Civil and Political Rights dealing with the abolition of the death penalty, the high water mark of the United Nations activities in this field.

Mr. Schabas concludes his examination of the trend towards abolition at the global level by analysing the treatment of capital punishment in international humanitarian law, notably in the Third and Fourth Geneva Conventions of 1949 and in the two 1977 Additional Protocols thereto.

Next, Professor Schabas turns his attention to the death penalty in European human rights law, notably to a discussion of the relevant provisions of the European Convention on Human Rights and its Sixth Protocol on abolition. He concludes with a thorough discussion of the development of the material on capital punishment in the American Declaration of the Rights and Duties of Man, the American Convention on Human Rights, and the Protocol to the American Convention abolishing the death penalty. On each of these he has some new insights to contribute, from an examination of the text and from an examination of the preparatory work. He contributes a shrewd political analysis of the balance of forces in the regional organizations at the relevant time.

A thoughtful conclusion draws all the threads together.

Professor Schabas endeavours to demonstrate that, since the 1940s, there has been a steady movement towards the creation of a norm of international law supporting the abolition of the death penalty. Insofar as practice is concerned, approximately half the countries of the world have become abolitionist *de facto* or *de jure* (p. 2). The offences for which it may be imposed are increasingly limited (p. 20). Categories of persons who may not be subjected to the death penalty are slowly being established (the pregnant, the insane, sometimes the old, and, in the 1980s, only Barbados, Iraq, Iran, Nigeria, Pakistan, Bangladesh, and the United States executed individuals convicted of murder for an offence occurring when they were under the age of eighteen)(p. 295). International human rights law continues to set higher standards for the procedural requirements that are essential before a trial may validly result in capital punishment (p. 20). These norms are in part entrenched by treaty and in part by customary law, the latter particularly crystallized in resolutions of the United Nations General Assembly and its Economic and Social Council.

Yet, the movement has had its setbacks. As the author notes (p. 152, n. 112), a resolution put forward at the Eighth United Nations Congress on the Prevention of Crime and the Treatment of Offenders recommending a three-year moratorium on carrying out the death penalty failed to garner the necessary two-thirds vote of the participating states. Any effort for further movement at the global level must run the formidable gauntlet of opposition from most of the Islamic states, with China and the United States in their tow.

Professor Schabas reminds us (p. 1) that when Uruguay objected to the inclusion of the death penalty in the Nuremberg Charter, it was accused of having Nazi sympathies. It is perhaps a measure of the progression of which this fine book speaks that the Tribunal set up to deal with crimes in the former Yugoslavia is not empowered to impose the death penalty.

ROGER S. CLARK
Rutgers University School of Law

Iraq and Koweit: The Hostilities and Their Aftermath. Edited by M. Weller. Cambridge International Documents Series, Volume 3. Cambridge: Grotius, 1993. Pp. xxx and 780. ISBN 0-949009-98-9; *Guerre du Golfe: Le dossier d'une crise internationale 1990-1992.* Par Brigitte Stern, Habib Ghérari et Olivier Delorme. Paris: La Documentation française, 1993. Pp. 626. ISBN 2-11-002825-4.

Pour quelques bonnes années encore à venir, juristes et chercheurs continueront à analyser cette Guerre du Golfe résultant de l'invasion du Koweit par l'Irak à un moment où les relations internationales avaient déjà pris le tournant de la fin de la guerre froide; avec les deux ouvrages que nous évoquerons ici, ils disposeront d'emblée d'un volume considérable de documents, réalisant de ce fait une fort appréciable économie de temps et de moyens.

Précisons, dès ores, que ces deux recueils, loin de constituer le dédoublement l'un de l'autre en versions anglaise et française, s'avèrent en fait être des outils complémentaires de travail et de réflexion sur les multiples aspects et dimensions d'un conflit dont la société internationale n'a pas fini — tant s'en faut — d'accuser les conséquences.

L'impressionnante collection de documents (plus de cinq cent) réunie par M. Weller, Research Fellow au Centre de recherche pour le Droit International de l'Université de Cambridge, a été organisée selon six parties distinctes correspondant aux principales séquences événementielles, à l'exception de la première partie de l'ouvrage qui regroupe l'ensemble des résolutions du Conseil de Sécurité pour les années 1990 et 1991 ainsi que des extraits de procès-verbaux des séances du Conseil durant 1991, le premier d'entre eux étant, par choix délibéré et significatif du concepteur de cette présentation, consacré à l'adoption d'une résolution des Nations Unies relative au Groupe d'Observation Militaire entre l'Iran et l'Irak. En fait, comme le remarque Brigitte Stern dans son introduction à l'ouvrage qui retient également notre attention: "La seconde 'guerre' du Golfe n'aurait peut-être pas eu lieu s'il n'y avait eu la première guerre du Golfe. . . ." Ces deux démarches tacitement concordantes montrent bien que toute appréhension juridique de la crise ne saurait se dispenser de l'éclairage par le contexte dans le cadre duquel elle s'est inscrite et déroulée.

C'est l'intérêt d'une lecture des débats du Conseil de Sécurité; c'est celui, pareillement, des différentes lettres que les représentants des États adressent aux instances de l'ONU au nom de leurs gouvernements respectifs, et qui abondent dans le recueil de M. Weller — émaillant les cinq autres parties de l'ouvrage de manière parfois prédominante lorsque les thématiques sont plus particulièrement tributaires du rôle assumé par les organes onusiens à mesure de l'évolution de la crise. Toutefois, la contexture documentaire de l'ensemble demeure assez variée.

Il en est ainsi de la deuxième partie: elle couvre la période située entre le début de l'occupation du Koweit par les troupes irakiennes et le démarrage de la contrainte armée contre l'Irak sur la base de la résolution 678 du Conseil de Sécurité; sa section consacrée à la question des droits de la personne à l'intérieur d'un Koweit occupé met l'accent sur les travaux de la Commission des Droits de l'Homme des Nations Unies — rapports, résumés, résolutions — examinant les allégations de violations commises par les autorités irakiennes; tandis que celle portant sur les propositions destinées à mettre fin pacifiquement à l'occupation du Koweit se compose d'une suite de positions gouvernementales exprimées surtout à travers le courrier adressé à cet égard au Secrétaire Général de l'ONU, mais aussi au moyen de quelque point de presse comme c'est le cas pour le Secrétaire d'État américain. Ces documents reflètent la problématique qui avait sous-tendu les différentes initiatives, en particulier celles du Secrétaire Général des Nations Unies, marquées par le lien alors établi entre la crise du Golfe et l'ensemble du conflit au Moyen-Orient avec son abcès de fixation autour de la question palestinienne.

La troisième partie du recueil est axée sur l'application de la force militaire contre l'Irak, en référence à trois aspects majeurs y afférents: le déclenchement et la conduite des hostilités; la mise en oeuvre du droit de la guerre; et les conséquences environnementales du conflit. Les documents relatifs à l'action armée proviennent de trois sources, distinctement traitées: les Nations Unies, bien sûr, mais surtout les États-Unis et la Grande-Bretagne dont les pièces au dossier permettent notamment de procéder à un examen affiné du montage géopolitique de la Coalition d'États ayant participé à la confrontation armée, des opérations militaires, de leurs finalités stratégiques et des conclusions qui peuvent en être tirées. Pour ce qui est du droit de la guerre applicable au cours de ce type d'hostilités, le document le plus important demeure le communiqué du CICR, en date du 21 janvier 1991, dans lequel l'organisme humanitaire définit le conflit, énonce les règles juridiques auxquelles sont assujettis les belligérants compte tenu à la fois de leurs engagements conventionnels et du droit coutumier en la matière et enfin, énumère les règles fondamentales que devraient observer les parties aux affrontements. En ce qui a trait aux dimensions du conflit reliées à l'environnement, il convient de noter que la reproduction de larges extraits de la Convention sur la protection de l'environnement marin dans la région du Golfe, conclue en 1978 et à laquelle l'Irak et le Koweit sont parties, ne manquera pas de soulever des interrogations quant à l'éventuelle portée de certaines dispositions (obligations générales, pollution à partir de sources terrestres y compris celles transportées par l'air, etc.) dans un contexte conflictuel et alors que l'Irak n'a pas ratifié La Convention "ENMOD" (Convention on the Prohibition of Military or Any Other Hostile Use of Environmental Modification Techniques) de 1977, dont il est pourtant signataire.

En exergue de la quatrième partie consacrée au cessez-le-feu et à sa mise en oeuvre, le Rédacteur rappelle que c'est le Président Bush qui a décrété l'arrêt des hostilités, et non le Conseil de Sécurité, lequel est intervenu quelques jours après pour adopter la résolution 686 du 2 mars 1991 énonçant un cessez-le-feu conditionnel qui n'est entré en vigueur que le 11 avril suivant, lorsque le Président du Conseil de Sécurité a certifié à l'Irak qu'il avait rempli certaines des exigences de la résolution 687 par laquelle sont établies les conditions désormais imposées à l'État irakien. Si la masse de documents formant les sections relatives à l'établissement du cessez-le-feu et à sa mise en oeuvre n'offre pas un intérêt toujours égal (on aurait pu éviter le dédoublement de textes de l'ONU ayant fait l'objet de réimpression technique), la sélection documentaire s'avère d'une meilleure utilité pour aborder les questions de délimitation des frontières entre l'Irak et le Koweit ainsi que d'instauration de la Mission d'Observation des Nations Unies entre les deux pays — MONUIK. En dehors des questions frontalières, la cessation des combats sera accompagnée d'une série de mesures concernant la détection, le contrôle ou la destruction de certains armements et installations irakiens, de même que les réclamations, sanctions et autres affaires financières, et sur lesquels l'ouvrage offre une entrée en matière efficace avec les textes de base ayant présidé à la mise en place de ces divers mécanismes.

Par ailleurs, des questions humanitaires et de droits de l'homme ont surgi dramatiquement dans la foulée de la crise et de la guerre du Golfe; la cinquième partie de l'ouvrage leur accorde, comme il se devait, une juste considération. Elle comprend une mise en perspective du problème Kurde sur sa toile de fond historico-juridique campée par une note de service du Foreign and Commonwealth Office, des extraits pertinents du traité de Sèvres du 10 août 1920 et d'un rapport de la Société des Nations de décembre 1925 suivi d'une décision du Conseil de la SDN adoptée à la même époque; à cela s'ajoutent quelques textes plus récents relatifs à l'agencement des rapports entre le gouvernement irakien et les mouvements Kurdes. Les sujets complétant cette partie sont la situation humanitaire en Irak à la fin des hostilités, la levée partielle des sanctions contre l'Irak et l'assistance humanitaire fournie par les Agences d'aide internationales (dont la diversité devrait susciter une réflexion sur l'efficacité de l'action menée dans ces conditions), les droits de la personne en Irak — incluant des descriptions sur la situation d'autres minorités non-Kurdes telles les Assyriens et

les Turcomans — et la réponse de Membres de la Coalition internationale caractérisée par l'établissement de zones de sécurité et
d'exclusion de survol aérien. À côté de cet ensemble de documents
relatifs à l'Irak, la section réservée à la situation à l'intérieur du
Koweit en matière de droits de la personne s'avère particulièrement
succincte quand on sait que les autorités koweitiennes se sont
distinguées par des pratiques discriminatoires et fréquemment bru-
tales à l'endroit de nombreuses catégories de résidents étrangers se
trouvant sur le territoire du Koweit, le rapport du Secrétaire Général de l'ONU reproduit dans le recueil révélant sur ce plan une
indulgence qui contraste avec le ton appliqué aux violations
irakiennes en la même matière. Or, faut-il le souligner, par delà les
motifs politiques qui peuvent expliquer cette différence de traitement, c'est le respect et l'application des dispositifs de protection
des personnes et de leurs droits qui perdent de leur crédibilité et de
leur efficacité: un autre danger à terme.

Enfin, dans une dernière partie — la sixième — le recueil rappelle que des hostilités ultérieures impliquant l'Irak ont ponctuelle-
ment eu lieu pour forcer le gouvernement irakien à se conformer
aux obligations résultant pour lui des résolutions du Conseil de
Sécurité. L'ouvrage se referme sur une section cartographique de
belle qualité et, bien sûr, les index facilitant le repérage des
documents.

D'une tout autre facture est le volume de documents présentés
par Brigitte Stern — Professeur à l'Université de Paris I, Directrice
du Centre de Droit International (CEDIN) — et rassemblés par
Habib Gherari et Olivier Delorme — respectivement Maître de
Conférence à l'Université de Paris X — Nanterre, et Agrégé de
l'Université, chargé de mission à la Documentation française.
Coiffé d'une courte introduction dense et pénétrante, qui en elle-
même offre de nombreuses voies de réflexion et d'analyse,
l'ouvrage s'inscrit résolument dans une approche de sociologie et
de droit des relations internationales qui favorise, à n'en pas douter,
une compréhension plus approfondie des événements, une
démarche critique éclairée des mécanismes juridiques sur lesquels
s'est adossée l'action de la Coalition internationale contre l'Irak ou
encore de ceux qui ont été instaurés pour gérer les conditions de
cessation des hostilités imposées à l'État irakien.

D'ailleurs, dans son introduction, Madame Stern soulève des
questions (parfois sous forme de constats) dont il faut vivement
souhaiter qu'elles susciteront les recherches appropriées: comment

expliquer l'insistance du Koweit à exiger de l'Irak un remboursement rapide et intégral des sommes qu'il lui avait prêtées alors que
l'Arabie Saoudite avait effacé la dette que lui devait l'Irak, ces deux
situations financières étant la conséquence de la guerre que le
régime irakien avait menée contre l'Iran pour défendre les monar-
chies du Golfe contre la poussée de l'intégrisme islamique; étonne-
ment, aussi, face à l'attitude de provocation du président irakien;
interrogation face à la "pusillanimité dérisoire" du Conseil de
Sécurité s'abstenant de qualifier d'agression les agissements de
l'Irak à l'égard du Koweit; les termes quelque peu neutres utilisés
par la résolution 678 du Conseil de Sécurité cachaient-ils des divergences entre la France et les États-Unis à propos de la nécessité
d'une action armée; compte tenu des ambiguïtés manifestées par le
Conseil de Sécurité dans la façon d'utiliser ses pouvoirs peut-on
dire que la guerre du Golfe a véritablement constitué un emploi de
la force par les Nations Unies; la paralysie de la société internationale face à la crise yougoslave ne démontre-t-elle pas que la
volonté de faire respecter le droit international par tous les États
manifestée à l'endroit de l'Irak n'est en définitive qu'une paren-
thèse déjà fermée.

À travers un tel prisme, le dossier de crise qu'entend présenter ce
recueil revêt tout son relief, avec cinq parties dont les quatre
premières tissent, en fait, la trame historique de cette suite d'événements qui finira par devenir le "tournant majeur dans les relations
internationales de la seconde moitié du XXe siècle," pour
reprendre les termes de Brigitte Stern; d'ailleurs, chacune de ces
quatre parties s'ouvre sur une chronologie des textes et des événements marquants pour la période considérée.

Ainsi, comme l'origine de la situation antagonique de l'Irak par
rapport au Koweit plonge ses racines dans la pénétration britannique de l'Empire Ottoman, la première partie de l'ouvrage s'em-
ploie à retracer ce qui est intitulé "Une longue histoire." La date
de départ est celle de 1756, année où la région du Koweit voit
s'établir son premier cheikh inaugurant en même temps la dynastie
des Sabah; cent quarante trois ans plus tard, est signé le traité de
protectorat entre le Royaume-Uni et le gouvernement du Koweit,
point de départ de l'imbroglio historico-juridique qui va sous-
tendre les revendications de l'Irak sur le Koweit. Deux séries de
documents vont donc composer cette partie: ceux relatifs au con-
tentieux historique, avec le traité de protectorat, l'échange de
messages mettant fin à ce régime et permettant l'accession du

Koweit à l'indépendance, et les textes exprimant au même moment la volonté irakienne de réaliser l'union avec le Koweit, qualifié de partie intégrante de l'Irak; l'autre volet documentaire est consacré aux récents éléments qui, en 1990, ont jalonné le cheminement vers la crise, c'est-à-dire les discours de Messieurs Saddam Hussein et Tarek Aziz dressant le catalogue des réclamations irakiennes notamment par rapport aux fluctuations des prix pétroliers et au manque à gagner que l'Irak a dû encourir du fait des changements dans les flux de pétrole à son détriment pendant la guerre contre l'Iran, la position koweitienne en réplique au mémorandum irakien adressé à la Ligue Arabe, et surtout, "les ambiguïtés américaines" manifestées lors de l'entretien du président Saddam Hussein avec l'ambassadeur des États-Unis en Irak, propos dont l'essentiel est reproduit et dont la teneur s'avère encore insondable à bien des égards.

Au fil de la deuxième partie du recueil est plantée la crise internationale dans son déroulement entre août 1990 et janvier 1991 et avec les prises de positions, institutionnelles et étatiques, qu'elle a suscitées. La section relative à l'ONU regroupe notamment les résolutions adoptées durant cette période par le Conseil de Sécurité, les discours de certains chefs d'État (France, Koweit, États-Unis) et ministres des affaires étrangères (Iran, URSS, Maroc, Irak) prononcés lors de la quarante cinquième session de l'Assemblée Générale des Nations Unies, les dispositions envisagées pour assister les pays touchés par l'application des sanctions à l'égard de l'Irak, et la déclaration du Secrétaire Général des Nations Unies en date du 15 janvier 1991 — date limite établie par la résolution 678 du Conseil de Sécurité pour ouvrir la voie à l'action armée contre l'Irak — adressant une ultime invitation au Président irakien à éviter la guerre imminente. Suivent, sous des sections clairement identifiées, des documents significatifs cherchant à restituer les traits des attitudes adoptées par l'Irak, par les autorités koweitiennes réfugiées en Arabie Saoudite et tentant d'organiser la continuité de leur État, par les États-Unis et l'Union Soviétique — individuellement et en commun —, par le monde arabe — tant dans le cadre de ses organismes régionaux que sont la Ligue des États Arabes, l'Organisation de la Conférence Islamique et le Conseil de coopération du Golfe, qu'au niveau de certains États — par les institutions européennes, par la France et, à travers le monde, par quelques pays (Allemagne, Chine, Grande-Bretagne, Iran, Israël, Japon, Turquie) et regroupements (Mouvement des non-alignés, OTAN). Une place est également faite aux ONG avec les problématiques du CICR, d'Amnesty International et des Ligues des Droits de l'Homme.

Structurée à l'instar de la précédente, la troisième partie est axée sur l'opération "Tempête du désert" qui domine l'échiquier international durant les mois de janvier et février 1991. Au cours de cette période, l'on assistera aux tirs de missiles SCUD irakiens sur Israël, l'on observera la retenue du Gouvernement israélien expliquée par son Premier Ministre devant le Knesset, l'on notera que le gouvernement chinois s'adresse aux "deux parties belligérantes" et l'on soulignera la désapprobation du Ministre français de la Défense, Jean-Pierre Chevènement, à l'égard de ce qu'il appelle "la manœuvre américaine" dans laquelle va s'insérer l'action militaire de la France ainsi que sa démission subséquente douze jours après le début des combats.

Réplique des deux autres dans son articulation générale, la quatrième partie de l'ouvrage s'attarde sur l'après-guerre tel qu'il s'organise entre mars 1991 et janvier 1993. Ce sont des mois qui fourmillent d'événements divers: imposition, par voie de résolutions du Conseil de Sécurité, de nombreuses obligations à l'Irak; affaire Kurde; déploiement de la MONUIK; difficultés rencontrées par les missions chargées d'appliquer les mesures relatives à certains types d'armements en possession de l'Irak, pour ne citer que cet ensemble de faits saillants. Face aux différents dispositifs contraignants pour l'État irakien, les réactions que ce dernier a exprimées dans ses échanges avec les instances onusiennes retiendront particulièrement l'attention: elles marquent, d'une certaine manière, les limites de l'acceptation par l'Irak de la teneur et des conséquences juridiques des énoncés résolutoires; plus spécifiquement, la lettre du Ministre irakien des Affaires étrangères informant le Secrétaire Général des Nations Unies que son gouvernement acceptait d'assumer les obligations lui incombant en vertu de la résolution 686 (1991) fait remarquer "La manière dont les Forces américaines et leurs partenaires dans les opérations militaires contre l'Irak ont appliqué La résolution 678 (1990) du Conseil de Sécurité et [les] dégâts importants qui ont été causés à l'infrastructure de l'Irak" et déplore qu'il n'en ait pas été tenu compte dans la résolution 686, laquelle inflige des obligations au seul État irakien. Le déséquilibre ainsi perçu par l'Irak comme une "injustice" servira de soutènement aux résistances extérieures que manifesteront les autorités irakiennes vis-à-vis de la mise en oeuvre des mesures résultant des différentes résolutions.

Avant de clore le recueil, une partie a été réservée aux éléments d'un bilan dont il est précisé qu'il ne saurait prétendre être fiable, ni exhaustif, notamment du fait que "La guerre médiatique qui s'est déroulée parallèlement à la crise politique et militaire pose de sérieux problèmes méthodologiques quand il s'agit de valider ou non les données transmises par les belligérants." Cet essai de bilan porte sur les opérations militaires, les pertes humaines et dommages subis par le Koweit, la catastrophe écologique et les conséquences économiques de la crise du Golfe sur le commerce mondial. L'impact du conflit sur l'Irak fait l'objet d'un renvoi à un rapport de l'ONU reproduit parmi les documents affectés à l'après-guerre.

Il convient de noter que le maniement de l'ouvrage est fort aisé: les chronologies sur lesquelles s'ouvrent les quatre premières parties par rapport aux périodes respectivement considérées mentionnent en caractères italiques les faits relativement auxquels des documents ont été retenus et opèrent le renvoi précis à cet effet. Ceci en permet une lecture contextuelle qui répond bien aux besoins de la réflexion. En outre, à côté du très utile index thématique, quelques pages d'orientations bibliographiques offrent aux chercheurs un appréciable point de départ pour les nombreux travaux que cette crise internationale va encore, très certainement, susciter.

KATIA BOUSTANY
Université du Québec à Montréal

Crisis in the Gulf. By John Norton Moore. Dobbs Ferry: Oceana Publications, 1992. Pp. xliii, 677. ISBN 0-379-20166-6; *Entre les Lignes: La Guerre du Golfe et le Droit International.* Edited by N. Servais. Brussels: Centre de Droit International U.L.B., 1991. Pp. 214.

The apparent unwillingness of the western powers to enforce effective no-fly zones in Bosnia or to take military action against the warring parties, including those responsible for "ethnic cleansing," has resulted in criticisms based on the different approach that was adopted at the time of the invasion of Kuwait and during Iraq's oppressive acts against its Kurdish population. For example, Ambassador Kampelman in his foreword to Professor Moore's book comments, "if we are serious about a new world order, it is crucial for the international community to stand firm against aggression.

Mildly condemning an attack while also opposing a defensive response is insufficient" (p. xxvi).

Even without this comparison, there has been some criticism of the efforts by the western coalition to impose its no-fly zone in northern Iraq while conducting bombing attacks on Iraqi targets in an effort to ensure Iraq's compliance with United Nations and Coalition demands. These criticisms have not only come from radical politicians or organizations who seem intent on describing the Gulf War as a purely western exercise, ignoring the fact that there were thirty-three Coalition states participating, including some Islamic and Communist states. For instance, in his statement to the General Assembly, Shevardnadze, then Foreign Minister of the Soviet Union, stated, "An act of terrorism has been perpetrated against the emerging new world order. This is a major affront to mankind. Unless we find a way to respond to it and cope with the situation, our civilization will be thrown back by half a century" (p. viii).

In this regard, three papers included in *Entre Les Lignes: La Guerre du Golfe et le Droit International* are useful. In Klein and Schaus's "Deux Poids, Deux Mesures? : L'Inégalité dans l'Application du Pouvoir du Conseil de Sécurité," the authors draw attention to the lack of or halfhearted response by the Council when its Resolutions have been disregarded in circumstances that the writers consider to be similarly reprehensible.

In Dr. Pierson-Mathy's paper "Non à la Guerre," the legality of the punitive attacks as well as of the original operation is questioned. Recommended at the same time is Pierre Mertens's cynical closing essay entitled "Cosi Fan Tutti," which performs an incisive "hatchet job" on the propaganda campaigns. It is useful, therefore, to have fully reasoned accounts of the legal issues involved in the Gulf War and its immediate aftermath.

Apart from the analysis that Professor Moore provides of the variety of legal problems involved, one of the great attractions of *Crisis in the Gulf* lies in its extensive collection of documents (some 230 pages) that cover the historic background, starting with the 1913 United Kingdom — Turkish Agreement relating to the "autonomy of the Sheikh of Koweit," through the 1932 papers relating to Iraq's admission to the League of Nations, and culminating in the 1963 Agreed Minutes between Kuwait and Iraq whereby the latter "recognized the independence and complete sovereignty of the State of Kuwait with its boundaries" (p. 39) as established in correspondence between Iraq and Kuwait in July and August 1932. In addition, the text includes all the Security Council Resolutions relating to the dispute from August 2, 1990, immediately after the invasion, until September 19, 1991, concerning "the nutritional and health situation of the Iraqi civilian population" (p. 451), as well as a variety of other relevant instruments, including an interesting map showing the vote of the Arab League at its Cairo meeting a week after the invasion. Normally, it would be necessary to seek these documents out in a variety of materials, but in this text all are conveniently brought together in one readily accessible form.

For those particularly concerned about the legality of the response of the United Nations and the international community to the Iraqi aggression, Moore's chapter 3 is of significance. Equally so are the papers included in *Entre Les Lignes* by Dr. Robert, "La Licéité des Sanctions des Nations Unies contre l'Irak," and by Dr. Klein, "Le Statut des Forces Coalisées."

However much one condemns Iraq's invasion of Kuwait and its behaviour in that country and towards its nationals as well as aliens and diplomats, it becomes a little difficult to share Moore's view that "these violations suggest, in their brutality, ruthlessness and inhumanity, [that] the actions of Saddam Hussein in the Gulf crisis were a throwback to the Dark Ages of fifteen hundred years ago" (p. 6). If this were true, how does one classify the Nazi behaviour in occupied Europe, together with the Holocaust? It is far easier to accept Moore's analysis of the illegality of Iraq's aggression and its violation of its obligations as a member of the United Nations and of the League of Arab States (pp. 21-49), a view largely shared by Professor Salmon in his essay "Droit International, Politique et Idéologique dans la Guerre du Golfe" in *Entre les Lignes*.

Ample evidence has been brought forward of the commission of war crimes in Bosnia, and the Security Council has called for the establishment of a tribunal to try those involved. In the Gulf, the Security Council condemned Iraq's breaches of the Geneva Conventions and called for the collection of evidence, but made no reference to any means of trying those involved and, as Moore shows (pp. 50-90), there is ample evidence that war crimes — crimes against humanity as well as a series of breaches of the law relating to the protection of aliens and diplomats — were committed by Iraq. It is unfortunate that, while discussing the illegality of treating alien civilians as hostages (pp. 86-88), Moore at no time mentions that, since Iraq was not a party to the Terrorist

Convention, there is little point in citing the latter as if it were binding law for all (p. 86). Perhaps the proposed war crimes tribunal, despite the restriction of its jurisdiction to Bosnia, may serve to strengthen the precedent set by Nuremberg, and its principles may assist those who contend that it is still not too late to proceed against any Iraqi who may fall into the hands of a member of the United Nations prepared to sustain the validity of the law of armed conflict.

Insofar as Iraq's activities were breaches of the law of war and of international criminal law as such, reference may be made to Dr. David's "La Guerre de Golfe au Regard du Droit des Conflits Armés at du Droit Pénal International." This paper should be read in conjunction with Moore's chapter 6, particularly Part B that deals with war crimes trials. One is perhaps a little surprised, however, to find an American lawyer, regardless of what happened at Nuremberg, supporting the possibility of trials *in absentia*. Such a proposal might be difficult for Canada to support in view of the Charter of Rights, even though this may be the only procedure possible in the case of major war criminals in Bosnia.

There has been much controversy as to the ecological effects of Iraq's destruction of oil wells and whether such action amounts to environmental war crimes. Moore has no hesitation in regarding them as such; in fact, he labels this policy "environmental terrorism" (pp. 76-82). By way of contrast, in their paper "La Guerre Sale: Les Règles du Droit International Applicables à la Protection de l'Environnement," Drs. Daems and Paye comment:

Dans le cadre du conflit actuel, les belligérants qui bombardent volontairement les installations pétrolières sur terre et sur mer comme les tankers violent certainement leurs obligations générales de prévention et de protection de l'environnement. *A fortiori*, s'il devait être prouvé que l'Irak a ouvert les vannes de plusieurs stations de pompage et que les coalisés ont bombardé des usines nucléaires, il s'agirait également de violations des interdictions spécifiques du temps de guerre. It reste que, comme c'est souvent le cas, il sera difficile d'établir clairement et distinctement les responsabilités respectives de chaque belligérant pour les atteintes causés à l'environnement. (p. 135)

None of the contributors to *Entre les lignes* is concerned with the future, nor do they attempt to draw any lessons from the experiences of the Gulf War. Professor Moore's text, on the other hand, includes a closing chapter on "Controlling the Scourge of War: Toward a More Peaceful Future." He points out that many of the recent wars with which the international community has been plagued have resulted from a lack of deterrence on the part of those who profess to be upholders of the rule of law, and continues:

[D]eterrence is strengthened by successful examples of effective collective security and community response against aggression. With respect to the rule of law in such systemic deterrence, deterrence is strengthened when the system clearly condemns aggression, clearly encourages defense against aggression, and understands the importance of this vital distinction between aggression and defense. And systemic deterrence is weakened — and the rule of law becomes progressively irrelevant for peace — to the extent that the system fails to meaningfully condemn aggression, focuses its displeasure on the defensive response instead, or fails in general to promote a vital distinction between aggression and defense. *(p. 338)*

Perhaps, in the light of the fiasco of the United Nations' response to the situation in Bosnia, this extract might with advantage be posted above the desk of every foreign minister and of the Secretary General.

The lessons from the Gulf War drawn by Professor Moore for the future include:

(1) the need to strengthen Chapter 7 of the Charter and the ability of the regional arrangements to deal with aggression and threats to the peace;

(2) the need "to prevent massive militarization of radical regimes", requiring a "new thinking" among the successor states of the Soviet Union;

(3) "[a]n international effort, aware of the relationship between war and extreme radical regimes . . . to work energetically and effectively to enhance the rule of law within nation States";

(4) [e]nhanced efforts to develop a real-world model that would be able to provide timely warning that the risk of conflict on a particular border or within a particular region is reaching critical levels, so that the international system might be able to take immediate supplemental deterrent or other effective actions to prevent war rather than having to fight it;

(5) the creation of a small UN "presence" force that the Secretary General could deploy in response to an urgent request from a threatened State;

(6) "[m]eans for revitalizing the critical prohibition against aggressive attack and for strengthening a rule of law that will meaningfully sanction such aggression," with a tough-minded application of sanctions, including reparations and war crimes trials (pp. 341-44).

There would probably be little expressed opposition to proposals of this kind, but the author does not pay due regard to the extent to which there is opposition to amending the Charter, and he ignores the hesitancy of the responsible powers to take the measures necessary to give effect to such proposals, as may be seen from the Bosnia situation.

L. C. GREEN
University of Alberta

Droit international public. Par Jean-Maurice Arbour. 2ème édition. Yvon Blais: Cowansville, 1992. Pp. xxxiv, 514.

Ainsi que son auteur le précise d'emblée, l'ouvrage commenté ici est avant tout un manuel d'enseignement destiné aux futurs juristes. Renonçant à l'exhaustivité d'un traité, le professeur Arbour a préféré concentrer son attention — et attirer celle de ses étudiants — sur un certain nombre de règles-clés qui gouvernent le droit international public contemporain. Celles-ci sont présentées en suivant un plan classique où sont successivement traités les sources et les sujets du droit des gens, les principes essentiels régissant la vie de l'État, le droit applicable aux espaces internationaux et les modalités de règlement des différends internationaux.

Les deux premières parties de l'ouvrage appellent peu de commentaires et constituent une très bonne présentation, synthétique et efficace, des sources et des sujets du droit des gens. On observera toutefois que l'étude des sources reste partielle, à la suite de la disparition — semble-t-il accidentelle — du chapitre consacré aux principes généraux du droit et aux actes unilatéraux[1] et que la notion de sujet de droit international aurait pu être abordée de manière plus extensive en réservant quelques développements à la place croissante de l'individu et des peuples dans l'ordre juridique international moderne.

En dépit de certains problèmes de structure — sur lesquels l'on reviendra plus loin, les troisième et cinquième parties fournissent une bonne introduction aux principes de base régissant les relations internationales. Ils ne sont toutefois pas sans receler quelques sources de confusion. Pour n'en prendre que ces exemples, aucune

[1] Annoncé à la page 33, ce troisième chapitre de la première partie ne se retrouve pas dans le corps de l'ouvrage.

distinction n'est opérée entre normes primaires et secondaires dans l'explication des mécanismes de base de la responsabilité internationale, et la guerre de Corée est assimilée à une opération de maintien de la paix des Nations Unies (p. 459). De même, le caractère contraignant de l'intervention et la nécessité qu'elle porte sur une matière appartenant au domaine réservé de l'Etat sont insuffisamment mis en évidence dans l'analyse de ce premier concept, ce qui ne permet pas à l'auteur d'aboutir à une définition suffisamment claire de l'intervention non armée (pp. 262 et 263). On soulignera en contrepoint la précision de l'étude de sujets tels que ceux de la compétence extra-territoriale des États ou de la délimitation maritime (dans la quatrième partie) qui parvient à rendre ces problèmes complexes aisément intelligibles au lecteur, même néophyte.

La quatrième partie offre, quant à elle, un excellent panorama des normes internationales applicables aux espaces, que ceux-ci soient ou non soumis à la souveraineté de l'État, en insistant particulièrement sur les espaces maritimes et extra-atmosphérique (le territoire de l'État étant en effet étudié, quoi que de manière moins approfondie, dans la partie consacrée aux sujets du droit international). L'étude est exhaustive, et ne néglige pas des aspects moins souvent traités dans ce type d'ouvrage mais qui n'en revêtent pas moins une importance cruciale à l'heure actuelle, comme celui de la pêche.

On notera aussi au fil de tous ces chapitres les références très utiles faites à la pratique canadienne dans des domaines aussi variés que l'application des différentes sources du droit international par les tribunaux canadiens, les mesures législatives concernant l'immunité des États et l'étendue des compétences extra-territoriales de ceux-ci ou les réserves à la déclaration d'acceptation de la juridiction de la Cour internationale de Justice.

Il faut observer de manière générale que l'option choisie par l'auteur pour le traitement de ce qu'il est convenu d'appeler les "principes touchant les relations amicales et la coopération entre Etats,"[2] soit les grands principes du droit international, n'est pas sans poser quelques problèmes de cohérence qui se ressentent dans l'exposé de plusieurs problématiques. Sa démarche apparaît en fait comme une tentative de présenter ces règles fondamentales de façon plus dynamique en les regroupant autour des concepts à fort contenu politique que sont la souveraineté et le règlement des conflits. En étant analysés uniquement en référence à ces derniers,

---

2 Résolution 2625 (XXV) de l'Assemblée générale des Nations Unies.

des principes aussi fondamentaux que le droit des peuples à disposer d'eux-mêmes ou la non-intervention ne font dès lors finalement l'objet que d'une étude parcellaire et fragmentée qui suscite elle aussi quelques regrets.

Ceci ne signifie toutefois assurément pas qu'il faille pour autant remettre en cause l'attention accordée par l'auteur de manière constante dans son étude tant aux enseignements de la science politique en elle-même qu'au cadre politique dans lequel le droit international se développe et s'applique. Bien au contraire, l'introduction de l'ouvrage, en présentant un certain nombre de caractères généraux de cette branche du droit et en soulignant ses spécificités par rapport au droit interne révèle déjà tout l'intérêt d'une telle approche. Cette vision "située" des règles essentielles se retrouve d'ailleurs tout au long de l'étude et contribue grandement à son intérêt.

Dans son ensemble, la matière fait l'objet d'une présentation claire, rigoureuse, précise et empreinte d'un réalisme de bon aloi,[3] dans laquelle les prises de positions personnelles de l'auteur ne sont pas exclues. Au-delà d'un simple choix en faveur de l'une ou l'autre des opinions doctrinales exposées, les options prises par le professeur Arbour sont le fruit d'un travail de réflexion que l'on sent nourri par une "pratique" non négligeable du sujet. Le seul sentiment d'incertitude qui continuera peut-être à habiter le lecteur résultera sans doute de l'oscillation de l'auteur entre les théories objectiviste et volontariste du droit international, sans que l'une ou l'autre ne semble emporter véritablement sa préférence.[4] On soulignera par ailleurs son souci de montrer le caractère évolutif du droit international (ainsi à propos des procédures de conclusion des traités, du critère de légitimité[5] ou des manifestations de l'égalité souveraine des États, par exemple), de même que la place qu'il

---

[3] La formule de l'auteur selon laquelle "l'égoïsme des Etats n'a d'égal que l'égoïsme individuel" (p. 13) en constitue à nos yeux une très bonne illustration. L'humour n'est par ailleurs pas absent non plus: ainsi à propos du "gentlemen's agreement" (p. 64).

[4] Si la théorie objectiviste semble initialement favorisée (p. 27), les choses apparaissent moins claires par la suite (pp. 203 et 248 e.a.).

[5] Même si les conclusions atteintes par l'auteur à ce propos font sans doute une part trop réduite au consensus qui semble se dégager sur le plan international pour considérer les élections "libres, périodiques et équitables" comme un critère reconnu de la légitimité démocratique (voy. e.a. les résolutions 45/150 et 46/137 adoptées par l'Assemblée générale des Nations Unies le 18 décembre 1990 et le 17 décembre 1991 respectivement).

accorde à certains débats très actuels, dont témoigne entre autres la note consacrée au "droit d'ingérence" humanitaire. A cet égard, le principal regret du lecteur naîtra sans doute du peu de place accordé à l'étude du Chapitre VII de la Charte,[6] dont plusieurs événements récents ont pourtant montré toute l'importance qu'il revêtait dans la réalité des faits.

De façon sans doute inévitable, les intérêts plus particuliers de l'auteur transparaissent dans le traitement plus méthodique de certaines questions. Il en va certainement ainsi pour la délimitation maritime, déjà mentionnée, ainsi que, par exemple, pour les pactes de sécurité collective. Malgré tout l'intérêt qu'ils suscitent, ces développements risquent toutefois de faire naître une certaine impression de déséquilibre chez le lecteur, que les restrictions exprimées par l'auteur dans son avant-propos risquent de ne pas convaincre entièrement lorsqu'il mettra dans la balance les six pages consacrées à l'OTAN, d'une part, les trois pages consacrées aux droits de la personne dans leur ensemble, de l'autre.

Il n'en reste pas moins que le professeur Arbour a sans aucun doute brillamment atteint l'objectif qu'il s'était fixé et qu'il offre aux étudiantes et étudiants en droit un manuel de premier ordre pour guider leurs premiers pas dans l'univers souvent déconcertant du droit international public. Les mérites de l'ouvrage ne s'arrêtent d'ailleurs pas là: au-delà des ambitions affichées de son auteur, son œuvre permettra aussi à des internationalistes plus confirmés de faire à plus d'une reprise le point avec bonheur sur certaines questions centrales du droit international contemporain.

PIERRE KLEIN
Centre de droit international
Université libre de Bruxelles

Principles of Water Law and Administration: National and International. By Dante A. Caponera. Rotterdam: A. A. Balkema, 1992. Pp. xix, 260 (U.S.$105).

The rapid growth in the population of the world and increasing industrialization inevitably will lead to higher consumption of water and thus to increasing scarcity of this vital substance. This trend

---

6 Que soit à titre d'exception à l'interdiction du recours à la force ou au principe de non-intervention (article 2, § 7 de la Charte).

towards scarcity bodes ill for the welfare of humankind. For, as Dr. Caponera warns, "the past history of water control and management should point out to present and future generations that an adequate management of water resources is a prerequisite for civilized progress and human survival," adding that "the softening of or the lack of respect for existing water regulations caused the decadence and eventual disappearance of . . . civilization" (p. 25).

With these sombre thoughts in mind, Dr. Caponera wrote his book with the purpose of providing "a tool for dealing with the legal and institutional aspects of water resources management." Thus, since the management of water resources is in the hands of administrators and not of lawyers, the form and content of the book are based on the assumption that most readers will have no knowledge of national or international water resources law. The presentation of the material, therefore, is for the most part general, descriptive, and simplified; it is intended and designed for non-lawyers and lawyers who have no knowledge of water law, not for specialists in national and international water resources law.

On the whole, the book achieves its purpose admirably. It sets forth in easily understood terms the history of the water law of the various regions of the world and gives an indication of the prevailing law there. Furthermore, the dominant theme is the urgent need for the rational management of the world's water resources. This management, it is argued, must be based on equitable and reasonable legal principles. The importance of laws and institutions is stressed, and guidelines for determining what is appropriate in this area are given. Dr. Caponera's views on these matters are especially valuable, since he has had a long and successful career as a water resources lawyer with FAO and more recently as an adviser to governments in various regions.

While simplicity and generality were necessary features of the book, given the readership for whom it was intended, they necessarily involved the risk of superficial treatment of some material. That is so in the case of the current principles of international water resources law, the exposition of which discloses some ambivalence. In particular, the relationship between the principle of equitable utilization and that of "no significant harm" is not adequately dealt with. At one point, the former seems to be regarded as the primary rule; at another, the latter seems to be so regarded. Moreover, in the discussion of these principles, references to the pertinent authorities are not always apt or accurate. In the light of the book's purpose and of the wide range of the material, however, these lapses may be expected and excused.

The book is composed of thirteen chapters. Its contents, however, fall into three parts: chapters 1 to 7 deal with the history of water law from earliest times to the present; chapters 8, 9, and some of 13 with national water law; and chapters 10 to 12 and part of 13 with international water resources. Within each part, attention is given both to the evolution of the law and to the administration and institutions of water resources management. More recent developments are treated in greater detail.

The book lacks an index. This shortcoming is, however, compensated for to some extent by a very detailed table of contents. And for those who wish to go into the subject more deeply, a full list of references to leading authorities is provided at the end of each chapter.

In a future of water shortages, then, those charged with the responsibility of providing for the needs of their communities will be well advised to take timely action in accordance with the guidelines recommended in this book. Dr. Caponera's proposals for the rational management of national and international water resources are well-founded and should be taken seriously.

CHARLES B. BOURNE
University of British Columbia

Droit de la Mer: Études dédiées au Doyen Claude-Albert Colliard. Edited by Institut du droit économique de la mer. Pedone: Institut du droit économique de la mer, Monaco, 1992. Pp. 120.

This collection of six studies is dedicated to the late Dean Colliard. The volume is brief, but the topics are diverse and several of the contributors are well known. Two of the authors — Professors Laurent Lucchini and Jean-Pierre Quéneudec — appeared as counsel for France in the recent arbitration between Canada and France respecting the maritime boundary in the St-Pierre and Miquelon area.

Two of the papers deal with maritime boundaries. Professor Quéneudec describes the historical evolution and final constitution of the France-Monaco delimitation in "Quelques Remarques sur la Délimitation Maritime Franco-Monégasque." This delimitation is more than a geopolitical curiosity for Canadian observers of the law of the sea. The configuration of the zone allotted to Monaco — a long and very narrow corridor corresponding to the breadth of the coastal front of Monaco — is strikingly similar to the offshore portion of the zone allotted to St-Pierre and Miquelon in the 1992 decision of the Canada-France Court of Arbitration. Although the France-Monaco delimitation was not referred to in the reasons given by the Court, it was discussed in the pleadings and it is reasonable to assume that the Court was not unmindful of the similarities in making its award. Professor Quéneudec points out that the negotiators had agreed, as early as 1973, on the principle that the territorial waters of Monaco should not be enclaved — a perspective that helps explain the strength of France's opposition to the Canadian enclave position with respect to St-Pierre and Miquelon. He concludes that, while the delimitation is highly favourable to Monaco, it is accompanied by a resource agreement that is "très satisfaisant pour la France" — an agreement, however, that is destined to remain confidential, apparently forever.

A paper entitled "Variations sur la Notion de Frontière Maritime" by Josette Beer-Gabel will be of interest mainly to specialists. It is densely packed with empirical data and doctrinal speculation. The central proposition appears to be that the purported trend towards single maritime boundaries (reflected in both the *Gulf of Maine* and the *St-Pierre-et-Miquelon* proceedings) has not become universal, and is perhaps unlikely to do so. Far from being or becoming the rule, a single maritime boundary can be established only where no particular circumstances, whether geographical, political, or socio-economic, would render it inappropriate. This is because there is, as yet, no rule of law respecting the merger of the exclusive economic zone and the continental shelf. In the course of reaching her conclusion, the author notes a number of apparent errors in the Canadian summary of state practice submitted to the International Court of Justice in the *Gulf of Maine* case, in which certain delimitations, in her view, were wrongly characterized as "single" maritime boundaries.

Professor Lucchini revisits the perennial issue of "creeping jurisdiction" in "Une Nouvelle Vague de Nationalisme Maritime? Quelques Réponses à la Pratique Étatique." On this matter, as always, European and Canadian perspectives are often at odds. He deals first with trends towards expansion of the content of the jurisdiction of coastal states. Here he instances, *inter alia*, laws that extend the totality of a coastal state's domestic legislation to extraterritorial zones such as the continental shelf and the EEZ. The Canadian Laws Offshore Application Act is not mentioned, and is probably invulnerable to his criticisms: its principal effect is to extend Canadian law to offshore installations clearly under Canadian jurisdiction, and the navigational and other rights of foreign states under international law are specifically protected. (See Ross Hornby, "The Canadian Laws Offshore Application Act: The Legislative Incorporation of Rights over the Continental Shelf," 29 *Canadian Yearbook of International Law* 355 (1991).)

A more extensive treatment is given to trends towards spatial expansions of coastal state jurisdiction. Professor Lucchini does not agree that the whole of Article 76 of the Montego Bay Convention — the new, distance-oriented definition of the continental shelf — has yet become part of general international law. Nevertheless, he does not specifically challenge the view that at least the basic concepts of Article 76 have replaced the 1958 definition of the shelf. He cites a number of baselines he considers questionable, the most intriguing being those of Bangladesh, which apparently has proclaimed baselines that follow the ten-fathom contour instead of the coastline. Much of his ammunition, however, is aimed at efforts to expand coastal state jurisdiction beyond 200 miles — an issue of intensive interest to Canadians. He describes these developments as a form of "quiet nibbling" ("sourd grignotage"). Referring to the meeting of scientific experts in St. John's, Newfoundland, in September 1990, he attacks as legally unfounded the theory that a coastal state may lawfully take unilateral measures with respect to straddling fish stocks in exceptional circumstances. Similarly, he suggests that a proposal on straddling stocks and highly migratory species co-sponsored by Canada at a preparatory conference for UNCED, and asserting the "special interest" of the coastal state, reflects a biased interpretation of the Convention.

Professor Lucchini concludes his paper by speculating on whether certain states might be hoping for jurisdictional gains through a partial renegotiation of the Montego Bay Convention in the context of a reopening of Part 11 on the deep seabed regime. He notes that, in any event, "maritime nationalism" is a permanent phenomenon that helps propel the evolution of the customary international law of the sea.

The other three papers deal with more technical issues. Professor van der Mensbrugghe's article on "Le Contrôle de Certains Navires entrant dans les Ports Maritimes de la Communauté ou en Sortant:

État de la Question," deals with the complex history of attempts in the European Community to regulate shipments of dangerous goods. While much of this is of no direct interest to Canadians, he refers to the negotiations leading to the 1989 Basel Convention, when Canada and other states apparently sought a "droit de regard" over ships transitting their territorial waters with cargoes of dangerous wastes.

"Les Cartes Marines dans la *Convention de Montego Bay*" by Michel Voelckel deals with marine charts both on a highly technical level and in terms of certain general legal concepts. The technical material — for example, the difficulties inherent in establishing the low water mark along the coast — will be of little interest to lawyers. He notes, however, that under the Montego Bay Convention marine charts have a dual role: they are used for navigation and they allow the international community to oversee claims to jurisdiction by coastal states, particularly those made by way of baselines. On the international level, the publication of charts by states can have direct legal effects on national claims through the doctrines of recognition, acquiescence, and estoppel. In domestic law, inaccuracies can lead to government liability.

Voelckel's observations on different types of cartographical projections are of interest. Both baselines and offshore delimitations between opposite or adjacent states depend significantly on the subjective appreciation of geography: that is, factors such as the "general direction of the coast"; the right of each state to the areas "directly in front of" its coast; or the objective of a roughly equal division, subject to a reasonable degree of proportionality. Intuitive reactions based on "a glance at the map" can be decisive, but can vary according to the projection used. The example that Voelckel gives is a Canadian one — the Canadian arctic archipelago apparently seems much more integrated into the general direction of the coast when the recent Robinson projection is used in place of the more traditional Mercator projection.

Both admiralty lawyers and generalists will benefit from a paper on recent developments in the law of salvage: "L'Assistance Maritime une institution en quête de reconnaissance," by Françoise Odier. The latter describes how the 1989 International Convention on Salvage has modified and broadened the law of salvage, particularly by taking account of environmental considerations. The most significant innovation, according to her account, is a relaxation of the "no cure, no pay rule." The remuneration of salvors under the new rules will no longer depend entirely on the success of the operation; some compensation will be payable, regardless of the outcome, in cases where salvors have acted in the interests of the environment. But Odier's overall assessment is pessimistic: the 1989 overhaul was "trop timide" in the light of the "disastrous" economic situation in which the salvage industry apparently now finds itself.

Since the topics covered in this collection are disparate, the volume as a whole is somewhat lacking in cohesiveness. While this volume is not an essential acquisition, a number of the individual contributions will be of interest to followers of the law of the sea.

L. A. WILLIS
Department of Justice, Ottawa

Moscow Symposium on the Law of the Sea. Edited by T. A. Clingan, Jr, and A. L. Kolodkin. Honolulu: The Law of the Sea Institute, 1991. Pp. xi, 394 including index.

This book contains the proceedings of a symposium co-sponsored by the Law of the Sea Institute, the Soviet Maritime Law Association, and the Soviet Peace Fund, held in Moscow between November 28 and December 2, 1988. Surprisingly, it was the first Soviet-American symposium on the law of the sea. The participants, who were not exclusively drawn from the Soviet Union and the United States, included many familiar to the followers of the various workshops and symposia on the law of the sea, including, to name but a few, Bernard Oxman, Ed Miles, William Burke, Edgar Gold, and Choon-ho Park.

The Moscow symposium was devoted to the following issues: the international legal regimes for navigation; fisheries, with particular emphasis on the legal difficulties surrounding highly migratory stocks; and marine scientific research. Of the issues treated, the book allocates the largest amount of space to navigation, which here embraces general subjects such as an assessment of the United Nations Convention on the Law of the Sea and its prospects for entry into force and specialist topics such as legal liability for oil pollution, the role of legal rules at sea during armed conflict, and the suppression of piracy.

The quality of the papers is diverse. Generally, the longer the paper the more useful it is, and the specialist papers are better than the general. This may be because the longer specialist papers have sufficient space to identify the particular positions taken by specific states on the relevant issues, something one cannot always find out elsewhere; the book's usefulness in this regard is assisted by its index. However, inevitably by virtue of the number of papers, there is a fair amount of repetition. Furthermore, looking at the book from today's perspective, the symposium's purpose, and certain papers such as Nikitina's on possible mechanisms for strengthening Soviet-American co-operation in marine research, seem anachronistic.

Overall this is a useful collection of papers, even if one suspects that, as is so often the case with conferences and symposia, the real contribution made by the Moscow Symposium on the Law of the Sea has been the links and thrust forged between the participants.

Finally, one cannot resist commenting on the number of errors of a typographical nature in this book, including, on page 1 of the first paper, reference to the "United States Convention on the Law of the Sea" — a somewhat ironic oversight in a paper devoted to the stabilization of the law of the sea through the Convention.

JEREMY A. THOMAS
Barrister at Law, London, England
Dalhousie Law School, Halifax

The Development of International Law by the European Court of Human Rights. By J. G. Merrills. 2d ed. Manchester: Manchester University Press, 1993. Pp. 265 including index and table of cases. ISBN 0-7190-3737-9.

Like the Canadian Charter of Rights and Freedoms, 1982, the European Convention on Human Rights, 1950, is less a code of definite legal rights than an expression of broad values and principles. The use of expansive guarantees allows for flexible interpretation and the development of case law that keeps pace with changing human needs, interests, and values. To get a clear picture of the precise content and scope of European Convention rights and obligations, it is therefore necessary to explore the rich jurisprudence of the European Court of Human Rights; a few case studies would not adequately serve this purpose. European Convention jurisprudence is now sufficiently voluminous, detailed, and complex that to obtain an accurate image of its full significance and import one must comprehend the principal doctrinal trends.

Professor Merrills's second edition, updating the first which appeared in 1988, aims "to identify issues of method and function relevant to the international judicial process generally, and specifically to the role of adjudication in developing an international law of human rights." It centres on decisions of the Court rather than on those of the European Commission on Human Rights. The adjudication of the Court is the more important in terms of doctrine and jurisprudence, whereas the Commission's main role is to consider questions of admissibility and to delimit the subject matter in issue to come before the Court.

The author's perspective sets the European Convention system against the backdrop of general international law rather than the other way around. The focus is thus fixed primarily on Convention jurisprudence and less on the effect that this jurisprudence might have on the evolving rules of general international law. Hence this book does not delve into such questions as to what effect jurisprudence might have on clarifying the normative content of *jus cogens*, the possible effect of the Convention on the changing position of the individual in general international law, or the significance of the Convention in transforming the classic doctrine of state responsibility. Nor was this book intended to be an exhaustive treatment of Convention jurisprudence. Nevertheless, the author makes clear and concise reference to many important cases, and his comment on dissenting opinions helps to illustrate the various approaches taken by the Court.

The book begins with a brief overview of the Court as an international institution, its composition, the scope of its work, and its relation to the Commission. Chapter 2 covers the form, content, and style of judgments. Various operational aspects such as the scope of individual procedural capacity, jurisdiction *ratione personae*, and friendly settlement are dealt with in Chapter 3. Chapter 4 examines the Court's chief methods of interpretation which, following those prescribed in the 1969 Vienna Convention on the Law of Treaties, place primary emphasis on the ordinary meaning of words viewed in the context of the treaty's objects and purposes.

Central to many problems of human rights implementation is the challenge to reduce the discrepancies between, on the one hand, the lofty ideals espoused by the state, and, on the other, the capacity of the individual to enforce human rights against the state. The Court has embraced the principle that Convention rights are intended to be practical and effective rather than theoretical or illusory, and this aspect is thoroughly explored in Chapter 5. Chapter 6 describes how the European Court has interpreted human rights to best preserve the rule of law and democratic values in general. The following chapter analyses the critical concept of the "margin of appreciation" applied by the European Court to limit its own jurisdiction *ratione materiae*, thereby affirming that the state ought to have discretion to exercise exclusive competence in certain areas. The author points out that the margin of appreciation has been elaborated on a case-by-case basis at the expense of some measure of consistency and predictability in the law. The chapters on interpretation, the margin of appreciation, and the Court's application of the principle of effectiveness are particularly well written and analytically incisive.

Chapters 8 and 9 explore the Court's use of such general principles as waiver, *égalité des armes*, and estoppel and describe those instances in which the Court has looked to principles of general international law for guidance on both procedural and substantive issues.

The final chapter puts forward two dichotomies — "judicial activism" versus "judicial restraint," and "tough conservatism" versus "benevolent liberalism" — to show how the ideological propensity of the judge affects the development of international law through the Court. While the concluding chapter uncovers ideological proclivities in judges' decision-making, the contrast between "tough conservatism" and "benevolent liberalism" seems to add little of explanatory value. Perhaps this distinction is overly broad, providing more of an ideological caricature than analytical insight.

In some instances the author mentions the respondent state by way of summarizing the facts, and in other instances the case is very well known. Yet, it would be useful if the book's references to European Convention cases were to mention the particular respondent state, either in the footnote citations or perhaps by inclusion of the full style of cause in the table of cases. This might ease reference for those students who are not already familiar with Convention jurisprudence.

Most works on the Convention written to date fail to take the reader very far beyond a grasp of the institutional and procedural aspects of the Convention. In contrast, Professor Merrills's treatment, with its sharp focus on the Convention's fundamental doctrinal principles, clearly demonstrates the wider influence of the

Convention on general international law, and vice versa. This feature makes the book especially valuable to lawyers who practise outside the European Convention system and to academics who wish to stay abreast of European Convention jurisprudence. As it continues to develop, European Convention jurisprudence will likely grow in importance as a source of arguments and approaches that apply generally to the judicial interpretation of domestic human rights codes. The Canadian Charter of Rights and Freedoms, for example, shares much in common with the European Convention in the catalogue and formulation of rights as well as in the wording of limitations and derogation clauses. Merrills's broad yet incisive approach is surely of value at a time when international law scholarship tends to neglect the larger context of general international law.

LYAL S. SUNGA
Ottawa

The United Nations Decade of International Law: Reflections on International Dispute Settlement. Edited by M. Brus et al. Dordrecht: Martinus Nijhoff, 1991. Pp. vii, 155 plus index.

This slim volume is one of the first published contributions to the United Nations Decade of International Law. The book is a compilation of ten essays by various, and sometimes distinguished, authors that were previously published in the special issue of the *Leiden Journal of International Law* for the year 1990 on the subject of the second purpose of the Decade — namely, the peaceful settlement of disputes. These essays are preceded by a short preface by the then Secretary-General of the United Nations, Dr. J. Perez de Cuellar, and an introductory essay to the Decade by two of the editors.

The thesis of the first essay by Sucharitkul is that "better law will inspire greater confidence among the states to settle their disputes by peaceful means." Accordingly, he sets himself the task of examining and assessing the past and potential performance of the International Law Commission. With implications also for implementing the third purpose of the Decade — the codification and progressive development of international law — he makes the point that the Commission "is handicapped by [a] shortage of expertise and scarcity of topics which appeal to the international community and which are sufficiently ripe for progressive development and codification." Subsequent developments during the last session of the United Nations might lead Sucharitkul to change this view of the Commission, although it is certainly true that under the auspices of the Decade, save for perhaps the environment, there is little enthusiasm for new projects.

Quintana's contribution provides some valuable insights into the origins of the Decade and the difficulties that face it. He draws our attention to the fact that the original draft of the Hague Declaration included provision for establishing a ministerial committee whose purpose was to visit each non-aligned country that had not yet declared its acceptance of the compulsory jurisdiction of the International Court of Justice, with a view to ensuring full acceptance of the Court's jurisdiction by the non-aligned countries before the end of the Decade. Significantly, this provision did not make it into the final draft of the Hague Declaration; we are told its deletion was the "most significant alteration made in the original text."

The third essay by Sohn picks up the proposal that the end to the Decade should see the convening of a third Hague Peace Conference that would "adopt appropriate international instruments for the enhancement of international law and the strengthening of methods for the peaceful settlement of international disputes." Sohn argues, as he has done elsewhere, that the best way for international law to assist the peaceful settlement of disputes is to provide a mix of binding and non-binding dispute mechanisms from which states, as they find appropriate, can choose. The Decade, in his view, provides an opportunity for a comprehensive convention to bring together the existing fragmented obligations of states to submit to the peaceful settlement of their disputes. The following essay by Shinkaretskaya on the changing attitude towards international adjudication in the Soviet Union suggests that Sohn may be right in this view that the time is now ripe for such a convention, at least with regard to what once was a superpower.

The fifth essay by Falk concerns the implementation of international law before the courts of the United States and is the first of a series of essays that considers the efficacy of invoking international law before national courts as a means of strengthening the international legal order. Falk's conclusion is that judicial deference and passivity prevails in the United States in the setting of foreign policy and national security concerns, a state of affairs that he subjects to a rigorous analysis.

Falk's conclusion is not unexpected, and the following essay by Schermers notes that the judiciary of Europe, with one notable exception, would concur with their colleagues in the United States that disputes concerning foreign policy and national security are best left alone. However, Schermers' principal focus is on that exception. His aspiration is that one day all national courts will follow the example set by the European Court of Justice in the early 1960s when, in the *Van Gend & Loos* case, it held that in respect of at least one treaty (the EEC Treaty), individuals had directly enforceable rights independent of the legislation of member states. In his words, "[i]nternational law could be enormously promoted if all courts in the world would take the same position."

The final four essays broadly concern the settlement of disputes in particular areas of international law. Kooijman deals with disputes in the field of human rights, Myjer in the area of arms control, Ostrihansky in the context of GATT, and Traa-Engelman in the field of space law. Generally the authors are concerned that more formal dispute settlement procedures should be introduced into their particular areas of interest, and their recommendations as to the degree of compulsion appropriate to their respective areas of interest do not necessarily vary, as one would expect, with the political circumstances prevailing in these areas. Kooijman, for instance, in the context of the follow-up to the Conference on Security and Cooperation in Europe (CSCE), suggests the establishment of "a committee of independent experts composed of nationals of all participating states. . . . Such a [non-] judicial committee . . . would first of all have a fact-finding mandate with the competence to report to the various subsequent CSCE meetings if no solution had been reached in the meantime." Myjer, however, in the more controversial area of arms control, again in the context of the CSCE, suggests a greater recourse to arbitration based upon the permanent Court of Arbitration. Certain other themes that appeared earlier in the book also reappear, such as the potential that individuals have for the effective supervision of international law, the direct effectiveness of international law in municipal courts, and the need for a mix of dispute settlement procedures.

As in many compilations, the articles in this volume vary in quality, and the more interesting articles tend to fill the first half. There is perhaps an insufficient attempt by contributors to relate their essays to the Decade; too often the reader feels that the contributor is summarizing his or her view on some aspect of the peaceful settlement of disputes without making a real effort to relate it practically to the special context of the Decade. For example, one theme that emerges in a number of essays is the need to invoke greater participation by individuals in the enforcement of international law. Nevertheless, little attention is given to how this aim might be achieved within the context of the Decade. This is unfortunate, since the involvement of individuals in international law is the very area in which the Decade might be most effective. It is perhaps too easy to expect the International Court of Justice to give *locus standi* to individuals to enforce international law in the manner followed by the European Court in *Van Gend & Loos*. In fact, this is unlikely to happen in the foreseeable future. What is needed is some suggestion as to some less radical changes that can increase the interest and participation of individuals in international law and thereby stimulate their demands for greater involvement.

Nevertheless, the book provides valuable insights into the potential of the Decade for advancing the peaceful settlement of disputes. Quintana's contribution on the failure to include a provision for the establishment of a "visitation team" to encourage all states to accept the compulsory jurisdiction of the International Court of Justice is, in particular, an illuminating warning of the difficulties to come.

Moreover, the editors must be congratulated on the alacrity of their response to the declaration by the United Nations of the Decade of International Law. It is perhaps symbolic of the enthusiasm of the Dutch law schools and government for international law in general and for the Decade in particular — an enthusiasm that hopefully will be infectious. Accordingly, in this context it is unfortunate to note the spelling of "enthousiasm" in the first sentence of the first page of the work.

JEREMY A. THOMAS
Barrister at Law, London, England
Research Associate, Dalhousie Law School, Halifax

International Law in Historical Perspective. Vol. XI, Part IX C. The Law of Maritime Prize. By J. H. W. Verzijl. Dordrecht: Martinus Nijhoff, 1992. Pp. xvi, 729. U.S.$220. ISBN 0-7923-0944-8.

In 1968 Professor Verzijl published the first volume of his *magnum opus, International Law in Historical Perspective.* At the time of his death in 1987 at the age of ninety-eight, ten volumes had been published, but the two volumes he intended to produce on the law of maritime prize were incomplete. About 60 per cent of what was to be the first volume dealing with the topic up to 1914 existed only in note form. At the request of the board of editors of the Institute for International Law of the University of Utrecht, of which Verzijl had been a member for many years, these notes were put into publishable form by Mrs. J. P. S. Offerhaus and Mr. W. P. Heere, Verzijl's long time collaborators, and issued as Volume XI of his history.

The breadth of Verzijl's research may be shown by mentioning the fact that the index of prize cases spans over twenty pages, while the treaty index, extending back to the Treaty of 1221 between Pisa and Arles, occupies five pages. In relation to the Treaty of 1221, he states:

As far as can be retraced, the oldest custom observed by seafaring nations during the thirteenth and fourteenth centuries admitted the double principle that enemy merchandise was subject to confiscation even if laden in a ship of "friends" (i.e. non-enemies), and that merchandise belonging to friends was to be respected even if laden in an enemy ship . . . [T]he right of confiscating enemy's goods on board neutral vessels seems to have been recognized, both by Christian and Mohammedan powers, in the early part of the twelfth century. . . . This customary system of *separatorum separata fit ratio* was, however, often modified by treaty or encroached upon in actual practice. It was laid down in . . . the *Consulado de Mar* . . . and was applied by early nineteenth century English prize courts. *(pp. 302-3)*

In his introductory chapter, Verzijl lists a number of regional prize codifications predating the *Laws of Oleron* and the *Black Book of the Admiralty* and names as the oldest surviving manuscript the *Judgments of the Sea*, part of the *Liber Memorandum* dating from the early fourteenth century and kept in the Record Room at the London Guildhall. He reproduces as one of the oldest texts the *Ordinance of Hastings* issued by King John in 1202 that declared as enemy and liable to seizure any ship failing to strike and lower its sails when called upon by the King's admiral or his lieutenant (p. 13). In chapter 1, Verzijl lists, as among the other sources of the law of prize, bilateral treaties, national laws and ordinances, instructions for the Admiral or for privateers, admiralty and prize decisions, customary practice, arbitral awards, and collective treaties.

More important from the point of view of the modern law is the brief history to be found in chapter 1, which covers the period from the Armed Neutrality Alliance beginning with Catherine II's proclamation of 1780 and ending with the Harvard draft of 1939. This general survey is followed by a far more detailed analysis of the entire law, covering such issues as those qualified to exercise the right of prize (pp. 148-72); when and where the right might be exercised (pp. 173-202); the enemy or non-enemy character of prizes, including such matters as a change of flag from enemy to non-enemy in anticipation of war; and the determination of ownership (pp. 203-72). The next 200 pages are devoted to the substantive law, including the problem of enemy goods of neutral ships and vice versa, contraband, blockade, unneutral service, and the Rule of the War of 1756.

Those concerned with maritime warfare law today recognize that there are limits as to the modalities of treating enemy vessels or seaborne enemy goods and they will find the ensuing eighty pages of interest, since they deal with the exercise of the right of capture. This section of the work should be read in conjunction with the final 100 pages of the text, which are concerned with prize jurisdiction, including a discussion of the significance of reprisal orders and the award of damages, and conclude with a short statement on the review of national prize decisions.

Even though the text of this volume does not deal with the law as it was applied and developed during both the world wars and in such conflicts as those affecting India and Pakistan, Israel and Egypt, or the Iran-Iraq war, it is of vital significance from the point of view of the development of the law and indicates the extent to which maritime practice has contributed to the customary law that applied in those wars. The editors must be congratulated on the way in which they have dealt with Verzijl's incomplete manuscript to produce a volume that serves admirably in bringing to a close Verzijl's great work on *International Law in Historical Perspective*.

L. C. GREEN
University of Alberta

ANALYTICAL INDEX /
INDEX ANALYTIQUE

THE CANADIAN YEARBOOK OF
INTERNATIONAL LAW

1993

ANNUAIRE CANADIEN
DE DROIT INTERNATIONAL

(A) Article; (NC) Notes and Comments;
(PR) Practice; (R) Review
(A) Article; (NC) Chronique; (PR) Pratique;
(R) Recension de livre

*Abolition of the Death Penalty in
International Law, The,* by
William A. Schabas (R),
reviewed by Roger S. Clark,
433-35
Agence internationale de
développement, l' (IDA), 327,
329
Arbour, Jean-Maurice, *Droit
international public,* 2ème
édition (R), reviewed by Pierre
Klein, 448-51

Bangkok Declaration, 151
Banque des règlements
internationaux (BRI), 330-31
Banque européene pour la
reconstruction et le
développement (BERD), 326,
328
Banque mondiale, 326, 329
Blais, Céline. *See* "Canadian Practice
in International Law / La
pratique canadienne en
matière de droit international
public: Treaty Action Taken by
Canada in 1992 / Mesures
prises par le Canada en
matière de traités en 1992"
(PR)

Blom, Joost. *See* "Canadian Cases in
International Law in 1992-93 /
La jurisprudence canadienne
en matière de droit
international en 1992-93"
Brus, M., et al., editors, *The United
Nations Decade of International
Law: Reflections on International
Dispute Settlement* (R), reviewed
by Jeremy A. Thomas, 461-64

Canada
actions bilatérales et multilatérales,
337-42
aid and development, 379-80
ALÉ, 318-23, 335
ALÉNA, 339-41, 352, 376-78
antidumping, 317
bancaires et financières, 329-33
beer exports, 314-17
bilateral treaties, 381-85, 387-90
conflict of laws, 395-423
customs tariff law, harmonized,
89-149
diplomatic relations, 343-44,
371-73
environmental law, 375-76
fishing, high seas, 46-86, 355-56
France, boundary dispute with,
265-81, 454-55

INDEX OF CASES /
INDEX DES AFFAIRES